SOLUTIONS M

INTRODUCTION TO MANAGEMENT ACCOUNTING

ELEVENTH EDITION

HORNGREN SUNDEM STRATTON

Prentice Hall, Upper Saddle River, NJ 07458

Acquisitions editor: Deborah Emry
Associate editor: Natacha St. Hill Moore
Senior editorial assistant: Jane Avery
Project editor: Richard Bretan
Manufacturer: Technical Communication Services

A Simon & Schuster Company
Upper Saddle River, New Jersey 07458

Printed in the United States of America

10 9 8 7 6 5 4 3

ISBN 0-13-274283-7

Prentice-Hall International (UK) Limited, *London*
Prentice-Hall of Australia Pty. Limited, *Sydney*
Prentice-Hall Canada Inc., *Toronto*
Prentice-Hall Hispanoamericana, S.A., *Mexico*
Prentice-Hall of India Private Limited, *New Delhi*
Prentice-Hall of Japan, Inc., *Tokyo*
Simon & Schuster Asia Pte. Ltd., *Singapore*
Editora Prentice-Hall do Brasil, Ltda., *Rio de Janeiro*

CONTENTS

Page

Solutions by Chapter

GENERAL COMMENTS

Please read the textbook preface before examining this material. The scope and depth of a particular assignment schedule largely depend on the instructor's personal evaluation of the relative importance of various topics. In turn, his or her evaluation will be influenced by students' backgrounds and other courses in the curriculum. Because this book may be used in a wide variety of courses, several sample assignment schedules have been prepared.

This edition contains both straightforward assignment material, homework that can be solved simply by referring to the presentations in the chapters, and more challenging problems, which require more thoughtful analysis.

This book's approach divorces product costing from planning and control. For example, Chapters 1 through 11 assume that no changes take place in the level of beginning and ending inventories. This sharpens the analysis of planning and control, enhances clarity, and eases the learning process. The problems of product costing are then considered in Chapters 12 through 15. This whole approach may be unconventional, but classroom experience and experimentation have convinced us of its superiority over the traditional approach, which interweaves product costing, planning, and control. If students raise thorny questions regarding inventory valuation when Chapters 1 through 11 are being covered, we usually ask them to postpone their queries until Chapters 12 through 15 are discussed. If desired, Chapters 12 through 14 may be studied at any time after Chapter 4; Chapter 15, any time after Chapter 8.

For comments on how to choose among the various problems in each chapter, see the section entitled "Comments on Choices of Problems in Each Chapter." Other teaching aids for use with this textbook are an Instructor's Resource Manual (which includes chapter overviews, chapter outlines organized by objectives, teaching tips, a chapter quiz, transparency masters, suggested readings and a video guide that carefully integrates the videos into classroom lectures), Solutions Transparencies (which includes acetates for all the end-of-chapter assignments), a Test Item File (including multiple choice, true/false, comprehensive problems, short-answer problems, and critical thinking questions), the Prentice Hall Custom Test (a computerized testing package), On Location Video Library (which includes segments on companies such as Grand Canyon Railway, McDonald's, Home Depot, and many more), the PH Professor: A Classroom Presentation on PowerPoint (includes over 50 PowerPoint slides for each chapter and can be downloaded from our website at www.prenhall.com/horngren/.

Available for students is a Study Guide that provides overviews, study tips and chapter reviews formatted for easy note-taking, and self-tests including a variety of test questions to prepare for examinations. Spreadsheet Templates are also available for selected exercises and problems are identified in the text by a spreadsheet icon. Solutions are available on disk to the instructor.

SAMPLE ASSIGNMENT SCHEDULES

Summary of Potential Assignments

Suggested alternative schedules are summarized here in terms of the relative percentage of time to be devoted to various chapters. Detailed assignment schedules are shown after this summary.

Alternative 1*				Alternative 2**			
Sequence A		Sequence B		Sequence A		Sequence B	
Chapter	Percentage of Time	Chapter	Percentage of Time	Chapter	Percentage of Time	Chapter	Percentage of Time
1	2%	1	2%	1	2%	1	2%
2	5	2	5	16	6	16	6
3	6	3	6	17	6	17	4
4	6	4	6	18	5	2	5
5 & 6	12	13	6	19	5	3	6
8	10	5 & 6	12	2	5	4	6
9	8	11	8	3	6	13	6
10	6	8	10	4	6	14	4
11	10	15	10	5 & 6	10	5 & 6	10
12	7	9	8	8	8	7	4
13	6	10	7	9	6	8	10
15	8	12	6	10	5	16	6
				11	10	9	6
				12	6	10	4
						11	7
Review or Exams	14	Review or Exams	14	Review or Exams	14	Review or Exams	14
Total	100%	Total	100%	Total	100%	Total	100%

*For students who have taken one term of elementary accounting immediately prior to this course.

** For students who have not taken elementary accounting recently. Students with no background in elementary accounting will have to spend more time on Chapters 16 and 17 than is suggested in the above tables.

Use of Fundamental Assignment Material

Some instructors may prefer to assign all the problems in either the A series or the B series of problems under "Fundamental Assignment Material". Each series includes a set of problems that covers the most important topics in the chapter. In addition to the A or B series, selected problems from "Additional Assignment Material" can be assigned as time allows. However, for those who wish to select particular problems in each chapter, some suggestions follow.

Alternative 1, Sequence A

Designed for one semester of 15 weeks with three 50-minute meetings per week. Note that longer semesters permit either more intensive or extensive coverage, depending on instructor preferences.

No. of Class Meeting	Chapter in Text	Problem Assignments: Normal: Based on Approximately Two Hours of Homework per session	Problem Assignments: Selected Additional Problems if Time Permits
1	Introduction.	See the section that follows shortly, "COMMENTS ON CHOICE OF PROBLEMS IN EACH CHAPTER."	
2	Ch. 1 - Perspective	A1, A3, 24	39
3	Ch. 2 - Excluding appendices	A1 (or 35 or 36) and A2 (or B1)	34, 38
4	Appendices to Ch. 2	47 (or 48), 49 (or 50)	Any of 28-31, 54 or 55
5	Ch. 3	A1 & A3 (or B1 & B3)	38
6	Review Ch. 3	A2 or B2	47
7	Review Ch. 3	33, 42	44, 45 (appendix)
8	Ch. 4	A1 (or B1)	
9	Review Ch. 4	A2 (or 27), B2, 28	B3 or 41
10	Review Ch. 4 (Consider jump to Ch. 12)	45 (or 46 or 47)	49
11	Ch. 5	A1, A2, 37 (or 39 or 40)	46
12	Review Ch. 5	B1	32 or 35
13	Review Ch. 5	50 (or B3)	42 or 43
14	Ch. 6	A1 (or B1 or 42)	41
15	Review Ch. 6	A2 (or 43), any of 32, 33, 36, or 37	40
16	Review Ch. 6 (Consider jump to Ch. 11)	39, 47	48, any of 21, 22, 33, or 34
17	Ch. 7	Start A1 or B1	26, 28, 29, 31
18	Review Ch. 7	Finish A1 or B1	33
19	Ch. 8, pp. 292-305	A1 (or B1 or 32 or 33)	Any of 20-23
20	Ch. 8, pp. 305 - end	A3 or B2, 38	Any of 25-27, 29
21	Review Ch. 8	39, 40	36, 42
22	Review Ch. 8	A2, B3, 35	28, 43
23	Review Ch. 8 (Consider jump to Ch. 15)	45, 48	47

No. of Class Meeting	Chapter in Text	Problem Assignments: Normal: Based on Approximately Two Hours of Homework per session	Selected Additional Problems if Time Permits
24	Review for Exam		
25	*Test on Ch. 1 thru Ch. 8		
26	Ch. 9	A1 or B1, A2 or B2	41
27	Review Ch. 9	A3, B3, 40	39, 42
28	Ch. 10	A2 or B1	A3, 31, 34, 36
29	Review Ch. 10	A1 or B2, A4	B3 (or 41), 45
30	Ch. 11	A1 or B1, 40 or 41	Any of 23-29
31	Review Ch. 11	31 or 32, 55	57
32	Review Ch. 11	43, 46	47, 61
33	Review Ch. 11	A3 (or B3), A4 (or B4)	A5 or B5 and any of 33-37
34	Review Ch. 11	38 or 39, 58	52, 59, 60
35	Ch. 12	A1 (or B1), B2 (or A2)	30 (or 31 or 32), 35
36	Review Ch. 12	A3 or B3	39
37	Review Ch. 12	A4 (or B4)	40
38	Ch. 13	A1 or B1, A2	Any of 26-33
39	Review Ch. 13	A3 or B2, 28 or 29	Any of 41-45
40	Review Ch. 13	38, 39, or 40	47, 48
41	Ch. 15 (exclude appendices)	A1 or B1, A2 or B2	Any of 20-22, 27, 29-31
42	Review Ch. 15	32, 35	28, 34
43	Review Ch. 15	38, 40 or 44	Any of 25, 26, 41-43
44	Final review		
45	Final examination		

*Some instructors devote time to discuss tests in subsequent sessions. We have found it more fruitful to hand out photocopied solutions and have students do their checking not on class time. See the later section, "PRESENTATION OF SOLUTIONS IN CLASS."

Alternative 1, Sequence B

This is the same as the above, except that many instructors may prefer to interweave product costing and corresponding material on planning and control. Assignments 35-40 may be used immediately after meeting 10. Furthermore, assignments 30 through 34 may be used immediately after 16, and assignments 41 through 43 may be used immediately after 23.

Alternative 2, Sequence A

No. of Class Meeting	Chapter in Text	Problem Assignments: Normal: Based on Approximately Two Hours of Homework per session	Problem Assignments: Selected Additional Problems if Time Permits
1	Introduction		
2	Ch. 1 - Perspective	A1, A3, 24	39
3	Ch. 16 - Basic Concepts	A1 or B1, 19, 22, 32, or 33	18, 23
4	Review Ch. 16	A2 or B2 or 24	A3 or B3
5	Ch. 17	A1 or 35, A2 or 42, A3 or 43, A4 or 44	B1, B2, B3
6	Review Ch. 17	48, 49	34, 47, 53, 55
7	Ch. 18, Part One	A1 or B1, B3	
8	Review Ch. 18, Part One	A2 or B2, 28	A3, A4
9	Ch. 18, Part Two	A5, B5, 36	37
10	Ch. 19, Part One	A1 or B1, B2 or 22, 23	25, 29, 35, 36
11	Ch. 19, Part Two	A2 or 31 or 32	B3, 30, 38
12-44	Same as alternative 1, Sequence A, from session 3 thru 36, omitting sessions 17 and 18.		
45	Final examination		

Students with no background in accounting will need to spend more time on Chapters 16, 17, and 18 than is suggested in the tables above. Some instructors may wish to omit parts of Chapters 17, 18, or 19.

Alternative 2, Sequence B

This is basically the same as Alternative 2, Sequence A, except that those instructors who wish to cover the chapters on planning and control earlier in the course may prefer to delay sessions 7 through 11 until the end of the course. Moreover, the sessions for Chapters 10, 18, and 19 may be deleted, whereas Chapters 7, 13, and 15 may be included.

Other Possibilities

Some instructors prefer to concentrate on a few chapters in greater depth and to delete other chapters. When we use this approach, we delete Chapters 12 through 19 and occasionally Chapters 7 and 11. Other instructors prefer to cover all the chapters. To do so effectively, an instructor must obviously concentrate on the Normal Problem Assignments above and condense the number of sessions per chapter.

LINKING OF 10TH EDITION PROBLEMS TO THOSE IN THE 11TH EDITION

Users of the 10th Edition of *Introduction to Management Accounting* may have favorite problems that they want to continue to use. To help select a problem in the 11th Edition that is similar, the following table links the problems in the two editions. The first column for each chapter lists the problem numbers from the 10th Edition, and the second column shows the corresponding problem in the 11th Edition. Problems from Chapters 12-20 of the 10th Edition have a different chapter number in the 11th Edition. The new chapter number is shown for these problems.

10th Ed. Chapter	Problems 10th Ed.	Problems 11th Ed.
1	A1	A1
	A2	A2
	A3	A3
	B1	B1
	B2	B2
	B3	B3
	22	24
	23	25
	24	26
	25	27
	26	28
	27	29
	28	30
	29	31
	30	32
	31	35
	32	37
	33	38
	34	39
2	A1	A1
	A2	A2
	B1	B1
	B2	B2
	21	--
	22	23
	23	24
	24	25
	25	26
	26	28
	27	29
	28	30
	29	31
	30	32
	31	33
	32	34

10th Ed. Chapter	Problems 10th Ed.	Problems 11th Ed.
2 (cont.)	33	35
	34	36
	35	37
	36	38
	37	39
	38	40
	39	41
	40	42
	41	43
	42	44
	43	45
	44	47
	45	48
	46	49
	47	50
	48	51
	49	52
	50	53
	51	54
	52	55
3	A1	A1
	A2	A2
	A3	A3
	B1	B1
	B2	B2
	B3	B3
	25	25
	26	26
	27	27
	28	28
	29	29
	30	30
	31	33
	32	34
	33	40

10th Ed. Chapter	Problems 10th Ed.	Problems 11th Ed.
3 (cont.)	34	36
	35	38
	36	39
	37	42
	38	35
	39	43
	40	46
	41	47
	42	44
	43	45
	44	48
4	A1	A1
	A2	A2
	A3	42
	B1	B1
	B2	B2
	B3	B3
	25	27
	26	28
	27	29
	28	30
	29	31
	30	32
	31	33
	32	34
	33	35
	34	36
	35	37
	36	38
	37	--
	38	--
	39	39
	40	40
	41	41
	42	A3

10th Ed. Chapter	Problems 10th Ed.	Problems 11th Ed.
4	43	43
(cont.)	44	44
	45	45
	46	46
	47	47
	48	--
	49	48
	50	49

10th Ed. Chapter	Problems 10th Ed.	Problems 11th Ed.
5	A1	A1
	A2	A2
	A3	A3
	B1	B1
	B2	B2
	B3	B3
	24	23
	25	24
	26	25
	27	26
	28	27
	29	28
	30	29
	31	30
	32	--
	33	31
	34	32
	35	33
	36	35
	37	36
	38	37
	39	38
	40	39
	41	40
	42	42
	43	43
	44	45
	45	46
	46	47
	47	48
	48	49
	49	50
	50	51
	51	--
	52	53
	53	54

10th Ed. Chapter	Problems 10th Ed.	Problems 11th Ed.
6	A1	B1
	A2	B2
	A3	A3
	A4	A4
	B1	A1
	B2	B3
	B3	B4
	20	29
	21	30
	22	23
	23	21
	24	22
	25	31
	26	24
	27	25
	28	26
	29	27
	30	32
	31	33
	32	36
	33	37
	34	38
	35	34
	36	40
	37	41
	38	42
	39	43
	40	--
	41	39
	42	35
	43	44
	44	47
	45	48

10th Ed. Chapter	Problems 10th Ed.	Problems 11th Ed.
7	A1	A1
	B1	B1
	22	23
	23	24
	24	25
	25	26
	26	27
	27	28
	28	29
	29	30
	30	31

10th Ed. Chapter	Problems 10th Ed.	Problems 11th Ed.
7	31	32
(cont.)	32	33
	33	37
	34	38
	35	39
	36	40

10th Ed. Chapter	Problems 10th Ed.	Problems 11th Ed.
8	A1	A1
	A2	A3
	A3	A2
	B1	B1
	B2	B2
	B3	B3
	20	20
	21	21
	22	22
	23	23
	24	29
	25	27
	26	25
	27	26
	28	24
	29	28
	30	30
	31	40
	32	37
	33	39
	34	32
	35	33
	36	35
	37	31
	38	36
	39	38
	40	43
	41	44
	42	42
	43	45
	44	47
	45	46
	46	48

10th Ed. Chapter	Problems 10th Ed.	Problems 11th Ed.
9	A1	A1
	A2	A2
	A3	A3
	B1	B1
	B2	B2
	B3	B3
	25	26
	26	27
	27	28
	28	29
	29	--
	30	31
	31	32
	32	34
	33	35
	34	36
	35	37
	36	39
	37	40
	38	41
	39	42
10	A1	A1
	A2	A2
	A3	A3
	A4	A4
	B1	B1
	B2	B2
	B3	B3
	21	--
	22	22
	23	23
	24	25
	25	26
	26	27
	27	28
	28	29
	29	30
	30	44
	31	31
	32	32
	33	33
	34	34
	35	36
	36	37
	37	38
10 (cont.)	38	39
	39	41
	40	43
	41	45
	42	46
	43	47
11	A1	A1
	A2	41
	A3	31
	B1	B1
	B2	40
	B3	32
	21	23
	22	24
	23	--
	24	25
	25	26
	26	--
	27	27
	28	28
	29	--
	30	--
	31	29
	32	30
	33	--
	34	--
	35	--
	36	--
	37	42
	38	43
	39	44
	40	47
	41	45
	42	--
	43	--
	44	55
	45	61
	46	46
	47	57
	48	--
	49	58
	50	59
12	A1	11-A3
	A2	11-A4
	A3	11-A5
	A4	11-38
	B1	11-B3
	B2	11-B4
	B3	11-B5
	B4	11-39
	20	--
	21	11-33
	22	11-34
	23	11-35
	24	--
	25	--
	26	--
	27	11-36
	28	--
	29	11-37
	30	--
	31	11-48
	32	--
	33	--
	34	11-54
	35	--
	36	11-49
	37	11-50
	38	11-51
	39	11-52
	40	--
	41	11-53
	42	11-60
13	A1	12-A1
	A2	12-A2
	A3	12-A3
	A4	12-A4
	B1	12-B1
	B2	12-B2
	B3	12-B3
	B4	12-B4
	22	12-23
	23	12-24
	24	12-26
	25	12-27
	26	12-28
	27	12-29

10th Ed. Chapter	Problems 10th Ed.	Problems 11th Ed.
13	28	12-30
(cont.)	29	12-31
	30	12-32
	31	12-33
	32	12-34
	33	12-35
	34	12-38
	35	12-29
	36	12-40
	37	12-41
14	A1	13-A1
	A2	13-A2
	A3	13-A3
	B1	13-B1
	B2	13-B2
	B3	13-B3
	21	13-22
	22	13-23
	23	13-24
	24	13-25
	25	13-26
	26	13-27
	27	13-28
	28	13-29
	29	13-30
	30	13-31
	31	13-32
	32	13-33
	33	13-34
	34	13-35
	35	13-36
	36	13-38
	37	13-39
	38	13-40
	39	13-41
	40	13-42
	41	13-43
	42	13-45
	43	13-46
	44	13-47
	45	13-48

10th Ed. Chapter	Problems 10th Ed.	Problems 11th Ed.
15	A1	14-A1
	A2	14-A2
	A3	14-A3
	B1	14-B1
	B2	14-B2
	B3	14-B3
	19	14-19
	20	14-20
	21	14-21
	22	14-22
	23	14-23
	24	14-24
	25	14-25
	26	14-26
	27	14-27
	28	14-28
	29	14-29
	30	14-30
	31	14-31
	32	14-33
	33	14-34
	34	14-35
	35	14-36
	36	14-37
	37	14-38
	38	14-39
	39	14-40
	40	14-41
16	A1	15-A1
	A2	15-A2
	B1	15-B1
	B2	B15-2
	20	15-20
	21	15-21
	22	15-22
	23	15-23
	24	15-24
	25	15-25
	26	15-26
	27	15-27
	28	15-28

10th Ed. Chapter	Problems 10th Ed.	Problems 11th Ed.
16	29	15-29
(cont.)	30	15-30
	31	15-31
	32	15-32
	33	15-34
	34	15-35
	35	15-36
	36	15-37
	37	15-38
	38	15-39
	39	15-40
	40	15-41
	41	15-42
	42	15-43
	43	15-44
	44	15-45
17	A1	16-A1
	A2	16-A2
	A3	16-A3
	B1	16-B1
	B2	16-B2
	B3	16-B3
	17	16-17
	18	16-18
	19	16-19
	20	16-20
	21	16-21
	22	16-22
	23	16-23
	24	16-24
	25	16-25
	26	16-26
	27	16-28
	28	--
	29	16-29
	30	16-30
	31	16-31
	32	16-32
	33	16-33
	34	16-34

10th Ed. Chapter	Problems 10th Ed.	Problems 11th Ed.
18	A1	17-A1
	A2	17-A2
	A3	17-A3
	A4	17-A4
	B1	17-B1
	B2	17-B2
	B3	17-B3
	36	17-34
	37	17-35
	38	17-36
	39	17-37
	40	17-38
	41	17-39
	42	17-40
	43	17-41
	44	14-42
	45	14-43
	46	17-44
	47	17-45
	48	17-46
	49	17-47
	50	17-48
	51	17-49
	52	17-50
	53	17-51
	54	17-52
	55	17-53
	56	17-54
	57	17-55
	58	17-56

10th Ed. Chapter	Problems 10th Ed.	Problems 11th Ed.
19	A1	18-A1
	A2	18-A2
	A3	18-A3
	A4	18-A4
	A5	18-A5
	B1	18-B1
	B2	18-B2
	B3	18-B3
	B4	18-B4
	B5	18-B5
	22	18-22
	23	18-23
	24	18-24
	25	18-25
	26	18-26
	27	18-27
	28	18-28
	29	18-29
	30	18-30
	31	18-31
	32	--
	33	18-33
	34	--
	35	18-34
	36	18-36
	37	18-37

10th Ed. Chapter	Problems 10th Ed.	Problems 11th Ed.
20	A1	19-A1
	A2	19-A2
	B1	19-B1
	B2	19-B2
	B3	19-B3
	23	19-21
	24	19-22
	25	19-23
	26	19-24
	27	19-25
	28	19-26
	29	19-27
	30	19-28
	31	19-29
	32	19-30
	33	19-31
	34	19-32
	35	19-33
	36	19-35
	37	19-36
	38	19-37
	39	19-38

COMMENTS ON CHOICES OF PROBLEMS IN EACH CHAPTER

Throughout the book, the "fundamental assignment material" contains two sets of problems, an "A" series (such as 1-A1 and 1-A2) and a "B" series (such as 1-B1 and 1-B2). To cover the basics of any chapter, you can assign either the "A" or the "B" series. To reinforce the basics or to explore issues in more depth, you can use items in the "additional assignment material". We especially encourage use of some of the cases at the end of the problem material. These are generally not overly long cases, but they allow discussion of material that is not straightforward. They are a good basis for class discussions.

Chapter 1: Managerial Accounting and the Business Organization

The distinctions between scorekeeping, attention directing, and problem solving are frequently subject to argument. We do not find such disputes fruitful, so we cut them short. Despite their fuzziness, these distinctions help the student to recognize that accounting is a rich discipline that is not confined solely to data accumulation.

Problems 1-30 and 1-31 stress the cost-benefit approach to the design of systems. Problems 1-35, 1-38, and 1-39 cover professional ethics.

Chapter 2: Introduction to Cost Behavior and Cost-Volume Relationships

Problems 2-A1 and 2-A2 (or 2-B1 and 2-B2) cover the basic techniques, but any of 2-33 through 2-40 may be viewed as likely substitutes. There are plenty of good choices. Many instructors may prefer not to assign the appendices.

Other problems in later chapters, such as 5-34 and 5-35 may be logically assigned in conjunction with Chapter 2. You may desire to examine Chapters 2 through 6 as a package before choosing particular assignments for each chapter.

Chapter 3: Measurement of Cost Behavior

Chapter 3 problems are designed with several purposes: (1) to measure fixed and variable cost behavior, (2) to stress the role of activity-based cost drivers, and (3) to predict costs with appropriate cost drivers. Problem 3-25 is a good, visual approach to cost behavior, and 3-30, 3-33, and 3-38 are different approaches to modeling cost behavior. Many of the problems involve non-output-volume-related cost drivers; these include 3-40, 3-43, 3-44, 3-45, 3-47, and 3-48. Problems 3-26, 3-28, 3-35, 3-36, 3-39, and 3-46 use cost behavior to predict costs. Several problems require least squares regression analysis: 3-43, 3-44, and perhaps 3-48. Two problems require understanding regression output but do not require the analysis itself: 3-33 and 3-42.

Chapter 4: Cost Management Systems and Activity-Based Costing

Problems 4-A1 and 4-A2 give a traditional overview. Problems 4-A3, 4-B1, 4-B2, and 4-B3 give a more contemporary view of cost systems. Problems 4-28 through 4-38 dwell on the fundamentals that many students seek. Problems 4-45 through 4-47 cover Chapters 2 through 4. They are interchangeable and were used originally as mid-term exam questions; a solid grasp of the material is needed to solve them.

Many instructors prefer to insert Chapters 12, 13, and 14 immediately after Chapter 4. This can be accomplished without breaking continuity. We prefer not to cover Chapter 14, the process costing chapter, in an introductory course. There are too many other important and stimulating topics that deserve attention. Therefore, give serious consideration to omitting Chapter 14 completely, or perhaps you may wish to assign only its first part.

Chapter 5: Relevant Information and Decision Making: Marketing Decisions

Chapters 5 and 6 can help students learn much about how accounting data bear on decision making. Careful selection of assignment material in these two chapters is critical. Depending on the time available, our preferences in Chapter 5 follow: 5-A1, 5-A2, and 5-B1. Others that deserve special mention are 5-35, 5-38 through 5-40, and 5-52 through 5-53. The answer to 5-32 is obvious to most students, but it drives home a lesson to many students who are harder to convince.

Chapter 6: Relevant Information and Decision Making: Production Decisions

Problem 6-A1 is a special favorite that we always follow up (see 6-43). Problem 6-41 is a practical example of 6-43. Problems 6-B1 and 6-B2 are shortened versions of 6-A1 and 6-43. Problems 6-32, 6-33, 6.36, and 6.37 are short items that warrant consideration. Cases 6-47 and 6-48 provide more opportunity for discussion.

Many instructors prefer to insert Chapter 11 immediately after Chapter 6.

Chapter 7: The Master Budget

The exercises, 7-24 through 7-30, cover relatively simple elements of the master budget. The fundamental assignment problems, 7-A1 and 7-B1, are complete master budgets. Because these are time consuming, it may be best to build up to these with assignments that cover parts of the master budget if time permits. If computer literacy is part of the course objectives, problems 7-37 and 7-38 should be assigned. Also consider a group assignment to create a spreadsheet that reproduces the master budget in the summary review problem at the end of the chapter, with a groundrule that only formulas, no numbers, can appear in any of the master budget cells.

Chapter 8: Flexible Budgets and Variance Analysis

If time is short or if you do not wish to emphasize calculation of detailed price and usage variances, you may wish to assign only the first half of the chapter. Exercises 8-20 through 8-23 and problems 8-30, 8-31 through 8-36, and 8-47 focus on flexible budgets without detailed variances. Most of these problems refer to textbook Exhibit 8-5, which provides a helpful template for solving this sort of problem. In addition, Case 8-48 introduces an activity approach to flexible budgeting that is worth considering given the current interest in activity analysis.

Problems that require detailed variance calculations refer to textbook Exhibits 8-8 or 8-9, which are concrete examples and useful templates for variance analysis. These references aid students by giving them a framework for organizing data and developing problem solutions.

Chapter 9: Management Control Systems and Responsibility Accounting

Chapter 9 problems focus on setting goals and objectives, developing incentives, and measuring performance toward objectives. Goals and objectives are covered in 9-26 through 9-29, 9-35, and 9-41. Incentives are covered in 9-29 and 9-37. Performance measurement is in 9-36, 9-39, and 9-40. Case 9-41 combines strategic pricing issues, cost behavior, and productivity; it is not a long case, but it is thought-provoking.

Chapter 10: Management Control in Decentralized Organizations

Many instructors will want to delay assigning Chapter 10 until the end of the course. Chapter 10 is easily divisible into two separate parts, one on transfer pricing and one on performance measurement. In any event, the material can be covered on either of two levels: a brisk survey, which would concentrate on 10-A1 and 10-A2 (or 10-B1 and 10-B2), or a deeper study, which would necessitate more than one class session.

There are several "nuts and bolts" problems: 10-A1, 10-A2, 10-B1, 10-B3, 10-22 through 10-28, and 10-31. Problem 10-41 deals with residual income. Problems 10-40 and 10-42 cover economic value added. Problem 10-34 provides perspective on transfer pricing, and 10-36 covers multinational transfer prices. Problem 10-37 introduces agency theory.

Case 10-47 (a special favorite) shows how the issues in Chapters 9 and 10 are closely related. We especially like 10-47 because it underscores the goal congruence and management effort aspects of designing management control systems. Too often, much material in this chapter is dismissed as being too "soft" or too qualitative for an accounting course. We disagree. We regard this chapter as the conceptual core of the course. It stresses the central questions that the designer of a control system must face, even though few pat answers are provided. Knowing what central questions to ask is an extremely important lesson for accountants and managers.

Chapter 11: Capital Budgeting

Many instructors want to introduce income taxes at the outset of capital budgeting. However, income tax considerations are not needed to grasp the essential ideas. The problem of determining what is relevant is far more imposing that any difficulties in using discounted cash flow tables. In addition to the fundamental assignment material, our favorite problems include 11-55, 11-43, 11-45, and 11-46. Problem 11-46 is of special interest because it has negative operating cash flows under both alternatives but a positive incremental operating cash flow. Cases 11-57, 11-58, and 11-59 address investment decisions in the new manufacturing environment. Problem 11-47 might be assigned in conjunction with Problem 11-51.

The "nuts and bolts" problems are 11-A1, 11-31, and 11-41 (or 11-B1, 11-32, and 11-40), 11-23 through 11-26, and 11-28.

Taxes and inflation complicate capital budgeting but do not change the basic concepts. Problems 11-A3 and 11-A4 (or 11-B3 and 11-B4) provide the most efficient way to drive the major points home regarding income taxes and discounted cash flow, but 11-A5 and 11-38 (or 11-B5 and 11-39) should also be used if there is time. Problems 11-33 through 11-35 provide informative basic exercises. Inflation is covered in 11-38, 11-39, and 11-51.

Chapter 12: Cost Allocation and Activity-Based Costing

Chapter 12 contains some technical details on cost allocation, and instructors who wish to avoid such detail can skip this chapter entirely. Others may want to insert this chapter and Chapter 13 immediately after Chapter 4.

Problems 12-A1 and 12 B1 contains the important basic ideas of cost allocation. Problems 12-A2, 12-B2, and 12-35 compare direct and step-down methods of cost allocation. Activity-based costing is the focus of problems 12-A3 and 12-B3. Choice of cost pools and allocation bases is covered in case 12-39, and case 12-40 presents multiple allocation bases. Joint product costs are the focus of problems 12-A4, 12-B4, 12-26, and 12-38.

Chapter 13: Job-Costing Systems

This chapter may be assigned as a package with Chapter 14 on process costing, or it can be assigned without assigning Chapter 14 (a subject we prefer to omit). Job costing may be studied at two levels or more. The first level would be confined to 13-A1 (or 13-B1) and 13-A3 (or 13-B2), which cover the basic points. At this first level, Problems 13-A2 and 13-31 or 13-32 might also be considered. Alternates for 13-A3 and 13-B2 include 13-34, 13-35, and 13-36.

The second level probes cost bookkeeping in more detail, including the chapter appendix. Consider 13-34 and 13-45.

There are many short straightforward exercises and problems. Consider 13-26, 13-27, 13-30, and 13-39. For a straightforward overview, consider 13-40.

Nonmanufacturing situations are presented in 13-41, 13-42, and 13-43. Problem 13-45 presses the student.

Chapter 14: Process-Costing Systems

The three major parts of this chapter may be studied independently. For example, many instructors may confine their coverage to pages 534-543. Pages 543-549 will be used by those instructors who wish to cover the weighted-average and first-in, first-out methods. Others will skip this second part but cover pages 549-552, which introduces backflush costing. The assignment material is divided accordingly. Problems 14-A1, 14-B1, 14-19 through 14-23, and 14-34 through 14-36 cover pages 534-543. Problems 14-A2, 14-B2, 14-24 through 14-31, 14-37 and 14-38 cover pages 543-549. Finally, problems 14-A3, 14-B3, and 14-39 cover backflush costing.

The appendix, which covers operation costing, can be assigned without necessarily assigning pages 543-552. Consider Problems 14-40 and 14-41.

Chapter 15: Overhead Application: Variable and Absorption Costing

This chapter may be assigned without assigning Chapters 12, 13, or 14. However, Chapter 8 should precede Chapter 15.

Assign this material carefully so that the student does some simple work first. Problems 15-A1 (or 15-B1), 15-A2 (or 15-B2 or 15-27), and 15-20 provide a basic introduction. Problems 15-21, 15-22, and 15-30 concentrate on essentials of absorption and direct costing. Cases 15-44 and 15-45 pursue the topic more deeply. The essentials of production volume variances are covered in 15-32. A recapitulation of all variances, as discussed in the first appendix, is presented in 15-36; additional practice is found in 15-25, 15-26, 15-41, and 15-42. Problem 15-37 covers the disposition of variances.

Please note the overall tone of this set of problems. The emphasis is on an overall perspective, not on detailed intricacies of variance analysis. In particular, consider the lessons that can be learned from 15-28, 15-40, and 15-45.

Special Note on Chapters 16-19

Much of the assignment material in Chapters 16-19 is also in this textbook's companion volume, *Introduction to Financial Accounting*. Students who have thoroughly studied that book will have little need to study Chapters 16-19 here, except as a review or to fill in gaps. For example, if there is time, many topics in the final two chapters of this book will deserve more careful study than may have been feasible in an earlier course. Consider intercompany investments, consolidations, and accounting for changing prices.

Chapter 16: Basic Accounting: Concepts, Techniques, and Conventions

This material can be used in a variety of ways, depending on the objectives of the course and the backgrounds of the students. For example, if we are teaching a class of managers some "financial accounting for non-financial executives," we usually assign either 16-A2 and 16-A3 (or 16-B2 and 16-B3). If we have more time, we also assign 16-A1 (or 16-B1), 16-18, and 16-19. For regular classes, we also like to assign 16-22 or 16-23.

The assignment material for Appendix 17B permits a study of the mechanics of bookkeeping and provides a deeper study of the general concepts of the chapter. If there is little time, it is unnecessary to cover the appendix on ledger accounts. *Subsequent chapters are not dependent on knowledge of T accounts.*

In sum, there is an ample supply of material that can be used for a quick survey or for a deep probing of basic accounting concepts and procedures. The amount of time devoted to the chapter will obviously depend on the instructor's purposes.

Chapter 17: Understanding Corporate Annual Reports: Basic Financial Statements

Although this chapter was not formally divided into major parts, instructors can pick and choose if they prefer. For instance, some instructors may wish to assign the earlier part, stopping on page 665,before covering the statement of cash flows. Consider the following pertinent assignment material that covers the highlights: 17-A1 (or 17-B1), 17-34, 17-35, 17-48 through 17-51.

The statement of cash flows is covered in the fundamental assignment material (17-A2 through 17-A4, 17-B2, and 17-B3) and also by 17-36 through 17-46 and 17-52 through 17-56.

Chapter 18: More on Understanding Corporate Annual Reports

Many instructors may not have time to cover the entire Fundamental Assignment Material. If so, Problem 18-B2 and 18-B3 may be the most serious candidates for homework assignments. Problem 18-28 provides a general overview of consolidated financial statements.

We always take a few minutes in class to stress the highlights of the consolidated balance sheet and income statement in the two big exhibits in the chapter.

To cover financial ratios, consider 18-A5, 18-B5, 18-29, and 18-37. We cover financial ratios only if the finance course does not.

Chapter 19: Difficulties in Measuring Net Income

Again, the instructor may use this chapter in various ways, covering Part One or Part Two or both, as preferred. There are fundamental problems on both Part One (19-A1, 19-B1, and 19-B2) and Part Two (19-A2 and 19-B3). Many angles of FIFO and LIFO may be emphasized, including the classic Chrysler illustration in 19-33.

There is a special note in the textbook at the start of the assignment material for Chapter 19. Problems 19-A1, 19-B1, and 19-22 are good basic problems that have solutions similar to the first exhibit in the chapter on this topic. Problem 19-A2, 19-31, and 19-32 have solutions similar to the exhibit in Part Two of the text.

When inflation is covered, there is a danger of getting too enmeshed in the *details* of how the four major methods differ. Some time should be devoted to the *measuring* of the differences, especially the strengths and weaknesses of the historical cost/constant dollar method in comparison with the other methods.

PRESENTATION OF SOLUTIONS IN CLASS

Instructors have a variety of views regarding the use of classroom time for homework solutions. Most instructors put solutions on a chalkboard or use overhead projectors. In turn, many students frantically copy the materials in their notes. Our practice is to reproduce the printed homework solutions for distribution either before, during, or after the discussion of a particular solution. The members of the class are glad to pay a modest fee to the school to cover the reproduction costs. In this way, students can spend more of their classroom time in thinking rather than writing. Furthermore, they have a complete set of notes.

Some instructors object to this procedure because it provides students with a "file" that can be passed along to subsequent classes. Students in subsequent classes will then use the "file" to avoid conscientious preparation of homework. There will always be some students who hurt themselves by not doing homework in an appropriate way. Why should the vast majority of students be penalized by withholding the printed solutions? The benefits of using printed solutions clearly outweigh the costs; we no longer fret about the few students who beat the system (and themselves).

Similarly, we distribute printed solutions to tests and examinations along with a summary of overall class performance. We do not devote class time to discussing these solutions. The students deserve feedback, but they have sufficient motivation to scrutinize the printed solutions and check their errors on an individual basis. In this way more class time is available for new material.

If students have complaints about grades, we usually ask them to cool off for 24 hours and then submit a written analysis of how they were unjustly treated. We then take these complaints in batches, regrade the papers, and return the papers. If the student then wants to have a person-to-person discussion of the matter, he or she is welcome to see us. This procedure may seem too impersonal, but we recommend it to those teachers (like us) who have been through some painful debates that have been inefficient and frustrating for both student and teacher.

CONDUCTING THE COURSE

From time to time we have received inquiries regarding how we teach a course in management accounting. The following "Notes on Classroom Procedures" explains our philosophy, and it can be handed out to students at the start of a course:

> The following describes my general teaching style. I am placing this description in writing to avoid any misunderstanding; in the past, a few students have been misled about why I operate classes in a particular way.
>
> In my view, the most effective and efficient use of classroom time aims at reinforcing or clarifying what the student has tried to learn on an individual basis (or sometimes a group basis) before entering the classroom. Therefore, optimal learning is achieved by (a) wholehearted preparation via studying the assigned readings and solving the assigned problems or cases; (b) discussion of the material by the students and teacher in class; and (c) the instructor's underscoring of the most important points via comments or short lectures (lecturettes). I rarely give lectures *per se*. My lectures are in the text or the readings.
>
> Obviously, problems or cases are not ends in themselves; instead they are the means of focusing on central issues, concepts, or knowledge.
>
> Given the foregoing, the success of this course depends on adequate preparation for classes by both students and teacher. It also requires participation during class--always participation of the mind and occasional participation of the mouth. Throughout the term, a variety of helpful questions arise from a variety of students. As in all situations throughout life, some individuals naturally speak more often than others. (We all realize that there is no necessary consistency between lots of talk and lots of comprehension of the subject matter.)
>
> I use a call list for two major reasons: (a) to get acquainted with all the students in class so that I can at least link faces with names; and (b) to provide motivation and ensure widespread participation.
>
> From time to time, you may come to class unprepared for a variety of reasons. In such instances, if you want to preclude the possibility of being called on, simply put your name on a slip of paper on the front desk before the session begins. In this way, everybody wins; I don't enjoy calling on students who are unprepared.
>
> Unless otherwise specified, no assignments need to be handed in. However, as you know, the best preparation entails writing solutions and

answers. Your contribution to the class via your solutions, comments, and questions is an essential part of the course. If you are absent from a particular class, you should hand in your solutions at the subsequent class. This requirement encourages an active rather than a passive role in the course.

Some of you may have unusually severe anxiety about being called on in class. If so, please see me after class during the first week of the quarter to discuss alternate arrangements. My use of a call list is not intended to be a terror tactic.

KEY AMOUNTS FROM SUGGESTED SOLUTIONS TO SELECTED PROBLEMS
For Students' Use in Checking Their Own Solutions

Introduction to Management Accounting, 11th Ed.
Horngren, Sundem, and Stratton

Chapter 1

1-A2	Tot. var., $178U	1-22	5. Financial
1-B2	Actual, $14,840	1-23	3. Staff
1-B3	1. T		

Chapter 2

2-A1	1. 15,000; $15,000	2-38	1. $900
2-A2	1. $40,000	2-39	3. $(840)
2-B1	2. $30,000	2-40	2. $144,000
2-B2	1. $1,120	2-41	1. 40,000
2-23	3. Sales, $940,000	2-42	1. 122
2-24	1. Net inc., $80,000	2-43	3. 69.7%
2-25	1. $50,000,000	2-44	1. 46%
2-26	2. 40,000 rooms	2-45	1. 40,000
2-27	1. $28	2-46	4. $3,213
2-28	1. 233	2-47	1. $70,000
2-29	2. 41,143	2-48	2. Net inc., $2,000,000
2-30	2. 66,000	2-49	2. 57%
2-31	$1,700,000	2-50	1. a
2-32	$1,320,000	2-51	1. 15,000
2-33	1. $503	2-52	2. a. $542,000
2-34	1. £2,310,000	2-53	1. Old, $15,000; New, $60,000
2-35	2. 2,500	2-54	1. B-E: L, 170; D, 85
2-36	2. 10,000	2-55	1. 275,000

Chapter 3

3-A1	1. b	3-32	Var., £20/ton
3-A2	1. Sign One, $180 and $120	3-35	2. $3,000 fixed cost/week
3-A3	1. Var., $5.00	3-36	1. Var., $10,400U
3-B2	Act. anal., Z15, $64	3-39	$4,000
3-B3	FC, $50,000,000/month	3-40	1. Act. anal., Blooms, $4,140
3-25	2. B	3-41	2. $4,223
3-26	1. $3,000/month	3-43	3. $340.33
3-27	Disc., $86,000	3-45	2. a. # of boards, $149,133
3-28	B-E, 50,000 orders	3-47	2. 19X7, $174.32/employee
3-29	2. Var., $2.22/unit		

Chapter 4

4-A1	2. $336,800
4-A2	2. $760
4-B1	2. $1,050,000
4-B3	1. CL3, $23,750
4-27	1. $32,000,000
4-30	1. I, V
4-31	1. d, e
4-32	WIP, $0
4-33	Tot. inv., $485,000
4-34	2. $320,000
4-35	3. ¥30,000,000
4-36	k. $180,000,000
4-37	Sales, $930,000
4-38	3. $80,000
4-40	Corresp., $12.64
4-41	2. X-1, $105,100
4-43	2. Tot. inv., $115,000
4-45	1. $25,000
4-46	1. $22,000
4-47	1. $18,000
4-49	2. a. FF129,000,000

Chapter 5

5-A1	2. 46.1%
5-A2	1. Plain: $16, 24%
5-A3	2. 50%
5-B1	4. $150,000 decline
5-B2	1. XY-7, 4/5 hour
5-25	Difference, $50
5-26	1. $300 increase
5-27	3. a. 30
5-28	1. 300
5-29	1. c. $24.80
5-31	1. SF 1,200 decrease
5-34	1. $10
5-35	1. 66.7%
5-36	3. $201,600
5-39	1. With, £103,000
5-41	1. 516,923
5-43	1. Op. inc. @300,000, $220,000
5-44	1. 2nd option by $80
5-45	1. Increase DM 1,200
5-46	1. $5
5-50	2. $2.40
5-51	1. $31.05
5-52	1. $1,550,000
5-54	4. $20,625

Chapter 6

6-A1	1. $22,000
6-A2	3. $64,000
6-A4	1. $42,000
6-B1	Difference, $7,500
6-B3	1. Difference, DM2.5/unit
6-B4	1. $300
6-23	1. Difference, $10,000
6-25	1. c
6-26	1. $250
6-27	1. Difference, $2,000
6-28	2. $14.50
6-29	$20,760
6-31	2. $20,160
6-32	2. 55.56%
6-33	2. 50%
6-34	1. Difference, $100,000
6-35	1. $312,000
6-36	1. With, $4,745,000
6-37	1. With, $9.07
6-38	1. FF48,350
6-39	1. $204,000
6-40	3. 30,000 units
6-42	1. Difference, $3,000
6-44	3. a. 468/show
6-45	2. $550,000
6-46	2. $150
6-47	2. $10.00
6-48	2. 50,000 units

Chapter 7

7-A1	1. Net inc., $61,370; cash bal., 8/31, $25,940
7-B1	1. Net inc., $16,367; cash bal., 3/31, $32,992
7-23	2. Sales
7-24	1. $1,632,000
7-25	3. $120,000
7-26	July collections, $428,000
7-27	March collections, ¥225,600,000
7-28	$398,350
7-29	July purchases, $260,000
7-30	1. $23,000
7-31	Cash, 6/30, $27,000
7-32	Cash, 4/30, $109,000
7-33	Cash, 10/31, $13,115
7-34	2. $594,000
7-39	3. $1,656,000
7-40	2. Total, $11,092,900

Chapter 8

8-A1	2. $960,000 + $.80X
8-A2	Activity-level var., $9,000U
8-A3	2. Mat. usage, $1,250U
8-B1	2. Flex.-bud. var., $27,500U
8-B2	1. Lab. price var., $30,000F
8-B3	2. 117,000
8-20	$282,500
8-21	@40,000, $12,000
8-22	Dir. mat., $8/unit
8-24	Flex.-bud. var., $12,500U
8-25	Mat. price var., $2,000F
8-26	1. $14.54
8-27	Lab. usage var., $4,500U
8-28	1. $13,000
8-29	Mat. usage var., $7,500F
8-30	Sales-act. var., $900,000U
8-31	Tot. flex.-bud. var., $25U
8-32	Act. op. inc., $111,400
8-34	Sales - act. var., B600,000
8-35	2. $11,880U
8-36	Tot actual, $13,042
8-38	Lab. usage var., $2,000U
8-39	1. e. 5,500SF U
8-40	2. Lab. price var., $1,140F
8-41	1. Mat. pr. var., $5,600F
8-42	1. a. Usage, $600U
8-43	Tot. cost, $135.10
8-44	Dir. mat., $48.00
8-45	1. a. $9,200U
8-47	1. Usage, $1,050U
8-48	1. Flex.-bud. var., $10,000U

Chapter 9

9-A3	1. 1998, National, $126,864
9-29	1. C, March, ¥398,500,000
9-37	1. 640,000
9-39	2. Eurotel, 19X6, 123
9-40	1. 19X7, 32.7 pounds/hr.
9-42	1. B-E, $705,128

Chapter 10

10-A1	1. a. $9.00	10-27	3. Y, $52,000
10-A2	1. $45,000 disadvantage	10-28	1. b. Ace, 36%
10-A3	$54,000 advantage	10-29	1. J, ROI, 28%
10-A4	3. B. $72,000	10-35	$20 to $50
10-B1	$3.30 per gallon	10-36	1. $27.50 saved
10-B2	1. c. 6.86%	10-38	2. C, ROI, 3%
10-B3	1. b. ROI, 33%	10-39	1. a. Pub./Info., 17.1%
10-22	1. a. Overall, $1.25	10-40	1997, $487,000,000
10-23	2. $9 if excess capacity	10-41	1. Shoes, RoA, repl. cost, 18%
10-24	1. $400	10-42	1. $1,944,255,000
10-25	3. 3.6%	10-45	1. $28,500 increase
10-26	A. 21%		

Chapter 11

11-A2	$6,885	11-38	1. $20,016
11-A3	1. $(8,159)	11-39	2. $83,336
11-A4	1. $(89,690)	11-40	2. $17,774
11-A5	@ $65,000, Cash up $60,500	11-41	2. $2,986
11-B1	1. a. $10,365.60	11-42	2. Difference, $7,994
11-B2	$37,808	11-43	Difference, $7,831
11-B3	1. $(1,761)	11-44	NPV, $3,996
11-B4	2. $10,280	11-45	Difference, £7,000
11-B5	1. Cash inflow, $11,600	11-46	1. $25,000
11-23	1. b. $21,216	11-47	2. 46.5 trips
11-24	1. $254,200,000	11-48	2. $8,856
11-25	2. a. $376,440	11-49	2. $3,061
11-26	1. $228,180	11-50	$4,433
11-27	$202,800	11-51	1. NPV, $3,272
11-28	IRR, 20 yrs., $2,225	11-52	2. $782
11-29	$(2,028)	11-53	NPV, $38,527
11-30	1. $17,232	11-54	6. ¥46,421,000
11-31	2. $9,069	11-55	1. $3,292
11-32	1. $6,862	11-56	1. $111,550
11-33	Net inc., $48,000	11-57	1. NPV, Skr 387,040
11-34	Sales, $2,150,000	11-58	2. $4,661,025
11-35	$480,000	11-59	NPV, $427,965
11-36	2. 2000, $2,560	11-60	Alt. C, NPV, $218,521
11-37	a. $45,046	11-61	Exp. NPV, ($558,070)

Chapter 12

12-A1	1. Northeast, $6 million	12-28	$12,870
12-A2	2. Tot., machining, $1,872,864	12-30	1. $.25
12-A3	1. II, $11,000	12-31	4. To East, $570,000
12-A4	2. B, $6,720,000	12-32	1. University, $8,700
12-B1	1. Business, $72,000	12-33	3. M1, $183.32
12-B2	3. a. $12.56	12-34	3. M1, $182.92
12-B3	1. Giant, $176.50	12-35	3. $6.875
12-B4	2. Oat bran, $225,000	12-36	1. $24,075
12-23	2. $3,000	12-37	1. $1,488
12-24	1. Sunnyville, $60,000	12-38	2. a. B, op. prof., $138
12.25	2. Mach., $633,904	12-39	4. c. Prod. A, $270
12-26	2. A, $160,000	12-40	1. Board L, £199.35
12-27	2. $35,000	12-41	1. $216,750

Chapter 13

13-A2	3. $482.50	13-33	2. Case 2, $333,000
13-A3	1. Underapplied, $8,000	13-34	3. Difference, $24,000
13-B2	2. Lower by $10,000	13-35	2. FF33 and FF38 million
13-B3	2. $20.00	13-36	Difference, $24,000
13-22	1. $6 million	13-38	1. 475
13-23	$6 million	13-39	2. 200%
13-24	2. $14 million	13-40	2. 80,000 hours
13-25	Tot. cost, $14,047	13-41	2. $326.62
13-26	3. $12,000	13-42	2. $515.63
13-27	1. c. Sept., $350,000	13-43	1. 200%
13-28	WIP, $5 million	13-45	d. $56,250
13-29	WIP, $22 million	13-46	1. 1st 6 mos., $11,000 overapplied
13-30	3. Rate, 80%	13-47	1. Tot. mfg. prod. cost, $95.03
13-31	Case A, 170%	13-48	2. b. K102, SF29,200
13-32	Case 1, c, 150%		

Chapter 14

14-A1	2. Transferred, $136,000
14-A2	1. $1,365,000
14-B1	2. Transferred, $1,680,000
14-B2	WIP, $3,960
14-19	2. WIP, $1,091,200
14-20	2. Completed, $571,200
14-23	Case B, 7,300
14-24	Conversion, current per., 33,700
14-25	b, 33,500
14-26	Dir. mat., FIFO, 47,800
14-27	Conversion, Feb. only, 85,000
14-28	¥8,000
14-29	$5.30
14-32	2. $2,525
14-34	3. $1,815,000
14-35	2. WIP, $140,000
14-36	Completed, $3,625,000
14-37	WIP, $4,046
14-38	1. Transferred, $1,374,097
14-39	2. $368,000
14-40	2. Std., cost/unit, $60
14-41	1. $4,000

Chapter 15

15-A1	1. $2,800
15-A2	1. Op. inc., $1,210
15-B1	2. $2,000
15-B2	Abs. op. inc., $28,500
15-20	Abs. net inc., 19X8, $12,000
15-21	4. 10,000 units
15-22	1. $15,000
15-23	¥1,260,000U
15-24	1. b. $10,500F
15-25	Flex.-bud. var., fixed, $1,700U
15-26	2. Eff. var., tot., $4,000U
15-27	2. c. $6 and $3
15-28	2. 1,600,000 gal.
15-29	2. Var. costing, 19X7, $210,0000
15-30	1. Abs. op. inc., $122,000
15-31	1. Abs. op. inc., $74,800
15-32	1. $l6 per unit
15-33	2. $7,500,000F
15-34	1. Prod.-vol. var., $72,000U
15-35	1. Base a, 19X5, $14.56
15-36	DL usage var., $18,000U
15-38	f. $196,500
15-39	1. b. $195,000
15-41	Var. OH sp. var., $1,000F
15-42	Var. OH eff. var., $1,100U
15-43	2. a. $720,000
15-44	1. 11,000 units

Chapter 16

16-A1	A, $30,000; H, $40,000
16-A2	2. Net inc., $3,000
16-A3	$40,000
16-B1	A, $878.7 million
16-B2	2. Net earn., ¥3 billion
16-B3	¥45 billion
16-16	1. F
16-22	3. B191,000
16-23	2. X, $2,000; Y, $6,000
16-24	2. Net inc., $7,900
16-25	1. Cr.
16-26	1. T
16-30	1. Accrual op. inc., $63,300
16-32	a. $142,445,000
16-33	1. a. Net inc., $1,966 million
16-34	Net inc., $3,415 million

Chapter 17

17-A1	Addl. paid-in-cap., $121,000
17-A2	Cash from op. act., $334,000
17-A4	1. Net inc., $200,000
17-B1	Ret. earn., $13,975 million
17-B3	$4,194 million
17-34	Tot. assets, DM2,640
17-35	Intang. assets, ¥21,000 million
17-36	$634,000
17-37	$352,000
17-38	$60,000
17-39	Cash from op. act., DK241,000
17-42	Cash from op. act., $218,000
17-44	Net inc., $12 million
17-45	Cash from op. act., $69 million
17-46	1. Cash from op. act., $31 mill.
17-48	b. $2 million
17-50	1. $449,723,000
17-51	Gain, $5,538,000
17-52	a. Investing
17-56	Cash, $39,901

Chapter 18

18-A2	2. Consol. net inc., $95 million
18-A3	2. Consol. net inc., $93 million
18-A4	2. $750,000; $6,000,000
18-A5	1. a. $60 million
18-B2	2. Consol. net. inc., $600 mill.
18-B3	1. ($13,200,000)
18-B4	1. 2.225 times
18-B5	1. 1.40
18-22	$94 million; $95 million
18-23	2. Consol. net inc., $260,000
18-26	1. $123 million
18-27	1. Tot. assets, $500 million
18-28	Consol. net inc., $115 million
18-29	1. a. 19X2, 6.0%
18-32	$1,184 million
18-34	1. $1,553,035
18-35	1. $3,594 million
18-36	1. 7.33%
18-37	2. a. 0.8

Chapter 19

19-A1	LIFO, GM, $150,000
19-A2	CC/CD, inc. fr. cont. ops., $300
19-B1	2. a. Lower, $92
19-B2	LIFO, taxes $48 lower
19-B3	1. c. HC/CD, $1,838 million
19-21	1. a. $5,650
19-22	2. $1,600
19-23	LIFO, save $680 of taxes
19-24	1. b. EPS, $.05
19-25	1. LIFO, GM, $168,000
19-26	1. Edmonton, $39,000
19-27	1. FIFO, yr. 1, net inc., R3,600
19-38	1. a. Net inc., $22,660
19-29	8/31/X1, $75,000
19-30	1. c. $18,000,000
19-31	1. Hold. gain, CC/ND, $120,000
19-34	1. Op. Inc., $1.33 billion
19-35	1997 op inc., $701.8 million
19-36	1. 1996, 4.9%
19-37	2. $8 million

CHAPTER 1
Managerial Accounting and the Business Organization

1-A1 (10-15 min.)

Because the accountant's duties are often not sharply defined, some of these answers could be challenged:

1. Problem solving. Helps a manager assess the impact of a decision.
2. Scorekeeping. Reports on the results of an operation.
3. Attention directing and problem solving. Budgeting involves making decisions about planned activities – hence, aiding problem solving. Budgets also direct attention to areas of opportunity or concern – hence, directing attention. Reporting against the budget also has a scorekeeping dimension.
4. Attention directing. Focuses attention on areas that need attention.
5. Attention directing. Helps managers learn about the information contained in a performance report.
6. Scorekeeping. The statement merely reports what has happened.
7. Problem solving. The cost comparison is apparently useful because the manager wishes to decide between two alternatives. Thus, it aids problem solving.
8. Attention directing. Variances point out areas where results differ from expectations. Interpreting them directs attention to possible causes of the differences.
9. Problem solving. Aids a decision about where the parts should be made.
10. Scorekeeping. Determining a depreciation schedule is simply an exercise in preparing financial statements to report the results of activities.

1-A2 (15-20 min.)

1.

	Budgeted Amounts	Actual Amounts	Deviations or Variances
Room rental	$ 150	$ 150	$ 0
Food	800	1,013	213U
Entertainment	600	600	0
Decorations	220	185	35F
Total	$1,770	$1,948	$178U

2. Because of the management by exception rule, room rental and entertainment require no explanation. The actual expenditure for food exceeded the budget by $213. Of this $213, $150 is explained by attendance of 15 persons more than budgeted (at a budget of $10 per person) and $63 is explained by expenditures above $10 per person.

   Actual expenditures for decorations were $35 less than the budget. If all desired decorations were purchased, the decorations committee should be commended for their savings.

1-A3 (5 min.)

1. Head of accounting for current planning and control, controller, president. Sometimes the cost records clerk also has a line responsibility to the head of general accounting, but Exhibit 1-9 does not show such a relationship.
2. Assembly manager, production superintendent, manufacturing vice-president, president.

1-B1 (15-20 min.)

Because the accountant's duties are often not sharply defined, some of these answers could be challenged:

1. Scorekeeping. Simply recording of what has happened.
2. Problem solving. Helps a manager decide between alternatives.
3. Attention directing. Directs attention to the use of overtime labor.
4. Scorekeeping. Records events.
5. Problem solving. Provides information to managers for deciding between alternatives.
6. Attention directing. Directs attention to why nursing costs increased
7. Attention directing. Directs attention to areas where actual results differed from the budget.
8. Problem solving. Helps the vice-president to decide which course of action is best.
9. Scorekeeping. Records costs in the department to which they belong.
10. Scorekeeping. Records actual overtime costs.
11. Attention directing. Directs attention to stores with either high or low ratios of advertising expenses to sales.
12. Attention directing. Directs attention to causes of returns of the drug.
13. Attention directing or problem solving, depending on the use of the schedule. If it is to identify areas of high fuel usage it is attention directing. If it is to plan for purchases of fuel, it is problem solving.
14. Problem solving. Provides information for deciding between two alternative courses of action.
15. Scorekeeping. Records items needed for financial statements.

1-B2 (10-15 min.)

1 & 2.

	Budget	Actual	Variance
Sales	$80,000	$79,860	$ 140U
Costs:			
Fireworks	$40,000	$44,000	$4,000U
Labor	15,000	13,000	2,000F
Other	8,000	8,020	20U
Profit	$17,000	$14,840	$2,160U

3. The cost of fireworks was $4,000 ÷ $40,000 = 10% over budget. Did fireworks suppliers raise their prices? Did competition cause retail prices to be lower than expected? There should be some explanation for the extra cost of fireworks. Also, the labor cost was $2,000 ÷ $15,000 =13% below budget. It would be useful to discover why this cost was saved. Both sales and other costs were very close to budget.

1-B3 (10 - 15 min.)

1. Treasurer. Allowing credit is a financial decision.
2. Controller. Advising managers aids operating decisions.
3. Controller. Advice on cost analysis aids managers' operating decisions.
4. Controller. Divisional financial statements report on operations. Financial statements are generally produced by the controller's department.
5. Treasurer. Financing the business is the responsibility of the treasurer.
6. Controller. Tax returns are part of the accounting process overseen by the controller.
7. Treasurer. Insurance, as with other risk management activities, is usually the responsibility of the treasurer.
8. Treasurer. Analysts affect the company's ability to raise capital, which is the responsibility of the treasurer.

1-1 Decision makers within and outside an organization use accounting information for three broad purposes:

1. Internal reporting to managers for planning and controlling operations.
2. Internal reporting to managers for special decision-making and long-range planning.
3. External reporting to stockholders, government, and other interested parties.

1-2 The emphasis of financial accounting has traditionally been on the historical data presented in the external reports. Management accounting emphasizes planning and control purposes.

1-3 The branch of accounting described in the quotation is management accounting.

1-4 Scorekeeping is the recording of data for a later evaluation of performance. Attention directing is the reporting and interpretation of information for the purpose of focusing on inefficiencies of operation or opportunities for improvement. Problem solving presents a concise analysis of alternative courses of action.

1-5 Additional regulation sometimes forces managers to rethink and redesign their accounting systems. Improvements in systems often result. The key question is whether the value of the improvements exceeds their costs.

1-6 Yes, but it covers more than that. The Foreign Corrupt Practices Act applies to all publicly-held companies and covers the quality of internal accounting control as well as bribes and other matters.

1-7 Three examples of service organizations are banks, insurance companies, and public accounting firms. Such organizations tend to be labor intensive, have outputs that are difficult to define and measure, and have both inputs and outputs that are difficult or impossible to store.

1-8 Two considerations are cost-benefit and behavioral effects. Cost-benefit refers to how well an accounting system helps achieve management's goals in relation to the cost of the system. The behavioral consideration specifies that an accounting system should be judged by how it will affect the behavior (that is, decisions) of managers.

1-9 Yes. The act of recording events has become as much a part of operating activities as the act of selling or buying. For example, cash receipts and disbursements must be traced, and receivables and payables must be recorded, or else gross confusion would ensue.

1-10 A budget is a prediction and guide; a performance report is a tabulation of actual results compared with the budget; and a variance reconciles the differences between budget and actual.

1-11 No. Management by exception means that management spends more effort on those areas that seem to be out of control and less on areas that are functioning as planned. This method is an efficient way for managers to decide where to put their time and effort.

1-12 No. There is no perfect system of automatic control, nor does accounting control anything. Accounting is a tool used by *managers* in their control of operations.

1-13 Information that is relevant for decisions about a product depends on the product's life-cycle stage. Therefore, to prepare and interpret information, accountants should be aware of the current stage of a product's life cycle.

1-14 The six functions are: (1) research and development; (2) product and service process design; (3) production; (4) marketing; (5) distribution; and (6) customer service.

1-15 No. Not all of the functions are of equal importance to the success of a company. Measurement and reporting should focus on those functions that enable a company to gain and maintain a competitive edge.

1-16 Line authority is held by those managers directly responsible for the production and sale of goods or services. Staff authority is held by persons who have an indirect responsibility for the production and sale of goods or services.

1- 17 A treasurer is concerned mainly with the company's financial matters, the controller with operating matters. In a small organization the same person might be both treasurer and controller.

1-18 The controller exercises control over the accounting and reporting systems in line departments by virtue of the approval given to his efforts and recommendations by top line management. He also exercises direct control over his own department.

1-19 The four parts of the CMA examination are: (1) economics, finance, and management, (2) financial accounting and reporting, (3) management reporting, analysis, and behavioral issues, and (4) decision analysis and information systems.

1-20 Changes in technology are affecting accounting in two main ways. First, the increasing capabilities and decreasing cost of computers are changing the way data are processed. Second, increased automation of manufacturing and other processes is changing the types of information managers find useful.

1-21 The essence of the just-in-time philosophy is the elimination of waste, accomplished by reducing the time products spend in the production process and trying to eliminate the time spent in processes that do not add value to the product.

1-22 The four major responsibilities are: (1) *competence* - develop knowledge; know and obey laws, regulations, and technical standards; and perform appropriate analyses, (2) *confidentiality* - refrain from disclosing or using confidential information, (3) *integrity* - avoid conflicts of interest, refuse gifts that might influence actions, recognize limitations, and avoid activities that might discredit the profession, and (4) *objectivity* - communicate information fairly, objectively, and completely, within confidentiality constraints.

1-23 Standards do not always provide the needed guidance. Sometimes an action borders on being unethical, but it is not clearly an ethical violation. Other times two ethical standards conflict. In situations such as these, accountants must make ethical judgments.

1-24 (5 min.)

1. Financial
2. Financial
3. Management
4. Management
5. Financial
6. Financial
7. Management

1-25 (5 min.)

1. Line
2. Staff
3. Staff
4. Line
5. Staff
6. Line

1-26 (30 min.)

The production departments appear on the bottom line of the organization chart shown on the next page in Exhibit 1-26. The factory service departments are in the middle of the chart.

EXHIBIT 1-26
ORGANIZATION CHART – A MANUFACTURING COMPANY

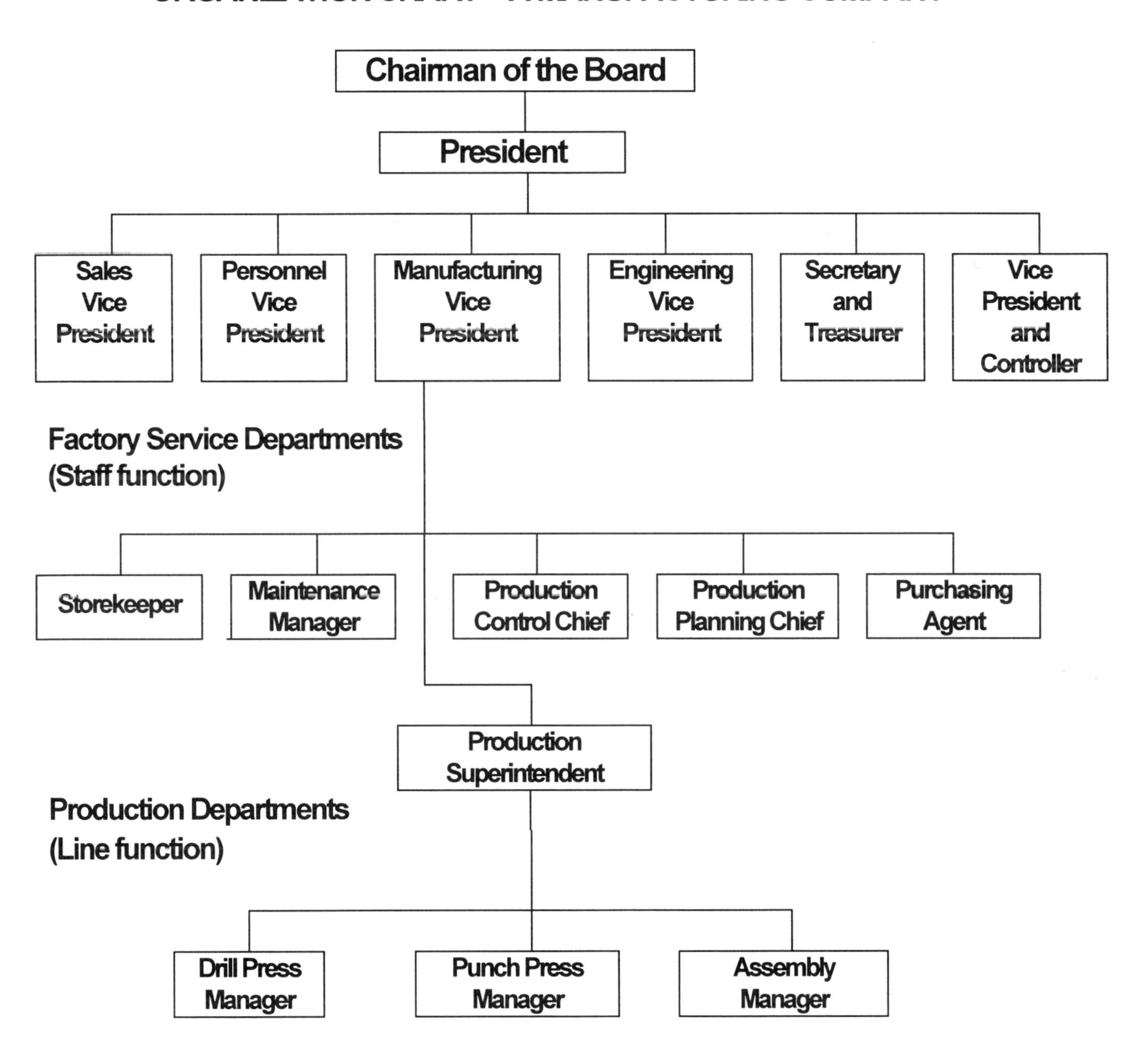

1-27 (15-20 min.)

The management accountant's major purpose is to provide information that helps *line managers* in making decisions regarding the planning and controlling of operations. The accountant supplies information for scorekeeping, attention directing, and problem solving. In turn, managers use this and other information for routine and non-routine decisions and for evaluating subordinates and the performance of sub-parts of the organization. Management accountants must walk a delicate line between (1) making sure that managers are properly using the pertinent information and (2) making sure that the managers, not the accountants, are doing the actual managing.

1-28 (15-20 min.)

This problem can form the basis of an introductory discussion of the entire field of management accounting.

1. The focus of management accounting is on helping internal users to make better decisions, whereas the focus of financial accounting is on helping external users to make better decisions. Management accounting helps in making a host of decisions, including pricing, product choices, investments in equipment, making or buying goods and services, and manager rewards.

2. Generally accepted accounting standards or principles affect both internal and external accounting. However, change in internal accounting is not inhibited by generally accepted principles. For example, if an organization wants to account for assets on the basis of replacement costs for internal purposes, no outside agency can prohibit such accounting. Of course, this means that organizations may have to keep more than one set of records. There is nothing immoral or unethical about having multiple sets of books, but they are

expensive. Accounting data are commodities, just like butter or eggs. Innovations in internal accounting systems must meet the same cost-benefit tests that other commodities endure. That is, their perceived increases in benefits must exceed their perceived increases in costs. Ultimately, benefits are measured by whether better decisions are forthcoming in the form of increased net profits or cost savings.

3. Budgets, the formal expressions of management plans, are a major feature of management accounting, whereas they are not as prominent in financial accounting. Budgets are major devices for compelling and disciplining management planning.

4. An important use of management accounting information is evaluation of performance, which often takes the form of comparison of actual results against budgets, providing incentive and feedback to improve future decisions.

5. Accounting systems have enormous influence on the behavior of individuals affected by them. Management accounting is more concerned with the likely behavioral effects of various accounting alternatives that may be adopted than is financial accounting.

1-29 (10 min.)

The main point of this question is that cost information is crucial for decisions regarding which products and services should be emphasized or de-emphasized. The incentives to measure costs precisely are far greater when flat fees are being received instead of reimbursements of costs.

Note too that nonprofit organizations and profit-seeking organizations have similar desires regarding management accounting. Accountability is now in fashion for many purposes, including justification of prices, cost control, and response to criticisms by investors (whether they be donors, taxpayers, or others).

When somebody's money is at stake, accounting systems get much love and attention. In a Price Waterhouse survey of 550 hospitals, hospital financial executives said that improved cost accounting systems "are crucial to responding to changes in hospital payment mechanisms and that better cost information is essential for more profitable and efficient operations." Hospitals will increasingly identify costs by product (type of case), not just by departments.

1-30 (10 min.)

Paperwork and systems often seem to become ends in themselves. However, the rationale that should underlie systems design is the cost-benefit philosophy or approach that is implied in the quotation. The aim is to get the managers and their subordinates collectively to make better decisions under one system versus another system – for a given level of costs.

1-31 (10 min.)

Anderson implies that technical skills are not enough for successful management. The understanding of the financial implications of management decisions is also required, particularly in a competitive environment.

Management accounting helps managers to weigh their alternatives in light of the ultimate tests, which are almost always financial. However, managers should not be so consumed by financial measures that important nonfinancial aspects are ignored.

1-32 (10-15 min.)

1. Boeing's competitive environment and manufacturing processes changed greatly during the 1980s and early 1990s. An accounting system that served them well in their old environment would not necessarily be optimal in the new environment. Boeing's management probably thought that changes in the accounting system were necessary to produce the kind of information necessary to remain competitive.

2. A cost-benefit criterion was probably used. Boeing's management may not have quantified the costs and the benefits, but they certainly assessed whether the new system would help decisions enough to warrant the cost of the system.

   Many of the benefits of a better accounting system are hard to measure. They affect many strategic decisions of an organization. Without accurate product costs, management will find it difficult to assess the consequences of their decisions. An accurate accounting system will help to price airplanes and other products competitively.

3. More accurate product costs will usually result in better management decisions. But if the cost of the accounting system that produces the more accurate costs is too high, it may be best to forego the increased accuracy. The benefit of better decisions must exceed the added cost of the system for a change to be desirable.

1-33 (10 min.)

1. There are many possible activities for each function of Nike's value chain. Some possibilities are:

   Research and development – Determining changes in customers' tastes and preferences for shoes and sportswear to come up with new products (maybe the next "Air Jordans").

   Product and service process design – Design a shoe to meet the increasing demands of competitive athletes.

   Production – Determine where products are to be produced and negotiate contracts with the companies producing them.

   Marketing – Signing prominent athletes to endorse Nike's products.

   Distribution – Select the best locations for warehouses for distribution to retail outlets.

   Customer service – Formulate return policies for products that customers perceive to be defective.

2. Accounting information that would aid managers' decisions includes:

   Research and development – Trends in sales for various products, to determine which are becoming more and less popular.

Product and service process design – Production costs of various shoe designs.

Production – Measure total costs, including both purchase cost and transportation costs, for production in various parts of the world.

Marketing – The added profits generated by the added sales due to product endorsements.

Distribution – Storage and shipping costs for different alternative warehouse locations.

Customer service – The net cost of returned merchandise, to be compared with the benefits of better customer relations.

1-34 (10-15 min.)

This problem can lead to a long or short discussion. Pointing out the problems can be done reasonably quickly. Formulating solutions can generate much discussion.

1. The appropriate accounting information presented correctly should be helpful to managers. It is clear that Belton does not regard the accounting performance reports as helpful. Some key problems are:

   - Belton refers to "their" budget, meaning that the budget belongs to the controller's department, not him and his department. Managers should help formulate the budget and should accept it as a reasonable target.
   - The controller's office shows up only when costs are over budget. Controllers should not be "policemen." They should be business advisors who provide continual assistance not occasional reprimand.

- Belton clearly does not understand the performance reports. An important role for the controller is education of managers in how to use accounting information.
- Belton believes the performance report has nothing to do with what happens on the shop floor. He may be right. Accounting reports often arrive too late and are not specific enough to be useful to front-line managers. If so, the reports should be changed or the results used differently.
- Paperwork takes time away from productive activity. This is especially a problem when the numbers have little value to those putting in the time.
- Budgeting is not taken seriously, so the numbers reported by Belton and his subordinates are not reliable.
- Things have gotten so bad that Belton had an attitude problem toward the controller's office. Palencia is meeting him for the first time, and he is already disrespectful of her.

2. Palencia has major problems. Her first task is to get the cooperation of Belton, his subordinates, and those like them in other departments. This will probably involve changing the accounting reports received by the line managers, and it will certainly involve changes in how these reports are presented and used. If the reports are not useful, she needs to find out why. Then she can change the reports so that the managers find them helpful. If they have useful information, she needs to show managers how they can use the information to make better decisions.

   Foremost, Palencia has to change the attitudes of the line managers toward the controller's department. This will take time, and will require some specific instances where the controller or her staff provide information that the managers perceive as useful. To do this, she may need to change the accounting system to produce better information, and she needs to teach her controller's department staff how to present information in a nonthreatening way.

There is no one solution to Palencia's problems. Different managers would handle it in different ways. If students have had experience, there will be many suggestions about how to proceed. For students with little experience, it may be sufficient to point out the variety of possible approaches.

1-35 (15-20 min.)

1. Because of the standard of confidentiality, the information in the geologist's report should not be revealed.
2. The standard of integrity would require one to reject the invitation.
3. This is a difficult ethical problem, one that deserves discussion. Two ethical standards apparently conflict. Confidentiality would lead to nondisclosure, provided there was no legal requirement to do so. But objectivity would indicate that the information about the additional losses should be used in making the earnings prediction. The authors think that objectivity should take precedence here, but others might disagree.
4. The standard of competence, and to some extent the standard of integrity, would lead one to research the tax law before deciding whether to deduct the item.

1-36 (10-15 min.)

Accountants become the information experts in many companies. In a company such as Marmon, with its many varied subsidiaries, the accounting system provides a link between the various operating companies. The accountants provide information about the operations on an indivdiual unit, and they also show how the units fit together as parts of the Marmon Group.

Management accountants should work together with managers to determine what information they would find useful. Then the accountants should help devise systems to produce that information, provided that its value is greater than its cost. As such, management accountants are information consultants to managers. Decisions are still the domain of managers, but the accountants provide advice to help managers make better decisions.

Once, accountants were considered "corporate cops," staff members who reported on the failings of managers. They were primarily scorekeepers, but when the score showed something awry, they became informants - carriers of bad news to corporate headquarters. Managers resented them. But today, good management accountants are allies of managers. They provide information that helps managers make better decisions, which makes the managers look good. Everyone is better off when management accountants focus on providing the information that aids management decisions.

1-37 (10-15 min.)

1. Line authority is held by those managers directly responsible for the production and sales of goods or services. Staff authority is held by persons who have an indirect responsibility for the production and sale of goods and services. Staff provide expertise, advice and support for line positions; line managers are directly responsible for achieving the basic objectives of the organization.

   Conflicts between line and staff can arise for many reasons, ranging from the types of people that are generally attracted to each type of position to their responsibilities in the organization. Among the reasons are:

   - Staff personnel tend to be younger, better educated, more professionally established.
   - Line managers see staff managers as threats to their authority.
   - Line managers are uncomfortable when they must rely on the knowledge and expertise of staff.
   - Line managers often think staff managers overstep their authority and have a narrow view of the world.
   - Staff managers often think line managers ignore their advice and resist their ideas.

2. Shores has a staff position, providing advice to the controller. His main conflicts will probably arise with the chief accountant and the managers under him. He reports to the chief accountant's superior, but he prepares reports that affect the operations in the chief accountant's area of responsibility.

   Shevlin is in a line position because she is an integral part of the company's main line of business, leasing equipment. Her main conflicts are likely to arise in areas such as requisitioning of equipment and billing of customers where she must rely on other departments over which she has no authority.

Paperman is in a staff position because accounting is not directly involved with sales or delivery of leasing services. He provides counsel and advice to all the line managers and most of the staff managers in the company. Conflicts may arise if he tries to exert authority instead of just giving advice or if the other managers ignore his advice.

Burgstahler is in a staff position and offers advice to most other managers in the company. Conflicts might arise if managers perceive her advertising of positions or screening of candidates as not fulfilling their needs, or if she tries to exert her preferences instead of the hiring department's preferences into the advertising and screening activities. Conflicts can also arise in the performance evaluation functions, where she may be enforcing an unpopular policy.

1-38 (10-15 min.)

1. Laughton's decisions violate standards of competence and integrity. Competence is violated because the most competent persons apparently are not being hired, jeopardizing the competence of the accounting department. Further, Laughton may be violating equal opportunity employment laws and regulations.

   Integrity requires an accountant to avoid conflicts of interest, but hiring the sons of personal friends certainly appears to be a conflict of interest. Such hiring was possibly for the personal gain of Laughton at the expense of the company. Further, this practice subverts the company's equal employment opportunity policy.

2. Myers's first step normally would be to discuss this situation with his boss. However, because the alleged unethical behavior is by his boss and Myers has already confronted him about it and been rebuffed, the next step seems warranted. This would involve going to Laughton's superior. (Alternately, some organizations have an individual, possibly called an ombudsman, to whom such concerns could be reported. Apparently Red Ball Berverage Company does not have such a person.) If the matter could not be resolved at that level, he should continue up the line until reaching Chiapello, the president. If equal employment opportunity is genuinely a company priority, Chiapello should be very concerned about Laughton's actions.

   What if the situation is not resolved to Myers's satisfaction after following the steps in the preceding paragraph? The final step is to go directly to the Board of Directors. If that is unsatisfactory, there may be no recourse but to resign, sending an explanatory memo to an appropriate high-level official of the company.

   Should Myers go to the press so that they will put on pressure to change the hiring practices? Such a step is generally not appropriate. It would put Myers in the position of violating the ethical standard of confidentiality. The only person external to the firm with whom it is appropriate to discuss this issue is a confidential objective advisor.

1-39 (20-30 min.)

1. In accordance with textbook Exhibit 1-10, "Standards of Ethical Conduct for Management Accountants," management accountants should not condone the commission of acts by their organization that violate the standards of ethical conduct. The specific standards that apply are:

   - competence. Management accountants have a responsibility to perform their professional duties in accordance with relevant laws and regulations.

   - confidentiality. Management accountants must refrain from disclosing confidential information unless legally obligated to do so. Rebecca Long may have a legal responsibility to take some action.

   - integrity. Management accountants have a responsibility to
     - refrain from either actively or passively subverting the attainment of the organization's legitimate and ethical objectives.
     - communicate favorable as well as unfavorable information and professional judgments or opinions.
     - refrain from engaging in or supporting any activity that would discredit the profession.

2. In accordance with Exhibit 1-10, the first alternative being considered by Rebecca Long, seeking the advice of her boss, is appropriate. To resolve an ethical conflict, the first step recommended is to discuss the problem with the immediate superior, unless it appears that this individual is involved in the conflict. In this case, it does not appear that Long's boss is involved.

   Releasing the information to the local newspaper would be an inappropriate course of action. Communication of confidential information to anyone outside of the company is inappropriate unless there is a legal obligation to do so, in which case Long should contact the proper authorities.

Contacting a member of the board of directors would be an inappropriate action at this time. In accordance with Exhibit 1-10, Long should report the conflict to successively higher levels within the organization and turn to the board of directors only if the problem is not resolved at lower levels.

3. Assuming there is no established company policy in place to resolve the conflict, Long should report the problem to successively higher levels of management until it is satisfactorily resolved. There is no requirement for Long to inform her immediate supervisor of this action, because he is involved in the conflict. Long could also clarify the situation by confidential discussion with an objective advisor to obtain an understanding of possible courses of action. If the conflict is not resolved after exhausting all courses of internal review, Long may have no other recourse than to resign from the organization and submit an informative memorandum to an appropriate representative of the organization.

1-40 (90 min. or more)

The purpose of this exercise is to learn about the practice of management accounting. Students often have the mistaken impression that accountants sit in the back room and prepare reports. These articles illustrate the varied skills and abilities that are necessary to be a successful management accountant.

The exercise also focuses on critical reading – identifying the most important points made in an article. It also shows how different students will focus on different aspects of each article. What one student considers important, others might think unimportant. Prioritizing the lessons will bring out differences in opinion, and create a need to form consensus from possibly conflicting views.

Finally, students should come away with a better understanding of why they are studying management accounting, whether they plan to be an accountant or simply a user of accounting information and services.

CHAPTER 2
Introduction to Cost Behavior and Cost-Volume Relationships

2-A1 (20-25 min.)

1. Let N = number of units

$$\begin{aligned} \text{Sales} &= \text{Fixed expenses} + \text{Variable expenses} + \text{Net income} \\ \$1.00\,N &= \$3{,}000 + \$.80\,N + 0 \\ \$.20\,N &= \$3{,}000 \\ N &= 15{,}000 \text{ units} \end{aligned}$$

Let S = sales in dollars

$$\begin{aligned} S &= \$3{,}000 + .80\,S + 0 \\ .20\,S &= \$3{,}000 \\ S &= \$15{,}000 \end{aligned}$$

Alternatively, the 15,000 units may be multiplied by the $1.00 to obtain $15,000.

In formula form:

In units

$$\frac{\text{Fixed costs} + \text{Net income}}{\text{Contribution margin per unit}} = \frac{(\$3{,}000+0)}{\$.20} = 15{,}000$$

In dollars

$$\frac{\text{Fixed costs} + \text{Net income}}{\text{Contribution margin percent}} = \frac{(\$3{,}000+0)}{.20} = \$15{,}000$$

2. The quick way: (18,000 - 15,000) x $.20 = $600

Compare income statements:

	Break-even Point	Increment	Total
Volume in units	15,000	3,000	18,000
Sales	$15,000	$3,000	$18,000
Deduct expenses:			
Variable	12,000	2,400	14,400
Fixed	3,000	—	3,000
Total expenses	$15,000	$2,400	$17,400
Effect on net income	$ 0	$ 600	$ 600

3. Total fixed expenses would be $3,000 + $576 = $3,576

$$\frac{(\$3{,}576)}{.20} = 17{,}880 \text{ units}; \quad \frac{(\$3{,}576)}{.20} = \$17{,}880 \text{ sales}$$

or 17,880 x $1.00 = $17,880 sales

4. New contribution margin is $.18 per unit; $3,000 ÷ $.18 = 16,667 units

16,667 units x $1.00 = $16,667 in sales

5. The quick way: (18,000 - 15,000) x $.16 = $480. On a graph, the slope of the total cost line would have a kink upward, beginning at the break-even point.

2-A2 (20-30 min.)

The following format is only one of many ways to present a solution. This situation is really a demonstration of "sensitivity analysis," whereby a basic solution is tested to see how much it is affected by changes in critical factors. Much discussion can ensue, particularly about the final three changes.

The basic contribution margin per revenue mile is $1.50 - $1.30 = $.20

	(1)	(2)	(3) (1) x (2)	(4)	(5) (3) - (4)
	Revenue Miles Sold	Contribution Margin Per Revenue Mile	Total Contribution Margin	Fixed Expenses	Net Income
1.	800,000	$.20	$160,000	$120,000	$ 40,000
2. (a)	880,000	.20	176,000	120,000	56,000
(b)	800,000	.35	280,000	120,000	160,000
(c)	800,000	.07	56,000	120,000	(64,000)
(d)	800,000	.20	160,000	132,000	28,000
(e)	840,000	.17	142,800	120,000	22,800
(f)	720,000	.275	198,000	120,000	78,000
(g)	840,000	.20	168,000	132,000	36,000

2-B1 (15-20 min.)

1. $$\frac{(\$6{,}000)}{(\$20 - \$15)} = \frac{(\$6{,}000)}{\$5} = 1{,}200 \text{ units}$$

2. Contribution margin: $$\frac{(\$40{,}000 - \$30{,}000)}{(\$40{,}000)} = 25\%$$

$$\$7{,}500 \div 25\% = \$30{,}000$$

3. $$\frac{(\$37{,}000 + \$7{,}000)}{(\$30 - \$14)} = \frac{(\$44{,}000)}{\$16} = 2{,}750 \text{ units}$$

4. $(\$50{,}000 - \$20{,}000)(110\%) = \$33{,}000$ contribution margin;
$\$33{,}000 - \$20{,}000 = \$13{,}000$

5. New contribution margin: $\$40 - (\$30 - 20\% \text{ of } \$30)$
$= \$40 - (\$30 - \$6) = \$16$;

New fixed expenses: $\$80{,}000 \times 110\% = \$88{,}000$;

$$\frac{(\$88{,}000 + \$24{,}000)}{\$16} = \frac{(\$112{,}000)}{\$16} = 7{,}000 \text{ units}$$

2-B2 (15-25 min.)

1. 176 x ($30 - $10) - $2,400 = $3,520 - $2,400 = $1,120

2. a. 198 x ($30 - $10) - $2,400 = $3,960 - $2,400 = $1,560
   or (22 x $20) + $1,120 = $440 + $1,120 = $1,560

   b. 176 x ($30 - $11) - $2,400 = $3,344 - $2,400 = $944
   or $1,120 - ($1 x 176) = $944

   c. $1,120 - $200 = $920

   d. [(9.5 x 22) x ($30 - $10)] - ($2,400 + $300) = $4,180 - $2,700 = $1,480

   e. [(7 x 22) x ($33 - $10)] - $2,400 = $3,542 - $2,400 = $1,142

2-1 This is a good characterization of cost behavior. Identifying cost drivers will identify activities that affect costs, and the relationship between a cost driver and costs specifies how the cost driver influences costs.

2-2 Examples of variable costs are the costs of merchandise, materials, parts, supplies, sales commissions, and many types of labor. Examples of fixed costs are real estate taxes, real estate insurance, many executive salaries, and space rentals.

2-3 Fixed costs, by definition, do not vary in total as volume changes. However, if fixed costs are allocated or spread over volume on a per-unit-of-volume basis, they decline *per unit* as volume increases.

2-4 Yes. Fixed costs per unit change as the volume of activity changes. Therefore, for fixed cost per unit to be meaningful, you must identify an appropriate volume level. In contrast, total fixed costs are independent of volume level.

2-5 No. Cost behavior is much more complex than a simple dichotomy into fixed or variable. For example, some costs are not linear, and some have more than one cost driver. Division of costs into fixed and variable categories is a useful simplification, but it is not a complete description of cost behavior in most situations.

2-6 No. The relevant range pertains to both variable and fixed costs. Outside a relevant range, some variable costs, such as fuel consumed, may behave differently per unit of activity volume.

2-7 The major simplifying assumption is linearity of costs and revenues with respect to a single measure of volume.

2-8 The same cost may be regarded as variable in one decision situation and fixed in a second decision situation. For example, fuel costs are fixed with respect to the addition of one more passenger on a bus because the added passenger has almost no effect on total fuel costs. In contrast, total fuel costs are variable in relation to the decision of whether to add one more mile to a city bus route.

2-9 No. Contribution margin is the excess of sales over all *variable* costs, not *fixed* costs. It may be expressed as a total, as a ratio, as a percentage, or per unit.

2-10 A "break-even analysis" does not describe the real value of a CVP analysis, which shows profit at any volume of activity within the relevant range. The break-even point is often only incidental in studies of cost-volume relationships.

2-11 No. break-even points can vary greatly within an industry. For example, Rolls Royce has a much lower break-even volume than does Chrysler (or Ford, Toyota, and other high-volume auto producers).

2-12 No. The CVP technique you choose is a matter of personal preference or convenience. The equation technique is the most general, but it may not be the easiest to apply. All three techniques yield the same results.

2-13 Three ways of lowering a break-even point, holding other factors constant, are: decrease total fixed costs, increase selling prices, and decrease unit variable costs.

2-14 No. In addition to being quicker, incremental analysis is simpler. This is important because it keeps the analysis from being cluttered by irrelevant and potentially confusing data.

2-15 Yes. Computers readily display various combinations of changes in selling prices, unit variable costs, fixed costs, and target profits.

2-16 Operating leverage is a firm's ratio of fixed to variable costs. A highly leveraged company has relatively high fixed costs and low variable costs. Such a firm is risky because small changes in volume lead to large changes in income.

2-17 No. In retailing, the contribution margin is likely to be smaller than the gross margin. For instance, sales commissions are deducted in computing the contribution margin but not the gross margin.

2-18 No. CVP relationships pertain to both profit-seeking and nonprofit organizations. In particular, managers of nonprofit organizations must deal with tradeoffs between variable and fixed costs. To many government department managers, lump-sum budget appropriations are regarded as the available revenues.

2-19 Contribution margin could be lower because of a decline in the proportion of the product bearing the higher unit contribution margin.

2-20

$$\text{Target income before income taxes} = \frac{\text{Target after-tax net income}}{1 - \text{tax rate}}$$

2-21

$$\text{Change in net income} = \text{Change in volume in units} \times \text{Contribution margin per unit} \times (1 - \text{tax rate})$$

2-22 No. The individual is confused. Definitions of variable and fixed cost behavior are based on *total* cost behavior, not *unit* cost behavior.

2-23 (5-10 min.)

1. Contribution margin = \$900,000 - \$500,000 = \$400,000
   Net income = \$400,000 - \$275,000 = \$125,000

2. Variable expenses = \$800,000 - \$350,000 = \$450,000
   Fixed expenses = \$350,000 - \$ 80,000 = \$270,000

3. Sales = \$600,000 + \$340,000 = \$940,000
   Net income = \$340,000 - \$260,000 = \$ 80,000

2-24 (10-20 min.)

1.

$$
\begin{aligned}
d &= c(a - b) \\
\$720,000 &= 120,000(\$30 - b) \\
b &= \$24 \\
f &= d - e \\
&= \$720,000 - \$640,000 = \$80,000
\end{aligned}
$$

2.

$$
\begin{aligned}
d &= c(a - b) \\
&= 100,000(\$10 - \$6) = \$400,000 \\
f &= d - e \\
&= \$400,000 - \$320,000 = \$80,000
\end{aligned}
$$

3.

$$
\begin{aligned}
c &= d \div (a - b) \\
&= \$100,000 \div \$5 = 20,000 \text{ units} \\
e &= d - f \\
&= \$100,000 - \$15,000 = \$85,000
\end{aligned}
$$

4.

$$
\begin{aligned}
d &= c(a - b) \\
&= 70,000(\$30 - \$20) \\
&= \$700,000 \\
e &= d - f \\
&= \$700,000 - \$12,000 = \$688,000
\end{aligned}
$$

5.

$$
\begin{aligned}
d &= c(a - b) \\
\$160,000 &= 80,000(a - \$9) \\
a &= \$11 \\
f &= d - e \\
&= \$160,000 - \$120,000 = \$40,000
\end{aligned}
$$

2-25 (10 min.)

1.

$$\text{Let TR} = \text{total revenue}$$
$$TR - .20(TR) - \$40,000,000 = 0$$
$$.80(TR) = \$40,000,000$$
$$TR = \$50,000,000$$

2. Daily revenue per patient = $50,000,000 ÷ 40,000 = $1,250. This may appear high, but it includes the room charge plus additional charges for drugs, x-rays, and so forth.

2-26 (15 min.)

1.

	100% Full	50% Full
Room revenue @ $50	$3,650,000 [a]	$1,825,000 [b]
Variable costs @ $10	730,000	365,000
Contribution margin	2,920,000	1,460,000
Fixed costs	1,600,000	1,600,000
Net income (loss)	$1,320,000	$ (140,000)

[a] 200 x 365 = 73,000 rooms per year
73,000 x $50 = $3,650,000

[b] 50% of $3,650,000 = $1,825,000

2.

$$\text{Let N} = \text{number of rooms}$$
$$\$50N - \$10N - \$1,600,000 = 0$$
$$N = \$1,600,000 \div \$40 = 40,000 \text{ rooms}$$
$$\text{Percentage occupancy} = 40,000 \div 73,000 = 54.8\%$$

2-27 (15 min.)

1. $28. To compute this, let X be the variable cost that generates $1 million in profits:

$$
\begin{aligned}
(\$48 - X) \times 800{,}000 - \$15{,}000{,}000 &= \$1{,}000{,}000 \\
(\$48 - X) &= (\$1{,}000{,}000 + \$15{,}000{,}000) \div 800{,}000 \\
\$48 - X &= \$160 \div 8 = \$20 \\
X &= \$48 - \$20 = \$28
\end{aligned}
$$

2. Loss of $600,000:

$$
\begin{aligned}
&(\$48 - \$30) \times 800{,}000 - \$15{,}000{,}000 \\
&= (\$18 \times 800{,}000) - \$15{,}000{,}000 \\
&= \$14{,}400{,}000 - \$15{,}000{,}000 \\
&= (\$600{,}000)
\end{aligned}
$$

2-28 (15-20 min.)

1. Let N = number of rooms per month

$$\$65N - \$15N - \$350{,}000 = \$0$$
$$N = \$350{,}000 \div \$50$$
$$N = 7{,}000 \text{ per month or } 233 \text{ per day}$$

2.

$$\$65N - \$15N - \$350{,}000 = \$120{,}000$$
$$N = \$470{,}000 \div \$50$$
$$N = 9{,}400 \text{ per month}$$

3. Let P = room rate per day

Other contribution margin = $70,000 + $40,000 + $32,400 + $30,000
= $172,400

$$[.80(400) \times 30 \times P] + \$172{,}400 - [.80(400) \times 30 \times \$15] - \$350{,}000 = \$120{,}000$$
$$9{,}600P + \$172{,}400 - \$144{,}000 - \$350{,}000 = \$120{,}000$$
$$9{,}600P = \$321{,}600$$
$$P = \$33.50$$

The latter answer indicates how hotels frequently may be inclined to reduce room rates if they can generate contribution margins from other hotel activities. The most prominent example is gambling conducted by hotels in Las Vegas and Atlantic City.

2-29 (15-20 min.)

1. Let R = pints of raspberries and 2R = pints of strawberries
sales - variable expenses - fixed expenses = zero net income

$$\$1.00(2R) + \$1.35(R) - \$.65(2R) - \$.85(R) - \$14,400 = 0$$
$$\$2.00R + \$1.35R - \$1.30R - \$.85R - \$14,400 = 0$$
$$\$1.2R - \$14,400 = 0$$

R = 12,000 pints of raspberries
2R = 24,000 pints of strawberries

2. Let S = pints of strawberries
($1.00 - $.65) x S - $14,400 = 0
.35S - $14,400 = 0
S = 41,143 pints of strawberries

3. Let R = pints of raspberries
($1.35 - $.85) x R - $14,400 = 0
$.50R - $14,400 = 0
R = 28,800 pints of raspberries

2-30 (10 min.)

1. $$\$.50N - \$.40N - \$6,000 = \frac{\$288}{1 - .2}$$

$$\$.10N = \$6,000 + \frac{\$288}{.8}$$

$.10N = $6,000 + $360
N = $6,360 ÷ $.10 = 63,600 units

2. $$\$.50N - \$.40N - \$6,000 = \frac{\$480}{1 - .2}$$

$$\$.10N = \$6,000 + \frac{\$480}{.8}$$

$.10N = $6,000 + $600
N = $6,600 ÷ $.10 = 66,000 units

2-31 (15 min.)

Several variations of the following general approach are possible:

$$\text{Sales - Variable expenses - Fixed expenses} = \frac{\text{Target after-tax net income}}{\text{1 - tax rate}}$$

$$S - .7S - \$440{,}000 = \frac{(\$42{,}000)}{(1 - .4)}$$

$.3S = \$440{,}000 + \$70{,}000$

$S = \$510{,}000 \div .3 = \$1{,}700{,}000$

Check:		
	Sales	$1,700,000
	Variable expenses (70%)	1,190,000
	Contribution margin	510,000
	Fixed expenses	440,000
	Income before taxes	$ 70,000
	Income taxes	28,000
	Net income	$ 42,000

2-32 (10-15 min.)

The answer is $1,320,000.

Refined analysis:

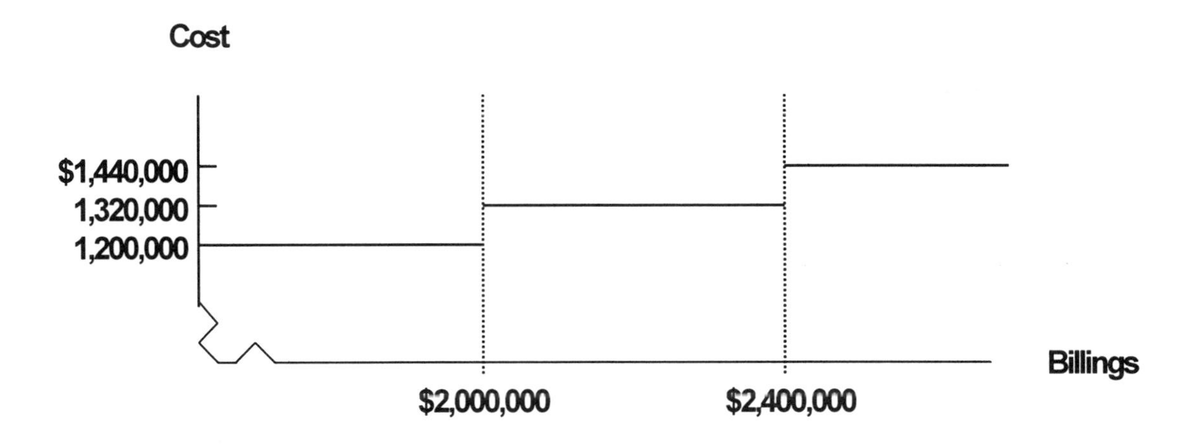

Practical analysis:

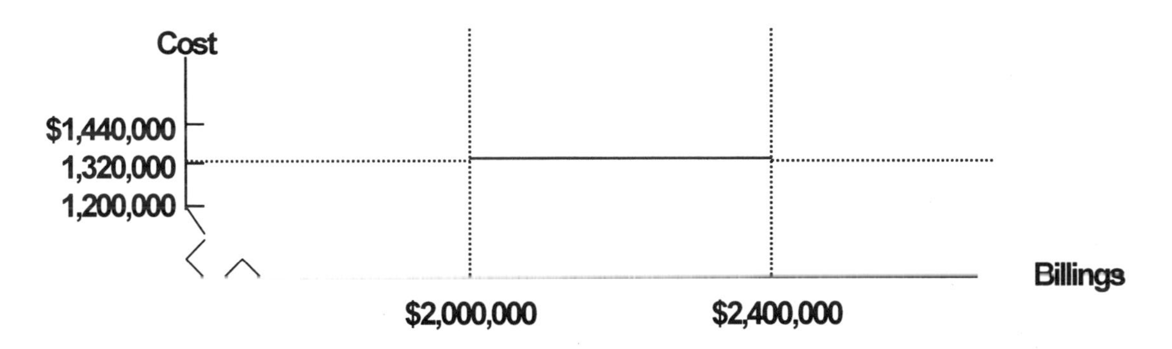

2-33 (15-20 min.)

1.

		Film	Refreshments	Total
Revenue from admissions		$2,250	$270 [b]	$2,520
Variable costs		1,125 [a]	162 [c]	1,287
Contribution margin		$1,125	$108	$1,233
Fixed costs:				
Auditorium rental	$330			
Labor	400			730
Operating income				$ 503

[a] .50 x $2,250 = $1,125
[b] .12 x $2,250 = $270
[c] .60 x $ 270 = $162

Some labor might be exclusively devoted to refreshments. Labor might be allocated, but such a discussion is not the major point of this chapter.

2.

		Film	Refreshments	Total
Revenue from admissions		$1,350	$162 [b]	$1,512
Variable costs		750 [a]	97 [c]	847
Contribution margin		$ 600	$ 65	$ 665
Fixed costs:				
Auditorium rental	$330			
Labor	400			730
Operating income (loss)				$ (65)

[a] Minimum is $750
[b] .12 x $1,350 = $162
[c] .60 x $162 = $97

3. The risk is shifted completely to the movie producer, whereas ordinarily a great deal of the risk is borne by the theater owner. The owner is assured of a specified income; the producer then reaps the rewards or bears the losses.

2-34 (15 min.)

1. Let X = amount of additional fixed costs for advertising

(1,100,000 x £13) +£300,000 -.30(1,100,000 x £13) - (£8,000,000 + X) = 0

£14,300,000 + £300,000 - £4,290,000 - £8,000,000 - X = 0

X = £14,600,000 - £12,290,000

X = £2,310,000

2. Let Y = number of seats sold

£13Y + £300,000 - .30(£13)Y - £9,000,000 = £500,000

£9.10Y = £9,200,000

Y = 1,010,989 seats

2-35 (20-30 min.)

Many shortcuts are available, but this solution uses the equation technique.

1. Let N = meals sold

Sales - Variable expenses - Fixed expenses = Profit before taxes

\$18N - \$9.60N - \$21,000 = \$8,400

N = \$29,400 ÷ \$8.40

N = 3,500 meals

2. \$18N - \$9.60N - \$21,000 = \$0

N = \$21,000 ÷ \$8.40

N = 2,500 meals

3. \$22N - \$11.50N - \$29,400 = \$8,400

N = \$37,800 ÷ \$10.50

N = 3,600 meals

4. Profit = $22(3,150) - $11.50(3,150) - $29,400
   Profit = $3,675

5. Profit = $22(3,450) -$11.50(3,450) - ($29,400 + $2,000)
   Profit = $36,225 - $31,400
   Profit = $4,825, an increase of $1,150.

   A shortcut, incremental approach follows:

Increase in contribution margin, 300 x $10.50 =	$3,150
Increase in fixed costs	2,000
Increase in profit	$1,150

2-36 (25-30 min.)

This problem raises more issues than are apparent at first glance. For instance, unless Andre is very wealthy and generous, he probably would not regard the five barbers as fixed costs over the entire possible range of volume. In short, if business declines precipitously, barbers would be discharged or laid off. Note how the later requirements demonstrate the effects of various mixes of variable and fixed costs on risks.

1. Selling price-Unit variable costs =Contribution margin

Selling price		Unit variable costs		Contribution margin
$12	-	0	=	$12

2. Fixed expenses (annual)

Barbers' salaries (5 x $9.90 x 40 x 50)	$ 99,000
Rent and other fixed expenses (12 x $1,750)	21,000
	$120,000

$$\text{B.E. Point} = \frac{\text{Total fixed expenses}}{\text{Contribution margin}} = \frac{(\$120{,}000)}{\$12} = 10{,}000 \text{ haircuts}$$

3. Two valid approaches:

(a)

Revenue (20,000 x $12)	$240,000
Fixed expenses	120,000
Operating income	$120,000

(b) Haircuts in excess of break-even point:

20,000 - 10,000 = 10,000 haircuts

10,000 haircuts @ $12 = $120,000

4. Even though fixed costs decline, the break-even point rises:

Contribution margin per haircut = $12 - $6 = $6

Fixed costs = (5 x $4 x 40 x 50) + (12 x $1,750) = $61,000

$$\text{Break-even point} = \frac{(\$61{,}000)}{(\$6.00)} = 10{,}167 \text{ haircuts}$$

5. Contribution margin = $12.00 - $7.00 = $5.00

Fixed costs = $21,000 given

$$\text{Break-even point} = \frac{(\$21{,}000)}{\$5} = 4{,}200 \text{ haircuts}$$

6.

Revenue (20,000 x $12.00)	$240,000
Variable expenses @ $7.00	140,000
Contribution margin	$100,000
Fixed expenses	21,000
Operating income	$ 79,000

Thus, if volume is 20,000 haircuts, the new arrangement would increase the barbers' compensation from $99,000 to $140,000 and decrease operating income from $120,000 to $79,000. Note the risk-sharing here of the sales commission plan. Generally, the lower the fixed costs, the lower the risks, but the lower the rewards. If the volume declines markedly, Andre would still have an operating income as long as the total volume exceeds 4,200 haircuts. However, if volume soars to 20,000, Andre's operating income would be less than that of the hourly wage plan.

7. Let X = rate of commission

$$
\begin{aligned}
20{,}000(\$12) - \$120{,}000 &= 20{,}000(\$12) - 20{,}000(\$12)X - \$21{,}000 \\
\$240{,}000 - \$120{,}000 &= \$240{,}000 - \$240{,}000X - \$21{,}000 \\
\$240{,}000X &= \$120{,}000 - \$21{,}000 \\
\$240{,}000X &= \$99{,}000 \\
X &= \frac{(\$99{,}000)}{(\$240{,}000)} = 41.25\%,
\end{aligned}
$$

or 41.25% x $12 = $4.95 per haircut

Proof:

Contribution margin: $12.00 - $4.95 = $7.05

Operating income: (20,000 x $7.05) - $21,000 = $120,000

2-37 (10-15 min.) Amounts are in millions.

Net sales (1.10 x $24,002)		$26,402
Variable costs:		
Cost of goods sold (1.10 x $20,442)		22,486
Contribution margin		3,916
Fixed costs		
Selling, administrative, and general expenses	$2,265	
Interest expense	277	
Total fixed costs		2,542
Operating income		$ 1,374

The percentage increase in operating income would be ($1,374 ÷ $1,018) - 1 = .35 or 35%, compared with a 10% increase in sales. The contribution margin would increase by 10% or .10 x ($24,002 - $20,442) = $356 million. Because fixed costs would not change (assuming the new volume is within the relevant range), operating income would also increase by $356 million, from $1,018 million to $1,374 million. If all costs had been variable, costs would have increased by an additional .10 x $2,542 = $254 million, making operating income $1,374 - $254 = $1,120 million, a 10% increase over the 1997 operating income of $1,018 million. Because of the existence of fixed costs, the percentage increase in operating income will exceed the percentage increase in sales.

2-38 (15-25 min.)

1.

Average revenue per person		$4.00 + 3($1.50) = $8.50
Total revenue, 200 @ $8.50 =		$1,700
Rent		800
Total available for prizes & operating income		$ 900

The church could award $900 and break even.

2.

Number of persons		100	200	300
Total revenue @ $8.50		$ 850	$1,700	$2,550
Fixed costs				
Rent	$800			
Prizes	900	1,700	1,700	1,700
Operating income (loss)		$ (850)	$ 0	$ 850

Note how "leverage" works. Being highly leveraged means having relatively high fixed costs. In this case, there are no variable costs. Therefore, the revenue is the same as the contribution margin. As volume departs from the break-even point, operating income is affected at a significant rate of $8.50 per person.

3.

Number of persons		100	200	300
Revenue		$ 850	$1,700	$2,550
Variable costs		200	400	600
Contribution margin		$ 650	$1,300	$1,950
Fixed costs:				
Rent	$400			
Prizes	900	1,300	1,300	1,300
Operating income		$ (650)	$ 0	$ 650

Note how the risk is lower because of less leverage. Fixed costs are less, and some of the risk has been shifted to the hotel. Note too that lower risk brings lower rewards and lower punishments. The income and losses are $650 instead of the $850 shown in part (2).

2-39 (15-25 min.)

1.

Let N	=	number of hamburgers per month
$1.10N	=	$.70N + $1,560
$.40N	=	$1,560
N	=	3,900 per month, or 3,900 ÷ 30 = 130 per day

2. Multiply the answers in (1) by $1.10

3,900 x $1.10 = $4,290 per month
130 x $1.10 = $143 per day

3. Hamburgers per month = (3,600 ÷ 2) = 1,800

Revenue per month, 1,800 x $1.10	$1,980
Variable expenses, 1,800 x $.70	1,260
Contribution margin	$ 720
Fixed expenses	1,560
Operating income (loss)	$ (840)

4. Contribution margin on extra beers:

Per day, 60 x $.60 = $36
Per month, 30 x 36 = $1,080

Income would increase by $1,080, which more than offsets the $840 loss on the hamburger operation, making the net increase in operating income $1,080 - $840 = $240.

5.		
	Operating loss on hamburgers	$(840)
	Desired contribution margin on extra beers	840
	Overall effect on operating income	$ 0

Desired number of extra beers to provide overall effect on operating income of zero:

Per month = $840 ÷ .60 = 1,400 beers
Per day = 1,400 ÷ 30 = 46.7 beers

Or, desired contribution margin per day is 840 ÷ 30 = $28
Daily number of beers = $28 ÷ $.60 = 46.7

Therefore, if Andy believed that the extra beers sold amounted to almost 47 daily instead of 60, the hamburger operation would have provided an overall effect on operating income of zero.

2-40 (40 min.)

1. Let N = the number of people to be admitted for the season

Revenue:

Rights for concession	$50,000
Admissions	$1.00N
Percentage of bets	10% of $27N = $2.70N

Total revenue = $50,000 + $3.70N

Expense:

Fixed costs:

Wages of cashiers	$ 160,000
Commissioner's salary	20,000
Maintenance	20,000
Utilities	30,000
Other expense	90,000
Purses	810,000
Total fixed costs	$1,130,000

Variable costs:

Parking is $6.00 per car or $1.00 per person
(6 persons attend for each car, so $6.00 ÷ 6 = $1.00)

Total expense = $1,130,000 + $1.00N

(a) Break-even point:

$$\$50,000 + \$3.70N - \$1,130,000 - \$1.00N = 0$$
$$\$2.70N = \$1,080,000$$
$$N = 400,000 \text{ people}$$

(b) Desired operating profit $270,000:

$$\$50,000 + \$3.70N - \$1,130,000 - \$1.00N = \$270,000$$
$$\$2.70N = \$1,350,000$$
$$N = 500,000 \text{ people}$$

2. Previous level of attendance 600,000 people
20% increase in attendance 720,000 people
Total bets: 720,000 x $27 $19,440,000

Revenue:		
Concession		$ 50,000
Admission		None
Percentage of bets (10% x $19,440,000)		1,944,000
Total revenue		$1,994,000
Expense:		
Fixed	$1,130,000	
Variable ($1.00 x 720,000)	720,000	$1,850,000
Operating profit		$ 144,000

3. The purses are doubled:

Previous fixed expense	$1,130,000
Additional purse money	810,000
New fixed expense	$1,940,000

Variable expense, $1.00 per person
Revenue, $50,000 + $3.70N

$$\$50{,}000 + \$3.70N - \$1{,}940{,}000 - \$1.00N = 0$$
$$\$2.70N = \$1{,}890{,}000$$
$$N = 700{,}000 \text{ people}$$

2-41 (30-40 min.)

1. Fixed costs:

Depreciation ($13,500 - $6,000) ÷ 3 =	$2,500
Insurance	700
Total fixed costs	$3,200
Variable costs:	
Gas, $1.70 ÷ 17 miles	$.10
Oil, $30.00 ÷ 3,000 miles	.01
Maintenance, $240 ÷ 6,000 miles	.04
Variable cost per mile	$.15

Let N = Number of miles to break-even
Revenue - Variable costs - Fixed costs = 0
$.23N - $.15N - $3,200 = 0
N = $3,200 ÷ $.08 = 40,000 miles

2. An "equitable" mileage rate might be based on the actual number of business-related miles expected. The days not on the road are:

	Days
Weekends, 52 x 2	104
Vacation	10
Holidays	6
Home office	15
Not on the road	135
On the road, 365 - 135 =	230
Miles, 230 x 120 =	27,600

Let X = Reimbursement per mile to break even
27,600X = $3,200 + 27,600($.15)
27,600X - $3,200 - $4,140 = 0
X = $7,340 ÷ 27,600 = $.266

Therefore, a rate of $.27 seems more equitable than $.23.

2-42 (15-20 min.) Note in requirements 2 and 3 how the percentage declines exceed the 15% budget reduction.

1. Let N = number of persons

Revenue - variable expenses - fixed expenses = 0

$$
\begin{aligned}
\$900{,}000 - \$5{,}000N - \$290{,}000 &= 0 \\
5{,}000N &= \$900{,}000 - \$290{,}000 \\
N &= \$610{,}000 \div \$5{,}000 \\
N &= 122 \text{ persons}
\end{aligned}
$$

2. Revenue is now .85($900,000) = $765,000

$$
\begin{aligned}
\$765{,}000 - \$5{,}000N - \$290{,}000 &= 0 \\
\$5{,}000N &= \$765{,}000 - \$290{,}000 \\
N &= \$475{,}000 \div \$5{,}000 \\
N &= 95 \text{ persons}
\end{aligned}
$$

Percentage drop: (122 - 95) ÷ 122 = 22.1%

3. Let y = supplement per person

$$
\begin{aligned}
\$765{,}000 - 122y - \$290{,}000 &= 0 \\
122y &= \$765{,}000 - \$290{,}000 \\
y &= \$475{,}000 \div 122 \\
y &= \$3{,}893
\end{aligned}
$$

Percentage drop: ($5,000 - $3,893) ÷ $5,000 = 22.1%

Regarding requirements 2 and 3, note that the cut in service can be measured by a formula:

$$\%\text{ cut in service} = \frac{\%\text{ budget change}}{\%\text{ variable cost}}$$

The variable-cost ratio is $610,000 ÷ $900,000 = 67.8%

$$\%\text{ cut in service} = \frac{15\%}{67.8\%} = 22.1\%$$

2-43 (20 - 30 min.)

1. 1996 revenue = 61,000 million x .681 x $.1310 = $5,442 million
   1995 revenue = 61,000 million x .656 x $.1251 = $5,006 million

2. a) $3,000 million ÷ ($.1310 - $.05) = 37,037 million revenue passenger miles
   37,037 ÷ 61,000 = 60.7 % load factor

   b) $3,000 million ÷ (.1251 - $.05) = 39,947 million revenue passenger miles
   39,947 ÷ 61,000 = 65.5% load factor

3. $3,400 million ÷ ($.13 - $.05) = 42,500 million revenue passenger miles
   42,500 ÷ 61,000 = 69.7% load factor

2-44 (15-20 min.) Answers are in millions.

1.

Sales		$15,968
Variable costs:		
Variable costs of goods sold	$6,526	
Variable other operating expenses	2,086	8,612
Contribution margin		$ 7,356

Contribution margin percentage = $7,356 ÷ $15,968 = 46%

The contribution margin is sales less all variable costs, while gross margin is sales less cost of goods sold. The variable costs will include part of the costs of goods sold and also part of the other operating costs. Note that contribution margin can be either larger than or smaller than the gross margin. If most of the cost of goods sold and a good portion of the other operating costs are variable, then variable costs may exceed the cost of goods sold, and the contribution margin will be smaller than the gross margin, as is the case for Kodak. However, if a large portion of both the cost of goods sold and the other expenses are fixed, cost of goods sold may exceed the variable cost, resulting in the contribution margin exceeding the gross margin.

2. Predicted sales increase = $15,968 x .10 = $1,596.8
Additional contribution margin = $1,596.8 x .46 = $734.5
Fixed costs do not change
Predicted 1997 operating income = $1,556 + $734.5 = $2,290.5
Percentage increase in operating income = $734.5 ÷ $1,556 = 47%

3. Assumptions include:
- Expenses can be classified into variable and fixed categories that completely describe their behavior within the relevant range.
- Costs and revenues are linear within the relevant range.
- 1997 volume is within the relevant range.
- Efficiency and productivity are unchanged.
- Sales mix is unchanged.
- Changes in inventory levels are insignificant.

2-45 (20-30 min.)

Variable costs per box are ($.14 + $.22 + $.09), ($.14 + $.14 + $.09), and ($.14 + $.05 + $.09), or $.45, $.37, and $.28, respectively.

1. Let N = volume level in boxes that would earn same profit
$8,000 + $.45N = $11,200 + $.37N
$.08N = $3,200
N = 40,000 boxes

2. As volume increases, the more expensive models would generate more profits. Compare the regular and super models:

Let N = volume level in boxes that would earn same profit
$20,200 + $.28N = $11,200 + .37N
$.09N = $9,000
N = 100,000 boxes

Therefore, the decision rule is as shown below.

Anticipated Annual Sales Between	Use Model
0 - 40,000	E5
40,000 - 100,000	R12
100,000 and above	S30

The decision rule places volume well within the capacity of each model.

3. No, management cannot use theater capacity or average boxes sold because the number of seats per theater does not indicate the number of patrons attending nor the popcorn-buying habits in different geographic locations. Each theater may have a different "boxes sold per seat" average with significant variations. The decision rule does not take into account variations in demand that could affect model choice.

2-46 (25 min.)

1. Break-even = \$950 million ÷ (\$70 million - \$45 million)
   = \$950 million ÷ \$25 million = 38 airplanes

   Sales = \$70 million x 38 = \$2.660 billion

2. There are two efficient ways to compute the profit:
   a) (42 - 38) x \$25 million = \$100 million
   b) (42 x \$25 million) - \$950 million = \$100 million

3. Operating profit = [42 x (\$70 million - \$43 million)] - \$1,034 million
   = (42 x \$27 million) - \$1,034 million = \$100 million

   Break-even = \$1,034 million ÷ (\$70 million - \$43 million)
   = \$1,034 million ÷ \$27 million = 38.3 airplanes

   Although the change in cost structure does not change the operating profit at the projected level of sales, the break-even point increases from 38 to 38.3 airplanes. The additional fixed costs add to the risk of not breaking even. However, it also adds to the potential rewards if sales exceed the projected level of 42 airplanes.

4. Break-even = \$950 million ÷ [\$70 million - (1.1 x \$45 million)]
   = \$950 million ÷ \$20.5 million
   = 46.3 airplanes

   Notice the substantial increase in the break-even point with a 10% increase in variable costs. Boeing might want an escalation clause in its contracts so that the price charged for airplanes increases with cost increases. They might want to enter into long-term contracts with suppliers to limit the possibilities for cost increases. Finally, they might want to undertake changes in their production process to limit cost increases.

2-47 (20-25 min.)

1. Net income (loss) = 250,000($3) + 125,000($4) - $1,320,000
= $750,000 + $500,000 - $1,320,000
= ($70,000)

2. Let V = number of units of veal to break even (V)
2V = number of units of chicken to break even (C)

Total contribution margin - fixed expenses = zero net income

$$
\begin{aligned}
\$4V + \$3(2V) - \$1{,}320{,}000 &= 0 \\
\$10V &= \$1{,}320{,}000 \\
V &= 132{,}000 \\
2V &= 264{,}000 = C
\end{aligned}
$$

The break-even point is 132,000 units of veal plus 264,000 units of chicken, a grand total of 396,000 units.

3. If veal, break-even would be $1,320,000 ÷ $4 = 330,000 units.
If chicken, break-even would be $1,320,000 ÷ $3 = 440,000 units.

Note that as the mixes change from 1 veal to 2 chicken, to 0 chicken to 1 veal, and to 1 chicken to 0 veal, the break-even point changes from 396,000 to 330,000 to 440,000.

4. Net income (loss) = 297,000($3) + 99,000($4) - $1,320,000
= $891,000 + $396,000 - $1,320,000
= ($33,000)

Let V = number of units of veal to break even (V)
3V = number of units of chicken to break even (C)

Total contribution margin - fixed expenses = zero net income

$4V + $3(3V) - $1,320,000 = 0
$13V = $1,320,000
V = 101,538
3V = 304,615 = C

The major lesson of this problem is that changes in sales mix change break-even points and net incomes. The break-even point is 101,538 units of veal plus 304,615 units of chicken, a total of 406,153 units. Thus, the unfavorable change in mix results in a net loss of $33,000 at the old total break-even level of 396,000 units. In short, the break-even level is higher because the sales mix is less profitable when chicken represents a higher proportion of sales. In this example, the budgeted and actual total sales in number of units were identical, but the proportion of product having the higher contribution margin declined.

2-48 (20-25 min.)

1. Let S = number of self-pay patients (S)
4S = number of other patients (G)

$$\begin{aligned}
\$1{,}000S + \$800(4S) - \$600S - \$600(4S) - \$48{,}000{,}000 &= 0\\
\$1{,}000S + \$3{,}200S - \$600S - \$2{,}400S &= \$48{,}000{,}000\\
\$1{,}200S &= \$48{,}000{,}000\\
S &= 40{,}000\\
4S &= 160{,}000 = G
\end{aligned}$$

The break-even point is 40,000 self-pay patient days plus 40,000 x 4 = 160,000 other patient days, a grand total of 200,000 patient days.

2. Contribution margins:
S = \$1,000 - \$600 = \$400 per patient day
G= \$ 800 - \$600 = \$200 per patient day

Patient days:
S = .25 x 200,000 = 50,000
G= .75 x 200,000 = 150,000

Net income = 50,000(\$400) + 150,000(\$200) - \$48,000,000
= \$20,000,000 + \$30,000,000 - \$48,000,000 = \$2,000,000

Let S = number of self-pay patients (S)
3S = number of other patients (G)

$$\begin{aligned}
\$1{,}000S + \$800(3S) - \$600S - \$600(3S) - \$48{,}000{,}000 &= 0\\
\$1{,}000S + \$2{,}400S - \$600S - \$1{,}800S &= \$48{,}000{,}000\\
\$1{,}000S &= \$48{,}000{,}000\\
S &= 48{,}000\\
3S &= 144{,}000 = G
\end{aligned}$$

The break-even point is now lower (192,000 patient days instead of 200,000 patient days). The more profitable mix produces a net income of \$2,000,000 at the 200,000 patient-day level.

2-49 (15-25 min.)

1. Let N = number of rooms

$$\$105N - \$25N - \$10,000,000 = \frac{(\$720,000)}{1-.4}$$

$$\$80N - \$10,000,000 = \$1,200,000$$

$$\$80N = \$11,200,000$$

$$N = 140,000 \text{ rooms}$$

$$\$80N - \$10,000,000 = \frac{(\$360,000)}{1-.4}$$

$$\$80N = \$10,600,000$$

$$N = 132,500 \text{ rooms}$$

2. $$\$105N - \$25N - \$10,000,000 = 0$$

$$\$80N = \$10,000,000$$

$$N = 125,000 \text{ rooms}$$

Number of rooms at 100% capacity = 600 x 365 = 219,000
Percentage occupancy to break even = 125,000 ÷ 219,000 = 57%

3. Using the shortcut approach described in the chapter appendix:

$$\text{Change in net income} = \text{Change in volume in units} \times \text{Contribution margin in units} \times (1 - \text{tax rate})$$

= 15,000 x $80 x (1 - .40)
= 15,000 x $48
= $720,000, a large increase because of a high contribution margin per dollar of revenue.

Note that a 10% increase in rooms sold increased net income by $720,000 ÷ $1,200,000 or 60%.

Rooms sold	150,000	165,000
Contribution margin @ $80	$12,000,000	$13,200,000
Fixed expenses	10,000,000	10,000,000
Income before taxes	2,000,000	3,200,000
Income taxes @ 40%	800,000	1,280,000
Net income	$ 1,200,000	$ 1,920,000

Increase in net income	$720,000
Percentage increase	60%

<u>2-50</u> (15-25 min.)

New variable costs per disk will be 130% of \$10, or \$13, plus \$2 = \$15.

1. a. Break-even point $= \dfrac{(\$600{,}000)}{\$16 - (\$10 + \$2)} = 150{,}000$ disks

2. d. Contribution margin: \$16 - (\$10 + \$2) = \$4
Increased after-tax income: 10% x 200,000 x \$4 x 60% = \$48,000;
or using formula at end of appendix:

$$\text{Change in net income} = \text{Change in volume in units} \times \text{Contribution margin in units} \times (1\text{-tax rate})$$

$$= 20{,}000 \times \$4 \times (1 - .40)$$

$$= \$48{,}000$$

3. a. Let N = target sales in units

$$\text{Target sales} - \text{variable expenses} - \text{fixed expenses} = \frac{\text{target after-tax net income}}{1 - \text{tax rate}}$$

$$\$16N - \$15N - \$600{,}000 = \frac{(\$120{,}000)}{1 - .40}$$

$$\$16N - \$15N - \$600{,}000 = \$200{,}000$$

$$N = 800{,}000 \text{ units}$$

$$\$16N = \$12{,}800{,}000$$

4. b. Let P = new selling price
Current contribution ratio is \$4 ÷ \$16 = .25
New contribution ratio is (P - \$15) ÷ P = .25

$$.25P = P - \$15$$

$$.75P = \$15$$

$$P = \$15 \div .75$$

$$P = \$20$$

2-51 (25-35 min.)

1. $$\frac{(\$12{,}000{,}000)}{\$800} = 15{,}000 \text{ patient-days}$$

2. $$\text{Variable costs} = \frac{(\$3{,}150{,}000)}{(15{,}000)} = \$210 \text{ per patient-day}$$

Contribution margin = $800 - $210 = $590 per patient-day

To recoup the specified fixed expenses:
$5,900,000 ÷ $590 = 10,000 patient-days

3. The fixed cost levels differ as the relevant range changes:

Patient-Days	Non-Nursing Fixed Expenses	Nursing Fixed Expenses	Total Fixed Expenses
10,000-12,000	$5,900,000	$1,350,000(a)	$7,250,000
12,001-16,000	5,900,000	1,575,000(b)	7,475,000

(a) $45,000 x 30 = $1,350,000
(b) $45,000 x 35 = $1,575,000

To break even on a lower level of fixed costs:
$7,250,000 ÷ $590 = 12,288 patient-days

This answer exceeds the lower-level maximum; therefore, this answer is infeasible. The department must operate at a $7,475,000 level of fixed costs to break even: $7,475,000 ÷ $590 = 12,669 patient-days.

4. The nursing costs would have been variable instead of fixed. The contribution margin per patient-day would have been \$800 - \$210 - \$200 = \$390. The break-even point would be higher: \$5,900,000 ÷ 390 = 15,128 patient-days.

   Some instructors might want to point out that hospitals have been under severe pressures to reduce costs. More than ever, nursing costs are controlled as variable rather than fixed costs. For example, more part-time help is used, and nurses may be used for full shifts but only as volume requires.

<u>2-52</u> (10-15 min.)

1. Total variable cost = \$10 x 75,000 = \$750,000
   Total fixed cost = \$1,000,000 - \$12,000 - \$750,000 = \$238,000

2. (a) Operating income = \$1,700,000 - (\$10 x 92,000) - \$238,000
   = \$1,700,000 - \$1,158,000
   = \$542,000

   (b) Operating income = \$1,870,000 - \$10 x 101,200 - \$238,000
   = \$1,870,000 - \$1,250,000
   = \$620,000

   (c) Operating income = \$1,530,000 - \$10 x 82,800 - \$238,000
   = \$1,530,000 - \$1,066,000
   = \$464,000

3. There are two reasons for the increased operating income: increased sales price and increased volume. In 1993 the sales price was \$1,000,000 ÷ 75,000 - \$13.33, creating a unit contribution margin of \$13.33 - \$10.00 = \$3.33. In 1994 the sales price is predicted to be \$1,700,000 ÷ 92,000 = \$18.48, creating a unit contribution margin of \$8.48. Even with no increase in sales volume, the extra contribution margin would increase operating income by (\$8.48 - \$3.33) x 75,000 = \$386,250. Further, each of the 17,000 additional units to be sold in 1994 would have a unit contribution margin \$8.48, creating additional operating income of \$8.48 x 17,000 = \$144,160. The total extra operating income in 1994 would be \$386,250 + \$144,160 = \$530,410, which is within a rounding error of the \$530,000 by which predicted 1994 operating income exceeds 1993 operating income.

<u>2-53</u> (15-20 min.)

1. Old: (Contribution margin x 600,000) - \$585,000 = Budgeted profit
[(\$3.10 - \$2.10) x 600,000] - \$585,000 = \$15,000

New: (Contribution margin x 600,000) - \$1,140,000 = Budgeted profit
[(\$3.10 - 1.10) x 600,000] - \$1,140,000 = \$60,000

2. Old: \$585,000 ÷ \$1.00 = 585,000 units
New: \$1,140,000 ÷ \$2.00 = 570,000 units

3. A fall in volume will be more devastating under the new system because the high fixed costs will not be affected by the fall in volume:

   Old: ($1.00 x 500,000) - $585,000 = -$85,000 (a $85,000 loss)
   New: ($2.00 x 500,000) - $1,140,000 = -$140,000 (a $140,000 loss)

   The 100,000 unit fall in volume caused a $15,000 - (- $85,000) = $100,000 decrease in profits under the old environment and a $60,000 - (- $140,000) = $200,000 decrease under the new environment.

4. Increases in volume create larger increases in profit in the new environment:

   Old: ($1.00 x 700,000) - $585,000 = $115,000
   New: ($2.00 x 700,000) - $1,140,000 = $260,000

   The 100,000 unit increase in volume caused a $115,000 - $15,000 = $100,000 increase in profit under the old environment and a $260,000 - $60,000 = $200,000 increase under the new environment.

5. Changes in volume affect profits in the new environment (a high fixed cost, low variable cost environment) more than they affect profits in the old environment. Therefore, profits in the old environment are more stable and less risky. The higher risk new environment promises greater rewards when conditions are favorable, but also leads to greater losses when conditions are unfavorable, a more risky situation.

2-54 (25-30 min.) This case is based on real data that has been simplified so that the numbers are easier to handle.

1. Daily break-even volume is 85 dinners and 170 lunches:

First compute contribution margins on lunches and dinners:
Variable cost percentage = ($1,246,500 + $222,380) ÷ $2,098,400
= 70%
Contribution margin percentage = 1 - variable cost percentage
= 1 - 70% = 30%

Lunch contribution margin = .30 x $20 = $6
Dinner contribution margin = .30 x $40 = $12

Annual fixed cost is $170,700 + $451,500 = $622,200

Let X = number of dinners and 2X = number of lunches

12(X) + 6(2X) - $622,200 = 0
24(X) = 622,200
X = 25,925 dinners annually to break even
2X = 51,850 lunches annually to break even

On a daily basis:
Dinners to break even = 25,925 ÷ 305 = 85 dinners daily
Lunches to break even = 85 x 2 = 170 lunches daily or $51,850 ÷ 305 = 170 lunches daily.

To determine the actual volume, let Y be a combination of 1 dinner and 2 lunches. The price of Y is $40 + (2 x $20) = $80, and total volume in units of Y is $2,098,400 ÷ $80 = 26,230 and daily volume is 26,230 ÷ 305 = 86. Therefore, 86 dinners and 2 x 86 = 172 lunches were served on an average day. This is 1 dinner and 2 lunches above the break-even volume.

2. The extra annual contribution margin from the 3 dinners and 6 lunches is:

3 x $40 x .30 x 305 =	$10,980
+ 6 x $20 x .30 x 305 =	10,980
Total	$21,960

The added contribution margin is greater than the $15,000 advertising expenditure. Therefore, the advertising expenditure would be warranted. It would increase operating income by $21,960 - $15,000 = $6,960.

3. Let Y again be a combination of 1 dinner and 2 lunches, priced at $80. Variable costs are .70 x $80 = $56, of which $56 x .25 = $14 is food cost. Cutting food costs by 20% reduces variable costs by .20 x $14 = $2.80, making the variable cost of Y $56 - $2.80 = $53.20 and the contribution margin $80 - $53.20 = $26.80. (This could also be determined by adding the $2.80 saving in food cost directly to the old contribution margin of $24.) The required annual volume in Y needed to keep operating income at $7,320 is:

$26.80 (Y) - $622,200 = $7,320
$26.80 (Y) = $629,520
Y = 23,490
Therefore, daily volume = 23,490 ÷ 305 = 77 (rounded)

If volume drops no more than 86 - 77 = 9 dinners and 172 - 154 = 18 lunches, using the less costly food is more profitable. However, there are many subjective factors to be considered. Volume may not fall in the short run, but the decline in quality may eventually affect repeat business and cause a long-run decline. Much may depend on the skill of the chef. If the quality difference is not readily noticeable, so that volume falls less than, say, 10%, saving money on the purchases of food may be desirable.

2-55 (25-30 min.)

1. Break-even in pounds = $\frac{\text{Annual fixed costs}}{\text{Contribution margin per pound}}$

$$= \frac{(\$550{,}000)}{\$5.00 - \$3.00} = 275{,}000 \text{ pounds}$$

2. Contribution margin ratio = $2.00 ÷ $5.00 = 40%

Old variable cost = $3.00

Only the cost of *salmon* is affected:
New variable cost = $3.00 + .15 ($2.50) = $3.375

Let S	= Selling price
Selling price - Variable costs	= Contribution margin
S - $3.375	= .40S
.60S	= $3.375
S	= $5.625

Check: ($5.625 - $3.375) ÷ $5.625 = 40%

3. Current income before taxes:
= 390,000 pounds ($5.00 - $3.00) - $550,000
= $780,000 - $550,000 = $230,000

Current income after taxes:
= $230,000(.60) = $138,000

The problem can be solved by using units and then converting to dollar sales.

Let N = sales in pounds

$$\text{Sales - Variable expenses - Fixed expenses} = \frac{\text{Net income}}{\text{1 - tax rate}}$$

$$\$5.00N - [(\$3.00 + .15(\$2.50)]N - \$550{,}000 = \frac{(\$138{,}000)}{1 - .4}$$

$$\$5.00N - \$3.375N - \$550{,}000 = \$230{,}000$$

$$\$1.625N = \$780{,}000$$

$$N = 480{,}000 \text{ pounds}$$

$$\$5.00N = \$2{,}400{,}000 \text{ sales}$$

An alternative way to get the solution is:

$$\text{New contribution margin ratio} = \frac{\$5.00 - \$3.375}{\$5.00} = .325$$

New variable-cost ratio = 1.000 - .325 = .675

Let S = Sales

$$S = .675S + \$550{,}000 + \frac{(\$138{,}000)}{1 - .4}$$

$$.325S = \$780{,}000$$

$$S = \$2{,}400{,}000$$

4. Strategies might include:
(a) Increase selling price by the $.375 cost increase.
(b) Decrease other variable costs by $.375 per pound.
(c) Decrease fixed costs by $.375 x 390,000 = $146,250.
(d) Increase unit sales by 480,000 - 390,000 = 90,000 pounds.
(e) Some combination of the above.

2-56 (30 min. or more)

The purpose of this problem is to develop an intuitive feel for the costs involved in a simple production process and to assess whether various costs are fixed or variable. Then students must assess the market to determine a price so that they can compute a break-even point.

Completing this problem can be done quickly or it can take much time. It might even be done in class, with students suggesting the various costs and predicting their levels. A complete analysis might involve finding the actual prices of the resources needed to make the product or service. This could lead to time-consuming research. Whatever approach is taken, students are led to see the real-world application of what they are learning.

CHAPTER 3
Measurement of Cost Behavior

3-A1 (20-25 min.)

Some of these answers are controversial, and reasonable cases can be built for alternative classifications. Class discussion of these answers should lead to worthwhile disagreements about anticipated cost behavior with regard to alternative cost drivers.

1. (b) Discretionary fixed cost.
2. (a) Purely variable cost with respect to revenue.
3. (a) Mixed cost with respect to passenger-miles.
4. (d) Mixed cost with respect to miles driven.
5. (c) Committed fixed cost.
6. (b) Discretionary fixed cost.
7. (c) Committed fixed cost.
8. (a) Purely variable cost with respect to cases of Coca-Cola.
9. (b) Discretionary fixed cost.
10. (e) Step cost.
11. (b) Discretionary fixed cost.

3-A2 (25-30 min.)

1. Support costs based on 60% of the cost of materials:

	Sign One	Sign Two
Direct materials cost	$300	$150
Support cost (50% of materials cost)	$180	$ 90

Support costs based on $40 per power tool operation:

	Sign One	Sign Two
Power tool operations	3	6
Support cost	$120	$240

2. If the activity analysis is reliable, by using the current method, Evergreen Signs is predicting too much cost for signs that use few power tool operations and is predicting too little cost for signs that use many power tool operations. As a result he could be losing jobs that require few power tool operations because his bids are too high – he could afford to bid less on these jobs. Conversely, he could be getting too many jobs that require many power tool operations, because his bids are too low – given what his "true" costs will be, he cannot afford these jobs at those prices. Either way, his sign business could be more profitable if he better understood and used activity analysis. Custom Signs would be advised to adopt the activity analysis recommendation, but also to closely monitor costs to see if the activity analysis predictions of support costs are accurate.

3-A3 (25-30 min.)

1. High-Low Method:

	Support Cost	Machine Hours
High month = September	$13,500	1,750
Low month = May	9,000	850
Difference	$ 4,500	900

$$\text{Variable cost per machine hour} = \frac{\text{Change in cost}}{\text{Change in cost driver}}$$

$$= \frac{\$4{,}500}{900} = \$5.00$$

Fixed support cost per month=Total support cost - Variable support cost

At the high point: = $13,500 - $5.00 x 1,750
= $13,500 - $8,750
= $ 4,750

or at the low point: = $ 9,000 - $5.00 x 850
= $ 9,000 - $4,250
= $ 4,750

2. The regression analysis results are somewhat different from the results of the high-low method. As a result, estimates of total support cost may differ considerably depending on the expected machine hour usage. For example, consider the following support cost estimates at three levels of machine hour usage (all within the relevant range):

		Machine Hour Usage		
		950 Hours	1,200 Hours	1,450 Hours
High-Low:				
Fixed		$4,750	$ 4,750	$ 4,750
Variable:	$5.00 x 950	4,750		
	$5.00 x 1,200		6,000	
	$5.00 x 1,450			7,250
Total		$9,500	$10,750	$12,000
Regression:				
Fixed		$2,728	$ 2,728	$ 2,728
Variable:	$6.77 x 950	6,432		
	$6.77 x 1,200		8,124	
	$6.77 x 1,450			9,817
Total		$9,160	$ 10,852	$12,545

Because the high-low approach has a lower variable cost estimate, the regression-based predictions exceed the high-low-based predictions by more at higher levels of machine usage. The high-low method used only two data points, so the results may not be reliable. Fernandez would be advised to use the regression results, which are based on all relevant data.

3-B1 (20-25 min.)

The following classifications are open to debate. With appropriate assumptions, other answers could be equally supportable. This problem provides an opportunity to discuss various aspects of cost behavior.

Cost	Cost Behavior	Likely Cost Driver(s)
1. Training cost	Discretionary fixed	Growth, cross-training*
2. Depreciation	Committed fixed	Capacity, service level*
3. Consulting	Discretionary fixed	Improvement policy*
4. Nursing supervisors	Step	Number of nurses, patients*
5. X-ray operating cost	Mixed	Capacity, number of patients
6. Insurance	Step	Number of employees*
7. Cancer research	Discretionary fixed	Research policy*
8. Repairs	Variable	Number of patients

*Not a required answer.

3-B2 (25-30 min.)

	Board Z15	Board Q52
Mark-up method:		
Material cost	$30	$55
Support costs (100%)	$30	$55
Activity analysis method:		
Manual Operations	16	7
Support costs (@$4)	$64	$28

The support costs are different because different cost behavior is assumed by the two methods. If the activity analyses are reliable, then boards with few manual operations are overcosted with the markup method, and boards with many manual operations are undercosted with the markup method.

3-B3 (25-30 min.)

$$\text{Variable cost per machine hour} = \frac{\text{Change in Repair Cost}}{\text{Change in Machine Hours}}$$

$$= \frac{(\$260{,}000{,}000 - \$190{,}000{,}000)}{(12{,}000 - 8{,}000)}$$

$$= \$17{,}500 \text{ per machine hour}$$

Fixed cost per month = total cost - variable cost
= $260,000,000 - $17,500 x 12,000
= $260,000,000 - $210,000,000
= $ 50,000,000 per month

or = $190,000,000 - $17,500 x 8,000
= $190,000,000 - $140,000,000
= $ 50,000,000 per month

3-1 A cost driver is an activity of an organization that is believed to cause costs to fluctuate in a predictable manner. For example, direct labor costs are probably driven by direct labor hours; materials costs are probably driven by levels of product output; and support costs may be driven by a variety of drivers, such as output levels, product complexity, number of different products and/or parts, and so on.

3-2 Linear cost behavior assumes that costs behave as a straight line. This line is anchored by an intercept, or fixed cost estimate, and total costs increase proportionately as cost driver activity increases. The slope of the line is the estimate of variable cost per unit of cost driver activity.

3-3 Whether to categorize a step cost either as a fixed cost or as a variable cost depends on the "size" of the steps (height and width) and on the desired accuracy of the description of step cost behavior. If the steps are wide, covering a wide range of cost driver activity, then within each range the cost may be regarded as fixed. If the steps are narrow and not too high, with small changes in cost, then the cost may be regarded as variable over a wide range of activity level, with little error. If the steps are narrow and high, covering big changes in cost, then the cost probably should not be regarded as variable, since small changes in activity level can result in large changes in cost.

3-4 Mixed costs are costs that contain both fixed and variable elements. A mixed cost has a fixed portion that is usually a cost per time period. This is the minimum mixed cost per period. A mixed cost also has a variable portion that is a cost per unit of cost driver activity. The variable portion of a mixed cost increases proportionately with increases in the cost driver.

3-5 In order to achieve the goals set for the organization, management makes critical choices – choices that guide the future activities of the organization. These choices include decisions about locations, products, services, organization structure, and so on. Choices about product or service attributes (mix, quality, features, performance, etc.), capacity (committed and discretionary fixed costs), technology (capital/labor considerations, alternative technologies), and incentives (standard-based performance evaluation) can greatly affect cost behavior.

3-6 Some fixed costs are called capacity costs because the levels of these fixed costs are determined by management's strategic decisions about the organization's expected levels of activities, or capacity.

3-7 Committed fixed costs are costs that are often driven by the planned scale of operations. These costs typically cannot be changed easily or quickly without drastically changing the operations of the organization. Typical committed fixed costs include lease or mortgage payments, property taxes, and long-term management compensation. Discretionary fixed costs are costs that may be necessary to achieve certain operational goals, but there are no contractual obligations to continue these payments. Typical discretionary fixed costs include advertising, research and development, and employee training programs. The distinction between committed and discretionary fixed costs is that discretionary fixed costs are flexible and could be increased or eliminated entirely on short notice if necessary, but committed fixed costs usually must be incurred for some time – greater effort is needed to change or eliminate them.

3-8 Committed fixed costs are the most difficult to change because long-term commitments generally have been made. These long-term commitments may involve legal contracts that would be costly to renegotiate or dissolve. Committed fixed costs also are difficult to change, because doing so may mean greatly changing the way the organization conducts its activities. Changing these committed fixed costs may also mean changing organization structure, location, employment levels, and products or services.

3-9 The primary determinants of both committed and discretionary fixed costs are elements of the organization's strategy relating to capacity, product attributes, and technology. These elements will determine long-term cost commitments (committed costs) and flexible spending responses to changes in the environment (discretionary costs).

3-10 Both planning for and controlling discretionary costs are important. It is hard to say that one is more important than the other, but certainly effective use of discretionary costs requires prior planning. One would not know, however, if these costs had been effective in meeting goals unless the organization has a reliable and timely control system – a means of checking accomplishments against goals.

3-11 High technology production systems often mean higher fixed costs and lower variable costs.

3-12 Incentives to control costs are means of making cost control in the best interests of the people responsible for making cost expenditures. A simple example will illustrate the use of incentives to control costs. Assume that you are an executive who travels for business, purchases professional literature, and keeps current with personal computer technology. Under one incentive system, you simply bill the organization for all your travel and professional expenses. Under another system, you are given an annual budget for travel and professional needs. Which system do you think would cause you to be more careful how you spend money for travel and professional needs? Most likely, the latter system would be more effective in controlling costs. Usually these incentives are economic, but other non-financial incentives may also be effective.

3-13 Use of cost functions, or algebraic representations of cost behavior, allows cost analysts or management to build models of the organization's cost behavior. These models can be used to aid planning and control activities. One common use of cost functions is in financial planning models, which are algebraic models of the cost and revenue behavior of the firm – extended C-V-P models similar to those discussed in Chapter 2.

3-14 A "plausible" cost function is one that is intuitively sound. A cost function is plausible if a knowledgeable analyst can make sound economic justifications why a particular cost driver could cause the cost in question. A "reliable" cost function is one that accurately and consistently describes actual cost behavior, past and future. Both plausibility and reliability are essential to useful cost functions. It is difficult to say that one is more important than the other, but one would not have much confidence in the future use of a cost function that is not plausible, even if past reliability (e.g., based on statistical measures) has been high. Likewise, one would not be confident using a cost function that is highly plausible, but that has not been shown to be reliable. The cost analyst should strive for plausible and reliable cost functions.

3-15 Activity analysis identifies underlying causes of cost behavior (appropriate cost drivers) and measures the relationships of costs to their cost drivers. A variety of methods may be used to measure cost functions, including engineering analysis and account analysis.

3-16 Engineering analysis is a method of identifying and measuring cost and cost driver relationships that does not require the use of historical data. Engineering analysis proceeds by the use of interviews, experimentation, and observation of current cost generating activities. Engineering analysis will be more reliable if the organization has had past experience with the activities.

Account analysis is a method of identifying and measuring costs and cost driver relationships that depend explicitly on historical cost data. An analyst selects a single volume-related cost driver and classifies each cost account as fixed or variable with respect to that cost driver. Account analysis will be reliable if the analyst is skilled and if the data are relevant to future uses of the derived cost function.

3-17 There are four general methods covered in this text to measure mixed costs using historical data: (1) cost account analysis, (2) high-low, (3) visual fit, and (4) regression.

- Account analysis looks to the organization's cost accounts and classifies each cost as either fixed, variable, or mixed with regard to an appropriate cost driver.
- High-low analysis algebraically measures mixed cost behavior by constructing a straight line between the cost at the highest activity level and that at the lowest activity level.
- Visual-fit analysis seeks to place a straight line among data points on a plot of each cost and its appropriate cost driver.
- Regression analysis fits a straight line to cost and activity data according to statistical criteria.

3-18 Engineering analysis and account analysis often are combined. One of the problems of account analysis is that historical data may contain past inefficiencies. Therefore, account analysis measures what costs were, not necessarily what they should be. Differences in future costs may be desired and/or anticipated, and cost account analysis alone usually will not account for these differences. Engineering analysis may be combined with cost account analysis to revise cost-account-based measures for desired improvements in efficiency and/or planned changes in inputs or processes.

3-19 The strengths of the high-low method are also its weaknesses – the method is simple to apply since it does not require extensive data or statistical sophistication. This simplicity also means that the method may not be reliable because it may not use all the relevant data that are available and choice of the two points to measure the linear cost relationship is subjective. The method itself also does not give any measures of reliability.

The visual-fit method is an improvement over the high-low method because it uses all the available (relevant) data. However, this method, too, may not be reliable since it relies on the analyst's judgment on where to place the line.

3-20 Regression analysis is usually preferred to the high-low method (and the visual-fit method) because regression analysis uses all the relevant data and because easy-to-use computer software does the analysis and provides useful measures of cost function reliability. The major disadvantage of regression analysis is that it requires statistical sophistication to use properly. Because the software is easy to use, many users of regression analysis may not be able to critically evaluate the output and may be misled to believe that they have developed a reliable cost function when they have not.

3-21 This is a deceptive statement, because it is true on the face of it, but regression also has many pitfalls for the unwary. Yes, regression software provides useful output that can be used to evaluate the reliability of the measured cost function. If one understands the assumptions of least-squares regression, this output can be used to critically evaluate the measured function. However, the regression software cannot evaluate the relevance or accuracy of the data that are used. Even though regression analysis is statistically objective, irrelevant or inaccurate data used as input will lead to unreliable cost functions, regardless of the strength of the statistical indicators of reliability.

3-22 Plotting data helps to identify outliers, that is, observations that are unusual and may indicate a situation that is not representative of the environment for which cost predictions are being made. It can also show nonlinear cost behavior that can lead to transformations of the data before applying linear regression methods.

3-23 R^2 is a goodness-of-fit test. It tells us the percentage of variation in cost that is associated with changes in the cost driver.

3-24 Control of costs does require measurement of cost behavior, either what costs have been or what costs should be. Problems of work rules and the like may make *changing* cost behavior difficult. There are tradeoffs, of course, and the instructor should expect that students could get into an impassioned debate over where the balance lies – union job protection versus improved efficiency. This debate gets to one of the major roles of accounting in organizations, and it is important that students realize that accounting does matter greatly to individuals, and, ultimately, to society.

3-25 (10-15 min.)

1. Quantity discounts: A, amount purchased
2. Raw material: B, units produced
3. Annual wage: C or E (depending on work levels), labor hours
4. Water bill: H, gallons used
5. Machining labor: G, number of units completed
6. Depreciation: E, capacity
7. Sheet steel: D or F (depending on purchasing), number of implements
8. Salaries: F, number of solicitors
9. Natural gas bill: C, energy usage

3-26 (10-15 min.)

1. Fuel costs: $.20 x 15,000 miles per month = $3,000 per month.
2. Equipment rental: $6,000 x 7 x 3 = $126,000 for five pieces of equipment for three months
3. Ambulance and EMT cost: $1,100 x (2,400/250) = $1,100 x 10 = $11,000 (must round up from 9.6 to 10)
4. Purchasing: $7,500 + $4 x 4,000 = $23,500 for the month.

3-27 (10-15 min.)

There may be some disagreement about these classifications, but reasons for alternative classifications should be explored.

Cost	Discretionary	Committed
Advertising	$20,000	
Depreciation		$ 47,000
Company health insurance		15,000
Management salaries		85,000
Payment of long-term debt		50,000
Property tax		32,000
Grounds maintenance	9,000	
Office remodeling	21,000	
Research and development	36,000	
Totals	$86,000	$229,000

3-28 (15-20 min.)

This problem extends the chapter analysis to preview short-run decision making and capital budgeting. This problem ignores taxes, investment cost and the time value of money, which are covered in Chapter 11.

	Alternative 1	Alternative 2
Variable cost per order	$8.00	$4.00
Expected number of orders	70,000	70,000
Annual variable costs	$560,000	$280,000
Annual fixed cost	200,000	400,000
Annual total costs	$760,000	$680,000

Therefore, Alternative 2 is less costly than Alternative 1 by $80,000.

Let X = the break-even number of orders, the level at which expected costs are equal.

Costs for Alternative 1	= Costs for Alternative 2
\$200,000 + \$8X	= \$400,000 + \$4X
\$4X	= \$200,000
X	= 50,000 orders

At 50,000 orders, the alternatives are equivalent. If order levels are expected to be below 50,000 orders, then Alternative 1 would have lower costs because fixed costs are lower. If orders are expected to be greater than 50,000, then Alternative 2 would have lower costs because variable costs are lower.

3-29 (20-25 min.) (A master of the scatter-diagrams with least-square regression lines and high-low lines appears on the following page.)

This exercise enables a comparison of the high-low and visual-fit methods of decomposing mixed-costs into fixed and variable parts. Students find it interesting to compare their best guesses to the least-squares regression results. They find it interesting that a fairly complete and accurate analysis is possible based on a scatter-diagram and a little common sense. We normally have the class determine a "class best guess" before showing the transparency of the regression results.

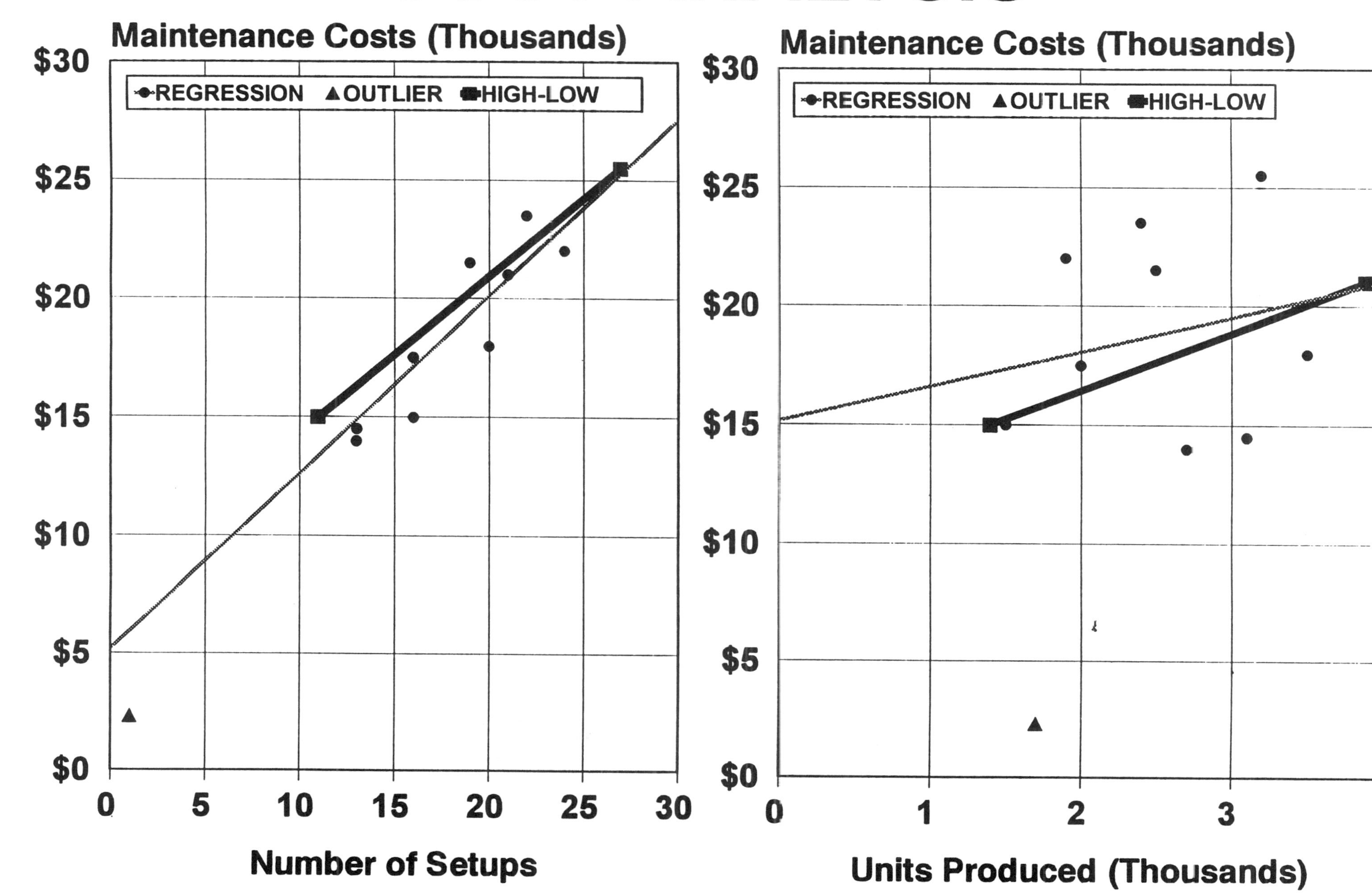
COST ANALYSIS
Maintenance Costs (Thousands)
REGRESSION
OUTLIER
HIGH-LOW
$30
$25
$20
$15
$10
$5
$0
0
5
10
15
20
25
30
Number of Setups
Maintenance Costs (Thousands)
REGRESSION
OUTLIER
HIGH-LOW
$30
$25
$20
$15
$10
$5
$0
0
1
2
3
Units Produced (Thousands)

The exercise also introduces students to the concept of a hierarchy of activity levels. The literature contains discussions of four general levels of activities. Recognizing each of these levels can be an aid in choosing appropriate cost drivers. These levels and example cost drivers are:

1. Unit-level activities – performed each time a unit is produced (units of product, machine hours, labor hours).
2. Batch-level activities – performed each time a batch of goods is processed or handled (number of orders processed, number of setups, pounds of material handled).
3. Product-level activities – performed as needed to support the production of each different type of product (number of tests, number of parts, number of engineering change notices, hours of design time, number of inspections).
4. Facility-level activities – sustain a facility's general manufacturing process (square footage, number of employees, hours of training).

In this exercise, a batch-level activity is involved – setups.

1. Student answers will vary somewhat. Least-squares regression lines are given as a standard for comparison. Based on regression, the cost functions are:

   Maintenance costs = $15,162 + $1.45 x Units produced (000s)

   Maintenance costs= $5,190 + $745 x Number of setups

   The April observation should be ignored since it does not represent a typical month – it is an example of an outlier. Other examples would be strikes, abnormal downtime, or scheduled plant closings.

2. The high-low method uses only the highest and lowest activity levels. These are shown on the graphs as squares. Note that using a scatter diagram, the high-low method can be used without knowing the exact figures. Fixed cost can be easily estimated using a straight edge and should be about $11,500 based on Units Produced and $7,500 based on Setups. Variable costs are determined using the following computations:

   Variable maintenance costs = (21,000 - 15,000)/(3,900 - 1,200) = $2.22 per unit

   Variable maintenance costs = (25,500 - 15,000)/(27 - 11) = $656 per setup

3. Both cost drivers appear, on the surface, to be plausible. However, if maintenance activity is primarily associated with a "batch-level" activity such as setups, the setup driver is preferred. Of the three costs associated with maintenance activity, supplies and energy are probably variable, so salaries are the primary fixed costs. The monthly salary of two mechanics is $4,167 [(2 x 25,000)/12]. The cost function based on setups estimates fixed costs of about $5,200 (visual-fit method). This is much more plausible than the $15,200 estimate based on units of production. Students may inquire as to the use of "setup time" as an alternative to number of setups. Setup time is an acceptable alternative that is often used when setup times differ among different products. Another consideration is data availability. Setup times by product may not be easily obtained.

   Reliability of cost drivers is measured by the coefficient of determination, R-Squared. Only 9% of the past year's variability in maintenance costs can be explained by changes in the volume of units produced, whereas 86% of past fluctuations in costs can be explained by the number of setups performed.

3-30 (15-20 min.)

Cost	Fixed per month	Variable per computer
Phone	$ 50	
Utilities	65	
Advertising	75	
Insurance	80	
Materials		$1,500
Labor	1,300	100
Totals	$1,570 per month	$1,600 per computer

Algebraically, y = $1,570 + $1,600x,
where y = total cost per month
x = number of computers

3-31 (5 min.)

All of the functions except (e) and (f) are linear cost functions. Both (c) and (d) are mixed costs. Note that (e) is not linear because X_1 and X_2 are multiplied, and (f) is not linear because it contains X_1^2.

3-32 (5-10 min.)

Variable cost per ton = (£1,100,000 - £900,000) ÷ (45,000 - 35,000)

$$= \frac{£200,000}{10,000} = £20/\text{ton}$$

Fixed cost = £1,100,000 - 45,000 x £20 = £200,000
or = £900,000 - 35,000 x £20 = £200,000

Cost function = £200,000 + £20 x Number of pounds

3-33 (10-15 min.)

The regression analysis results show that more was spent on building maintenance in months of low production volume than in months of high volume. The assistant controller erred in not thinking about the economic logic of this result. The result does not imply that intensive use of the building decreases maintenance costs. When production volume is low, workers do maintenance rather than work on production. When volume is high, little maintenance is done because workers are busy on production. This is a case where the regression analysis does not correctly separate costs into fixed and variable components. Considering the economic plausibility of a negative variable maintenance cost should make this readily apparent. A more correct analysis would probably show that maintenance costs are not related to direct labor, or, if there is a relationship, more labor should cause more maintenance because it implies more intensive use of the production facilities.

3-34 (50-60 min.) (Masters of the line graph and pie charts appear on the next two pages.)

1. The line graph shows the plot of the total cost for each of the two options at various levels of capacity utilization. The outsource/overtime option has a steeper slope due to the larger proportion of variable costs, especially beyond the 100% level of production when overtime premiums and outsourcing are required (note the kink in the line). At production (sales) levels below 100% of capacity, total costs are lower with the outsource/overtime option. At production levels above 100%, the build option becomes the low-cost option.

2. Controlling risk usually means reducing the financial exposure of a company when business conditions turn unfavorable. Companies attempt to control this risk through various means – diversifying their product lines and markets and reducing fixed (committed) costs or converting fixed costs into variable costs. In this case, the outsource/overtime option avoids converting variable production

TOTAL COSTS

BUILD VERSUS OUTSOURCE/OVERTIME OPTIONS

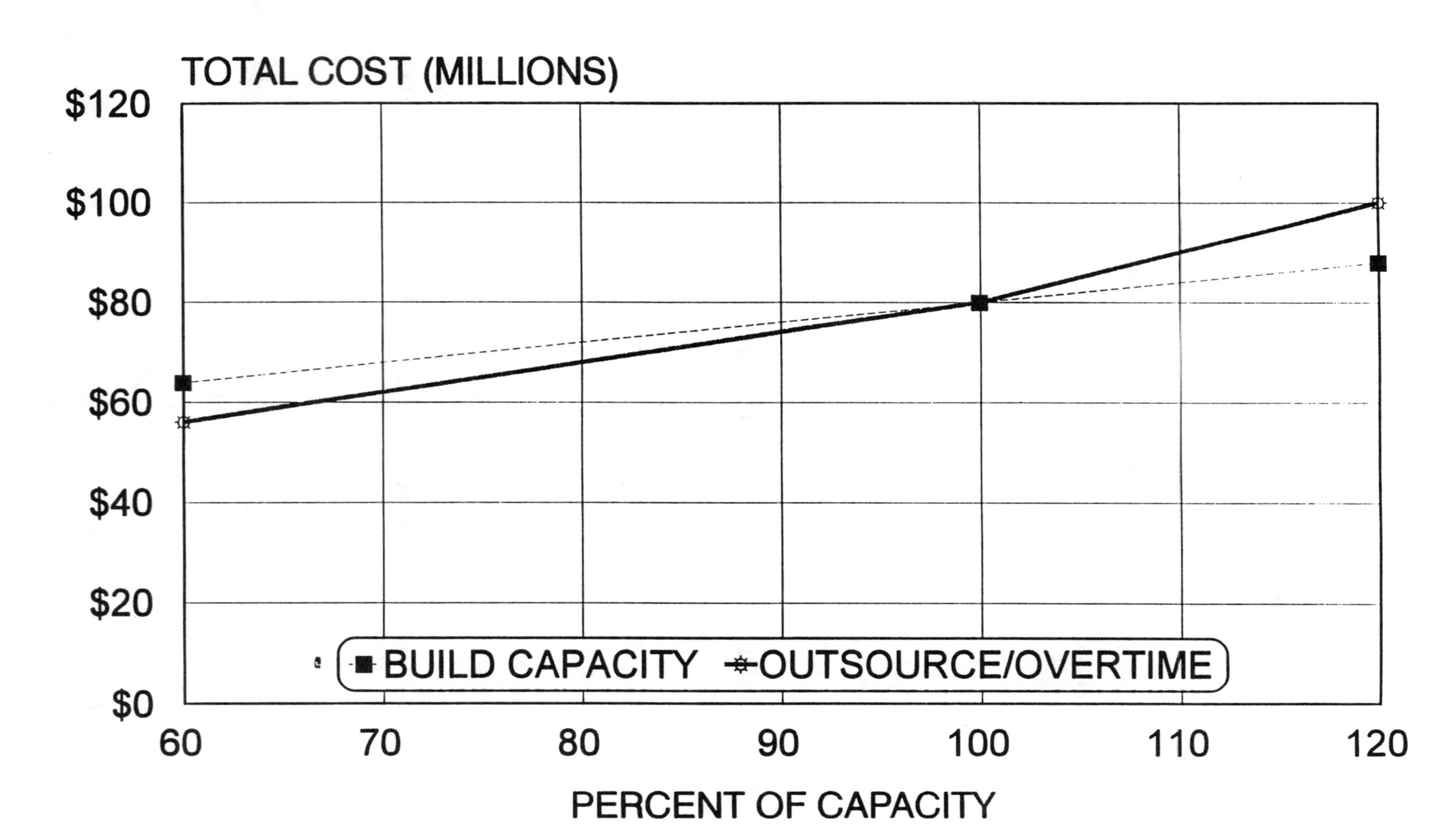

COST BEHAVIOR OF CAPACITY COSTS [Millions]

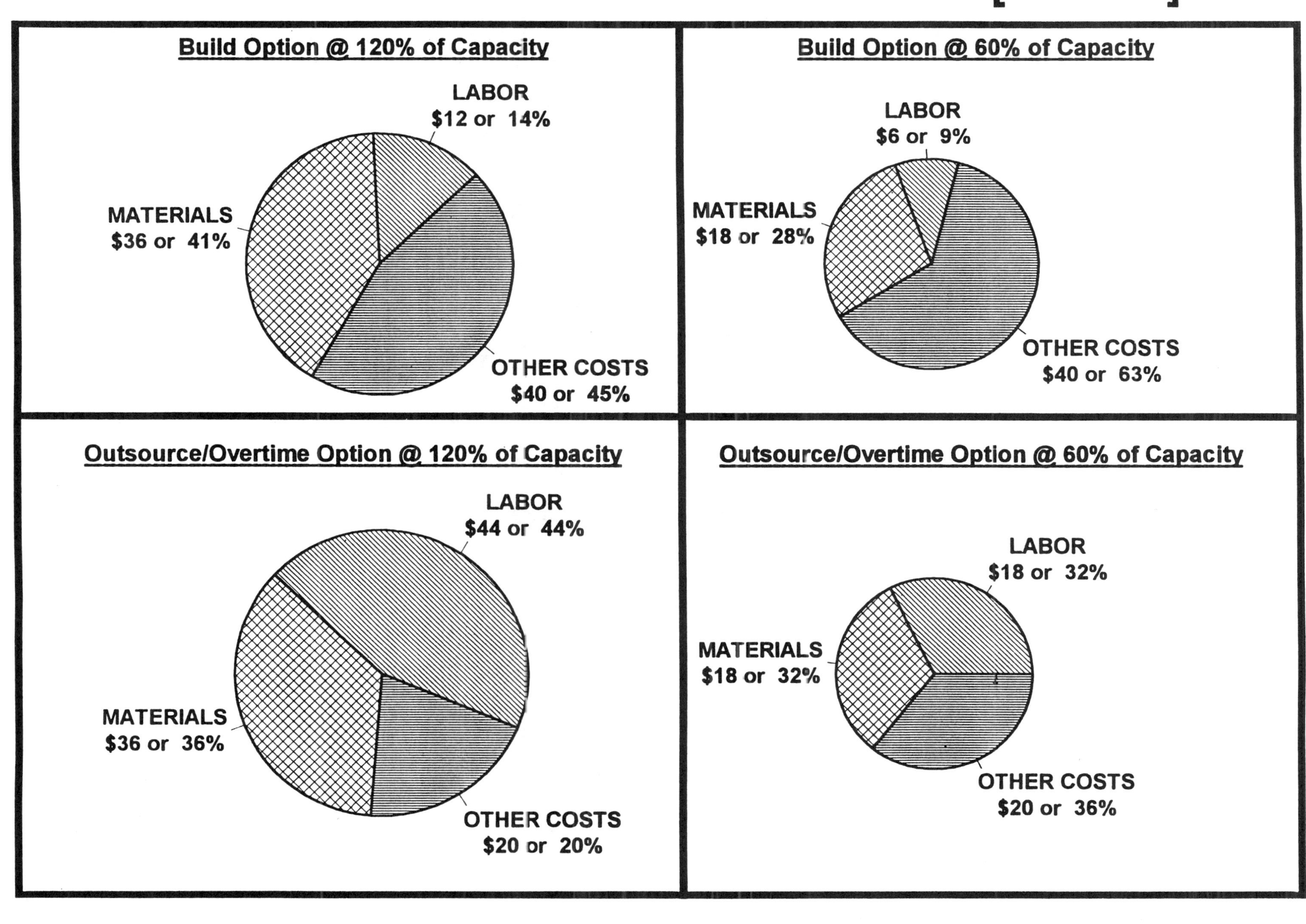

costs into committed fixed (capacity) costs in order to retain cost control and hence reduce financial exposure.

As can be readily seen from the graph or the table, the benefit of the outsource/ overtime option is the decreased financial exposure when production is low. Total costs of the outsource/overtime option at the 60% level of production are $8 million less than those of the build option. The cost of the outsource/ overtime option is the lost profit when demand is high – total costs are $12 million higher at the 120% level. In essence, by choosing the outsource/ overtime option, Ford is willing to forego $12 million of profit in the near term in order to reduce its financial exposure to an $8 million loss in the future. Why? Perhaps Ford's assessment of the probability of continued high demand is less than the probability of a future downturn, or perhaps Ford's key decision makers prefer to avoid risk.

3. Students' answers to this question will vary depending on their attitudes toward risk. This part of the problem helps students realize the value of different forms of analysis. We use pie charts to demonstrate one form of analysis – tables can also be used. The pie charts bring out the importance of fixed costs more readily than the line graph. The four pie charts can be used to point out the value of proportional pie charts. First, focus attention on the two build-option pies. Point out that fixed-cost percentages range from 45% to 63% of total costs if Ford builds automated facilities. This range of fixed costs is reduced to 20-36% of total costs if Ford continues to use overtime and outsourcing. However, comparing the size of the two 120% pies, it can be easily seen that Ford will sacrifice profits by not building if volume approaches the 120% level.

3-35 (30-35 min.)

1. The graph of weekly planned cost of jail guards versus number of prisoners shows that this cost is a step cost beyond 16 prisoners.

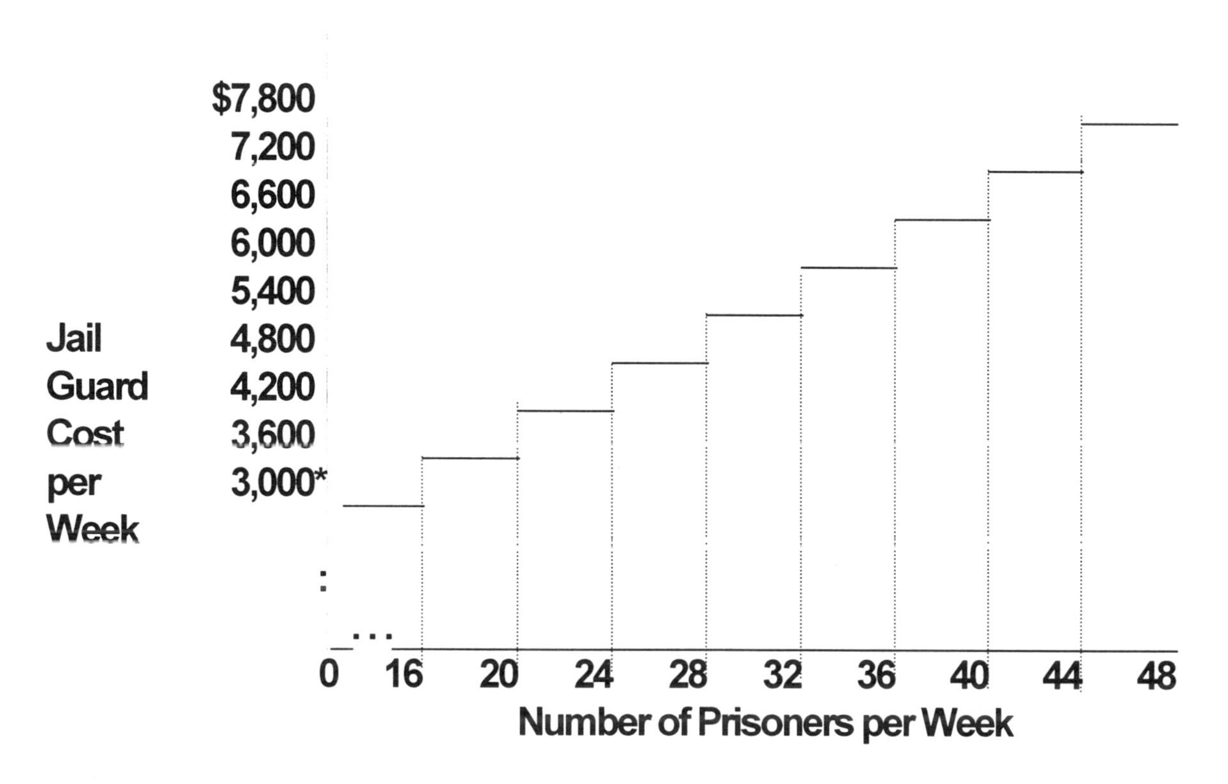

*($36,000/48) x 4

2. In January up to 16 prisoners are expected; therefore, $3,000 should be planned for jail guard costs. This represents the minimum staffing level, and would represent a fixed cost.

3.

Week	Actual Prisoners	Minimum Guard Cost
1	25	$ 4,800
2	38	6,600
3	26	4,800
4	43	7,200
Total		$23,400
Actual		$19,800
Variance		$ 3,600 under

This report indicates that Atlantic County spent less than planned for jail guards during July. It might appear that the county was extremely efficient because it spent less than planned. However, another interpretation of this report is that the jail was understaffed during the critical "busy" summer season. This could mean that prisoners were not adequately monitored and safeguarded during this time. The $3,600 savings might be small compared to damages awarded by the court to a prisoner who was harmed during the time of understaffing.

4. The $3,000 fixed amount is the total weekly salary paid to the permanent guard staff. Each four prisoners (or portion thereof) above 16 requires an additional guard at a cost of $600 per week. On average, each additional prisoner costs $600 ÷ 4 or $150.

5.

Week	Actual Prisoners	Minimum Guard Cost	
1	25	$ 3,000+$150(25-16) =	$ 4,350
2	38	3,000+$150(38-16) =	6,300
3	26	3,000+$150(26-16) =	4,500
4	43	3,000+$150(43-16) =	7,050
Total			$22,200
Actual			$19,800
Variance			$ 2,400 under

Even though the variance of this report is much less than the previous one, this report is not necessarily more accurate. The average cost function predicted actual costs more closely, but if the cost behavior described in 3 above represents *committed* step costs due to state or federal regulations, then the amounts calculated in 3 are costs that the county should have incurred. On the other hand, the administrator of the county jail may try to hire guards according to the simplification of the minimum staffing cost behavior presented in 4, and expect that on average the jail will not be understaffed.

3-36 (25-30 min.)

1.

	Actual Costs	Planned Costs	Variance
Salaries	$66,400	8,000 x 7 = $56,000	$10,400 Unfavorable

2. If the cost measurements are reliable, then the audit office is overstaffed by approximately three auditors. Each auditor should be able to process 4 weeks x 5 days per week x 8 hours per day x 3 returns per hour or 480 returns during the 4-week period. The 8,000 returns should have been processed by 8,000 ÷ 480 or less than 17 auditors, three less than were employed. Alternatively, the $10,400 variance represents $10,400 ÷($830 x 4 weeks) or approximately 3 excess auditors.

3. The variance may be due to inefficiency of the auditors, improperly trained or inexperienced auditors, inaccuracy of the cost measures, a batch of unusually complex returns, or a combination of all these factors. The role of the cost variance is to identify where something is different than planned. The variance itself usually does not identify the *cause* of the variance, only that management attention may be required.

4. Besides number or returns, alternative cost drivers might include number of individual forms included in filed returns, number of pages of returns processed, and amount of taxes shown on returns filed.

<u>3-37</u> (10-15 min.)

One possible cost driver is shown, with cost behavior with respect to the cost driver in parentheses. Other costs drivers are also possible.

a. Pilots' salaries – Hours of flight time (variable)
b. Flight attendants' salaries – Passenger miles (variable)
c. Baggage handlers' salaries – Number of flights (variable)
d. In-flight meals – Number of passengers (variable)
e. Airplane fuel – Flight miles (variable)
f. Airplane depreciation – Flight miles (fixed)
g. Advertising – This is a discretionary fixed cost for which identifying a cost driver is difficult.

3-38 (25-30 min.)

The first temptation may be to measure the cost behavior with the high-low method, using the cost and activity levels from 19X4 and 19X6 since they are the lowest and highest cost and activity levels given. However, Dr. Mueller has indicated that drug test procedures are both more numerous and more complex than they were in the past. Accordingly, if more and more expensive equipment has been acquired and more complex testing is commonplace to meet this new demand, then the past data may not be a relevant base for cost-behavior measurement. A simple graph of cost and activity illustrates the possible problems:

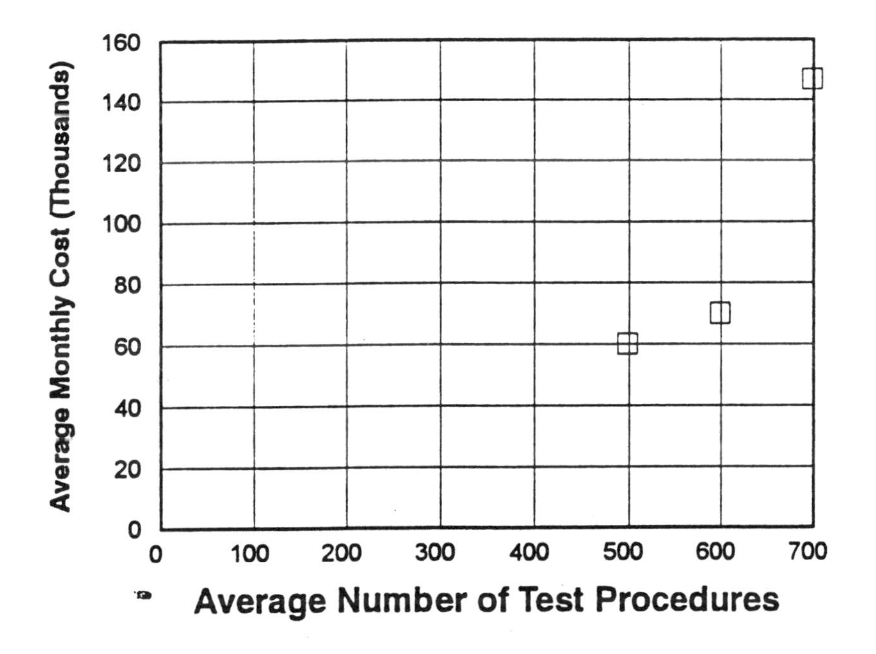

A line drawn through the points for the first two years will have a much different slope and intercept than that implied by the most recent year's experience. It is likely that cost behavior has changed significantly, and this cost behavior may not be revealed by the data currently available. New cost behavior probably has a higher intercept (greater fixed costs per month) and a steeper slope (greater variable cost per procedure) than in the past. More current data are required. Since the data given are monthly averages, the raw monthly data are probably available. One recommendation would be to disregard data from the first two years and to use monthly data from the third year to measure current cost behavior. It could well be that this analysis will indicate a need for the price increase demanded by Dr. Mueller.

3-39 (30-35 min.)

The data should be used to first determine variable expenses as a function (percentage) of tuition revenue. Then fixed expenses can be calculated. Since only two data points are available, the high-low method is the appropriate approach.

$$\text{Variable expenses} = \frac{\text{Change in expenses}}{\text{Change in revenues}} = \frac{(\$730{,}000 - \$710{,}000)}{(\$770{,}000 - \$720{,}000)}$$

$$= \frac{\$20{,}000}{\$50{,}000} = \underline{\underline{.4 \text{ or } 40\% \text{ of tuition revenue}}}$$

Fixed expenses = Total expenses - Variable expenses
= $730,000 - .4 x $770,000
= $730,000 - $308,000
= $422,000 per year

or = $710,000 - .4 x $720,000
= $710,000 - $288,000
= $422,000 per year

Income for 19X9 may be predicted as follows:

METRO BUSINESS COLLEGE
Projected Income
19X9

Tuition revenue		$710,000
Less: Variable expenses (.4 x $710,000)	$284,000	
Fixed expenses	422,000	206,000
Net Income		$ 4,000

Algebraically, Net Income = Tuition revenue - variable expenses - fixed expenses

= $710,000 - .4 x $710,000 - $422,000
= .6 x $710,000 - $422,000 = $4,000

Break-even tuition revenue may be found by setting Net Income = 0 and solving for the unknown tuition revenue, TR, as below:

0 = TR -.4TR - $422,000
0 = .6TR - $422,000
$422,000 = .6TR
TR = $703,333 at break-even

3-40 (20-25 min.)

1. Support cost measurement:

	Customer	
	West Acres Plants	Beautiful Blooms
Fixed charge method:		
Basic cost of FertMix	$12,000	$12,000
Support cost @ 50%	$ 6,000	$ 6,000
Activity Analysis method:		
Lines of customized code	490	180
Estimated cost per line of customized code	x $23	x $23
Activity support cost	$11,270	$ 4,140

2. The activity analysis approach indicates that products requiring large amounts of customizing incur much more support cost than those that require relatively little customizing. The old approach leads to distorted costs that might lead to poor planning and control and either lost sales or unprofitable sales.

   The benefits of adopting the activity analysis approach are (1) more accurate measures of support costs, (2) more competitive cost-based prices, (3) better planning of support costs, and (4) better control of support costs. The disadvantages are that the activity analysis will be more costly to implement and monitor (and may not be necessary for pricing if Des Moines Softuare's industry is not a competitive one).

3-41 (10-15 min.)

1. Variable cost/unit = ($1,1131 - $655) ÷ (136 - 72) = $476 ÷ 64 = $7.4375
   Fixed cost = $1,131 - (163 x 7.4375) = $1,131 - $1,011.50 = $119.50
   Predicted cost for 500 units = ($119.50 x 4) + (500 x $7.4375) = $4,196.75

   Notice that the data are quarterly observations. Thus, the annual fixed cost is 4 times the computed (quarterly) fixed cost.

2. Predicted cost for 500 units = ($337 x 4) + (500 x $5.75) = $4,223.00

3. The regression analysis gives better cost estimates because it uses all the data to form a cost function. The two points used by the high-low method may not be representative of the general relation between costs and volume.

3-42 (35-40 min.)

If supplies cost is at least partly fixed with regard to production volume, then treating supplies cost as if it were purely variable (e.g., using the average supplies cost per unit of production as the variable cost rate) will result in predicting too little supplies cost at low levels of production and too much at high levels of production. See the graph below:

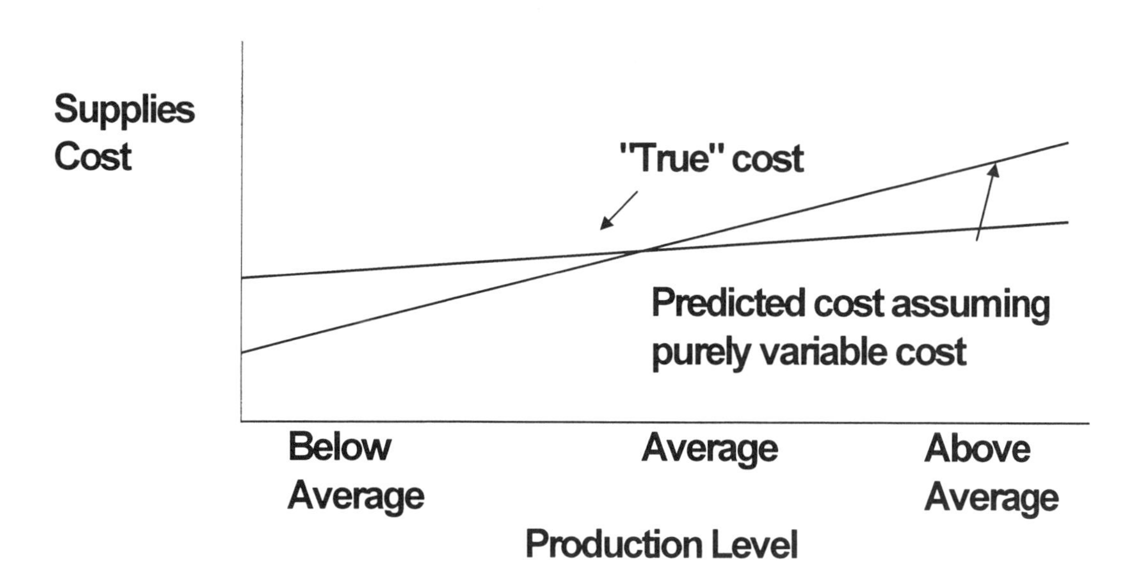

1. The preferred cost function uses "square feet of material used" as the cost driver for supplies cost. Although many other statistical criteria could be (should be) used to make this determination, this choice is based on the relative R-Squared values. The R-squared measures the amount (percentage) of fluctuation (variation) in historical supplies cost that is associated with either number of sleeping bags or with square feet of material used. The cost function using square feet of material used has a much higher R-squared value and, therefore, is more closely associated with historical variations in supplies cost.

The interpretation of the preferred cost function is that, based on past data, supplies cost has a fixed component, $1,900 per month, and a variable component, $0.072 per square foot of material used in a month. The total supplies cost function can be written as:

Total supplies cost = $1, 900 per month + $0.072 x Square feet of material used

2. Approximately 68.6% of the variation in historical supplies cost is associated with variations in square feet of materials. The other 31.4% of variation in supplies cost (100% - 68.6%) depends on other factors, not included in the cost function. Square feet of materials used does not explain this 31.4% of supplies cost.

3-43 (40-45 min. unless data supplied by instructor, then 25-30 min.)

1. The accompanying graphs can be used to discuss requirements 1-4.

2. Regression Output:

Constant	24.42553
Std Err of Y Est	15.54677
R Squared	0.955692
No. of Observations	10
Degrees of Freedom	8
X Coefficient	10.53191
Std Err of Coeff.	0.801764

3. Support costs = fixed cost + variable cost
= $24.43 + $10.53 x 30
= $340.33

4.

	Support cost	Batch size
High Level	$320	30
Low Level	110	9
Difference	$210	21

$$\text{Variable cost} = \frac{\text{Change in cost}}{\text{Change in activity}} = \frac{210}{21} = \underline{\$10 \text{ per unit in batch}}$$

Fixed Cost = total cost - variable cost
= $320 - $10x30 = $20 per batch

Support costs of a batch of size 30 = $20 + $10 x 30 = $320

Although the cost functions and cost estimates are fairly close, the manager would probably be better off using the regression result. The regression results appears to be very reliable and plausible. Since regression uses all the data and no data appear to be unusual (per the graph), there is little reason not to use the regression.

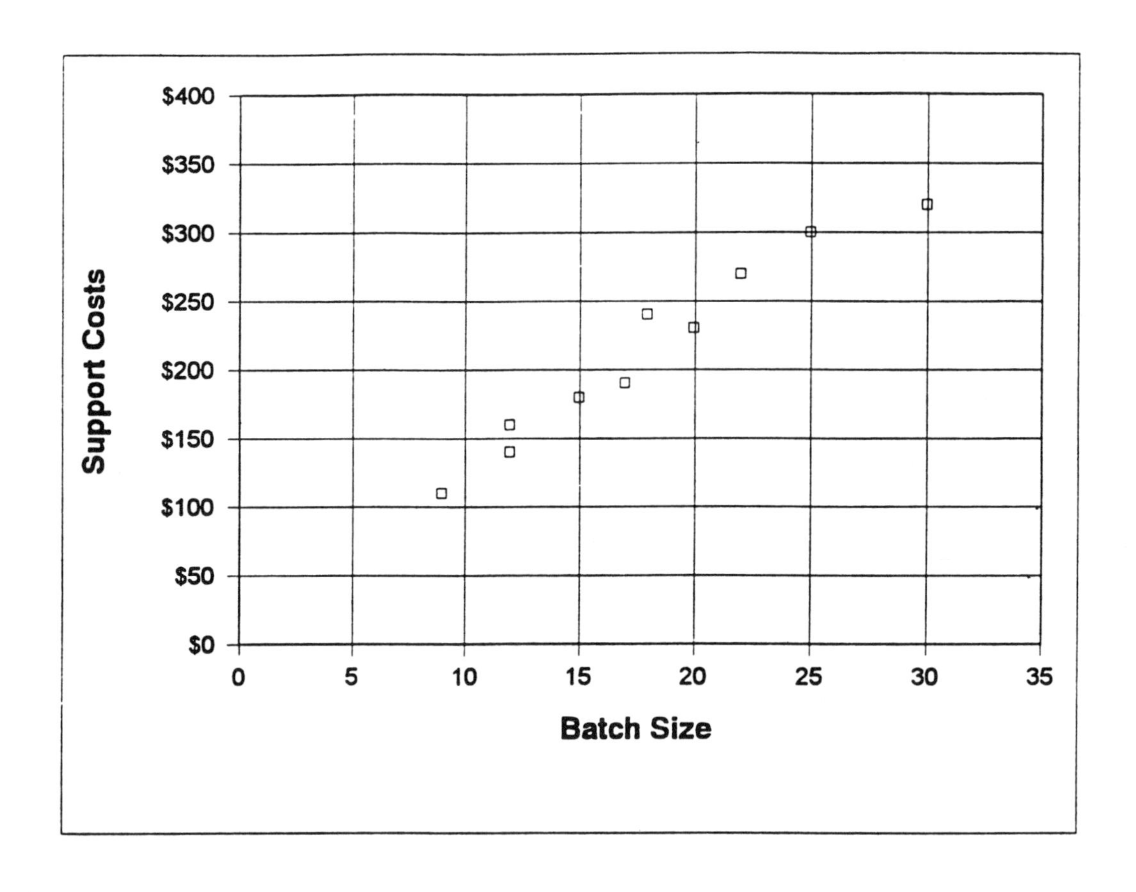
$400
$350
$300
$250
$200
$150
$100
$50
$0
0
5
10
15
20
25
30
35
Support Costs
Batch Size

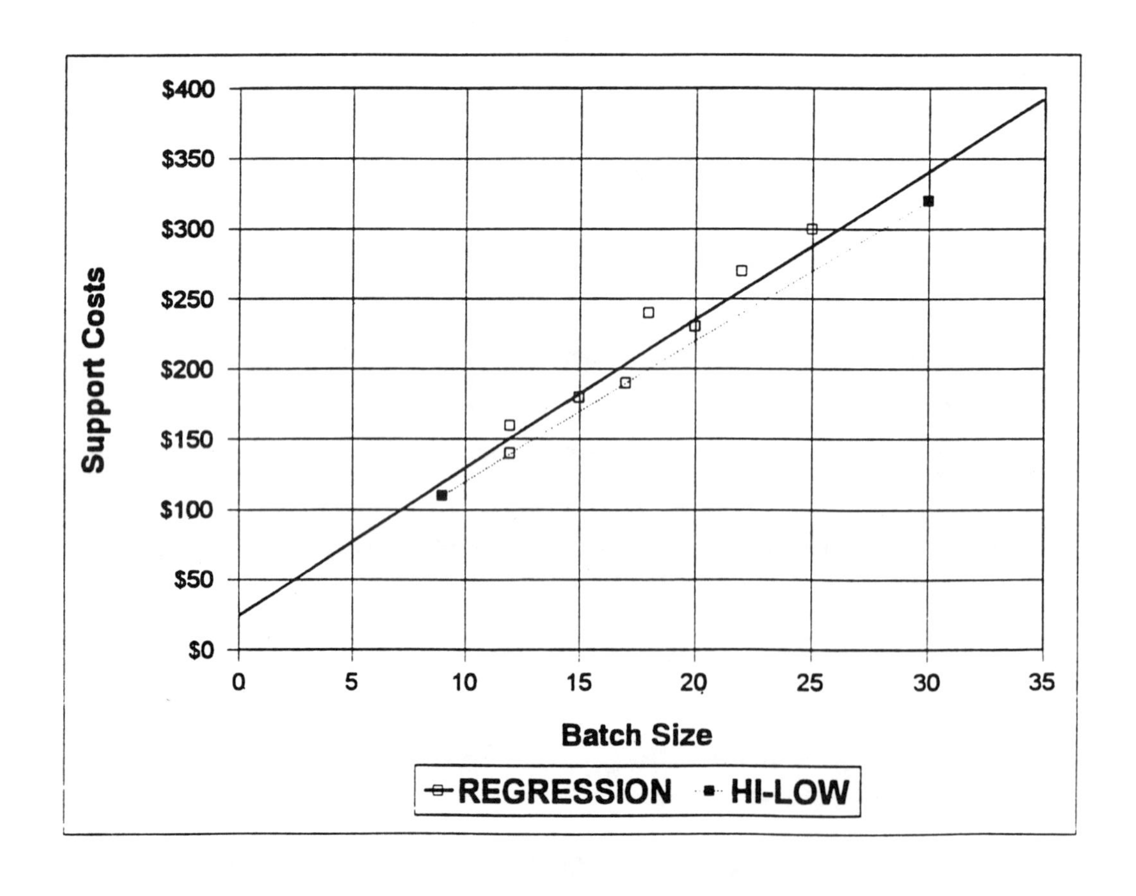
$400
$350
$300
$250
$200
$150
$100
$50
$0
0
5
10
15
20
25
30
35
Support Costs
Batch Size
REGRESSION
HI-LOW

3-44 (35-50 min.)

1. See graphs on the following page.

2. This output is generated by a spreadsheet. Regressions of circuit board support costs using the following as cost drivers:

Regression Output:	Direct Labor Hours
Constant	9466.871
Std Err of Y Est	9308.949
R Squared	0.0059439
No. of Observations	25
Degrees of Freedom	23
X Coefficient(s)	5.960404
Std Err of Coef.	16.06578

Regression Output:	Number of Boards Completed
Constant	21810.742
Std Err of Y Est	8234.805
R Squared	0.2219548
No. of Observations	25
Degrees of Freedom	23
X Coefficient(s)	13.9454396
Std Err of Coef.	5.443818

Regression Output:	Cycle Time
Constant	6572.774
Std Err of Y Est	3567.643
R Squared	0.8540626
No. of Observations	25
Degrees of Freedom	23
X Coefficient(s)	330.4828626
Std Err of Coef.	28.49517

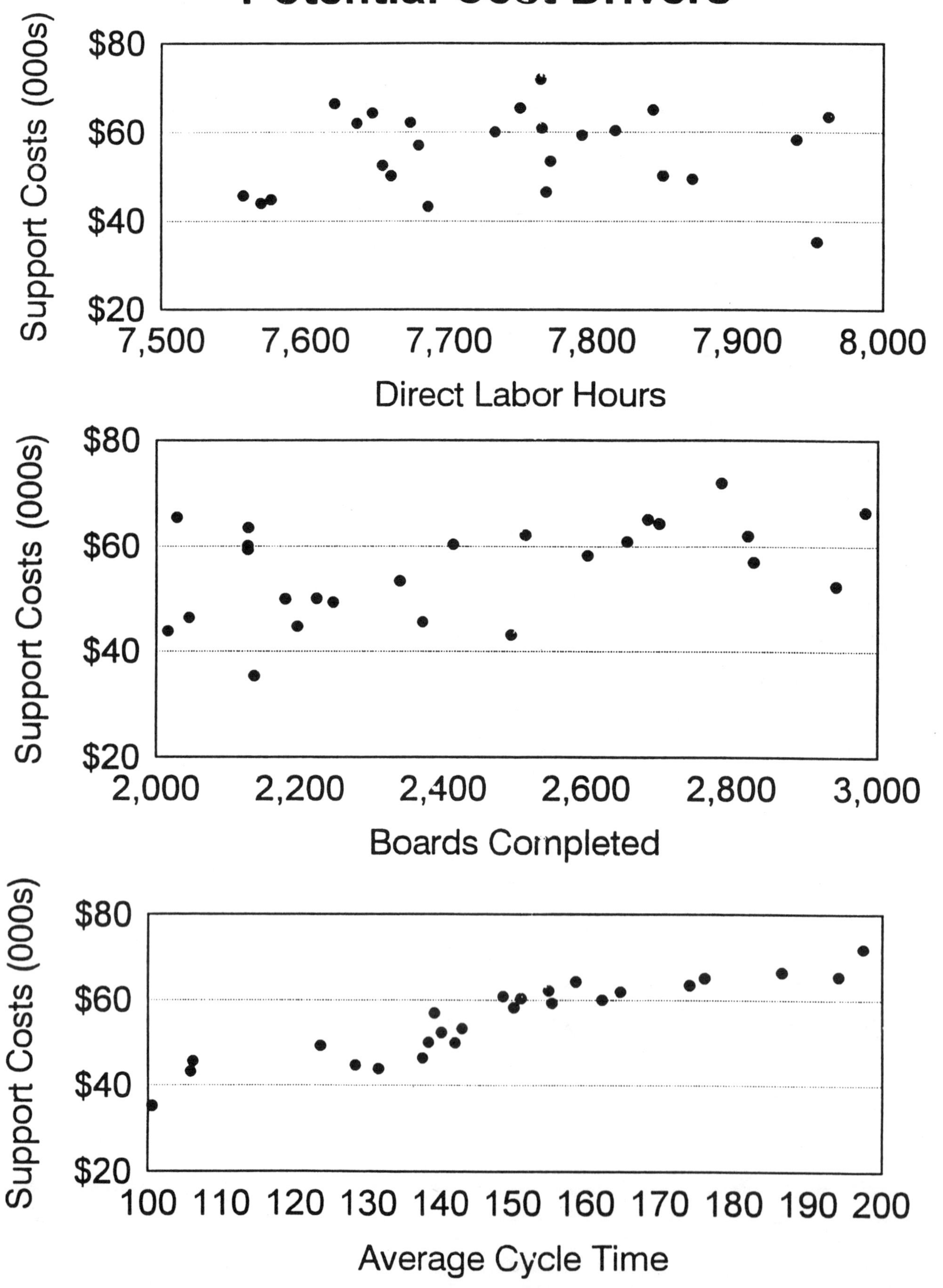
Circuit-Board Assembly Support Costs and Potential Cost Drivers
Support Costs (000s)
$80
$60
$40
$20
7,500
7,600
7,700
7,800
7,900
8,000
Direct Labor Hours
Support Costs (000s)
$80
$60
$40
$20
2,000
2,200
2,400
2,600
2,800
3,000
Boards Completed
Support Costs (000s)
$80
$60
$40
$20
100
110
120
130
140
150
160
170
180
190
200
Average Cycle Time

3. The most plausible and reliable regression function, identifying the best single cost driver for Micro Devices's circuit board support costs, appears to be the one that uses cycle time as the cost driver. (A multiple regression using both cycle time and number of boards is even better.) All of the functions are plausible – they indicate increasing support cost as the cost driver increases. The bases for choosing among the functions are the relative R-squareds of each function. Using cycle time as the cost driver generates the highest R-squared value of all the models using a single cost driver.

4. The economic meaning of the function using cycle time as the cost driver is that circuit board support costs have a fixed component of $6,573 per week and a variable component of $330.48 per hour of average cycle time. Reducing cycle time by an average of one hour should reduce support costs by about $330.

3-45 (30-35 min.)

This problem anticipates the use of cost functions for pricing purposes. Alternatively, the instructor may wish to use this problem in conjunction with Chapter 5.

1. One would expect that the third cost function, using average cycle time as the cost driver, would be the most reliable for explaining and predicting support costs. Although all the functions are plausible, average cycle time as a cost driver generates the highest R-squared, which means that it best explains past support costs. If the process remains unchanged, then this function should be reliable for predicting future support costs.

2. The first part of this solution uses the cost function developed in problem 3-44. The second part uses the cost function given in the problem.

(a) Cost function from 3-44:

Cost using Direct Labor Cost as the cost driver:

Fixed cost:	$9,467/wk x 3 weeks =	$ 28,401
Variable cost:	$5.96 x 20,000 hours =	119,200
Total		$147,601

Cost using Number of Boards as the cost driver:

Fixed cost:	$21,811/wk x 3 weeks =	$ 65,433
Variable cost:	$13.95 x 6,000 boards =	83,700
Total		$149,133

Cost using Average Cycle Time as the cost driver:

Fixed cost:	$6,573/wk x 3 weeks =	$ 19,719
Variable cost:	$330.48 x 180 hours x 3 weeks =	178,459
Total		$198,178

(b) Cost function from the problem:

Cost using Direct Labor Cost as the cost driver:

Fixed cost:	$9,000/wk x 3 weeks =	$ 27,000
Variable cost:	$6 x 20,000 hours =	120,000
Total		$147,000

Cost using Number of Boards as the cost driver:

Fixed cost:	$20,000/wk x 3 weeks =	$ 60,000
Variable cost:	$14 x 6,000 boards =	84,000
Total		$144,000

Cost using Average Cycle Time as the cost driver:

Fixed cost:	$5,000/wk x 3 weeks =	$ 15,000
Variable cost:	$350 x 180 hours x 3 weeks =	189,000
Total		$204,000

3. For this three-week period and the particular boards manufactured, the cycle time cost function yields materially different cost predictions. We know from the regression analyses that the direct labor function and, to a lesser degree, the number of boards function are not reliable functions. Unless there was something unusual about the production activity of those three weeks, Micro Devices should use the cost estimates from the cycle time regression.

4. In a highly competitive environment, the market may have much more influence over prices than does cost. Therefore, setting prices by marking up costs, even if costs are accurate, is not a sufficient pricing policy. At a minimum, Micro Devices should examine its prices compared to those of its competition in addition to comparing them to its costs.

3-46 (30-35 min.)

1. This is only a first pass; obviously Dr. Black would be able to specify more precisely which are committed or discretionary costs.

Program Area	Committed	Discretionary
Administration:		
Salaries		
Administrator	$ 60,000	
Assistant		$30,000
Two secretaries	42,000	
Supplies	35,000	
Advertising and Promotion		9,000
Professional meetings, dues, and literature		14,000
Purchased Services		
Accounting and billing	15,000	
Custodial and maintenance	13,000	
Security	12,000	
Professional consulting		10,000
Community mental health services		
Salaries (two social workers)	46,000	
Transportation	5,000	5,000
Out patient mental health treatment		
Salaries		
Psychiatrist	85,000	
Two social workers	70,000	
Totals	$383,000	$68,000

2. If all discretionary costs were eliminated, perhaps at least $68,000 could be saved. However, some of these "discretionary" cuts may

seriously affect the ability of the health center to deliver its services. There does not seem to be much "fat" in this budget to begin with, and eliminating such items as transportation for social workers would mean that the community would have to come to the clinic rather than vice-versa. Cutting down on professional development opportunities of the staff could mean losing quality staff or reducing their quality over time. Dropping advertising and promotion may be the least painful since the center is apparently at capacity now. However, this could mean that individuals who really need the services will not find out about them. Eliminating the consulting may mean that the center cannot refer individuals with unique problems to specialists. Reducing levels of maintenance and custodial care may mean that more costly problems will develop in the future. Finally, eliminating the administrative assistant will mean a greater burden for Dr. Black and the limited secretarial staff. Cutting these "discretionary" expenses may be necessary, but they will be painful.

3. Dr. Black should prepare for the worst but begin now to build her case for even higher resources given the past budget cuts and increasing demand for services at the center. Documentation of community needs, benefits provided by the center, and needs not being met are necessary. A good-faith effort to first eliminate any possible waste may convince budgetary authorities that no further budget cuts are necessary and even that some budget enhancement is desirable.

3-47 (45-50 min.)

This problem extends the use of activity analysis for control and transfer-pricing purposes. The instructor may wish to use this problem as a preview of later applications or in conjunction with Chapter 10.

1. The number of employees may be an indicator of service department costs in general. If all users of service departments have roughly the same per capita usage of services, then using number of employees may be a simple and reasonably accurate and equitable means of charging for these costs. However, more specialized services may have more specific cost drivers that are not distributed according to number of employees, as is apparently the case of SS department costs at Southeast Pulp and Paper. Whether activity analysis is justified to identify and measure this cost behavior more accurately depends, of course, on the costs and benefits of the effort. This case is similar to the experience of Weyerhaeuser, cited in the text. Weyerhaeuser felt the effort was worthwhile, and while we do not have post-audit type information on the continued viability of activity analysis of service costs at Weyerhaeuser, we will assume that the benefits continue.

2. 19X7 SS Cost per Employee $= \dfrac{\text{19X7 SS Costs}}{\text{Number of Employees}}$

$= \dfrac{(\$300,000)}{(1,721)} = \$174.32$

19X7 SS Cost per Report $= \dfrac{\text{19X7 SS Costs}}{\text{Number of Reports}}$

$= \dfrac{(\$300,000)}{(1,232)} = \$243.51$

19X8 SS Cost per Employee $= \dfrac{\text{19X8 SS Costs}}{\text{Number of Employees}}$

$= \dfrac{(\$385,000)}{(1,295)} = \$297.30$

19X8 SS Cost per Report $= \dfrac{\text{19X8 SS Costs}}{\text{Number of Reports}}$

$= \dfrac{(\$385,000)}{(1,556)} = \$247.43$

	Total	Forest Mgmt	Lumber Products	Paper Products
19X7 Number of Employees	1,721	762	457	502
19X7 SS Costs Charged to Divisions via Employees ($174.32 x 762, etc.)		$132,832	$ 79,664	$ 87,509
19X7 Number of Reports	1,232	410	445	377
19X7 SS Costs Charged to Divisions via Reports ($243.51 x 410, etc.)		$99,839	$108,362	$91,803
19X8 Number of Employees	1,295	751	413	131
19X8 SS Costs Charged to Divisions via Employees ($297.30 x 751, etc.)		$223,272	$122,785	$38,946
19X8 Number of Reports	1,556	412	432	712
19X8 SS Costs Charged to Divisions via Reports ($247.43 x 412, etc.)		$101,941	$106,890	$176,170

It is clear that the other divisions have what they see are legitimate complaints. Each of the other divisions, Forest Management and Lumber Products, has reduced the number of employees, but not as drastically as the Paper Products division. The result has been that more of the SS department costs have been shifted to Forest Management and Lumber Products, even as Paper Products has increased its demands for SS services. It would appear that Paper Products is not paying its fair share of SS costs.

3. Charging for SS department costs on the basis of number of employees creates an incentive to reduce the number of employees or to add employees only if the added benefits exceed the wage/salary cost plus SS (and other service) department costs. Charging for SS costs based on the number of reports creates the incentive to demand additional reports only if their value to the division exceeds the cost charged. This latter form of charge, based on the department's cost driver(s), probably will permit planning and control of service department costs more effectively than using generic charges.

4. It appears that activity analysis should be extended to all of Southeast's service departments. Using number of employees as the basis for charging for service costs probably distorts incentives for divisions to control costs.

3-48 (35-50 min.)

1. See the accompanying graph. One can discern two different cost behaviors that appear to mirror changes in the cost time series. Matching the cost table and the graph shows that both the intercept and the slope of the cost function have changed after week 13. After week 13, fixed costs have increased at the same time that variable costs per order have decreased. In fact, logistics costs seems to be an almost purely fixed cost after week 13.

2. The first 13 weeks of data appear to be irrelevant to current cost behavior. Any measures of cost behavior that are to be used for current and future use should be based on the most recent data (weeks 14-25) only.

3. See the accompanying graph. The data do support Hudson's expectations: Fixed costs have increased, and variable costs have decreased. Regression analyses (though on limited numbers of observations) bear this out.

Regression Output: Weeks 1-13	
Constant	5497.172
Std Err of Y Est	870.0801
R Squared	0.8401874
No. of Observations	13
Degrees of Freedom	11
X Coefficient(s)	12.9031643
Std Err of Coef.	1.784237

Regression Output: Weeks 14-25	
Constant	20337.16
Std Err of Y Est	266.7286
R Squared	0.1282178
No. of Observations	12
Degrees of Freedom	10
X Coefficient(s)	0.5556408
Std Err of Coef.	0.559401

However, average total logistics costs do not appear to have decreased. On logistics cost behavior alone, the switch does not seem to be justified. However, the new ordering system may be more flexible and may contribute to cost and quality savings in other departments. A full analysis of the benefits of the new ordering system should try to capture those benefits as well. If the ordering activity should increase greatly, the new system may be able to operate at lower total cost than the old system, but this level of activity would be well outside the relevant range of experience.

ANALYSIS OF LOGISTICS COSTS AND NUMBER OF ORDERS

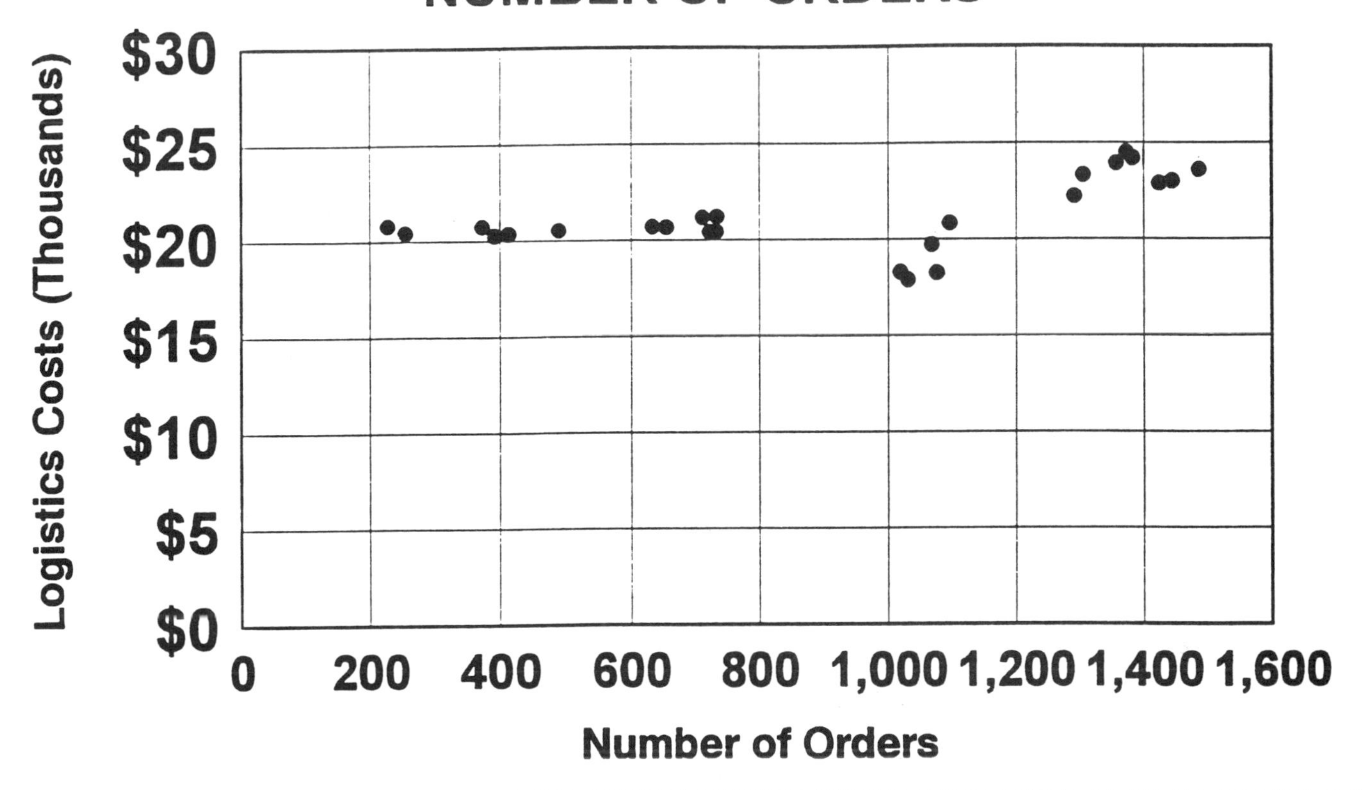

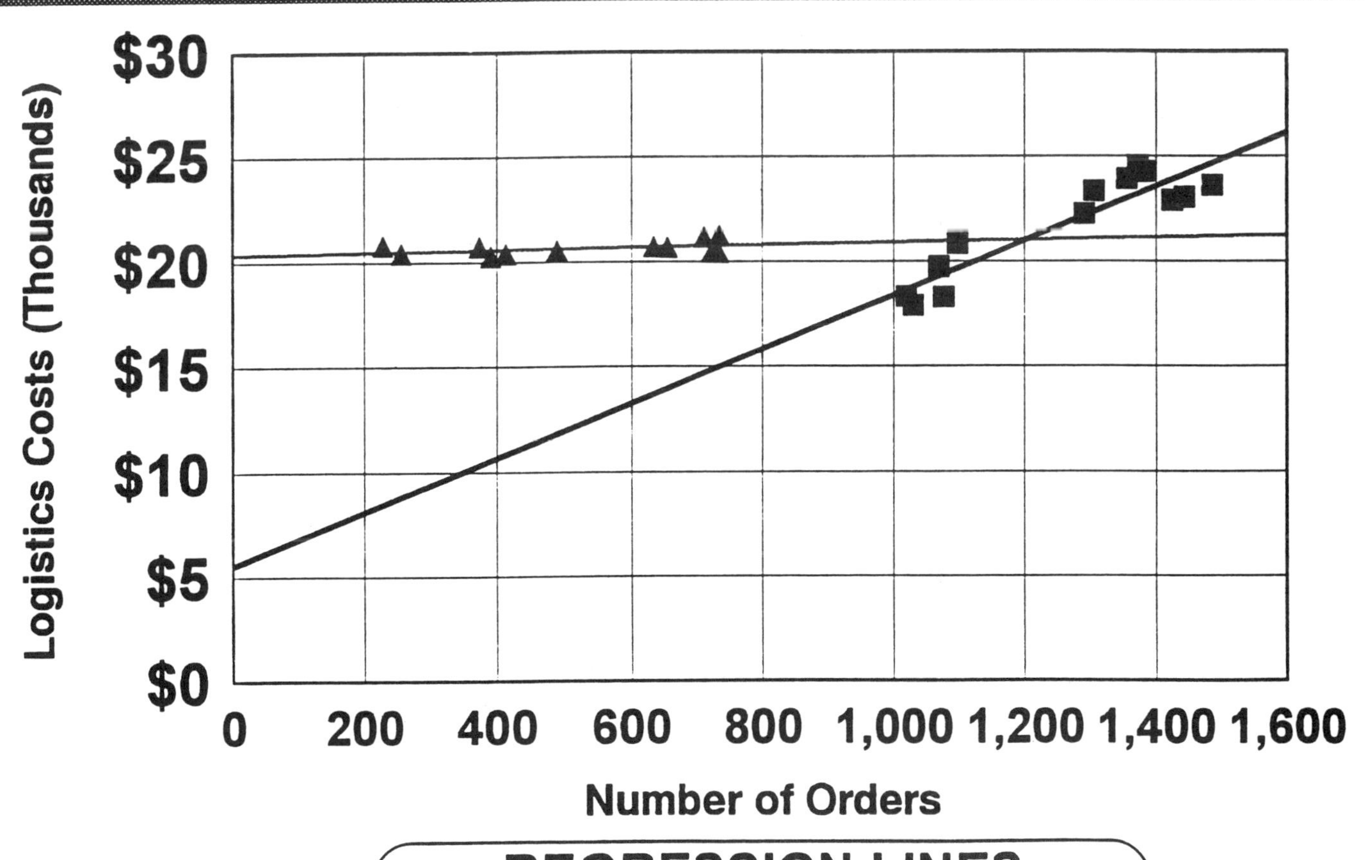

3-49 (10-30 min.)

The purpose of this exercise is to develop an understanding of different types of costs and their behavior. Assigning the problem ahead of time allows students to prepare lists of each type of cost, forcing them to think about types of cost and their behavior. However, the game could be played without advance preparation, especially if many students have some business experience.

CHAPTER 4
Cost Management Systems and Activity-Based Costing

4-A1 (40-50 min.)

1.

COLUMBIA COMPANY
Contribution Income Statement
For the Year Ended December 31, 19X9
(in thousands of dollars)

Sales		$1,800
Less variable expenses		
Direct material	$400	
Direct labor	330	
Variable manufacturing overhead (Schedule 1)	150	
Total variable manufacturing cost of goods sold	$880	
Variable selling expenses	60	
Variable administrative expenses	24	
Total variable expenses		964
Contribution margin		$ 836
Less fixed expenses:		
Fixed manufacturing overhead (Schedule 2)	$232	
Selling expenses	240	
Administrative expenses	120	
Total fixed expenses		592
Operating income		$ 244

COLUMBIA COMPANY
Absorption Income Statement
For the Year Ended December 31, 19X9
(in thousands of dollars)

Sales		$1,800
Less manufacturing cost of goods sold:		
Direct material	$400	
Direct labor	330	
Manufacturing overhead (Schedules 1 and 2)	382	
Total manufacturing cost of goods sold		1,112
Gross margin		$ 688
Less:		
Selling expenses	$300	
Administrative expenses	144	444
Operating income		$ 244

COLUMBIA COMPANY
Schedules of Manufacturing Overhead
For the Year Ended December 31, 19X9
(in thousands of dollars)

Schedule 1: Variable Costs		
Supplies	$ 20	
Utilities, variable portion	40	
Indirect labor, variable portion	90	$150
Schedule 2: Fixed Costs		
Utilities, fixed portion	$ 12	
Indirect labor, fixed portion	40	
Depreciation	110	
Property taxes	20	
Supervisory salaries	50	232
Total manufacturing overhead		$382

2. Change in revenue $200,000

Change in total contribution margin:

Contribution margin ratio in part 1 is $836 ÷ $1,800 = .464

Ratio times increase in revenue is .464 x $200,000

$ 92,800

Change in revenue	$200,000
Change in total contribution margin: Contribution margin ratio in part 1 is $836 ÷ $1,800 = .464; Ratio times increase in revenue is .464 x $200,000	$ 92,800
Operating income before change	244,000
New operating income	$336,800

This analysis is readily done by using data from the contribution income statement. In contrast, the data in the absorption income statement must be analyzed and split into variable and fixed categories before the effect on operating income can be estimated.

4-A2 (10 min.)

1. $400 + $330 = $730
2. $330 + $382 = $712
3. $382
4. $382
5. $382
6. $382

4-A3 (30-35 min.)

1.

Cost/Activity Center: Cost Drivers	Annual Traceable Cost	Annual Cost Driver Activity	Cost per Driver Unit	Cost Driver Consumption Part T151A	Total Cost, Part T151A
Quality: Pieces scrapped	$ 800,000	10,000	$ 80	1,000	$ 80,000
Production scheduling: Setups	50,000	500	100	12	1,200
Setup: Setups	600,000	500	1,200	12	14,400
Shipping: Containers shipped	300,000	60,000	5	500	2,500
Shipping admin.: Shipments	50,000	1,000	50	100	5,000
Production: Machine hours	1,500,000	10,000	150	500	75,000
Total indirect cost	$3,300,000				$178,100
Direct materials					150,000
Direct labor					86,000
Total Cost of Part T151A					$414,100
Number of units produced					100,000
Cost per unit					$4.141
Selling price					6.000
Gross margin					$1.859
Gross margin percentage					31.0%

2. Assuming that the results of the activity analysis are accurate, Product T151A is much more profitable than RMP's existing costing system estimates. The existing system is overcosting product T151A by $1.659 or 40%! Chrysler's proposal can be accepted as long as the reduction in price is not significant. RMP should be aware, however, that the existing costing system is also *undercosting* some products, since all indirect costs are allocated (for example, see problem 4-42 and the related charts). The activity-based costing system should be used to cost all product lines in order to identify RMP's "winners" as well as "losers."

Benefits of activity-based cost implementation include:

- More accurate costing of activities, product, customers, and other cost objects
- A solid foundation for activity-based management – using ABC information as a management tool for budgeting, planning, and control purposes
- An effective communication tool, since successful ABC implementation should involve all functional areas of the company

Costs of implementing ABC include:

- The cost of a pilot study includes salaries of managers who are dedicated to the study.
- Consultants are often necessary.
- Data collection is extensive since operational and financial data are often not available as required to support the new ABC system.
- It may be necessary to maintain an ABC system separate from the accounting system used for external reporting.

(Note to instructor: See solution to problem 4-42 for a graph that depicts product cross-subsidation.)

4-B1 (40-50 min.)

1. KINGLAND COMPANY
Contribution Income Statement
For the Year Ended December 31, 19X9
(In thousands of dollars)

Sales			$10,000
Less variable expenses:			
Direct material		$4,000	
Direct labor		2,000	
Variable indirect manufacturing costs (Schedule 1)			960
Total variable manufacturing cost of goods sold			$6,960
Variable selling expenses:			
Sales commissions	$500		
Shipping expenses	300	800	
Variable clerical salaries		400	
Total variable expenses			8,160
Contribution margin			$ 1,840
Less fixed expenses:			
Manufacturing (Schedule 2)		$ 582	
Selling (advertising)		200	
Administrative-executive salaries		100	
Total fixed expenses			882
Operating income			$ 958

KINGLAND COMPANY
Absorption Income Statement
For the Year Ended December 31, 19X9
(In thousands of dollars)

Sales			$10,000
Less manufacturing cost of goods sold:			
Direct material		$4,000	
Direct labor		2,000	
Indirect manufacturing costs (Schedules 1 and 2)		1,542	7,542
Gross profit			$ 2,458
Selling expenses:			
Sales commissions	$500		
Advertising	200		
Shipping expenses	300	$1,000	
Administrative expenses:			
Executive salaries	$100		
Clerical salaries	400	500	1,500
Operating income			$ 958

KINGLAND COMPANY
Schedules 1 and 2
Indirect Manufacturing Costs
For the Year Ended December 31, 19X9
(In thousands of dollars)

Schedule 1: Variable Costs		
Cutting bits	$ 60	
Abrasives for machining	100	
Indirect labor	800	$ 960
Schedule 2: Fixed Costs		
Factory supervisors' salaries	$100	
Factory methods research	40	
Long-term rent, factory	100	
Fire insurance on equipment	2	
Property taxes on equipment	10	
Depreciation on equipment	300	
Factory superintendent's salary	30	582
Total indirect manufacturing costs		$1,542

2. Operating income would increase from $958,000 to $1,050,000, computed as follows:

Increase in revenue	$500,000
Increase in total contribution margin:	
Contribution margin ratio in contribution income statement is $1,840 ÷ $10,000 = .184.	
Ratio times revenue is .184 x $500,000	$ 92,000
Increase in fixed expenses	0
Operating income before increase	$958,000
New operating income	$1,050,000

The above analysis is readily calculated by using data from the contribution income statement. In contrast, the data in the absorption income statement must be analyzed and divided into variable and fixed categories before the effect on operating income can be estimated.

4-B2 (15-20 min.)

1.

Value-Added Activities	Non-Value-Added Activities
Rear wheel assembly	Materials receiving and inspection
Assemble handlebars	Production scheduling
Install speedometer	Production setup
	Move engine from fabrication to assembly building
	Paint inspection
	Rework defective brake assemblies
	Put completed motorcycle in finished goods storage

2.

- Materials receiving and inspection. Inspection costs can be reduced by forming good relations with suppliers so that they guarantee quality. Receiving costs can be reduced by setting up the receiving area so that minimal handling is necessary. If materials are received just when they are needed, time to place them in inventory storage and then retrieve them is eliminated.

- Production scheduling. Scheduling time is reduced by simplifying the production process and letting the receipt of orders drive the production schedule.

- Production setup. Simplifying products and processes may reduce the number of setups required. Changing the production process and training production employees to perform setups can reduce the time and cost of the setups.

- Move engine from fabrication to assembly building. Changing the production flow to minimize move times and waiting times, and automating production flow can reduce these costs.

- Paint inspection. An emphasis on quality in the painting operation may make inspection unnecessary, or at least less costly.

- Rework defective brake assemblies. Again, emphasis on quality may make much of this rework unnecessary. Rework can often be done more cheaply directly on the production line if employees are trained to spot defects and know how to fix them.

- Put completed motorcycle in finished goods storage. A JIT system is driven by customer orders. If an order is received for a motorcycle before it is produced, it will be shipped immediately upon completion instead of being put into storage, saving costs of handling and storing finished goods.

4-B3 (20-30 min.)

1. The first step is to determine the cost per cost-driver unit for each activity:

Activity Center [Cost Driver]	Monthly Manufacturing Overhead	Cost-Driver Activity	Cost per Driver Unit
Material Handling [Direct materials cost]	$ 8,000	$200,000	$ 0.04
Engineering [Engineering change notices]	20,000	20	1,000.00
Power [Kilowatt hours]	16,000	400,000	0.04
Total Manufacturing Overhead	$44,000		

Next, the costs of each activity can be allocated to each of the three products:

Cost	PHYSICAL FLOW/ALLOCATED COST SA2		SA5		SA9	
Material Handling	$.04 x 25,000	=$ 1,000	$.04 x 50,000	=$ 2,000	$.04 x 125,000	=$ 5,000
Engineering	$1,000 x 13	= 13,000	$1,000 x 5	= 5,000	$1,000 x 2	= 2,000
Power	$.04 x 50,000	= 2,000	$.04 x 200,000	= 8,000	$.04 x 150,000	= 6,000
Total		$16,000		$22,000		$13,000

2. Overhead rate based on direct labor costs:

$$\text{Rate} = \frac{\text{Total manufacturing overhead}}{\text{Total direct labor cost}} = \frac{\$44{,}000}{\$8{,}000} = \$5.50/\text{DL\$}$$

Overhead allocated to each product is:

SA2:	$5.50 x 4,000 =	$22,000
SA5:	$5.50 x 1,000 =	5,500
SA9:	$5.50 x 3,000 =	16,500
Total		$44,000

Notice that much less manufacturing overhead cost is allocated to SA5 using direct labor as a cost driver. Why? Because SA5 uses only a small amount of labor but large amounts of other resources, especially power.

3. The product costs in requirement 1 are more accurate if the cost drivers are good indicators of the causes of the costs – they are both plausible and reliable. For example, kilowatt hours is certainly a better measure of the cost of power costs than is direct labor hours. Therefore, the allocation of power costs in requirement 1 is certainly better than in requirement 2. Materials handling and engineering are likewise more accurate in requirement 1. A manager would be much more confident in the manufacturing overhead allocated to products in requirement 1. Remember, however, that there are incremental costs of data collection associated with the more accurate ABC system. The benefit/cost criteria must be applied in deciding which costing system is "best."

4-1 Cost objectives or cost objects include departments, products, territories, miles driven, bricks laid, patients seen, and potholes repaired.

4-2 Cost accounting systems become more detailed as management seeks more accurate data for decision making.

4-3 No. Departments are objects of costing because they represent a logical grouping of activities for which a separate determination of costs is desired.

4-4 Yes, the same cost (for example, the department supervisor's salary) can be direct with respect to a department but indirect with respect to the variety of products flowing through a department (e.g., tables, chairs, and cabinets).

4-5 Yes. Economic feasibility means being "cost effective." That is, managers do not want cost accounting to be more expensive than its expected benefits.

4-6 Some costs can be physically linked with a department (or a product), but not in an economically feasible way. An example is the use of departmental meters for measuring power usage. Such devices would measure power costs as direct costs of a department. Otherwise, factory power costs usually are regarded by managers as indirect costs of individual departments. Managers often decide whether the resulting increased accuracy provided by individual power meters is worth their additional cost; thus, the test of economic feasibility will decide whether a particular cost is regarded as direct or indirect.

4-7 Prime costs are direct labor plus direct materials costs. Conversion costs are direct labor plus manufacturing overhead costs.

4-8 *For financial statement purposes*, the typical accounting system does not allocate costs associated with value-chain functions other than production to the physical units produced. However, for guiding decisions regarding product-pricing and product-mix decisions, many companies allocate all costs, including R&D, design, marketing, distribution, and customer service costs. However, the allocations of these costs may not be embedded in the system that generates financial statements.

4-9 No. They are direct as far as the physical product is concerned, but in accounting for their cost it would usually be impractical to keep records of the amount of glue or tacks used in each unit of product. A more feasible method would be to consider these as supplies (indirect material).

4-10 The two-fold category consists of direct materials and conversion costs. Some companies use factory overhead instead of conversion costs to describe the second element. The important point to recognize is that direct labor vanishes as a major cost element. Instead, it is subsumed as a part of factory overhead. The label is of secondary importance.

4-11 Depreciation related to manufacturing activities is a product cost, not a period cost. Hence, it will become an expense as a part of manufacturing cost of goods sold. Thus, depreciation is not always an immediate expense.

4-12 "Expenses" denote all costs deducted from (matched against) revenues in a given period. "Costs" is a much broader term; for example, "cost" is used to describe an asset (the cost of inventory) and an expense (the cost of goods sold).

4-13 Unexpired costs are not confined to inventory costs. Other examples are plant, equipment, and miscellaneous deferred or prepaid costs such as insurance premiums.

4-14 Direct labor costs are incurred at the same time the direct labor is used in production. It is not purchased and stored for future use. Therefore, there is no direct labor inventory account.

4-15 The contribution approach has several advantages over the absorption approach, including a better analysis of cost-volume-profit relationships, clearer presentation of all variable costs, and more relevant arrangement of data for such decisions as make-or-buy or product expansion.

4-16 Manufacturing is the transformation of materials into other goods through the use of labor and factory facilities. In contrast, merchandising companies (retailers or wholesalers) sell goods without changing their basic forms.

4-17 The terms that describe an income statement that emphasizes the differences between variable or fixed costs are *contribution approach*, *variable costing*, or *direct costing*.

4-18 A cost driver is an output measure for a resource or activity. In an ABC system, the costs of overhead resources that are consumed when activities are performed are allocated to these activities using appropriate output measures (cost drivers A, B, and C). Thus, these cost drivers are referred to as resource cost drivers (or simply cost drivers).

After the costs of all resources consumed by an activity are accumulated into an activity cost pool, this cost must be allocated to products (or services or even other activities). This is done using the most appropriate (plausible or reliable) output measure. In practice, these measures are often referred to as cost drivers but they are more appropriately called activity cost drivers (D, E, and F).

4-19 The simplest answser is to recommend a traditional costing system for the Youngstown plant and an ABC costing system for the Salem plant. Why? Because the purpose of any costing system is to provide as accurate cost information as possible subject to the benefit-cost criterion. There is always a tradeoff between the accuracy of a system and the costs to implement and maintain it. Generally, as the operations of a company become more complex, the diversity of demands upon resources increases across products (services). In order to accurately track resource costs in such a diverse operating environment, many cost pools are used – that is, an ABC system. Because the Youngstown plant operations are not complex, a simple (traditional) costing system probably provides sufficiently accurate cost information. Due to the complexity and diversity of the Salem plant operations, an ABC costing system should be considered.

4-20 The four steps are:

Step 1. Determine cost objectives, key activities, resources and related cost drivers.
Step 2. Develop a process-based map representing the flow of activities, resources, and their interrelationships.
Step 3. Collect relevant data concerning costs and physical flow of cost-driver units among resources and activities.
Step 4. Calculate and interpret the new activity-based information.

4-21 A fixed-cost resource is a resource with costs that do not change with changes in the amount of cost-driver units. A variable-cost resource is a resource with costs that change in direct proportion to changes in the amount of the cost-driver units. In Exhibit 4-11, paper, telecommunications, and computer resources are probably variable-cost resources. We assume that the computer resource is leased and thus the cost is based on transactions (or minutes used). If Portland Power owns its computer, the resource cost would be fixed.

4-22 Six factors that explain why more and more organizations are adopting activity-based costing systems are:

1. Fierce competitive pressure has resulted in shrinking margins making accurate cost determinations essential. While companies may know their overall (annual basis) margin is shrinking, they often do not have faith in the accuracy of the margins for *individual* products or services. Some are winners and some are losers – but which ones?
2. Business complexity has increased, resulting in greater diversity in the types of products and services as well as customer classes. This means that the consumption of a company's shared resources also varies substantially across products and customers.
3. New production techniques have increased the indirect proportion of total costs – that is, indirect costs are far more important in today's world-class manufacturing environment. In many industries direct labor is being replaced by automated equipment. It is not unusual for indirect cost to be over 50% of total cost.
4. The rapid pace of technology change has shortened product life cycles. This means that companies do not have time to make price or cost adjustments once costing errors are discovered.
5. The costs associated with bad decisions that result from inaccurate cost determinations are substantial (bids lost due to overcosted products, hidden losses from undercosted products, failure to detect activities that are not cost effective, etc.).
6. Computer technology has reduced the costs of develping and operating cost systems that track many activities.

4-23 Activity-based management is using activity-based cost information to improve the operations of an organization. Managers use ABC information for decision making, planning, and controlling purposes. Cost information is vital for each of these purposes. The accuracy level of the cost information is a critical factor in determining the effectiveness of decision making, planning, and controlling.

4-24 Managers seek to eliminate, or at least reduce as much as possible, non-value-added activities. Separating these from value-added activities helps focus attention on the costs that should be examined for potential reductions.

4-25 Just-in-time production systems require 1) short production cycle times, 2) smooth flow of production, 3) focus on quality, and 4) flexible production operations.

4-26 The goal of ABC and JIT is the same – improve competitiveness. However, the means used to achieve competitive improvements are very different. JIT focuses on operational improvements such as reduction in inventories, reduced cycle times, cellular manufacturing, focus on quality, flexible production operations, and a customer orientation.

Activity-based costing systems focus on identifying opportunities for improvement by providing more accurate costs of activities, products, customers, and other cost objects.

In many cases, JIT systems reduce the total amount of indirect costs because of the use of dedicated work cells. This reduces the need for ABC. However, many companies use both JIT and ABC since indirect cost is still an important component of total costs. In addition, nonmanufacturing costs are largely indirect and often significant in amount. For the same reasons mentioned above, ABC applied to all indirect costs enables many companies to gain and maintain the competitive edge.

4-27 (5-10 min.)

1. $20,000,000 + $12,000,000 = $32,000,000
2. $12,000,000 + $8,000,000 = $20,000,000
3. $8,000,000
4. Same answer as in (3).

4-28 (25-30 min.)

1.

Model Income Statement
Manufacturing Company

Sales (8,000,000 units at $10)			$80,000,000
Cost of goods manufactured and sold:			
Beginning finished goods inventory		$ 0	
Cost of goods manufactured:			
Direct materials used	$20,000,000		
Direct labor	12,000,000		
Factory overhead	8,000,000		
Manufacturing costs incurred during the year	$40,000,000		
Less ending work-in-process inventory	3,000,000	37,000,000	
Cost of goods available for sale		$37,000,000	
Less ending finished goods inventory		5,000,000	
Cost of goods sold (an expense)			32,000,000
Gross margin or gross profit			$48,000,000
Less other expenses:			
Selling costs (an expense)		$30,000,000	
General and administrative costs (an expense)		8,000,000	38,000,000
Operating income (also net income in this example)			$10,000,000

2. In Exhibit 4-5, the numbers on the line entitled "Complete production" would change from 40 million to 37 million. The ending balance of Work in Process Inventory would be 3 million instead of 0. The ending balance of Finished Goods Inventory would be 5 million instead of 8 million.

4-29 (10 min.)

Nature of Classification	Objectives of Costing: Assembly Department	Objectives of Costing: Products Assembled
Materials used	D	D
Supplies used	D	D or I*
Assembly labor	D	D
Material-handling labor	D	D or I*
Depreciation, building	I	I
Assembly supervisor's salary	D	D or I*
Building and grounds supervisor's salary	I	I

D = Direct

I = Indirect

*Whether such costs are direct or indirect depends on the types of products in question. For example, a one-product, one-department operation would have many more direct product costs than a multi-product, multi-department operation.

The terms *direct* and *indirect* have no meaning unless they are related to an objective of costing. Traceability is the essence of the distinction. The word *direct* refers to the practicable, obvious, physical tracing of cost as incurred to a given cost objective. A cost may be direct with respect to an activity but indirect with respect to a product. For example, the salary cost of a production supervisor may be a direct charge to a department but an indirect charge to a variety of products being manufactured in that department.

4-30 (10 min.)

This exercise emphasizes how a given cost item may be seen from different viewpoints. Classroom use of such exercises will get students *thinking* instead of *memorizing*. Surely, classroom discussion at this early stage of the course will not settle the student's mind on many issues. Exceptions can be cited for nearly every answer. The class will rarely be able to discuss more than half the items. This should not disturb the instructor; to accomplish the purpose of these problems, every item need not be discussed in prolonged detail.

	Manufacturing Costs	
	Direct (D) or Indirect (I)	Variable (V) or Fixed (F)
1.	I	F
2.	I	V
3.	I	V
4.	I	V
5.	I	F
6.	I	F
7.	I	V
8.	D	V
9.	D	V
10.	I	V

4-31 (20 min.)

1. c,f	7. c,e	13. a,f
2. a,f	8. c,e	14. e,partly d, partly c
3. a,e	9. c,e	15. b**,f
4. c,f	10. d,e	16. c,e
5. g*	11. c,f	17. c,f
6. c,f	12. c,f	18. a,e

*Non-recurring items such as this are not classified as either variable or fixed.

**Could possibly be (f) if immaterial.

This problem emphasizes how a given cost item may be seen from different viewpoints. Classroom use of such problems causes students to *think* instead of *memorize*. Surely, classroom discussion at this early stage of the course will not settle the student's mind on many issues. Exceptions can be cited for nearly every answer. The class will rarely be able to discuss more than half the items. This should not disturb the instructor; to accomplish the purpose of these problems, every item need not be discussed in prolonged detail.

4-32 (15 min.)

SLIDER COMPANY
Inventory Transactions

Transaction:	Direct Materials Inventory	Work-in-process Inventory	Finished Goods Inventory
Beginning Balance	$ 0	$ 0	$ 0
Purchase direct materials	+350	-	-
Use direct materials	-300	+300	-
Acquire and use direct labor	-	+160	-
Acquire and use factory overhead	-	+200	-
Complete production	-	-660	+660
Sell goods and record cost of goods sold	-	-	-330
Ending Balance	$ 50	$ 0	$ 330

The ending inventory balances are:

Direct materials inventory	$ 50,000
Work-in-process inventory	0
Finished goods inventory	330,000
Total inventories	$380,000

4-33 (10-15 min.)

The only changes in the preceding solution would be the presence of Work-in-process Inventory of $100. The transaction entitled "Complete production" would be for $560 instead of $660. Therefore, cost of goods sold would be 1/2($560) = $280 instead of $330. The balances would be:

Direct materials inventory	$ 50,000
Work-in-process inventory	100,000
Finished goods inventory	280,000
Total inventories	$430,000

4-34 (10 min.) This is a basic exercise. Answers are in thousands of dollars.

1. 210 + 150 + 170 = 530
2. 700 - 530 = 170
3. 170 - 150 = 20
4. 210 + 150 = 360
5. 150 + 170 = 320

4-35 (10-15 min.) This is a basic exercise.

Sales		¥770
Variable expenses:		
Direct materials	¥290	
Direct labor	140	
Variable factory overhead	60	
(1) Variable manufacturing cost of goods sold	¥490	
Variable selling and admin. expenses	100	
Total variable expenses		590
(2) Contribution margin		¥180
Fixed expenses:		
Fixed factory overhead	¥120	
Fixed selling and administrative expenses	45	165
(3) Operating income		¥ 15

4-36 (15-20 min.)

This is a straightforward exercise in basic terms and relationships. To fill all the blanks, both absorption and contribution income statements must be prepared. Data are in millions of dollars.

	Absorption Approach		Contribution Approach	
Sales		$920		$920
Direct materials used	$350		$350	
Direct labor	210		210	
Variable indirect manufacturing costs	100		100	
f. Variable manufacturing cost of goods sold			660	
Variable selling and administrative expenses			90	
Total variable expenses				750
k. Contribution margin				170
Fixed factory overhead	50		50	
g. Manufacturing cost of goods sold		710		
j. Gross profit		210		
Fixed selling and administrative expenses	80		80	130
Variable selling and administrative expenses	90	170		
n. Operating income		$ 40		$ 40

l. Prime costs are 350 + 210 = 560

m. Conversion costs are 210 + 100 + 50 = 360

4-37 (10-20 min.) Answers are in thousands of dollars.

Prime costs = Direct material + Direct labor
600 = 370 + DL
DL = 230

The body of a model income statement follows. The computations are explained for each item that was originally blank. Numbers given in the problem are in bold.

Sales, 780 + 120		$900
Direct materials	$370	
Direct labor, 600 - 370	230	
Factory overhead, 780 - (370 + 230)	180	
Manufacturing cost of goods sold		780
Gross margin		$120
Selling and administrative expenses*		100
Operating income		$ 20

*120 - 20

Conversion costs are $230 + $180 = $410

4-38 (15-20 min.) The data are placed in the format of the income statement, and the unknowns are computed as shown:

Sales		$970
Variable expenses		
Direct materials	$210	
Direct labor	170	
Variable factory overhead	110	
Variable manufacturing cost of goods sold		490 [1]
Variable selling and administrative expenses		280 [2]
Total variable expenses (970 - 200)		770
Contribution margin		200
Fixed expenses		
Fixed factory overhead	90 [3]	
Fixed selling and administrative expenses	100	190
Operating income		$ 10

[1] 210 + 170 + 110 = 490

[2] 970 - 200 = 770; 770 - 490 = 280

[3] Total fixed expenses = 200 - 10 = 190
Fixed factory overhead = 190 - 100 = 90

4-39 (40-50 min.) This exercise is a good review of value-added costing, but it is challenging. The distinction between value-added cost and (*value-added*) activities is important. As defined in the text, a *value-added cost is the necessary cost of a (value-added) activity that cannot be eliminated without affecting a product's (service's) value to the customer.* From the viewpoint of PPC's customers, *value* can be defined as receiving power and related services, including billing, in a manner that exceeds their expectations for quality, cost, and service. Hence, it is necessary to identify the activities of the billing department as a first step in answering the exercise. From Exhibit 4-12, there are five activities that should be classified as value-added (V), non-value-added essential (NV-E), or non-value-added discretionary (NV-D). These classifications are:

Activity	Classification
Supervision[1]	NV-E
Account Inquiry	NV-E[2]
Correspondence	NV-E
Account Billing	V
Accounting Verification	NV-D

[1] Point out to students that only four "key" activities were identified in the text discussion. Supervision – an activity and resource combined – was not identified as a key activity in the text discussion, since the study team did not believe it to be a significant activity for the ABC study.

[2] Some students will argue that account inquiry activity is value-added because it provides service to customers. However, we must consider the reason for inquiries. Often, inquiries are due to customers questioning the accuracy of their bill or not understanding the bill. Errors in billing or poorly designed bills are not a valued service attribute from the perspective of a customer.

Students need to determine what we call the flow-cost-assignment paths for each resource/activity. Flow-cost-assignment paths trace the physical flow of resources and related costs. The "best" management control method to use depends on the type of activity within each flow-cost-assignment path. For example, the costs of resources (or portions thereof) that support activities that are non-value-added discretionary (NV-D) are NV-D costs and are managed by striving to eliminate the NV-D activity. Point out to students that classification of activities as value-added or non-value-added is not easy in some situations. It is not uncommon that half of the activities in an organizational unit cannot be easily classified as V or NV. One benefit of a process map such as Exhibit 4-12 is facilitating value-added analysis. The suggested classifications and appropriate managerial actions are (CI=Continuous Improvement):

Resource/Activity	Flow-Cost-Assignment Paths (from Exhibit 4-12) and Activity Classification	Management Response
Telecommunications (T)	1. T→Account Inquiry Activity (NV-E)→Correspondence Activity (NV-E)	1. CI
	2. T→Account Inquiry Activity (NV-E)	2. CI
	3. T→Billing Labor→Account Billing Activity (V)	3. CI[3]
	4. T→Billing Labor→Account Verification Activity (NV-D)	4. Eliminate
Paper (P)	1. P→Account Billing Activity (V)	1. CI
Computer (C)	1. C→Account Verification Activity (NV-D)	1. Eliminate
	2. C→Account Inquiry Activity (NV-E)	2. CI
	3. C→Account Inquiry Activity (NV-E)→Correspondence Activity (NV-E)	3. CI
	4. C→Account Billing Activity (V)	4. CI
Supervisors (S)	1. S→Billing Labor→Account Verification Activity (NV-D)	1. Eliminate
	2. S→Billing Labor→Account Billing Activity (V)	2. CI
	3. S→Account Inquiry Activity (NV-E)	3. CI
	4. S→Account Inquiry Activity (NV-E)→Correspondence Activity (NV-E)	4. CI
Account Inquiry Activity (A)	1. Account Inquiry Activity (NV-E)	1. CI
	2. A→Correspondence Activity (NV-E)	2. CI
Billing Labor (B)	1. B→Account Verification Activity (NV-D)	1. Eliminate
	2. B→Account Billing Activity (V)	2. CI

[3] Value-added activities and related value-added costs are also subject to continuous improvement efforts. For example, paper wasted during the account billing activity should be minimized.

4-40 (10 min.)

This exercise provides students with an example of cost object costing under an activity-based costing system. Note that the cost for these "trouble" customers is more than double the cost of the average commercial account ($14.57).

Activity	Cost per Driver Unit	Physical Flow Driver Units	Cost/Account
Account Inquiry Labor	$62.22/Hour	5/60	$ 5.19
Correspondence	$12.64/Letter	1	12.64
Bill Printing	$ .097/Line	75	7.28
Account Verification	$ 4.44/Account	1	4.44
			$29.55

4-41 (20-30 min.)

This problem provides an overview of cost accumulation and allocation without getting bogged down in the intricacies of bookkeeping. Some instructors may prefer to assign the problem in conjunction with Chapter 13. In particular, note that the complication of under- and over-applied overhead is avoided in Chapter 4. For a fuller discussion, see Chapter 13.

1. Figures are in dollars.

	Machining	Finishing	Total
Direct material	96,000	24,000	120,000
Direct labor	18,000	42,000	60,000
Manufacturing overhead	36,000	42,000	78,000
Total	150,000	108,000	258,000

2.

	X-1		
	Direct Material	Direct Labor	Mfg. Overhead
Machining	48,000	6,000	12,000*
Finishing	8,000	16,800	16,800
Totals	56,000	22,800	28,800

	Y-1		
	Direct Material	Direct Labor	Mfg. Overhead
Machining	24,000	6,000	12,000*
Finishing	8,000	16,800	16,800
Totals	32,000	22,800	28,800

	Z-1		
	Direct Material	Direct Labor	Mfg. Overhead
Machining	24,000	6,000	12,000*
Finishing	8,000	8,400	8,400
Totals	32,000	14,400	20,400

Total Costs:	
X-1 (56,000 + 22,800 + 28,800)	$107,600
Y-1 (32,000 + 22,800 + 28,800)	83,600
Z-1 (32,000 + 14,400 + 20,400)	66,800
Accounted for	$258,000

*(33 1/3% x 36,000)

4-42 (30-35 min.)

1.

Cost/Activity Center: Cost Drivers	Annual Traceable Cost	Annual Cost Driver Activity	Cost per Driver Unit	Cost Driver Consumption, Part H707	Total Cost, Part H707
Quality: Pieces scrapped	$ 800,000	10,000	$ 80	120	$ 9,600
Production scheduling: Setups	50,000	500	100	4	400
Setup: Setups	600,000	500	1,200	4	4,800
Shipping: Containers shipped	300,000	60,000	5	10	50
Shipping admin.: Shipments	50,000	1,000	50	5	250
Production: Machine hours	1,500,000	10,000	150	15	2,250
Total indirect cost	$3,300,000				$17,350
Direct materials					5,000
Direct labor					1,000
Total Cost of Part H707					$23,350
Number of units produced					2,000
Cost per unit					$11.675
Selling price					7.500
Gross margin					$ (4.175)
Gross margin percentage					55.7%

2. Assuming that the results of the activity analysis are accurate, product H707 is much more costly than RMP's existing costing system estimates. The existing system is under costing product H707 by $6.675 per unit or 57%! General Motor's proposal should be rejected unless GM is willing to increaes the price or RMP can significantly reduce its costs. RMP should be aware, however, that the existing costing system is also *overcosting* some products since all indirect costs are allocated (for example, see problem 4-A3). The activity-based costing system should be used to cost all product lines in order to identify RMP's "winners" as well as "losers."

Benefits of activity-based implementation include:

- More accurate costing of activities, products, customers, and other cost objects
- A solid foundation for activity-based management – using ABC information as a management tool for budgeting, planning, and control purposes

- An effective communication tool since successful ABC implementation should involve all functional areas of the company
- The cost of a pilot study includes salaries of managers who are dedicated to the study.
- Consultants are often necessary.
- Data collection is extensive since operational and financial data are often not available as required to support the new ABC system.
- It may be necessary to maintain an ABC system separate from the accounting system used for external reporting.

(Note to instructor: The graph on the next page shows the results for problem 4-42 and problem 4-A3. Both of these problems use the same base data for RMP. These graphs can be used to demonstrate that product "cross-subsidation" often is substantial. We show the top graph first (covering the bottom graph), explaining the derivation of the bars. Then we ask students for a "gut" feeling about the unit cost of both products using an ABC system. That is, "Will the ABC unit cost of H707 be higher, about the same, or lower than the existing cost of $5.00? What about T151A?"

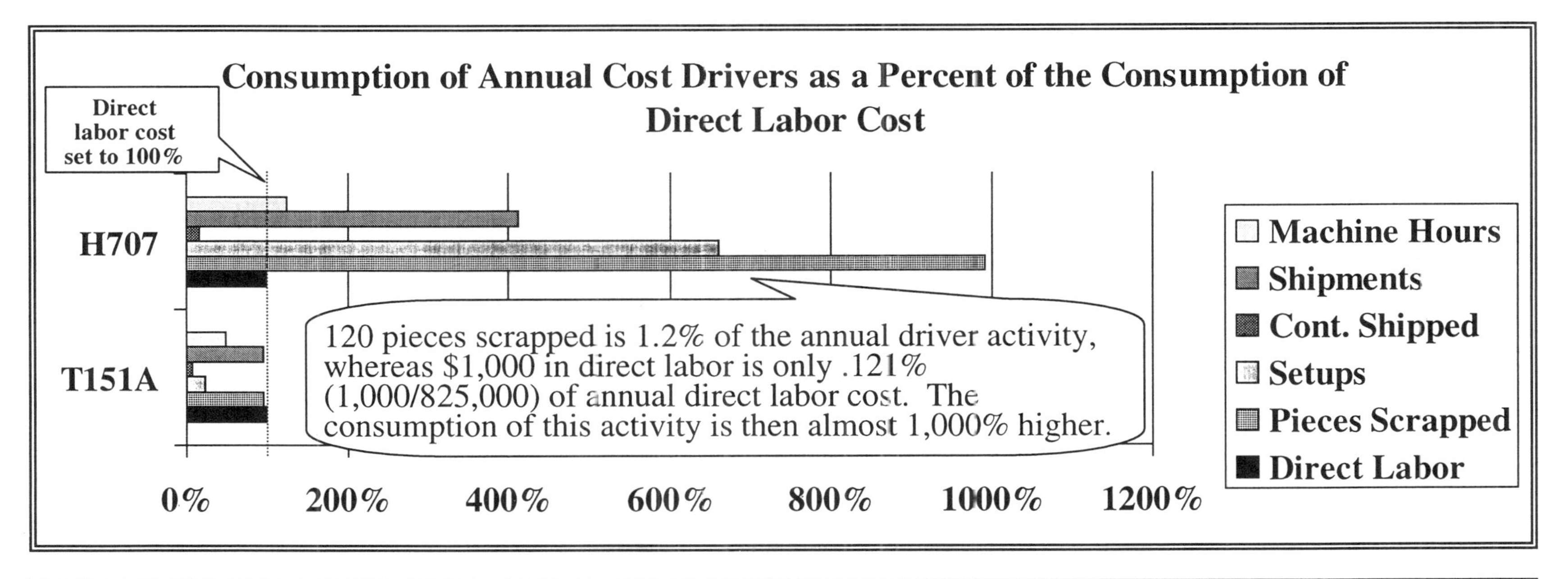

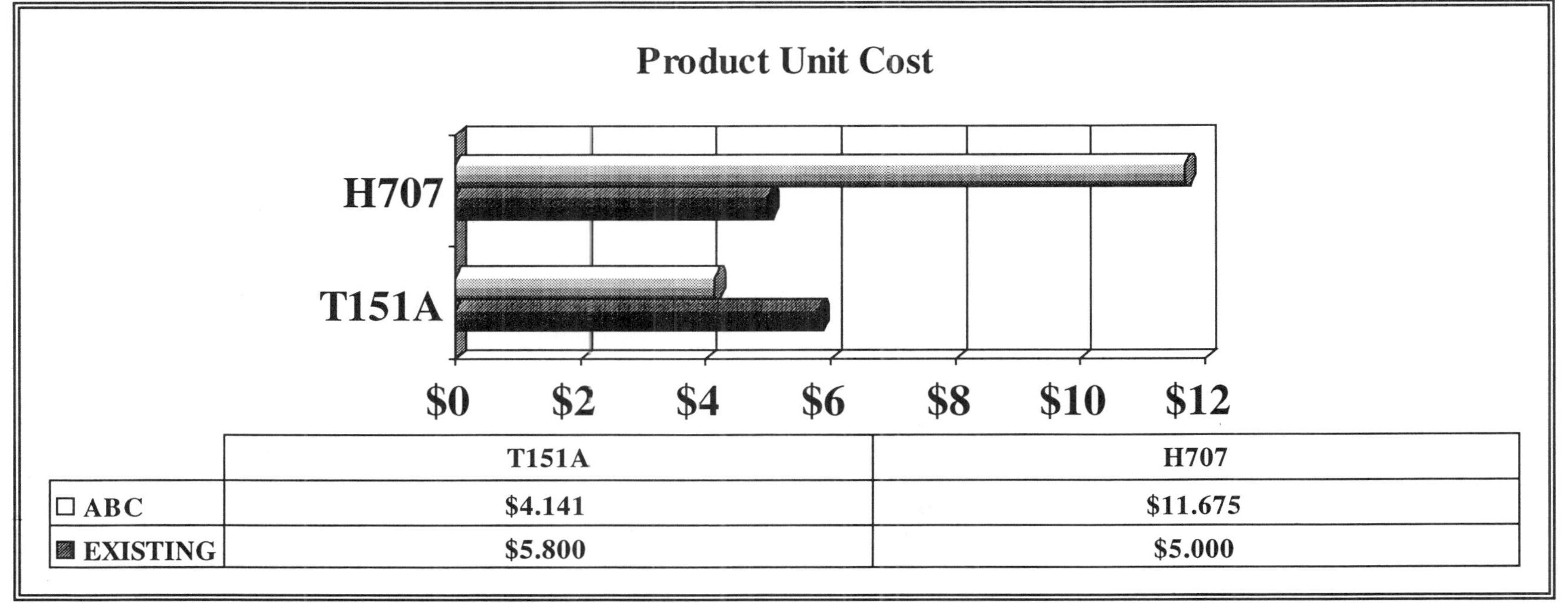

	T151A	H707
ABC	$4.141	$11.675
EXISTING	$5.800	$5.000

4-43 (25-30 min.)

1. Merchandise Inventories, 1,000 tents @ $90 — $90,000

2.

Direct materials inventory	$ 15,000
Work-in-process inventory	0
Finished goods inventory	90,000
Total inventories	$105,000

3.

Sales (9,000, units at $120)		$1,080,000
Cost of goods sold:		
Beginning finished goods inventory	$ 0	
Purchases	900,000	
Cost of goods available for sale	$900,000	
Less ending finished goods inventory	90,000	
Cost of goods sold (an expense)		810,000
Gross margin or gross profit		$ 270,000
Less other expenses: selling & administrative costs		150,000
Operating income (also income before taxes in this example)		$ 120,000

4.

Sales (9,000, units at $120)			$1,080,000
Cost of goods manufactured and sold:			
Beginning finished goods inventory		$ 0	
Cost of goods manufactured:			
Direct materials used	$ 520,000		
Direct labor	260,000		
Factory overhead	120,000		
Manufacturing costs incurred during the year	$900,000		
Less ending work-in-process inventory	0	900,000	
Cost of goods available for sale		$900,000	
Less ending finished goods inventory		90,000	
Cost of goods sold (an expense)			810,000
Gross margin or gross profit			$ 270,000
Less other expenses: selling and administrative costs			150,000
Operating income (also income before taxes in this example)			$ 120,000

5. The balance sheet for the merchandiser (OEC) has just one line for inventories, the ending inventory of the items purchased for resale. The balance sheet for the manufacturer (MSI) has three items: direct materials inventory, work-in-process inventory, and finished goods inventory.

The income statements are similar except for the computation of cost of goods available for sale. The merchandiser (OEC) simply shows purchases for the year. In contrast, the manufacturer (MSI) shows the three categories of cost that comprise manufacturing cost: direct materials, direct labor, and factory (or manufacturing) overhead. The manufacturer also shows a deduction from the costs of manufacturing for any ending work-in-process, which was zero in this example.

4-44 (60 min. or more)

The purpose of this exercise is to force students to look beyond the textbook. The library has many examples of applications of management accounting that show that topics presented in textbooks are of interest in the "real world".

The expectation in this exercise should not be for a detailed understanding of how a company applied JIT or activity-based costing. At this point in the course students should get a general impression of how textbook topics are being applied. Look for some expression of understanding the article, making sure that students are expressing the information in their own words. A brief, intuitive explanation is much better than a detailed description taken nearly verbatim from the article.

4-45 (20-30 min.)

This problem reviews Chapters 2 through 4. It attempts to nail down some terms that often give students trouble. Sharp distinctions should be made among gross profit, contribution margin, manufacturing cost of goods sold and variable manufacturing cost of goods sold. This and the succeeding problem were used originally as exam questions.

1, 3, 5. Answers (1), (3), and (5) can be computed without knowing either the contribution margin or the break-even point. Probably the easiest way to compute the answers is to prepare an income statement, filling in the known items, and then solving for the unknowns. The following are in thousands of dollars:

Sales		$100
Cost of goods manufactured and sold (i.e., manufacturing cost of goods sold):		
Direct material	$35	
Direct labor	25	
Variable manufacturing overhead	5**	
Fixed manufacturing overhead	15	
Total manufacturing cost of goods sold		80*
Gross profit		20
Selling and administrative expenses:		
Variable	15 ***	
Fixed	10	25
Net loss		$ (5)

*Answer (5) is simply 100 - 20 = 80.
**Answer (3) is 80 - (35 + 25 + 15) = 5.
***Total selling and administrative expenses = 5 + 20 = 25.
Then answer (1) is 25 - 10 = 15.

2.

Sales	$100
Direct materials	(35)
Direct labor	(25)
Variable manufacturing overhead	(5)
Variable selling and administrative	(15)
Contribution margin	$ 20

4. $$\text{Break-even} = \frac{\text{Fixed mfg. overhead+Fixed sell.\&adm.}}{\text{Contribution margin \%}}$$

$$= \frac{(\$25{,}000)}{(.20)} = \$125{,}000$$

4-46 (35-45 min.)

Probably the easiest way to compute the answers is to prepare an income statement, filling in the known items, and then solving for the unknowns.

1. The answer is $18,000, computed as follows, in thousands of dollars:

Sales		$100
Cost of goods sold:		
Direct material	$24	
Direct labor	28	
Variable manufacturing overhead	5	
Fixed manufacturing overhead	18[b]	
Total cost of goods sold		75[a]
Gross profit		$ 25

[a] 100 - 25 = 75.

[b] 75 - (24 + 28 + 5) = 18.

2. The answer is $13,000, computed using the following data in thousands of dollars:

Sales		$100
Variable costs:		
Direct material	$24	
Direct labor	28	
Variable manufacturing overhead	5	
Variable selling and administrative expenses	13[b]	
Total variable costs		70[a]
Contribution margin		$30

[a] 100 - 30 = 70.

[b] 70 - (24 + 28 + 5) = 13. Note that this can be computed without having to know the gross profit, the break-even point, or the fixed manufacturing overhead computed in part (1).

3. The answer is $2,000, computed as follows:

Break-even point = Total fixed costs ÷ Contribution margin percentage

∴ Total fixed costs = Break-even point x Contribution margin percentage
= $66,667 x .30
= $20,000

Now, Total fixed costs = Fixed manufacturing + Fixed selling and overhead administrative expense

$20,000 = $18,000 + X
X = $2,000

Therefore, the answer is $2,000. Alternatively, full credit can be given for an answer equal to $2,000 minus the answer in part (1), if that happened to be wrong.

An alternate approach to part (3) is:

Let F = Total fixed expenses

Break-even point sales = Variable expenses + Fixed expenses

$66,667 = .70($66,667) + F

F = $66,667 - $46,667

= $20,000

Then the fixed expenses can be analyzed as before.

4-47 (30-35 min.)

This problem tests knowledge of both the contribution format and the absorption format. It also reviews cost-volume-profit analysis.

		In Dollars
Sales		100,000
Variable expenses:		
Direct materials used	21,000	
Direct labor	16,000	
Variable manufacturing overhead	13,000	
Variable selling and administrative expenses	X	
Total variable expenses (100,000 - 40,000)		60,000
Contribution margin		40,000
Fixed expenses:		
Fixed manufacturing overhead	14,000	
Fixed selling and administrative expenses	Y	
Total fixed expenses (40,000 - 22,000)		18,000
Operating income		22,000

1. X = 60,000 - (21,000 + 16,000 + 13,000)
   = 10,000

2. Y = 18,000 - 14,000
   = 4,000

3. An absorption income statement would show a cost of goods sold of 21,000 + 16,000 + 13,000 + 14,000 = 64,000.

4. a. ($14,000 + $14,000) ÷ ($40,000 ÷ 1,000) = $28,000 ÷ $40 = 700 units

b. Let U = units

$40U - $28,000 = $12,000

U = 1,000 units

c. Let P = selling price

Variable costs per unit = $60,000 ÷ 1,000 = $60

Contribution margin per unit = P - $60

900(P - $60) - $28,000 = $17,000

900P - $54,000 - $28,000 = $17,000

900P = $99,000

P = $110

4-48 (30 min.)

Activities/Resources	Cost Behavior	Cost Drivers
Setups	Activity	No. of setups
Molding process	Activity	Machine hours
Maintenance mechanics	Fixed	Mechanic hours
Supervisors	Fixed	No. of people
Molding machine operators	Fixed	Operator hours
Machine supplies	Variable	Machine hours
Energy	Variable	Kilowatt hours
Building	Fixed	Square footage
Molding machines	Fixed	Machine hours

4-49 (25-35 min.)

1.

LaGRANDE CORPORATION
Contribution Income Statement
For 19X9
(In millions of French francs)

Sales		FF900
Less variable expenses:		
Manufacturing cost of goods sold	FF400	
Selling and administrative expenses	140	540
Contribution margin		360
Less fixed expenses:		
Manufacturing costs	180	
Selling and administrative expenses	60	240
Operating income		FF120

2. (a)

Sales: FF900 x 90% x 130%	FF1,053
Variable expenses: FF540 x 130%	702
Contribution margin	351*
Fixed expenses	240
Operating income	FF 111

*Alternative computation of contribution margin:

Sales after a 10% reduction in prices:		
FF900 x 90%	FF810	
Variable expenses	540	
Contribution margin before volume change		270
Add 30% of FF270	81	
Estimated new contribution margin	FF351	

(b)	Contribution margin: FF360 x 110%		FF396
	Fixed expenses: FF240 + FF30		270
	Operating income		FF126

(c)	Sales		FF900
	Variable expenses:		
	Manufacturing: FF400 x 85%	FF340	
	Selling and administrative	140	480
	Contribution margin		420
	Fixed expenses: FF240 + FF80		320
	Operating income		FF100

(d)	Sales: FF900 x 120% x 105%		FF1,134
	Variable expenses:		
	Manufacturing: FF400 x 120%	FF480	
	Selling and administrative:		
	FF140 x 120% x 125%	210	690
	Contribution margin		444**
	Fixed expenses:		
	Manufacturing	FF200	
	Selling and administrative: FF60 x 2	120	300
	Operating income		FF 144

**Alternate computation of contribution margin:

Sales after a 5% increase in prices: FF900 x 105%		FF945
Variable expenses:		
Manufacturing	FF400	
Selling and administrative after a 25% increase in unit costs: FF140 x 125%	175	575
Contribution margin before volume change		370
Add 20% of FF370		74
Estimated new contribution margin		FF444

(e) These computations are good examples of "sensitivity analysis"– testing various inputs to a model to measure the effects on estimated outputs. This is a planning procedure. An important point to make with students is that the contribution form of income statement is much more appropriate for these purposes than the absorption form.

The analysis is readily calculated by using data from the contribution income statement. In contrast, the data in the absorption income statement must be analyzed and split into variable and fixed categories before the effect on operating income can be estimated.

3. Alternatives (a) and (c) are clearly undesirable because they produces less operating income than the status quo. Either alternative (b) or alternative (d) would be better than the status quo. However, if both alternatives cannot be undertaken simultaneously, and if there is no subjective reason to favor alternative (b), alternative (d) seems best. It produces FF144 - FF126 = FF18 (or 18 million French francs) more operating income than alternative (b). It would also be worth looking into the possibility of conducting the sales promotion campaign in alternative (b) together with the redesign of selling and administrative operations mentioned in alternative (d)

4-50 (60 min. or more)

1. Before implementing the process modeling approach to ABC, AT&T allocated some billing costs on the basis of *number of invoices* produced.

2. The business billing center was selected for the pilot study at AT&T. The overall goals of the pilot study from the managers' perspective included gaining an understanding of the center's operations and identifying value-adding activities.

3. Cost objects were the product and service types. Activities included printing, sorting, dispatching, validating data, correcting errors, and monitoring the billing process. Resources included labor pools, computers, facilities, and paper. Cost dirvers included square feet, pages printed, printer hours, and labor hours.

4. The "billing" activity (cost driver is "pages printed") consumes billing labor time (cost driver is "labor hours") at some rate. If it takes 1 labor hour for every 400 pages printed, the rate, or consumption characteristic is $1 \div 400 = 0.0025$ labor hours per page.

5. AT&T considered the flowchart "critical" because it "revealed how the organization conducted business. Managers were able to see how cost flows are a function of operations (activities) and how they (activities) consume costly resources." Recall that this was one of the overall goals for the pilot study.

6. There were 1,800 labor hours (driver units) for the inquiry activity and each hour costs $62.22 for a total of $111,996. A similar calculation would be made for the correspondence and billing activities. The sum of these three activity costs is the total cost to support residential customers.

7. Using data from Exhibit 4-14, the percent of billing department costs associated with inquiry investigation (both account inquiry and correspondence) is 42.6% [($111,999 + $93,333 + $22,747 + $12,637) ÷ $565,340].

8. Account inquiry associates were given access to additional operating systems allowing end-to-end responsibility for inquiry investigation. Training was also given to associates in the use of these systems. The elmination of referrals to other working groups resulted in reductions in investigation time, improved service, and cost reductions. This is a good example of ABM – how ABC is used to improve operations.

4-51 (60 min. or more)

Answers will vary based on the industry and particular company chosen.

CHAPTER 5
Relevant Information

5-A1 (25-30 min.)

1. A contribution format, which is similar to Exhibit 5-3, clarifies the analysis.

	Without Special Order	Effect of Special Order		With Special Order
Units	2,000,000	150,000		2,150,000
		Total	Per Unit	
Sales	$10,000,000	$660,000	$4.40[1]	$10,660,000
Less variable expenses:				
Manufacturing	$ 3,600,000	$300,000	$2.00[2]	$ 3,900,000
Selling & administrative	800,000	37,500	.25[3]	837,500
Total variable expenses	$ 4,400,000	$337,500	$2.25	$ 4,737,500
Contribution margin	$ 5,600,000	$322,500	$2.15	$ 5,922,500
Less fixed expenses:				
Manufacturing	$ 2,400,000	0	0.00	$ 2,400,000
Selling & administrative	2,500,000	0	0.00	2,500,000
Total fixed expenses	$ 4,900,000	0	0.00	$ 4,900,000
Operating income	$ 700,000	$322,500	$2.15	$ 1,022,500

[1] $660,000 ÷ 150,000 = $4.40

[2] Regular unit cost = $3,600,000 ÷ 2,000,000 =	$1.80
Logo and assembly	.20
Variable manufacturing costs	$2.00
[3] Regular unit cost = $800,000 ÷ 2,000,000 =	$ .40
Less sales commissions not paid (3% of $5)	.15
Regular unit cost, excluding sales commission	$ .25

2. Operating income from selling 7.5% more units would increase by \$322,500 ÷ \$700,000 = 46.1%. Note also that the average selling price on regular business was \$5.00. The full cost, including selling and administrative expenses, was \$4.65. The \$4.65, plus the 20¢ per clip, less savings in commissions of 15¢ came to \$4.70. The president apparently wanted \$4.70 + .08(\$4.70) = \$4.70 + .376 = \$5.076 per calculator.

Most students will probably criticize the president for being too stubborn. The cost to the company was the forgoing of \$322,500 of income in order to protect the company's image and general market position. Whether \$322,500 was a wise investment in the future is a judgment that managers are paid for rendering.

5-A2 (10 min.)

1. Contribution margins:
   Plain = \$66 - \$50 = \$16
   Fancy = \$100 - \$70 = \$30

   Contribution margin ratios:
   Plain = \$16 ÷ \$66 = 24%
   Fancy = \$30 ÷ \$100 = 30%

2.

	Plain	Fancy
a. Units per hour	2	1
b. Contribution margin per unit	\$16	\$30
Contribution margin per hour	\$32	\$30
Total contribution for 20,000 hours	\$640,000	\$600,000

3. For a given capacity, the criterion for maximizing profits is to obtain the greatest possible contribution to profit for each unit of the limiting or scarce factor. Moreover, fixed costs are irrelevant unless their total is affected by the choice of products.

5-A3 (15-20 min.)

The purpose of this problem is to underscore the idea that any of a number of general formulas might be used that, properly employed, would achieve the *same* target selling prices. Desired sales = \$7,500,000 + \$1,500,000 = \$9,000,000.

The target markup percentage would be:

1. 100% of prime costs of \$4,500,000.

   Computation is: $\frac{(\$9,000,000 - \$4,500,000)}{(\$4,500,000)} = 100\%$

2. 50% of the full cost of jobs of \$6,000,000.

   Computation is: $\frac{(\$9,000,000 - \$6,000,000)}{(\$6,000,000)} = 50\%$

3. $\frac{(\$9,000,000-(\$3,500,000+\$1,000,000+\$900,000))}{(\$5,400,000)} = 66.67\%$

4. $\frac{(\$9,000,000 - \$7,500,000)}{(\$7,500,000)} = 20\%$

5. $\frac{(\$9,000,000 - (\$3,500,000 + \$1,000,000 + \$900,000 + \$300,000))}{(\$5,700,000)}$

   $= \frac{(\$3,300,000)}{(\$5,700,000)} = 57.9\%$

If the contractor is unable to maintain these profit percentages consistently, the desired operating income of \$1,500,000 cannot be obtained.

5-B1 (30-40 min.)

1.

HUNTER COMPANY
Income Statement
For the Year Ended December 31, 19X7

		Total	Per Unit
Sales		$40,000,000	$20.00
Less variable expenses:			
Manufacturing	$19,000,000		
Selling & administrative	9,000,000	28,000,000	14.00
Contribution margin		$12,000,000	$ 6.00
Less fixed expenses:			
Manufacturing	$ 5,000,000		
Selling & administrative	5,000,000	10,000,000	5.00
Operating income		$ 2,000,000	$ 1.00

2. Additional details are either in the statement of the problem or in the solution to requirement 1:

	Total	Per Unit
Absorption cost = full manufacturing cost	$24,000,000	$12.00
Variable cost:		
Manufacturing	$19,000,000	$ 9.50
Selling and administrative	9,000,000	4.50
Total variable cost	$28,000,000	$14.00
Full cost = fully allocated cost*		
Full manufacturing cost	$24,000,000	$12.00
Selling and administrative expenses	14,000,000	7.00
Full cost	$38,000,000	$19.00
Gross margin ($40,000,000 - $24,000,000)	$16,000,000	$ 8.00
Contribution margin ($40,000,000 - $28,000,000)	$12,000,000	$ 6.00

* Students should be alerted to the loose use of these words. Their meaning may not be exactly the same from company to company.

Thus, "fully allocated cost" in some companies may be used to refer to manufacturing costs only.

3. Ricardo's analysis is incorrect. He was on the right track, but he did not distinguish sufficiently between variable and fixed costs. For example, when multiplying the additional quantity ordered by the $12 absorption cost, he failed to recognize that $2.50 of the $12 absorption cost was a "unitized" fixed cost allocation. The first fallacy is in regarding the total fixed cost as though it fluctuated like a variable cost. *A unit fixed cost can be misleading if it is used as a basis for predicting how total costs will behave.*

   A second false assumption is that no selling and administrative expenses will be affected except commissions. Shipping expenses and advertising allowances will be affected also – unless arrangements with Costco on these items differ from the regular arrangements.

   The following summary, which is similar to Exhibit 5-3, is a correct analysis. The middle columns are all that are really necessary.

	Without Special Order	Effect of Special Order		With Special Order
Units	2,000,000	100,000		2,100,000
		Total	Per Unit	
Sales	$40,000,000	$1,700,000	$17.00	$41,700,000
Less variable expenses:				
Manufacturing	$19,000,000	$ 950,000	$ 9.50	$19,950,000
Selling and administrative	9,000,000	350,000	3.50*	9,350,000
Total variable expenses	$28,000,000	$1,300,000	$13.00	$29,300,000
Contribution margin	$12,000,000	$ 400,000	$ 4.00	$12,400,000
Less fixed expenses:				
Manufacturing	$ 5,000,000	0	0.00	$ 5,000,000
Selling and administrative	5,000,000	0	0.00	5,000,000
Total fixed expenses	$10,000,000	0	0.00	$10,000,000
Operating income	$ 2,000,000	$ 400,000	$ 4.00	$ 2,400,000

* Regular variable selling and administrative expenses, $9,000,000 ÷ 2,000,000 =	$4.50
Average sales commission at 6% of $20 =	1.20
Regular variable selling and administrative expenses, less commission	$3.30
Special commission, $20,000 ÷ 100,000	.20
Selling and administrative expenses	$3.50

Some students may wish to enter the $20,000 as an extra fixed cost. The final result would be the same; in any event, the cost is relevant because it would not exist without the special order.

Some instructors may wish to point out that a 5% increase in volume would cause a 40% increase in operating income, which seems like a high investment by Hunter to maintain a rigid pricing policy.

4. Ricardo is incorrect. Operating income would have declined from $1,000,000 to $850,000, a decline of $150,000. Ricardo's faulty analysis follows:

Old fixed manufacturing cost per unit, $5,000,000 ÷ 2,000,000 =	$2.50
New fixed manufacturing cost per unit, $5,000,000 ÷ 2,500,000 =	2.00
"Savings"	$ .50
Loss on variable manufacturing costs per unit, $9.20 - $9.50	.30
Net savings per unit in manufacturing costs	$ .20

The analytical pitfalls of unit-cost analysis can be avoided by using the contribution approach and concentrating on the totals:

	Without Special Order	Effect of Special Order	With Special Order
Sales	$40,000,000	$4,600,000[a]	$44,600,000
Variable manufacturing costs	$19,000,000	$4,750,000[b]	$23,750,000
Other variable costs	9,000,000	0	9,000,000
Total variable costs	$28,000,000	$4,750,000	$32,750,000
Contribution margin	$12,000,000	$ (150,000)[c]	$11,850,000

[a] 500,000 x $9.20 selling price of special order
[b] 500,000 x $9.50 variable manufacturing cost per unit of special order
[c] 500,000 x $.30 negative contribution margin per unit of special order

No matter how fixed manufacturing costs are unitized, or spread over the units produced, their total of $5,000,000 remains unchanged by the special order.

5-B2 (15 min.)

1. If fixed manufacturing cost is applied to product at $1.00 per machine hour, it takes $.80 ÷ $1.00, or 4/5 of an hour to produce one unit of XY-7. Similarly, it takes $.20 ÷ $1.00 or 1/5 of an hour to produce XZ-8.

2. If there are 100,000 hours of capacity:

   XY-7: 100,000 hours ÷ 4/5 = 125,000 units.
   XZ-8: 100,000 hours ÷ 1/5 = 500,000 units.

   Total contribution margins show that XZ-8 should be produced:

	Per Unit	Units	Total
XY-7	$6.00 - ($3.00 + $2.00) = $1.00	125,000	$125,000
XZ-8	$4.00 - ($1.40 + $2.00) = $ .60	500,000	$300,000

5-B3 (15-20 min.)

All amounts are in thousands of British pounds.

The major lesson is that a product that shows an operating loss based on fully allocated costs may nevertheless be worth keeping. Why? Because it may produce a sufficiently high contribution to profit so that the firm would be better off with it than any other alternatives.

The emphasis should be on totals:

		Replace Magic Department With	
	Existing Operations	General Merchandise	Electronic Products
Sales	6,000	-600 + 300 = 5,700	-600 + 200 = 5,600
Variable expenses	4,090	-390 + 210[a] = 3,910	-390 + 100[b] = 3,800
Contribution margin	1,910	-210 + 90 = 1,790	-210 + 100 = 1,800
Fixed expenses	1,110	-100 + 0 = 1,010	-100 + 25 = 1,035
Operating income	800	-110 + 90 = 780	-110 + 75 = 765

[a](100% - 30%) x 300
[b](100% - 50%) x 200

The facts as stated indicate that the magic department should not be closed. First, the total operating income would drop. Second, fewer customers would come to the store, so sales in other departments may be affected adversely.

5-1 Precision is a measure of the accuracy of certain data. It is a quantifiable term. Relevance is an indication of the pertinence of certain facts for the problem at hand. Ideally, data should be both precise and relevant.

5-2 Decisions may have both quantitative and qualitative bases corresponding to the nature of the facts being considered before deciding. Quantitative implications of alternative choices can be expressed in monetary or numerical terms, such as variable costs, initial investment, etc. Other relevant features may not be quantifiable, such as the quality of life in a choice between locating in Chicago or New York. The advantage of quantitative information is that it is more objective and often easier to compare alternatives than with qualitative judgments.

5-3 The accountant's role in decision making is primarily that of a technical expert on relevant information analysis, especially relevant costs. The accountant is usually an information provider, not the decision maker.

5-4 No. Only future costs that are different under different alternatives are relevant to a decision.

5-5 Past data are unchangeable regardless of present or future action and thus would not differ under different alternatives.

5-6 Past costs may be bases for formulating predictions. However, past costs are not inputs to the decision model itself because past costs cannot be changed by the decision.

5-7 The commonalty of approach is the focus on the differences between expected outcomes of different available alternatives.

5-8 The lesson here is important. No matter how fixed costs are spread for *unit* product costing purposes, the *total* fixed costs will be unchanged (even though fixed costs *per unit* may change).

5-9 No. There is a confusion between total fixed costs and unit fixed costs. Increasing volume will decrease unit fixed costs, but not total fixed costs.

5-10 Yes. The costs that make a difference when a product or department is being deleted are the avoidable costs.

5-11 No. Avoidable costs are all costs (both variable and fixed) that will not continue if an ongoing operation is changed or deleted.

5-12 Four examples of scarce factors are: (a) labor hours, (b) money (investment capital), (c) supervisory hours, (d) computer hours.

5-13 Marginal cost is the additional cost resulting from producing and selling one additional unit. It changes as production volume changes, often decreasing up to a point and then increasing. Variable cost is the accountant's approximation to marginal cost. It remains constant over the relevant range of volume.

5-14 Four major factors influencing pricing decisions are: the law, customers, competitors, and costs.

5-15 Customers are one of the factors influencing price decisions because they can buy or do without the product, they can make the product themselves, or they can usually purchase a similar product from another supplier.

5-16 In target costing, managers start with a market price. Then they try to design a product with costs low enough to be profitable at that price. Thus, prices essentially determine costs.

5-17 The variable costs of a job can be misused as a guide to pricing. However, the adjusted markup percentages based on variable costs can have the same price result as those based on total costs, plus they have the advantage of indicating the minimum price at which any sale may be considered profitable even in the short run.

5-18 Three examples of pricing decisions are (1) pricing new products, (2) pricing products sold under private labels, and (3) responding to new prices of a competitor's products.

5-19 Four popular markup formulas are (1) as a percentage of variable manufacturing costs, (2) as a percentage of total variable costs, (3) as a percentage of full costs, and (4) as a percentage of absorption costs.

5-20 Two long-run effects that inhibit price cutting are (a) the effects on longer-run price structures and (b) the effects on longer-run relations with customers.

5-21 Full costs are more popular than variable costs for pricing because price stability is encouraged and in the long run all costs must be recovered to stay in business.

5-22 Executives usually use full costs for setting "normal" prices and the contribution approach for special, non-recurring orders.

5-23 (5 min.)

All the data given are historical costs. Most students will identify the $6 and $7 prices as relevant. They will also declare that the $2 price of popcorn is irrelevant. Press them to see that the relevant admission prices are expected *future* costs that will differ between the alternatives. The past prices are being used as a basis for *predicting* the future prices.

Similarly, the *past* prices of popcorn were not different. Hence, they are regarded as irrelevant under the assumption that the *future* prices will not differ.

5-24 (20 min.) Some students will forget to apply the 10% wage rate increase to both alternatives.

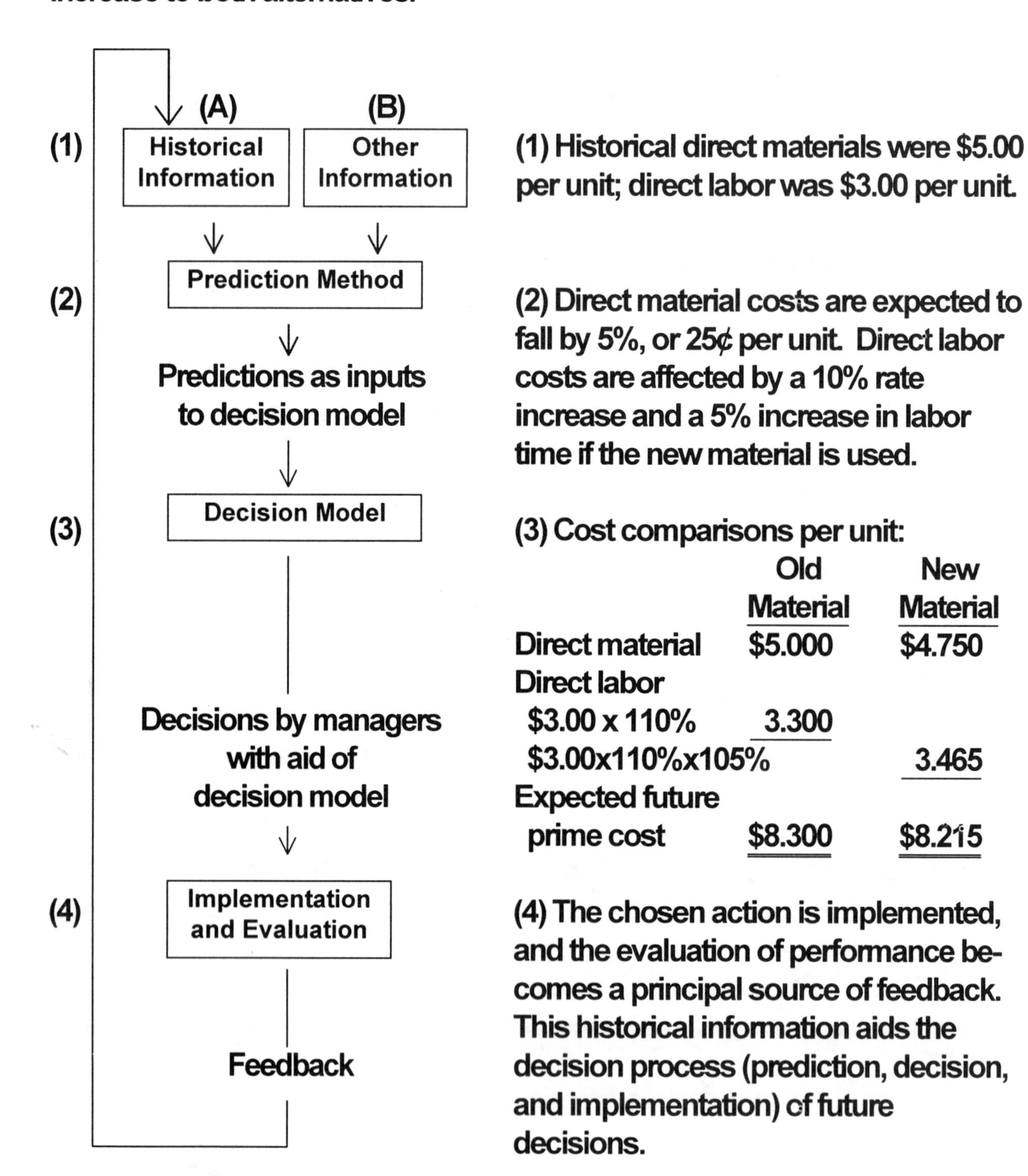

(1) Historical direct materials were $5.00 per unit; direct labor was $3.00 per unit.

(2) Direct material costs are expected to fall by 5%, or 25¢ per unit. Direct labor costs are affected by a 10% rate increase and a 5% increase in labor time if the new material is used.

(3) Cost comparisons per unit:

	Old Material	New Material
Direct material	$5.000	$4.750
Direct labor		
$3.00 x 110%	3.300	
$3.00x110%x105%		3.465
Expected future prime cost	$8.300	$8.215

(4) The chosen action is implemented, and the evaluation of performance becomes a principal source of feedback. This historical information aids the decision process (prediction, decision, and implementation) of future decisions.

5-25 (10 min.)

Relevant costs are the future costs that differ between alternatives. Among the irrelevant costs are the cost of tickets to the symphony, automobile costs, and baby-sitting cost for the first four hours. The relevant costs are:

	Symphony	Game	Difference
Tickets, 2 @ $20 each	$0	$40	$40
Parking	0	6	6
Baby-sitting, 1 extra hour @ $4	0	4	4
Total	$0	$50	$50

The baseball game is $50 more costly to the Ramaswamys than is the symphony.

5-26 (10-15 min.)

1. Operating income would increase by $300 if the order is accepted.

	Without Special Order	Effect of Special Order	With Special Order
Units	2,000	100	2,100
Sales	$36,000	$1,500	$37,500
Purchase cost	20,000	1,000	21,000
Variable printing cost	4,000	200	4,200
Total variable cost	24,000	1,200	25,200
Contribution margin	12,000	300	12,300
Fixed cost	8,000	0	8,000
Operating income	$ 4,000	$ 300	$ 4,300

2. If maximizing operating income in the short run were the only goal, the order should be accepted. However, if qualitative considerations favoring rejection are worth more than the $300 increase in operating income, the manager would reject the offer. For example, accepting the offer from F. C. Kitsap may generate similar offers from other clubs who now willingly pay the $18 normal price. Lost profits on such business might more than offset the $300 gain on this sale. On the other hand, this might be a way of gaining F. C. Kitsap as regular customers who will then buy other items that generate a profit well in excess of the $300.

5-27 (20 min.)

1.

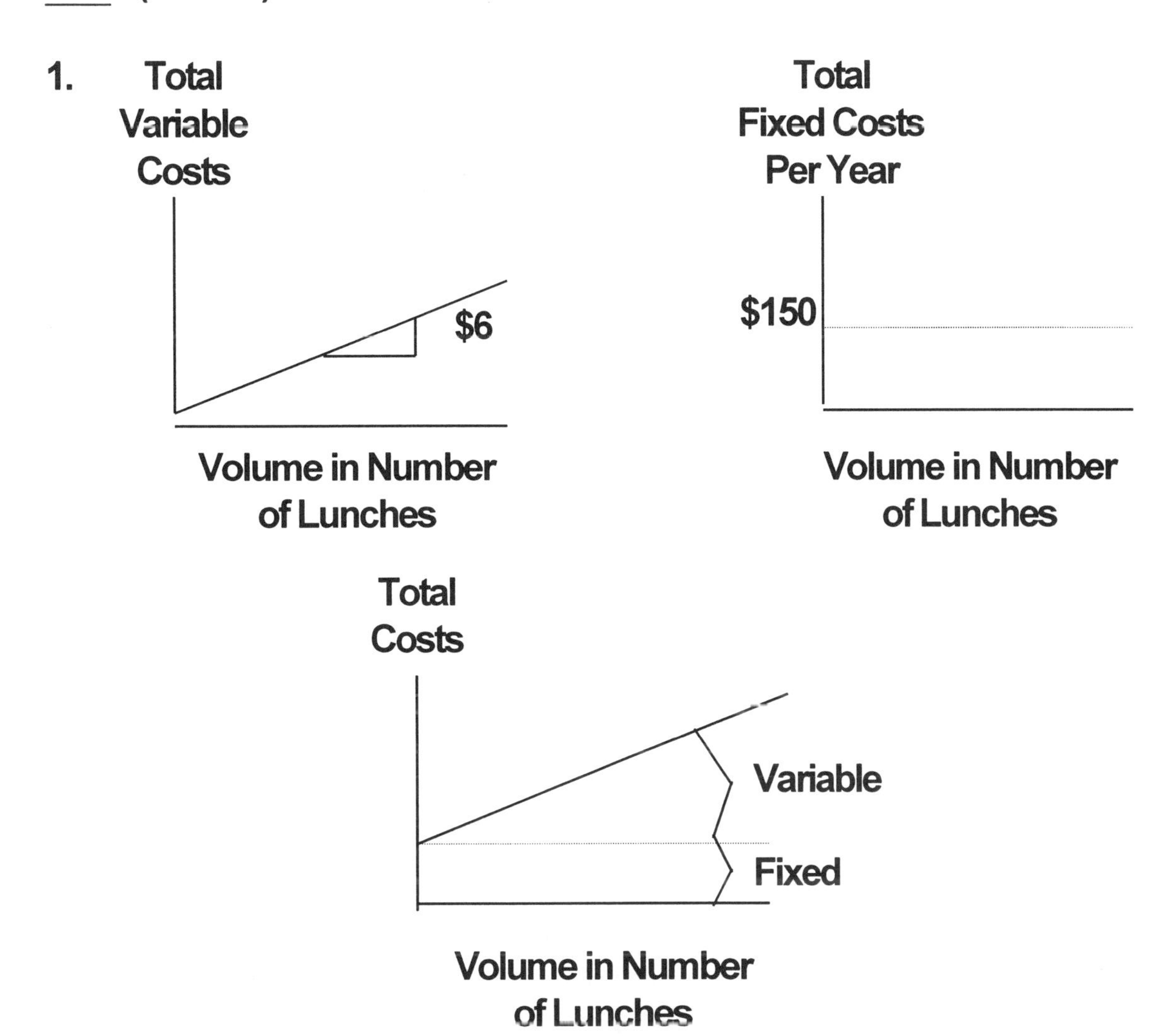

2. There are correct ways and incorrect ways to analyze the data. A correct way follows:

Total cost	= Total FC + Total VC
	= $150 per year + $6 per lunch
Let X	= The number of lunches
Then, Unit cost	= ($150÷ X) + $6
If 1 lunch, Unit cost	= ($150÷ 1) + $6 = $156.00 per lunch
If 12 lunches, Unit cost	= ($150÷ 12) + $6 = $ 18.50 per lunch
If 200 lunches, Unit cost	= ($150÷ 200) + $6 = $ 6.75 per lunch

3. (a) The CPA can compare either total annual costs or unit costs. Let X = the total number of lunches in question.

	Total Costs		Unit Costs	
	Elsewhere	At Club	Elsewhere	At Club
In general	$ 11X	$150+$ 6X	$11.00	($150÷X)+$6
For 1 lunch	$ 11	$150+$ 6 =$ 156	$11.00	$156.00
For 12 lunches	$ 132	$150+$ 72 =$ 222	$11.00	$ 18.50
For 200 lunches	$2,200	$150+$1,200 =$1,350	$11.00	$ 6.75

Let X = Number of lunches
$11X = $150 + $6X
X = 30 lunches is point of indifference.

(b)		
	Elsewhere, 250 x $11	$2,750
	At Club, $150 + 250($6)	1,650
	Savings	$1,100

The preceding parts concentrated on how total costs behave in relation to chosen volume levels. *Generally, the decision maker should take a straightforward, analytical approach by thinking in terms of total costs rather than unit costs.* By keeping an eye on the total picture, the manager is less likely to fall into some analytical traps that come from misinterpreting *unit* costs. In addition, of course, the qualitative aspects should not be ignored. For example, there may be an intangible benefit of dining with actual and potential clients at the luncheon club.

5-28 (15 min.)

1. Except for the advertising costs, the fixed costs are irrelevant in this situation.
   The contribution margin per student is $15,000 - $8,900 = $6,100
   Break-even point for the campaign is $1,830,000 ÷ $6,100 = 300 students.

2. 360 x $6,100 = $2,196,000

3. 90 x $6,100 = $549,000

5-29 (10 min.)

1.

	Cost per Unit of Product		
Variable manufacturing cost	$10.00	$10.00	$10.00
Variable selling and administrative cost	3.00		3.00
(a) Total variable cost	$13.00		
Fixed manufacturing cost		6.00*	6.00
(b) Absorption cost		$16.00**	
Fixed selling and administrative cost			5.80*
(c) Full cost			$24.80

* Fixed manufacturing cost, $3,000,000 ÷ 500,000 = $6.00
Selling and administrative cost, $2,900,000 ÷ 500,000 = $5.80

** This amount must be used by U.S. companies for inventory valuation in reports to shareholders.

2. Full cost is often called fully allocated cost.

5-30 (20 min.)

1. These warehouse stores attempt to maximize profits by cutting prices and increasing turnover. Since profit is the product of contribution margin and total sales, it can be affected by changing either. Total profit can be increased if the added turnover brought about by a lowering of price brings in more contribution margin than was lost by the price cut. They also try to minimize fixed costs by limiting their investment in buildings and equipment.

   Characteristics: (a) choose product lines and sizes that move quickly and avoid stocking slow-moving items and sizes, (b) stock lower cost, lower quality items, (c) rely heavily on self service, (d) attempt to cut costs by providing fewer services, and (e) build low-cost buildings in a place where property costs are not too high.

2. Such a criterion by itself gives no indication what net income can be expected. Sales turnover or volume must be used also, for the rate of return on assets is determined by

$$\text{Rate of return} = \frac{\text{Contribution margin x Total sales}}{\text{Average assets}}$$

   If sales turnover can be assumed to be fairly constant among items, then such a figure as a 20% average target gross profit might be meaningful.

5-31 (10-15 min.)

1. The key is to focus on lost revenues and avoidable costs:

Revenues, 600 hours @ SF12 per hour		SF7,200
Avoidable costs*:		
Teacher salaries	SF5,200	
Supplies	800	6,000
Decrease in operating income		SF1,200

*In addition to the avoidable costs shown, there might be some savings in sanitary engineering (less cleaning necessary) and depreciation (less wear and tear on equipment). Unless these savings are more than the SF1,200 decrease in operating income, the school will be worse off financially without the after-school care program.

2. Among the qualitative factors to consider are that the after-school care program might attract students to the regular program, it provides additional compensation to teachers, and there is a social need for such programs.

5-32 (20 min.)

This solution may be obvious to most students. However, the use of this problem in executive programs and regular classes has shown that some students need this exercise before they become convinced that the "unitization" of fixed costs can be misleading. Moreover, in decision-making in general, the use of *total* rather than *unit* cost is nearly always less confusing.

This special order increases revenue by $390,000 and variable costs by $420,000. Total fixed costs are unchanged at $300,000. This $300,000 is unaffected regardless of how they are allocated to units of product. Therefore, net income will be affected only by the changes in revenue and variable costs.

Summary of regular operations:

	Per Unit	Total
Revenue	$2.00	$600,000
Variable costs	1.40	420,000
Contribution margin	$ .60	$180,000
Fixed costs	1.00	300,000
Net income	$ -.40	$-120,000

The new business would alter the picture as follows, assuming fixed costs are "spread" on a 50/50 basis:

	Regular	Special	Total
Revenue	$600,000	$ 390,000	$ 990,000
Variable costs	420,000	420,000	840,000
Contribution margin	$180,000	$ -30,000	$ 150,000
Fixed costs	150,000	150,000	300,000
Net income	$ 30,000	$-180,000	$-150,000

No matter how the fixed costs are spread, the total fixed costs will be $300,000 and the total net loss will be $150,000. This is true despite the fact that fixed costs *per unit* have fallen from $1.00 to $.50. The moral is: beware of unit costs.

Some instructors may want to emphasize how the unitization of fixed costs differs. That is, the unit cost depends on the production volume chosen as the denominator.

$$\text{Fixed costs per unit} = \frac{\text{Total fixed costs}}{\text{Production volume}} = \frac{(\$300{,}000)}{(300{,}000 \text{ units})} = \$1$$

$$\text{or } \frac{(\$300{,}000)}{(600{,}000 \text{ units})} = \$.50$$

The *total* fixed cost is unaffected by what volume is chosen as the denominator for computing the cost per unit.

Using the graphs like those in the chapter:

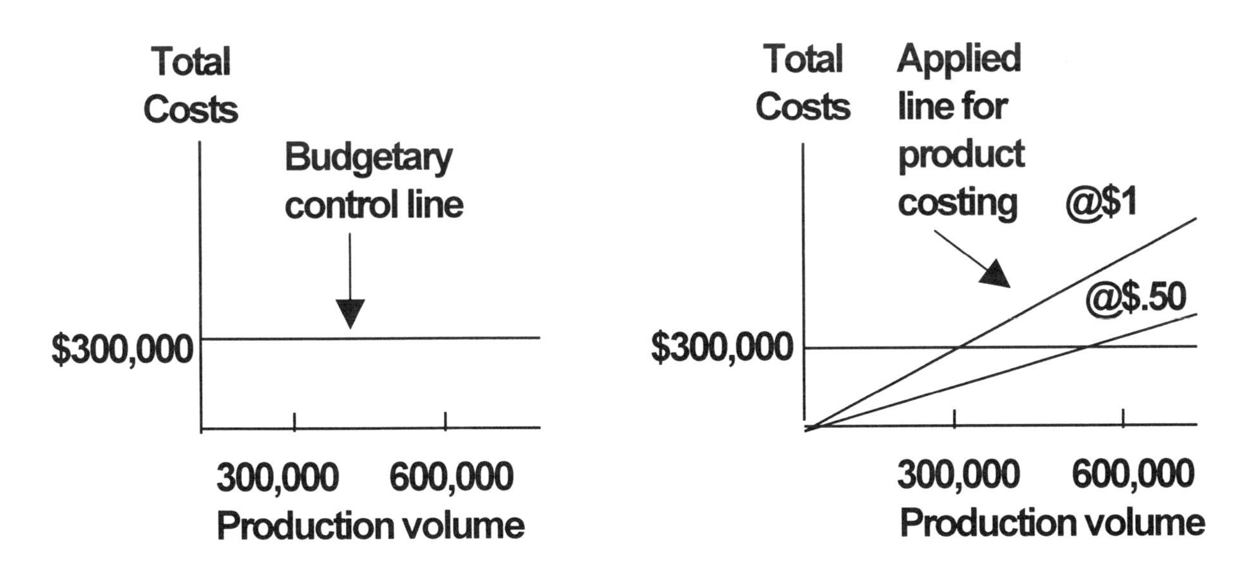

5-33 (10-15 min.)

Pricing policies always seem to spark much student interest. This "break-even" philosophy is similar to the "base or bulk volume" philosophy favored by many executives. That is, the "normal" pricing applies to the bulk or base of the business, but price cutting can be applied to incremental business.

In the case of the auto business, this normal-incremental pricing is applied by many dealers in the manner described in the problem. Many observers think such pricing is nonsense, unless it is a response to changes in demand and in competitor pricing.

Why is such pricing nonsense? Because prices should be influenced by customer demand and competition, not by where sales happen to be on a break-even graph. Ordinarily, a pricing strategy should aim to maximize the contribution margin, all other things being equal. Some critics maintain that it is foolhardy to cut a price to the same potential customer just because he or she appears on, say, May 27 rather than on May 23.

As prospective customers, most rational people would shop for a car during the final two or three days of the month.

5-34 (15 min.)

1. Assuming that total fixed costs are the same at production levels of 6,000 and 10,000 units, the analysis can focus on contribution margins:

   CM@ $12: 6,000 units x ($12-$6) = $36,000
   CM@ $10: 10,000 units x ($10 - $6) = $40,000

   Profits will be $40,000 - $36,000 = $4,000 higher at the $10 price.

2. Subjective factors include image in the marketplace (higher price may give image of quality), market penetration (satisfied customers may become repeat customers), and effects on the sales force.

5-35 (10 min.)

1. ($60,000 - $36,000) ÷ $36,000 = 66.7%
2. ($60,000 - $50,000) ÷ $50,000 = 20%
3. ($60,000 - $30,000) ÷ $30,000 = 100%
4. [$60,000 - ($30,000 + $8,000)] ÷ ($30,000 + $8,000) = 58%

5-36 (10-15 min.)

1. (150% x $28,000) + ($75 x 2,000 hours) = $42,000 + $150,000 = $192,000

2 & 3.

Materials and supplies, at cost	$ 28,000
Hourly pay for consultants	72,000
Fringe benefits for consultants	24,000
Total variable cost	$124,000
Avoidable fixed costs	9,000
Minimum bid	$133,000
Unavoidable fixed costs	35,000
Total cost	168,000
Desired mark-up, 20% x $168,000	33,600
Bid to achieve desired profit	$201,600

5-37 (10 min.)

This problem raises issues for which there are no right answers. Determining the types of product promotion activities that are ethically and legally appropriate is not an easy question, and the role of price discrimination is especially difficult.

For a company to legally charge different prices to different customers, it usually must show a cost difference in serving the customers. But many companies promote their products by charging a zero price (i.e., giving free samples for a limited amount of the product). Is this case any different than a breakfast cereal company sending free samples through the mail? If so, how? Further, establishing physicians' confidence in the medication has a potential long-run benefit; does this justify giving the drug free to physicians? In addition, physicians need to know how to adminster the drug and how to look for possible side effects, so are the free samples justified as an educational investment? Or are the free drug samples essentially bribes to convince physicians to prescribe the new drug?

What about the difference in price between hospital and retail pharmacies? GLPI may think that if a hospital pharmacy starts a patient on the new drug, he or she will stay on it even if further purchases are from a retail pharmacy. Does this justify a price differential? Or it may be that distribution costs are less to hospital pharmacies than to retail pharmacies. Is this difference enough to justify a $15 difference in price?

Students are likely to disagree on the appropriateness of the policies, and some may feel passionately about their opinion. At some time the discussion should be turned to the effect of cost on the pricing policies. For example, a lead-in question may be whether the eventual price of $50 is fair for a product whose production cost is only $12. Then it can proceed to considering whether a cost differential can justify the $15 difference between the prices to hospital and retail pharmacies. Finally, the issue of price and incentives to physicians can be addressed. This last issue may be the first one students want to focus on, and it may be the one with the most ethical content, but it should not be the sole issue discussed.

5-38 (10-15 min.)

	Contribution Approach	Fully Allocated Cost Approach
1. Sales	$39,000	$39,000
Fully allocated operating expenses		45,000
Variable operating expenses (80% x $45,000)	36,000	
Apparent change in operating income	$ 3,000	$ (6,000)

2. A decision not to accept the order means that short-run income would be $3,000 lower. In effect, Transnational invests $3,000 to maximize long-run benefits. Goldmark can find the contribution approach helpful because he can weigh decisions of this sort by asking whether the probability of long-run benefits (not encouraging price-cutting by competitors, not encouraging customers to expect lower prices) is worth a quantifiable present investment equal to the contribution margin ($3,000 in this case).

   Students should be alerted to the fact that, by itself, the contribution approach does *not* say "go forth and cut prices." All it does is quantify a manager's options more sharply.

5-39 (20-25 min.)

1. Net income would be increased by £3,000 if the order were taken:

	Without the Order	Effect of the Order	With the Order
Sales	£1,100,000	£19,800	£1,119,800
Direct material	£ 280,000	£ 5,600	£ 285,600
Direct labor	320,000	6,400	326,400
Variable overhead	240,000*	4,800	244,800
Fixed overhead	160,000	0	160,000
Total costs	£1,000,000	£16,800	£1,016,800
Operating income	£ 100,000	£ 3,000	£ 103,000

* Variable overhead is total overhead - fixed overhead, or £400,000 - £160,000 = £240,000. Variable overhead rate = £240,000 ÷ £320,000 = 75% of direct labor.

2. A contribution approach to pricing might appear as follows:

Selling price		£19,800
Direct materials	£5,600	
Direct labor	6,400	
Variable overhead at 75% of direct labor	4,800	
Total variable cost		16,800
Contribution margin		£ 3,000

The contribution approach essentially attempts to provide a measure of the decrease in immediate net income that would result from rejecting an order. This is the contribution margin forgone. Traditional approaches to pricing do not supply such a number. In part (1), the £3,000 tells Smythe that she is *investing* £3,000 now to uphold her pricing policies. She can then assess whether preserving such policies and the long-run pricing structure is worth an investment of such magnitude. She also may assess whether accepting marginal business will cause this customer to seek such concessions regularly. Alternatively, Smythe may want to make such concessions occasionally to attract new customers.

A possible contribution margin formula may be illustrated as follows:

Direct material	£ 5,600
Direct labor	6,400
Variable overhead at 75% of direct labor	4,800
Total variable cost	£16,800
Markup at 30.95%* of £16,800	5,200
Target selling price	£22,000

*Normal markup percentage = (£22,000 - £16,800) ÷ £16,800 = 30.95%

Note that the markup of 30.95% is much higher than the 10% used previously because the markup must provide for the recovery of fixed overhead as well as the making of net income. The key to the contribution approach is its intelligent use with full recognition that total variable cost is *not* total cost.

An alternative way to compute the target selling price would provide for a two-step markup:

Total variable cost	£16,800
Fixed costs, 19.0%* of £16,800	3,200
Total costs	£20,000
Markup, 11.9%** of £16,800	2,000
Target selling price	£22,000

* 160 ÷ (280 + 320 + 240) = 19.0%

** 100 ÷ 840 = 11.9%

5-40 (15-20 min.)

1.

	Year to Date	Final Course Enrollment 30	10 More	Grand Totals
Tuition revenues	$2,000,000	$6,000	$1,000	$2,007,000
Costs of courses	800,000	4,000	600	804,600
Contribution margin	1,200,000	2,000	400	1,202,400
General administrative expenses	400,000	0	0	400,000
Operating income	$ 800,000	$2,000	$ 400	$ 802,400

2. The same general considerations influence pricing decisions in profit-seeking and nonprofit organizations. The exception is price-setting by many government-owned entities, which often is heavily affected by legislative bodies. The familiar three Cs – customers, costs, and competition – do influence price setting.

Executive education is highly competitive; the rates for top-flight teachers are relatively high; and customers often do without or conduct their own in-house training. The offering of discounts is often risky. It may alienate full-paying customers, may lead to widespread price-cutting, and may encourage the particular customers to bargain hard regarding course after course.

The setting of tuition in private universities is similar to setting prices in private industry. *Customers* may go to the *competition* – to other private or public universities. *Costs* must be recovered if the institution is to survive. Of course, tuition is only one part of a university's revenue. Private institutions are especially dependent on endowment income and on donations from friends and alumni.

5-41 (15 min.)

1. Contribution margin from direct sales = $15 - $2 = $13
   Contribution margin from sales to distributor = $50 - $2 = $48

   Total contribution from sales to distributors
   = (14,000 x 10) x $48 = $6,720,000
   Tape sales @ $15 to get CM of $6,720,000 = $6,720,000 ÷ $13 = 516,923

2. The cost of producing and promoting the movie is irrelevant to this decision.

3. Total contribution from direct sales = 30 million x ($15.50 - $2) = $405 million

   Sales at CM of $48 to get contribution of $405 million:
   $405,000,000 ÷ $48 = 8,437,500 tapes
   Sales per store = 8,437,500 ÷ 14,000 = 603 tapes

   It is unlikely that Disney would have been able so sell 580 tapes per video store. The decision to sell directly to consumers appears to have been wise.

5-42 (20 min.)

This is a classic problem of the application of the contribution approach.

	Basic	Marginal	Total
Number of flights per month	3,000	120	3,120
Available seats	300,000	12,000	312,000
Seats filled	156,000	2,400	158,400
Percent filled	52%	20%	51%
Revenue	$31,200,000	$240,000	$31,440,000
Variable expenses	21,840,000	120,000	21,960,000
Contribution margin	$ 9,360,000	$120,000	$ 9,480,000

Continental's approach was described by Chris F. Whelan, vice president in charge of economic planning, who makes the scheduling decisions. He uses a marginal (variable cost) approach, which was described as follows:

> Whelan considers that the bulk of his scheduled flights have to return at least their fully allocated costs. Overhead, depreciation, and insurance are very real expenses and must be covered. The out-of-pocket approach comes into play, says Whelan, only after the line's basic schedule has been set.
>
> "Then you go a step farther," he says, and see if adding more flights will contribute to the corporate net. Similarly, if he's thinking of dropping a flight with a disappointing record, he puts it under the marginal microscope: "If your revenues are going to be more than your out-of-pocket costs, you should keep the flight on."
>
> By "out-of-pocket costs" Whelan means just that: The actual dollars that Continental has to pay out to run a flight. He gets the figure not by applying hypothetical equations but by circulating a proposed schedule to every operating department concerned and finding out just what extra

expenses it will entail. If a ground crew already on duty can service the plane, the flight isn't charged a penny of their salary expense. There may even be some costs eliminated in running the flight; they won't need employees to roll the plane to a hanger, for instance, if it flies on to another stop.

Most of these extra flights, of course, are run at off-beat hours, mainly late at night. At times, though, Continental discovers that the hours aren't so unpopular after all. A pair of night coach flights on the Houston-San Antonio-El Paso-Phoenix-Los Angeles leg, added on a marginal basis, have turned out to be so successful that they are now more than covering fully allocated costs.

Alternative. Whelan uses an alternative cost analysis closely allied with the marginal concept in drawing up schedules. For instance, on his 11:11 p.m. flight from Colorado Springs to Denver and a 5:20 a.m. flight the other way, Continental uses Viscounts that, though they carry some cargo, often go without a single passenger. But the net cost of these flights is less than would be the rent for overnight hangar space for the Viscount at Colorado Springs.

And there's more than one absolute-loss flight scheduled solely to bring passengers to a connecting Continental long-haul flight; even when the loss on the feeder service is considered a cost on the long-haul service, the line makes a net profit on the trip.

Continental's data handling system produces weekly reports on each flight, with revenues measured against both out-of-pocket and fully allocated costs. Whelan uses these to give each flight a careful analysis at least once a quarter. But those added on a marginal basis get the fine-tooth-comb treatment monthly.

The business on these flights tends to be useful as a leading indicator, Whelan finds, since the off-peak traffic is more than normally sensitive to economic trends and will fall off sooner than that on the popular-hour flights. When he sees the night coach flights turning in consistently poor showings, it's a clue to lower his projections for the rest of the schedule.

5-43 (15-20 min.)

1. Total variable costs are $.90 + $.20 = $1.10 per boomerang.
   Total fixed costs are $300,000 + $50,000 = $350,000

Volume in units	200,000	250,000	300,000
Sales @ $3.00	$600,000	$750,000	$900,000
Total variable costs @ $1.10	220,000	275,000	330,000
Contribution margin	380,000	475,000	570,000
Fixed costs	350,000	350,000	350,000
Operating income	$ 30,000	$125,000	$220,000
Operating income percentage of sales	5.0%	16.7%	24.4%

2. Note the significant difference in predictions. For example, the correct analysis indicates $30,000 operating income at a 200,000 volume level; the incorrect analysis indicates $100,000 operating income. The manager's tabulation is incorrect because it assumes that all costs are variable. The presence of a larger proportion of fixed costs causes much wider swings in operating income when volume deviates from the volume used to develop the full costs per boomerang.

5-44 (15-20 min.)

1. Extra revenue from option 1: ($30 - $15) x 30 passengers = $450
   Extra costs for option 1: ($2.20 - $.20) x 65 mi + $400 = $530
   Therefore, the second option (adding a car to an existing train) is more profitable by $530 - $450 = $80.

   Costs that are the same for both alternatives are irrelevant. These include the cost of the tour guide, cost of moving the car or car and engine to the main track, and depreciation.

2. This depends on the total additional revenues and costs for option 2:

Revenues: $30 x 30	$900.00
Costs: Fuel - 65 mi x $.20/mi	$ 13.00
Tour guide	150.00
Moving car	40.00
Total additional cost	$203.00

   This option is definately profitable, generating extra profit of $900 - $203 = $697. The cost of the tour guide and the cost of moving the car to the main track are relevant for this decision because they would be incurred only if the agreement with the tour agent is accepted. The depreciation remains irrelevant as long as excess cars are available.

5-45 (15-20 min.)

1. Net income will be increased by 300 x (DM40 - DM26 - DM10) = DM1,200.

2. The variable manufacturing costs per unit: DM26.

3. DM180,000, DM60,000, DM30,000, DM10; i.e., all numbers are irrelevant except DM26.

4. Selling price: DM180,000 ÷ 2,000 units = DM90

Total sales: 2,400 x 2 x DM90 =		DM432,000
Less expenses:		
Fixed: DM60,000 + DM30,000 + 100,000* =	DM190,000	
Variable: 2,400 x 2 x (DM26 + DM10) =	172,800	362,800
Net income		DM 69,200

*Depreciation: DM500,000 ÷ 5 = DM100,000.

5-46 (15-25 min.)

1. Budgeted fixed manufacturing overhead per unit = $1,000,000 ÷ 200,000 = $5

2. Relevant items:

Additional sales	$120,000
Additional manufacturing costs, 10,000 x $10	$100,000
Additional selling and administrative expenses	1,000
Total relevant costs	$101,000
Additional operating income	$ 19,000

Fixed manufacturing costs are irrelevant because their total will be the same regardless of the special order being accepted or rejected.

3. Students may raise many points, including:

   a. Whether the president is willing to "invest" $19,000 in forgone operating income now to preserve a marketing policy or to prevent a general weakening of prices among competitors.

   b. Whether accepting the order now may lead to more profitable orders from the same customer subsequently.

4. Budgeted fixed manufacturing overhead rate would be $1,000,000 ÷ 100,000 = $10. However, the *additional* operating income in requirement 2 would be unaffected by how fixed costs are "unitized." (Of course, the original budgeted operating income would have been different, but that is irrelevant in requirement 2.)

5-47 (20-30 min.)

When this problem was used in an exam, it was well done by students who used contribution margin analysis or pro forma income statement methods, in total dollars. A number of students attempted to force a decision by means of analysis of unit costs or by break-even analysis, failing to consider the effect of sales volume on profits. A number of good solutions were marred by failure to draw specific conclusions.

Output and pricing:

Volume	Price	C/M	Total Contribution
50,000	$25	9	$450,000
60,000	24	8	480,000
70,000	23	7	490,000
80,000	22	6	480,000

The C/M per unit decreases as volume increases.

Output of 70,000 at selling price of $23 yields the largest contribution margin. However, this is in excess of capacity.

Maximum at present capacity: 60,000 units output at $24
= Contribution margin of $480,000

To increase capacity:

Investment	$200,000
Useful life	10 years
Cost per year ($200,000 ÷ 10)	$ 20,000

By increasing capacity to 70,000 units, which is maximum C/M, the company gains an additional $10,000 in C/M but incurs an additional fixed cost of $20,000.

Conclusions: Do not invest in new capacity.
Sell at $24.
Produce 60,000, the maximum capacity now available.

5-48 (15-20 min.)

1.	Designer	Moderately Priced
Items that can be displayed in 8,000 square feet	300	400
Contribution margin per item	$120	$65
Contribution margin per turnover of inventory	$36,000	$26,000
Relative number of turnovers for a given time period	2	3
Total contribution margin for a given time period	$72,000	$78,000

Students should recognize that square feet of floor space is the limiting or scarce factor. Note that the contribution margin *percentage* and the contribution margin *per item* are greater for the designer items. Nevertheless, the moderately priced items will generate a larger contribution margin *in total*. Why? Because more moderately priced dresses are sold in any given period of time. The analysis above implies sales of 300 x 2 = 600 designer dresses versus 400 x 3 = 1,200 moderately priced dresses. The designer items should be dropped.

2. The solution in requirement 1 assumes that moderately priced items can outsell designer items 3 to 2 and that the store will be 100% full of such items. Interdependencies between the items are ignored. If these factors do not hold, some combination of the two items may be preferable.

Additional considerations include the investment in inventories, the number of sales personnel, the skills and training of sales personnel, and the degree of substitutability between the types of items.

This problem could also be addressed on a unit basis. Suppose one designer dress is displayed and sold in a given time period. How many moderately priced dresses could be sold in the same period? First, compute how many moderately priced dresses would be displayed:

Moderate priced dresses displayed = 4/3 x designer dresses displayed
= 4/3 x 1 = 1 1/3

For each dress displayed, 1 1/2 moderately priced dresses would be sold in the same time period that 1 designer dress is sold. Why? Because turnover of designer items is 2/3 that of moderately priced dresses, which implies that turnover of moderately priced dresses is 1 1/2 times that of designer dresses. Therefore,

Moderate priced dresses sold = 1 1/2 x 1 1/3 x designer dresses sold
= 2 x designer dresses sold

Gulf Coast Fashions can use a given amount of space to sell either 1 designer dress or 2 moderately priced dresses. Contribution margins are:

Designer dresses	Moderately priced dresses
1 x $120 = $120	2 x $65 = $130

The contribution is greater from selling 2 moderately priced dresses than from selling 1 designer dress.

Allied Signal - 1993 (Valuation)
(Assumes persistent ROE)
($ in Millions except per share amounts)

Cost of capital	0.14
Initial book value - 12/31/93	$ 2,251
Dividend payout	0.25

Year ahead	YR. 1	YR. 2	YR. 3	YR. 4	YR. 5	YR. 6	YR. 7	YR. 8	YR. 9	YR. 10
Predicted net income	$ 405 [(1)]	460	522	592	672	763	866	983	1,116	1,267
End-of-year book value	2,555 [(2)]	2,900	3,291	3,736	4,240	4,812	5,462	6,199	7,036	7,986
Predicted abnormal net income	90 [(3)]	102	116	132	149	170	192	218	248	281
Discount factor	0.8772	0.7695	0.6750	0.5921	0.5194	0.4556	0.3996	0.3506	0.3075	0.2697
PV of abnormal net income	79 [(4)]	79	78	78	78	77	77	77	76	76

Initial book value	$ 2,251
PV of abnormal net income	774
Estimated value	3,025
Shares (millions)	283
Predicted price	**11.35**
Actual high	$ 40.00
Actual low	$ 35.00

[1] $2,251 (12/31/93 equity book value) × 18% (ROE) = $450

[2] Beginning equity book value	$2,251
+ Estimated net income	405
- Estimated dividend payment (25% × $405)	(101)
Ending equity book value	$2,555

[3] Predicted net income	$405
- "Normal" earnings (14% × $2,251)	(315)
Predicted abnormal earnings	$90

[4] Abnormal earnings at end of Year 1	$90
× PV of sum for 1 period @ 14%	x .8772
PV of abnormal earnings at 12/31/93	$79

C5-2. General Motors (CW): Income statement discussion

Optional Note to Instructors:

Included as part of the solution are edited (i.e., shortened versions) of General Motors' balance sheets, income statements, and cash flow statements for the period covered by the case. When covering the case, you might consider handing these out in advance of covering the case in class or, alternatively, handing them out on the day you cover the case in class.

5-50 (30-50 min.)

This might be assigned at the end of the next chapter as a review of two chapters. This problem is more challenging than nearly all of the others in this chapter. Accordingly, this solution is more elaborate than is really necessary to answer the question.

1. The total amount of fixed overhead is common to all alternatives. Therefore, it is irrelevant to this analysis. The scarce resource is hours of capacity. The objective is to maximize the contribution per hour:

	Subcomponents	Plug-in Assemblies	Difference
Revenue per unit	$2.20	$5.30	
Variable cost per unit	1.40	3.30	
Contribution per unit	$ .80	$2.00	$-1.20
Contribution per hour	$ 48.00*	$ 40.00**	$ 8.00
Hours available	x 600,000	x 600,000	
Total contribution	$28,800,000	$24,000,000	$4,800,000

* $.80 x 60 units per hour = $48.00
** $2.00 x 20 units per hour = $40.00

Plug-in assemblies should be dropped because it is diverting the limited resource from a more profitable use. Note that the sales manager is incorrect. These decisions should not be reached by "all-costs" allocations and consequent computations of net profits or losses on units of product. Each plug-in assembly is making $2.00 contribution to profit and to the recovery of fixed costs, but it takes three times as long to get a plug-in assembly.

2. The lowest price must yield a contribution of $28,800,000. The contribution per unit would be $28,800,000 divided by the number of units produced in one year, or:

$28,800,000 ÷ (600,000 hours x 20 unit per hour)
= $28,800,000 ÷ 12,000,000 units = $2.40 per unit

Because the contribution is currently $2.00 per unit at a selling price of $5.30, the minimum acceptable price must be $5.70 in order to provide a unit contribution of $2.40.

To double check, consider the following:

	100% of Capacity	
	To Subcomponents	To Plug-in Assemblies
Sales in units	36,000,000	12,000,000
Sales at $2.20 and $5.70	$79,200,000	$68,400,000
Variable costs at $1.40 and $3.30	50,400,000	39,600,000
Contribution margin	$28,800,000	$28,800,000
Fixed costs*	21,600,000	21,600,000
Operating income	$ 7,200,000	$ 7,200,000

*36,000,000 x Unit fixed overhead rate of $.60, and 12,000,000 x Unit fixed overhead rate of ($1.20 + the $.60 transferred-in), respectively.

3. Note that this increase in variable cost per hour is common to both alternatives. That is, the variable processing cost would rise by $14.40 per hour:

Variable overhead = 40% of old fixed overhead
= .4 x $21,600,000 = $8,640,000

Variable overhead rate per hour = $8,640,000 ÷ 600,000 = $14.40

The contribution per hour is therefore reduced from $48 to $33.60 for subcomponents and from $40 to $25.60 for plug-in assemblies. Note that the crucial difference per hour is still $8.00. The critical question in relevant cost analysis is: what difference does it make?

Incidentally, many individuals often jump to the conclusion that relevant cost analysis is simple: variable costs are always relevant, and fixed costs are irrelevant. This is an example where the variable cost is irrelevant. (For that matter, in this case, the labor cost, another variable cost, is also irrelevant.) Irrelevant costs can be included in the analysis. But, *if they are analyzed correctly*, they will not make any *difference* between alternatives. If analyzed incorrectly, they will provide misleading information.

In short, the answer here is the same as the answers to (1) and (2). The lowest acceptable price is still $5.70. To prove this, use the same format as in (2):

	100% of Capacity	
	To Subcomponents	To Plug-in Assemblies
Sales in units	36,000,000	12,000,000
Sales at $2.20 and $5.70	$79,200,000	$68,400,000
Variable costs* at $1.64 and $4.02	59,040,000	48,240,000
Contribution margin	$20,160,000	$20,160,000
Fixed costs**	12,960,000	12,960,000
Operating income	$ 7,200,000	$ 7,200,000

*$1.40 + ($14.40 ÷ 60 units) = $1.64, and
$3.30 + ($14.40 ÷ 20 units) = $4.02
**.6 x $21,600,000 = $12,960,000

Finally, note that the fixed costs could be ignored completely in all of the above requirements. If you want to include them, you may – but, if the fixed costs are analyzed correctly, they won't affect the decisions. In part (2), $21.6 million of fixed costs would be deducted no matter what product mix is chosen; in part (3), $12.96 million of fixed costs would be deducted under any alternative.

5-51 (10-15 min.)

1.

Manufacturing cost	\$27.00
Gross margin, 15% x \$27.00	4.05
Price	\$31.05

Knoxville would not produce a motor because they would not be able to sell them at \$31.05, assuming that market research is right about the market price of \$25.00 Even with no profit margin, the cost of \$27 exceeds the price of \$25.

2. Using target costing, Memphis would begin with the market price of \$25.00. From this, managers would compute the largest acceptable manufacturing cost:

Price	\$25.00
Less gross margin	3.26*
Manufacturing cost	\$21.74

*Price = Cost + (.15 x Cost)
\$25.00 = 1.15 x Cost
Cost = \$25.00 ÷ 1.15 = \$21.74
Margin = \$25.00 - \$21.74 = \$3.26

3. Memphis managers would have to determine if they could design the garage-door-opener motor and its production process in a way that manufacturing costs were below \$21.74. Both the design specifications for the motor and the production process would need to be looked at. If there is no way to reduce production costs to \$21.74 or below, the product should not be produced. However, target costing forces managers to examine ways to lower the production costs through product and process design. Instead of taking the design and process as givens and then examining the market to see if the product can be sold for a high enough price, Memphis managers will try to design a product and process that meets the constraints of the market.

5-52 (20 min.)

1. Contribution margin = \$800 - (\$475 + \$25) = \$300
   Total contribution = \$300 x 44,000 mowers = \$13,200,000
   Total fixed costs = 7 years x (\$900,000 + \$50,000) = \$6,650,000
   Development costs = \$5,000,000

   Life cycle profit = \$13,200,000 - \$6,650,000 - \$5,000,000
   = \$1,550,000

2. Desired profit = .10 x (\$800 x 44,000) = \$3,520,000

   The life cycle profit is \$3,520,000 - \$1,550,000 = \$1,970,000 short of what is desired. Therefore, unless some changes can be made, Southeast will not enter the riding lawn mower market.

3. A target costing company does not quit when the first cost estimate comes in too high. Managers establish a target cost and try to adjust design, production and marketing processes to meet the target cost. In this case, the target cost is:

Revenue	\$35,200,000
Desired profit	3,520,000
Target cost	\$31,680,000

Expected costs are:

Variable production costs	\$20,900,000
Fixed production costs	6,300,000
Variable selling costs	1,100,000
Fixed selling costs	350,000
Development costs	5,000,000
Total costs	\$33,650,000

If total costs can be reduced by \$1,970,000, to \$31,680,000 by changes in the product's design, the production process design, or production or selling methods, this will be a profitable product.

5-53 (30 min.)

Fixed overhead allocation rate per machine hour
= FF2,160,000 ÷ 90,000 = FF24
Variable overhead allocation rate = FF40 - FF24 = FF16

St. Tropez should not accept either order. The company does not have adequate plant capacity to manufacture the order of 20,000 jewelry cases from Lyon Inc. without subcontracting. The order from Avignon Co. does not yield St. Tropez a positive contribution margin.

The calculations showing that the St. Tropez does not have the necessary plant capacity in the third quarter to produce the order for 20,000 jewelry cases are as follows:

Annual plant capacity	90,000 machine hours
Monthly plant capacity	7,500 machine hours
Estimated monthly capacity use .8 x 7,500	6,000 machine hours
Excess capacity per month	1,500 machine hours
Period involved, third quarter	x 3 months
Total excess capacity available	4,500 machine hours

Machine hours required to produce 20,000 jewelry cases
= Number of cases x machine hours per case
= 20,000 x .25 = 5,000 hours.

The Lyon Inc. order for 20,000 jewelry cases would require 5,000 machine hours, but only 4,500 machine hours are available in the third quarter.

Computations related to the order from Avignon Co. are as follows:

Price offered per case		FF 85.0
Production cost per case:		
Raw materials	FF42.5	
Direct labor, .5 hours @ FF60	30.0	
Overhead, .5 machine hours @ FF16*	8.0	80.5
Contribution margin per case		FF 4.5
Number of cases		x 7,500
Total contribution margin		FF33,750
Fixed costs related to the order:		
Setup costs	FF15,000	
Special device	25,000	40,000
Loss from taking the order		FF (6,250)

*Fixed costs are not relevant in this case and should be omitted.

The Avignon Co. order should be rejected because it is unprofitable in the short run with the present price and cost structure.

5-54 (40-60 min.) Some instructors may prefer to omit some requirements.

1. SAN JUAN BOTTLING COMPANY
Income Statement
For the Year Ended December 31, 1998

	Totals (in 000's of dollars)		Per Unit	
Sales		900		$.60
Variable expenses:				
Direct material	450		$.300	
Direct labor	90		.060	
Variable factory overhead	18		.012	
Variable selling:				
Sales commissions	45*		.030*	
Shipping and other	90		.060	
Variable administration	12	705	.008	.47
Contribution margin		195		$.13
Fixed expenses:				
Factory overhead	50			
Selling	110			
Administrative	40	200		
Operating income		-5		

*5% of sales *dollars*.

2. All of the variable costs apparently increase in relation to physical volume except that sales commissions are related to dollar sales. Dollar sales are expected to increase by $100,000, apparently consisting of a unit increase of 10% ($90,000 ÷ $900,000) and a price increase of 1.01% ($10,000 ÷ $990,000). In addition, fixed selling expenses are expected to increase by $28,000 or 25%.

3.

SAN JUAN BOTTLING COMPANY
Budgeted Income Statements
For the Year Ended December 31, 1999
(in 000's of dollars)

	3(a)	3(b)	3(c)
Sales	1,026.0[a]	850.500[b]	1,023.0[c]
Variable expenses:			
Direct material @ $.30 unit	540.0	405.000	495.0
Direct labor @ $.06	108.0	81.000	99.0
Variable factory overhead @ $.012	21.6	16.200	19.8
Variable selling:			
Sales commissions @ 5% of sales	51.3	42.525	102.3[d]
Shipping and other @ $.06	108.0	81.000	99.0
Variable administrative @ $.008	14.4	10.800	13.2
Total variable expenses	843.3	636.525	828.3
Contribution margin	182.7	213.975	194.7
Fixed expenses:			
Factory overhead	50.0	50.0	50.0
Selling	110.0	110.000	110.0
Administrative	40.0	40.000	40.0
Total fixed expenses	200.0	200.000	200.0
Operating income	- 17.3	+13.975	- 5.3

[a] 1,800,000 units x $.57
[b] 1,350,000 units x $.63
[c] 1,650,000 units x $.62
[d] Sales commissions of 10% x $1,023,000

4. Proofs of answers to Requirements 4, 5, and 6 are at the end of this solution.

Selling price		$.660
Variable costs, excluding sales commissions	$.440	
Sales commissions, .05 x $.66	.033	.473
Contribution margin per unit		$.187
Units to be sold	1,875,000	
Total contribution margin, 1,875,000 x $.187	$ 350,625	
Fixed expenses, $200,000 + $130,000	330,000	
Operating income	$ 20,625	

5. The needed contribution must be high enough to make up for the loss of last year and provide sufficient margin for this year. Therefore, the contribution needed on the incremental business must be $15,000 if an overall target operating income of $10,000 is to be obtained. The variable costs would be $.47 - $.09 = $.38 per unit. Add the contribution margin needed per unit, $15,000 ÷ 300,000 = $.05; the selling price would be $.43 per unit. A more elaborate explanation follows:

	300,000 Units		From Part (1) Regular	Grand
	Per Unit	Total	Business	Total
Sales	$?	$?	$900,000	$?
Variable costs:				
Per requirement (1),				
$.47 less commissions				
($.03) and shipping ($.06)	.38	114,000	705,000	819,000
Contribution margin	$.05	$ 15,000	$195,000	$210,000
Fixed expenses		0	200,000	200,000
Operating income		$+15,000	$ -5,000	$+10,000

Selling price = ($15,000 + $114,000) ÷ 300,000 = $.43 or $.38 + $.05 = $.43

Then, sales on incremental order = \$129,000 and a grand total sales = \$1,029,000.

An alternative approach is the equation technique:

Let X = Desired selling price on special order

Sales = Variable expenses + Fixed expenses + Operating income

$$\$900{,}000 + 300{,}000X = \$705{,}000 + \$.38(300{,}000) + \$200{,}000 + \$10{,}000$$
$$300{,}000X = \$705{,}000 + \$114{,}000 + \$200{,}000 + \$10{,}000 - \$900{,}000$$
$$300{,}000X = \$129{,}000$$
$$X = \$.43$$

6. Let X = Number of units

Sales = Variable expenses + Fixed expenses + Operating income

$$\$.60X = (\$.47 + \$.03)X + \$200{,}000 + \$10{,}000$$
$$\$.60X - \$.50X = \$210{,}000$$
$$X = 2{,}100{,}000 \text{ units}$$

Proof of answers 4, 5, and 6:

4.			
	Sales	1,875,000 @ \$.66 =	\$1,237,500
	Variable expenses	1,875,000 @ \$.473 =	886,875
	Contribution margin	1,875,000 @ \$.187 =	350,625
	Fixed expenses		320,000
	Net income		\$ 20,625

5.

Sales	300,000 @ $.43	=	$129,000
Variable expenses	300,000 @ $.38	=	114,000
Contribution margin			15,000
Contribution margin on regular business			195,000
Total contribution margin			210,000
Fixed expenses			200,000
Net income			$ 10,000

6.

Sales	2,100,000 @ $.60	=	$1,260,000
Variable expenses	2,100,000 @ $.50	=	1,050,000
Contribution margin			210,000
Fixed expenses			200,000
Net income			$ 10,000

The decision would be based on whether the total contribution margin with the flavoring is greater than the total contribution margin without the flavoring. Of course, subjective factors may also influence the decision.

CHAPTER 6

Relevant Information and Decision Making: Production Decisions

6-A1 (30-40 min.)

Problem 6-43 is an extension of this problem. The two problems make a good combination.

1. Operating inflows for each year, old machine:

$910,000 - ($810,000 + $60,000)	$40,000
Operating inflows for each year, new machine:	
$910,000 - ($810,000 + $25,000*)	$75,000
* $60,000 - $35,000	

Cash flow statements (in thousands of dollars):

	Keep			Buy		
	Year 1	Years 2 & 3	Three Years Together	Year 1	Years 2 & 3	Three Years Together
Receipts, inflows from operations	40	40	120	75	75	225
Disbursements:						
Purchase of "old" equipment	(87)*	–	(87)	(87)	–	(87)
Purchase of "new" equipment:						
Total costs less proceeds from disposal of "old" equipment ($99,000-$16,000)	–	–	–	(83)	–	(83)
Net cash inflow (outflow)	(47)	40	33	(95)	75	55

*Assumes that the outlay of $87,000 took place on January 2, 19X9, or sometime during 19X9. Some students will ignore this item, assuming correctly that it is irrelevant to the decision. However, note that a statement for the entire year was requested.

The difference for three years taken together is $22,000 ($55,000 - $33,000). Note particularly that the $87,000 book value can be omitted from the comparison. Merely cross out the entire line; although the column totals will be affected, the net difference will still be $22,000.

2. Income statements (in thousands of dollars):

	Keep		Buy		
	Years 1, 2 & 3	Three Years Together	Year 1	Years 2 & 3	Three Years Together
Sales	910	2,730	910	910	2,730
Expenses:					
Other expenses	810	2,430	810	810	2,430
Operating of machine	60	180	25	25	75
Depreciation	29	87*	33	33	99
Total expenses	899	2,697	868	868	2,604
Loss on disposal:					
Proceeds ("revenue")	–	–	(16)	–	(16)
Book value ("expense")	–	–	87	–	87*
Loss	–	–	71	–	71
Total charges	899	2,697	939	868	2,675
Net income	11	33	(29)	42	55

*As in part (1), the $87,000 book value can be omitted from the comparison without changing the $22,000 difference. This would mean dropping the depreciation item of $29,000 per year (a cumulative effect of $87,000) under the "keep" alternative, and dropping the book value item of $87,000 in the loss on disposal computation under the "buy" alternative.

Difference for three years together, $55,000 - $33,000 = $22,000.

Note the motivational factors here. A manager may be reluctant to replace simply because the large loss on disposal will severely harm the profit performance in Year 1.

3. The net difference for the three years taken together would be unaffected because the item is a past cost. Any number may be substituted for the original $87,000 figure without changing this answer.

   For example, examine how the results would change in part (1) by inserting $1 million where the $87,000 now appears (in thousands of dollars):

		Keep: Three Years Together	Buy: Three Years Together	Difference
Receipts		120	225	105
Disbursements:				
Purchase of old equipment		(1,000)	(1,000)	0
Purchase of new equipment:				
Gross price	99			
Disposal proceeds of "old"	16	–	(83)	(83)
Net cash outflow		(880)	(858)	22

   In sum, this may be a horrible situation. The manager really blundered. But keeping the old equipment will compound the blunder to the cumulative tune of $22,000 over the next three years.

4. Diplomatically, Lee should try to convey the following. All of us tend to indulge in the erroneous idea that we can soothe the wounded pride of a bad purchase decision by using the item instead of replacing it. The fallacy is believing that a current or future action can influence the long-run impact of a past outlay. *All* past costs are down the drain. Nothing can change what has already happened.

The $87,000 has been spent. Subsequent accounting for the item is irrelevant. The schedules in parts (1) and (2) clearly show that we may *completely* ignore the $87,000 original outlay and still have a correct analysis. The important point is that the $87,000 is not an element of difference between alternatives and, therefore, may be safely ignored. The only relevant items are those expected future items that will *differ* between alternatives.

5. The $87,000 purchase of the original equipment, the sales, and the other expenses are irrelevant because they are common to both alternatives. The relevant items are the following (in thousands of dollars):

	Three Years Together		
	Keep		Buy
Operating of machine (3 x $60; 3 x $25)	$180		$ 75
Incremental cost of new machine:			
Total cost		$99	
Less proceeds of old machine		16	
Incremental cost	–		83
Total relevant costs	$180		$158
Difference in favor of buying			$ 22

6-A2 (20 min)

1. The key to this question is what will happen to the fixed overhead costs if production of the boxes is discontinued. Assume that all $60,000 of fixed costs will continue. Then, Sunshine State will lose $36,000 by purchasing the boxes from Georgia-Pacific:

Payment to Georgia-Pacific, 80,000 x $2.40	$192,000
Costs saved, variable costs	156,000
Additional costs	$ 36,000

2. Some subjective factors are:
   - Might Georgia-Pacific raise prices if Sunshine State closed down its box-making facility?
   - Will sub-contracting the box production affect the quality of the boxes?
   - Is a timely supply of boxes assured, even if the number needed changes?
   - Does Sunshine State sacrifice proprietary informatin when disclosing the box specifications to Georgia-Pacific?

3. In this case the fixed costs are relevant. However, it is not the depreciation on the old equipment that is relevant. It is the cost of the new equipment. Annual cost savings by not producing the boxes now will be:

Variable costs	$156,000
Investment avoided (annualized)	100,000
Total saved	$256,000

The payment to Georgia-Pacific is $256,000-$192,000 = $64,000 less than the savings, so Sunshine State would be $64,000 better off subcontracting the production of the boxes.

6-A3 (15-20 min.)

The first tabulation is probably easier to understand, but the choice of a tabulation is a matter of taste:

	(a) Expand Laboratory Testing	(b) Expand Eye Clinic	(c) Rent to Gift Shop
Revenues	$320,000	$500,000	$11,000
Expenses	290,000	480,000	0
Income effects per year	$ 30,000	$ 20,000	$11,000

Treating the gift shop as the forgone (rejected) alternative, the tabulation is:

	(a) Expand Laboratory Testing		(b) Expand Eye Clinic	
Revenue		$320,000		$500,000
Expenses:				
Outlay costs	$290,000		$480,000	
Opportunity cost, rent forgone	11,000	301,000	11,000	491,000
Income effects per year		$ 19,000		$ 9,000

The numbers favor laboratory testing, which will generate a contribution to hospital income that is $10,000 greater than the eye clinic's.

The numbers have been analyzed correctly under both tabulations. Both answer the key query: What difference does it make? As a general rule, we prefer using the first tabulation. It is a straightforward presentation.

6-A4 (15 min.) Table is in thousands of dollars.

1,2.

	(a) Sales Beyond Split-Off	(b) Sales at Split-Off	(a)-(b) Incremental Sales	(c) Separable Costs Beyond Split-Off	(a)-(b)-(c) Incremental Gain or (Loss)
A	230	54	176	190	(14)
B	330	28	302	300	2
C	175	54	121	100	21
Increase in overall operating income from further processing of A, B, and C					9

The incremental analysis indicates that Products B and C should be processed further, but Product A should be sold at split-off. The overall operating income would be $42,000, as follows:

Sales: $54,000 + $330,000 + $175,000		$559,000
Joint cost of goods sold	$117,000	
Separable cost of goods sold:		
$300,000 + $100,000	400,000	517,000
Operating income		$ 42,000

Compare this with the present operating income of $28,000. That is, $230,000 + $330,000 + $175,000 - ($190,000 + $300,000 + $100,000 + $117,000) = $28,000. The extra $14,000 of operating income comes from eliminating the $14,000 loss resulting from processing Product A beyond the split-off point.

6-B1 (15-20 min.)

1.

	Three Years Together		
	Keep	Replace	Difference
Cash operating costs	$42,000	$22,500	$19,500
Old equipment, book value:			
Periodic write-off as			
depreciation	18,000	-	
or			-
lump-sum write-off	-	18,000*	
Disposal value		-3,000*	3,000
New equipment, acquisition cost		15,000**	-15,000
Total costs	$60,000	$52,500	$ 7,500

*In a formal income statement, these two items would be combined as "loss on disposal" of $18,000 - $3,000 = $15,000.

**In a formal income statement, written off as straight-line depreciation of $15,000 ÷ 3 = $5,000 for each of three years.

2.

	Three Years Together		
	Keep	Replace	Difference
Cash operating costs	$42,000	$22,500	$19,500
Disposal value of old equipment	-	-3,000	3,000
New equipment, acquisition cost	-	15,000	-15,000
Total relevant costs	$42,000	$34,500	$ 7,500

This tabulation is clearer because it focuses on only those items that affect the decision.

3. The prospective benefits of the replacement alternative:

3 x ($14,000 - $7,500) =	$19,500
Deduct initial net cash outlay required,	
$15,000 - $3,000 =	12,000
Difference in favor of replacement	$ 7,500

Of course, the new equipment is likely to be faster, thus saving operator time. The latter is important, but it is not quantified in this problem.

6-B2 (10 min.)

1. The replacement alternative would be chosen because the county would have $7,500 more cash accumulated in three years.

2. The keep alternative would be chosen because the higher overall costs of photocopying for the first year would be shown for the replacement alternative (under accrual accounting):

	First Year	
	Keep	Replace
Cash operating costs	$14,000	$ 7,500
Depreciation	6,000	5,000
Loss on disposal		15,000
Total costs	$20,000	$27,500

Thus, the performance evaluation model might motivate the manager to make a decision that would be undesirable in the long run.

6-B3 (15-20 min.)

1.

	Make		Buy	
	Total	Per Unit	Total	Per Unit
Purchase cost			DM10,000,000	DM50
Direct material	DM5,500,000	DM27.5		
Direct labor	1,900,000	9.5		
Factory overhead, variable	1,100,000	5.5		
Factory overhead, fixed avoided	1,000,000	5.0		
Total relevant costs	DM9,500,000	DM47.5	DM10,000,000	DM50
Difference in favor of making	DM 500,000	DM 2.5		

The numerical difference in favor of making is DM500,000 or DM2.5 per unit. The relevant fixed costs are DM1,000,000, not DM2,500,000.

2.

	Make	Buy and Leave Capacity Idle	Buy and Rent
Rent revenue	DM –	DM –	DM 1,250,000
Obtaining of components	(9,500,000)	(10,000,000)	(10,000,000)
Net relevant costs	DM(9,500,000)	DM(10,000,000)	DM(8,750,000)

The final column indicates that buying the components and renting the vacated capacity will yield the best results in this case. The favorable difference is DM9,500,000 - DM8,750,000 = DM750,000.

6-B4 (15 min.)

1.

Sales ($400 + $600 + $100)		$1,100
Costs:		
Raw materials	$700	
Processing	100	
Total		800
Profit		$300

2.

Sales ($860 + $850 + $175)		$1,885
Costs:		
Joint costs	$800	
Frozen dinner costs	470	
Salisbury steak costs	200	
Tanning costs	80	
Total costs		1,550
Profit		$ 335

Although it is more profitable to process all three products further than it is to sell them all at the split-off point, it is important to look at the economic benefit from further processing of each individual product.

3.

Steaks to frozen dinners:

Additional revenue from processing further ($860 - $400)	$460
Additional cost for processing further	470
Increase (decrease) in profit from processing further	$ (10)

Hamburger to Salisbury steaks:

Additional revenue from processing further ($850 - $600)	$250
Additional cost for processing further	200
Increase (decrease) in profit from processing further	$ 50

Untanned hide to tanned hide:

Additional revenue from processing further ($175 - $100)	$75
Additional cost for processing further	80
Increase (decrease) in profit from processing further	$ (5)

Only the hamburger should be processed further, because it is the only product whose additional revenue for processing further exceeds the additional cost. The resulting profit would be $350:

Sales ($400 + $850 + $100)		$1,350
Costs:		
Joint costs	$800	
Further processing of hamburger	200	
Total cost		1,000
Profit		$ 350

6-1 An opportunity cost does not entail a disbursement of cash at any time, whereas an outlay cost does entail a disbursement sooner or later.

6-2 The $800 represents an opportunity cost. It is the amount forgone by rejecting an opportunity. It signifies that the value to the owner of keeping those strangers out of the summer house for that two-week period is at least $800.

6-3 Accountants do not ordinarily record opportunity costs in accounting records, because those records are traditionally concerned with real transactions rather than possible transactions. It is impossible to record data on all lost opportunities.

6-4 Basically, incremental costs and differential costs are indistinguishable. They are synonyms. However, incremental costs are ordinarily linked with increases in the volume of activity, as distinguished from broader uses of the term.

6-5 No. Incremental cost has a broader meaning. It is the addition to total costs by the adoption of some course of action. Another term, marginal cost, is used by economists to indicate the addition to costs from the manufacture of *one* additional unit. Of course, marginal cost is indeed the incremental cost of one unit.

6-6 The decline in costs would be called differential or incremental savings.

6-7 Not necessarily. Qualitative factors can favor either making or buying. Often factors such as product quality and assurance of delivery schedules favor making. However, sometimes establishing long-term relationships with suppliers is an important qualitative factor favoring the purchase of components.

6-8 The choice in many cases is not really whether to make or buy. Instead, the choice is how best to use available capacity.

6-9 The split-off point is where the individual products produced in a joint process become separately identifiable. Costs before the split-off point are irrelevant for decisions about the individual products. They affect the decision about whether to undertake the entire production process, but they do not influence decisions about what to do with the individual products.

6-10 Yes. Techniques for assigning joint-product costs to individual products are useful only for product costing, not for deciding on further processing after the split-off point. The product must be considered separately at that point apart from its historical cost. The proper basis of the decision on further processing is a comparison of incremental revenue versus incremental expense between the alternatives of selling at the split-off point and processing further.

6-11 No. Once inventory has been purchased, the price paid is a sunk cost. It is true that selling at a price less than $5,000 would produce a reported loss. However, a sale at any price above $0 is economically beneficial provided that the only alternative is to scrap the inventory.

6-12 No. Sunk costs are irrelevant to the replacement decision.

6-13 No. Past costs are not relevant because they cannot be affected by a decision. Although past costs are often indispensable for formulating predictions, past costs themselves are not the predictions that are the inputs to decision models. Clear thinking is enhanced by these distinctions.

6-14

a. Book value of old equipment is *irrelevant* to a replacement decision because it does not change under any alternative and cannot be realized.
b. Disposal value of old equipment is *relevant* to a replacement decision because it can either be realized (by replacement) or forgone (by continued use).
c. Cost of new equipment is *relevant* to a replacement decision because it can be incurred (by replacement) or avoided (by continued use).

6-15 Yes. Some expected future costs may be irrelevant because they will be the same under all feasible alternatives.

6-16 Yes. The statement is correct in terms of *total* variable costs.

6-17 Two reasons why units costs should be analyzed with care in decision making are:

1. Most unit costs are stable only over a certain range of output, and care must be taken to see that allowances are made when alternatives are considered outside that range.
2. Some unit costs are an allocation of fixed costs; thus when a higher volume of output is being considered, unit cost will decrease proportionately, and vice versa.

Two other reasons are mentioned in the text:

1. Some unit costs are based on both relevant and irrelevant factors and should be broken down further before being considered.
2. Unit costs must be reduced to the same base (denominator) before comparing or combining them.

6-18 Sales personnel sometimes neglect to point out that the unit costs are based on outputs far in excess of the volume of their prospective customer.

6-19 An inconsistency between a decision model and a performance evaluation model occurs when a decision about whether to replace a piece of equipment is based on the cash flow effects over the life of the equipment but a manager's performance evaluation is based on the first year's reported income. The loss on disposal of the equipment is irrelevant for decision purposes, but it affects the first year income, hence the performance evaluation.

6-20 The wide use of income statements to evaluate performance may overly influence managers to maximize short-run performance that may hurt long-run performance. They may pass up profitable opportunities to replace equipment because of the large loss on disposal shown on the first year's income statement.

6-21 (10-15 min.)

1.

	Independent Practice	Employee	Difference
Operating revenues	$320,000	$90,000	$230,000
Operating expenses	220,000	–	220,000
Income effects per year	$100,000	$90,000	$ 10,000

		Choose Independent Practice
Revenues		$320,000
Expenses:		
Outlay costs	$220,000	
Opportunity cost of employee compensation	90,000	310,000
Income effects per year		$ 10,000

Each tabulation produces the key difference of $10,000. As a general rule, we favor using the first tabulation. It offers a straightforward presentation of inflows and outflows under sharply stated alternatives.

2.

		Choice as Employee
Revenue		$ 90,000
Expenses:		
Outlay costs	$ 0	
Opportunity cost of accounting practice	100,000	100,000
Income effects per year		$ (10,000)

If the employee alternative is selected, the key difference in favor of becoming a sole practitioner is again $10,000. Bridgeman is sacrificing $10,000 to avoid the risks of an independent practice.

6-22 (10-15 min.)

	Alternatives Under Consideration		
	(1)	(2)	(1) - (2)
	Sell, Rent, and Invest in Bonds	Hold Present Home	Difference
Revenue	$16,000	$ -	$16,000
Less: Outlay cost	14,000	6,000	8,000
Income effects per year	$ 2,000	$(6,000)	$ 8,000

Advantage of selling home is $2,000 + $6,000 = $8,000. Obviously, if rent is much higher, the advantage may become negative.

The above analysis does not contain explicit opportunity costs. If opportunity costs were a part of the analysis, the following presentation applies (whereby the interest on investment in bonds is not listed as a separate alternative but is regarded as a forgone alternative):

	Alternative Chosen: Hold Present Home
Opportunity cost	$2,000
Outlay cost	6,000
Income effects per year	$8,000

As before, the advantage of selling the home and renting is $8,000. The opportunity cost of home ownership is $16,000 - $14,000 = $2,000.

6-23 (15 min.)

1. It is easiest to analyze total costs, not unit costs.

	Make	Purchase
Direct materials	$300,000	
Avoidable overhead costs:		
Indirect labor	30,000	
Supplies	20,000	
Allocated occupancy cost	0	
Purchase cost		$340,000
Total relevant costs	$350,000	$340,000

The difference in favor of purchasing is $350,000 - $340,000 = $10,000.

2. Because the quantitative difference is small, qualitative factors may dominate the decision. As described in Chapter 4, companies using a just-in-time system need assurance of both quality and timeliness of supplies of materials, parts, and components. A small, local company may not be reliable enough for NEC. In essence, NEC may be willing to "invest" $10,000, the quantitative advantage of purchasing, in order to have more control over the supply of the components.

The division manager may have made the right decision for the wrong reason. He incorrectly ignored avoidable fixed costs, leading to a mistaken belief that making the components was less costly by $.40 per unit or $40,000 in total. The $50,000 of avoidable fixed costs makes the purchase option less costly by $10,000. If the manager's decision is to make the component, it should be because forgoing profits of $10,000 has a long-run qualitative benefit of more than $10,000, not because the bid is greater than the variable cost.

6-24 (10 min.)

Product M should not have been processed further. The only valid approach is to concentrate on the separable costs and revenues *beyond* split-off:

	Sell at Split-off as M	Process Further as Super M	Difference
Revenues, 2,500,000 gallons @30¢ & 38¢	$750,000	$950,000	$200,000
Separable costs beyond split-off	–	225,000	225,000
Income effects for April	$750,000	$725,000	$ (25,000)

The joint costs do not differ between alternatives and are irrelevant to the question of whether to sell or process further. The next table (not required) confirms the results (in thousands):

	Alternative 1			Alternative 2			
					Super		Differential
	L	M	Total	L	M	Total	Effects
Revenues	$1,000	$750	$1,750	$1,000	$950	$1,950	$200
Joint costs			$1,600			$1,600	—
Separable costs			—		225	225	225
Total costs			$1,600			$1,825	$225
Income effects			$ 150			$ 125	$ (25)

6-25 (10 min.)

1. Answer (c): $8,000 ÷ 2,000 = $4.00

2. Answer (a): Product A is the only product that produces an incremental profit ($42,000 - $25,000) - $9,000 = $8,000.

6-26 (5-10 min.)

1. The only relevant item is the $250 to be received for the calendars. No additional costs will be incurred. Therefore, profit will be $250 higher if the offer is accepted than if it is rejected.

2. The amount paid for the calendars is irrelevant. Even if $1 million had been paid for the calendars, the added profit from selling them for $250 is $250. The $900 paid is a past cost, a sunk cost, that will not be affected by the decision.

6-27 (15-20 min.)

1. The difference in total costs over the five years is $2,000 in favor of replacement, computed as follows:

	Five Years Together		
	Keep	Replace	Difference
Cash operating costs	$22,500	$10,000	$ 12,500
Old machine (book value):			
Depreciation	5,000	–	
or			–
Lump-sum write-off	–	5,000	
Disposal value	–	-2,000	2,000
New machine: Acquisition cost	–	12,500	-12,500
Total costs	$27,500	$25,500	$ 2,000

2. The loss on disposal of the old machine combines the lump-sum write-off (an irrelevant item) with the disposal value (a relevant item), $5,000 - $2,000 = $3,000 loss on disposal. Because of the inclusion of an irrelevant item, this amount does not affect the computation in requirement 1. It is best to keep the lump-sum write-off and the disposal value separate, as is done in the table in requirement 1.

6-28 (10 min.)

1.

Variable cost	$ 90,000
Fixed cost	110,000
Total cost	$200,000
Cost per unit, $200,00 ÷ 10,000	$ 20.00

2.

Variable cost	$180,000
Fixed cost	110,000
Total cost	$290,000
Cost per unit, $290,000 ÷ 20,000	$ 14.50

3. The two unit costs are equally accurate (or, more appropriately, equally inaccurate). Unit costs that include unitized fixed costs are always suspect. A unit cost that includes fixed costs will be accurate at only one volume; using it at any other volume will be misleading.

6-29 (10 min.)

The original investment is the "cash equivalent" cost. "Excess" trade-in allowances, such as the $1,500 in this instance, are really reductions in the "list price." The $1,260 sales tax is added to the original cost. The problem is silent regarding how the sales tax is computed. The original investment is:

List price	$21,000
Less price allowance, $4,500 - $3,000	1,500
Cash equivalent cost before sales tax	$19,500
Sales tax	1,260
Cash equivalent cost	$20,760

The annual cash operating costs are irrelevant. Another way of computing the $20,760 is:

Cash payment ($21,000 - $4,500 + $1,260)	$17,760
Opportunity cost of truck traded in	3,000
Total cost	$20,760

6-30 (10 min.)

The $9 million is gone. It is irrelevant for decision purposes. The relevant comparison is whether to invest $5 million in the division or to invest it elsewhere:

	Sell Division	Hold Division
Investment required	$5 million	$5 million
Income generated	?	$500,000 yearly*

*This assumes that the division has truly "turned around" and will now make a net profit of $500,000 per year for the foreseeable future.

The $5 million is relevant because Lake Forest is forgoing the opportunity to invest it elsewhere for some return. If projects or divisions of comparable risk can be expected to generate more than $500,000 yearly, the division should be sold.

6-31 (10-15 min.) The purpose of this problem is to sharpen the student's concept of "opportunity cost." Daily fees are $140 x 6 hours, or $840.

1. The difference in annual income is $241,920 - $221,760 = $20,160:

	(a) Work	(b) Don't Work
Work, $840 x 6 days x 48 weeks	$241,920	
Don't work on every other Saturday:		
$840 x 5 days x 24 weeks		$100,800
$840 x 6 days x 24 weeks		120,960
Totals	$241,920	$221,760

2. The calculation in (1) seems awkward and unnecessary. The opportunity cost is the maximum amount forgone by not working on every other Saturday, which is $840 x 1 day x 24 weeks, or $20,160. This is really the key number because it answers the crucial question, "What difference does it make?" Opportunity cost is defined as the maximum available contribution to profit forgone by using limited resources for a particular purpose.

3. If she has already decided to take the day off, her opportunity cost is zero because in any case she would not see patients. Note that opportunity cost is a "situation-specific" concept. If one of the possible alternatives is not even allowed into the feasible set by the decision maker, its financial effects are irrelevant. On the other hand, if she decided to repair her car instead of keeping the appointments with patients on a *working* Saturday, her opportunity cost for the day would be $840; for half a day, $420.

6-32 (15-25 min.)

1.

	With Northwest Airlines Personnel	Without Northwest Airlines Personnel
Revenue for October 20:		
$100 x 50	–	$5,000
$ 50 x 50	$2,500	–

Opportunity cost is a slippery term, so we are reluctant to be overly rigid about its definition during classroom sessions. The strict definition would be that the opportunity cost is $5,000–the maximum profit (in this instance, revenue, because the variable costs of servicing the rooms would be identical) forgone by rejecting the best forsaken alternative. Nevertheless, some students will insist that the $5,000 - $2,500 = $2,500 difference between the alternatives is the opportunity cost.

On December 28, the opportunity cost would be 10 x $80 = $800.

2. The simplest approach is:

Let X = % of occupancy
Then $90X = $50
X = $50 ÷ $90 = 55.56%

A longer approach follows. To be indifferent, Marriott would have to generate the same rent as the Northwest Airlines contract which is $50 x 50 rooms x 365 days = $912,500.

Let Y = Number of rooms per day @ $90
$90(Y)365 = $912,500
$32,850Y = $912,500
Y = 27.777 rooms per day

Percentage of occupancy of the 50 rooms = 27.77 ÷ 50
= .55555
= 55.56%

To check the answer:
\$90 x .556(50) x 365 = \$912,573 (higher than \$912,500 because of rounding of .55555 to .5556)

6-33 (10-15 min.)

1. Contribution margin from airlines: (\$50 - \$10)(50)(365) = \$730,000
General contribution margin: (\$90 - \$10)(50)(365)(.53) = \$773,800
Marriott should reject the contract.

Compare the answers to 6-32 and 6-33. Note that the answer to requirement 2 of 6-32 (55.56%) implies that the answer to 6-33 should be to accept the contract. Why? Because general occupancy (53%) is expected to be less than the indifference point. However, when variable costs are considered, Marriott should reject the contract.

2. Let X = occupancy rate
(\$90 - \$10)(50)(365)(X) = \$730,000
\$1,460,000X = \$730,000
X = .50 or 50% occupancy rate

6-34 (10-20 min.)

The point of requirement 2 is to emphasize that the essence of make or buy is how to best utilize facilities.

1.

	Make		Buy	
	Total	Per Unit	Total	Per Unit
Purchase cost			$1,050,000	$21
Direct material	$400,000	$ 8		
Direct labor	300,000	6		
Variable factory overhead	150,000	3		
Fixed factory overhead that canbe avoided by not making	100,000	2		
Total relevant costs	$950,000	$19	$1,050,000	$21
Difference in favor of making	$100,000	$ 2		

2.

	Make	Buy and Leave Facilities Idle	Buy and Rent	Buy and Use Facilities for Oil Filters
Rent revenue	$ -	$ -	$ 65,000	$ -
Contribution from other products	-	-	-	200,000
Obtaining of parts	(950,000)	(1,050,000)	(1,050,000)	(1,050,000)
Net relevant costs	$(950,000)	$(1,050,000)	$ (985,000)	$ (850,000)

The analysis indicates that buying the parts and using the vacated facilities for the production of other products is the alternative that should yield the best results in this instance. The advantage over making the parts is $950,000 - $850,000, = $100,000.

6-35 (35-50 min.)

Requirement 2 of this problem usually gives trouble to students; because Requirement 2 takes considerable class time for a clear explanation, you may prefer to assign Requirement 1 only.

1. There are several ways to approach this problem. The easiest is probably to concentrate on the difference in the total contribution margin. The total fixed costs of $780,000, before considering the increase in advertising, will be unaffected and may be ignored. Production and sales will decline by 10%, from 60,000 to 54,000 units:

	60,000 Units	54,000 Units	Difference
Sales at $90 and $98, respectively	$5,400,000	$5,292,000	
Variable costs at $70*	4,200,000	3,780,000	
Contribution margin	$1,200,000	$1,512,000	$312,000

*$35 + $12 + $8 + $15

Advertising may be increased by $312,000 without affecting the current operating income level of $420,000 (contribution margin of $1,200,000 minus fixed expenses of $780,000).

2. If the total fixed costs do not change, the company will need a total contribution margin of $1,200,000 from the two products together. How many units of the new product can be sold? The clue to the production capacity of the plant is in how fixed factory overhead was unitized: $300,000 ÷ $6 per unit = 50,000 units of expected sales.

New product budget @ 50,000 Units:

Sales at $40	$2,000,000
Variable costs at $30*	1,500,000
Contribution margin, new product	$ 500,000

*Direct material	$ 6
Direct labor	12
Variable factory overhead	8
Variable selling expense, 10% x $40	4
Total variable costs per unit	$30

Therefore, the needed contribution margin on the old product is $1,200,000 - $500,000, or $700,000.

Sales, 60,000 units at $90	$5,400,000
Contribution margin needed	700,000
Total variable costs that can be sustained	$4,700,000
Variable selling costs at $9*	540,000
Maximum that may be paid to the supplier	$4,160,000

*$15 less 40% = $9 or 60% ($15 x 60,000) = $540,000

Maximum unit purchase price, $4,160,000 ÷ 60,000 = $69.33.

If students do not accept the above analysis, the following proof may be helpful (in thousands):

	Old	Difference	New Product 1	New Product 2
Sales	$5,400	$2,000	$5,400	$2,000
Variable costs	4,200	2,000	4,700*	1,500
Contribution margin	$1,200	$ -	$ 700	$ 500
Fixed manufacturing costs	300	-	-	300
Fixed selling costs	480	-	380**	100**
Total fixed costs	$ 780	$ -	$ 380	$ 400
Operating income	$ 420	$ -	$ 320	$ 100

*An alternate approach to this whole solution is to use the above format and solve toward the unknown purchases figure. The $4,700,000 is the maximum allowable variable cost. Because $540,000 of the $4,700,000 represents selling expense, the remainder, $4,160,000 must be the maximum that may be paid to the supplier.

**This allocation uses the $2.00 unit cost figure for the new product and assigns the remaining fixed costs to the old product. Note, however, that how the total fixed selling costs are allocated is irrelevant because total fixed costs are unaffected by allocation methods or by how such costs are assigned to products.

6-36 (15-25 min.)

1.

	Alternative	
	Without Contract	With Contract
Contribution margin:		
(200 rooms x 365 days)($85 - $10)(.85)	$4,653,750	
(200 - 40)(365)($85-$10)(.95)		$4,161,000
(40)(365)($50 - $10)		584,000
Total contribution margin	$4,653,750	$4,745,000
Difference in favor of contract	$91,250	

2. Let X = contribution margin per room

(40)(365)(X) + $4,161,000 = $4,653,750

14,600X = $492,750

X = $33.75

Add back variable cost: $33.75 + $10.00 = $43.75

Note how this room rate is the "point of indifference." The manager has $50.00 - $43.75 = $6.25 of leeway to bargain on contract rates.

6-37 (10-20 min.)

The basic message here is that airlines can maintain the same revenue per mile even in the face of switching by some passengers to lower fares.

1.

	Without Discount	With Discount
Revenue, 75 @ $.12	$9.00	
Revenue		
72 @ $.12		$8.64
6 @ $.072		.43
Total per airplane mile	$9.00	$9.07

Note that a minor (4%) gain in passengers will be beneficial. Note, too, that airlines have negligible variable costs of adding a few passengers in otherwise empty seats.

Some instructors may want to use the language of "opportunity costs" here, but such language is not really necessary and may be confusing. For example, some observers would say that the three passengers who switch cause an opportunity cost of 3 x $.12 or $.36 that is more than offset by the added revenue of 6 x $.072 or $.43.

2. Let X = number of passengers who switch

Revenue with discount	= Revenue without discount
50(.60)($.12)	= X($.12)
50($.072)	= $.12(X)
$3.60	= $.12(X)
X	= $3.60 ÷ $.12 = 30 passengers

Check:	Without Discount	With Discount
Revenue, 75 @ $.12	$9.00	
Revenue:		
(75 - 30) @ $.12		$5.40
50 @ $.072		3.60
Total per airplane mile	$9.00	$9.00

Therefore, if at least 21 of the 50 discount passengers are "new," that is, they would not have flown without the discount, there is more revenue with the discount plan.

6-38 (25-40 min.)

1. Sets result in a 20% sales increase: 1,250 x 1.20 = 1,500 dresses.

	Percent of Total	Total Number of Dresses	Capes	Handbags	Total
Complete sets	70%	1,050	1,050	1,050	
Dress and cape	6	90	90		
Dress and handbag	15	225		225	
Dress only	9	135			
Total units if accessories are introduced	100%	1,500	1,140	1,275	
Unit sales if accessories are not introduced		1,250	—	—	
Incremental sales		250	1,140	1,275	
Incremental contribution margin per unit		FF 650	FF 40	FF 20	
Total incremental contribution margin		FF162,500	FF45,600	FF25,500	FF233,600

Additional costs		
Additional cutting cost (1,500 x FF36)	FF54,000	
Additional material cost (250 x FF300)	75,000	
Cutting cost on additional dresses (250 x FF100)	25,000	
Lost remnant sales (1,250 x FF25)	31,250	
		185,250
Incremental profit		FF48,350

2. Nonquantitative factors that could influence management in its decision to manufacture matching capes and handbags include:
   - accuracy of forecasted increase in dress sales.
   - accuracy of forecasted product mix.
   - company image from dress manufacturer only to a more extensive supplier of women's apparel.
   - competition from other manufacturers of women's apparel.
   - whether there is adequate capacity (labor, facilities, storage, etc.).

6-39 (15-30 min.)

1.

Sales: 10,000 x 12 x $12			$1,440,000
Less expenses:	Direct materials	$ 4.10	
	Direct labor	.60	
	Overhead	1.50	
	Selling	4.10	
	10,000 x 12 x	$10.30	1,236,000
Operating income [or: (10,000 x 12) ($12 - $10.30)]			$ 204,000

2.

Sales	
10,000 x 12 x 120% x $11 = 144,000 x $11	$1,584,000
Less variable expenses:	
($4.10 + $.60 + $.70 + $3.00)(144,000)	1,209,600
Contribution margin	$ 374,400
Less fixed expenses: ($.80 + $1.10)(120,000)	228,000
Operating income	$ 146,400

(A common student error is to use 144,000 units at old fixed costs per unit.)

3.

Cost to obtain order: $6,000 ÷ 5,000	$1.20
Direct materials	4.10
Direct labor	.60
Variable overhead	.70
Variable selling expenses: 60% of $3.00	1.80
Minimum price for special order	$8.40

4. The variable selling expenses only $3.00

6-40 (15-20 min.)

1. The salesman's analysis is faulty because it includes depreciation on the old equipment, which is irrelevant. Moreover, both the total and unit costs are based on an annual volume of 40,000 units, which may not necessarily be accurate.

2.

	New Machine	Old Machine
Units	20,000	20,000
Variable costs	$ 80,000	$120,000
Straight-line depreciation	60,000	-
Total cost	$140,000	$120,000
Unit cost	$7.00	$6.00

3. Let X = Number of units

$60,000 + $4X = $6X

X = 30,000 units

6-41 (15 min.)

Marketing management misjudged the life of the old freight cars. This may raise questions about the accuracy of the estimated useful life of the new freight cars. However, the unexpired costs of the old freight cars are not relevant to this decision. The conceptual error being made by the operating manager is the failure to distinguish between two decisions: the original decision and the current decision. Instead, he is mixing the two so that neither is evaluated correctly.

The current decision should be influenced solely by expected future outlays, including the capital investment, and revenues. The book value of the old equipment is *per se* irrelevant. The current decision should not carry the burden of past blunders.

The past decision should be audited. In this instance, hindsight reveals that marketing management was overly optimistic. The key question is whether unwarranted optimism is being used again to justify additional outlays.

Some instructors may wish to point out how decisions such as these might be affected by the long-term relationships with a big customer at this and other locations. Many decisions have such interdependencies.

6-42 (15-30 min.)

1. Cost Comparison–Replacement of Equipment
Relevant Items Only

	Three Years Together		
	Keep	Replace	Difference
Cash operating costs	$30,000	$18,000	$12,000
Disposal value of old equipment		-3,000	3,000
Depreciation–new equipment		12,000	-12,000
Total relevant costs	$30,000	$27,000	$ 3,000

The advantage of replacement is $3,000 for the three years together.

2. Cost Comparison–Replacement of Equipment
Including Relevant and Irrelevant Items

	Three Years Together		
	Keep	Replace	Difference
Cash operating costs	$30,000	$18,000	$12,000
Old equipment (book value):			
Periodic write-off as depreciation	9,000		
or			—
Lump-sum write-off		9,000*	
Disposal value	—	-3,000*	3,000
New equipment, acquisition cost	—	12,000**	-12,000
Total costs	$39,000	$36,000	$ 3,000

*In a formal income statement, these two items would be combined as "loss on disposal" of $9,000 - $3,000 = $6,000.

** In a formal income statement, written off as straight-line depreciation of $12,000 ÷ 3 = $4,000 for each of the three years.

3.

	Keep	Replace
Cash operating costs	$10,000	$ 6,000
Depreciation	3,000	4,000
Loss on disposal ($9,000 - $3,000)	—	6,000
Total charges against revenue	$13,000	$16,000

Assuming the manager is evaluated on the basis of the division's profitability, the performance evaluation model for the first year indicates a difference *in favor of keeping*: $16,000 - $13,000 = $3,000. As indicated earlier in this solution, such a decision would result in $3,000 less income over the next three years together. However, many managers would adhere to the short-run view and not replace the equipment.

6-43 (10 min.)

This problem extends problem 6-A1. It should not be assigned without also assigning 6-A1.

1. The "replace" alternative would be chosen because it enhances cumulative wealth.

2. The division would show lower income for the first year under the "replace" alternative. The manager who wants to show better short-run performance will oppose replacement.

3. The answers to the first two parts probably would be unaffected. The point is that decision models and performance evaluation models may conflict in nonprofit organizations too. Moreover, the money in the budget appropriation may have been spent. In addition, there is a higher likelihood of unfavorable publicity and also a danger of cuts in subsequent budget appropriations.

6-44 (20 min.)

The numbers in this case are a slight modification of those given in an article in the *New York Times*, November 21, 1994.

1.

	On Broadway	Off Broadway
Attendance	400	400
Revenue	$176,000	$128,000
Expenses	206,000*	82,000
Net profit (loss)	$ (30,000)	$ 46,000

*$82,000 + $124,000 = $206,000

2.

	On Broadway	Off Broadway
Attendance	750	375
Revenue	$330,000	$120,000
Expenses	206,000	82,000
Net profit	$124,000	$ 38,000

3. a. $206,000 ÷ $55 = 3,745 weekly attendance
3,745 ÷ 8 = 468 per show attendance

b. $82,000 ÷ $40 = 2,050 weekly attendance
2,050 ÷ 8 = 256 per show attendance

4.

	On Broadway	Off Broadway
Attendance	600	400
Revenue	$264,000	$128,000
Expenses	206,000	82,000
Net profit	$ 58,000	$ 46,000

Total profit for a 26-week run:
On Broadway: ($58,000 x 26) - $1,295,000 = $213,000
Off Broadway: ($46,000 x 26) - $ 440,000 = $756,000

5. Total profit for a 100-week run:
   On Broadway: ($58,000 x 100) - $1,295,000 = $4,505,000
   Off Broadway: ($46,000 x 100) - $ 440,000 = $4,160,000

6. a. $1,295,000 ÷ 58,000 = 22.3 weeks
   b. $ 440,000 ÷ 46,000 = 9.6 weeks

7. Let X be the length of run in weeks at which on Broadway profit equals off Broadway profit:
   $58,000 X - $1,295,000= $46,000 X - $440,000
   12,000 X = $855,000
   X = 71.25 weeks

8. Mr. Simon's decision depends on both his predictions of attendance on Broadway versus off Broadway and his attitude toward risk. The on-Broadway production has more risk because of its bigger up-front investment. If the attendance figures in requirements 4 and 5 are accurate (400 off-Broadway and 600 on-Broadway), the off-Broadway alternative is better for any runs less than 68.25 weeks. Because this is a long run and many successful shows have shorter runs than 50 weeks, it appears that the off Broadway alternative might be best. However, if attendance on Broadway can exceed 600 per show, especially if it approaches the capacity of 1,000 per show, there is much more money to be made on Broadway.

   There is a trend for non-musical plays to be produced off Broadway because of the large investment required on Broadway. Many plays do not last beyond a few weeks, and even filling a theater to capacity would require more than a 5-week run just to recoup the initial investment. ($55 x 1,000 x 8 - $206,000 = $234,000 weekly profit; $1,295,000 ÷ $234,000 = 5.5 weeks to break even.) There is less risk off Broadway, especially because it takes many fewer theater-goers to reach the break-even point. For example, at capacity operations it takes 5.5 x 8 x 1,000 = 44,000 attendees to break even on Broadway. Off Broadway it requires only a little more than half that number:

($40 x 500 x 8) - $82,000 = $78,000 weekly profit
$440,000 ÷ $78,000 = 5.6 weeks to break even
5.6 x 8 x 500 = 22,400 attendees to break even.

6-45 (15-20 min.)

1. The opportunity cost of the land is 10% x $150,000,000 = $1,500,000.

2. Costs saved by closure of tomato farm:

Variable production costs	$ 550,000
Shipping costs	200,000
Saved fixed costs	300,000
Opportunity cost of land	1,500,000
Total	$2,550,000

Cost of purchasing tomatos:
8,000,000 lbs. x $.25/lb. = $2,000,000

Net savings to Agribiz from closing the tomato farm and buying tomatos on the market is $2,550,000 - $2,000,000 = $550,000.

3. The main ethical issue involves the impact of the plant closure on employees and on the community.

6-46 (10–15 min.)

1. Starbucks should process the beans because it gererates more profit than selling them as-is.

Sell as is:	$2.75 x 1,000 = $2,750	
Reprocess:	Revenue, $3.70 x 1,000	$3,700
	Reprocessing cost	(600)
	Shipping cost	(200)
	Total	$2,900

2.

Sell as is	$2,750
Reprocess	2,900
Advantage to reprocessing	$ 150

3. The costs of buying and roasting the original beans is irrelevant.

6-47 (30-40 min.)

1. Minnetonka Corporation should *make* the bindings.

Cost saved by purchasing bindings:	
Material, 20% x $30	$ 6.00
Labor, 10% x $35	3.50
Overhead, 10% x $5*	.50
Total	$10.00
Cost to buy per pair	$10.50

*Total overhead $15 per pair
Allocated overhead $10 per pair ($100,000 ÷ 10,000).
Variable overhead $5 per pair.

2. Minnetonka Corporation would *not pay more than* $10 each because that is the cost to make the product internally.

3. At a volume of 12,500 pair, Minnetonka should *buy* the bindings. The cost of buying 12,500 pair is $131,250. The cost of making 12,500 pair is:

12,500 x $10	$125,000	
Added fixed costs	10,000	
Total	$135,000	
Buying the bindings will save		$ 3,750

Making the bindings saves variable costs of $.50 per pair. If sales exceed $10,000 ÷ $.50 = 20,000 pair, it is cheaper to make the bindings.

4. Minnetonka Corporation needs 12,500 pair of bindings. The cost to buy 12,500 pair is $131,250. The cost to make 10,000 and buy 2,500 is:

Cost to make 10,000 pair	$100,000
Cost to buy 2,500 pair	26,250
Total	$126,250

Therefore, Minnetonka should choose this latter course of action, which saves $5,000.

5. There are many nonquantifiable factors that Minnetonka should consider in addition to the economic factors calculated above. Among such factors are:

   1. The quality of the purchased bindings as compared to Minnetonka -produced bindings.
   2. The reliability of delivery to meet production schedules.
   3. The financial stability of the supplier.
   4. Development of an alternate source of supply.
   5. Alternate uses of binding manufacturing capacity.
   6. The long-run character and size of the market.

6-48 (30-45 min.)

1. The $10,000 disposal value of the old equipment is irrelevant because it is the same for either choice. This solution assumes that the direct department fixed overhead is avoidable. You may want to explicitly discuss this assumption.

Cost Comparison for Make or Buy Decision

	At 60,000 Units Normal Volume	
	Make	Buy
Outside purchase cost at $1.00	-	$60,000
Direct material at $.30	$18,000	–
Direct labor and variable overhead at $.10	6,000	–
Depreciation ($188,000 - $20,000) ÷ 7	24,000	–
Direct departmental fixed overhead** at $.10 or $6,000 annually	6,000	–
Totals	$54,000*	$60,000

*On a unit basis, which is very dangerous to use unless proper provision is made for comparability of volume:

Direct material	$.30
Direct labor and variable overhead	.10
Depreciation, $24,000 ÷ 60,000	.40
Other fixed overhead**, $6,000 ÷ 60,000	.10
Total unit cost	$.90

Note particularly that the machine sales representative was citing a $.24 depreciation rate that was based on 100,000 unit volume. She should have used a 60,000 unit volume for the Rohr Company.

**Past records indicate that $.05 of the old unit cost was apportioned fixed overhead that probably will be unaffected regardless of the decision. *This assumption could be challenged.* This total of $3,000 ($.05 x 60,000 units) could be included under *both* alternatives, causing the total costs to be $57,000 and $63,000, and the unit costs to be $.95 and $1.05, respectively. Note that such an inclusion would have no effect on the difference between alternatives.

Also, this analysis assumes that any idle facilities could not be put to alternative profitable use. The data indicate that manufacturing rather than purchasing is the better decision–before considering required investment.

2.

	At 50,000 Units		At 70,000 Units	
	Make	Buy	Make	Buy
Outside purchase cost @ $1.00	-	$50,000	-	$70,000
Direct material at $.30	$15,000	–	$21,000	–
Direct labor and variable overhead at $.10	5,000	–	7,000	–
Depreciation	24,000	–	24,000	–
Other direct fixed overhead	6,000	–	6,000	–
Totals	$50,000	$50,000	$58,000	$70,000

At 70,000 units, the decision would not change. At 50,000 units, Rohr would be indifferent. The general approach to calculating the point of indifference is:

Let X = Point of indifference in units

Total costs of making = Total costs of buying

$$\$.30X + \$.10X + \$24{,}000 + \$6{,}000 = \$1.00X$$

$$\$\text{-}.60X = \$\text{-}30{,}000$$

$$X = 50{,}000 \text{ units}$$

3. Other factors would include: Dependability of estimates of volume needed, need for quality control, possible alternative uses of the facilities, relative merits of other outside suppliers, ability to renew production if price is unsatisfactory, and the minimum desired rate of return. Factors that are particularly applicable to the evaluation of the outside supplier include: short-run and long-run outlook for price changes, quality of goods, stability of employment, labor relations, and credit standing.

6-49 (60 min. or more)

This exercise provides experience searching the literature of a particular subject as well as developing a better understanding of outsourcing decisions. Students will research the literature individually and then share their findings with their group.

Requirements 2 and 3 help develop critical thinking. The articles are not likely to answer these questions directly, but students will probably be able to infer answers from the information given.

The short report in requirement 4 will help develop an ability to select the most important points from the literature and report them in a way that is helpful to others.

CHAPTER 7
The Master Budget

7-A1 (60-90 min.)

1. Exhibit I

COMPUTER SUPERSTORES, INC.
Las Vegas Store
Budgeted Income Statement
For the Three Months Ending August 31, 19X6

Sales		$1,500,000
Cost of goods sold (.60 x $1,500,000)		900,000
Gross profit		$ 600,000
Operating expenses:		
Salaries, wages, commissions	$300,000	
Other expenses	60,000	
Depreciation	7,500	
Rent, taxes and other fixed expenses	165,000	532,500
Income from operations.		$ 67,500
Interest expense*		6,130
Net income		$ 61,370

*From Exhibit II, $318,000 of principal is outstanding during June and July, and $318,000 - $212,000 = $106,000 is outstanding during August. The interest expense accrued is then

$318,000 x .10 x 2/12 + $106,000 x .10 x 1/12
= $5,300 + $830 = $6,130.

Note that this accrual is independent of the cash interest actually paid ($3,530 and $1,530).

Exhibit II
COMPUTER SUPERSTORES, INC.
Las Vegas Store
Exhibit 2: Budgeted Statement of Cash Receipts and Disbursements
For the Three Months Ending August 31, 19X6

	June	July	August
Cash balance, beginning	$ 29,000	$ 25,000	$ 25,470
Cash receipts, collections & cash sales (schedule b)	376,000	607,000	454,000
(a) Total cash available before financing	$ 405,000	$ 632,000	$479,470
Cash disbursements:			
Merchandise (schedule d)	$ 420,000	$ 240,000	$240,000
Fixtures	55,000	-	-
Salaries, wages, commissions, @ 20% x sales	140,000	80,000	80,000
Other variable expenses, @ 4% x sales	28,000	16,000	16,000
Fixed expenses	55,000	55,000	55,000
(b) Total disbursements	$ 698,000	$ 391,000	$391,000
Minimum cash balance desired	25,000	25,000	25,000
Total cash needed	$ 723,000	$ 416,000	$416,000
Excess (deficiency)	$(318,000)	$ 216,000	$ 63,470
Financing:			
Borrowing, at beginning of period	$ 318,000	$ -	$ -
Repayment, at end of period.	-	(212,000)	(61,000)
Interest, 10% per annum	-	(3,530)*	(1,530)**
(c) Total effects of financing	$ 318,000	$(215,530)	$ (62,530)
(d) Cash balance (a + c - b)	$ 25,000	$ 25,470	$ 25,940

*10% x $210,000 x 2/12 = $3,500

**10% x $ 61,000 x 3/12 = $1,525, rounded to $1,530.

Exhibit III
COMPUTER SUPERSTORES, INC.
Las Vegas Store
Budgeted Balance Sheet
August 31, 19X6

Assets		Equities	
Cash (Exhibit II)	$ 25,940	Accounts payable	$180,000
Accounts receivable*	432,000	Notes payable	45,000
Merchandise inventory	180,000	Accrued interest payable	1,070
Total current assets	$637,940	Total current liabilities	$226,070
Net fixed assets:		Owners' equity:	
$168,000 less		$511,000 plus net	
depreciation of $7,500	160,500	income of $61,370	572,370
Total assets	$798,440	Total equities	$798,440

*July sales, 20% x 90% x $400,000	$ 72,000
August sales, 100% x 90% x $400,000	360,000
Accounts receivable (to Exhibit III)	$432,000

Schedule a: Sales Budget	June	July	August	Total
Credit sales	$630,000	$360,000	$360,000	$1,350,000
Cash sales	70,000	40,000	40,000	150,000
Total sales (to Exhibit I)	$700,000	$400,000	$400,000	$1,500,000

Schedule b: Cash Collections

Cash sales	$ 70,000	$ 40,000	$ 40,000	
On accounts receivable from:				
April sales	54,000	-	-	
May sales	252,000	63,000	-	
June sales	-	504,000	126,000	
July sales	-	-	288,000	
Total collections (to Exhibit II)	$376,000	$607,000	$454,000	
Schedule c: Purchases Budget	May	June	July	August
Desired purchases:				
60% x next month's sales	$420,000	$240,000	$240,000	$180,000
Schedule d: Disbursements for Purchases				
Last month's purchases (to Exhibit II)		$420,000	$240,000	$240,000
Accounts payable, August 31, 19X6				
(to Exhibit III)				$180,000
Cost of goods sold (to Exhibit I)		$420,000	$240,000	$240,000
Schedule e: Operating Expense Budget				
and				
Schedule f: Payments for Operating Expenses				
Salaries, wages, commissions,				
other @24% of sales		$168,000	$ 96,000	$ 96,000

2. This is an example of the classical short-term, self-liquidating loan. The need for such a loan often arises because of the seasonal nature of many businesses. In times of peak sales, the payroll and suppliers must be paid in cash that is not then available. The basic source of cash is proceeds from sales to customers. However, credit is extended to customers so that there is a lag between the sale and the collection of the cash. When the cash is collected, it in turn may be used to repay the loan. The amount of the loan and the timing of the repayment are heavily dependent on the credit terms that pertain to both the purchasing and selling functions of the business.

7-B1 (60-120 min.)

1. See Exhibits I, II, and III and supporting schedules a, b, c, d.

2. The cash budget and balance sheet clearly show the benefits of moving to just-in-time purchasing (though the transition would rarely be accomplished as easily as this example suggests). However, the company would be no better off if it left so much of its capital tied up in cash – it has merely substituted one asset for another. At a minimum, the excess cash should be in an interest bearing account – the interest earned or forgone is one of the costs of inventory.

	January	February	March
Schedule a: Sales Budget			
Total sales (100% on credit)	$62,000	$75,000	$38,000
Schedule b: Cash Collections			
60% of current month's sales	$37,200	$45,000	$22,800
30% of previous month's sales	7,500	18,600	22,500
10% of second previous month's sales	2,500	2,500	6,200
Total collections	$47,200	$66,100	$51,500

	December	January	February	March
Schedule c: Purchases Budget				
Desired ending inventory	$39,050	$ 6,000	$ 6,000	$ 6,000
Cost of goods sold	12,500	31,000	37,500	19,000
Total needed	$51,550	$37,000	$43,500	$25,000
Beginning inventory	16,000	39,050	8,050	6,000
Purchases	$35,550	$ -	$35,450	$19,000
Schedule d: Disbursements for Purchases				
100% of previous month's purchases		$35,550	$ -	$35,450
March 31 accounts payable				$19,000

Exhibit I

VICTORIA KITE

Budgeted Statement of Cash Receipts and Disbursements

For the Three Months Ending March 31, 19X9

	January	February	March
Cash balance, beginning	$ 5,000	$ 5,100	$37,692
Cash receipts, collections from customers (Schedule b)	47,200	66,100	51,500
(a) Total cash available before financing	$ 52,200	$ 71,200	$89,192
Cash disbursements:			
Merchandise (Schedule c)	$ 35,550	$ -	$35,450
Rent	8,050	250	250
Wages and salaries	15,000	15,000	15,000
Miscellaneous expenses	2,500	2,500	2,500
Dividends	1,500	-	
Purchase of fixtures	-	-	3,000
(b) Total disbursements	$ 62,600	$ 17,750	$56,200
Minimum cash balance desired	5,000	5,000	5,000
Total cash needed	$ 67,600	$ 22,750	$61,200
Excess (deficiency)	$(15,400)	$ 48,450	$27,992
Financing:			
Borrowing, at beginning of period	$ 15,500	$ -	$ -
Repayment, at end of period	-	(15,500)	
Interest, 10% per annum	-	(258)	
(c) Total effects of financing	$ 15,500	$(15,758)	$ -
(d) Cash balance, end (a + c - b)	$ 5,100	$ 37,692	$32,992

Exhibit II

VICTORIA KITE

Budgeted Income Statement

For the Three Months Ending March 31, 19X9

Sales (Schedule a)		$175,000
Cost of goods sold (Schedule c)		87,500
Gross margin		$ 87,500
Operating expenses:		
Rent*	$17,250	
Wages and salaries	45,000	
Depreciation.	750	
Insurance	375	
Miscellaneous	7,500	70,875
Net income from operations		$ 16,625
Interest expense		258
Net income		$ 16,367

*(January-March sales less $10,000) x .10 plus 3 x $250

Exhibit III
VICTORIA KITE
Budgeted Balance Sheet
March 31, 19X9

Assets		
Current assets:		
Cash (Exhibit I)	$32,992	
Accounts receivable*	22,700	
Merchandise inventory (Schedule c)	6,000	
Unexpired insurance	1,125	$62,817
Fixed assets, net: $12,500 + $3,000 - $750		14,750
Total assets		$77,567
Liabilities and Stockholders' Equity		
Liabilities:		
Accounts payable (Schedule d)	$19,000	
Rent payable.	16,500	
Dividends payable	1,500	$37,000
Stockholders' equity**		40,567
Total liabilities and stockholders' equity.		$77,567

*February sales (.10 x $75,000) plus March sales (.40 x $38,000) = $22,700

**Balance, December 31, 19X6	$25,700
Add: Net income.	16,367
Total	$42,067
Less: Dividends declared.	1,500
Balance, March 31, 19X7	$40,567

7-1 Budgeting is primarily attention directing because it helps managers to focus on operating or financial problems early enough for effective planning or action.

7-2 Budgets are often used to limit expenditures. But the budget has a much larger role in the effective and efficient management of an organization. It helps managers make decisions by projecting the results of those decisions, and it aids adapting to changing conditions.

7-3 Strategic planning covers no specific time period, is quite general, and often is not built around financial statements. Long-range planning usually has a 5- or 10-year horizon and consists of financial statements without much detail. Budgeting usually has a horizon of one year or less, and consists of financial statements with much detail.

7-4 No. Capital relates to the investment in productive assets, and capital budgeting is a method of planning and controlling these investments.

7-5 Continuous budgets add a month in the future as the month just ended is dropped. The target for the next eleven months need not be changed. Therefore, each monthly budget, or target, is established twelve months ahead of time. Some companies revise the budgets for the next eleven months in addition to adding a month. However, most such companies compare results to the original budget (a fixed target) in addition to comparing them to the latest revised budget.

7-6 No. Continuous budgets cover a constant future planning period by dropping the current month and adding a future month to the budget as each month passes. Pro forma statements are defined as those which include not actual figures but estimated or forecasted figures. All budgets are thus pro-forma statements.

7-7 Budgeted performance is better than past performance as a basis for judging current performance because the budget contains no hidden inefficiencies and can be founded on current rather than past economic conditions.

7-8 Budgets are especially important in environments that are rapidly changing. They force managers to look forward. Budgets allow systematic reactions to change. They force analysis of the factors that are bringing about the changes.

7-9 Budgeting is beneficial because it encourages careful planning, allows both continuous and periodic evaluation of current operation, and facilitates coordination between subunits.

7-10 No. When budgeting in done correctly, it is an important aid to managers. Managers need time to plan and coordinate their various activities. Budgeting forces them to take time from the day-to-day problems and focus on longer-term issues.

7-11 An operating budget is used as a guide for production and sales, while a financial budget is used to control the receipt and disbursement of funds.

7-12 The sales forecast is the starting point for budgeting because all other operating activities of the company are affected by the volume of sales.

7-13 The sales forecast is the ultimate cost driver in most organizations. For example, in manufacturing firms, forecasts of sales lead to production schedules. Production schedules lead to cost driver activity forecasts, which lead to forecasts of manufacturing, distributing, and administrative costs.

7-14 Operating expenses are costs charged to the income statement in a particular period. Some operating expenses may be associated with the sales of the period, and others may be costs of being in business for the period. Disbursements for these operating expenses, that is, the cash payments for them, may come in a previous period (assets purchased in one period and depreciated over future periods) or a future period (wages accrued in a period but paid in the next period), as well as during the period.

7-15 A cash budget is an attempt to regulate the flow of cash in optimum fashion.

7-16 A sales forecast is simply a prediction of sales under a given set of conditions. A sales budget reflects a commitment to establish the conditions to generate the predicted level of sales.

7-17 The sales forecast is influenced by past patterns of sales, estimates made by the sales force, general economic conditions, competitors' actions, changes in prices, market research studies, and advertising and sales promotion plans.

7-18 Budgeting will be effective only if it is accepted by those managers who are responsible for controlling costs; but, since their performance will be measured against the budget, they must be educated in the assumptions underlying the budget and convinced of its objectivity and relevance.

7-19 Financial planning models are mathematical statements of the relationships in the organization among all the operating and financial activities and of other major internal and external factors that may affect the financial results of decisions.

7-20 No. Financial planning models can help simplify the process of budgeting. But planning models are only as good as the assumptions and inputs used to build them. Managers must understand the models to provide appropriate assumptions and inputs. If managers do not understand budgeting, using financial planning models can result in GIGO (garbage in, garbage out).

7-21 Setting up the master budget on a spreadsheet is time-consuming – the first time. However, if it is done properly, with maximum flexibility, then the ease of subsequent use probably will more than offset that initial cost. Ultimately, though, the master budget system must meet the cost-benefit test. Improved budgeting systems are only worthwhile if they offer net benefits. It is also a fact that all large, well-managed companies have computerized master budget systems. Preparing and revising the master budget of a large company just would not be feasible without the aid of a computer.

7-22 Spreadsheets can be used to make a mathematical model of an organization. It may take much effort to create the model, but once it is in place it can be used over and over again with minimal effort. Such a model is especially useful for sensitivity analysis, the asking of "what if" questions.

7-23 (5 min.)

1. a. Budget income statement
   b. Budgeted balance sheet
   c. Cash flow budget
   d. Capital budget
2. Sales budget
3. Sales budget
4. Continuous (rolling)
5. Overall goals of the organization

7-24 (10-15 min.)

1.

Cost + (.25 x Cost)	= Sales
1.25 x Cost	= $2,040,000
Cost	= $1,632,000

2. Best path to success is to sketch the Cost of Goods Sold section of an income statement. Start with the cost of goods sold and work backwards.

July Cost of Goods Sold Schedule	
Beginning inventory (.30 of July cost of goods sold)	$ 520,800
Add: Purchases	X
Cost of goods available for sale	$2,288,000
Less: Final inventory (.30 of August cost of goods sold)	552,000
Cost of goods sold ($2,170,000 ÷ 1.25)	$1,736,000

X = $1,736,000 + $552,000 - $520,800 = $1,767,200

7-25 (25-30 min.)

1. July collections include:

May sales billed June 10, .18 x .5 x $750,000	$ 67,500
June sales billed July 10, .80 x .5 x $800,000 x .98	313,600
June sales billed June 20, .18 x .5 x $800,000	72,000
July sales billed July 20, .80 x .5 x $900,000 x .98	352,800
Total	$805,900

2. September collections from August sales:

August sales billed September 10, .80x.5x$900,000x.98	$352,800
August sales billed August 20, .18 x .5 x $900,000	81,000
Total	$433,800

3. .80 x .25 x $600,000 = $120,000

4.

Ending inventory, .80 x .25 x next month's sales	$180,000
Merchandise needed for current month's sales, .80 x sales	640,000
Total needs	820,000
Beginning inventory, .80 x .25 x $800,000	160,000
Purchases	$660,000

5.

	July	August
Ending inventory, .80 x .25 x next month's sales	$180,000	$120,000
Merchandise needed for current month's sales, .80 x sales	720,000	720,000
Total needs	900,000	840,000
Beginning inventory, .80 x .25 x current month's sales	180,000	180,000
Purchases	$720,000	$660,000
Payments, 1/2 of current purchases, 1/2 of preceding month's purchases, .5 x $720,000 + .5 x $660,000		$690,000

7-26 (15 min.) This is straightforward. It follows the illustration in the chapter very closely. All amounts are in dollars.

	June	July	August
Sales budget			
Credit sales, 30%	120,000	132,000	150,000
Cash sales, 70%	280,000	308,000	350,000
Total sales, 100%	400,000	440,000	500,000
Cash collections budget			
Cash sales this month	280,000	308,000	350,000
100% of last month's credit sales	120,000	120,000	132,000
Total collections	400,000	428,000	482,000

7-27 (15-25 min.) This problem is slightly more complex than 7-26. All amounts are in thousands of Japanese yen.

	January	February	March
Sales budget			
Credit sales, 80%	144,000	168,000	192,000
Cash sales, 20%	36,000	42,000	48,000
Total sales	180,000	210,000	240,000
Cash collections budget			
Cash sales this month	36,000	42,000	48,000
50% of this month's credit sales	72,000	84,000	96,000
40% of last month's credit sales	62,400	57,600	67,200
10% of next-to-last month's credit sales	18,000	15,600	14,400
Total collections	188,400	199,200	225,600

7-28 (10-15 min.)

Collections from:		
January sales:	$300,000 x 12%	$ 36,000
February sales:	$400,000 x 10% x 99%	39,600
	$400,000 x 25%	100,000
March sales:	$450,000 x 50% x 99%	222,750
Total cash collections		$398,350

7-29 (15-20 min.) This is straightforward. It follows the illustration in the chapter very closely. All amounts are in dollars. Some students need to be reminded that merchandise inventories are carried at cost, not at selling prices.

FERNANDEZ FURNITURE MART

	June	July	August
Purchases budget			
Ending inventory	220,000	270,000	250,000
Cost of goods sold, 60% of sales	264,000	210,000	240,000
Total needed	484,000	480,000	490,000
Beginning inventory	250,000	220,000	270,000
Purchases	234,000	260,000	220,000
Disbursements for purchases			
10% of this month's purchases	23,400	26,000	22,000
80% of last month's purchases	144,000*	187,200	208,000
10% of second-last month's purchases	25,000**	18,000	23,400
	192,400	231,200	253,400

*.80 x 180,000 = 144,000
**.10 x 250,000 = 25,000

7-30 (20-25 min.) This is straightforward. Except for requirement 1, it follows the illustration in the chapter very closely. All amounts are in British pounds.

1. 200,000 - [15,000 + .9(.6 x 300,000)] = 200,000 - [15,000 + .9(180,000)]
= 200,000 - 177,000
= 23,000

2. BELFAST APPLIANCE COMPANY

	June	July	August
Purchases budget			
Ending inventory*	166,200	198,600	231,000
Cost of goods sold, 60% of sales	180,000	168,000	204,000
Total needed	346,200	366,600	435,000
Beginning inventory	200,000	166,200	198,600
Purchases	146,200	200,400	236,400
Disbursements for purchases			
80% of last month's purchases	120,000	116,960	160,320
20% of this month's purchases	29,240	40,080	47,280
Disbursements for purchases	149,240	157,040	207,600

*Inventory targets, end of month:
June: 15,000 + .9(0.6 x 280,000) = 15,000 + .9(168,000) = 166,200
July: 15,000 + .9(0.6 x 340,000) = 15,000 + .9(204,000) = 198,600
August: 15,000 + .9(0.6 x 400,000) = 15,000 + .9(228,000) = 231,000

7-31 (20 min.) This is a straightforward exercise.

RALEIGH COMPANY
Cash Budget
For the Month Ended June 30, 19X6
(in thousands)

Cash, May 31, 19X6		$ 15
Receipts:		
Collections from customers from:		
June sales (.80 x $290)	$232	
May sales (.5 x 24)*	12	
April sales	16	260
Cash available for needs		$275
Disbursements:		
On accounts payable of May 31	$145	
On June purchases, .25 x $192	48	
Wages	36	
Utilities	5	
Advertising	10	
Office expenses	4	248
Cash, June 30, 19X6		$ 27

*$24,000 = 20% of May sales, 10% of which or half the remainder will be collected in June. All of April's remaining sales will be collected in June.

7-32 (20-25 min.) The collections from March sales are a bit tricky. Note that the *receivable* balance from March sales at March 31 is $450,000; therefore, four fifths (because 40/50 will be collected in April and 10/50 will be collected in May) will be received in April.

KATE'S GIFTS
Budgeted Statement of Cash Receipts and Disbursements
For the Month Ending April 30, 19X7

Cash balance, March 31, 19X7		$ 80,000
Add receipts, collections from customers:		
From April sales, 1/2 x $1,000,000	$500,000	
From March sales, 4/5 x $450,000	360,000	
From February sales	60,000	920,000
Total cash available before current financing		$1,000,000
Less disbursements:		
Merchandise purchases, $500,000 x 40%	$200,000	
Payment on accounts payable	460,000	
Payrolls	90,000	
Insurance premium	1,500	
Other expenses	45,000	
Repayment of loan and interest	94,500	891,000
Cash balance, April 30, 19X7		$ 109,000

7-33 (40-60 min.)

AQUARIUS COMPANY
Statement of Estimated Cash Receipts and Disbursements
For the Month of October 19X7

Cash balance, September 30, 19X7		$ 4,800
Receipts, collections of receivables (Schedule 1)		29,340
Total cash available		$34,140
Less disbursements:		
Merchandise purchases (Schedule 2)	$17,000	
Variable expenses (Schedule 3)	3,125	
Fixed expenses (Schedule 3)	900	21,025
Cash balance, October 31, 19X7		$13,115

Schedule 1, Collections of Accounts Receivable:

		Collected in October	
	Sales	Percent	Amount
From August sales	$12,000	6%	$ 720
From September sales	$36,000	30%	10,800
From October sales	$30,000	60% x 99%	17,820
Total October collections			$29,340

Schedule 2, Payments for Merchandise:

	September	October
Target ending inventory	$ 9,000*	$ 6,600*
Goods sold	21,600	18,000
Total needs	$30,600	$24,600
Beginning inventory	10,800*	9,000*
Purchases	$19,800	$15,600
Payments, 2/3 x $15,600 October purchases		$10,400
Accounts payable, end of September, 1/3 x $19,800 purchases		6,600
Total payments in October		$17,000

* (12/20)(.5)(30,000) = $9,000; (12/20)(.5)(36,000) = $10,800; (12/20)(.5)(22,000) = $6,600

Schedule 3, Selling and General Administrative Expenses:

Total selling and general administrative expenses	$55,500
Less fixed expenses	18,000
Total variable expenses for year (vary with sales)	$37,500

October variable expenses:

$37,500 x (October sales ÷ Year's sales) =

$37,500 x ($30,000 ÷ $360,000) $ 3,125

Total fixed expenses	$18,000
Less depreciation (no current cash outlay)	7,200
Total cash required for fixed expenses for year	$10,800

October cash required for fixed expenses:

$10,800 ÷ 12 $ 900

7-34 (30 - 40 min.)

1. The Ritz-Carleton's monthly cash budget is:

	January	February	March	April	May	June
Revenues	$2,137,500	$2,137,500	$1,912,500	$1,912,500	$1,575,000	$1,575,000
Collections:						
Previous Mo. Sales	$ 598,500	$ 598,500	$ 598,500	$ 535,500	$ 535,500	$ 441,000
This Mo. Sales	1,282,500	1,282,500	1,147,500	1,147,500	945,000	945,000
Next Mo. Sales	213,750	191,250	191,250	157,500	157,500	157,500
Total collections	2,094,750	2,072,250	1,937,250	1,840,500	1,638,000	1,543,500
Disbursements:						
Variable costs	256,500	256,500	229,500	229,500	189,000	189,000
Fixed salaries	400,000	400,000	400,000	400,000	400,000	400,000
Fixed operating costs	120,000	120,000	120,000	120,000	120,000	120,000
Interest payments						3,000,000
Total disbursements	776,500	776,500	749,500	749,500	709,000	3,709,000
Net cash inflow	$1,318,250	$1,295,750	$1,187,750	$1,091,000	$ 929,000	($2,165,500)

	July	August	September	October	November	December	Total
Revenues	$1,575,000	$1,575,000	$1,575,000	$1,575,000	$1,912,500	$2,137,500	$21,600,000
Collections:							
Previous Mo. Sales	$ 441,000	$ 441,000	$ 441,000	$ 441,000	$ 441,000	$ 535,500	$ 6,048,000
This Mo. Sales	945,000	945,000	945,000	945,000	1,147,500	1,282,500	12,960,000
Next Mo. Sales	157,500	157,500	157,500	191,250	213,750	213,750	2,160,000
Total collections	1,543,500	1,543,500	1,543,500	1,577,250	1,802,250	2,031,750	21,168,000
Disbursements:							
Variable costs	189,000	189,000	189,000	189,000	229,500	256,500	2,592,000
Fixed salaries	400,000	400,000	400,000	400,000	400,000	400,000	4,800,000
Fixed operating costs	120,000	120,000	120,000	120,000	120,000	120,000	1,440,000
Interest payments						3,000,000	6,000,000
Total disbursements	709,000	709,000	709,000	709,000	749,500	3,776,500	14,832,000
Net cash inflow	$ 834,500	$ 834,500	$ 834,500	$ 868,250	$1,052,750	($1,744,750)	$ 6,336,000

2. Increase in revenues: 6 mo. x .05 x 300 rooms x $250 x 30 days = $675,000
   Increase in costs: 6 mo. x .05 x 300 rooms x $30 x 30 days - $81,000
   Increase in profit = $675,000 - $81,000 = $594,000

7-35 (15 min.)

1. Possible cost-saving actions would probably focus on one or more of the activities of the Warehousing Department. Procter might start with the non-value added activities, handling and record-keeping. For example, if the number of moves could be cut by 40%, the entire $43,200 could be saved. Reorganizing the warehouse is one way to try to achieve such savings. The activity-based budget also shows that the highest-cost activity is shipping, so that might be the best place to look for cost savings from changing processes.

2. Regardless of what methods are selected to achieve cost savings, the activity-based budget seems to be a better starting point. The traditional budget does not show directly how changes in activities might affect costs, whereas the activity-based budget does.

7-36 (25-30 min.)

1. An optimistic preliminary budget might be as follows, assuming level sales volume, a $.94 per pound price, and a 2% decrease in variable costs.

Sales, 1.6 million pounds @ $.94/pound	$1,504,000
Variable costs	862,400
Fixed costs, primarily depreciation	450,000
Pretax profit	$ 191,600

This budget does not meet the $209,000 profit goal. Masur has a dilemma of submitting a realistic budget that does not meet Legree's goal or preparing an unrealistic budget. To meet the profit target, she might assume that prices will not fall, sales levels will be maintained, and some fixed costs will be saved. Although the following budget is not one Masur believes in, she might be forced to submit it (or something similar) to headquarters:

Sales, 1.6 million pounds @ $.95/pound	$1,520,000
Variable costs	862,400
Fixed costs, primarily depreciation	448,600
Pretax profit	$ 209,000

2. Two major problems are the arbitrary setting of budget targets by top management and the draconian measures used when a budget is not met, even if the shortfall is small or reasonable explanations for the shortfall are given.

3. Apparently the preliminary financial results are as follows:

Sales, 1.6 million pounds @ $.945/pound	$1,512,000
Variable costs	862,400
Fixed costs, primarily depreciation	450,000
Pretax profit	$ 199,600

Extending the depreciable lives of fixed assets by 2 years could increase this profit to $214,600, well above the target. But doing so would be manipulating the accounting system to achieve desirable results. When the estimates of depreciable lives was first make, there may have been much uncertainty in the estimates. However, changing the accounting method to make the financial results look better is an ethical violation.

Managers should not be able to change accounting methods just to make their performance look better (or in this case, to save their job). Although changing the depreciation schedule is not ethical, it is easy to see how the budgeting process creates an incentive for such unethical behavior. If the budget and reporting process makes excellent performance appear deficient, there will be great temptation for managers to manipulate the system.

7-37 (50-90 min.) This spreadsheet is constructed so that only formulas are entered in the disbursements and operating income schedules. You can compare the total operating income figures at the bottom of each spreadsheet to assess the effects of each scenario.

1 and 2.

Table of Budget Data	June	July	August	
Sales forecasts	$375,000	$330,000	$420,000	
Growth	0%	0%	0%	
	$375,000	$330,000	$420,000	
Cost of goods sold percentage			70%	
Misc. expense percentage			6%	
Sales commissions			10%	
Employee salaries per month			$22,000	
Rent per month			6,000	
Insurance expense per month			450	
Depreciation per month			2,850	
Disbursements for Operating Expenses (2a)				
Cost of goods sold	$262,500	$231,000	$294,000	$787,500
Commissions	37,500	33,000	42,000	112,500
Salaries	22,000	22,000	22,000	66,000
Miscellaneous	22,500	19,800	25,200	67,500
Rent	6,000	6,000	6,000	18,000
Total	$350,500	$311,800	$389,200	$1,051,500

Operating Income (2b)	June	July	August	Total
Sales	$375,000	$330,000	$420,000	$1,125,000
Cost of goods sold	262,500	231,000	294,000	787,500
Gross margin	$112,500	$99,000	$126,000	$337,500
Operating expenses				
Commissions	37,500	33,000	42,000	112,500
Salaries	22,000	22,000	22,000	66,000
Miscellaneous	22,500	19,800	25,200	67,500
Rent	6,000	6,000	6,000	18,000
Insurance	450	450	450	1,350
Depreciation	2,850	2,850	2,850	8,550
Total	$91,300	$84,100	$98,500	$273,900
Operating income	$21,200	$14,900	$27,500	$63,600

3a.

Table of Budget Data	June	July	August	
Sales forecasts	$375,000	$330,000	$420,000	
Growth	5%	5%	5%	
	$393,750	$346,500	$441,000	
Cost of goods sold percentage			70%	
Misc. expense percentage			6%	
Sales commissions			10%	
Employee salaries per month			$22,000	
Rent per month			6,000	
Insurance expense per month			450	
Depreciation per month			2,850	
Disbursements for Operating Expenses				Total
Cost of goods sold	$275,625	$242,550	$308,700	$826,875
Commissions	39,375	34,650	44,100	118,125
Salaries	$22,000	$22,000	$22,000	66,000
Miscellaneous	23,625	20,790	26,460	70,875
Rent	6,000	6,000	6,000	18,000
Total	$366,625	$325,990	$407,250	$1,099,875

Operating Income	June	July	August	Total
Sales	$393,750	$346,500	$441,000	$1,181,250
Cost of goods sold	275,625	242,550	308,700	826,875
Gross margin	$118,125	$103,950	$132,300	$354,375
Operating expenses				
Commissions	39,375	34,650	44,100	118,125
Salaries	$22,000	$22,000	$22,000	66,000
Miscellaneous	23,625	20,790	26,460	70,875
Rent	6,000	6,000	6,000	18,000
Insurance	450	450	450	1,350
Depreciation	2,850	2,850	2,850	8,550
Total	$94,300	$86,740	$101,860	$282,900
Operating income	$23,825	$17,210	$30,440	$71,475

3b.

Table of Budget Data	June	July	August	
Sales forecasts	$375,000	$330,000	$420,000	
Growth	-2%	-2%	-2%	
	$367,500	$323,400	$411,600	
Cost of goods sold percentage			70%	
Misc. expense percentage			6%	
Sales commissions			0%	
Employee salaries per month			$52,500	
Rent per month			6,000	
Insurance expense per month			450	
Depreciation per month			2,850	
Disbursements for Operating Expenses				Total
Cost of goods sold	$257,250	$226,380	$288,120	$771,750
Commissions	0	0	0	0
Salaries	52,500	52,500	52,500	157,500
Miscellaneous	22,050	19,404	24,696	66,150
Rent	6,000	6,000	6,000	18,000
Total	$337,800	$304,284	$371,316	$1,013,400

Operating Income	June	July	August	Total
Sales	$367,500	$323,400	$411,600	$1,102,500
Cost of goods sold	257,250	226,380	288,120	771,750
Gross margin	$110,250	$97,020	$123,480	$330,750
Operating expenses				
Commissions	0	0	0	0
Salaries	52,500	52,500	52,500	157,500
Miscellaneous	22,050	19,404	24,696	66,150
Rent	6,000	6,000	6,000	18,000
Insurance	450	450	450	1,350
Depreciation	2,850	2,850	2,850	8,550
Total	$83,850	$81,204	$86,496	$251,550
Operating income	$26,400	$15,816	$36,984	$79,200

7-38 (50-90 min.) These spreadsheets contain data from the problem in the top of the space. Computations of operating expenses are accomplished with formulas that reference the table. Comparing the summary calculations of operating expenses (labeled TOTAL OPERATING EXPENSE) allows the user to assess the effects of alternate scenarios.

1. Table of Budget Data

Cost behavior					
Cost	Fixed	Variable	Quantity / drive		
10X components		$100	5		
5X components		$40	5		
Indirect	$40,000	$16/component			
Packaging	$8,000	$4 / drive			
Shipping	$8,000	$2 / drive			
TOTAL OPERATING EXPENSE	$19,206,000				

Sales forecasts		10X drives	5X drives		
	Sales mix	1	1.25		
Month	Sales growth	1	1		
1 October	3,200	3,200	4,000		
2 November	2,400	2,400	3,000		
3 December	5,600	5,600	7,000		
4 January	3,200	3,200	4,000		
5 February	3,200	3,200	4,000		
6 March	2,400	2,400	3,000		
7 April	2,400	2,400	3,000		
8 May	2,800	2,800	3,500		
Operating expenses					
Month	Components	Indirect	Packaging	Shipping	Total
1 October	$2,400,000	$616,000	$36,800	$22,400	$3,075,200
2 November	1,800,000	472,000	29,600	18,800	2,320,400
3 December	4,200,000	1,048,000	58,400	33,200	5,339,600
4 January	2,400,000	616,000	36,800	22,400	3,075,200
5 February	2,400,000	616,000	36,800	22,400	3,075,200
6 March	1,800,000	472,000	29,600	18,800	2,320,400
Totals	$15,000,000	$3,840,000	$228,000	$138,000	$19,206,000

2. Table of Budget Data

Cost behavior					
Cost	Fixed	Variable	Quantity / drive		
10X components		$100	5		
5X components		$40	5		
Indirect	$40,000	$16 / component			
Packaging	$8,000	$4 / drive			
Shipping	$8,000	$2 / drive			
TOTAL OPERATING EXPENSE	$16,639,680				
Sales forecasts		10X drives	5X drives		
Sales mix		1	1.25		
Month	Sales growth	0.9	0.9		
1 November	2,400	2,160	2,700		
2 December	5,600	5,040	6,300		
3 January	3,200	2,880	3,600		
4 February	3,200	2,880	3,600		
5 March	2,400	2,160	2,700		
6 April	2,400	2,160	2,700		
7 May	2,800	2,520	3,150		

Operating expenses					
Month	Components	Indirect	Packaging	Shipping	Total
1 November	$1,620,000	$428,800	$27,440	$17,720	$2,093,960
2 December	3,780,000	947,200	53,360	30,680	4,811,240
3 January	2,160,000	558,400	33,920	20,960	2,773,280
4 February	2,160,000	558,400	33,920	20,960	2,773,280
5 March	1,620,000	428,800	27,440	17,720	2,093,960
6 April	1,620,000	428,800	27,440	17,720	2,093,960
Totals	$12,960,000	$3,350,400	$203,520	$125,760	$16,639,680

3. Table of Budget Data

Cost behavior					
Cost	Fixed	Variable	Quantity / drive		
10X disk components		$100	5		
5X disk components		$40	5		
Indirect	$40,000	$16 / component			
Packaging	$8,000	$4 / drive			
Shipping	$8,000	$2 / drive			
TOTAL OPERATING EXPENSE	$18,240,600				

Sales forecasts		10X drives	5X drives		
Sales mix		1	1.5		
Month	Sales growth	0.9	0.9		
1 December	5,600	5,040	7,560		
2 January	3,200	2,880	4,320		
3 February	3,200	2,880	4,320		
4 March	2,400	2,160	3,240		
5 April	2,400	2,160	3,240		
6 May	2,800	2,520	3,780		
7	0	0	0		
8	0	0	0		
Operating expenses					
Month	Components	Indirect	Packaging	Shipping	Total
1 December	$4,032,000	$1,048,000	$58,400	$33,200	$5,171,600
2 January	2,304,000	616,000	36,800	22,400	2,979,200
3 February	2,304,000	616,000	36,800	22,400	2,979,200
4 March	1,728,000	472,000	29,600	18,800	2,248,400
5 April	1,728,000	472,000	29,600	18,800	2,248,400
6 May	2,016,000	544,000	33,200	20,600	2,613,800
Totals	$14,112,000	$3,768,000	$224,400	$136,200	$18,240,600

7-39 (40-60 min.)

1.

MERCY HOSPITAL
Budgeted Cash Receipts
For the Quarter Ending September 30, 19X7
(in thousands)

	Calculation	July	August	September
May: 3rd-party billings	.9 x 6000 x .2	$1,080		
May: patient billings	.1 x 6000 x .4	240		
June: 3rd-party billings	.9 x 6000 x .2		$1,080	
June: patient billings	.1 x 6000 x .4		240	
June: 3rd-party billings	.9 x 6000 x .5	2,700		
June: patient billings	.1 x 6000 x .4	240		
July: 3rd-party billings	.9 x 5400 x .2			$ 972
July: patient billings	.1 x 5400 x .4			216
July: 3rd-party billings	.9 x 5400 x .5		2,430	
July: patient billings	.1 x 5400 x .4		216	
July: 3rd-party billings	.9 x 5400 x .2	972		
July: patient billings	.1 x 5400 x .1	54		
August: 3rd-party billings	.9 x 6000 x .5			2,700
August: patient billings	.1 x 6000 x .4			240
August: 3rd-party billings	.9 x 6000 x .2		1,080	
August: patient billings	.1 x 6000 x .1		60	
Sept: 3rd-party billings	.9 x 6600 x .2			1,188
Sept: patient billings	.1 x 6600 x .1			66
Total receipts from billings		$5,286	$5,106	$5,382
Endowment fund income		210	210	210
Total cash receipts		$5,496	$5,316	$5,592

2. Budgeted Cash Disbursements
For the Quarter Ending September 30, 19X7
(in thousands)

		July	August	September
Salaries:	$1,800 + .2 x $5,400	$2,880		
	$1,800 + .2 x $6,000		$3,000	
	$1,800 + .2 x $6,600			$3,120
Purchases, previous month		1,450	1,500	1,800
Interest				540
Total cash disbursements		$4,330	$4,500	$5,460

3. Budgeted Cash Receipts and Disbursements
For the Third Quarter, 19X7
(in thousands)

Beginning cash balance	$ 350
Budgeted cash receipts ($5,496 + $5,316 + $5,592)	16,404
Less budgeted cash disbursements ($4,330 + $4,500 + $5,460)	(14,290)
Budgeted cash balance, September 30, 19X7	$ 2,464
Minimum cash balance (.1 x $2,200)	(220)
Cash available for capital expenditures	$ 2,244
Budgeted capital expenditures	(3,900)
Borrowing needed on October 1, 19X7	$ (1,656)

7-40 (50-60 min.)

1.

WESTERN WYOMING STATE UNIVERSITY
Projected Enrollment, Credits, and Faculty
Academic Year 19X8-X9

	Undergraduate	Graduate	Total
Expected enrollment[a]	3,528	1,890	5,418
Average credit hours	25	20	-
Total credit hours[b]	88,200	37,800	126,000
Full-time-equivalent enrollment[c]	2,940	1,575	4,515
Credit hours per faculty member[d]	720	360	1,080
Total faculty needed[e]	122.5	105	227.5

[a] 98% x 3,600 = 3,528; 105% x 1,800 = 1,890
[b] 25 x 3,528 = 88,200; 20 x 1,890 = 37,800
[c] 88,200/ 30 = 2,940; 37,800 /24 = 1,575
[d] 24 x 30 = 720; 18 x 20 = 360
[e] 88,200 / 720 = 122.5; 37,800/360 = 105

2.

WESTERN WYOMING STATE UNIVERSITY
Faculty Salaries Budget
Academic Year 19X8-X9

	Faculty Needed	Average Salary	Total Faculty Salaries
Undergraduate	122.5	$48,760	$ 5,973,100
Graduate	105.0	48,760	5,119,800
Total	227.5		$11,092,900

3.

WESTERN WYOMING STATE UNIVERSITY
Tuition and Legislative Revenue Budget
Academic Year 19X8-X9

	Undergrad Division	Graduate Division	Total
Total credit hours	88,200	37,800	126,000
Less: Scholarship credit hours*	900	1,200	2,100
Tuition paying credit hours	87,300	36,600	123,900
Tuition per credit hour	x $70	x $70	x $70
Total tuition budget	= $6,111,000	= $2,562,000	= $8,673,000
Full time equivalent students	2,940	1,575	4,515
Legislative apportionment per full-time equivalent student	x $780	x $780	x $780
Total legislative apportionment	= $2,293,200	= $1,228,500	= $3,521,700

*30 x 30 = 900; 50 x 24 = 1,200

4.

WESTERN WYOMING STATE UNIVERSITY
Annual Budget Shortfall
Academic Year 19X8-X9

Budgeted operating expenditures:	
Faculty salaries	$11,092,900
Operation and maintenance of facilities:	
Salaries and wages (1.06 x $240,000)	254,400
Other ($260,000 + $12,000)	272,000
General Administrative	525,000
Library:	
Acquisitions	155,000
Operations	200,000
Health Services	50,000
Intramural athletics	60,000
Intercollegiate athletics	245,000
Insurance and retirement	560,000
Interest	75,000
Total budgeted operating expenditures	$13,489,300
Budgeted revenues:	
Tuition	$ 8,673,000
Legislative apportionment	3,521,700
Endowment income	210,000
Auxiliary services	335,000
Intercollegiate athletics	300,000
Total budgeted operating revenues	$13,039,700
Deficit from operations	$ 449,600
Budgeted capital expenditures	550,000
Total cash needed from fund-raising*	$ 999,600

*13,489,300 + 550,000 - 13,039,700

7-41 (30-60 min.)

The purpose of this exercise is to prepare a budget for an organization (an individual student) that is familiar to all students and to see the effect of assumptions on the budget. Each student will have some ideas about both the revenue and expense budgets of a typical student, but these ideas will likely vary across students. They will experience the process of negotiation needed to get a budget that the group can agree on.

When the groups get together and compare budgets, it will be instructive to see how different groups make different assumptions that lead to different budgets. This should reinforce the importance of assumptions to the budget process and show how decisions made during the budget process affect the resulting budget.

CHAPTER 8
Flexible Budgets and Variance Analysis

8-A1 (30-45 min.) Amounts are in thousands.

1.

	Flexible Budget Amounts		
Revenue	$7,000	$8,000	$9,000
Fuel	$ 140	$ 160	$ 180
Repairs and maintenance	70	80	90
Supplies and miscellaneous	700	800	900
Variable payroll	4,690	5,360	6,030
Total variable costs	$5,600	$6,400	$7,200
Supervision	$ 160	$ 160	$ 160
Rent	160	160	160
Depreciation	480	480	480
Other fixed costs	160	160	160
Total fixed costs	$ 960	$ 960	$ 960
Total costs	$6,560	$7,360	$8,160
Operating income	$ 440	$ 640	$ 840

2. $960,000 per quarter plus .80 of revenue.

3. Variances are defined as deviations of actual results from plans. The total variances in the problem can be subdivided to provide answers to two broad questions:

   (a) What portion is attributable to not attaining a predetermined level of volume or activity? This variance is called the *sales activity variance*.

(b) What portion is attributable to nonvolume effects? This variance is often called the *flexible budget variance*, which is composed of *price* and *efficiency* variances.

The existing performance report, which is based solely on a *static* budget, cannot answer these questions clearly. It answers (a) partially, because it compares the revenue achieved with the original targeted revenue. But the report fails to answer (b). A complete analysis follows:

Summary of Performance
(in thousands)

	(1) Actual Results at Actual Activity Level	(2) (1)-(3) Flexible Budget Variances	(3) Flexible Budget for Actual Sales Activity	(4) (3)-(5) Sales Activity Variances	(5) Master (Static) Budget
Net revenue	$7,600	$ -	$7,600	$400	$8,000
Total variable costs	6,223	143	6,080	320	6,400
Contribution margin	$1,377	$143U	$1,520	$ 80U	$1,600
Fixed costs	962	2U	960	-	960
Operating income	$ 415	$145U	$ 560	$ 80U	$ 640

U = Unfavorable

Column (4) focuses on the effects of sales volume. It shows that a $400,000 drop in sales activity caused a $80,000 decrease in contribution margin and hence a $80,000 drop in operating income.

Column (2) generally focuses on efficiency. Without a flexible budget, operating inefficiencies cannot be isolated from the effects of changes in sales activity. Cost control performance may be reported in more detail, where the focus is on efficiency (in thousands):

	Actual Costs	Flexible Budget Allowance*	Budget Variance
Fuel	$ 157	$ 152	$ 5U
Repairs and maintenance	78	76	2U
Supplies and miscellaneous	788	760	28U
Variable payroll	5,200	5,092	108U
Supervision	164	160	4U
Rent	160	160	-
Depreciation	480	480	-
Other fixed costs	158	160	2F
Totals	$7,185	$7,040	$145U

U = Unfavorable
*For $7,600,000 revenue.

8-A2 (20-30 min.)

	A	B	C
	Actual Overhead Costs Incurred	Flexible Budget Based on Actual Outputs x Expected Prices	Master Budget Based on Standard Inputs Allowed for Planned Outputs Achieved x Expected Prices
Systems consulting, variable	$45,000	90 requests x $600 = $5,400	(75 requests x $60)= $45,000
	Flexible-budget variance (A - B) $45,000 - $54,000 = $9,000 F	Activity-level variance (B - C) $54,000 - $45,000 = $9,000 U	
	Master budget variance (A - C) $45,000 -$45,000 = 0		
Systems consulting, fixed	$78,000 (given)		$70,000
	Master budget variance (A -C) $78,000 - $70,000 = $8,000 U		

8-A3 (20 - 30 min.)

1. Direct materials: 10 lb x \$ 5.00 = \$ 50.00
   Direct labor: 5 x \$25.00 = 125.00
   Total \$175.00

Direct materials:	10 lb x \$ 5.00 =	\$ 50.00
Direct labor:	5 x \$25.00 =	125.00
Total		\$175.00

2. The standard costs expected are based on actual output achieved, not scheduled or budgeted output.

	A	B	C
	Actual Cost Incurred: Actual Inputs x Actual Prices	Flexible Budget Based on Actual Inputs x Expected Prices	Flexible Budget Based on Expected Inputs for Actual Outputs Achieved x Expected Prices
In general:	\$xxx	\$xxx	\$xxx

Price variance (A - B)	Usage variance (B - C)
Flexible-budget variance (A - C)	

	A	B	C
Direct Materials	5,500 lbs x \$4.25 = \$23,375	5,500 lbs x \$5.00 = \$27,500	525 units x 10 x \$5.00 = \$26,250

Price variance (A - B)	Usage variance (B - C)
\$23,375 -\$27,500 = \$4,125 F	\$27,500 - \$26,250 = \$1,250 U
Flexible-budget variance (A - C) \$23,375 - \$26,250 = \$2,875 F	

Direct Labor	2,850 hr x \$26.00 = \$74,100	2,850 hr x \$25.00 = \$71,250	525 units x 5 hr x \$25.00 = \$65,625
	Price variance (A - B) = \$74,100 - \$71,250 = \$2,850 U		Usage variance (B - C) = \$71,250 - \$65,625 = \$5,625 U
	Flexible-budget variance (A - C) \$74,100 - \$65,625 = \$8,475 U		

3. Among the possible explanations for the performance are:

   (a) Were substandard materials used because they were cheaper, resulting in higher waste than usual? (Note the tradeoff resulted in a net favorable materials variance.)

   (b) Net savings in material costs may be undesirable if they cause inefficient use of direct labor too.

   (c) Direct labor is expensive. A wage rate that is 4% above the standard rate can be significant in total amount.

8-B1 (15-20 min.)

1. EXPRESS TAX PREPARATION SERVICES, INC.

Summary Performance Report

	Actual Results at Actual Activity Level	Flexible Budget Variances	Flexible Budget for Actual Activity Level	Sales Activity Variances	Master Budget
Physical units (clients)	3,000	-	3,000	500F	2,500
Sales	$1,080,000	$30,000F	$1050,000	$175,000F	$875,000
Variable costs	800,000	50,000U	750,000	125,000U	625,000
Contribution margin	$ 280,000	$20,000U	$ 300,000	$ 50,000F	$250,000
Fixed costs	157,500	7,500U	150,000	-	150,000
Operating income	$ 122,500	$27,500U	$ 150,000	$ 50,000F	$100,000

2.

Master budget operating income		$100,000
Variances:		
Sales activity variances	$50,000F	
Flexible-budget variances	27,500U	22,500F
Actual operating income		$122,500

8-B2 (20-30 min.)

1.

	A Actual Cost Incurred: Actual Inputs x Actual Prices	B Flexible Budget Based on Actual Inputs x Expected Prices	C Flexible Budget Based on Standard Inputs for Actual Outputs Achieved x Expected Prices
Direct Materials	56,000 lb x $16 = $896,000	56,000 lb x $14 = $784,000	14,400 units x 5 x $14 = $1,008,000

Price variance (A - B) =	Usage variance (B - C)
$896,000 - $784,000 = $112,000 U	$784,000 - $1,008,000 = $224,000 F
Flexible-budget variance (A - C) = $896,000 - $1,008,000 = $112,000F	

	A	B	C
Direct Labor	30,000 hr x $12 = $360,000	30,000 hr x $13 = $390,000	14,400 units x 2 hr x $13 = $374,400

Price variance (A - B) =	Usage variance (B - C)
$360,000-$390,000 = $30,000 F	$390,000-$374,400 = $15,600 U
Flexible-budget variance (A - C) $360,000 - $374,400 = $14,400 F	

2. Tradeoffs may have been made in each category. More expensive materials may have been acquired with the hope of achieving less waste. Less expensive labor may have been used that caused more inefficiency. The overall effects were favorable, at least as measured by these variances. Management also should be concerned with effects of these tradeoffs on quality, on-time delivery, customer satisfaction, and so on.

8-B3 (20-30 min.) If the total overhead incurred is $202,200, of which $133,500 is fixed, then variable overhead was $202,200 - $133,500 = $68,700. The following analysis should be helpful. All given items are designated by an asterisk (*).

	A	B	C
	Actual Overhead Costs Incurred	Flexible Budget Based on Actual Inputs x Expected Prices	Flexible Budget Based on Standard Inputs Allowed for Actual Outputs Achieved x Expected Prices
Billing department, variable	$68,700	$68,700 + $1,500* = $70,200; 117,000 hr x 10* x $.06* = $70,200	$70,200 - $7,500 = $62,700 = 104,500 hr x 10* x $.06*
	Spending variance $1,500* F	Efficiency variance $6,000 U - $1,500 F= $7,500 U	
	Flexible-budget variance (A - C) $6,000* U		

1. $7,500U. The efficiency variance is computed by subtracting the price variance from the flexible-budget variance, $6,000 - (-$1,500). Note that this computation can be made independently of the next two requirements.

2. 117,000 hours. The actual hours can be computed by adding the price variance to the actual variable overhead and then dividing the result by $.60: ($68,700 + $1,500) ÷ $.60 = 117,000 hours. Alternatively, this answer could be obtained by taking the answer in part (3) and adding 12,500 hours because the unfavorable efficiency variance represents 12,500 hours of work ($7,500 ÷ $.60).

3. 104,500 hours. The standard hours allowed for output achieved can be computed in one of two ways:

   (a) Take the answer in part (2) and deduct 12,500 hours: 117,000 - 12,500 = 104,500 hours.

   (b) Deduct the efficiency variance from the $70,200 and then divide the result, $62,700, by $.60: ($70,200 - $7,500) ÷ $.60 = 104,500 hours.

8-1 Favorable variances arise when actual costs are less than budgeted costs (or actual revenue exceeds budgeted revenue). Unfavorable variances mean that actual costs are greater than budgeted costs (or actual revenue falls short of budgeted revenue).

8-2 Yes. Flexible budgets are flexible only with respect to variable costs. There is no point in scaling down the fixed cost budget in proportion to actual output when the actual fixed costs don't behave that way.

8-3 No. A flexible budget adjusts costs as the *level of activity* changes, not as prices change.

8-4 The use of flexible budgeting requires cost formulas or functions to predict what costs should be at different levels of cost driver activity. These flexible-budget cost formulas are possible only if cost behavior is understood.

8-5 A "flex" in a flexible budget generally refers to adjustments made because of changes in volume. Activities that have variable costs will therefore generate "flexes" in the budget, but those activities that drive only fixed costs will not have a "flex".

8-6 No. Performance can be either effective or efficient or both. For example, the targeted sales level (effectiveness) may be achieved or not, independent of whether the actual level of operations used the appropriate amount of resources (efficiency).

8-7 A master budget variance is the difference between the originally planned (master budget) amount and the actual amount. A flexible-budget variance is the difference between the actual amount and the amount that is expected for the actual level of output achieved.

8-8 Favorable and unfavorable variances to not necessarily mean good and bad performance, respectively. They mean simply that actual results differed from the standards. Differences may arise from inaccurate standards, or they may be the result of factors that are beyond the control of management. Variances should be a signal to ask the question "why", but they do not automatically give the answer.

8-9 No. The primary function of a control system is *explanation*, not fixing blame.

8-10 Sales activity variances are most often the responsibility of sales personnel. However, if factors such as quality of product and meeting of delivery schedules impact the volume of sales, production managers who affect quality and delivery may also affect the sales activity variance.

8-11 A perfection (or ideal) standard disregards all imperfections and human errors and thus is rarely attained. A currently attainable standard can be closely approached by keeping all inefficiencies down to a minimum level, and it can be occasionally surpassed by exceptional effort.

8-12 The first interpretation is that standards are set just tightly enough so that employees regard their fulfillment as highly probable if normal effort and diligence are exercised. The second interpretation is that standards are set more tightly so that employees regard their fulfillment as possible though unlikely.

8-13 There is much room for measurement error when a standard is set. Consequently, random fluctuations around the standard can really be conceived of as defining the band of acceptable outcomes rather than as variances from a precise standard. The standard is often the midpoint of the band of acceptable outcomes.

8-14 Price variances should be computed even if prices are outside of company control because the use of a standard price will still be helpful for measuring production performance. By separating price effects from efficiency effects, the efficiency variances are not affected by price changes.

8-15 Some common causes of usage or efficiency variances are improper handling, poor quality of material, poor workmanship, changes in methods, new workers, slow machines, breakdowns, and faulty designs.

8-16 Failure to meet price standards is often the responsibility of the purchasing officer, but responsibility may be shared with the production manager if he or she has frequent rush orders for materials. Of course, market conditions may be such that it is beyond the control of anyone in the company to attain the price standard.

8-17 Direct material price variances are generally recognized at the time of purchase to give feedback as early as practical to those responsible for acquiring materials.

8-18 Overhead control techniques are different from direct material cost control techniques because:

1. Cost drivers are generally more complex and less obvious.
2. Responsibility is split among various people.
3. A large percentage of overhead costs may be fixed or joint in nature.

8-19 The variable overhead spending variance is not the result of only price changes, as is the labor price variance, but also includes such factors as inadequate attention to cost control and imperfect identification and measurement of cost drivers for cost estimates.

8-20 (10 min.)

Variable cost is $170,000/20,000 units = $8.50 per unit
Budgeted cost = $8.50(25,000) + $70,000 = $282,500

8-21 (10 min.)

Mileage	30,000	40,000	50,000
Fuel @ $.15	$ 4,500	$ 6,000	$7,500
Depreciation	6,000	6,000	6,000
Total	$10,500	$12,000	$13,500

8-22 (10 min.) Answers are in *italics*.

	Budget Formula per Unit	Various Levels of Output		
Units		6,000	7,000	8,000
Sales	$18	*$108,000*	*$126,000*	*$144,000*
Variable costs:				
Direct material	*8*	48,000	*56,000*	*64,000*
Fuel	2	*12,000*	*14,000*	*16,000*
Fixed costs:				
Depreciation		*15,000*	15,000	*15,000*
Executive salaries		*40,000*	*40,000*	40,000

8-23 (10-15 min.)

The manager's delight is unjustified. A more informative analysis is obtained when a flexible budget is introduced:

	Actual Costs	Flexible-Budget Variance	Flexible Budget	Sales Activity Variance	Master Budget
Units of product	6,800	-	6,800	1,200	8,000*
Direct materials	$ 90,000	$ 8,400U	$ 81,600	$14,400F	$ 96,000
Direct labor	37,600	3,600U	34,000	6,000F	40,000
Total	$127,600	$12,000U	$115,600	$20,400F	$136,000

*$96,000/$12 = 8,000 or $40,000/$5 = 8,000

Note that the manager should have expected lower costs when volume was 15% less than the master budget. But the manager was unable to bring the costs below the amounts in the flexible budget. Costs of $20,400 were saved by producing 1,200 fewer units than planned, but the manager spent $12,000 more than expected to produce 6,800 units.

8-24 (10-15 min.)

	A	B	C
	Actual Results at Actual Activity Level	Flexible Budget for Actual Pounds of Activity	Master Budget
Materials support:	$175,000 (given)	650,000 lb x $.25 = $162,500	750,000 lb x $.25 = $187,500

Flexible-budget variance (A - B)	Materials-activity variance (B - C)
$175,000 - $162,500 = $12,500 U	$162,500-$187,500 = $25,000 F

Master-budget variance (A - C)
$175,000-$187,500
= $12,500 F

8-25 (10-15 min.) This simple problem highlights the calculation of material price variance at the time of purchase and the material usage variance at the time of use of the materials.

Cost Incurred: Actual Inputs x Actual Prices	Flexible Budget Based on Actual Inputs x Expected Prices	Flexible Budget Based on Standard Inputs Allowed for Actual Outputs Achieved x Expected Prices
10,000 sq. yd x $6.90 = $69,000	10,000 sq. yd. x $7.10 = $71,000	
10,000 x ($6.90 - $7.10) = Price variance, $2,000F		
	7,900 sq. yds. x $7.10 = $56,090	7,600 sq. yds. x $7.10 = $53,960
	(8,000 - 7,600) x $7.10 = Usage variance, $2,130U	

8-26 (15-20 min.)

1. Price variance per hr. = Total price variance/ Actual hrs.
= $945/1,750
= $.54, unfavorable

Actual labor rate (price) = Standard price + Price variance
= $14.00 + $.54
= $14.54

2. Flexible-budget labor variance = Price variance + Usage variance
$1,855 = $-945 + X
X = $2,800, favorable

Usage variance = Standard price x Difference in hours
$2,800 = $14.00 x Difference in hours

Difference in hours = $2,800 ÷ $14.00
= 200

Because the variance is favorable, the standard hours allowed must be 1,750 + 200 = 1,950.

The analytical framework follows. All given items are designated by an asterisk (*).

Actual Hours x Actual Price	Actual Hours x Expected Price	Standard Hours x Expected Price
1,750 hrs.* x $14.54 = $25,445	1,750 hrs.* x $14.00* = $24,500	1,950 hrs. x $14.00* = $27,300

1,750* x $.54 = Price variance, $945U*	200 x $14.00* = Usage variance, $2,800F
Flexible-budget variance, $1,855F*	

8-27 (10 min.)

Material usage variance
= Difference in pounds x Standard price
= (17,000 - 18,000) x $3
= $3,000, favorable

Labor usage variance
= Difference in hours x Standard price
= (46,500 actual hours - 45,000 standard hours) x $3
= $4,500, unfavorable

8-28 (10-20 min.)

1. Usage variance = (Actual hours - Standard hours) x Standard rate

$13,500	= (Actual hours - 12,000) x $13.50
$13,500	= $13.50(Actual hours) - $162,000
Actual hours	= $175,500 ÷ $13.50 = 13,000

or

Excess hours, $13,500 ÷ $13.50	1,000
Standard hours	12,000
Total actual hours	13,000

2. Price variance

= Actual quantity purchased x (Actual price - Standard price per unit)

$-288	= 1,800(Actual price - $4.50)
$-288	= 1,800(Actual price) - $8,100
Actual price	= $7,812 ÷ 1,800 = $4.34

or

Standard price	$4.50
Variance per unit, $288 ÷ 1,800	.16F
Actual price	$4.34

8-29 (10-15 min.)

Direct material:
Price variance: $153,000 - $165,000 = $12,000F
Usage variance: $165,000 - $172,500 = $7,500F
Flexible-budget variance: $153,000 - $172,500 = $19,500F

Direct labor:
Price variance: $79,000 - 74,000 = 5,000U
Usage variance: $74,000 - $71,300 = $2,700U
Flexible-budget variance: $79,000 - $71,300 = $7,700U

You may wish to call the students' attention to tradeoffs. For example, more efficient use of materials may be attained by more careful work that takes more time than allowed by the labor standard.

8-30 (10-15 min.) (in thousands)

	(1)	(2) (1)-(3)	(3)	(4) (3)-(5)	(5)
	Actual Results at Actual Prices	Flexible-Budget Variances	Flexible Budget for Actual Sales Output Achieved	Sales Activity Variances	Master Budget
Revenue	$ 4,000	$ -	$4,000	$1,000U	$5,000
Variable costs	400	-	400	100F	500
Contribution margin	$ 3,600	$ -	$3,600	$ 900U	$4,500
Fixed costs	4,860	360U	4,500	-	4,500
Operating income	$(1,260)	$360U	$ (900)	$ 900U	$ -

U = Unfavorable

Note that this is an example of a "high fixed cost" or "highly leveraged" organization. This means a high sensitivity of operating income in relation to changes in revenue. Income plummeted in this case, but would have soared if the change in revenue had been $1,000,000 in the opposite direction.

8-31 (15-25 min.)

1.

	Actual Results	Flexible-Budget Variance,	Flexible Budget	Sales Activity Variance	Master Budget
Attendees	90	-	90	5F	75
Revenue	$3,255	$105F	$3,150	$525F	$2,625
Chicken dinners	1,668	84U	1,584	264U	1,320
Beverages	466	74F	540	90U	450
Club rental	81	0	81	0	81
Music	840	120U	720	0	720
Profit	$ 200	$ 25U	$ 225	$171F	$ 54

2. If all costs had behaved as budgeted, the extra 15 attendees would have produced an extra $171 of profit ($525 more revenue and $264 + $90 = $354 more cost). The sales activity variance summarizes this effect of volume. Revenue was $105 over budget for the number of attendees. Three tickets must have been sold to persons who did not attend. Costs ran $84 + $120 - $74 = $130 more than the budget for 90 attendees. Dinner cost was $84 over budget; this is not easily explained – did the caterer charge extra costs?. Beverages were under budget by $74. The band seems to have played (or at least was paid for) an extra half hour.

8-32 (20-30 min.)

1.

	Actual Results at Actual Prices	Flexible-Budget Variances	Flexible Budget	Sales Activity Variances	Static (Master) Budget
Physical units	80,000	-	80,000	8,000[a]	72,000
Sales	$806,400[c]	$ 6,400F	$800,000[b]	$80,000F	$720,000
Variable costs	492,000	12,000U	480,000	48,000U	432,000[g]
Contribution margin	314,400[d]	5,600U	320,000	32,000F	288,000
Fixed costs	203,000[e]	8,000U	195,000	-	195,000
Operating income	$111,400[f]	$13,600U	$125,000	$32,000F	$ 93,000

[a]80,000 - 72,000
[b]720,000/72,000 = $10 per unit; $10 x 80,000 = 800,000
[c]800,000 + 6,400
[d]806,400 - 492,000
[e]195,000 + 8,000
[f]314,400 - 203,000
[g]480,000/800,000 = .60; 720,000 x .60 = 432,000

2. Sales were 8,000 units higher than originally budgeted. This higher sales volume should have produced an operating income of $125,000 (up from $93,000 by $80,000(1 - .6) = $32,000). However, only $111,400 was achieved. Sales prices were higher by $6,400, but costs exceeded the flexible budget by $12,000 + $8,000 = $20,000:

Actual operating income		$111,400
Variances:		
Sales prices	6,400F	
Sales volume	32,000F	
Variable costs	12,000U	
Fixed costs	8,000U	18,400F
Master budgeted operating income		$ 93,000

8-33 (20-30 min.) There is a need to work from the knowns to the unknowns.

DIAZ CREDIT SERVICES
Analysis of Income Statement
For the Year 19X8
(in thousands)

	(1) Actual	(2) (1)-(3) Flexible-Budget Variances	(3) Flexible Budget	(4) (3)-(5) Sales Activity Variances	(5) Master Budget
Reports	700	-	700	100U	800
Sales @ $50	$35,000	$ -	$35,000	$5,000U	$40,000
Variable costs @ $15	11,400	900U	10,500	1,500F	12,000
Contribution margin	$23,600	$ 900U	$24,500	$3,500U	$28,000
Fixed costs	22,200	700U	21,500	-	21,500
Operating income	$ 1,400	$1,600U	$ 3,000	$3,500U	$ 6,500

Note: The variance in fixed costs is properly a flexible budget variance–not a sales volume variance. The variances in Column (4) are traceable *solely* to changes in volume: The effects of price and efficiency changes and any other types of spending changes are presented in Column (2).

The $6,500,000 budgeted income was not attained because (a) *volume* was down by 100,000 returns, causing a $3,500,000 shortfall in contribution margin. In addition, our *prices* paid for services (commissions) were higher, and the *efficiency* of our workers receiving wages was lower; together these totaled $900,000. Finally, we spent $700,000 in excess of our advertising budget.

8-34 (15-20 min.)

1. The sales activity variance is B600,000 favorable, and the flexible-budget variance is B390,000 unfavorable (in millions of Thai Baht):

	Actual Results at Actual Activity Level	Flexible-Budget Variances	Flexible-Budget for Actual Sales Activity	Sales Activity Variances	Master Budget
Sales	9.30	—	9.30	2.00 F	7.30
Variable costs	6.90	.39 U	6.51	1.40 U	5.11
Contribution margin	2.40	.39 U	2.79	.60F	2.19
Fixed costs	1.80	.00	1.80	—	1.80
Operating income	.60	.39 U	.99	.60 F	.39

2. The B210,000 favorable variance in 1996 resulted from the increase in volume. In fact, if there had been no cost overruns in 1996, profits would have increased by B600,000. In 1997 sales volume falls to its 1996 budgeted level, and if the franchise maintains the cost structure of 1997, its profits would fall well below the level budgeted for 1996. If another B390,000 unfavorable flexible-budget variance occurrs in 1997, profit would be zero.

8-35 (20-25 min.)

1. Monetary amounts are in thousands of dollars

	Actual Results at Actual Prices	Flexible-Budget Variance	Flexible Budget	Sales Activity Variances	Master Budget
Millions of passenger miles	1,650	-	1,650	150	1,500*
Revenue	303,600**	26,400U	330,000	30,000F	300,000
Variable expenses	200,000	14,500F	214,500***	19,500U	195,000
Contribution margin	103,600	11,900U	115,500	10,500F	105,000
Fixed expenses	77,000	2,000U	75,000	-	75,000
Operating income	26,600	13,900U	40,500	10,500F	30,000

*300,000 /$.20 = 1,500,000
**330,000 - .08(330,000) = 303,600
***(195,000 ÷ 300,000) x 330,000 = 214,500

2.	Jet fuel	110,880	11,880U*	99,000	9,000U	90,000

*Price variance of .12 x 99,000 = 11,880U

8-36 (20-30 min.) This is an excellent basic problem in flexible budgeting.

1. LIVERPOOL UNIVERSITY MOTOR POOL
Monthly Budget Report
For March 19X6

	March Actual	Monthly Budget	Under (over)
Gasoline	£ 7,500	£ 7,000	£(500)
Oil, minor repairs, parts and supplies	1,300	1,400	100
Outside repairs	50	234	184
Insurance	416	416	-
Salaries and benefits	1,800	1,800	-
Depreciation	1,976	1,976	-
Totals	£13,042	£12,826	£ (216)
Number of automobiles	26	26	-
Actual kilometers	140,000	140,000	-
Cost per kilometers	£ .0932	£ .0916	£(.0016)

Supporting Calculations for Monthly Budget Amounts:
Gasoline: (140,000 km ÷ 8 km per liter) x £.40 per liter = £7,000
Oil, et al.: 140,000 km x £.01 per km = £1,400
Outside repairs: (£108 per auto x 26 autos) ÷ 12 months = £234
Insurance:
Annual cost for one auto = £4,800 ÷ 25 autos = £192 per auto
Annual cost for 26 autos = 26 x £192 = £4,992
Monthly cost = £4,992 ÷ 12 = £416
Salaries and benefits:
No change, monthly cost = £21,600 annual cost ÷ 12 months = £1,800
Depreciation:
Annual depreciation per auto = £22,800 ÷ 25 autos = £912
Annual depreciation for 26 autos = £912 x 26 = £23,712
Monthly depreciation = £23,712 ÷ 12 = £1,976

2. Outside automobile repairs are a function of the use of the automobile over its lifetime. However, these repairs occur irregularly throughout the year and the life of the car. A monthly budget figure based upon a per mile charge becomes questionable. Therefore, the use of one-twelfth of the estimated annual outside repair costs adjusted for the number of cars in operation during a month would appear to be more reasonable.

8-37 (50-70 min.)

The following notation applies to requirements 1-3.

TC = Total cost
F_I = Fixed costs of the Account Inquiry activity center
F_C = Fixed costs of the Correspondence activity center
F_B = Fixed costs of the Account Billing activity center
F_V = Fixed costs of the Bill Verification activity center
V_I = Variable cost per labor hour in the Account Inquiry activity center
V_C = Variable cost per letter in the Correspondence activity center
V_B = Variable cost per line in the Account Billing activity center
V_V = Variable cost per account in the Bill Verification activity center
HR = Account Inquiry labor hours
LR = Letters of correspondence issued
LN = Lines printed
AC = Commerical accounts verified

1\.

Activity Center	Flexible-Budget Formula		
Account Inquiry	$F_I + V_I \times HR$	=	\$155,270 + \$24.22(1) x HR
Correspondence	$F_C + V_C \times LR$	=	25,584 + \$ 3.50(2) x LR
Account Billing	$F_B + V_B \times LN$	=	81,400 + \$ 0.063(3) x LN
Bill Verification	$F_V + V_V \times AC$	=	78,050 + \$ 0.54(4) x AC

(1) 79,910 ÷ 3,300
(2) 9,800 ÷ 2,800
(3) 154,377 ÷ 2,440,000
(4) 10,797 ÷ 20,000

2\.

Flexible Budget – Account Inquiry Activity Center

	Budget Formula:	Cost Driver – Number of Labor Hours (HR) 3,000	4,000	5,000
Variable Costs	\$24.22/HR	\$ 72,660	\$ 96,880	\$121,100
Fixed Costs	\$155,270	155,270	155,270	155,270
Total Flexible Budget		\$227,930	\$252,150	\$276,370

Flexible Budget – Correspondence Activity Center

	Budget Formula:	Cost Driver – Number of Letters (LR) 2,500	3,000	3,500
Variable Costs	\$3.50/LR	\$ 8,750	\$10,500	\$12,250
Fixed Costs	\$25,584	25,584	25,584	25,584
Total Flexible Budget		\$34,334	\$36,084	\$37,834

Flexible Budget – Account Billing Activity Center

	Budget Formula:	Cost Driver – Number of Lines (LN) 2,000,000	2,500,000	3,000,000
Variable Costs	$0.063/LN	$126,000	$157,500	$189,000
Fixed Costs	$81,400	81,400	81,400	81,400
Total Flexible Budget		$207,400	$238,900	$270,400

Flexible Budget – Bill Verification Activity Center

	Budget Formula:	Cost Driver – Number of Letters (LR) 15,000	20,000	25,000
Variable Costs	$0.54/AC	$ 8,100	$10,800	$13,500
Fixed Costs	$78,050	78,050	78,050	78,050
Total Flexible Budget		$86,150	$88,850	$91,550

3. $TC = F_I + F_C + F_B + F_V + V_I \times HR + V_C \times LR + V_B \times LN + V_V \times AC$
$= 340{,}304 + 24.22 \times V_I + 3.50 \times LR + .063 \times LN + .54 \times AC$

4.

Activity Center	Actual Costs	Flexible Budget	Flexible-Budget Variances
Account Inquiry	$229,890	$261,838(1)	$31,948F
Correspondence	38,020	36,959(2)	1,061U
Account Billing	285,000	264,100(3)	20,900U
Bill Verification	105,320	90,200(4)	15,120U
Total Costs	$658,230	$653,097	$ 5,133U

(1) 155,250 + (24.22 x 4,400) = $261,838
(2) 25,584 + (3.50 x 3,250) = $36,959
(3) 81,400 + (0.063 x 2,900,000) = $264,100
(4) 78,050 + (0.54 x 22,500) = $90,200

8-38 (25-30 min.)

	Cost Incurred: Actual Inputs x Actual Prices	Flexible Budget Based on Actual Inputs x Expected Prices	Flexible Budget Based on Standard Inputs Allowed for Actual Outputs Achieved x Expected Prices
Direct materials	3,400 lbs. x $.95 = $3,230	3,400 lbs. x $1.00 = $3,400	3,000 lbs. x $1.00 = $3,000
	3,400 x ($.95 - $1.00) = Price variance $170F		(3,400 - 3,000) x $1.00 = Usage variance $400U
	Flexible-budget variance, $230U		
Direct labor	5,500 hrs. x $3.80 = $20,900	5,500 hrs. x $4.00 = $22,000	5,000 hrs x $4.00 = $20,000
	5,500 x ($3.80 - $4.00) = Price variance $1,100F		(5,500-5,000) x $4.00 = Usage variance, $2,000U
	Flexible-budget variance, $900U		
Variable overhead	5,500 hrs x $.8691 = $4,780	5,500 hrs. x $.80 = $4,400	5,000 hrs. x $.80 = $4,000
	5,500 x ($.8691 - $.80) = Price variance, $380U		(5,500-5,000) x $.80 = Efficiency variance, $400U
	Flexible-budget variance, $780U		

U = Unfavorable, F = Favorable

* The average variable overhead price is unnecessary to comply with the requirements of the problem. It was computed by dividing $4,780 by 5,500 hours.

8-39 (30-35 min.) The format of the solution may seem awkward at first, but students find that it provides perspective on the analysis of variances. SF = Swiss Franc.

1.

Cost Incurred: Actual Inputs x Actual Prices	Flexible Budget Based on Actual Inputs x Expected Prices	Flexible Budget Based on Standard Inputs Allowed for Actual Outputs Achieved x Expected Prices
6,400 lbs. x 15.5F = 99,200SF	6,400 lbs. x 16SF = 102,400SF	
6,400 x .5SF = Price variance, 3,200SF F		
	4,300 lbs x 16SF = 68,800SF	4,000 lbs. x 16SF = 64,000SF
	300 x 16SF = Usage variance, 4,800SF U	
6,400 hrs. x 30.5SF = 195,200SF	6,400 hrs. x 30SF = 192,000SF	6,000 hrs. x 30SF = 180,000SF
6,400 x .5SF = Price variance, 3,200SF U	400 x 30SF Usage variance, 12,000SF U	
Flexible-budget variance, 15,200SF U		
69,500SF	6,400 hrs. x 10SF = 64,000SF	6,000 hrs. x 10SF = 60,000SF
Spending variance, 69,500 - 64,000 = 5,500SF U	400 x 10SF = Efficiency variance, 4,000SF U	
Flexible-budget variance, 9,500SF U		

2. The flexible-budget allowance for any *variable* cost is the *same as* (is equal to) the total standard quantity allowed for the good units produced x the standard price.

The budget allowance under standard costing for variable costs always depends on *output*, the units produced. Therefore, the budget for 4,000 units is, as shown above, 4,000 units x 1 1/2 hours x 30SF = 180,000SF. For 5,000 units, the budgetary allowance would be 5,000 units x 1 1/2 hours x 30SF = 225,000SF. Note again that a budget can be established *after the fact* – after the number of units produced is known.

8-40 (30-50 min.)

1. Department Performance Report
Direct Labor and Variable Overhead

Actual hours	5,700
Standard hours allowed, 2/3 hour x 8,100 units	5,400
Excess hours	300

	Actual Costs Incurred	Budget Based on 5,400 Standard Direct Labor Hours Hours Allowed for 8,100 Good Units Produced	Flexible Budget Variance to be Explained
Direct labor	$28,785	$28,350	$435F
Variable overhead:			
Lubricants @$.60	$ 2,940	$ 3,240	$300F
Other supplies @$.30	1,845	1,620	225U
Rework @$.60	3,690	3,240	450U
Other indirect labor @ $1.50	8,550	8,100	450U
Total variable overhead	$17,025	$16,200	$825U

2. **Summary explanation:**

	Incurred: Actual Hours x Actual Price	Flexible Budget: Actual Hours x x Expected Price	Flexible Budget: Standard Hours Allowed x Expected Price
Direct labor	5,700 hrs. x $5.05 = $28,785	5,700 hrs. x $5.25 = $29,925	5,400 hrs. x $5.25 = $28,350

5,700 x $.20 = Price variance, $1,140F	300 x $5.25 = Usage variance, $1,575U
Flexible-budget variance, $435U	

Variable overhead	$17,100 less spending variance = $17,100 - $75F = $17,025	5,700 hrs. x $3.00 = $17,100	5,400 hrs. x $3.00 = $16,200

Spending var. = flexible-budget var. - usage var. = $825 U - $900 U = $75 F	Efficiency variance = $17,100 - $16,200 = $900 U
Flexible-budget variance, $825U	

3. The subdivision of the budget variance for variable overhead into *spending* and *efficiency* variances is similar to the split of the total direct labor variance into a *price* variance and a *usage* variance.

The efficiency variance for variable overhead measures the extra overhead costs (or savings) incurred solely because direct labor usage exceeded (or was less than) the standard direct labor hours allowed. When variable overhead is closely related to labor time, fluctuations in overhead costs should correspond with variations in labor time. Both the labor usage and overhead efficiency variances are measured by multiplying a standard price times the difference between actual hours and standard hours allowed.

The variable overhead *spending* variance is similar to the labor *price* variance, but its causal factors encompass more than price changes alone. Other causes include poor budget estimates for one or more individual overhead items, variation in attention and control regarding individual costs, and erratic behavior of specific overhead items that have been squeezed for convenience into a budget formula that assumes strictly variable behavior and relation to one volume base – labor hours. For example, material handling within the factory (getting material to the workbench) is more closely related to goods *started* during a period than to standard hours allowed for work done.

8-41 (30-40 min.)

1. Material price variance = ($5.50 - $5.30) x 28,000 = $5,600 F
   Material usage variance = $5.50 x (27,000 - (60 x 430)) = $6,600 U

   Labor rate variance = ($15.90 - $16.00) x 660 = $66 F
   Labor usage variance = $16.00 x (660 - (1.5 x 430)) = $240 U

   Overhead flexible budget variance = $5,320 - (($5.76 x 430) + $2,808)
   = $35.20U

2. The person in charge of purchasing saved $5,600 by purchasing direct materials for $.20 below standard cost. However, more of the material was used, causing an unfavorable variance of $6,600. If the excess usage was caused by the purchase of low-quality materials, the net effect was an unfavorable variance of $1,000.

   There was a small savings of $66 because the average wage rate was $.10 below standard. However, more than the standard amount of labor was used, costing $240. If the entire excess usage was caused by hiring lower quality (and therefore lower paid) workers, the net effect is $174 unfavorable.

   The excess labor might also have been related to the excess use of materials. If some processing is complete before the defective materials are identified, some labor would also be wasted in the process. Thus, the $240 unfavorable labor usage variance might be caused by the purchase of low quality materials.

   The overhead variance is not large, but it too is unfavorable; more overhead costs were incurred than would be expected for the production of 430 kayaks.

3. Suppose overhead varies with total labor hours. Then the overhead variance can be broken into and overhead efficiency variance and an overhead spending variance:

Var. OH/DLH = \$5.76 ÷ 1.5 = \$3.84

Overhead efficiency variance = \$3.84 x (660 - (1.5 x 430)) = \$57.60 U
Overhead spending variance = \$5,320 - ((\$3.84 x 660) + \$2,808)= \$22.40 F

The unfavorable overhead efficiency variance indicates that \$57.60 of overhead costs were incurred because of the excess use of labor. Whatever caused the extra labor hours also caused this variance. Control of overhead itself was good, as shown by the favorable \$22.40 overhead spending variance.

Note: None of the variances indicate <u>why</u> actual costs differed from standard costs. The variances point toward possible causes and lead managers to ask the right questions about possible causes. The explanations above are possible causes, but they cannot be known for sure until managers do further exploration.

8-42 (15-20 min.)

1. **Direct Materials:**

Price variance = ($7.80 - $8.00) x 2,775 = $555F

Usage variance = (2,775 - 2,700) x $8 = $600U

Total direct materials variance = $21,645 - (900 x $24)
= $21,645 - $21,600 = $45U

Overhead:

	Actual Results at Actual Prices	Flexible Budget for Actual Output Achieved	Flexible-Budget Variances
Supplies	$ 2,125	$ 2,250	$125F
Power	1,612	1,572	40U
Rent and other building services	2,775	2,815	40F
Factory labor	1,625	1,500	125U
Depreciation	4,500	4,500	0
Total overhead	$12,637	$12,637	$ 0

2. Ohio Precision Machine does not account separately for the price (rate) and quantity of labor. Therefore, labor price and usage variances cannot be computed. Many highly automated companies account for labor this way. Because labor is a small proportion of cost in some automated manufacturing processes, it is not worth the cost to monitor price and efficiency effects. Ohio Precision Machine treats labor as a fixed overhead cost. Therefore, the company does not expect to adjust the amount of labor used as volume changes. The actual labor cost is compared to a fixed monthly budget of $1,500.

8-43 (10-20 min.)

Raw material	(a) Initial mix	(b) Allowance for reduction	(c) Required quantity a ÷ b*	(d) Unit cost	Standard material cost (c x d)
Altium	24 kg	.8	30 kg	$2.05	$ 61.50
Bollium	19.2 ltr	.8	24 ltr	1.90	45.60
Credix	10 kg	1.0	10 kg	2.80	28.00
Standard material cost – 10-liter container					$135.10

* Instead of being divided by the 0.8, the first two items could be multiplied by 1.25 to obtain the same answer.

8-44 (25-35 min.) This problem is not straightforward. It is complicated by the need to include an allowance for defective units in the standard costs. Note that many accountants now object to standard costing because of the "acceptability" of allowing for defects in the standards.

Direct Materials	
Pounds in final product	2.8
Allowance for normal scrap	.4
Total pounds per finished unit	3.2
Allowance for defective units	.8*
Total pounds per good unit	4.0
Standard price per pound	$12.00**
Standard direct material cost per good unit	$48.00

*Defective units = 20% x total units or 25% of good units; Material allowance for defectives = .25 x 3.2 lb. = .8 lb.

**$11.25 price of materials + $.75 shipping and handling

Direct Labor

Hours of actual machining per unit	4.00
Allowance for nonproductive time	1.00*
Total hours per finished unit	5.00
Allowance for defective units	1.25**
Total hours per good unit	6.25
Standard rate per hour	$ 29.20***
Standard direct labor cost per good unit	$182.50

*For every 4 hours worked there is 1 hour of nonproductive time.

**Defective units = 20% x total units or 25% of good units;
Direct labor allowance for defectives = .25 x 5 hr = 1.25 hr.

***Basic rate	$22.00
Fringe benefits	5.00
Payroll taxes	2.20
Total labor rate	$29.20

8-45 (50-75 min.)

1. a. Sales-activity variance = Budgeted unit contribution margin x Difference between the master budget sales in units and the actual sales in units

= \$9.20 x (9,000 - 8,000)

= \$9,200, unfavorable

This variance is labeled as a sales-activity variance because it quantifies the impact on income of the deviation from an original sales target – while holding price and usage factors constant. Of course, the failure to reach target sales may be traceable to a number of causes beyond the control of the marketing force, including strikes, material shortages, and storms.

b. The budget formulas in Exhibit 8-2 are the basis for the following answers. The alert student will note that budgeted contribution margin and operating income are in the 8,000-unit column of Exhibit 8-2.

Budgeted contribution margin = \$9.20 x 8,000 = \$73,600
Budgeted operating income
= \$73,600 - \$70,000 fixed costs = \$ 3,600
Budgeted direct material = \$10.00 x 8,000 = \$80,000
Budgeted direct labor = \$8.00 x 8,000 = \$64,000

2.

	Cost Incurred Actual Inputs x Actual Prices	Flexible Budget Based on Actual Inputs x Expected Prices	Flexible Budget Based on Standard Inputs Allowed for Actual Output Achieved x Expected Prices
Direct Materials	42,000 lbs. x $1.85 = $77,700	42,000 lbs. x $2.00 = $84,000	(8,000 units x 5) x $2.00 = $80,000
	42,000 x ($1.85-$2.00) = Price variance, $6,300F		(42,000 - 40,000) x $2.00 = Usage variance, $4,000U
	Flexible-budget variance, $2,300F		
Direct Labor	4,125 hrs. x $16.40 = $67,650	4,125 hrs. x $16.00 = $66,000	(8,000 units x .5 hrs. x $16.00) or (4,000 hrs. x $16) = $64,000
	4,125 x ($16.40-$16.00) = Price variance, $1,650U		(4,125 - 4,000) x $16.00 = Usage variance, $2,000U
	Flexible-budget variance, $3,650U		

3. Whether the variance analysis in (2) would change depends on how the information system is designed. In many organizations, price variances for materials are isolated at the most logical control point – time of purchase rather than time of use. In turn, the production or operating departments that later use the materials are always charged at some predetermined so-called budget or standard unit price, never at actual unit prices. Under this procedure the price variance analysis would be conducted in the purchasing department and the usage variance analysis in the production department. This represents a slight modification of the approach in (2) as follows:

Control Point	Cost Incurred: Actual Inputs x Actual Price	Flexible Budget Based on Actual Inputs x Expected Price	Flexible Budget Based on Standard Inputs Allowed for Actual Output Achieved x Expected Price
Purchasing Department	60,000 lbs. x $1.85 = $111,000	60,000 lbs. x $2.00 = $120,000	
	60,000 x ($1.85 - $2.00) = Price variance, $9,000F		
Production Department		42,000 lbs. x $2 = $84,000	40,000 lbs. x $2 = $80,000
		(42,000 - 40,000) x $2.00 = Usage variance, $4,000U	

Note that the usage variance is the same in parts (2) and (3).

8-46 (30 min.) The solution is given in the textbook after the problem itself.

8-47 (30-45 min.) The computations of variances are straightforward, although the context is different from that in the text. The explanation of variances is potentially complex and difficult.

1. Nursing price variance = Actual cost - (Actual hours x Standard rate)
= $31,050 - (2,075 x $14)
= $31,050 - $29,050 = $2,000U

Nursing usage variance = (Actual hours - Standard hours allowed) x Standard rate
= [2,075 - (4,000 x .5)] x $14
= 75 x $14 = $1,050U

2. Efficiency variance
= (Actual hours - Std. hours allowed) x Variable overhead rate
= (2,075 - 2,000) x $10* = $750U

Spending variance = Actual cost - Actual hours x Variable overhead rate
= $20,320 - (2,075 x $10)
= $20,320 - $20,750 = $430F

*19,000 ÷ 1,900 = $10

3. The nursing price and usage variances are unfavorable. This may be due to inefficient scheduling. More nurses are being used than are required, and a higher proportion than is normal are in the high wage rate categories.

But this might be exactly what is expected when volume increases. The nurses who perform the extra work that physicians usually handle are probably highly skilled, and, therefore, are paid more than average. Thus, the average pay rate for nurses increases. Further, as additional patients are seen, nearly the entire added load may be borne by nurses. Why? Because physicians may already be at capacity. Therefore, although at a volume of 3,800 patients nurses average .5 hours per patient, they put in more than .5 hours with each additional patient because they pick up some physician tasks as well as their own normal tasks. Suppose a physician spends an average of .5 hours on each patient case. Since additional physician time may not be available, nurses might average a full hour for each additional patient, the .5 hour that they normally spend plus the .5 hour a physician usually spends.

It appears that Dr. McCaffrey has controlled supplies and other variable costs quite well. Of the $1,320 unfavorable variance, $1,000 is due to the added volume. An additional $750 is due to the use of extra nursing hours; that is, the variable overhead efficiency variance arises solely due to the use of extra nursing hours. The spending for supplies and other variable overhead is $430 less than expected. This reflects both price and quantity effects for the supplies and other variable overhead.

8-48 (35-45 min.)

1. Printing department costs for the first month:

	A	B	C
	Actual Cost Incurred: Actual Inputs x Actual Prices	Flexible Budget Based on Standard Inputs Allowed for Actual Outputs Achieved x Expected Prices	Master Budget
Printing	$50,000	40,000 pages x $1.00 = $40,000	35,000 pages x $1.00 = $35,000

Flexible-budget variance (A - B) = $50,000 - $40,000 = $10,000 U	Printing activity variance (B - C) = $40,000 - $35,000 = $5,000 U
Static budget variance (A - C) $50,000 - $35,000 = $15,000 U	

2. The static budget was inaccurate for the reasons given in the problem: all types of jobs requested more printing, and both government and central administration jobs used more four-color and graphics printing. Printing activity was higher, and the mix of types of jobs differed from what was expected. Likely explanations are that (1) the $1.00 charge per page is an average printing cost, but costs per page can differ greatly with relative complexity, (2) the printing department has not identified the appropriate cost drivers to enable it to charge for the costs the department incurs. All the users recognize that four-color, graphic printing is a bargain, and simple printing is too expensive. As a result, everyone wishes to use more of the low-price, high complexity printing.

3. a. The ABC analysis is an attempt to measure the costs of printing complexity. If the analysis is accurate, then four-color printing jobs will cost at least $1.30 per page ($.30 + $1.00) plus pre-press costs. Simple, one-color jobs will cost only $.30 per page. Costs charged for the various jobs will reflect their complexity and should result in more efficient use of printing services. Since the costs of different types of jobs will vary under this new system, it is critical that the ABC estimates are accurate. Methods for measuring cost behavior are discussed in Chapter 3.

b. These cost estimates are themselves averages per type of cost because some portions of the printing department costs are fixed in the short run. There is some controversy over whether these fixed costs should be spread over normal or expected levels of cost driver activity. Not "unitizing" these costs preserves the distinction between fixed and variable cost behavior. Under this approach, fixed costs would be recovered by an annual or monthly charge based on expected usage. An objection is that this merely passes the fixed cost problem along to the line units who are selling products or services to external customers. An alternative approach is to unitize these costs over expected or normal cost driver activity and charge users as if all costs were variable. If cost driver activity expectations are accurate, there should not be significant static budget variances. Large errors in forecasting, however, will lead to large budgeting errors because total fixed costs charged will not equal total fixed costs incurred.

c. Costs of government jobs:

	Old System	ABC System
27,500 pages	@$1/page = $27,500	@$.30/page =$8,250
27,500 use color	–	@ $1.00/color page = $27,500
Total cost	$27,500	$35,750

8-49 (60 min. or more)

The purpose of this exercise is to understand the difficulty of setting standard costs for even simple products or services. For many products or services, identifying the direct material and direct labor inputs may not be hard, but even identifying the overhead support can be a challenge. Students are likely to make various assumptions, which can lead to very different standard costs in all cost categories.

Requirements 2 and 3 also lead to considerationd (albeit it implicitly) of many of the behavioral issues organizations may have in setting standards. Different managers have different objectives and different levels of knowledge. These must be combined into a single standard cost estimate.

If class time allows, it may be useful to have one or more groups present their standard costs to the class and describe how they were determined. The class may have suggestions that the group failed to consider – possibly some implicit assumptions that would not necessarily hold true.

CHAPTER 9
Management Control Systems and Responsibility Accounting

9-A1 (20 min.)

Admittedly, GL Interiors may have a legitimate claim against the supplier, but for the sake of discussion assume that the supplier has a smart attorney and would win the case.

The penalty of $30,000 should be charged to the purchasing department. Leesa Martinson may have done everything in her power to see that the special part was delivered on time, but she must realize that she is the one who is responsible for purchasing necessary material when it is needed. Martinson may not have control over her suppliers and subsequent delivery, but it is her responsibility, and hers alone as far as GL Interiors is concerned, to have the purchased parts when they are needed. (She is the one person in the organization who has the most influence over delivery.) Everybody makes mistakes. (The important point is to minimize the number of mistakes and also to understand fully that the extensive control reflected in responsibility accounting is the necessary balance to the great freedom of action that individual executives are given.)

Other questions to discuss are: Did the sales department behave responsibly in accepting the order with penalty? Is it conceivable that a careful statistical study of delays by suppliers would permit the development of an "expected amount" of penalty to be incurred in a probabilistic sense, which then could be budgeted as part of the purchasing department's costs?

Discussions of this problem have again and again revealed a tendency among students (and among accountants and managers) to "fix the blame" – as if the variances arising from a responsibility accounting system should pinpoint misbehavior and provide answers. The point is that no accounting system or variances can provide answers ipso facto. However, variances can ask questions. In this case, in deciding where the penalty should be assigned, the student might inquire who should be asked in this situation – not who should be blamed.

9-A2 (30-40 min.) See Exhibit 9-A2.

9-A3 (15-20 min.)

1. Without adjusting for inflation, it appears that both companies had large increases in productivity in terms of revenues per employee.

	1992		1998	
National Food and Beverage	$\frac{(\$7,658,000,000)}{(75,900)}$	= $100,896	$\frac{(\$9,667,000,000)}{(76,200)}$	=$126,864
Lakeland Foods	$\frac{(\$5,924,000,000)}{(56,600)}$	= $104,664	$\frac{(6,764,000,000)}{(54,800)}$	= $123,431

However, the 1992 productivity measures should be expressed in 1998 dollars for comparability:

	1992		1998
National Food and Beverage	$\frac{(1.2 \times \$7,658,000,000)}{(75,900)}$	= $121,075	126,864*
Lakeland Foods	$\frac{(1.2 \times \$5,924,000,000)}{(56,600)}$	= $125,597	123,431*

*Same as above for 1998.

2. Using the productivity measures that are correctly adjusted for inflation, we see that Lakeland had a drop in productivity between 1992 and 1998. In contrast, National increased its productivity by $126,864 - $121,075 = $5,789 per employee, an increase of 5,789 ÷ 121,075 = 4.8%. Although Lakeland had a decrease in number of employees and National had an increase, the larger sales increase for National led to a higher productivity number. While Lakeland had higher productivity in 1992, National has the higher productivity in 1998.

EXHIBIT 9-A2 Answers are in thousands of dollars.

	Company as a Whole	Breakdown into Two Divisions		Breakdown of Denver Division			Breakdown of Colorado Springs Division			
		Denver Division	Colorado Springs Division	Not Allocated	Downtown	Littleton	Not Allocated	Downtown	Plaza	Airport
Net Sales	6,000	2,400	3,600		1,800	600		1,800	900	900
Variable costs:										
Cost of merchandise sold	3,750	1,500	2,125		1,125	375		1,125	562.5	562.5
Variable operating expenses	480	210	270		180	30		180	45	45
Total variable costs	4,230	1,710	2,520		1,305	405		1,305	607.5	607.5
Contribution margin	1,770	690	1,080		495	195		495	292.5	292.5
Less: Fixed costs controllable by segment managers	720	251	469	97	94	60	135	94	120	120
Contribution controllable by segment managers	1,050	439	611	(97)	401	135	(135)	401	172.5	172.5
Less: Fixed costs controllable by others	372	112	260	28	56	28	52	52	78	78
Contribution by segments	678	327	351	(125)	345	107	(187)	349	94.5	94.5
Less: Unallocated costs	78									
Income before income taxes	600									

9-B1 (15-20 min.)

1. It is not possible to determine the validity of Roberta Dahl's claim. It would be valid only if, on a proportional basis, the number of unidentified rejects caused by the other departments were greater than their proportionate number of identified rejects. Although the claims cannot be substantiated, a legitimate issue has been raised. The rejects charged to all the departments contain amounts not clearly attributable to the respective departments. This violates the concept that performance measures should not contain items outside the control of the manager. Further, a manager's effort to control the variation will be influenced by the result she can get from her actions. The fact that some of the variation could be caused by other departments will reduce the amount of the reported rejects within her control.

2. There are two solutions to this problem. First, remove the apportioned rejects from the reports and charge the managers with only the rejects identified with their department. Second, if the number of unidentified rejects is large and represents a large dollar value (which could be reduced if adequate information as to cause were available), then inspection at the end of each department should be considered.

9-B2 (30-35 min.)

1.

ATLANTIC COAST RAILROAD
Income Statement
For the Year Ended December 31, 19X8
(in thousands of dollars)

	Railroad as a Whole	Company Breakdown into Two Divisions: Freight Traffic	Company Breakdown into Two Divisions: Passenger Traffic	Possible Breakdown of Passenger Traffic Only: Not Allocable	Division No.1	Division No.2	Division No.3
Revenue....................	80,000	72,000	8,000	-	4,000	3,200	800
Variable costs.........	45,000	36,000	9,000	-	3,300	2,800	2,900
Contribution margin......................	35,000	36,000	(1,000)	-	700	400	(2,100)
Separable discretionary fixed costs..........................	8,000	7,600	400	80	240	60	20
Contribution controllable by segment managers.....	27,000	28,400	(1,400)	(80)	460	340	(2,120)
Separable committed costs..................	25,000	22,500	2,500	500	1,500	350	150
Contribution by segments................	2,000	5,900	(3,900)	(580)	(1,040)	(10)	(2,270)
Unallocated costs..........................	750						
Income before income taxes.........	1,250						

2. The incremental costs of running such sightseeing tours can be identified with much more confidence than in many other instances. Net income will be improved by the excess of tour revenue over such

costs; routine allocations of other operating costs and indirect costs do not seem relevant to the decision to run such tours. Those railroads that do not run such tours either:

(a) Do not expect incremental revenue to exceed incremental costs; or
(b) Even if profits could be enhanced, may not want to engage in any activity that will improve short-run profits because their long-run objective may be to reduce their passenger business as much as possible.

3. If the entire $60,000 of separable discretionary fixed costs can be avoided by dropping No. 2, net income would decrease by the controllable contribution of $340,000. If not, net income would decrease by between $340,000 and $400,000. In contrast, net income might increase by the amount of the separable committed costs that might be saved.

9-B3 (20-30 min.)

1. (a) Prevention cost – This includes costs incurred to prevent the production of defective products, such as programs to train personnel, simplified production processes, and improved production planning. These costs have increased between 19X5 and 19X7, both in absolute amount and as a percent of total quality cost. Apparently more attention is now being given to the prevention of defects.

   (b) Appraisal cost – These costs are incurred to identify defective products. They include testing, inspection, and various other quality control procedures. Although these costs were a larger percentage of total quality costs in 19X7 than 19X5, their total amount has increased in almost direct proportion to the increase in product cost. Therefore, appraisal procedures have probably remained much the same as in 19X5.

   (c) Internal failure cost – These are the costs of items scrapped and the costs of rework to correct defects in products. Although up slightly as a percentage of total quality costs, these costs are down significantly in absolute amount. Despite higher product costs, significantly less is being spent on defective units. Most likely this means that the money spent on prevention has decreased the number of defective units being scrapped or reworked.

   (d) External failure cost – These are costs caused by delivery of defective units, including warranty expenses and sales returns and allowances. There has been a dramatic decrease in this cost, probably because fewer defective units are being delivered to customers.

2. The overall costs of quality are much lower in 19X7 than in 19X5. The decrease comes primarily in two categories, internal and external failure costs. Dayton Manufacturing is following a popular approach

to modern quality control: preventing defects is less costly than identifying and correcting them. By increasing spending on prevention of defects, Dayton has reduced overall quality costs.

In addition to the costs in the quality cost report, companies should be concerned with potential lost sales if customers receive a large proportion of defective units. Dayton's decrease in external failure costs probably means that fewer defective units are being delivered, and therefore there will also be smaller opportunity costs due to lost sales.

9-1 A management control system aids and coordinates the process of making decisions and motivates individuals throughout the organization to act in the best interests of the organization.

9-2 Goals without performance measures may not be completely useless, but performance measure greatly enhance the achievement of goals. They provide signals to managers about whether goals are being achieved.

9-3 Some typical corporate objectives other than profit are (a) growth, (b) quality, (c) market domination, (d) social service, (e) prestige, and (f) productivity

9-4 Key success factors are those aspects of performance that are essential to achieve if the organization is to be successful. Management examines an organization's strategic plan and major goals and decides what factors are most important to achieving its goals. These are the key success factors.

9-5 Examples of sacrificing long-range goals to short-run performance gain are:

1. Wasteful disposal of inventory to improve the turnover rate.
2. Wasting prime materials by adhering to restrictive goals for by-products.
3. Maintaining peak personnel efficiency by refusing to rotate assignments for long-range flexibility and individual improvement.
4. Postponing desirable maintenance and repairs.

9-6 Three types of responsibility centers are:

- Cost center - responsibility for control of costs
- Profit center - responsibility for both costs and revenues
- Investment center - responsibility for both profit and investment.

9-7 Investment centers go a step farther than profit centers. Both measure profits, but an investment center also compares that profit to investment using measures such as return on investment or residual income.

9-8 Performance evaluation provides feedback to managers about how well they are achieving their goals. Goal congruence and motivation are two aspects important to achieving an organization's goals through managers' actions and decisions. Goal congruence is achieved if managers seek the goals sought by top management – that is, managers aim in the direction that is best for the organization. Managerial effort is exertion toward a goal. A good performance evaluation system provides the managers with appropriate goals and the incentive to achieve the goals.

9-9 A major purpose of management control systems is to motivate managers. To provide proper motivation, accountants must predict the effect of the system on managers, essentially a behavioral exercise.

9-10 Good performance measures will:

- Relate to the organization's goals.
- Balance long-term and short-term considerations.
- Reflect key activities of the organization.
- Be affected by managers' actions.
- Be easily understood by managers.
- Be used in evaluating and rewarding managers.
- Be reasonably objective and easily measured.
- Be used consistently.

9-11 Managers are expected to explain the entire profit of a profit center. They have the best information to assess the causes of the profit. But they should be evaluated on controllable profit. The objective in evaluation is to measure the effect of the manager's actions on the profit, and changes in profit due to factors beyond a manager's control do not indicate anything about the impact of the manager's actions.

9-12 A balanced scorecard is a performance report that contains measures of all the key financial and nonfinancial variables that are important for a company to prosper.

9-13 Some nonfinancial measures of performance are percentage of products delivered on time, number of defective units produced, setup time for a batch of production, average time from order to delivery, and pounds of output per direct labor hour.

9-14 No. Variable costs vary in direct proportion to output, and fixed costs do not. However, a fixed cost may be controllable by some person or group, and is almost always controllable in the long run. Variable costs may be uncontrollable for very short periods once a decision has been made to perform some activity.

9-15 No. By deducting separable discretionary costs from the contribution margin a better measure of short-run performance is obtained, which might be called the "short-run performance margin."

9-16 Examples of segments are divisions, territories, branches, product lines, and stores.

9-17 Managers should be judged on how well they attain their currently attainable objectives, whereas the subunit should be judged on its performance as an economic investment.

9-18 No. The contribution margin format does not ignore items that are not a part of the contribution margin. Rather, it separates costs by their behavior (variable and fixed) and by who can control the cost.

9-19 The four categories are:

(a) prevention – costs incurred to prevent the production of defective products or services,
(b) appraisal – costs incurred to identify defective products or services,
(c) internal failure – costs of defective products that are scrapped or reworked, and
(d) external failure – costs caused by delivery of defective products or services to customers.

9-20 Many companies are finding that it is less costly to prevent defects than it is to identify and correct defects.

9-21 Quality, cycle time, and productivity are related because improvements in cycle time and productivity are dependent upon high quality processes and inputs. High quality depends on good product (or service) and process designs, highly trained employees, and commitment to continuous improvement. These factors also lead to improvements in cycle time and productivity.

9-22 Control of nonfinancial performance requires setting objectives, measuring results, and evaluation of results by comparing outcomes to expectations (or objectives). This is the same sequence indicated by control of financial performance.

9-23 Three measures of productivity are:

(a) $$\frac{\text{Standard direct labor hours allowed for good output achieved}}{\text{Actual direct labor hours of input}}$$

(b) $$\frac{\text{Sales revenue}}{\text{Direct labor cost}}$$

(c) $$\frac{\text{Sales revenue}}{\text{Number of employees}}$$

9-24 Comparing profitability measures over time is complicated by changes in the production process and by inflation. Changes in the production process that substitute one input for another and make productivity with respect to the replaced input appear to increase, but productivity with respect to the input that is increased will appear to decrease. Further, if either input or output (but not both) are measured in monetary terms, inflation can distort productivity measures across time.

9-25 Yes. There are several reasons that developing control systems in nonprofit organizations is more difficult than in profit-seeking organizations, including:

(a) There are often multiple goals, and often the goals are not explicit.
(b) The types of people in nonprofit organizations, frequently professionals, are often less receptive to the demands imposed by control systems.
(c) There is no single, measurable objective such as profit.
(d) The relationship of inputs to outputs is hard to specify.
(e) A large portion of the costs are discretionary fixed costs, which are the hardest to manage through a control system.

<u>9-26</u> (15-25 min.)

This question cannot be answered directly from the text. It requires students to think about an issue closely related to those in the text.

An article in *FE: The Magazine for Financial Executives* (Vol. 1, No. 8) addresses these questions. After studying several large firms that encourage innovation, the author concluded that such firms had not abandoned sound financial controls or even watered them down. "The companies surveyed had achieved superior financial results and had sound financial systems in place ...The CFO [Chief Financial Officer] in each firm knew the key financial factors needed for the company's success, and had a financial control system to carefully track that success" (p.36).

Two structure-oriented and five process-oriented suggestions were made to adapt a financial control system to foster innovation. Regarding structure:

1. "The primary focus should be on setting up profit centers. A decentralized organization allows for expanding profit center accounting. Profit center accountability in turn permits more discretion and enhances innovation. Our study indicated that flexibility and entrepreneurial decision-making can be fostered by a well-structured profit center reporting system."

2. "A second structural factor in a large, decentralized organization committed to innovation calls for divisional financial executives to have a direct, solid-line reporting to the divisional general manager. However, a solid-line reporting of divisional financial executives to a corporate senior financial executive virtually precludes an entrepreneurial spirit at the division level."

The process-related suggestions are these:

1. Planning – "The successful entrepreneurial firms...have a well-developed strategy...The strategy is well understood through all levels of management...Highly structured, precisely quantified planning is not done...Planning is directed toward allowing flexibility and changes dictated by the changing business environment."

2. Budgeting – "An annual budget, with interim breakouts, is well accepted as essential for any successful business. An entrepreneur is not greatly burdened by and accepts the need for stating in numbers his or her program for the coming 12 months."

3. Resource allocation – "Approval systems for capital expenditures frequently require extensive reporting to higher levels of management...The CFO should measure the needs for capital controls against the driving force of an innovation entrepreneur. Achieving a fair balance is not easy."

4. Reporting – "A profit center seeking to be independent and innovative can lose its thrust if it perceives that every action is being followed by corporate headquarters through the monthly financial reporting. The challenge is to provide a system that maintains financial strength while allowing the flexibility and independence that produce superior results through innovation and entrepreneurism."

5. Analyzing operating results – "One factor in this area stood out: the frequent reference to comparisons of actual results to budget, giving full weight to noncontrollable factors and to changed conditions."

9-27 (10-15 min.)

A municipality is similar to many other organizations. When decisions are delegated to middle-managers, top management should be informed about activities and motivate managers to act in the best interests of the municipality. A responsibility accounting system can be a great aid. Identifying responsibility centers is an important first step. Developing a system to report the financial results of each responsibility center enables top management to know the city's financial situation. In 1975, New York City officials did not know exactly why the desperate financial situation had developed. IFMS allows them to anticipate financial demands. It also allows a check on managers who might tend to be fiscally irresponsible. Performance evaluation can be affected by the financial results of a responsibility center. Of course, non-financial matters also affect evaluations. But New York City provides a good case study in the consequences of not identifying and measuring the financial responsibilities of managers.

9-28 (20 min.)

Plant maintenance should be charged the standard rate of $13.00. The $7.00 hourly rate difference ($20.00 - $13.00) could be charged to Loss from Idle Capacity or some similar account, or from a control viewpoint, the $7.00 rate difference should be charged to the individual who is primarily responsible for deciding to retain the welders rather than to lay them off.

Charging plant maintenance the standard rate of $13.00 assumes that the welders are qualified to do the normal plant maintenance work. It is up to the plant maintenance supervisor to get $13.00 worth of work from the welders. The $7.00 hourly rate difference should certainly not be charged to plant maintenance since the regular help need be paid only $13.00.

Because the welders must be retained in order to maintain high quality workmanship, and perhaps the reputation and sales position of the company, a conceptual case could even be made for treating the $7.00 as an asset because the decision to keep high-priced personnel implies a future cost saving, possibly in hiring and training new employees, or a future revenue enhancement. This is rarely done in practice.

9-29 (35 min.)

1. Compensation = (¥45,000+¥58,000+.05 x (actual-quota), if quota is met)
(¥45,000, if quota is not met)

	Clerk		
	A	B	C
January	¥ 45,000	¥103,000	¥178,000
February	175,750	103,000	45,000
March	211,000	45,000	398,500
April	45,000	103,250	45,000

2. Notice the wide variation in month-to-month sales, which are under the control of the salesclerks, and the absurdity of the method of figuring sales quotas in relation to this salary bonus plan. The salesclerks would naturally be tempted to manipulate their sales to maximize their personal income.

Realizing the above mentioned points and the hopelessness of continually increasing sales by 3% a month, the salesclerks would try to just meet their quota or surpass it by a substantial amount.

With the relatively small-volume sales territory, salesclerk B would just try to meet his or her quota several months running and then have a low volume month to bring the quota down in preparation for another run of months of just meeting the quota.

Salesclerks A and C, with larger volume territories, are better off financially to surpass their sales quotas by substantial amounts and then have a slack month to bring down their quotas in preparation for a large bonus the following month.

Given sales quotas of 103% of the previous month's actual sales, the bonus of ¥58,000 plus 5% commission on sales over quota is extremely high and provides incentive for manipulation rather than overall sales effort.

The bonus system should be eliminated, and the base salary should be increased. If an incentive is to be provided, the quotas should reflect a normal month's sales and not be related directly to the previous month's sales. Any bonus payment should be small in relation to basic compensation and should be related to actual sales effort rather than to clever manipulation. Moreover, any bonus plan should be tied to performance over a longer time span than one month. A yearly span would not tempt nearly as much manipulation.

9-30 (10-15 min.) Students will suggest many different goals and measures in each category. This solution lists one possibility for each of the five areas.

Customer Satisfaction -
Goal: Reduce customer waiting time
Measure: Average time from check-in until seeing a physician

Efficient use of lab tests -
Goal: Reduce unnecessary lab tests
Measure: Lab tests per patient (possibly by diagnosis)

Usage of physician time -
Goal: Decrease time physicians spend on administrative and clerical tasks
Measure: Patients seen per hour of physician time or, better, percentage of physician time spent with patients

Maintain state-of-the-art facilities -
Goal: Provide patients with access to latest technology
Measure: Amount of capital expenditures or, better, percent of equipment below standard

Overall financial performance -
Goal: ROI exceeding the 75th percentile in the industry
Measure: Return on investment

This is a good time to discuss the cost/benefit tradeoff with possible performance measures. Sometimes the best performance metric is just too costly to measure. For example, use of physician time is better measured by the percentage of their working time that is spent seeing patients than by number of patients per hour of physician time. But the better measure requires physicians to log the time they spend on various activities. This may be too costly, both in terms of the time it takes and the resistance from physicians, so a less desirable surrogate such as patients per hour, might be used.

9-31 (15-20 min.)

Increasing sales activity can be related to increased number of new accounts; thus many stock brokerages set objectives for its brokers to make a set number of "cold calls" to solicit investments from potential clients. However, a large number of small accounts probably do not have the same impact on sales as a few large accounts. The brokerage firm must be careful not to divert its employees' energies so much to finding new accounts that research, analysis, and existing accounts are neglected. Service firms have found that it is much more profitable to retain existing customers than to find new customers. Therefore, customer retention has become a major objective, and performance is measured on activities that are believed to aid in retaining profitable customers. These measures include how quickly phones are picked up, how quickly inquiries are answered, accessibility of data bases, and so on.

9-32 (10-15 min.)

The figure on the next page can be used as both a solution to this exercise and point of further discussion by making a transparency or duplicating copies for students. It represents the current reality as espoused by "total-quality" guru Deming and attested to by most firms today. Note how the total cost of quality is higher for firms producing inferior quality products or services. Deming predicted this by pointing to the close relationship between quality and costs such as waste, rework, returns, lost sales, and inspection. Refer students to the boxed company examples in the text as examples of both approaches (theories) to quality.

In the TQM approach *all* phases of the company's operations are incorporated in the quality program. For example, the quality of incoming materials and parts is higher. This reduces (or eliminates) the need for appraisal (and associated costs), while failures that result from poor quality are also reduced. Another example of a win-win scenario is training

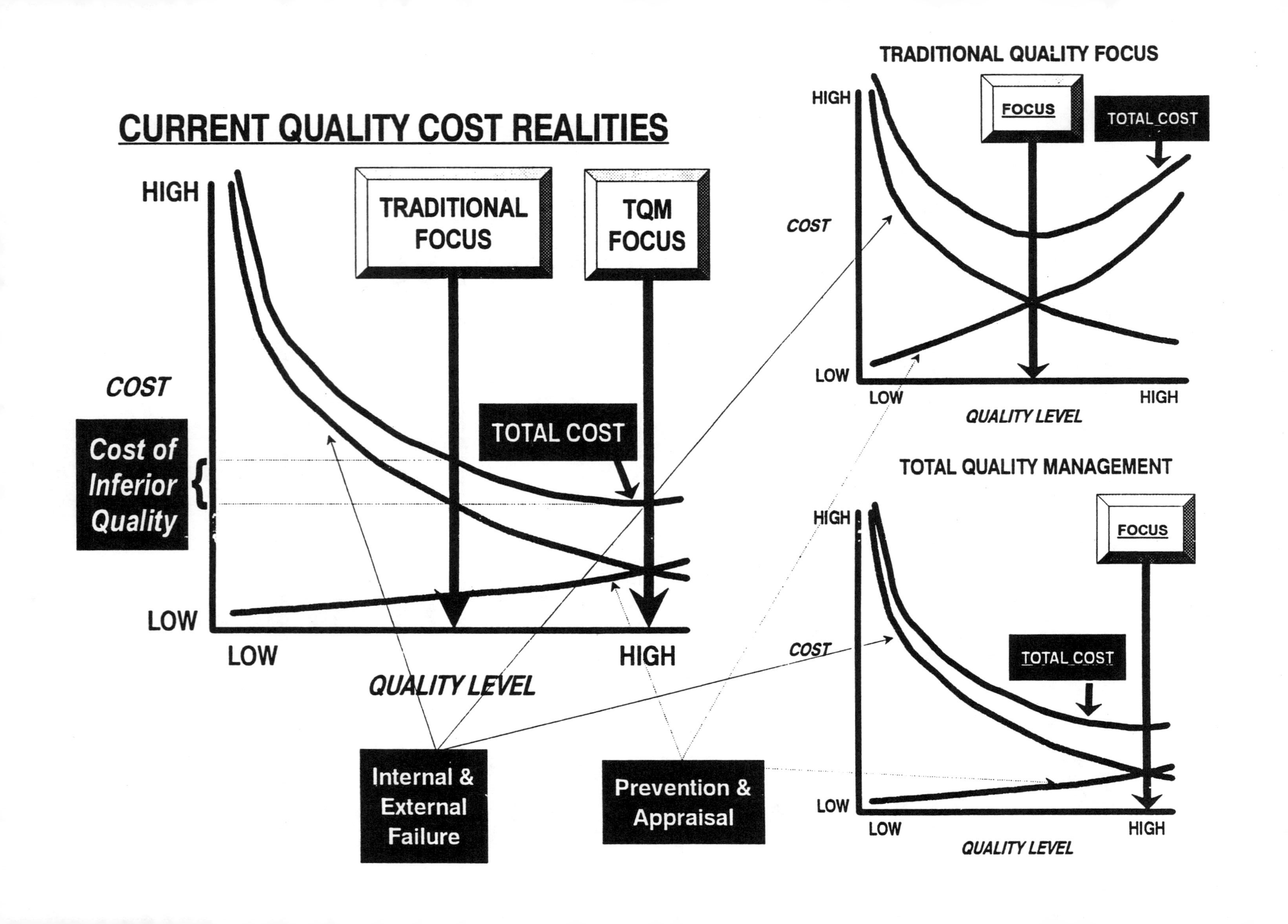

CURRENT QUALITY COST REALITIES
HIGH
COST
LOW
Cost of Inferior Quality
TRADITIONAL FOCUS
TQM FOCUS
TOTAL COST
LOW
HIGH
QUALITY LEVEL
Internal & External Failure
Prevention & Appraisal
TRADITIONAL QUALITY FOCUS
HIGH
COST
LOW
FOCUS
TOTAL COST
LOW
HIGH
QUALITY LEVEL
TOTAL QUALITY MANAGEMENT
HIGH
COST
LOW
FOCUS
TOTAL COST
LOW
HIGH
QUALITY LEVEL

employees to reduce errors resulting in cost savings from reduced inspection (appraisal) and internal and external failures. If the cost savings from reduced appraisal activity exceeds the training costs (prevention), the prevention and appraisal cost curve will shift downward while the internal and external failure costs also are lower.

9-33 (10-15 min.)

1. One trend is the overall upward trend in defective units. The overall rate of defective units has about doubled in the 8 weeks, from about .75% to 1.4%.

   A second trend is a weekly trend, with low defects on Monday and increasing each day of the week, with the most defects produced on Friday.

2. It is essential to arrest and reverse the overall trend toward more defective units. Even by the first week of this eight-week period, the defective rate was well above the target of .5%, and it grew each of the eight weeks. The control chart will not tell what actions are needed to reverse this trend, but it focuses attention on the problem and allows managers to explore potential solutions.

   The weekly pattern is also disturbing. There is no reason that defect rates must increase as the week goes on. Apparently employees come in refreshed on Monday and are quite attentive to quality. This attentiveness drops steadily until, by Friday, they don't seem to pay much attention to quality. Incentives for better quality late in the week might work, or the company may try changing the work patters so that employees are not bored, tired, or whatever else besets them by Friday.

9-34 (20-30 min.)

Week	Units completed	Total cycle time	Average cycle time
1	564	14,108	25.0
2	544	14,592	26.8
3	553	15,152	27.4
4	571	16,598	29.1
5	547	17,104	31.3
6	552	16,673	30.2

The cycle time objective was met only in the first week. After that, however, cycle time generally has steadily increased. With knowledge of the acceptable control limit, an analyst probably could determine within the third or fourth week that cycle time is tending to be out of control. Corrective action could have been initiated before increased cycle times lead to higher costs and possible difficulty in meeting schedules.

A control chart approach shows the increasing cycle time graphically:

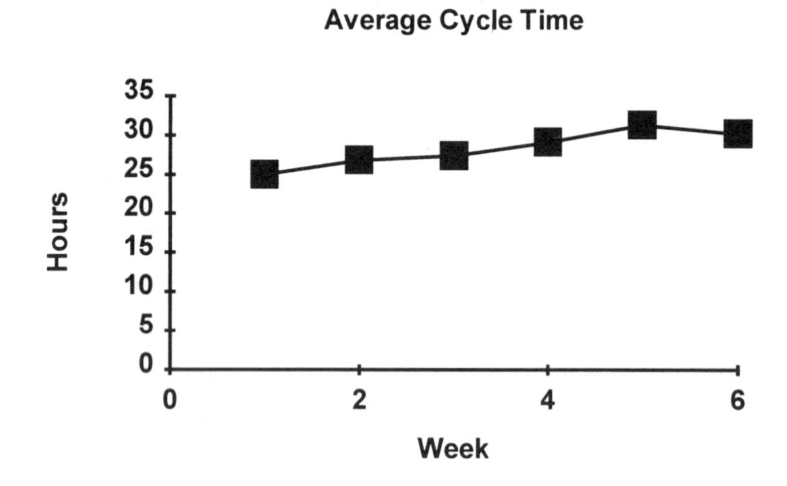

9-35 (20-35 min.)

The purpose of this problem is to force the student to recognize that measurements affect behavior and that accounting measurements tend to place too much focus on short-run results. An exhaustive study of the eight goals is impossible and unwarranted at this stage of the course. The aim is to provide an overview, a perspective on where accounting often fits in management control.

1. Students may add many alternative measurements in each of the following categories.

   a. Profitability. Total dollars of profit. Percentage of profit on sales. Rate of return on investment. Residual income. General Electric chose residual income, which is described in Chapter 10. The imputed interest rate should be established as closely as possible to the point at which discontinuance of the business would be considered. Using residual income, a manager maximizes an absolute amount (residual income) rather than a rate.

      Regardless of the alternative chosen, another question is whether the measurement should be based on historical costs, replacement costs, net realizable value, or some other alternative.

   b. Market position. Share of served markets. How is a market defined? For example, should the market consist of that served by the electric-range industry only? Or should it consist of all ranges, including gas ranges? Note that this area is important because a division could be showing handsome profitability and simultaneously be losing its share of the market.

   c. Productivity. This measure attempts to gauge efficiency. Productivity focuses on physical and/or financial relationships between inputs and outputs. Through the years, there have been various attempts, both by General Electric and others, to measure productivity for a division (as opposed to an individual worker or small cost center, where the measurement difficulties are less imposing). G.E. has changed its approach through the years, and it still has not found a completely satisfactory measure. As a rule, all measures should be adjusted for changes in unit prices because price changes should not affect measures of productivity. G.E. believes that productivity must be tied to all the factors of production, not just labor alone. For example, the company has used the following measure:

$$\frac{\text{Sales Billed}}{\text{Employee Compensation} + \text{Facilities Charge} + \text{Direct Materals Costs} + \text{Business Services Costs}}$$

d. Product leadership. This still tends to be a qualitative evaluation, but at least it should be conducted routinely on a standard evaluation form. Among the questions asked are: How does each product compare with its competition and general company standards? Where is the research conducted? Who introduced the basic product (for example, did G.E. or Westinghouse introduce the electric toothbrush)? Trends are important.

e. Personnel development. The objective of this area is to assure the steady flow of promotable employees. An inventory of various executive positions is taken to see whether orderly succession in the hierarchy is likely. Among the various programs that are evaluated are: recruitment, training, review, and counseling.

f. Employee attitudes. Among these measurements are employee turnover, absenteeism, and results of attitude surveys.

g. Public responsibility. Measures are routine but less precise, as you might expect. Explicit surveys of executive participation in community affairs and public attitudes are used.

h. Balance between short-range and long-range goals. This balance is not measured separately. It is included in the eight-point list to reinforce the basic idea of the entire measurements project. Note that areas (2) through (7) essentially counteract the built-in tendency of the accounting profitability measurements to stress short-range results.

2. By its very reliance on the other goals, G.E. must believe that profitability cannot encompass all the other goals. Nevertheless, profitability is usually dominant and other goals play a secondary (though still important) role.

9-36 (30 min.)

1. Operating Statement

	Parts and Service	Vehicles
Sales	$600,000	$2,600,000
Cost of sales	$ -	$2,120,000
Parts and service materials	180,000	-
Parts and service labor	240,000	-
Sales commissions	-	48,000
Subtotal	$420,000	$2,168,000
Mark-up on "variable" material and labor*	$180,000	$ 432,000
Parts and service overhead	$ 60,000	$ -
Advertising	-	120,000
Sales salaries	-	60,000
General dealership overhead	120,000	-
Operating expenses	$180,000	$ 180,000
Net income	$ 0	$ 252,000

*Roughly equivalent to contribution margin.

2. The operating statement by departments would be the same as (1) through "mark-up on variable material and labor." At that point an effort should be made to allocate general overhead to the two departments insofar as such allocations can be accomplished without reliance on arbitrary assumptions. The remaining general overhead should not be allocated at all. Assume that $75,000 of the $120,000 general overhead can be allocated with confidence, and that $45,000 cannot. The bottom of the income statement could appear as follows:

	Parts and Service	Vehicles	Total
Markup on "variable" material and labor	$180,000	$432,000	$612,000
Parts and service overhead	$ 60,000	$ -	
Advertising	-	120,000	
Sales salaries	-	60,000	
Direct allocation of general overhead	15,000	60,000	
Total expenses directly charged to departments	$ 75,000	$240,000	315,000
Departmental contribution to net income	$105,000	$192,000	$297,000
General overhead not allocable			45,000
Net income of the dealership as a whole			$252,000

3. The first approach is artificial in the sense that only one function of the dealership is regarded as a source of net income. An alternative approach is to view a dealership as a department store with three or more *profit centers* (segments of a business that have revenue as well as expenses): new vehicle, parts and service. Each is regarded as an independent venture. Each contributes its individual segment margin to the overall dealership overhead, which cannot be directly or obviously assigned to a specific profit center.

9-37 (35-45 min.)

1. A = 800,000 X = .50
F = 800,000 Y = .80
Z = 1.00

Performance = (Y x F) + X(A - F)
= (.80 x 800,000) + .50(800,000 - 800,000)
= 640,000

2. A = 800,000
F = 700,000

Performance = (Y x F) + X(A - F)
= (.80 x 700,000) + .50(800,000 - 700,000)
= 560,000 + 50,000
= 610,000

A = 800,000
F = 900,000

Performance = (Y x F) - Z(F - A)
= .80(900,000) - 1.00(900,000 - 800,000)
= 720,000 - 100,000
= 620,000

Notice that when F < A, increasing F by one auto gains Y and loses X, a net gain of Y - X = .80 - .50 = .30. When Nicolai predicts production 100,000 autos below actual, it costs him a .30 x 100,000 = 30,000 point drop in the performance measure. Therefore, there is an incentive not to predict a volume below the expected actual volume. Likewise, when F > A, decreasing F by one auto gains Z and loses Y, a net gain of Z - Y = 1.00 - .80 = .20. The overly optimistic forecast causes a .20 x 100,000 = 20,000 point drop in the performance measure. There is an incentive not to predict a volume above the expected actual volume. The system motivates a forecast equal to the expected actual volume.

3. When actual volume falls short of target, additional production increases the performance measure by Z = 1.0 per auto. It is worthwhile to achieve as much production as possible. When actual volume exceeds forecast, additional production increases the production measure by .50 per auto, still creating an incentive for continued production.

9-38 (15-20 min.) Students will suggest a variety of measures. There is not a right measure for each objective. Listed below are some possible measures:

1. Maintain strong financial health
   a. Daily cash balance
   b. Percentage increase in sales and income
   c. Return on investment or residual income (or EVA)
2. Provide excellent service to customers
   a. Customer satisfaction surveys
   b. Average time from receipt of order to shipping
   c. Percent of products returned by customers, or amount of allowances for quality defects.
   d. Number and dollar amount of exclusive supplier agreements.
3. Be among the industry leaders in product and process innovations
   a. Percent of sales from products less than 2 years old
   b. Dollars (or percent of sales) spend on process improvements
4. Develop and maintain efficient, state-of-the-are production processes
   a. Cost per unit
   b. Lead time from beginning of design to final production
   c. Average delay from projected date of availability (six-months before introduction) to actual delivery

9-39 (20-30 min.) This problem is similar to the problem in the chapter, with a slight difference. The purchase of Eurotel Corporation and the pooling of its operating statistics may be misleading because of fundamental differences in operations. The approach to the problem is to back out Global Telecom's normal growth from the 19X6 figures.

1.

Global Telecom only	19X5	19X6
Customer lines	14,315,000	15,054,000
Employees	70,866	74,520
Lines per employee	202	202

Productivity in 19X6 remained at the same level as in 19X5.

2.

	Global Telecom with Eurotel	Eurotel Only
Customer lines	19,994,000	19,994,000 - 15,054,000 = 4,940,000
Employees	114,590	114,590 - 74,520 = 40,070
Lines per employee	174	123

The low productivity of Eurotel reduces the productivity of the combined company.

3. The employees of the acquired company probably will not be able to immediately achieve the level of productivity achieved by Global Telecom's other employees. A rapid change to increase their productivity could lead to labor unrest and political difficulties. A dramatic increase in productivity at Eurotel probably also will require considerable investment in improved technology and in education and training of employees.

9-40 (20-30 min.)

1. The best productivity measure based on the physical measures given is: pounds of laundry processed ÷ direct-labor-hours worked. Comparing 19X4 and 19X7:

19X4	19X7
$\frac{680{,}000}{22{,}550}$ = 30.2 pounds/hour	$\frac{762{,}500}{23{,}325}$ = 32.7 pounds/hour

Productivity has increased by 32.7 - 30.2 = 2.5 pounds/hour, an increase of 2.5 ÷ 30.2 = 8.3%.

2. The best productivity measure based on the financial measures given is: sales revenue ÷ direct labor cost. Comparing 19X4 and 19X7:

19X4	19X7
$\frac{\$360{,}000}{\$158{,}000}$ = 2.28	$\frac{\$697{,}000}{\$249{,}000}$ = 2.80

By this measure, productivity has increased by .52 ÷ 2.28 = 22.8%. There are three explanations for this large increase: 1) increase in physical productivity, as shown in requirement 1, 2) increase in revenue per pound at a rate greater than inflation ($360,000 ÷ 680,000 = $.53 in 19X4 compared to $697,000 ÷ 762,500 = $.91 in 19X7, an increase of (.91 - .53) ÷ .53 = 72%), and 3) increase in wage rates per hour less than the rate of increase in revenue ($158,000 ÷ 22,550 = $7.01 in 19X4 compared to $249,000 ÷ 23,325 = $10.68 in 19X7, an increase of ($10.68 - $7.01) ÷ $7.01 = 52%).

3. This productivity measure mixes financial and physical measures. Therefore, it is essential to adjust for inflation. Expressing both 19X4 and 19X7 productivity measures in 19X7 dollars:

$$\frac{\$360,000 \times 1.4}{22,550} = \$22.35/\text{hour} \quad (19X4)$$

$$\frac{\$697,000}{23,325} = \$29.88/\text{hour} \quad (19X7)$$

This measure shows an increase in productivity of (\$29.88 - \$22.35) ÷ \$22.35 = 33.7%. It incorporates the increase in physical productivity and the revenue increase at greater than the inflation rate, but it excludes the effect of wage rate changes that was included in the solution to requirement 2.

9-41 (30 min.) There are numerous solutions to this case. Here is one possible solution.

1 & 2. Rico Estrada is faced with difficult tradeoffs. His subgoal of retaining a skilled and motivated work force is threatened by new, competitive pressures. As Estrada loses accounts, he is spreading his (discretionary fixed) labor costs over fewer accounts, and the average cost rises. If he tries to maintain his customary 25% markup, Estrada will become less competitive and probably will lose even more accounts. This has been termed the cost "death spiral," and if left unchecked could lead to bankruptcy. Estrada must find a solution or he eventually will not be able to cover his costs.

It is likely that Estrada can maintain quality service and customer satisfaction with a reduced work force. By November it appears that Estrada has (680÷20) - 41 = 7 excess employees unless this is a temporary downturn in business. This excess employment is costing Estrada 7 x \$3,000 = \$21,000 per month (ignoring taxes and fringe benefits). If Estrada could save this amount, he could reduce the average cost per account as shown:

Number of accounts	680
Average monthly cost per account	$191
Total monthly cost (680 x $191)	$129,880
Less: salary savings	$ 21,000
Revised monthly cost	$108,880

CDS's current price:

Average cost	$191.00
Markup @ 25%	47.75
CDS's price	$238.75

Competitor's price, 80% x $238.75	$191.00

Possible CDS Responses:

a. Maintain current markup of 25%:

Target cost	$191 ÷ 1.25 = $152.80
Total cost	680 x $152.80 = $103,904
Required cost reduction	$108,880 - $103,904 = $4,976
Required employee reduction @ $3,000 each	Approximately 2

b. Reduce markup to 15%:

Target cost	$191 ÷ 1.15 = $166.09
Total cost	680 x $166.09 = $112,941
Required cost reduction	None

To maintain the current 25% markup, Estrada would have to achieve a target cost of $152.80, but that would entail further cost savings of $4,976, or about two more employees. Estrada could avoid further layoffs by reducing his desired markup, but then the business may not be as attractive to him.

It is likely that the business will become even more competitive on the service dimensions, so a skilled, motivated work force will be critical to keeping current customers and regaining lost customers. Can Estrada reduce his work force and maintain the loyalty of the remaining employees? This will be difficult, but may be necessary, and may be at least partly accomplished through attrition and/or early retirements.

The equipment lease in August was probably in response to business growth, which now appears to be unnecessary. Can Estrada get out of the lease? If so, he may be able to cut costs further and/or retain some employees that otherwise would be laid off. Perhaps the best approach would be for Estrada to present the work force with the magnitude of the problem and enlist their aid in solving it. There are numerous stories in the business press about innovative solutions developed by employees who are able to achieve significant productivity increases. This could even lead to a purchase of the company by the employees.

9-42 (60-90 min.)

This problem provides a comprehensive review of many of the techniques and terms that were introduced in previous chapters. It might be used as a final examination. *You may wish to skip part (7).*

Some answers are based on the following detailed master budget:

	Product		
	A	B	Division
Sales, 50,000 at $10.00 and 70,000 at $5.00	$500,000	$350,000	$850,000
Variable manufacturing costs at $7.50 and $2.00	375,000	140,000	515,000
Contribution margin	$125,000	$210,000	$335,000
Fixed discretionary manufacturing costs	4,500	8,500	13,000
Contribution controllable by product managers	$120,500	$201,500	$322,000
Fixed committed manufacturing costs	40,500	76,500	117,000
Contribution by products*	$ 80,000	$125,000	$205,000
Unallocable fixed costs:			
Manufacturing (committed)			$ 25,000
Selling and administrative (discretionary)			72,000
Selling and administrative (committed)			48,000
Total unallocable fixed costs			$145,000
Operating income			$ 60,000

*This is the answer to part (2).

Note: Fixed manufacturing costs = $670,000 - $515,000 = $155,000, subdivided into components of $13,000 + $117,000 + $25,000 = $155,000.

Answers to requirements:

1. Contribution margin ratio: $335,000 ÷ $850,000 = .39
   Break-even point: ($145,000 + $130,000) ÷ .39 = $705,128
   Contribution margin per unit, A: $10.00 - $7.50 = $2.50
   Contribution margin per unit, B: $ 5.00 - $2.00 = $3.00

2. See the footnote to the analysis above.

3.

	Product		
	A	B	Total
Selling and administrative expenses:			
Discretionary, 53/117 and 64/117	$32,615	$39,385	$ 72,000
Committed, 50/120 and 70/120	20,000	28,000	48,000
Totals	$52,615	$67,385	$120,000

There is an arbitrary distinction between the allocation bases. The purpose of this part is to ask whether *budgeted* or *actual* numbers should be used as bases for allocating these costs. The chapter discusses this issue. Another point worth discussing is whether the *actual* costs or only the *budgeted* costs should be allocated. The answer often depends on the extent of controllability by the product managers (if any controllability exists). Of course if the product managers have zero influence over the level of costs, they should not be allocated.

4. This raises the issue of incentives and goal congruence. Product A has the higher selling price but the lower contribution margin ($10.00 and $2.50 for A versus $5.00 and $3.00 for B). The resulting incentives to push the higher-priced product will likely contribute less to the firm's overall profit performance (all other things equal).

5. Actual results were:

		Product A	Product B	Total
Sales, 53,000 units at $10.00 and 64,000 units at $5.00		$530,000	$320,000	$850,000
Variable manufacturing costs:				
Material		$134,500	$ 38,400	
Labor		156,350	50,000	
Overhead		108,650	50,000	
Total variable manufacturing costs		$399,500	$138,400	537,900
Contribution margin				$312,100
Fixed manufacturing costs*	$147,300			
Fixed selling and administrative costs	116,000			263,300
Operating income				$ 48,800

*The $685,200 given in the problem minus $537,900, also given, equals $147,300.

The "controllable contribution" is the actual contribution margin less the fixed *discretionary* costs, which would be:

Actual contribution margin		$312,100
Total actual fixed costs	$263,300*	
Committed fixed costs, which are the same as those budgeted (because there are no variances), $117,000 + $25,000 + $48,000	190,000	73,300
Contribution controllable by segment managers		$238,800

*Selling & administrative expenses	$ 116,000
Fixed manufacturing costs, $685,200 - $537,900	147,300
Total actual fixed costs	$263,300

6. The analysis rests *solely* on master budgeted sales and costs versus actual sales and costs *at budgeted unit prices*:

	Actual Sales at Budgeted Prices	Budgeted Sales at Budgeted Prices	Sales Activity Variance
Product A:			
Sales	$530,000	$500,000	
Variable costs	397,500*	375,000	
Contribution margin	$132,500	$125,000	$ 7,500F
Product B:			
Sales	$320,000	$350,000	
Variable costs	128,000**	140,000	
Contribution margin	$192,000	$210,000	$18,000U
Contribution margin for both products	$324,500	$335,000	$10,500U

*53,000 units x $7.50
**64,000 units x $2.00

7.

	Cost Incurred: Actual Inputs x Actual Prices	Flexible Budget Based on Actual Inputs x Expected Prices	Flexible Budget Based on Standard Inputs Allowed for Actual Outputs Achieved x Expected Prices
Product A			
Direct materials	538,000 pieces x $.25 = $134,500	538,000 pieces x $.25 = $134,500	530,000 pieces x $.25 = $132,500

Price variance, 0 | Usage variance, $2,000U

Flexible-budget variance, $2,000U

Labor	53,000 hours x $.2.95 = $156,350	53,000 hours x $3.00 = $159,000	53,000 hours x $3.00 = $159,000

Price variance, $2,650F | Usage variance, 0

Flexible-budget variance, $2,650F

Variable overhead	53,000 hours x $2.05 = $108,650	53,000 hours x $2.00 = $106,000	53,000 hours x $2.00 = $106,000

Spending variance, $2,650U | Efficiency variance, 0

Flexible-budget variance, $2,650U

Product B

Direct materials

320,000 lbs. x $.12 = $38,400	320,000 lbs. x $.10 = $32,000	320,000 lbs. x $.10 = $32,000
	Price variance, $6,400U	Usage variance, 0
	Flexible-budget variance, $6,400U	

Labor

20,000 hours x $2.50 = $50,000	20,000 hours x $2.50 = $50,000	19,200 hours x $2.50 = $48,000
	Price variance, 0	Usage variance, $2,000U
	Flexible-budget variance, $2,000U	

Variable overhead

20,000 hours x $2.50 = $50,000	20,000 hours x $2.50 = $50,000	19,200 hours x $2.50 = $48,000
	Spending variance, 0	Efficiency variance, $2,000U
	Flexible-budget variance, $2,000U	

Check:

	Product A	Product B	Total
Material	$2,000U	$ 6,400U	
Labor	2,650F	2,000U	
Variable overhead	2,650U	2,000U	
Totals	$2,000U	$10,400U	$12,400U

Total actual variable costs		
[item (8) in problem statement]		$537,900
Standard variable costs:		
Product A: 53,000 x $7.50	$397,500	
Product B: 64,000 x $2.00	128,000	525,500
Total variance		$ 12,400U

Summary of all variances:			
Budgeted operating income			$60,000
Variances:			
Sales activity variance		$10,500U	
Price and efficiency variances for variable costs		12,400U	
Budget variance for fixed costs:			
Actual*	$263,300		
Budgeted**	275,000	11,700F	
Total variances			11,200U
Actual operating income			$48,800

*See actual results in solution to requirement 5.
**$13,000 + $117,000 + $145,000.

9-43 (60 min. or more)

The purpose of this exercise is to develop goals and objectives for a familiar organization. By working in teams, students may see the possibly conflicting objectives of various stakeholder groups. They will also see how difficult it can be to develop measures for some seemingly obvious goals. For example, quality of education is certainly a goal of a university department. But how does one measure this quality? Standardized tests are often suggested, but they may motivate "teaching to the test" rather than generating overall quality. Eventual success in a career might be used, but it is available only after a long delay.

If the optional interview is obtained, it will be useful to see how the faculty member's goals and objectives differ from those of the student group. Does the faculty member have a different perspective? Would legislators (for a state university) or a board of trustees (for a private college or university) have an even different perspective? What about the staff of the university? The interview might lead to a better understanding of how difficult it is to set goals and objectives for an organization with many diverse stakeholders.

CHAPTER 10
Management Control in Decentralized Organizations

10-A1 (30-35 min.)

1. a. 25% of $900,000 = $225,000 target net income

Let X = Unit sales price
Dollar sales = Variable expenses + Fixed expenses+ Operating income
75,000X = 75,000($2) + $300,000 + $225,000
X = $675,000 ÷ 75,000 = $9.00

b. Expected asset turnover = $675,000 ÷ $900,000 = .75

c. Operating income percentage on dollar sales = $225,000 ÷ $675,000
= 33 1/3%

2. a, b.

	Sales Volume		
	75,000 Units*	90,000 Units	60,000 Units
Sales, at $9.00	$675,000	$810,000	$540,000
Variable expense, at $2.00	$150,000	$180,000	$120,000
Fixed expenses	300,000	300,000	300,000
Total expenses	$450,000	$480,000	$420,000
Operating income	$225,000	$330,000	$120,000
Rate of return on $900,000 assets	25.0%	36.7%	13.3%

*Column not required.

A summary analysis of these three cases, in equation form, follows:

	Operating Income Percentage on Sales	x	Asset Turn-over	=	Rate of Return
Volume 75,000	33.33%	x	.75	=	25.0%
Volume 90,000	40.74%	x	.90	=	36.7%
Volume 60,000	22.22%	x	.60	=	13.3%

3. Average available assets would decrease by $150,000, from $900,000 to $750,000. Fixed overhead would be $300,000 - $22,500 = $277,500. Results would be:

	Sell 52,500 Units	Sell 75,000 Units	Difference 22,500 Units
Sales, 52,500 units at $9.00 and 22,500 at $4.50	$472,500	$573,750	$101,250
Variable expenses, at $2.00	$105,000	$150,000	$ 45,000
Fixed expenses	277,500	300,000	22,500
Total expenses	$382,500	$450,000	$ 67,500
Operating income	$ 90,000	$123,750	$ 33,750
Total assets needed	$750,000	$900,000	$150,000
Rate of return on assets	12.0%	13.8%	22.5%

Based on the information given, he should sell at the $4.50 price. Both divisions and the company as a whole will benefit from such a decision. Although the original overall target rate of return of 25% is unattainable, the division will nevertheless earn a better rate of return with the intracompany business than without it. The additional units will earn a 22.5% *incremental* rate of return, which exceeds the 12.0% rate earned on 52,500 units. As a result, the overall rate of return would increase from 12.0% to 13.8%, as shown in the schedule above.

Despite this economic analysis, the manager may still decide against transferring goods at such a low price. For example, he may feel entitled to a higher profit. This would mean that the company would undoubtedly be worse off if the incremental costs of the other division are $4.50. Should top management interfere and force a transfer at $4.50? Such intervention would weaken the decentralization structure. Obviously, authoritarian action sometimes may be needed to prevent costly mistakes. But recurring interference and constraints simply transform a decentralized organization into a centralized organization. Of course, if managers repeatedly make costly dysfunctional decisions, the costs of decentralization may exceed the benefits. Then a more centralized organizational design may be desirable.

10-A2 (30 min.)

1. Assume that fixed costs are unaffected. Company as a whole will not benefit if the Tractor Division buys from outsiders:

Purchase costs from outsider, 3,000 units at $300	$900,000
Less: Savings in variable costs by reducing Iowa's output, 3,000 units at $285	855,000
Disadvantage to company as a whole	$ 45,000

2. The company will benefit if the Tractor Division buys from outsiders:

Purchase costs from outsider, 3,000 units at $300	$900,000	
Less:		
Savings in variable costs as above	$855,000	
Savings related to other production operations	61,000	916,000
Advantage to company as a whole		$ 16,000

3. The company will benefit if the Tractor Division buys from outsiders:

Purchase costs from outsiders, 3,000 units at $270	$810,000
Less: Savings in variable costs as above	855,000
Advantage to company as a whole	$ 45,000

4. As president, I probably would not want to become immersed in these disputes. If arbitration is necessary, it probably should be conducted by some other officer on the corporate staff. One possibility is to have the immediate line boss of the two managers make a decision.

If decentralization is to be strictly adhered to, the arbitrator should probably do nothing under any of the conditions described. If no forced transfer were made, the Tractor Division would go outside, resulting in an optimal decision for the overall company in parts (2) and (3) but not in part (1).

Of course, in part (1) if the manager of the Iowa Division understood cost-volume-profit relationships, and if he wanted to maximize his short-run net income, he would probably accept a price of $300. This would bring a contribution to the divisional profit of 3,000 x ($300 - $285), or $45,000.

Suppose, however, that he refuses to meet the price of $300. This would mean that the company will be $45,000 poorer in the short run. Should top management interfere and force a transfer at $300? This would undercut the philosophy of decentralization. Many managers would not interfere because they would view the $45,000 as the price that has to be paid for mistakes made under decentralization. But how high must this price go before the temptation to interfere would be irresistible? $60,000? $100,000? How much? On the other hand, the Iowa manager may realize that $45,000 is being sacrificed but may have decided that it is worth more than $45,000 to achieve some long-term subjective benefits.

In sum, the point of this question is that any super-structure that interferes with lower-level decision-making weakens decentralization. Of course, such interference may occasionally be necessary to prevent horrendous blunders. But recurring interference and constraints simply transform a decentralized organization into a centralized organization.

10-A3 (10 min.)

The company as a whole would benefit because the $45,000 disadvantage from purchasing on the outside would be more than offset by the additional contribution margin on sales to other customers:

Iowa's sales to other customers, 3,000 units at $330	$990,000
Variable costs, at $297	891,000
Contribution margin	$ 99,000

The net advantage would be $99,000 minus $45,000, or $54,000.

10-A4 (10-15 min.) Dollar amounts are in thousands.

	Division		
	A	B	C
Income percentage of revenue:			
$180 ÷ $3,600	5%		
$126 ÷ $1,800		7%	
$ 80 ÷ $8,000			1%
Capital turnover:			
$3,600 ÷ $1,000	3.6		
$1,800 ÷ $600		3	
$8,000 ÷ $800			10
Rate of return on invested capital:			
$180 ÷ $1,000 (or 3.6 x 5%)	18%		
$126 ÷ $600 (or 3 x 7%)		21%	
$ 80 ÷ $800 (or 10 x 1%)			10%

2. If ROI is used for judging relative performance, B is best for this period. Other factors deserving discussion include the risks faced by each division and the short-run versus long-run implications of current performance.

3.

	Division		
	A	B	C
Income	$180	$126	$80
Imputed interest	90	54	72
Residual income	$ 90	$ 72	$ 8

Division A has the highest residual income. Although its ROI is less than that of Division B, its investment base is sufficiently high and its ROI is sufficiently above the imputed interest rate to make Division A's residual income higher.

10-B1 (20 min.)

The appropriate transfer price is $3.30 per gallon. In general, internal profit centers should conduct both buying and selling at bona fide market price quotations. As long as the market prices are met, the buying divisions must purchase from the internal divisions. In this way, both divisions and the corporation as a whole will maximize operating income:

	Ice Cream Machine	
	Including Sales to Cape Drive-In	Excluding Sales to Cape Drive-In
Sales, 6,500 gallons @ $4; 1,500 gallons @ $3.30	$30,950	$26,000
Variable costs @ $2.10	16,800	13,650
Contribution margin	$14,150	$12,350
Fixed costs	6,800	6,320
Operating margin	$ 7,350	$ 6,030

Purchase should be kept inside because the overall company operating income will be higher by $1,320.In other words, Burger-Rama Enterprises is better off by $1,320 with sales to the Cape Drive-In:

Purchases from outside	$4,950
Less: Savings in fixed costs	(480)
Savings in variable costs by reducing Burger-Rama's output, 1,500 gallons @ $2.10	(3,150)
Net savings from inside purchases	$1,320

10-B2 (30-45 min.)

1. a. Contribution margin per unit = KRW 11,000
   Total contribution = KRW 11,000 x 3,400 units = KRW 37,400,000
   Operating income = KRW 37,400,000 - KRW 30,400,000
   = KRW 7,000,000
   ROI = KRW 7,000,000 ÷ KRW 62,500,000 = 11.2%

   b. Revenue = KRW 30,000 x 3,400 units = KRW 102,000,000
   Capital turnover = KRW 102,000,000 ÷ KRW 62,500,000 = 1.632

   c. Operating income percentage of sales
   = KRW 7,000,000 ÷ KRW 102,000,000 = 6.86%

2. a. Desired operating income
   = 20% x KRW 62,500,000 = KRW 12,500,000
   Let X = units to be sold to reach desired return
   KRW 11,000 x X units = KRW 30,400,000 + KRW 12,500,000
   X = KRW 42,900,000 ÷ KRW 11,000 = 3,900 units

b. Let Z = required decrease in total assets

Operating income	÷	total assets = .20
(7,000,000 + .1Z)	÷	(62,500,000 - Z) = .20
.3Z	=	5,500,000
Z	=	KRW 18,333,333
Operating income	=	7,000,000 + .1 (18,333,333) = KRW 8,833,333
Total assets	=	62,500,000 - 18,333,333 = KRW 44,166,667
ROI	=	8,833,333 ÷ 44,166,667 = 20%

3. Examine the operating income and rate of return on assets with and without the 1,400-unit transfer:

(amounts are thousands of Korean Won)

	Sell 2,400 units	Sell 3,800 units	Difference 1,400 units
Sales, 2,400 units @ KRW 30,000 and 1,400 units @ KRW 25,000	72,000	107,000	35,000
Variable costs, KRW 19,000/unit	45,600	72,200	26,600
Fixed costs	24,500	30,400	5,900
Total costs	70,100	102,600	32,500
Operating income	1,900	4,400	2,500
Total assets needed	50,000	62,500	12,500
Rate of return on assets	3.8%	7.0%	20%

Based on the information given, the Seoul division should sell 1,400 units to the American Marketing division at the KRW 25,000 price. Both divisions and the company as a whole will benefit from such a decision. Although the original overall target rate of return of 20% is unattainable, the division will nevertheless earn a better rate of return with intracompany business than without it. The additional units will earn a 20% incremental rate of return which exceeds the 3.8% rate earned on 2,400 units. As a result, the overall rate of return will increase from 3.8% to 7.0%, as shown in the schedule above.

Despite this economic analysis, the manager may still decide against transferring goods at such a low price. For example, he may feel entitled to a higher profit. This would mean that the company would undoubtedly be worse off in the short run if the American Marketing division must pay the equivalent of KRW 25,000 to purchase the games elsewhere. Should top management interfere and force a transfer at KRW 25,000? Such intervention would weaken the decentralization structure. Obviously, top management intervention sometimes may be needed to prevent costly mistakes. But recurring interference and constraints simply transform a decentralized organization into a centralized organization. Of course, if managers repeatedly make costly dysfunctional decisions, the costs of decentralization may exceed the benefits. Then a more centralized organizational design may be desirable. Further, the Seoul manager may acknowledge the KRW12.5 million loss by not transferring but feel that some long-run objective is worth the KRW 12 million short-term sacrifice.

10-B3 (30-45 min.)

1. The percentage return for each project is as follows:

Project	Percentage Return
1	25%
2	33%
3	13%
4	16%
5	21%
6	30%

a. Under assumption (a), projects 1, 2, 5, and 6 would be taken.

Total investment	$7,650,000
Total return	$2,053,500
Return on investment	26.8%
Residual income	$ 906,000*

*$2,053,500 - ($7,650,000 x .15)

The manager in taking the above projects would be following the company rule.

b. Under assumption (b), the rational manager will take only project 2, since this gives him a return on investment of 33% (and a residual income of $627,000 - ($1,900,000 x .15)=$342,000). To take any further projects at lower returns would lower his overall return on capital invested. It should be noted that if this were not a new division with no capital at this time, the manager under this alternative would take only those projects which would not lower his expected rate of return on presently-invested capital.

c. Under assumption (c), the manager will take projects 1, 2, 4, 5 and 6.

Total investment	$8,600,000
Total return	$2,205,500
Return on capital invested	25.6%
Residual income	$ 915,500*

*$2,205,500 - ($8,600,000 x .15)

2. To maximize the earnings of the company as a whole, the division manager should be instructed to maximize residual income. The essence of the concept of residual income is that it requires the manager to take all projects which promise a positive return to the company over and above the cost of the capital invested. This will maximize total *return* to the company for the capital it has available. To maximize ROI or to use a target rate above the cost of capital means that the company (assuming that it has the money to invest) is passing up profitable opportunities. Note that by taking project 4, the division manager lowered his ROI from assumption (a) but *raised* the residual income. Project 3 would lower residual income since its gross return on investment is less than the cost of the capital needed.

10-1 Benefits of decentralization include: 1) lower-level managers may make better decisions because they have better knowledge of local conditions, 2) managers develop their management skills so that there are more managers qualified to move up in the organization, and 3) managers have higher status and therefore are more highly motivated.

Costs of decentralization include: 1) managers may make decisions that are not in the best interest of the organization because they are not aware of or not interested in facts that don't pertain to their own segment, 2) managers may perform functions at the division level that would be less costly if centralized, and 3) the cost of information to coordinate and control activities may increase with decentralization.

10-2 One of the limitations in decentralization is lack of knowledge in segments of the organization. This is especially true in geographically decentralized operations. Accounting systems give a common language and structure for sharing information throughout an organization. Sophisticated communications systems make this information available without delay. Many companies have "data warehouses" that let managers anywhere in the organization have immediate access to whatever accounting information they want.

10-3 No. Profit centers facilitate decentralization, but one can exist without the other. They are different concepts, as the chapter explains.

10-4 It is more difficult to hold managers of nonprofit organizations responsible for performance because inputs and outputs are generally more difficult to measure. Without reliable performance measures, granting managerial freedom is more risky.

10-5 Decentralization is usually most successful in organizations where segments are relatively independent. If segments buy from or sell to one another, or if there are many common customers or suppliers, decentralization is less likely to be desirable.

10-6 Transfer-pricing systems are needed to accurately determine the efficiency of various divisions of a company's operation. If inefficiency exists somewhere in a corporation but no transfer - pricing system is employed, it is much harder to pin down the area or process that is most directly responsible. In addition, transfer pricing is an attention-directing device that highlights good performance and motivates personnel to maintain efficiency.

10-7 Using full costs can mask the real behavior of a cost. Any transfer price that includes a fixed cost element makes a fixed cost in the producing department look like a variable cost to the buying department. Using actual costs can pass on inefficiencies and make planning difficult for the buying department. The amount of the transfer is not known until actual costs are available, and it can be affected by factors beyond the control of the buying department.

10-8 If a producing division has idle capacity, a transfer price at or close to the variable cost will usually be optimal. Why? Because it costs the firm as a whole only the variable costs to produce the item to be transferred. If the buying division is willing to pay more than the variable cost for the item, the benefit from the transfer must exceed the cost. However, if there is not idle capacity, the selling (producing) division, and hence the firm as a whole, gives up the contribution it would obtain from selling to outside customers. A higher transfer price would be optimal in order to assure that the value to the buying division is at least as great as the sacrifice made by the selling division to transfer the item internally.

10-9 Variable-cost transfer prices can also lead to dysfunctional decisions. For example, the chapter includes an illustration of a situation where the producing division has no excess capacity and variable-cost transfers may cause dysfunctional decisions.

10-10 Negotiated transfer prices are likely to lead to better transfer pricing decisions because those with the best knowledge are making the decisions. On the other hand, valuable time and effort can be lost in the negotiating process.

10-11 When top management second-guesses divisional managers frequently, many advantages of decentralization are lost. Segment autonomy disappears. Essentially, top management intervention implies that top managers know more about the local market conditions than do segment managers. If this is indeed the case, a decentralized operation is not appropriate.

10-12 Multinational transfer prices are influenced by the relative income-tax rates in the countries in which the producing and purchasing divisions are located. They are also influenced by import duties and restrictions on flows of capital between countries.

10-13 Agency theory specifies how to trade off incentive, risk, and the cost of measuring performance.

10-14 The major advantage of the rate of return analysis of performance is its attention to the required asset investment in relation to operating income.

10-15 ROI is affected by a division's income and the amount of its investment.

10-16 No. ROI and residual income create different motivations for managers. Goal congruence and managerial effort would usually be accomplished better by residual income.

10-17 Division A's manager would reject the project because it would *decrease* the division's ROI. Division B's manager would accept it, because it would *increase* the division's ROI. If residual income were used with an imputed interest rate of 11%, both managers would accept the project. Why? Because the residual income of either division would be increased by accepting a project with a rate of return greater than the imputed interest rate.

10-18 Four possible definitions of invested capital are:

1. Total assets
2. Total assets employed
3. Total assets less current liabilities
4. Stockholders' equity

10-19 No. Using a historical cost accounting system *with budgets* is not backward looking. Budgets force managers to plan for the future, including predicting future prices.

10-20 The use of gross book value rather than net book value of assets to compute ROI may affect the speed with which managers replace assets. Gross book value leads to more rapid replacement. A manager who suggests using gross book value probably has assets that are relatively new compared to those in other divisions. When net book value is used, the manager's relatively new assets are valued considerably higher than older assets because they have little accumulated depreciation. When gross book value is used, accumulated depreciation is irrelevant and there is less difference between the values of older assets and newer assets.

10-21 In organizations using management by objectives (MBO), managers and their superiors jointly formulate and agree on the goals and plans for the forthcoming period. Managers are then evaluated against these agreed-upon goals and plans.

10-22 (10 min.)

1.

		(b) Process Further		(a) Sell to Outsiders at Transfer Point		
		Binding Division Performance	Overall Performance	Binding Division Performance		Overall Performance
Selling Price		$8.50	$8.50	$—		$6.25
Variable costs:						
Printing Division	$5.00				$5.00	
Binding Division	2.80				—	
Total variable costs		7.80	7.80	—		5.00
Contribution to net income		$ .70	$ .70	$—		$1.25

2. If the transfer price is based on variable cost, the manager of the Binding Division would want the product processed further. But this would hurt overall company performance. The essential question is whether the Binding Division should offer the final product in the market at all. The incremental revenue of $2.25 is less than the incremental cost of $2.80.

10-23 (10-15 min.)

1. If wheels were available for $14 each in the market, Minneapolis would not be willing to pay more than $14 to St. Paul. If wheels could not be purchased in the market, the maximum price would be $21.50, computed as follows:

Sales price	$175
Variable costs (except for wheels)	132
Contribution available for wheels and to cover fixed costs and profit	$ 43

The $43 must pay for two wheels, so the most that can be paid per wheel is $43÷2 = $21.50. The manager of the Minneapolis Division would likely not pay the entire amount of $21.50 per wheel, because that would leave no contribution to fixed costs plus profit. However, any price less that $21.50 would produce a positive contribution margin and therefore be better than not producing the bicycles.

2. Because there is excess capacity, any transfer price above the variable cost of $9 would result in a positive contribution margin. No price below $9 would be acceptable. If there were no excess capacity, the minimum transfer price would be the market price of $14. Why? Because the St. Paul division would have to forgo $14 of revenue from an external sale in order to transfer a wheel internally.

10-24 (10 min.)

1. Global is better off using a \$400 transfer price. A \$400 transfer price places an extra \$400 - \$200 = \$200 of income in Japan instead of Sweden, while a \$200 transfer price places an extra \$200 of income in Sweden instead of Japan. In addition, the \$400 transfer price adds to the import taxes paid to Sweden. The net affect is as follows:

Japanese income is \$200 higher, .3 x \$200 more taxes	\$(60)
Swedish income is \$200 lower, .6 x \$200 less taxes	120
Swedish import tax, .1 x \$200 more taxes	(20)
Net reduction in taxes from \$400 transfer price	\$(40)

2. The total taxes saved by the \$400 transfer price is \$40 per unit.

10-25 (10 min.) Dollar amounts are in thousands.

1. Turnover of capital = Sales ÷ Invested capital
= \$140,000 ÷ \$50,000
= 280%, or 2.8 times

2. Net income = 10% of \$50,000 = \$5,000

3. Net income as a percent of sales = \$5,000 ÷ \$140,000
= 3.6%

10-26 (5 min.)

The basic equation: ROI = Income percentage of revenue x Capital turnover

A:	7%	x 3	=	21%
B:	24%	÷ 3%	=	8
C:	20%	÷ 5	=	4%

10-27 (15-20 min.)

1. The filled-in blanks are underscored:

	Division		
	X	Y	Z
Invested capital, $182,000 ÷ .14	$2,000,000	$1,300,000	$1,250,000
Income, .025 x $4,000,000	$ 100,000	$ 182,000	$ 125,000
Revenue, $1,250,000 x 3	$4,000,000	$3,640,000	$3,750,000
Income percentage of revenue, $182,000 ÷ $3,640,000	2.5%	5%	3.33%*
Capital turnover, $4,000,000 ÷ $2,000,000; $3,640,000 ÷ $1,300,000	2	2.8	3
Rate of return on invested capital	5%**	14%	10%***

*$125,000 ÷ $3,750,000 = 3.33%
**2.5% x 2.0 = 5.0% or $100,000 ÷ $2,000,000 = 5.0%
***$125,000 ÷ $1,250,000 = 10% or 3.33% x 3 = 10%

2. If the criterion for judging relative performance is ROI, Division Y is best for this period. Other factors deserving attention include the relative risks faced by each division and the short-run versus long-run implications of current performance.

3.

	Division		
	X	Y	Z
Income	$ 100,000	$182,000	$125,000
Imputed interest	200,000	130,000	125,000
Residual income	$-100,000	$ 52,000	$ 0

10-28 (20 min.)

1.

	Ace Auto Rental	Richards Rental Service
Assets	$2,000,000	$2,000,000
Liabilities	800,000	0
Stockholders' equity	1,200,000	2,000,000
Income before interest	500,000	500,000
8% interest	64,000	0
Net income	$ 436,000	$ 500,000
Rate of return on:		
Assets	25%	25%
Stockholders equity	36%	25%

2. When an asset base is used for measuring return, the investor sources for the assets are ignored and so is interest. Rate of return, as used here, means 25% gross rate of return (that is, before interest expense) on total assets. The use of long-term debt can have an impact on the return based on stockholders' equity. However, the 36% rate of return on stockholders' equity does not distinguish between the basic earnings rate on total assets and the various costs of obtaining and using the funds. In other words, top management has two major functions: operating and financing. Measures of operational performance (how assets are employed) should not be influenced by financing decisions (how funds for investing are obtained). Ace Auto Rental in effect has paid 8% for the use of $800,000, which in turn has earned a gross return of 25%. This method of financing benefited the stockholders handsomely.

10-29 (20-30 min.) This problem presses the student more than those immediately preceding it.

1.

	Division		
	J	K	L
Income: .20 x $4,000,000; .15 x $16,000,000	$ 140,000	$ 800,000	$ 2,400,000
Revenue: $140,000 ÷ .07; $800,000 ÷ .04; 3 x $16,000,000	$2,000,000	$20,000,000	$48,000,000
Invested capital: $2,000,000 ÷ 4	$ 500,000	$ 4,000,000	$16,000,000
Income percentage of revenue, 15% ÷ 3	7%	4%	5%
Capital turnover, 20% ÷ 4%	4	5	3
Rate of return on invested capital, $140,000 ÷ $500,000	28%	20%	15%
Imputed interest rate on invested capital	20%	12%	12%*
Residual income, $140,000-(.20 x $500,000); $800,000 - (.12 x $4,000,000)	$ 40,000	$ 320,000	$ 480,000

*$2,400,000 - $480,000 = $1,920,000; $1,920,000 ÷ $16,000,000 = 12%

2. This requirement can generate much discussion or little discussion, as the instructor desires. Using ROI as the criterion, J is the best performer. Using residual income as the criterion, L is the best performer. Note that this company uses different interest rates for different divisions, probably because of wide variations in risks. Note too that residual income, an absolute amount, is always easier to generate by large divisions.

10-30 (20-30 min.)

Where market prices are not available as a foundation for setting transfer prices, the prices bear an artificiality that severely limits the significance of rate-of-return or other performance measures. The whole idea of decentralization is the manager's independence; unless a manager can resort to buying and selling outside the company, his or her profit center is essentially in a centralized company. Nevertheless, profit centers may promote more goal congruence than cost centers.

The rule to be used is that goods and services should be transferred at a price equivalent to that prevailing in an outside market at the time of transfer. Where the internal division meets these selling prices, the buying division must purchase internally. Market prices establish the ceiling for transfer-pricing. In many instances, a lower price may easily be justified, particularly where high-volume purchases are made or where selling costs are less.

In the two cases cited, the transfer prices should be no higher than those that could be obtained consistently by buying the used cars, parts, or services from outside parties.

10-31 (30 min.)

1. Both the Propeller Division and the company as a whole will benefit if the $30.00 price is met. If not, 75% of the propeller volume will disappear, and gross margin will fall to $500,000 as follows:

Sales, 250,000 at $40		$10,000,000
Variable costs, at $26	$6,500,000	
Fixed costs	3,000,000	
Total costs		9,500,000
Gross margin		$ 500,000

If the $30 price is met, the Propeller Division will show a gross margin of $3,500,000 as follows:

	To Outboard Motor Division	To Outsiders	Total
Sales:			
750,000 at $30	$22,500,000		
250,000 at $40		$10,000,000	$32,500,000
Variable costs	$19,500,000	$6,500,000	26,000,000
Fixed costs	2,250,000	750,000	3,000,000
Total costs	$21,750,000	$7,250,000	$29,000,000
Gross margin	$ 750,000	$2,750,000	$ 3,500,000

The rejection of intracompany business will slash margins by $2,250,000, the amount of fixed expenses that will continue regardless of any decision, plus the $750,000 margin on the sales to the Outboard Motor Division. Alternately, the acceptance of intracompany business will result in a contribution margin of $4.00 per propeller ($30 less $26 variable costs) or $3,000,000 which otherwise will be forgone.

2. Yes, the division should reject intracompany sales and concentrate on outside sales since the gross margin would be $4,000,000, whereas the gross margin if outboard motor division business were accepted would be $3,500,000. The gross margin would increase by $500,000 as follows:

Sales, 1,000,000 at $38		$38,000,000
Variable costs, at $29.00	$29,000,000	
Fixed costs	5,000,000	
Total costs		34,000,000
Gross margin (new proposal)		$ 4,000,000
Gross margin (accepting intracompany business)		3,500,000
Difference		$ 500,000

10-32 (30 min.)

1. Nashville should not supply Memphis with Part #A45K for the $6.90 per unit price. Nashville is operating at capacity and would lose $3.10 ($10.00 - $6.90) for each part sold to Memphis. The management performance of Nashville is measured by return on investment and dollar profits; selling to Memphis at $6.90 per unit would adversely affect those performance measures.

2. General Electronics would be $6.90 better off, in the short run, if Nashville supplied Memphis the part for $6.90 and the boom-box was sold for $62.50. Assuming the $10.00 per unit for fixed overhead and administration represents an allocation of costs Memphis incurs regardless of the boom-box order, General Electronics would lose $3.10 in cash flow for each part sold to Memphis but gain at least $10.00 from each boom-box sold by Memphis, a net gain of $10.00 - $3.10 = $6.90.

3. In the short run there is an advantage to General Electronics of transferring the part at the $6.90 price and thus selling the boom-box for at least $62.50. To make this happen, General Electronics could overrule the decision of the Nashville management. This action would be counter to the purposes of decentralized decision-making. If such action were necessary on a regular basis the decentralized decision-making inherent in the divisionalized organization would be a sham.

   Alternatively, the problem could be placed back with Memphis. Even if Memphis had to pay the market price of $10.00, the contract would increase its profit. The variable cost would be $28.10 + $10.00 + $17.50 = $55.60. As long as Memphis has excess capacity, its profit would increase by at least $6.90 (i.e., $62.50 - $55.60) per boom-box. Therefore, both the Memphis division and General Electronics as a whole would be better off if the transfer were made at market price. It is up to Memphis managers to find a way to price the boom-box at $62.50 or more even when Part #A45K is transferred at $10.00.

10-33 (20-25 min.)

1. The Grand Rapids Division manager would not buy the lumber for $70 and would not produce the chairs. The division would lose $5 on each chair produced at that price:

Revenue per chair		$92
Division cost per chair:		
Lumber	$70	
Manufacturing	21	
Selling	6	97
Division loss per chair		$ (5)

However, the company as a whole would benefit by $17 per chair if the chairs were produced and sold:

Revenue per chair		$92
Additional costs per chair:		
Lumber	$48	
Manufacturing	21	
Selling	6	75
Total contribution per chair		$17

Therefore, the policy to transfer at fully allocated costs motivates the manager to make a decision not in the best interests of the company as a whole.

2. When there is no idle capacity at the Northwoods Mill, transferring lumber to the Grand Rapids Division causes the Mill to pass up sales to outside customers. Compare the total contribution from selling the lumber to the total contribution from using the lumber to build chairs and selling the chairs:

Sell Lumber

Revenue		$72
Total additional costs:		
Variable cost of lumber		$48
Total contribution margin		$24

Build and Sell Chair

Revenue		$92
Total additional costs:		
Variable cost of lumber	$48	
Manufacturing	21	
Selling	6	75
Total contribution margin		$17

The company is $7 better off with the contribution of $24 from selling lumber rather than $17 from selling the chair.

Another way to view this problem is that, if the lumber can be sold for $72, using it to build a chair adds $92 - $72 = $20 of additional revenue. The additional costs are $21 + $6 = $27. The company is $7 worse off if it spends $27 to gain $20 in revenue.

10-34 (25-30 min.)

1. Cost of Kwik Print:

($.25 x 120 pages) + (100 copies per page x $.014 x 120 pages)
= $30.00 + $168.00 = $198.00

Thus Jiffy Press at a bid price of $180.25 is the least expensive. In addition, the reports would be ready sooner. If the San Jose office is not directed by top management to do otherwise, Galaxy - San Jose would choose Jiffy Press. If Kwik Print got the business that would occupy idle capacity, Galaxy would have .60 x $198.00 = $118.80 contribution to fixed costs, which it would not have if Kwik Print didn't get the business. Thus, giving the business to Jiffy Press is not an optimal economic decision from the entire corporation's point of view. If the decision maker at San Jose gives the business to Kwik Print due to top management's encouragement, his decision would be optimal economically.

2. If Kwik Print has idle capacity, the minimum transfer price is its variable costs, .40 x $198.00 = $79.20. If Kwik Print can get other orders outside at $198.00, the minimum transfer price should be $198.00.

3. The optimal decision might be to go with Jiffy Press since one to two days may be saved in getting the reports to the client. Potential future earnings for consulting services would be greater than the contribution forgone. However, it is uncertain whether the delay would affect the client's decision to utilize Galaxy's services in the future. The client's goodwill towards Galaxy is also determined by other factors such as the competence of the individuals in Galaxy, the quality of the report, the price of the report, and the time required for the report to be prepared up until the time of printing.

4. Top management has decreased the sense of autonomy of Galaxy - San Jose in suggesting that Kwik Print be utilized. This could affect morale and cause dysfunctional behavior, particularly since Kwik Print's quality is poor.

10-35 (10 - 15 min.)

The minimum transfer price is $20. Any price below $20 would cause the Fabricating Division to lose profit. In fact, the minimum transfer price could be slightly above $20 if the Fabricating Division, despite its current situatuion with excess capacity, would limit its future flexibility by agreeing to the production and transfer.

The maximum price is $50, the price at which the Assembly Division could buy the subassembly on the market. It might be slightly less than $50 if the Assembly Division can save some transportation or handling costs by buying internally, or if it can be more confident in the quality when purchasing internally.

10-36 (15 min.)

1. The optimal transfer price is $600 per unit:

   (a) Additional taxes with $350 transfer price:
   .60 x ($600 - $350) - .34 x ($600 - $350)
   = $150 - $85 = $65

   (b) Additional duty with $600 transfer price:
   .15 x ($600 - $350) = $37.50

   (c) Advantage of $600 transfer price over $350 transfer price:
   $65 - $37.50 = $27.50

2. The changes make the $350 transfer price optimal:

   (a) Additional taxes with $350 transfer price:
   .50 ($600 - $350) - .34 ($600 - $350)
   = $125 - $85 = $40

   (b) Additional duty with $600 transfer price:
   .20 ($600 - $350) = $50

   (c) Advantage of $350 transfer price over $600 transfer price:
   $50 - $40 = $10

   Multinational transfer pricing is heavily affected by the constraints of various countries' laws on taxes and tariffs. Moreover, the resulting transfer prices complicate the evaluation of the performance of the managers and the economic investments in a particular country.

10-37 (20-25 min.)

1. The two contracts illustrate the tradeoff between incentive and risk in employment contracts. The bonus contract provides more incentive to generate profits than does the straight salary. This should benefit London Trading Company. On the other hand, it may cause the manager to focus too much on short-run profitability. Further, it imposes risk on the manager. A manager demands extra compensation to bear this risk. If the vice-president/personnel is correct, the expected cost to London Trading of this risk is £14,000 (the amount by which the expected compensation with the bonus plan exceeds the straight salary). The choice should be based on whether the extra incentive under the bonus plan is likely to be worth at least £14,000 to London Trading.

   Another factor to consider is what type of manager will be attracted by each type of contract. Sometimes it is hard to determine a manager's qualifications at the time of hiring. The manager knows his or her abilities better than does the company. Highly qualified managers would seek contracts with a bonus. Why? They would be confident that they would do better than average and therefore receive compensation above what the firm expects an average manager to receive. The opposite is true for less qualified managers. Because London Trading receives £9 of every £10 of extra profit generated, attracting a highly qualified manager is likely to be advantageous.

2. Managers are generally risk averse. This means that they prefer a contract with less risk to one with more risk if the expected compensation does not differ. It does not mean that managers avoid risks, only that they want to be compensated for such risk seeking. If a risky contract has an expected compensation high enough, it will be preferred to a given risk-free contract. For London Trading Company, a quality manager willing to accept a straight-salary contract at £36,000 might not accept a risky bonus contract with an expected

compensation of £36,000. Extra compensation must be paid to offset the added risk.

The London Trading Company should recognize that besides normal operating risk, they have imposed an added risk in the bonus contract. Because the contract is in British currency, possible movement in exchange rates adds to the noncontrollable factors affecting the bonus, hence it increases the risk.

10-38 (25 min.)

1. The two separate components highlight certain features of profitability that are not revealed by the single calculation.
   a. The importance of turnover as a key to profits is stressed.
   b. The importance of sales volume is explicitly recognized.
   c. It reduces important elements to ratios instead of dollar figures. This often enhances comparability of different divisions, businesses, and time periods.
   d. The breakdown stresses the possibility of trading off turnover for margin so as to increase the average rate of return at a given level of output.

2.

	Company		
	A	B	C
Return on sales	15%	15%	1%
Turnover on capital	x 2	x .2	x 3
Return on investment	30%	3%	3%

Income and investment alone shed little light on comparative performance because of disparities in size between Company A and the other two companies. Thus, it is impossible to say whether B's low rate of return in comparison with A's is attributable to its larger capital or to its lower income. The fact that Companies B and C have identical income and capital suggests that the same conditions underlie the low rate of return, but this conclusion is erroneous.

Introducing sales to measure level of operations helps to disclose specific areas for more intensive investigation. Company B does as well as Company A in terms of profit margin, both companies earn 15% on sales. But Company B has a much lower turnover of capital than does Company A. Whereas a dollar of investment in Company A supports two dollars in sales each period, a dollar investment in Company B supports only 20 cents in sales each period. This suggests that the analyst should look carefully at Company B's investment. Is the company keeping an inventory larger than necessary for its sales volume? Are receivables being collected promptly? Or did Company A acquire its fixed assets at a price level which was much lower than that at which Company B purchased its plant?

On the other hand, C's turnover is higher than A's, but C's margin on sales is much lower. Why? Are its operations inefficient, are its material costs too high, or does its location entail high transportation costs?

Analysis of return on capital raises questions such as the foregoing. When answers are obtained, basic reasons for differences between rates of return may be discovered. For example, in Company B's case, it is apparent that the emphasis will have to be on increasing turnover by reducing investment or increasing sales. Most likely, B cannot appreciably increase its rate of return simply by increasing its earnings as a percent of sales. In contrast, Company C's management should concentrate on increasing the percentage of profit to sales.

10-39 (15-20 min.)

1. (a) Entertainment 223.0 ÷ 1,272.2 = 17.5%
Publishing/Information 120.4 ÷ 705.5 = 17.1%
Consumer/Commercial Finance 244.6 ÷ 1,235.0 = 19.8%

(b) Entertainment 1,272.2 ÷ 1,120.1 = 1.14
Publishing/Information 705.5 ÷ 1,308.7 = .54
Consumer/Commercial Finance 1,235.0 ÷ 924.4 = 1.34

(c) Entertainment 223.0 ÷ 1,120.1 = 19.9%
Publishing/Information 120.4 ÷ 1,308.7 = 9.2%
Consumer/Commercial Finance 244.6 ÷ 924.4 = 26.5%

2. This requirement can lead to a lengthy discussion of what causes differences in the three measures computed in requirement 1. The obvious difference is the low return on investment in the Publishing/ Information segment. It is worth noting that this difference arises primarily because of the low capital turnover in the segment. The Publishing/Information segment is generating less than half as much sales revenue per dollar of invested capital as either of the other two segments.

10-40 (10-15 min.) Amounts are in millions.

1. 1997 EVA = $9,187 - $7,807 - $499 - (12.5% x $3,156) = $487

1996 EVA = $6,471 - $5,495 - $346 - (12.5% x $2,431) = $326

2. As Phillip H. Knight said in his letter to shareholders, "It was the best year we have ever had, the best anybody has ever had in our business." EVA increased from $326 million to $487 million. This is a significant increase in the EVA.

10-41 (20-30 min.) Dollar amounts are in thousands.

	Shoes	Clothing	Accessories
Historical Cost:			
Net assets	$15,000	$45,000	$30,000
Operating income	2,700	6,750	4,800
Imputed interest	1,500	4,500	3,000
Residual income	1,200	2,250	1,800
Rate of return on net assets	18%	15%	16%
Replacement Cost:			
Net assets	$15,000	$55,000	$48,000
Operating income	2,700	6,150	3,900
Imputed interest	1,500	5,500	4,800
Residual income	1,200	650	(900)
Rate of return on net assets	18%	11%	8%

Neither base is foolproof regarding the evaluation of an individual *manager's* performance. First, the short-run emphasis of such measures includes only a part of the activities that promote profitability in the long-run. Second, the environmental conditions facing a particular division plus unfavorable carryover of past mistakes may severely hamper *divisional* performance even though the *manager* is clearly superior by any test other than rate of return or residual income. That is, the "best" managers are often deliberately given the sickest divisions precisely because they have the most ability to improve a sad situation. *Improvement* or *fulfilling tailor-made budgeted targets* may be the best tests of *management* performance as distinguished from *divisional* performance.

2. The following rankings exist:

	Rate of Return		Residual Income	
	On Historical Cost	On Replacement Cost	On Historical Cost	On Replacement Cost
First	Shoe	Shoe	Clothing	Shoe
Second	Accessories	Clothing	Accessories	Clothing
Third	Clothing	Accessories	Shoe	Accessories

3. In this case, if historical cost is the base, the use of rate of return ranks Shoes first, whereas residual income ranks Clothing first. Used indiscriminately, each method has its drawbacks, regardless of whether historical cost or replacement cost is used as a base. Rate of return inhibits divisions with high rates from expansion, whereas residual income tends to favor large divisions that earn in excess of the cut-off rates.

   Replacement costs are more helpful than historical costs as indicators of the relative profitability of *divisions* because they are usually good approximations of the current economic sacrifice being made to conduct such operations. As for managers, their ability to meet *budgeted* goals, however measured, is paramount. Students, professors, and managers have disagreements regarding which asset base is preferable.

10-42 (10-15 min.)

1. Weighted-average cost of capital:

30% x 5% = 1.5
70% x 12% = 8.4
9.9%

EVA = $3,915,000,000 - $1,104,000,000 - 9.9% x $8,755,000,000
= $1,944,255,000

2. Coca-Cola's EVA of nearly $2 billion is very high. Stern Stewart, the consulting company that first promoted EVA, ranks companies based on EVA. In 1997, Coca-Cola was ranking number 1.

10-43 (50-60 min.)

1. See Exhibit 10-43 on the following page.

2. Some major companies, including du Pont and Monsanto Chemical, have used gross assets as an investment base. One reason often cited for using undepreciated cost is that it partially compensates for the impact of the changing price level on historical cost. However, if a company desires to use replacement cost as a base, it should not try to tailor historical costs to the measurement problems of changing prices; the results of such hybrid attachments can be unreliable.

The reasoning in support of the gross assets base must be aligned with the purpose for its use: appraisal of company results as a whole (column 12 of the answer to requirement 1) or appraisal of a plant's or division's performance (column 7). A company's performance as a whole is the responsibility of top management. When profits are

EXHIBIT 10-43

Rate of Return on Assets Using Original Cost of Fixed Assets vs. Using Net Book Value of Fixed Assets

	Fixed Assets				Plant Performance			Company Performance					
						Rate of Return				Gross Assets		Net Assets	
Year	Gross Cost	Accumulated Depreciation	Net Value, End of Year	Average Book Value for Year*	Annual Net Income	On Gross Cost	On Average Book Value	Total Cash Accumulation**	Average*** Cash for Year	Base	Rate of Return	Base	Rate of Return
1	$800,000	$200,000	$600,000	$700,000	$80,000	10.0%	11.4%	$200,000	$100,000	$ 900,000	8.9%	$800,000	10.0%
2	800,000	400,000	400,000	500,000	80,000	10.0%	16.0%	400,000	300,000	1,100,000	7.3%	800,000	10.0%
3	800,000	600,000	200,000	300,000	80,000	10.0%	26.7%	600,000	500,000	1,300,000	6.2%	800,000	10.0%
4	800,000	800,000	0	100,000	80,000	10.0%	80.0%	800,000	700,000	1,500,000	5.3%	800,000	10.0%

* 1/2 (Beginning balance plus Ending balance), e.g., 1/2($600,000+$400,000) or $500,000 for year 2.

** Assume that sales and expenses except depreciation are on a cash basis, and that dividends equal net income. Thus cash in the amount of the depreciation charge will accumulate each year.

*** This situation is unrealistic in the sense that idle cash is being accumulated without being reinvested to earn a return.

made, depreciation is recouped out of sales revenue. If dividends are paid in the amount of net income, cash may accumulate in the amount of the annual $100,000 depreciation (column 9). (No cash is kept in the business from earnings, but there is a conversion of fixed assets into cash as measured by depreciation.) To count original cost plus the cash accumulation as a part of the investment base (column 11) is duplication; it does not provide as useful a base as net assets. In contrast, a plant manager's or division manager's performance often is best analyzed by using gross assets as the investment base (column 7). The reinvestment of the cash accumulation in the amount of depreciation charges may be beyond the manager's control.

Those who favor gross asset base state that it facilitates comparisons among plants or divisions. If income moves downward as a plant ages, the decrease in earning power will be evident under a gross asset base, while the constantly decreasing net asset base will reflect a possibly deceiving higher rate of return in later years (column 8).

The proponents of using net book value as a base maintain that it is less confusing because (a) it is consistent with the total assets shown on the conventional balance sheet and (b) it is consistent with net income computations, which include deductions for depreciation. Using net book value prevents duplication of the same asset in the base and shows a constantly rising rate of return on plant performance. See column (8). Note that the inclusion of the cash accumulation and *gross fixed assets* duplicates the same item, so that the total fixed and current gross asset base rises from year to year.

The definition of income should be consistent with the definition of the capital base to which it is related. Thus interest expense is ordinarily excluded in computing incomes that are related to asset bases, while interest expense is deducted in computing income that is related to stockholders' equity bases. Nonrecurring items are ordinarily excluded when current operating performance is to be appraised.

10-44 (30-40 min.)

The issues in this problem are covered briefly in a section in the chapter. This problem was originally used on a final examination. In particular, note that the quotation is dealing with *how to evaluate performance*, as distinguished from decisions to buy, hold, or sell assets.

A basic question, then, is why we bother to evaluate performance. Fundamentally, it is to assist future decisions and to provide managers with incentives toward organizational goals. One set of numbers may be appropriate for evaluating the economic performance of a segment, whereas a different set may be appropriate for appraising an individual manager's performance. The last sentence in the problem clearly recognizes this distinction, but students tend to pay insufficient attention to it in their solutions. Of course, the major reason for the distinction is that events uncontrollable by the manager sometimes dominate the economic performance of an entity; simultaneously, the manager may be doing either a superhuman or an abysmal job with respect to the critical factors under his or her control.

The issues couched in the statement assume the following logical pattern:

1. Economic values are the best for performance measurement.
2. Replacement values will probably be less than economic value throughout an asset's life.
3. Market (exit) value is inherently less than or equal to (usually the former) economic value for a given company.
4. Use of economic value is infeasible; hence, replacement value should be used.
5. Replacement value will facilitate the evaluation of the division's performance more easily than the division manager's performance.

The statement correctly establishes economic value as the "ideal" measure of an asset's value. The statement fails to disclose the characteristics of economic value that make it "infeasible." Infeasibility probably refers to the difficulty of determining (a) cash flows in the future and (b) the appropriate discount rate to be applied to those flows in the present value process.

The statement presents a reasonable case in favor of replacement value over exit value.

Some remarks might be made about the fact that replacement costs of highly specialized assets may be more difficult to obtain than a direct approximation of their economic values via discounted cash flow techniques.

The biggest defect of the commentary is its failure to mention the cost and value of information tradeoffs in deciding whether some "current" value basis for evaluation of performance is superior to continuing to use historical cost.

10-45 (15-20 min.)

1. 1,500 units x ($36 - $17) = $28,500 increase in operating income if units are purchased inside.

2. Variable manufacturing costs of $17 per unit.

3. Currently available outside purchase price of $36 per unit.

4. (a) Benefit of $28,500 from the Indianapolis Division's viewpoint, but disadvantage of 1,500 units x ($37 - $17) = $30,000 from the Fort Wayne Division viewpoint. Therefore, net decrease in Indiana Instruments Company operating income of $1,500.

   (b) Benefit of zero to the Indianapolis Division, but disadvantage of ($37 - $36) (1,500) = $1,500 to the Fort Wayne Division. Net decrease in Indiana Instruments Company operating income of $1,500.

5. (a) Fort Wayne Division's current ROI = $36,000 ÷ $300,000 = 12%. Proposed investment earns an ROI = $2,200 ÷ $20,000 = 11%. Therefore, the Fort Wayne Division's ROI will decrease if the proposal is accepted.

   (b) $2,200 - .09($20,000) = $400 increase in the Fort Wayne Division residual income, so the Fort Wayne Division would accept proposal.

10-46 (20-30 min.)

1. Management by Objectives (MBO) is a formal system for developing and making measurable the goals for each position in the organization for a given time period. Mutually agreed upon goals are set for each subordinate with his or her superior. Both agree on the objectives to be met and how they will be measured.

   Advantages most often claimed for the MBO system include:

   1. Increased subordinate motivation to accomplish goals.
   2. Channeling of subordinate efforts toward organizationally recognized goals rather than individual goals.
   3. Increased development of subordinate abilities through the systematic establishment of goals by subordinates.
   4. Improved performance appraisal accuracy over time because substantive measures are used rather than subjective supervisor evaluation.
   5. Increased communication between subordinate and superior.

   Disadvantages associated with MBO include:

   1. Likely emphasis on short-run rather than long-run consequences.
   2. Difficulty in dealing with non-quantifiable factors.
   3. Emphasis on organizational rather than personal goals, needs, and wants.
   4. The increased emphasis on counseling often requires too much time.
   5. Limited effectiveness in turbulent or less-structured environments.

2. The human value premises of MBO suggest that subordinates will attempt 100% achievement if they accept a clear and tangible set of

objectives. Inherent in MBO is the premise that goal formation is a joint process, where individual subordinates are involved in setting goals for their activities and developing programs that lead to attainment of organizational goals. In addition, the MBO system allows for adjustments to be made in goals to account for errors that may have occurred during the formation of them. During the appraisal process of MBO, recognition should be given for partial achievement of goals as well as for reaching the various goals.

Roger Brandt does not incorporate the human value premises of MBO in his management style for the following reasons:

1. Goal setting at Langston Company is not a joint process. Brandt assumes that only he can establish organizational and individual goals. Subordinates apparently are not consulted.
2. Brandt has assumed that no errors have been made in assigning objectives.
3. Apparently no analysis was conducted to determine the cause for any lack of achievement.
4. It is likely that Brandt failed to use periodic review sessions to help subordinates find ways to meet their goals.

10-47 (25-35 min.)

This is a favorite problem. In a short space, it gets to the heart of the problems of a control system: goal congruence and effort. In particular, it focuses on how the widespread accounting convention of writing off engineering costs as immediate expenses may inhibit wise investments. It is also a good problem on the motivational impact of cost allocations, so it might be assigned in conjunction with Chapter 12.

1. The strong points of the present plan include the tendency of the ECD manager to hire the optimal number of engineers and to use them efficiently. At first glance, the production managers will also tend to behave in similar fashion. In addition, the user receives no surprises because the total cost of each "contract" is known in advance.

   The weakest point of the present plan is not explicitly pinpointed in the case. (We usually do not raise this point until the proposed plan is discussed.) Why is top management considering a switch to a "no-charge" system? To encourage greater use of ECD services! Such services are evidently being under-used. A likely reason for small usage is that the "expense" borne in the first year may exceed the prospective savings for the first year. Therefore, even if the investment is justified on a longer-run basis, the production managers feel too much pressure for short-run performance to look beyond the current year. (Moreover, many managers are transferred or promoted nearly every year.)

   Under the proposed plan, the ECD manager may continue to hire engineers until their marginal cost exceeds the marginal savings. But a tenser atmosphere is likely. ECD services would be a "free good." When the selling price is zero, the production managers will increase their demand. The ECD manager (or some committee) will have to determine priorities. In contrast, the present plan uses a "market price" system of sorts. Priorities are determined by a negotiated contract at a predetermined price.

2. Most students will favor the present system, although a vocal minority will like the proposed system. Of course, other systems are possible. For example, an *internal* accounting system could capitalize the ECD costs and amortize them over the "useful life" of the expected cost savings. The latter system would then provide a method of performance evaluation (incentive) that would be consistent with the decision model (long-run net savings) apparently favored by top management.

   Again, in the final analysis, the choice of a system will depend on top management's prediction of the impact of the particular method on the collective decisions of the affected managers. In this instance, incidentally, top management adopted the proposed plan.

   A major lesson here is that internal accounting systems are neither inherently good nor inherently bad. The role of *timing* and the wishes of *top management* dramatically affect the choice of a system. Thus, a particular system may solve the problems of goal congruence and effort for a year or two or more. However, as time passes, the system invariably warrants correction or revamping.

   For example, after a class discussion of this case in an executive program, a French executive said in effect:

   > "This case is one that I've experienced. A few years ago, our top management adopted the no-charge system to spur heavier use of our central research and development department. Five years later we returned to a charge system, because our central staff had ballooned to an intolerable level."

In *both* instances, the choice of the system could have been correct.

Finally, the economic literature on agency theory emphasizes risk congruence. That is, the system of incentives may be designed to encourage or discourage the assumption of risk. In this case, the existing system discourages risk-taking on the part of individual managers, because they have less chance to have a diversified portfolio of projects. The newly proposed system shifts the risk to the ECD manager. Because this manager can attain a diversified portfolio, some riskier projects are more likely to be accepted. The latter may be desired by top management.

10-48 (40 min. or more)

The purpose of this exercise is to recognize that return on investment, a summary performance measure, is composed of two parts that may differ greatly by company and by industry. It also requires students to find publicly available information about a company, possibly using the Internet to do so.

Requirement 1 is an individual exercise in information gathering and analysis. Requirement 2 brings in the group aspect. By comparing results across companies, students should be able to see that some businesses generate returns on their investment through large margins (e.g., computer software companies), while some have high capital turnover (e.g. grocery stores). Strategies to improve ROI can emphasize either increasing margins or turnover.

If class time permits, reports from the groups would be worthwhile. In as little as 10 minutes of class time, students can see the variety in margins and turnover. They can also be reminded that the ultimate objective is return of investment, so focus on either margins or turnover without at least maintaining the other is not productive.

CHAPTER 11
Capital Budgeting

11-A1 (15-25 min.) Answers are printed in the text at the end of the assignment material.

11-A2 (20-30 min.) This is a straightforward exercise.

1. The model indicates that the computers should be acquired because the net present value is positive.

	16% Discount Factor	Total PV @ 16%	Sketch of Cash Flows (in thousands) 0	1	2	3
Cash effects of operations, $150,000	2.2459	$336,885		150	150	150
Investment		(330,000)	(330)			
Net present value		$ 6,885				

11-A3 (20-30 min.) This is a straightforward exercise.

1. The model indicates that the computers should not be acquired.

	12% Discount Factor	Total PV @ 16%	Sketch of Cash Flows (in thousands) 0	1	2	3
Cash effects of operations, $150,000(1-.40)	2.4018	$216,162		90	90	90
Cash effect of depreciation, savings of income taxes: $110,000 x .40 = $44,000	2.4018	105,679		44	44	44
Total after-tax effect on cash		321,841				
Investment		(330,000)	(330)			
Net present value		$ (8,159)				

2. The computers should be acquired. The net present value rises, and now it is positive:

After-tax impact of disposal on cash: .60($40,000 - 0) =	$24,000
PV is $24,000 x .7118 =	$17,083
Net present value as above	(8,159)
New net present value	$ 8,924

3. This requirement demonstrates that the choice of a discount rate often is critical to a decision.

Applying 8% discount factor:	
$150,000(1 - .40) x 2.5771 =	$231,939
$110,000 x .40 x 2.5771 =	113,392
	$345,331
Investment	(330,000)
NPV is positive, so acquire.	$ 15,331

11-A4 (25-30 min.)

1. Cash effects of operations:

Before tax annual cash inflow	$ 360,000
Taxes @ 40%: 360,000 x .4	144,000
After-tax cash inflow	$ 216,000
Present value @ 16%: $216,000 x 4.8332	$1,043,971

Cash effects of depreciation*:

Year	Tax Savings**	PV factor	Present Value
1	.1429 x $1,500,000 x .4 = $ 85,740	.8621	$73,916
2	.2449 x 1,500,000 x .4 = 146,940	.7432	109,206
3	.1749 x 1,500,000 x .4 = 104,940	.6407	67,235
4	.1249 x 1,500,000 x .4 = 74,940	.5523	41,389
5	.0893 x 1,500,000 x .4 = 53,580	.4761	25,509
6	.0892 x 1,500,000 x .4 = 53,520	.4104	21,965
7	.0893 x 1,500,000 x .4 = 53,580	.3538	18,957
8	.0446 x 1,500,000 x .4 = 26,760	.3050	8,162
Total present value			$366,339

*Short-cut using Exhibit 11-7: .6106 x .40 x $1,500,000 = $366,360, which differs from the $366,339 computed above only because of a rounding error.

**Factors .1429, .2449, etc. are from Exhibit 11-6.

Summary:

Present value of cash effects of operations	$1,043,971
Present value of cash effects of depreciation	366,339
Total after-tax effect on cash	$1,410,310
Investment	(1,500,000)
Net present value is negative, so don't acquire.	$ (89,690)

2. The 7-year MACRS analysis will apply regardless of the economic life of the equipment. The only change from requirement 1 will be the added five years of cash effects from operations:

PV of $216,000 per year for 5 years at 16%	
= 3.2743 x 216,000 = $707,249	
To account for the delay of 10 years before	
savings begin: $707,249 x .2267	$160,333*
NPV as above	(89,690)
NPV is positive, so acquire.	$ 70,643

*Or, $216,000(5.5755 - 4.8332) = $216,000 x .7423 = $160,337, which differs from $160,333 only because of a rounding error.

11-A5 (5-10 min.)

Many students forget to add the cash proceeds to the tax effect. Answers are in dollars.

(a) Cash proceeds	65,000	30,000
Book value	50,000	50,000
Gain (loss)	15,000	(20,000)
Effect on income taxes at 30%:		
(b) Tax saving (inflow effect)		6,000
(c) Tax paid (outflow effect)	(4,500)	
Total after-tax effect on cash		
(a) plus (b)		36,000
(a) minus (c)	60,500	

11-B1 (15-20 min.)

1. Using the right table is essential. Factors for this part are from Table 1:
   (a) PV = $12,000 x .8638 = $10,365.60
   (b) PV = $12,000 x .7513 = $9,015.60
   (c) PV = $12,000 x .6086 = $7,303.20

2. Use Table 2: (a) PV = $15,000 x 4.3295 = $64,942.50
   (b) PV = $15,000 x 3.7908 = $56,862.00
   (c) PV = $15,000 x 3.1272 = $46,908.00

3. Use Table 2: (a)
   PV = annual withdrawal x F
   $400,000 = annual withdrawal x 7.3601
   Annual withdrawal = $400,000 ÷ 7.3601 = $54,347.09
   (b)
   PV = annual withdrawal x F
   $400,000 = annual withdrawal x 6.1446
   Annual withdrawal = $400,000 ÷ 6.1446 = $65,097.81

4. Contract B has the higher present value:

Year	Present Value @14% From Table 1	Present Value of Contract A	Present Value of Contract B
1	.8772	$175,440	$394,740
2	.7695	230,850	269,325
3	.6750	270,000	202,500
4	.5921	296,050	118,420
Total		$972,340	$984,985

11-B2 (20-30 min.) This is a straightforward exercise.

1 & 2. The model indicates that the equipment should be acquired because the net present value is positive.

	18% Discount Factor	Total PV @ 14%	Sketch of Cash Flows (in thousands) 0	1	2	3	4	5
Cash effects of operations, $140,000	3.1272	$ 437,808		140	140	140	140	140
Investment		(400,000)	(400)					
Net present value		$ 37,808						

11-B3 (20-30 min.) This is a straightforward exercise.

1. The model indicates that the equipment should not be acquired.

	14% Discount Factor	Total PV @ 14%	Sketch of Cash Flows (in thousands) 0	1	2	3	4	5
Cash effects of operations, $140,000(1-.40)	3.4331	$ 288,380		84	84	84	84	84
Cash effect of depreciation, savings of income taxes*:	3.4331	109,859		32	32	32	32	32
Total after-tax effect on cash		$ 398,239						
Investment		(400,000)	(400)					
Net present value		$ (1,761)						

*Depreciation is $400,000 ÷ 5 = 80,000 per year;
annual tax savings is $80,000 x .40 = $32,000.

2. The equipment should be acquired. The net present value is positive.

After-tax impact of disposal on cash:	
.60($25,000 - 0) = $15,000	
PV is $15,000 x .5194=	$ 7,791
Net present value as above	(1,761)
New net present value	$ 6,030

3. Applying 10% discount factors:

$140,000(1 - .40)(3.7908) =	$ 318,427
$80,000(.40)(3.7908) =	121,306
	$ 439,733
Investment	(400,000)
NPV is positive, so acquire.	$ 39,733

11-B4 (25-30 min.)

1. See Exhibit 11-B4 on the following page for requirement 1.

2. The major reason for this requirement is to underscore the fact that the present value of the depreciation tax savings is unchanged regardless of the length of the economic life of the asset.

PV of the $54,600 to be received in the 6th year,	
$54,600 x .4104 factor =	$22,408
NPV as above	(12,128)
NPV is positive, so acquire.	$10,280

EXHIBIT 11-B4

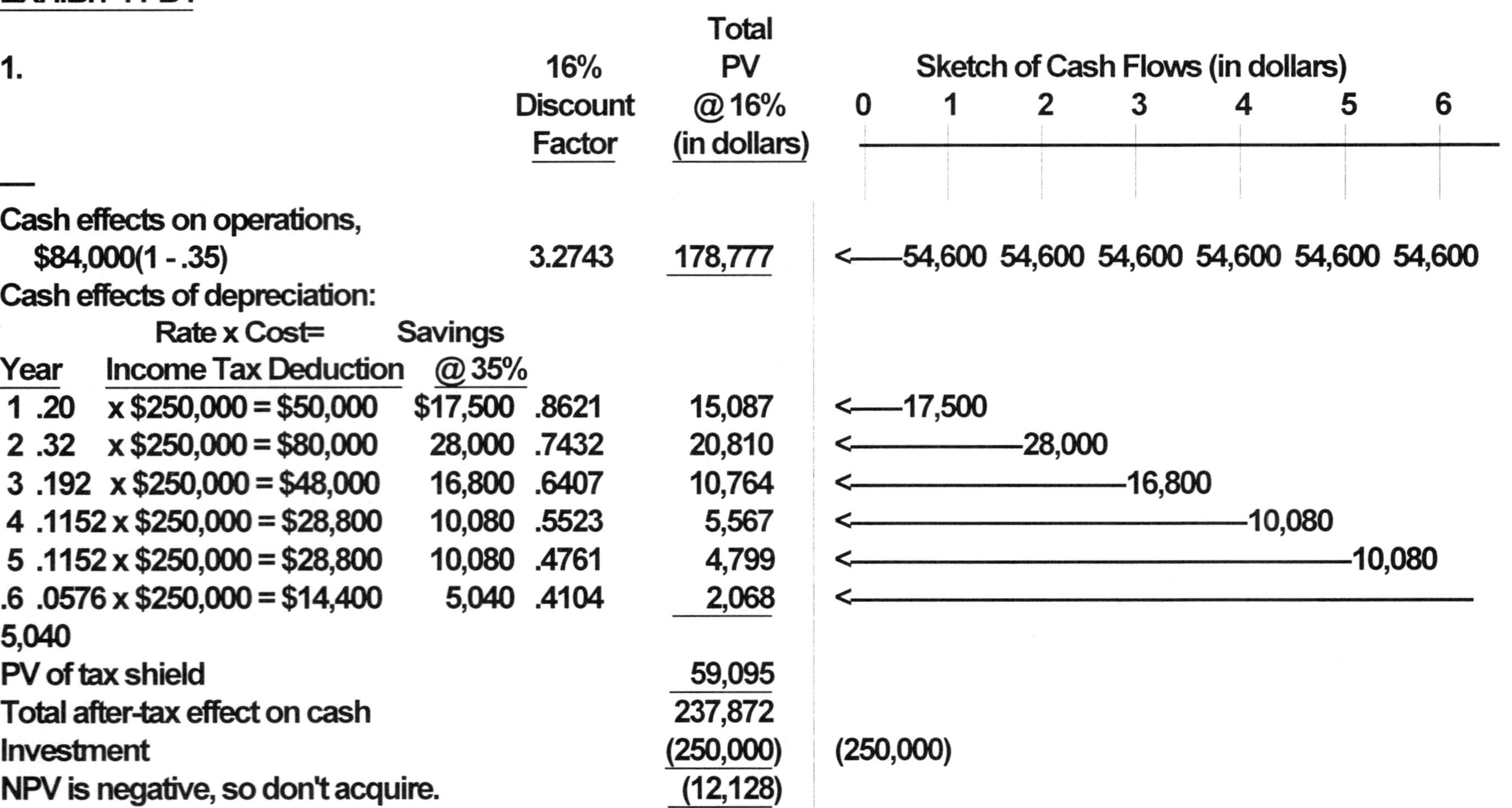

1.

	Savings @ 35%	16% Discount Factor	Total PV @ 16% (in dollars)	0	1	2	3	4	5	6
Cash effects on operations, $84,000(1 - .35)		3.2743	178,777	←	54,600	54,600	54,600	54,600	54,600	54,600
Cash effects of depreciation:										
Year / Rate x Cost= Income Tax Deduction										
1 .20 x $250,000 = $50,000	$17,500	.8621	15,087	←	17,500					
2 .32 x $250,000 = $80,000	28,000	.7432	20,810	←		28,000				
3 .192 x $250,000 = $48,000	16,800	.6407	10,764	←			16,800			
4 .1152 x $250,000 = $28,800	10,080	.5523	5,567	←				10,080		
5 .1152 x $250,000 = $28,800	10,080	.4761	4,799	←					10,080	
.6 .0576 x $250,000 = $14,400	5,040	.4104	2,068	←						5,040
PV of tax shield			59,095							
Total after-tax effect on cash			237,872							
Investment			(250,000)	(250,000)						
NPV is negative, so don't acquire.			(12,128)							

Note: The cash effects of MACRS depreciation can be computed more easily using Exhibit 11-7. Present value of tax savings = Original cost x Tax rate x Factor from 11-7 = $250,000 x .35 x .6753 = $59,089. This differs slightly from the $59,095 calculated above because of rounding error.

11-B5 (5-10 min.)

1.

Book value	$20,000	
Sale price	8,000	$ 8,000
Net loss	$12,000	
Tax savings	x .30	3,600
Net immediate cash inflow, including tax savings		$11,600

2.

Sales price	$35,000	$35,000
Book value	20,000	
Net gain	$15,000	
Income tax	x .30	(4,500)
Net immediate cash inflow, after taxes		$30,500

11-1 The accountant has a limited role in the project identification phase. In the selection phase, accountants provide information for predicting cash inflows and outflows and often are in charge of summarizing the information using a capital budgeting model. The postaudit phase uses information about the results of investment projects; this information usually comes from the accounting system.

11-2 Discounted cash flow is a superior method for capital budgeting because it measures profitability and takes into account the time value of money.

11-3 No. A higher minimum desired rate of return reduces the present value of future cash inflows and outflows, and hence the difference between them. The initial investment (at time zero) is unaffected. Therefore, the net present value is less. Higher discount rates reduce the price a company should be willing to pay.

11-4 No. It is true that the DCF model assumes certainty and perfect capital markets. But all practical capital budgeting models make even more limiting assumptions. The DCF model is not perfect, but in most situations it is the best practical alternative.

11-5 Yes, double counting does occur if depreciation expense is considered separately. The cost of an investment is represented by its cash outflow at year zero. An additional consideration of depreciation would be double counting.

11-6 Sensitivity analysis is especially appropriate for organizations that do not have accurate cash flow predictions. Sensitivity analysis can help a manager decide whether it is worth gathering information to improve cash flow predictions.

11-7 The differential approach should lead to the same choice between alternatives as the total approach because it merely disregards the factors that are constant for each alternative: those that make no difference.

11-8 The NPV model is appropriate for all types of investments. However, with some types of investments, such as those in advanced technology, NPV must be carefully applied. Many qualitative effects should be either quantified as best as possible and included in the model, or they should be considered as subjective factors in addition to the NPV analysis.

11-9 The marginal tax rate is the rate paid on *additional* amounts of pretax income. In contrast, the average tax rate is the total taxes paid divided by the total pretax income.

11-10 No. Two sets of books are appropriate. The objectives of tax reporting and shareholder reporting differ; therefore, the rules for reporting to each differ. If tax rules were used for financial reporting, users of the statements would not receive the information they judge to be most useful. Likewise, if tax authorities accepted financial reporting rules, certain social goals sought by the taxation system would not be met.

11-11 Tax avoidance is the achieving of a reduction in income tax payments through legal means; tax-evasion achieves the same end through illegal means. Tax avoidance is considered moral; tax evasion, immoral. Tax avoidance uses the rules of the system (tax laws) in an optimum way; tax evasion disregards the rules.

11-12 Accelerated rather than straight-line depreciation is to be preferred for tax purposes because it provides a bigger present value of tax savings by reducing taxable income more during the earlier years of an asset's life. Because of the time value of money, immediate tax savings are more important than tax savings in the future.

11-13 Yes. Two streams may be identified: (a) inflows from operations and (b) savings of income tax outflows (which are often regarded in capital budgeting as additions to inflows).

11-14 Because of the time value of money, the earlier a company takes tax deductions and thereby saves taxes, the larger the present value of the tax savings.

11-15 Yes. MACRS treats assets as if they were purchased at midyear, so they have depreciation effects for one tax year more than the number of years of their depreciable lives. For example, if a three-year MACRS asset is purchased during 1996 by a company that pays taxes on a calendar year basis, its depreciation begins July 1, 1996, and extends through June 30, 1999, affecting taxes in 4 years (1996 through 1999).

11-16 No. Depreciation is never a cash outlay. The depreciation amount is used to predict the income tax cash effect, but depreciation itself is not a cash effect.

11-17 The three components of the market or nominal interest rate are: 1) risk-free element, or pure rate of interest, 2) business-risk element, and 3) inflation element.

11-18 The correct analysis in inflation (a) uses a required rate that includes an element attributable to inflation and (b) explicitly adjusts the predicted operating cash flows for the effects of inflation.

11-19 The statement is erroneous. The increase in operating cash inflows is offset by using a larger discount rate to calculate their present value. In fact, the opposite of the statement is true. Why? Because tax savings due to depreciation *do not* increase with inflation. Still, a discount rate including an inflation element should be used to compute the present value. The larger the inflation, the larger the discount rate, and the smaller the present value of tax savings.

11-20 It is useful to learn the "payback" and "accounting rate-of-return" methods of capital budgeting because they are widely used today. In addition, the payback method may give a rough indication of riskiness, and the accounting rate of return shows a project's effect on an accrual accounting income statement. The comparative advantage of discounted cash flow can also be seen by contrast.

11-21 The basic flaw in the payback method is that it does not compare the total profitability of alternative projects, but only the quickest rate of recoupment of the initial investment.

11-22 If capital-budgeting decisions are made using DCF, and performance evaluations use accrual accounting numbers, a conflict may arise. Often accrual accounting can show low profits in the early years of a project's life because of high depreciation, write-offs of old equipment that is being replaced, or slow growth in revenues as new markets are being penetrated. Such low accrual accounting profits might discourage managers from making investments that have a positive net present value.

11-23 (10-15 min.)

1. The present value is $200,000 and the annual payments are an annuity, requiring use of Table 2:
   (a) $200,000 = annual payment x 11.2578
   annual payment = $200,00 ÷ 11.2578 = $17,765
   (b) $200,000 = annual payment x 9.4269
   annual payment = $200,000 ÷ 9.4269 = $21,216
   (c) $200,000 = annual payment x 8.0552
   annual payment = $200,000 ÷ 8.0552 =$24,829

2. (a) $200,000 = annual payment x 8.5595
   annual payment = $200,00 ÷ 8.5595 = $23,366
   (b) $200,000 = annual payment x 7.6061
   annual payment = $200,000 ÷ 7.6061 = $26,295
   (c) $200,000 = annual payment x 6.8109
   annual payment = $200,000 ÷ 6.8109 =$29,365

3. (a) Total payments = 30 x $21,216 = $636,480
   Total interest paid = $636,480 - $200,000 = $436,480
   (b) Total payments =15 x $26,295 = $394,425
   Total interest paid = $394,425 - $200,000 = $194,425

11-24 (10 min.) The initial step on solving present value problems focuses on a basic question: Which table should I use? No computations should be made until you are convinced that you are using the correct table.

1. Use Table 1, row 4, 12% column. Bank of America will lend $254,200,000. The $400 million is a future amount. Its present value is:

   PV = $400,000,000 x .6355 = $254,200,000

2. Use Table 2, row 4, 12% column. Bank of America will lend $303,730,000. The $100 million is a uniform periodic payment at the end of a series of years. Therefore, it is an annuity. Its present value is:

   PV_A = $100,000,000 x 3.0373 = $303,730,000

   In particular, note that Bank of America is willing to lend more than in requirement 1 even though the interest rate is the same. Why? Because the bank will get its money back more quickly.

11-25 (10-20 min.)

1. a. PV = $600,000(.6355) = $381,300
   b. PV = $600,000(.4823) = $289,380

2. The annual rates would be halved and the periods doubled. Present values decline:

   a. PV = $600,000(.6274) = $376,440
   b. PV = $600,000(.4665) = $279,900

3. Present values rise because the money is repaid more quickly:

   a. PV = $150,000(3.0373) = $455,595
   b. PV = $150,000(2.5887) = $388,305

11-26 (10-15 min.)

1. $80,000 = Future amount x .3506

   Future amount = $80,000 ÷ .3506
   = $228,180

2. $80,000 = Future annual amount x 4.6389

   Future annual amount = $80,000 ÷ 4.6389
   = $17,245

11-27 (10 min.)

The deferral cost Pippin $202,800 in present value, computed as follows:

Present value of $1,000,000 in 2 years	$ 797,200
Present value of $1,000,000 today	1,000,000
Sacrifice in present value	$ 202,800

A more detailed analysis follows:

Year	Present Value @ 12% from Table 1	Present Value of Original Contract	Present Value of Revised Contract
19X7	1.0000	$3,000,000	$2,000,000
19X8	.8929	3,125,150	3,125,150
19X9	.7972	3,188,800	3,986,000
Total		$9,313,950	$9,111,150

Difference ($9,313,950 - $9,111,150) = $202,800

11-28 (20-25 min.) This basic exercise develops comfort with the tables and the NPV method.

Number of years	8	18	20	28
Amount of annual cash inflow	$10,000	$13,751[b]	$ 9,000	$ 7,000
Required initial investment	$40,776[a]	$80,000	$65,000	$29,099
Minimum desired rate of return	14%	20%	12%[c]	26%
Net present value	$ 5,613	($13,835)	$2,225	($ 2,218)[d]

[a](4.6389 x $10,000) - $5,613 = $46,389 - $5,613 = $40,776

[b](4.8122 x CF) - $80,000 = ($13,835); CF = ($80,000 - $13,835) ÷ 4.8122 = $13,749

[c](F x $9,000) - $65,000 = 2,225; F = $67,225 ÷ $9,000 = 7.4694
On the 20 year row, the factor 7.4694 is a 12% rate

[d]PV Factor for 26% on 28-year row is 3.8402
$7,000 x 3.8402 = $26,881
NPV = $26,881 - $29,099 = $(2,218)

11-29 (10 min.)

Do not buy. The net present value is negative.

Initial outlay (Note 1)	$(33,000)
Present value of cash operating savings, from 12-year, 12% column of Table 2, 6.1944 x $5,000	30,972
Net present value	$(2,028)

Note 1: The trade-in allowance really consists of a $3,000 adjustment of the selling price and a bona fide $6,000 cash allowance for the old equipment. The relevant amount is the incremental cash outlay, $33,000. The book value is irrelevant.

11-30 (10-15 min.)

1. The quickest solution is to "net" the flows for each year:

1. $200,000 - $150,000 =	$ 50,000	
2. 250,000 - 200,000 =	50,000	an annuity of 3 payments (a)
3. 300,000 - 250,000 =	50,000	
4. 400,000 - 300,000 =	100,000	an annuity of 2 payments deferred
5. 450,000 - 350,000 =	100,000	three years (b)

(a) 50,000 x 2.3216	$116,080
(b) 100,000 x 1.6467 x .6750	111,152
Total	$227,232
Less initial investment	210,000
Net Present Value (NPV)	$ 17,232

Various other approaches would reach the same answer, but they would involve more computations.

2. The NPV is positive because at a 12% rate, the present value of the net inflows will be higher than at 14%, so NPV will increase.

11-31 (30-45 min.)

This problem deals essentially with sensitivity analysis, which asks how the basic forecasted results will be affected by changes in the critical factors (useful life, cash flows) that influence rate of return.

1. $25,000 ÷ $5,000 = 5 years

2. NPV=($5,000 x 6.8137) - $25,000 = $9,069

3. a) NPV = ($5,000 x 4.3553) - $25,000 = ($3,224)
   b) NPV = ($5,000 x 8.5136) - $25,000 = $17,568

4. NPV = ($3,000 x 6.8137) - $25,000 = ($4,559)

5. NPV = ($4,000 x 5.3349) - $25,000 = ($3,660)

11-32 (15-20 min.)

1. NPV = ($15,000 x 3.7908) - $50,000 = $56,862 - $50,000 = $6,862

2. (a) NPV = ($15,000 x 3.1699) - $50,000 = $47,549 - $50,000 = $(2,451)
   (b) NPV = ($15,000 x 4.8684) - $50,000 = $73,026 - $50 000 = $23,026

3. (a) NPV = ($11,000 x 3.7908) - $50,000 = $41,699 - $50,000 = $(8,301)
   (b) NPV = ($18,000 x 3.7908) - $50,000 = $68,234 - $50,000 = $18,234

4. (a) NPV = ($18,000 x 4.8684) - $50,000 = $87,631 - $50,000 = $37,631
   (b) NPV = ($11,000 x 3.1699) - $50,000 = $38,039 - $50,000 = $(15,131)

5. (Savings x 3.7908) - $50,000 = 0
   Savings = $50,000 ÷ 3.7908
   Savings = $13,190

11-33 (5-10 min.) In thousands of dollars.

(S)	Sales	530
(E)	Expenses excluding depreciation	350
(D)	Depreciation	100
	Total expenses	450
	Income before income taxes	80
(T)	Income taxes at 40%	32
(I)	Net income	48
	Cash effects of operations:	
(S - E)	Cash inflow from operations, 530 - 350 =	180
	Income tax outflow at 40%	72
	After-tax inflow from operations	108
	Effect of depreciation:	
(D)	Depreciation, $100	
	Income tax savings at 40%	40
	Total after-tax effect on cash	148

Total after-tax effect on cash is
either S - E - T = 530 - 350 - 32 = 148 or I + D = 48 + 100 = 148

11-34 (10-15 min.) Compute income before income taxes first. Amounts are in thousands of dollars.

(S)	Sales (800 + 1,350)	2,150
(E)	Expenses excluding depreciation, (1,350 - 300)	1,050
(D)	Depreciation	300
	Total expenses	1,350
	Income before income taxes (480 ÷ .6)	800
(T)	Income taxes at 40% (800 x .4)	320
(I)	Net income	480
	Cash effects of operations:	
(S - E)	Cash inflow from operations, 2,150 - 1,050 =	1,100
	Income tax outflow at 40%	440
	After-tax inflow from operations	660
	Effect of depreciation:	
(D)	Depreciation, $300	
	Income tax savings, .4 x $300	120
	Total after-tax effect on cash	780

Total after-tax effect on cash is
either S - E - T = 2,150 - 1,050 - 320 = 780 or I + D = 480 + 300 = 780

11-35 (5-10 min.)

Cash effects of operations:	
Cash inflow from operations: $1,200,000 - $600,000	$600,000
Income tax outflow @ 40%	240,000
After-tax inflow from operations (excluding depreciation)	$360,000

Effects of depreciation:	
Depreciation	$300,000
Income tax savings @ 40%	120,000
Total after-tax effect on cash	$480,000

11-36 (10 min.)

The month and day on which an asset is acquired does not affect its tax depreciation. The half-year convention is applied to all assets.

	1999	2000
1. 3-year property: 33.33% and 44.45% of $40,000	$13,332	$17,780
2. 5-year property: 20% and 32% of $8,000	1,600	2,560
3. 5-year property: 20% and 32% of $5,000	1,000	1,600
4. 7-year property: 14.29% and 24.49% of $4,000	572	980

11-37 (10 min.)

This problem could be solved by specifying appropriate schedules of tax savings and computing the present values. However, the process would be extremely time-consuming. The steps outlined in the chapter make the computations quite simple.

(a) $160,000 x .35 x .8044 = $ 45,046
(b) $560,000 x .40 x .7733 = $172,219
(c) $ 55,000 x .50 x .6106 = $ 16,792
(d) $910,000 x .35 x .7059 = $224,829
(e) $430,000 x .25 x .5492 = $ 59,039

11-38 (30 min.)

1 & 2. See Exhibit 11-38 on the following page for requirements 1 and 2.

The footnotes for the exhibit follow:

[a] Be sure to use a nominal discount rate, which includes an element attributable to inflation, and adjust the predicted cash flows for inflationary effects. Each year is adjusted for anticipated inflation: $68,750 x 1.04, $68,750 x 1.04^2,$68,750 x 1.04^3, etc.

[b] The annual savings in income taxes will be unaffected by inflation. Why? Because the income-tax deduction must be based on original cost of the asset in year 0 dollars. Amounts are 45% of (.20 x 300,000), (.32 x 300,000), (.192 x 300,000), (.1152 x 300,000), (.1152 x 300,000), and (.0576 x 300,000).

[c] Shortcut using Exhibit 11-7: .6211 x .45 x $300,000 = $83,849, which differs from the $83,852 calculated above only because of rounding error.

[d] A common error is to adjust the discount rate as above but *not* adjust the predicted cash inflows.

3. The method of Requirement 1 is correct. The required rate of return includes an inflation element, and the cash inflows are adjusted for inflation. In Requirement 2 the required rate of return includes an inflation element, but the cash inflows are not adjusted for inflation. This understates the cash flows, so the net present value is understated. The incorrect method would lead to underinvestment, because desirable investments would be rejected.

EXHIBIT 11-38

		At 20 Percent P.V. Factor	At 20 Percent Present Value	Sketch of Relevant Cash Flows (in dollars) 0	1	2	3	4	5	6
1. Correct Analysis										
Cash operating inflows:[a]										
Pretax inflow in year-0 dollars	$125,000									
Tax effect at 45%	56,250									
After-tax effect	$ 68,750									
		.8333	$ 59,581	<—	71,500					
		.6944	51,636	<—		74,360				
		.5787	44,753	<—			77,334			
		.4823	38,790	<—				80,428		
		.4019	33,617	<—					83,645	
Subtotal			$228,377							
Cash effect of depreciation:[b]										
Savings in income taxes		.8333	22,499	<—	27,000					
		.6944	29,998	<—		43,200				
		.5787	15,000	<—			25,920			
		.4823	7,501	<—				15,552		
		.4019	6,250	<—					15,552	
		.4019	2,604	<—						7,776
			83,852[c]							
Investment in equipment		1.0000	(300,000)	(300,000)						
Net present value			$ 12,229							
2. Incorrect Analysis										
Cash operating inflows after taxes[d]		2.9906	$205,604	<—	68,750	68,750	68,750	68,750	68,750	
Tax effect of depreciation (same as above)			91,639							
Investment in equipment		1.0000	(300,000)	(300,000)						
Net present value			$ (2,757)							

See footnotes on the previous page.

11-39 (30-40 min.) Answers are in Mexican pesos.

1. After-tax cash operating savings,
.6 x 160,000 = 96,000

PV of cash operating savings, 96,000 x 3.1272	300,211
Income tax savings from depreciation .4 x (410,000 ÷ 5) = .4 x 82,000 = 32,800	
PV = 32,800 x 3.1272	102,572
PV of total savings	402,783
Required outlay at time zero	410,000
Net present value	(7,217)

Note how income taxes have a two-edged effect. They chop the present value of the cash operating savings by 40%, but the depreciation deduction provides income tax savings.

2. See Exhibit 11-39 on the following page for requirement 2.

3. The analysis in Requirement 2 is correct. The cash flows and the required rate of return incorporate the 10% rate of inflation. In Requirement 1, the 18% required rate of return includes an inflation element, but the predicted cash flows ignore inflationary effects.

EXHIBIT 11-39

All numbers are expressed in Mexican pesos.

2.	18% PV Factor	Total Present Value	Sketch of Relevant Cash Flows (in thousands) 0	1	2	3	4	5
Cash operating savings:*	.8475	89,496		105,600				
	.7182	83,426			116,160			
	.6086	77,764				127,776		
	.5158	72,498					140,554	
	.4371	67,580						154,609
Total		390,764						
Income tax savings from depreciation *not* changed by inflation, see 1	3.1272	102,572		32,800	32,800	32,800	32,800	32,800
Total		493,336						
Required outlay at time zero	1.0000	(410,000)	(410,000)					
Net present value		83,336						

*Amounts are computed by multiplying (160 x .6) = 96,000 by 1.10, 1.10^2, 1.10^3, etc.

11-40 (10-15 min.)

Annual addition to profit = 40% x $50,000 = $20,000.

1. Payback period is $60,000 ÷ $20,000 = 3 years. It is not a good measure of profitability because it ignores returns beyond the payback period and it does not account for the time value of money.

2. NPV = $15,997. Accept the proposal because the NPV is positive.
Computation: NPV = ($20,000 x 3.8887) - $60,000
= $77,774 - $60,000 = $17,774

3. $$\text{ARR} = \frac{\text{increase in average cash flow - increase in depreciation}}{\text{initial investment}}$$
$$= (\$20{,}000 - \$10{,}000) \div \$60{,}000 = 16.7\%$$

11-41 (15 min.)

1. $20,000 ÷ $4,000 = 5 years

2. $4,000 x 5.7466, which is the P.V. of an annuity of $1.00 for 8 years, is $22,986. The company should buy because the net present value is a positive $22,986 - $20,000 = $2,986.

3. $$R = \frac{(\$4{,}000 - (\$20{,}000\,,\,8\text{ years}))}{(\$20{,}000)} = \frac{\$1{,}500}{\$20{,}000} = 7.5\%$$

11-42 (30-35 min.)

1. Annual Operating Cash Flows

	Xerox	Kodak	Difference
Salaries	$49,920(a)	$41,600(b)	$ 8,320
Overtime	1,728(c)	–	1,728
Repairs and maintenance	1,800	1,050	750
Toner, supplies, etc.	3,600	3,300	300
Total annual cash outflows	$57,048	$45,950	$11,098

(a) ($ 8 x 40 hrs.) x 52 weeks x 3 employees = $320 x 52 x 3 = $49,920
(b) ($10 x 40 hrs.) x 52 weeks x 2 employees = $400 x 52 x 2 = $41,600
(c) ($12 x 4 hrs.) x 12 months x 3 machines = $ 48 x 12 x 3 = $ 1,728

Initial Cash Flows

	Xerox	Kodak	Difference
Purchase of Kodak machines	$ –	$49,000	$49,000
Sale of Xerox machines	–	-3,000	-3,000
Training and remodeling	–	2,000	2,000
Total	$ –	$48,000	$48,000

	PV of $1.00 Discounted at 12%	Present Value of Cash Flows 0	Annual Cash Flows 1	2	3	4	5
Total Project Approach:							
Kodak:							
Initial cash outflow	1.0000	$(48,000)					
Operating cash flows	3.6048	(165,641)	(45,950)	(45,950)	(45,950)	(45,950)	(45,950)
Total		$(213,641)					
Xerox:							
Operating cash flows	3.6048	$(205,647)	(57,048)	(57,048)	(57,048)	(57,048)	(57,048)
Difference in favor of retaining Xerox		$(7,994)					
Incremental Approach							
Initial investment	1.0000	$(48,000)					
Annual operating cash savings	3.6048	40,006	11,098	11,098	11,098	11,098	11,098
Net present value of purchase		$(7,994)					

2. The Xerox machines should not be replaced by the Kodak equipment.

Net savings = (Present value of expenditures to retain Xerox machines) less (Present value of expenditures to convert to Kodak machines)

= $205,647 - $213,641 = $(7,994)

3. a. How flexible is the new machinery? Will it be useful only for the presently intended functions, or can it be easily adapted for other tasks that may arise over the next 5 years?
   b. What psychological effects will it have on various interested parties?

11-43 (40 min.)

	At 10% for 7 Years			Sketch of Cash Flows (in thousands)						
Total project Analysis	PV Factor	Present Value	0	1	2	3	4	5	6	7
Replace (A)										
Recurring cash maintenance cost	4.8684	$ (4,868)		(1.0)	(1.0)	(1.0)	(1.0)	(1.0)	(1.0)	(1.0)
Disposal value of old machine	1.0000	3,500	3.5							
Initial investment	1.0000	(72,000)	(72.0)							
Overhaul, end of 4th yr.	0.6830	(4,781)					(7.0)			
Disposal value of new machine	0.5132	2,566								5.0
Present value of net cash outflows		$(75,583)								
Keep (B)										
Recurring cash maintenance cost	4.8684	$ (5,842)		(1.2)	(1.2)	(1.2)	(1.2)	(1.2)	(1.2)	(1.2)
Recurring cash operating cost savings*	4.8684	(73,026)		(15.0)	(15.0)	(15.0)	(15.0)	(15.0)	(15.0)	(15.0)
Overhaul at end of 6th yr. (Machine 5 yrs. old)	0.9091	(4,546)		(5.0)						
Present value of net cash outflows		$(83,414)								
Difference in favor of replacement		$ 7,831								

*Some students will challenge this item as not being a "real" saving, because the laborer will merely be transferred to other work. However, this solution assumes that the laborer will engage in some productive work somewhere in the organization; therefore, the railroad will indeed be able to avoid hiring other people for such productive work and will save the overall organization $15,000, one-half of the laborer's annual compensation.

Differential Analysis	At 10% for 7 Years PV Factor	Present Value	0	1	2	3	4	5	6	7
				Sketch of Cash Flows (in thousands)						
Replace (A)										
Recurring cash maintenance savings	4.8684	$ 974		.2	.2	.2	.2	.2	.2	.2
Disposal value of old machine	1.0000	3,500	3.5							
Initial investment	1.0000	(72,000)	(72.0)							
Overhaul, end of 4th yr.	0.6830	(4,781)					(7.0)			
Disposal value of new machine	0.5132	2,566								5.0
Recurring cash operating savings	4.8684	73,026		15.0	15.0	15.0	15.0	15.0	15.0	15.0
Overhaul avoided at end of 6th year	0.9091	4,546		5.0						
Net present value of replacement		$ 7,831								

11-44 (30 min.)

The initial purchase cost of the golf course and the operating receipts and disbursements for the first season of ownership are irrelevant to the present decision. The relevant annual costs which Ms. Paar should take into consideration are:

Electricity, (150 x 1 kw) x (130 x 5 hrs.) x $.032 per kw hr.	$ 3,120
Labor cost, 130 x $15	1,950
Light bulb cost	300
Repairs and maintenance of lighting system, .04 x $20,000	800
Property taxes, .017 x $20,000	340
Total additional operating expenses	$ 6,510

Annual revenue from night operations:	
Years 1 and 2: 130 x $90	$11,700
Years 3, 4, and 5: 130 x $60	$ 7,800

One-time cash flows:	
Present value of initial investment	$20,000
Salvage value, year 5	$ 7,000

Example of Cash Flow Analysis

	Revenue		Expenses		Net Flow	PV Factor	PV of Cash Flows
Year 1	$11,700	-	$6,510	=	$5,190	.9091	$ 4,718
Year 2	11,700	-	6,510	=	5,190	.8264	4,289
Year 3	7,800	-	6,510	=	1,290	.7513	969
Year 4	7,800	-	6,510	=	1,290	.6830	881
Year 5	14,800	-	6,510	=	8,290	.6209	5,147
Present value of cash flows							$16,004

Since the present value of the annual cash flows is less than the initial investment of $20,000, the proposed lighting system should not be installed. If significant increases in revenue were predictable, the plan might become attractive to Ms. Paar.

11-45 (35-45 min.)

	PV Factor	Total Present Value	0	1	2	3	4	5
			Sketch of Cash Flows (in thousands)					
Old machine:								
Operating cash outflows	3.00	£(150,000)		(50)	(50)	(50)	(50)	(50)
Investment in inventories	1.00	(200,000)	(200)					
Liquidation of inventories at terminal date	.40	80,000						200
Disposal value*	.40	1,600						4
Present value		£(268,400)						
Speedo machine:								
Net cash outlay (£62,000-£15,000)	1.00	£ (47,000)	(47)					
Operating cash outflows	3.00	(120,000)		(40)	(40)	(40)	(40)	(40)
Investment in inventories	1.00	(160,000)	(160)					
Liquidation of inventories at terminal date	.40	64,000						160
Disposal value*	.40	1,600						4
Present value		£(261,400)						
NPV in favor of Speedo		£ 7,000						

*Could be excluded from both alternatives because they are the same amounts.

Speedo minimizes the present value of future costs by £7,000. Variations of the above analysis might exclude the £4,000 disposal values and show the cash flow for inventories at £40,000 and zero in year 0 and in year 5. The net quantitative difference between the alternatives should be the same no matter what approach is used, as long as such approach is used correctly.

Some students will assert that the £40,000 reduction in inventory represents an immediate offset to the cost of the new machine. That is exactly what the above solution does. We feel that this solution is the clearest approach because it regards all outlays alike regardless of whether they are for inventories or plant assets. Note that the old machine requires an "outlay" of £200,000 for inventories, but the new machine requires an "outlay" of £160,000. Thus, the £40,000 difference indeed shows up as an "offset" to the cost of the new machine.

Another way to show the effect of the investment in inventories would be via incremental analysis only. That is, the £40,000 difference in required investment would appear as a cash inflow at time zero and as a cash outflow at the end of year 5 because the recoupment then would be £160,000 instead of £200,000:

	PV Factor	Total Present Value	Sketch of Cash Flows (in thousands) 0	1	2	3	4	5
Speedo machine:								
Net cash outlay (£62,000-£15,000)	1.00	£(47,000)	(47)					
Liquidation of inventory at time zero	1.00	40,000	40					
Difference in recoupment of cash from inventory liquidation at terminal date	.40	(16,000)						(40)
Operating savings	3.00	30,000		10	10	10	10	10
Net present value in favor of Speedo		£ 7,000						

11-46 (30-35 min.) This is one of our favorite problems. The heart of the solution extends through the first paragraph of the response to requirement 2. The remainder is amplification.

		Analysis of Cash Flows		
	Present		Proposed	Difference
Revenue		$200,000	$15,000*	
Expenses:				
Miscellaneous	$100,000			
Salaries	110,000	210,000	13,000	
Net cash flow from operations		$ (10,000)	$ 2,000	$12,000
Required investment:				
Equipment		$ -	$19,000**	
Termination pay		-	28,000	
Total		$ -	$47,000	$47,000

*10% x $150,000 = $15,000 commission.

** An acceptable alternative would be to show $3,000 and $22,000 respectively. The incremental investment would still be $19,000.

1.

Present value of $12,000 per year for 10 years at 10% = $12,000 x 6.000	$72,000
Required investment	47,000
Net present value	$25,000

The requirements of the problem focus on the incremental approach. The total project approach could view the problem as choosing the alternative that minimizes the net present value of the future costs:

Present:	
Operating cash outflows, \$10,000 x 6.000	\$(60,000)
Proposed:	
Operating cash inflows, \$2,000 x 6.000	\$ 12,000
Termination pay	(28,000)
Equipment	(19,000)
Total	\$(35,000)
Difference in favor of proposed investment	\$ 25,000

2. The minimum amount of annual revenue that Amtrak would have to receive to justify the investment would be that amount yielding an incremental net present value of zero. As the initial investment is constant, any change in the incremental net present value is due solely to a change in the amount of revenue. Therefore, the maximum drop in the incremental net present value of \$25,000 equals the maximum drop in the present value of the revenue stream. This implies a maximum drop of \$25,000 ÷ 6 = \$4,167 in *annual* revenue and a minimum amount of annual revenue of \$15,000 - \$4,167 = \$10,833.

Let X = Revenue at point of indifference, where net present value is zero

NPV = PV of (New annual cash flows - Old annual cash flows) - Required investment

$$0 = 6.000[(X - 13{,}000) - (-10{,}000)] - 47{,}000$$
$$0 = 6.000(X - 13{,}000 + 10{,}000) - 47{,}000$$
$$0 = 6.000(X - 3{,}000) - 47{,}000$$
$$0 = 6.000X - 18{,}000 - 47{,}000$$
$$6.000X = 65{,}000$$
$$X = 10{,}833$$

Part 2 demonstrates sensitivity analysis, where the manager may see the potential impact of the possible errors in the forecasts of revenue. Such analysis shows how much of a margin of safety is available. In this case, his "best guess" is revenue of $15,000 (part 1). Sensitivity analysis shows him that a decline of revenue would have to occur from $15,000 to $10,833 before the rate of return on the project would decline to the minimum acceptable level.

The following alternate approach to solving requirement 2 is longer, but it may be clearer for many students:

If 10% is the minimum acceptable rate of return, the minimum acceptable net present value must be zero, using the 10% rate:

NPV = PV of future cash flows - Initial investment
Let X = Annual cash inflow
Then 0 = 6.000(X) - $47,000
X = $47,000 ÷ 6.000 = $7,833

Present value of $7,833 per year for 10 years at 10% = $7,833 x 6.000	$47,000
Required investment	47,000
Net present value	$ 0

Many students will stop at this point, giving an answer of $7,833. But the requirement asks for the minimum amount of *revenue*, as distinguished from the *difference in cash flows*. The following analysis shows that revenue can fall to $10,833. Note also that there can be negative cash flows under both alternatives; the alternative with the least negative cash flow is preferable:

	Present	Proposed	Difference in Cash Flows
Revenue	$200,000	$10,833	
Expenses	210,000	13,000	
Net cash flow from operations	$ (10,000)	$ (2,167)	$7,833

11-47 (30-40 min.)

1.

End of Year	PV of $1.00 Discounted at 20%	Present Value of Cash Flows	Sketch of Cash Flows (thousands) 0	1	2	3	4	5
A. Continue with common carriers:								
500,000 lbs. @ $.25	2.9906	$(373,825)		(125)	(125)	(125)	(125)	(125)
B. Purchase truck:								
Cost of truck	1.0000	(35,000)	(35)					
Cash operating costs*	2.9906	(672,885)		(225)	(225)	(225)	(225)	(225)
Back-haul revenue, 50 trips @ $2,400	2.9906	358,872		120	120	120	120	120
Present value of net cash flows		$(349,013)						
Difference in favor of truck		$ 24,812						

*500,000 lbs. ÷ 10,000 lbs. = 50 trips
50 trips x 5,000 miles x $.90 per mile = $225,000

2. The PV of back-haul revenue must fall by $24,812 before the net present value equals zero. Therefore, the total present value of back-haul revenue would be $358,872 less $24,812, or $334,060.

Let X = number of trips

$$(2.9906) \times (\$2,400) \times (X) = \$334,060$$
$$\$7,177\, X = \$334,060$$
$$X = 46.5 \text{ trips}$$

Consequently 46 trips would be slightly insufficient, and 47 trips would have to be guaranteed to yield a non-negative present value.

3. The greatest difficulty is the reliability of the numbers in a world of uncertainty. Although "the numbers" indicate the truck is a favorable alternative, the following other factors could influence the final decision:

(a) If the back-haul agreement can be canceled by Retro at any time, the truck becomes a more risky investment since the back-haul revenue is needed to make the investment produce a return of 20% or more.

(b) What is the outlook for other investments over the life of the truck investment? Does purchasing the truck preclude taking advantage of more favorable opportunities during the 5-year life of the truck?

(c) Does the management have the required expertise to run the truck operation efficiently?

(d) Will the truck give the company better service than common carriers?

(e) How certain are the predicted cash flows? Are shipment figures and operating cost predictions considered to be relatively accurate?

11-48 (15 min.)

1. Straight-line depreciation:
   Annual depreciation = $30,000 ÷ 5 = $6,000 per year
   PV of tax savings = $6,000 x .40 x 3.6048 = $8,652

2. MACRS depreciation:

Year	Tax Savings	PV factor	Present Value
1	.2000 x $30,000 x .4 = $2,400	.8929	$2,143
2	3200 x 30,000 x .4 = 3,840	.7972	3,061
3	1920 x 30,000 x .4 = 2,304	.7118	1,640
4	1152 x 30,000 x .4 = 1,382	.6355	878
5	1152 x 30,000 x .4 = 1,382	.5674	784
6	0576 x 30,000 x .4 = 691	.5066	350
Total present value of tax savings			$8,856

You can also use Exhibit 11-7: .7381 x $30,000 x .4 = $8,857 The difference between this and $8,856 is due to rounding error.

3. Immediate write-off:
   30,000 x .4 = $12,000

4. Mr. Tamura would prefer immediate write-off. Note that the total tax savings is $12,000 under all three methods. However, only the immediate write-off provides the entire savings immediately. Straight-line depreciation delays receipt of the tax savings the longest, and therefore it has the lowest present value.

11-49 (30 min.)

1. See Exhibit 11-49 on the next page for the solution to requirement 1.

2.		
	Net present value as above	$(1,656)
	Add Year 6 operating cash savings, $5,500 x .5066	2,786
	Add Year 7 operating cash savings, $5,500 x .4523	2,488
	Deduct PV of residual value	(557)
	Net present value is positive, so buy.	$3,061

11-50 (30 min.)

Investment		$(45,000)
Cash operating savings		
Annual savings	$13,500	
Income taxes @ 40%	5,400	
After-tax effect on cash	$ 8,100	
Present value ($8,100 x 4.5638)		36,967
PV of tax savings from depreciation:		
Investment x PV factor (Exhibit 11-7) x Tax rate =		
$45,000 x .7381 x .40		13,286*
Overhaul required:		
Total cost	$ 5,000	
Less income tax savings @ 40%	2,000	
Total after-tax effect	$ 3,000	
Present value ($3,000 x .6355)		(1,906)
Residual value:		
Cash received	$ 4,000	
Book value	0	
Gain	$ 4,000	
Income tax @ 40%	1,600	
Total after-tax effect	$ 2,400	
Present value ($2,400 x .4523)		1,086
Net present value of all cash flows		$ 4,433

EXHIBIT 11-49

1. There is a net disadvantage in purchasing because the net present value is slightly negative. However, such a slight quantitative disadvantage could be more than offset by positive factors not quantified here.

		Present Value Discount Factors, @ 12%	Total Present Values
Recurring operating cash savings	$10,000		
Income taxes, @ 45%	4,500		
After-tax operating cash savings	$ 5,500	3.6048	$ 19,826
Tax savings due to depreciation:			
5-year property @ $33,000			10,961*
Residual value, all subject to tax			
because book value will be zero	$ 2,000		
Less: 45% income tax on disposal gain	900		
Net cash inflow	$ 1,100	.5066	557
Initial required investment			(33,000)
Net present value of all cash flows			$ (1,656)

*The tax savings due to MACRS depreciation can be calculated as follows:

(1) Year	(2) MACRS Percentage	(3) Income Tax Deduction $33,000x(2)	(4) Present Value Savings, .45x(3)	(5) Total Present Factors, @ 12%	(6) Values (4)x(5)
1	.2000	$ 6,600	$2,970	.8929	$ 2,652
2	.3200	10,560	4,752	.7972	3,788
3	.1920	6,336	2,851	.7118	2,030
4	.1152	3,802	1,711	.6355	1,087
5	.1152	3,802	1,711	.5674	971
6	.0596	1,901	855	.5066	433
					$10,961

Sketch of Cash Flows at End of Year

0	1	2	3	4	5	6
	2,970					
		4,752				
			2,851			
				1,711		
					1,711	
						855

The tax savings due to MACRS depreciation can also be computed using Exhibit 11-7: .7381 x 33,000 x .45 = $10,961.

The investment is desirable

*The PV of the tax savings from depreciation can also be calculated as follows:

Year	Tax Savings	PV factor	Present Value
1	.2000 x $45,000 x .4 = $3,600	.8929	$ 3,214
2	.3200 x 45,000 x .4 = 5,760	.7972	4,592
3	.1920 x 45,000 x .4 = 3,456	.7118	2,460
4	.1152 x 45,000 x .4 = 2,074	.6355	1,318
5	.1152 x 45,000 x .4 = 2,074	.5674	1,177
6	.0576 x 45,000 x .4 = 1,037	.5066	525
Total present value of tax savings			$13,286

11-51 (40-50 min.)

1. See Exhibit 11-51 for the solution to requirement 1.
2. The greatest difficulty is the reliability of the numbers in a world of uncertainty. Although "the numbers" indicate the truck is a favorable alternative, the following other factors could influence the final decision:
   (a) If the back-haul agreement can be canceled by Retro at any time, the truck becomes a more risky investment since the back-haul revenue is needed to make the investment produce an after-tax return of 20% or more.
   (b) What is the outlook for other investments over the life of the truck investment? Does purchasing the truck preclude taking advantage of more favorable opportunities during the 5-year life of the truck?
   (c) Does the management have the required expertise to run the truck operation efficiently?
   (d) Will the truck give the company better service than common carriers?
   (e) How certain are the predicted cash flows? Are shipment figures and operating cost predictions considered to be relatively accurate?

EXHIBIT 11-51

		Total Present Value	After-Tax Cash Flows Year 0	Year 1	Year 2	Year 3	Year 4	Year 5	Year 6
Alternative 1: Continue w/ common carrier									
500,000 lbs @ 25¢	$125,000								
Income tax savings @ 40%	(50,000)								
After-tax (Year 0)	$ 75,000								
Adjust $75,000 for 10% inflation									
$75,000 x 1.1; x 1.1²; x 1.1³; x 1.1⁴; x 1.1⁵				(82,500)	(90,750)	(99,825)	(109,808)	(120,788)	
Present value factor @ 20%				.8333	.6944	.5787	.4823	.4019	
Present value		$(291,038)		(68,747)	(63,017)	(57,769)	(52,960)	(48,545)	
Alternative 2: Purchase truck									
Initial cash investment			(35,000)						
Depreciation deductions:									
Year % Deduction	Tax Savings								
1 20 $ 7,000	$2,800			2,800					
2 32 11,200	4,480				4,480				
3 19.2 6,720	2,688					2,688			
4-5 11.52 4,032	1,613						1,613	1,613	
6 5.76 2,016	806								806
Back-haul revenue*									
50 trips** @ $2,400	$120,000								
Income tax @ 40%	(48,000)								
After-tax	$ 72,000			72,000	72,000	72,000	72,000	72,000	
Cash operating costs:									
250,000 miles† @ 90¢	$225,000								
Income tax savings	(90,000)								
	$135,000								
Adjust $135,000 for inflation after Year 1									
$135,000 x 1.1; x 1.1²; x 1.1³; x 1.1⁴				(135,000)	(148,500)	(163,350)	(179,685)	(197,654)	
Total cash flow			(35,000)	(60,200)	(72,020)	(88,662)	(106,072)	(124,041)	806
Present value factors @ 20%			1.0000	.8333	.6944	.5787	.4823	.4019	.3349
Present value		(287,226)	(35,000)	(50,165)	(50,011)	(51,309)	(51,159)	(49,852)	270
PV difference in favor of purchasing truck		$ 3,812							

*Not subject to inflation due to 5-year agreement. **500,000 lbs ÷ 10,000 lbs/trip = 50 trips †50 trips @ 5,000 round-trip miles = 250,000 miles

11-52 (20-30 min.)

1 & 2. See Exhibit 11-52 for the solution to requirements 1 and 2.

3. Correct analysis of inflation can affect decisions. Using a required rate of return that includes an inflation element but neglecting to adjust cash inflows for inflation will understate the present value, causing possible rejection of desirable projects.

11-53 (45-60 min.)

A. Investment: $155,000 + (20 x $6,000) = $275,000

B. PV of cash inflows from operations:
Monthly rental payments = ($190 x 12) + ($220 x 8) = $4,040
Repair and maintenance = .15 x $4,040 = $606
Annual before-tax cash inflow = 12 x ($4,040 - $606) = $41,208
Annual after tax cash inflow = .62 x $41,208 = $25,549
Present value of inflows @ 10% = 25,549 x 6.1446 = $156,988

C. PV of tax savings:
Annual depreciation = $275,000 ÷ 27.5 = $10,000
Annual tax savings = $10,000 x .38 = $3,800
PV of tax savings for 10 years = $3,800 x 6.1446 = $23,349

D. PV of cash effects of disposal:

Cash received	$450,000
Book value [$275,000 - (10 x $10,000)]	175,000
Gain	$275,000
Income taxes @ 38%	$104,500
Net cash received at disposal ($450,000 - $104,500)	$345,500
Time 0 present value ($345,500 x .3855)	$133,190

EXHIBIT 11-52

Description	14% PV Factor	Total Present Value	Sketch of Relevant Cash Flows (in dollars)					
			19X6	19X7	19X8	19X9	19Y0	19Y1
1. Per Problem Instructions (But that is an incorrect analysis, which includes an inflation element in the discount rate but does not adjust the predicted cash flows for inflation.)								
Cash operating savings	3.4331	6,866		2,000	2,000	2,000	2,000	2,000
New machine, investment	1.0000	(7,300)	(7,300)					
Net present value		(434)						
2. Correct Analysis: (Includes an inflation element in both the discount rate and the predicted cash flows.)								
Cash operating savings:	.8772	1,860		2,120*				
	.7695	1,729			2,247			
	.6750	1,608				2,382		
	.5921	1,495					2,525	
	.5194	1,390						2,676
		8,082						
New machine, investment	1.0000	(7,300)	(7,300)					
Net present value		782						

*2,000 x 1.06, then 2,000 x $(1.06)^2$, then 2,000 x $(1.06)^3$, etc.

E. Net present value at time 0:

A. Investment	$(275,000)
B. PV of operating cash inflows	156,988
C. PV of income tax savings	23,349
D. PV of cash effect of disposal:	
PV of net cash received	133,190
Net present value	$ 38,527

The net present value is positive, so the NPV model indicates that Ramirez should purchase the apartment complex.

11-54 (15-20 min.) Amounts are in thousands of Japanese yen.

1. Depreciation expense: (¥400,000 - ¥50,000) ÷ 10 = ¥35,000

2. Net income:

Revenues		¥320,000
Less expense:		
Depreciation	¥ 35,000	
Other	165,000	200,000
Operating income		¥120,000
Less income tax (60%)		72,000
Net income		¥ 48,000

3. Cash flow: ¥48,000 + ¥35,000 = ¥83,000 per year
or ¥320,000 - ¥165,000 - ¥72,000 = ¥83,000

4. Payback period: ¥400,000 ÷ ¥83,000 = 4.8 years

You might note that 4.8 years is a reasonably long payback period for United States companies, and many companies would be inclined to reject such a project. However, in Japan managers tend to take a longer-run point of view, and a 4.8-year payback period is often acceptable.

5. Accounting rate of return: ¥48,000 ÷ ¥400,000 = 12%
(or, if average investment is used:
(¥400,000 + ¥50,000) ÷ 2 = ¥225,000 average investment;
¥48,000 ÷ ¥225,000 = 21.3%)

6. NPV:

Annual cash flows, ¥83,000 x 5.2161 =	¥432,936
Salvage value, ¥50,000 x 0.2697 =	13,485
Gross present value	¥446,421
Less: Investment	400,000
Net present value	¥ 46,421

11-55 (20-35 min.)

1.

$50,000 x 3.8887 factor =	$194,435
($22,000 + $15,000) x .4556 factor =	16,857
Total present value	$211,292
Less initial investment:	
$193,000 + $15,000 =	208,000
Net present value (NPV)	$ 3,292

3. a. Annual depreciation is ($193,000 - $22,000) ÷ 6 = $28,500
Increase in expected average annual operating income = $50,000 - $28,500 = $21,500
Initial investment is $208,000
Rate of return is $21,500 ÷ $208,000 = 10.3%

b. Note the rate of return is not twice the 10.3%. Why? Because the investment at the end of six years is not zero:

Investment at end of 6 years: $22,000 + $15,000 =	$ 37,000
Initial investment	208,000
Total	$245,000

"Average" investment: $245,000 ÷ 2 = $122,500
Rate of return is $21,500 ÷ $122,500 = 17.6%

4. The models in requirements 1 and 2 would induce a positive decision. However, the 10.3% accounting rate of return based on an initial investment might induce a negative decision because it is less than 14%. An administrator's reluctance to buy would be understandable if there is no reasonable consistency between the decision model and the performance evaluation model. If decisions are supposed to be based on DCF models, and performance is evaluated on accrual accounting models, the latter tend to be persuasive.

11-56 (20 min.)

1. Investment = \$2,000,000 + \$1,200,000 = \$3,200,000
Annual cash inflow = 300 skiers x 40 days x \$55/skier-day = \$660,000
Annual cash outflow
= (200 days x \$500/day)+(\$5/skier-day x 300 x 40) = \$160,000

PV of cash flows @ 14% = (\$660,000 - \$160,000) x 6.6231 = \$3,311,550

NPV = \$3,311,550 - \$3,200,000 = \$111,550

The new lift will create value of \$111,550, so it is a profitable investment.

2. After-tax cash flows = \$500,000 x .6 = \$300,000

PV of after-tax cash flows @ 8% = \$300,000 x 9.8181 = \$2,945,430

PV of tax savings = \$3,200,000 x .4 x .7059 (from Exhibit 11-7) = \$903,552

NPV after-tax = \$2,945,430 + \$903,552 - \$3,200,000 = \$648,982

The investment in the lift is more profitable on an after-tax basis than on a pretax basis.

3. Subjective factors that might affect this decision include:
   - Profits on sales of food, rental of equipment, and other items purchased by the additional skiers.
   - More satisfied customers because of less crowding on the days that the additional lift does not result in additional skiers being attracted to Deer Valley.
   - Additional skiers may not be as high as estimated if the weather is poor.

11-57 (25-30 min.) Amounts are in Swedish Kroner (SKr).

Annual cash savings (SKr 260,000 x 5)	SKr 1,300,000
Additional operating expenses	(900,000)
Net annual savings	SKr 400,000
Investment	SKr 1,600,000

1. NPV = (SKr 400,000 x 4.9676*) - SKr 1,600,000
   = SKr 1,987,040 - SKr 1,600,000
   = SKr 387,040

   *From Table 2, 12% column, 8-year row.

   The system should be purchased because the NPV is positive.

2. Pessimistic:
   Annual savings = SKr 400,000 - SKr 260,000 = SKr 140,000
   Economic life = 5 years
   NPV = (SKr 140,000 x 3.6048) - SKr 1,600,000
   =SKr 504,672 - SKr 1,600,000 = SKr (1,095,328)

Optimistic:

Annual savings = SKr 400,000 + SKr 260,000 = SKr 660,000
Economic life = 10 years

NPV = (SKr 660,000 x 5.6502) - SKr 1,600,000
= SKr 3,729,132 - SKr 1,600,000 = SKr 2,129,132

Most likely: NPV = SKr 387,040 (from requirement 1)

This analysis shows that predictions of savings and economic life can greatly affect the decision. Although the expected NPV is SKr 387,040, it is possible that the realized NPV might be as low as (SKr 1,095,328). It might be worthwhile to gather more information about the savings and economic life before making the decision.

3. Investment in new technology often has many effects that are difficult to quantify. A special report in *Business Week* reported that most companies do not provide a quantitative cost justification for the purchase of computers. However, the article goes on to point out that analyses such as NPV are being increasingly demanded by top management to justify investment in new technology.

The company should be concerned with the amount of investment specified. The system can be purchased for SKr 1,600,000, but might additional costs be incurred in implementing the system?

Will the quality of design be improved by the new system? Or might the system be incapable of meeting current standards?

Maybe most important, the analysis is based on the implementation of CAD only. Is there any chance that the CAM portion will be used? If so, the purchase has more value than shown in the analysis of CAD only.

11-58 (30-40 min.)

This case focuses on the appropriate baseline for NPV analysis for an investment in a high technology production system. It highlights the possible loss of competitive position if the investment is not undertaken. The potential magnitude of errors from omission of some factors in an NPV analysis is shown.

1. This is a straightforward NPV analysis:

Year	Present Value @ 12% from Table 1	Differential Net Cash Flow	Present Value of Differential Cash Flow
1997	1.0000	$(6,000,000)	$(6,000,000)
1998	.8929	(400,000)	(357,160)
1999	.7972	1,600,000	1,275,520
2000	.7118	1,600,000	1,138,880
2001	.6355	1,600,000	1,016,800
2002	.5674	1,600,000	907,840
2003	.5066	1,600,000	810,560
Total			$(1,207,560)

The investment in the CIM has a negative NPV of more than $1.2 million. It appears that it would be a mistake to invest.

2. An additional advantage of the CIM must be recognized in this analysis. In the absence of investment in the CIM, some of the existing contribution margin will be lost each year. Investment avoids this loss, so the amount of the contribution margin that would have been lost is in essence a savings from investment in the CIM.

The current market share of 40% and sales of $12 million implies that each 1% of the market is worth sales of $12,000,000 ÷ 40 = $300,000. Current sales are $12,000,000 and variable costs are $4,000,000 +

$2,000,000 = $6,000,000, making the contribution margin percentage 50%. Therefore, for each $1 of lost sales, Wisconsin Auto Parts loses $.50 in contribution margin. The loss of $300,000 in sales results in a loss of $150,000 in contribution margin.

Therefore, the potential lost contribution margin each year is:

Year	Lost Market Share	Lost Sales	Lost Contribution Margin
1998	3%	$ 900,000	$ 450,000
1999	6	1,800,000	900,000
2000	9	2,700,000	1,350,000
2001	12	3,600,000	1,800,000
2002	15	4,500,000	2,250,000
2003	18	5,400,000	2,700,000

Combining the savings from variable costs with the savings in contribution margin, the NPV becomes a positive $4,661,025, computed as follows:

Year	Present Value @ 12% from Table 1	Savings in Variable Costs	Savings in Contribution Margin	Total Differential Cash Flow	Present Value of Differential Cash Flow
1997	1.0000	$(6,000,000)			$(6,000,000)
1998	.8929	(400,000)	450,000	50,000	44,645
1999	.7972	1,600,000	900,000	2,500,000	1,993,000
2000	.7118	1,600,000	1,350,000	2,950,000	2,099,810
2001	.6355	1,600,000	1,800,000	3,400,000	2,160,700
2002	.5674	1,600,000	2,250,000	3,850,000	2,184,490
2003	.5066	1,600,000	2,700,000	4,300,000	2,178,380
Total					$ 4,661,025

The picture has changed radically from that in requirement 1. Avoiding the lost contribution margin has made the CIM a very desirable investment.

3. To the Board of Directors:

I recommend that Wisconsin Auto Parts invest in the new CIM system. I have made two net present value analyses, the first one showing a negative NPV of more than $1.2 million and the second showing a positive NPV of over $4.6 million. Let me explain why the second analysis is better.

The first analysis compares revenues and costs under the CIM to those that would be incurred if operations continue exactly as they did in 1997. However, if we do not invest in CIM, operations will not continue the way they are today. Many of our competitors are investing in technologically sophisticated production systems, and if we do not invest, they will have advantages over us in quality of products, response to design changes desired by our customers, and flexibility of delivery schedules. Investment in the CIM will not only save variable costs of production, it will allow us to maintain our market share.

The second analysis uses the correct baseline for comparisons. It compares the costs and revenues with the CIM to those we expect if we do not invest. It includes consideration of the lost sales, and therefore lost contribution margin, that we would experience if our competitors gain a competitive advantage by investing in CIM while we do not. If we do not upgrade to CIM or some similar system in the next six years, we risk losing nearly half our business. This risk is much greater than that of not achieving all the cost savings projected for the CIM.

In addition to the items included in my analysis, there are other potential benefits to investing in the CIM. First, it encourages our employees to think about the production process and places where we might eliminate or reduce non-value-added activities. It also introduces technologically sophisticated operations so that future expansion of similar activities may be easier.

In summary, cost savings alone do not justify investment in the CIM. But cost savings are not the only advantage of investment. When we add the extra contribution margins from business we will maintain only if we invest in the CIM, plus other qualitative advantages, the investment is certainly desirable.

11-59 (30-40 min.)

This problem includes a complex analysis of relevant costs in addition to its focus on an investment decision. This solution will first identify the relevant costs in four categories:

1. Initial investment
2. Current annual quality control costs
3. Annual quality control costs with new process
4. Forgone profits if quality is not improved

Initial investment:

Worker training	$900,000	
X-ray machine	200,000	
Total investment		$1,100,000

Current annual quality control costs:

Inspection cost	$ 40,000	
Correction of defects (1,500 x $85)	127,500	
Refunds to customers (500 x $210)	105,000	
Total current quality control costs		$ 272,500

Annual quality control costs with new process:

Inspection cost ($40,000 + $50,000)	$ 90,000	
Correction of defects (450 x $50)	22,500	
Refunds to customers (50 x $315)	15,750	
Total new quality control costs		128,250

Net savings in quality control costs	$ 144,250

Difference in contribution margin if quality is not improved:

19X1	$ 0	
19X2	350,000	(5,000 x $70)
19X3	700,000	(10,000 x $70)
19X4	1,050,000	(15,000 x $70)

Therefore, the total annual cash flows from the change in the quality control process are:

	Net Savings in Quality Control Costs	Differences in Total Contribution Margin	Net Cash Flow from Operations
19X1	$144,250	$ 0	$ 144,250
19X2	144,250	350,000	494,250
19X3	144,250	700,000	844,250
19X4	144,250	1,050,000	1,194,250

The net present value of the investment in the new quality control is positive, so invest:

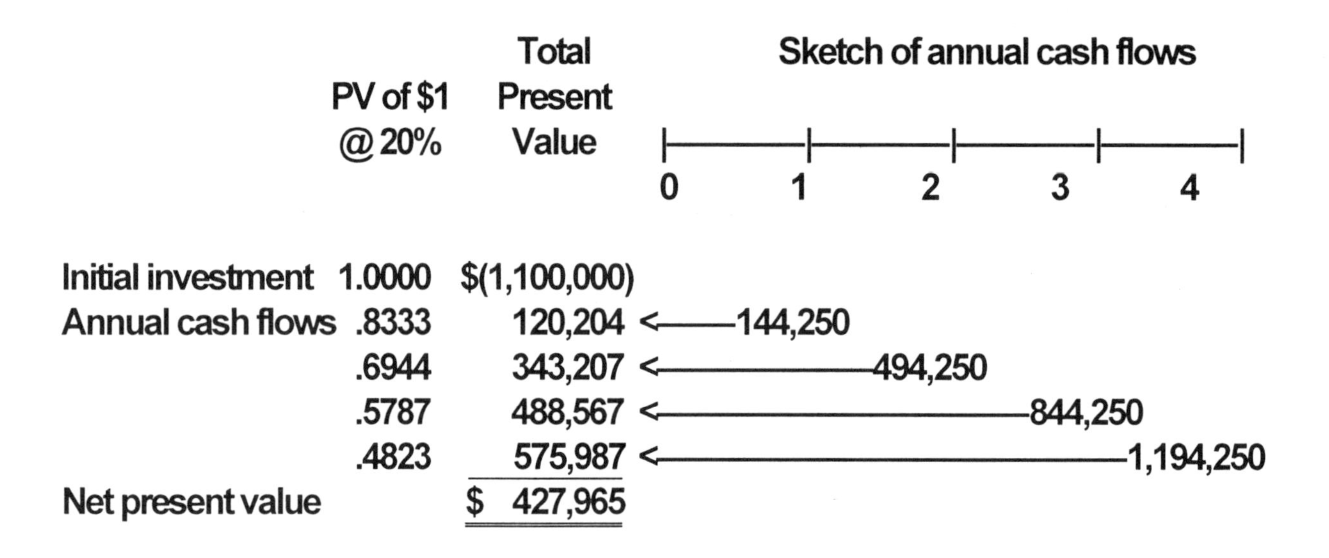

	PV of $1 @ 20%	Total Present Value	Sketch of annual cash flows 0	1	2	3	4
Initial investment	1.0000	$(1,100,000)					
Annual cash flows	.8333	120,204	<—	144,250			
	.6944	343,207	<—		494,250		
	.5787	488,567	<—			844,250	
	.4823	575,987	<—				1,194,250
Net present value		$ 427,965					

11-60 (50-75 min.)

This is a complex problem because it requires comparing three alternatives. It reviews Chapter 6 as well as covering several of the topics of Chapter 11. The following answer uses the total project approach. The total net future cash outflows are shown for each alternative.

1. Alternative A: Continue to manufacture the parts with the current tools.

Annual cash outlays		
Variable cost, $.92 x 80,000	$73,600	
Fixed cost, 1/3 x $.45 x 80,000 x .6	7,200	
Tax savings, .4 x ($73,600 + $7,200)	(32,320)	
After-tax annual cost	$48,480	
Present value, 3.6048 x $48,480		$174,761
PV of remaining tax savings on MACRS:		
11.52% x $200,000 x .4 x .8929		(8,229)
5.76 x $200,000 x .4 x .7972		(3,673)
Total present value of costs, Alternative A		$162,859

Alternative B: Purchase from outside supplier

Annual cash outlays		
Purchase cost, $1.10 x 80,000	$88,000	
Tax savings, $88,000 x .4	(35,200)	
After-tax annual cost	$52,800	
Present value, $52,800 x 3.6048		$190,333
Sale of old equipment:		
Sales price	$30,000	
Book value [(11.52% + 5.76%) x 200,000]	34,560	
Loss		$ 4,560
Taxes @ 40%	1,824	
Total after-tax effect ($30,000 + $1,824)		(31,824)
Total present value of costs, Alternative B		$158,509

Alternative C: Purchase new equipment

Investment		$180,000
Annual cash outlays		
Variable cost, $.73 x 80,000	$58,400	
Fixed cost, (same as A)	7,200	
Tax savings, .4 x ($58,400 + $7,200)	(26,240)	
After-tax annual cost	$39,360	
Present value, $39,360 x 3.6048		141,885
Tax savings on new equipment*		(57,922)
Effect of disposal of new equipment		
Sales price	$40,000	
Book value	0	
Gain		$40,000
Taxes @ 40%	16,000	
Total after-tax effect	$24,000	
Present value, $24,000 x .5674		(13,618)
Effect of disposal of old equipment (see Alternative B)		(31,824)
Total present value of costs, Alternative C		$218,521

*Using the MACRS schedule for tax depreciation, the depreciation rate for each year of a 3-year asset's life is shown in Exhibit 11-6:

Year	Depreciation Rate	Tax Savings	PV Factor	Present Value
1	33.33%	.3333 x 180,000 x .40 = $23,998	.8929	$21,427
2	44.45%	.4445 x 180,000 x .40 = 32,004	.7972	25,514
3	14.81%	.1481 x 180,000 x .40 = 10,663	.7118	7,590
4	7.41%	.0741 x 180,000 x .40 = 5,335	.6355	3,391
Total present value of tax savings				$57,922

Using Exhibit 11-7, we get .8044 x $180,000 x .4 = $75,917, which differs from $57,922 by a $5 rounding error.

The alternative with the lowest present value of cost is Alternative B, purchasing from the outside supplier.

2. Among the major factors are (1) the range of expected volume (both large increases and decreases below 70,000 make the purchase of the parts relatively less desirable), (2) the reliability of the outside supplier, (3) possible changes in material, labor, and overhead prices, (4) the possibility that the outside supplier can raise prices before the end of five years, (5) obsolescence of the products and equipment, and (6) alternate uses of available capacity (alternative uses make Alternative B relatively more desirable).

11-61 (20 min.)

The purpose of this exercise is to see how financial analyses and behavioral issues interact in decision making. We first present the NPV analysis that should form the basis of LaGrande's meeting with Osterland. Then we discuss other items that are likely to surface in the meeting.

To gain a 16% rate of return, the net present value at 16% must be positive. For Krispie Krinkles, optimistic, expected, and pessimistic present values of predicted cash inflows, assuming cash flows at the end of each year, are (in thousands of dollars):

Year	(1) PV of $1 at 16%	(2) Optimistic Cash Flow	(3) Optimistic Present Value (1) x (2)	(4) Expected Cash Flow	(5) Expected Present Value (1) x (4)	(6) Pessimistic Cash Flow	(7) Pessimistic Present Value (1) x (6)
1	.8621	800	690	600	517	400	345
2	.7432	1,800	1,338	1,200	892	600	446
3	.6407	2,500	1,602	1,500	961	500	320
4	.5523	4,000	2,209	2,200	1,215	400	221
5	.4761	5,000	2,380	2,600	1,238	200	95
Total			8,219		4,823		1,427

The investment and salvage values do not depend on the optimistic and pessimistic forecasts:

Investment (1.0000 x $6,000,000)	$(6,000,000)
Salvage value of facilities (.4761 x $800,000)	380,880
Salvage value of working capital (.4761 x $500,000)	238,050
Total	$(5,381,070)

Therefore, net prevent values are:

Optimistic ($8,219,000 - $5,381,070)	$ 2,837,930
Expected ($4,823,000 - $5,381,070)	$ (558,070)
Pessimistic ($1,427,000 - $5,381,070)	$(3,954,070)

If you believe the expected amounts, the product has a negative present value and should not be launched.

Osterland might raise some of the following issues supporting the project:

- The required rate of return is less than 16%.
- The optimistic scenario is more likely than the pessimistic scenario, making the expected cash flows more than those listed.
- The cash flow predictions for either the optimistic or pessimistic scenarios (or both) are understated.
- The contribution margin is 58% rather than 50%.
- The investment is less than $6 million.

For example, she might maintain that the required rate of return for a project of this risk should be 12% instead of 16%. Then the product's net present value would be $5,434,000 - ($6,000,000 = .5674 x $800,000 = .5674 x $500,000) = $171,620:

	(1)	(2)	(3)	(4)	(5)	(6)	(7)
		Optimistic		Expected		Pessimistic	
Year	PV of $1 at 12%	Cash Flow	Present Value (1) x (2)	Cash Flow	Present Value (1) x (4)	Cash Flow	Present Value (1) x (6)
1	.8929	800	714	600	536	400	357
2	.7972	1,800	1,435	1,200	957	600	478
3	.7118	2,500	1,779	1,500	1,068	500	356
4	.6356	4,000	2,542	2,200	1,398	400	254
5	.5674	5,000	2,837	2,600	1,475	200	113
Total			9,307		5,434		1,558

Or she might maintain that each expected cash flow should be $200,000 higher, making the net present value $4,823,000 + ($200,000 x 3.2743) = $5,381,070 = $96,790.

Or if the contribution margin were 58% rather than 50%, the net present value would be [$4,823,000 x (58/50)] - $5,381,070 = $213,610.

Finally, if the investment is less than $6,000,000 by at least $558,070, the net present value would be positive.

Osterland could use some combination of these changes to make the net present value of the product positive.

The ethical issues in this exercise can be revealing. If LaGrande believes his information is accurate, it would be unethical to produce biased numbers just to satisfy Osterland. Among the ethical requirements for management accountants are to "communicate information fairly and objectively," "disclose fully all relevant information," and "prepare concise and clear reports and recommendations after appropriate analyses of relevant and reliable information." These standards would be violated if LaGrande were to change his analysis just to satisfy Osterland.l

Therefore, it is important that LaGrande report numbers that he believes are accurate. This may upset his supervisor, Osterland, and that may create problems for LaGrande. Nevertheless, more serious problems are created when biased information is presented in order to justify a manager's pet projects.

CHAPTER 12
Cost Allocation and Activity-Based Costing

12-A1 (15-20 min.)

1. Allocations are in millions:

	Actual Revenue	Allocated Costs
Divisions:		
Northeast	$120	$ 6
Mid-Atlantic	200	10
Southeast	280	14
Total	$600	$30

2. Northeastern's manager would probably be indifferent, Mid-Atlantic's would be pleased, and Southeast's would be displeased.

   The major weakness of using revenue as a basis for cost allocation is that it often fails to portray underlying cause-and-effect relationships. The major point of this problem is to show how strange results occur when the costs being allocated to *a given* segment are dependent on the activity of some *other* segment. The Southeast Division has done the most to reduce the unit cost of central services, but it is being charged with a heavier dose of common costs. Indeed, Mid-Atlantic may have received more rather than less attention because of its current competitive troubles.

   Most of the central costs are discretionary. Pinpointing cause-and-effect relationships is hard. Such costs are usually predetermined by management fiat or by *budgeted* revenue.

Serious consideration should be given to one or more of the following:

a. No allocation, because no convincing allocation base is available.
b. Dividing the services into sub-categories and allocating by the use of several different cost drivers.
c. Using budgeted revenues rather than actual revenues as a cost driver for allocation. Of course, the use of budgeted revenues may induce more "gamesmanship" than is typically encountered during the budgetary process. There is a tendency to "under-budget" whenever a lower cost allocation will result.

3. Allocations are in millions:

	Budgeted Revenue	Allocated Costs
Divisions:		
Northeast	$120	$ 5.6
Mid-Atlantic	240	11.3
Southeast	280	13.1
Total	$640	$30.0

Many managers prefer this method because it portrays causes and effects somewhat better than in requirement (1). That is, at least the overall level of costs tend to be planned rather than just happen after the fact.

In requirement (1), the allocated costs were each 5% of *actual* revenue. However, in requirement (3), the allocation is predetermined, and therefore the percentages of actual revenue vary:

	(1) Actual Revenue	(2) Allocated Costs	(3) Percentage (2) ÷ (1)
Divisions:			
Northeast	$120	$ 5.6	4.7%
Mid-Atlantic	200	11.3	5.7%
Southeast	280	13.1	4.7%
Total	$600	$30.0	

Note that Mid-Atlantic 's budgeted percentage would have been $11.3 ÷ $240 = 4.7%. The resultant deviation of the actual percentage (5.7%) from the budgeted percentage (4.7%) would highlight the effects of Mid-Atlantic 's troubles.

4. Many accountants and managers oppose allocating any central costs when no convincing causes and effects can be established in any economically feasible way. The opponents of cost allocation feel that the managers of subunits will have better attitudes and will make better decisions if no allocation occurs.

12-A2 (30-50 min.)

The numerical answers for requirements 1 and 2 are in Exhibit 12-A2.

Most students will favor the direct method because the final allocations are not affected significantly.

EXHIBIT 12-A2

	Total	General Factory Administration	Cafeteria	Engi-neering	Machining	Assembly	Finishing and Painting
Total labor hours	1,296,000	-	36,000	120,000	300,000	720,000	120,000
Percentage	100.0%	-	2.8%	9.3%	23.1%	55.5%	9.3%
Employees	780	-	-	60	120	540	60
Percentage	100.0%	-	-	7.7%	15.4%	69.2%	7.7%
Engineering hours	80,000	-	-	-	50,000	20,000	10,000
Percentage	100.0%	-	-	-	62.5%	25.0%	12.5%
Cost Driver							
Cost Drivers		Total Labor Hours	Employees	Engineering Hours			
Method 1, Direct Method							
Total department overhead before allocation		$950,000	$150,000	$2,500,000	----------	Not Given	----------
General factory administration		(950,000)	-	-	$ 250,000[1]	$ 600,000	$100,000
Cafeteria		(150,000)	-	25,000	112,500[2]	12,500	
Engineering				(2,500,000)	1,562,500[3]	625,000	312,500
Totals					$1,837,500	$1,337,500	$425,000
Method 2, Step-Down Method							
Total department overhead before allocation		$950,000	$150,000	$2,500,000	----------	Not Given	----------
General factory administration		(950,000)	26,600[4]	88,350	$219,450	$527,250	$88,350
Cafeteria			(176,600)	13,598[5]	27,197	122,207	13,598
Engineering				(2,601,948)	1,626,217[6]	650,487	325,244
Totals					$1,872,864	$1,299,944	$427,192

[1] 300 + 720 + 120 = 1,140; 300/1,140 x 950,000 = 250,000; 720/1,140 x 950,000 = 600,000; etc.

[2] 120 + 540 + 60 = 720; 120/720 x 150,000 = 25,000; 540/720 x 150,000 = 112,500; etc.

[3] 50 + 20 + 10 = 80; 50/80 x 2,500,000 = 1,562,500; 20/80 x 2,500,000 = 625,000; etc.

Rounding in (4), (5), and (6) can cause discrepancies of hundreds of dollars:

[4] 2.8% x 950,000 = 26,600; 9.3% x 950,000 = 88,350; etc.

[5] 7.7% x 176,600 = 13,598; 15.4% x 176,600 = 27,196; etc.

[6] 62.5% x 2,601,948 = 1,626,218; 25.0% x 2,601,948 = 650,487; etc.

Special Note: As an example of rounding errors, reconsider footnote (4) in Table 12-A2. If fractions were used instead of percentages, the allocations would become:

36/1,296	x	950,000	=	26,389
120/1,296	x	950,000	=	87,963
300/1,296	x	950,000	=	219,907
720/1,296	x	950,000	=	527,778
120/1,296	x	950,000	=	87,963
Total				950,000

In turn, the computations in footnotes (5) and (6) would also be changed.

12-A3 (15-25 min.)

1.

	Model I	Model II	Model III
Direct materials	¥ 400,000	¥ 600,000	¥ 800,000
Materials handling	20,000	30,000	40,000
Assembly	300,000	200,000	100,000
Soldering	150,000	150,000	150,000
Quality assurance	200,000	120,000	80,000
Total for 100 circuit boards	¥1,070,000	¥1,100,000	¥1,170,000
Cost per circuit board	¥ 10,700	¥ 11,000	¥ 11,700

2. The cost is ¥677,000 for 100 Model I circuit boards:

	Model I
Direct materials	¥400,000
Materials handling	20,000
Assembly	150,000
Soldering	150,000
Quality assurance	120,000
Total for 100 circuit boards	¥840,000
Cost per circuit board	¥ 8,400

12-A4 (20-30 min.)

Note that total joint costs are $10 x 800,000 + $4 x 800,000 = $11,200,000.

1. Physical units method:

	Pounds	Weighting	Allocation of Joint Costs
A	200,000	(200 ÷ 800) x $11,200,000	$ 2,800,000
B	600,000	(600 ÷ 800) x $11,200,000	8,400,000
	800,000		$11,200,000

2. Relative sales value method:

Relative Sales Value at Split-off	Weighting	Allocation of Joint Costs
A $30.00 x 200,000 = $ 6,000,000	(6 ÷ 15) x $11,200,000	$ 4,480,000
B $15.00 x 600,000 = $ 9,000,000	(9 ÷ 15) x $11,200,000	6,720,000
$15,000,000		$11,200,000

3. The sales value of B at the split-off point must be approximated:

Sales value of B = Final sales value - Separable costs
= ($21.50 x 600,000) - [$300,000 + ($1 x 600,000)]
= $12,900,000 - $900,000
= $12,000,000

	Relative Sales Value at Split-off	Weighting	Allocation of Joint Costs
A	$ 6,000,000	(6 ÷ 18) x $11,200,000	$ 3,733,333
B	12,000,000	(12 ÷ 18) x $11,200,000	7,466,667
	$18,000,000		$11,200,000

12-B1 (10-15 min.)

1.

	Business	Engineering
Fixed costs per month:		
210÷700, or 30% of $100,000	$30,000	
490÷700, or 70% of $100,000		$ 70,000
Variable costs @ $200 per hour:		
210 hours	42,000	
390 hours		78,000
Total costs	$72,000	$148,000

2.

	Business	Engineering
Fixed costs per month:		
210/600 x $100,000	$35,000	
390/600 x $100,000		$ 65,000
Variable costs, as before	42,000	78,000
Total costs	$77,000	$143,000

The dean of Business would probably be unhappy. The Business School has operated exactly in accordance with the long-range plan. Nevertheless, Business is bearing an extra $5,000 of fixed costs because of what *another* consumer is using. The dean would prefer the method in Requirement 1 because it insulates Business from short-run fluctuations in costs caused by the actions of other users.

12-B2 (30-40 min.)

1. Direct method:

	Personnel	Administrative	Residential	Commercial
Direct departmental costs before allocation	$ 70,000	$ 90,000	$240,000	$400,000
Personnel	(70,000)		28,000	42,000
Administrative		(90,000)	33,750	56,250
Total costs after allocation			$301,750	$498,250

Calculations:

12 + 18 = 30

(12 ÷ 30) x $70,000 = $28,000

(18 ÷ 30) x $70,000 = $42,000

240,000 + 400,000 = 640,000

(240,000 ÷ 640,000) x $90,000 = $33,750

(400,000 ÷ 640,000) x $90,000 = $56,250

2. Step-down method:

	Personnel	Administrative	Residential	Commercial
Direct departmental cost before allocation	$ 70,000	$ 90,000	$240,000	$400,000
Personnel	(70,000)	10,000	24,000	36,000
Administrative		$(100,000)	37,500	62,500
Total cost after allocation			$301,500	$498,500

Calculations:

5 + 12 + 18 = 35

(5 ÷ 35) x $70,000 = $10,000

(12 ÷ 35) x $70,000 = $24,000

(18 ÷ 35) x $70,000 = $36,000

240,000 + 400,000 = 640,000

(240,000 ÷ 640,000) x $100,000 = $37,500

(400,000 ÷ 640,000) x $100,000 = $62,500

3. (a) Residential: $301,500 ÷ 24,000 hours = $12.56 per direct-labor hr
   (b) Commercial: $498,500 ÷ 9,970,000 sq. ft. = $.05 per square foot

12-B3 (20-30 min.)

1.

Unit costs:	Standard Kiwis	Giant Kiwis
Direct materials	$1.30	$2.20
Materials receiving and handling	.24	.48
Production setup (60/600, 60/240)	.10	.25
Cutting, sewing, and assembly	.40	.40
Total unit cost	$2.04	$3.33
x Number of units	100	50
Cost before packing and shipping	$204.00	$166.50
Packing and shipping	10.00	10.00
Total cost	$214.00	$176.50

2. This requirement calls for an understanding of cost drivers. Instead of setup costs being added as an average unit cost, they are added as a total cost for each product in this order. In essence, setup costs are driven by the order because the new requirements call for one setup for each product in each order:

Unit costs:	Standard Kiwis	Giant Kiwis
Direct materials	$1.30	$2.20
Materials receiving and handling	.24	.48
Cutting, sewing, and assembly	.40	.40
Total unit cost	$1.94	$3.08
x Number of units	100	50
Cost before setup and packing and shipping	$194.00	$154.00
Setup	60.00	60.00
Packing and shipping	10.00	10.00
Total cost	$264.00	$224.00

3. The activity-based costing system recognizes the behavior of the costs. Because Maori Novelty has no category for direct labor, it apparently is not a significant cost. Therefore, it is unlikely to have a cause-effect relationship with the other costs. The activity-based costing system allocates costs based on their causes. Therefore, Maori can better assess the costs of individual products. In addition, special situations such as the setups needed in requirement 2 can be costed more easily and accurately.

12-B4 (15 min.)

The joint costs include the purchase cost of $1,000,000 x $.60 = $600,000 and the processing cost before the split-off point of $.30 x 1,000,000 = $300,000, a total of $900,000.

1.

	Pounds	Weighting	Allocation of Joint Costs
Oat flour	800,000	800/1,000 x $900,000	$720,000
Oat bran	200,000	200/1,000 x $900,000	180,000
	1,000,000		$900,000

2.

	Relative Sales Value at Split-off*	Weighting	Allocation of Joint Costs
Oat flour	$1,200,000	1,200/1,600 x $900,000	$675,000
Oat bran	400,000	400/1,600 x $900,000	225,000
	$1,600,000		$900,000

*$1.50 x 800,000 and $2.00 x 200,000

3. Estimated value of oat flour at split-off:

Sales value of oat flakes, $2.90 x 800,000 pounds	$2,320,000
- Processing cost after split-off point, ($.60 x 800,000 pounds) + $240,000	720,000
	$1,600,000

	Relative Sales Value at Split-off	Weighting	Allocation of Joint Costs
Oat flour	$1,600,000	1,600/2,000 x $900,000	$720,000
Oat bran	400,000	400/2,000 x $900,000	180,000
	$2,000,000		$900,000

12-1 A cost accounting system collects and classifies costs and assigns them to cost objects in order to measure the cost of designing, developing, producing (or purchasing), selling, distributing, and servicing particular products or services.

12-2 No. The costs in a cost pool are not *physically traced* to cost objectives. They are *allocated* to cost objectives using a single cost driver as a base.

12-3 Reallocate, trace, assign, distribute, redistribute, load, apportion, reapportion, attribute, burden.

12-4 The four purposes of cost allocation are (1) to predict the economic effects of planning and control decisions, (2) to obtain desired motivation, (3) to compute income and asset valuations, and (4) to justify costs or obtain reimbursement.

12-5 The three types of allocation are (1) allocation of costs to the appropriate organizational unit, (2) reallocation of costs from one organizational unit to another, and (3) allocation of the costs of a particular organizational unit or activity to products or services.

12-6 The preferred guidelines for allocating service department costs are:

a. Evaluate performance using budgets for each service (staff) department, just as they are used for each production or operating (line) department. When feasible, maintain distinctions between variable-cost pools and fixed-cost pools.

b. Allocate variable- and fixed-cost pools separately. This is sometimes called the dual method of allocation. Note that one service department (such as a computer department) can contain a variable-cost pool and a fixed-cost pool. That is, costs may be pooled within and among departments if desired.

c. Establish part or all of the details regarding cost allocation in advance of rendering the service rather than after the fact.

12-7 Using budgeted rather than actual cost rates protects the using departments from inefficiencies in the service departments and from intervening price fluctuations.

12-8 Fixed costs are often allocated separately from variable costs because they are caused by different activities. Fixed costs are affected primarily by long-range decisions about the overall level of service. In contrast, variable costs depend on short-run fluctuations in actual usage.

12-9 The motivation to underestimate long-run usage is a common problem with allocation methods using lump-sums based on long-range plans. To counteract this tendency, management can evaluate predictions of long-run usage and provide rewards for accurate predictions.

12-10 Sales dollars are often a poor basis for allocation of costs because they reflect efficiency of sales effort and variations in pricing margins, neither of which is related to costs.

12-11 One way to allocate national advertising costs to territories is on the basis of *expected* sales in each territory, computed by some formula combining population, income, appeal, competition, and supply capability.

12-12 Two methods of allocating service department costs are the *direct method* and the *step-down* method. The direct method ignores other service departments when any given service department's costs are allocated. No costs are allocated from one service department to another. The step-down method recognizes that some service departments provide services to other service departments as well as to producing departments. The costs of the first service department are allocated to all other service departments. Then the second service department's costs are allocated to *the remaining* service departments (i.e., all service departments *except* those whose costs have already been allocated) and the producing departments. Once a service department's costs have been allocated, no subsequent service department's costs are allocated back to it. This procedure continues until all service department costs have been allocated.

12-13 No. Both the direct and step-down methods allocate the same total amount of costs to the producing departments.

12-14 The terms *apply* or *absorb* tend to have the narrower meaning of costs traced to *products* or services rather than to *departments*.

12-15 Non-volume-related cost drivers are causes of costs that are not proportional to the volume of output. For example, number of hours of engineering design services is a non-volume-related cost driver that can be used to allocate engineering costs. Another non-volume-related cost driver is product complexity - more specifically, possibly number of components in a final product.

12-16 First, managers identify the key activities in the organization, and they collect overhead costs for each activity. Cost drivers are then selected for each activity, and those cost drivers are used to allocate the costs to the cost objects.

12-17 It would be ideal if every cost pool would contain only fixed or only variable costs. This should be the goal. In practice, there are many reasons why this goal may not be achieved. For example, the identification of fixed and variable costs is not perfect; most costs have some fixed and some variable cost characteristics. Perfect separation into fixed and variable cost categories may not be possible. In addition, it may not be economically feasible to have separate cost pools for fixed and variable costs if most (but not all) of the cost fits into one of the categories. For example, if 90% of a cost is variable and 10% is fixed, it may be best to treat the entire cost as variable.

12-18 Some possible activities and cost drivers are:

Activity	Cost driver
Group of machines	Machine hours
Set-up costs	Number of set-ups
Quality inspection	Units passing inspection point
Personnel department	Number of employees

12-19 No. The main reasons that activity-based costing is becoming so popular relate to planning and control, not product costing: (1) decisions about product mix, prices, and other product-related decisions, and (2) control of costs focused on managing activities instead of products. The term activity-based management refers to the use of activity-based costs for planning and control purposes.

12-20 Joint costs are allocated to products or services for purposes of inventory valuation and income determination.

12-21 The *physical units* method allocates joint costs in proportion to some physical property of the products (e.g., weight or volume) at the split-off point. The *relative sales value* method allocates joint costs in proportion to the amounts for which the products can be sold at the split-off point.

12-22 By-products, like joint products, are not separately identifiable before the split-off point. However, by-products have relatively insignificant sales values compared to main products. Only separable costs are applied to by-products; no joint costs are allocated to them. Revenues from by-products, less separable costs, are deducted from the cost of the main product.

12-23 (10-15 min.)

1. Rate = $\frac{[\$2,500 + (\$.05 \times 100,00)]}{(100,000)}$ = $.075 per copy

Cost allocated to City Planning in August = $.075 x 42,000 = $3,150.

2. Fixed cost pool allocated as a lump sum depending on predicted usage:

To City Planning: (36,000 ÷ 100,000) x $2,500 = $900 per month

Variable cost pool allocated on the basis of actual usage:
$.05 x number of copies

Cost allocated to City Planning in August: $900 + ($.05 x 42,000) = $3,000.

3. The second method, the one that allocated fixed- and variable-cost pools separately, is preferable. It better recognizes the causes of the costs. The fixed cost depends on the size of the photocopy machine, which is based on predicted usage and is independent of actual usage. Variable costs, in contrast are caused by actual usage.

12-24 (10 - 15 min.)

	Sunnyville	Wedgewood	Independence
1. Allocation based on budgeted sales*	$60,000	$100,000	$40,000
2. Allocation based on actual sales**	66,667	77,778	55,556

*$200,000 x (600/2,000); $200,000 x (1,000/2,000); $200,000 x (400/2,000)
** $200,000 x (600/1,800); $200,000 x (700/1,800); $200,000 x (500/1,800)

3. The major argument against using actual sales as a cost driver for cost allocation is that a department's allocation depends on the success of other departments. Here, Sunnyville is allocated an extra $6,667 because sales in the Wedgewood store are below budget, even though Sunnyville's sales came in right on target. Further, stores with poor sales results probably do not cause reduced central office costs. If anything, a department with poor performance requires more central attention. Also, using budgeted sales reduces surprises; managers know what amount of allocated cost to expect. Often managers are more upset by unexpected changes in allocated amounts than by the size of the allocation itself.

12-25 (15-20 min.)

1. Direct method:

	Personnel	Custodial	Machining	Assembly
Direct department costs before allocation	$32,000	$70,000	$600,000	$800,000
Personnel*	(32,000)		14,222	17,778
Custodial**		(70,000)	20,000	50,000
Total cost after allocation	$ 0	$ 0	$634,222	$867,778

* (200 ÷ 450) x $32,000; (250 ÷ 450) x $32,000
**(10 ÷ 35) x $70,000; (25 ÷ 35) x $70,000

2. Step-down nethod:

	Personnel	Custodial	Machining	Assembly
Direct department costs before allocation	$32,000	$70,000	$600,000	$800,000
Personnel*	(32,000)	2,000	13,333	16,667
Custodial**		(72,000)	20,571	51,429
Total cost after allocation	$ 0	$ 0	$633,904	$868,096

* (30 ÷ 480) x $32,000; (200 ÷ 480) x $32,000; (250 ÷ 480) x $32,000
**(10 ÷ 35) x $72,000; (25 ÷ 35) x $72,000

12-26 (10 min.)

1.

	Gallons	Weighting	Allocation of Joint Costs
Solvent A	20,000	20/30 x $400,000	$266,667
Solvent B	10,000	10/30 x $400,000	133,333
	30,000		$400,000

2.

	Relative Sales Value at Split-off*	Weighting	Allocation of Joint Costs
Solvent A	$ 400,000	400/1,000 x $400,000	$160,000
Solvent B	600,000	600/1,000 x $400,000	240,000
	$1,000,000		$400,000

* $20 x 20,000 and $60 x 10,000

12-27 (10-15 min.)

1. *None.* The entire joint cost is allocated to the main product.

2. $35,000. The total inventory cost of the pulp is the separable cost, that is, the cost incurred after the split-off point.

3. Inventory cost of apples:

Direct materials (apples)	$1,000,000
Pressing cost	130,000
Filter, pasteurize, and pack cost	150,000
Total	$1,280,000
Less: Revenue less separable costs of by-product ($50,000 - $35,000)	(15,000)
Net cost of apple juice	$1,265,000

12-28 (20 min.)

This problem is based on a description in *Cost Finding and Rate Setting for Hospitals* (Chicago: American Hospital Association), p. 6 and p. 74. It illustrates the idea of using a weighted average, which is really a version of equivalent units (explained in the chapter on process costing). If process costing is covered in this course, the applicability of equivalent units in a hospital context is important to see.

The cost driver would be "weighted number of pounds processed" instead of "number of pounds processed." The new computations are:

Laundry department costs		$180,000
Weighted number of pounds processed:		
Radiology, (7,500 x 5) and (7,500 x 1)	45,000	
Other centers, 600,000 - 15,000	585,000	
Divided by total weighted pounds		630,000
Cost per weighted pound		$ .286

Total costs to radiology:	
Using unweighted base, 15,000 x $.30	$ 4,500
Using weighted base, 45,000 x $.286	$12,870

The practical problems of cost allocation are described in the cost-finding publication (pp. 73-74):

> One basis for the allocation of laundry costs is pounds of soiled laundry. This is a good basis provided it is possible for the hospital to identify the source of soiled linens by department. However, because of the use of linen chutes, or for other reasons, many hospitals cannot identify the source of laundry by department. In smaller hospitals the use of an outside commercial laundry service also is common, and some hospitals do not have weighing facilities.

In every hospital there must be a linen distribution function, and a study of the amount and type of linen distributed to the various departments of the hospital will produce a reliable basis for allocation. As a minimum, the number of pieces, adjusted for weight differentials, should be tallied for a period of perhaps two weeks, two or three times a year. The weight factor, however, needs to be established only once. Reliable weight factors can be developed by simply weighing the various pieces and establishing standard piece weights for each type of laundry. The average of the several two-week tests can be used as the basis for distributing laundry costs for cost-finding purposes.

Another method is to use commercial laundry prices as a weighting factor for the different types of pieces. This method has the advantage of allowing for the relative difficulty of different processing functions, such as pressed versus mangle finishing.

Hospitals can conduct very refined studies if they so desire. It may be appropriate, especially in larger institutions, to give special consideration to refinements. For example, where the laundry processes a large volume of uniforms for student nurses and doctors, and for dietary, housekeeping, and other service personnel, it may be desirable to separate washing and pressing costs and to develop separate allocation bases for each of these functions based on the production statistics. Furthermore, it may be desirable to consider the effect of different processing cycles, such as the special rinse cycles for operating room linens or the special cold wash cycles for woolen blankets. Through discussions with the laundry manager, it is possible to determine whether further analysis is justified. Another example of possible refinements is the personal laundry done for medical interns, residents, student nurses, and others; if the volume is large, it might have to be recognized in the departmental operations.

12-29 (15 min.)

1. What is the purpose of this cost allocation? Primarily, it is to help set a "fair" price. (Note the SP representative's reference to "it is not fair.") Regulatory authorities set prices based on cost allocations in many industries, including utilities, natural gas, and railroads, where free markets are allowed to reign only to a limited degree. The most troublesome problems usually arise when there is a significant amount of common costs.

   Obviously, this specific illustration will not lead to any clear-cut answers. Those commissioners who favor "full costing" will be sympathetic to the SP position, while those commissioners who favor "incremental costing" will be sympathetic to the PUC staff.

   Those who favor full costing should nevertheless be cautious in applying "system-wide" overhead rates to a small operation. The problem is akin to using plant-wide overhead rates for a particular factory department's operations; sometimes the final results are not affected significantly, but big potential differences lead toward developing departmental rates.

   Those who favor incremental costing should be concerned about more costs than just "above-the-rail" costs like fuel, labor, and equipment maintenance. The SP representative cited two examples of "common" costs that would indeed be affected if commuter service were discontinued. In addition, if regulatory commissions allowed only incremental costs to be covered by prices, companies would eventually go out of business. In the long run all costs must be covered.

2. This question was raised to demonstrate the dangers of having a cost allocation to one segment be heavily dependent on what is happening in another segment. Commuter passenger traffic is unlikely to be as sensitive to changes in business conditions as is freight traffic. Therefore, a sudden decline in freight traffic would result in passenger traffic's bearing a higher fraction of common costs.

12-30 (20-25 min.)

1. Annual costs for 24,000 miles:

Annual costs for 24,000 miles:	Fixed	$3,600
	Variable ($.10 x 24,000)	2,400
		$6,000

Cost per mile = $6,000 ÷ 24,000 miles = $.25 per mile

2. Two factors caused the April allocation of $.48 per mile to exceed the average of $.25 per mile:

(1) The motor pool's operating inefficiencies are passed on to the user departments. The cost of 50,000 miles in April should have been [($3,600 ÷ 12 months) x 50 autos] + ($.10 x 50,000 miles) = $15,000 + $5,000 = $20,000. Therefore, $4,000 of "unnecessary" cost was assigned to user departments, which is $4,000 ÷ 50,000 miles = $.08 per mile.

(2) April was a month of low general usage. In an average month, 100,000 miles are driven (2,000 miles per auto), and the fixed cost per mile is ($3,600 ÷ 12 months) ÷ 2,000 miles = $300 ÷ 2,000 miles = $.15 per mile. In April the $300 fixed cost of each auto was spread over only 1,000 miles, so fixed cost per mile was $300 ÷ 1,000 = $.30 per mile. This factor accounts for an extra $.15 per mile.

3. Undesirable behavioral effects include:

(a) The total *actual* motor pool cost is allocated. The manager is not motivated to control these costs.
(b) Allocated costs are affected by auto usage in other departments. A department is better off if its auto usage happens to fall in a month when other departments have high mileage.

(c) Decisions about whether driving another mile is worth its cost are not appropriately made. The city incurs only $.10 more expense for an additional mile, but departments are charged more.

(d) The cost allocation is affected only by miles driven, not number of autos assigned to a department. A department with two autos each being driven 15,000 miles per year is allocated the same cost as one with one auto driven 30,000 miles per year. But each auto causes the same average fixed costs, so fixed costs should be allocated on the basis of number of autos rather than miles driven. This may be the reason the city planner was continually concerned with her auto costs. Her department's autos were driven an average of 3,000 miles per month, but the city's average was only 2,000 miles. Because both fixed and variable costs are allocated on a per-mile basis, her department's autos are allocated more fixed cost than the average auto in the city. If fixed costs were allocated on the basis of number of autos, each auto would be charged $300 per month. This becomes $.10 per mile for the city planner's autos compared to $.15 for the average auto in the city.

4. Two basic principles should be applied:

(a) Allocate budgeted, not actual, costs. Inefficiencies of the motor pool should not be passed on to user departments.

(b) Separate costs into fixed and variable cost pools. The fixed costs should be allocated on the basis of number of autos assigned to a department or long-run predicted use of autos. Variable costs are appropriately assigned on a per-mile-driven basis.

This cost-allocation method illustrates why the city planner has a legitimate complaint. In April she paid $.08 per mile extra because of motor pool inefficiency, $.15 per mile extra because other departments had light usage in April, and $.05 per mile extra because fixed costs are charged on a per-mile basis rather than a per-auto basis.

12-31 (20-30 min.)

1.

Actual costs	$750,000 + $.80(500,000)	= $1,150,000
Rate per ton-mile*	$1,150,000 ÷ 500,000	= $2.30
To East	250,000 x $2.30	= $575,000
To West	250,000 x $2.30	= $575,000

*Rate is per thousand net ton-miles

2.

Actual costs	$750,000 + $.80(400,000)	= $1,070,000
Rate per ton-mile	$1,070,000 ÷ 400,000	= $2.675
To East	150,000 x $2.675	= $401,250
To West	250,000 x $2.675	= $668,750

Note that West 's costs increased from $575,000 to $668,750 or 16.3%, solely because East 's volume declined.

3.

Rate per ton-mile	$1,275,000 ÷ 500,000	= $2.55
To East	250,000 x $2.55	= $637,500
To West	250,000 x $2.55	= $637,500

Such allocation seems unjustified because the operating departments have to bear another department's cost of inefficiency. Note that the use of a predetermined or budgeted total amount geared to the various levels of activity of the operating departments would eliminate this difficulty. For example, the $2.30 rate of part (1) would be used here despite the excess of actual costs over budgeted costs.

4. Basic maximum capacity: 360,000 + 240,000 = 600,000 ton miles.

Fixed costs:	East	West
To East, 36/60 x $750,000	$450,000	$ -
To West, 24/60 x $750,000	-	300,000
Variable costs:		
To East, $.80 x 150,000	120,000	-
To West, $.80 x 250,000	-	200,000
Total costs	$570,000	$500,000

Note that East 's costs are $570,000 rather than the $401,250 in part (2).

This method has the following advantages:

a. The use of a predetermined unit rate for variable costs prevents the total charges from being affected by the efficiency of price changes of the service department.

b. The use of a predetermined lump-sum for fixed costs prevents the total charges from being affected by the consumption of service or the activity levels of other operating departments or the activity level of the service department.

12-32 (20-30 min.)

1. Basic long-run usage:

    75 + 50 = 125 x-rays per month

   Total costs incurred:

    $12,000 + 100 x-rays ($30) = $15,000

	University Hospital	Children's Hospital
Fixed costs:		
75/125 x $12,000	$ 7,200	
50/125 x $12,000		$4,800
Variable costs:		
50 x $30	1,500	
50 x $30		1,500
Total allocated costs	$8,700	$6,300

2. For budgetary control and motivation purposes, it is best not to allocate the $1,500 efficiency variance ($16,500 minus the $15,000 computed above). For cost recovery purposes, if reimbursement is based on actual costs, it should be allocated.

3.

	University Hospital	Children's Hospital
Total costs incurred, $15,000:		
50/100 x $15,000	$7,500	
50/100 x $15,000		$7,500

Children's Hospital bears $1,200 more costs than in part (1) despite the fact that its volume was exactly in accordance with its long-run average usage. In short, Children's Hospital's costs have increased *solely* because of a fellow consumer's actions, not its own actions.

University Hospital's failure to reach its predicted usage results in shifting $1,200 more fixed costs to Children's Hospital.

A behavioral effect of this method would be toward more erratic scheduling (to the extent this discretion exists). For instance, if University Hospital had a relatively light month, it would be motivated toward not scheduling procedures during the final week and bunching them in the first week of the second month. In this way, its unit costs of the second month would be lowered.

4. Both University and Children's Hospitals would be induced to underestimate usage. Of course, if both play the same game, the final fraction borne by each would be little changed. One way to counteract these tendencies is to exert higher arbitrary (and unreimburseable) cost allocations to both University and Children's Hospitals if they consistently exceed their predicted usage. Also, first priority on scarce resources can be extended to those consumers who are committed to the higher fractions.

12-33 (20-30 min.)

1.

	Building Services	Materials Receiving and Handling	Mechanical Instruments	Electronic Instruments
Direct department costs before allocation	$150,000	$120,000	$680,000	$548,000
Building services	(150,000)		100,000	50,000
Materials receiving and handling		(120,000)	40,000	80,000
Total costs after allocation			$820,000	$678,000

Calculations:

50,000 + 25,000 = 75,000

(50,000 ÷ 75,000) x $150,000 = $100,000

(25,000 ÷ 75,000) x $150,000 = $50,000

No. of components: 10 x 8,000 = 80,000; 16 x 10,000 = 160,000

80,000 + 160,000 = 240,000

(80,000 ÷ 240,000) x $120,000 = $40,000

(160,000 ÷ 240,000) x $120,000 = $80,000

2. Mechanical instruments:

$820,000 ÷ 30,000 hours = $27.33 per direct-labor hour

Electronic instruments:

$678,000 ÷ 160,000 components = $4.24 per component

3. Total cost = direct materials cost + manufacturing cost:

M1: $74 + ($27.33 x 4) = $74 + $109.32 = $183.32

M2: $86 + ($27.33 x 8) = $86 + 218.64 = $304.64

E1: $63 + ($ 4.24 x 10) = $63 + 42.40 = $105.40

E2: $91 + ($ 4.24 x 15) = $91 + 63.60 = $154.60

12-34 (20-30 min.)

1.

	Building Services	Materials Receiving and Handling	Mechanical Instruments	Electronic Instruments
Direct department costs before allocation	$150,000	$ 120,000	$680,000	$548,000
Building services	(150,000)	9,375	93,750	46,875
Materials receiving and handling		$(129,375)	43,125	86,250
Total costs after allocation			$816,875	$681,125

Calculations:

5,000 + 50,000 + 25,000 = 80,000
(5 ÷ 80) x $150,000 = $9,375
(50 ÷ 80) x $150,000 = $93,750
(25 ÷ 80) x $150,000 = $46,875
No. of components: 10 x 8,000 = 80,000; 16 x 10,000 = 160,000
80,000 + 160,000 = 240,000
(80 ÷ 240) x $129,375 = $43,125
(160 ÷ 240) x $129,375 = $86,250

2. Mechanical instruments:

$816,875 ÷ 30,000 hours = $27.23 per direct-labor hour

Electronic instruments:

681,125 ÷ 160,000 components = $4.26 per component

3. Total cost = direct materials cost + manufacturing cost

M1: $74 + ($27.23 x 4) = $74 + $108.92 = $182.92
M2: $86 + ($27.23 x 8) = $86 + $217.84 = $303.84
E1: $63 + ($ 4.26 x 10) = $63 + $ 42.60 = $105.60
E2: $91 + ($ 4.26 x 15) = $91 + $ 63.90 = $154.90

12-35 (40 min.)

1 & 2. The solution to requirements 1 and 2 is in Exhibit 12-35.

3. Single Plantwide Rate: $165,000 ÷ 24,000 = $6.875 per direct-labor hour.

4. Comparison of methods:

Step-down method:

Job K10,	19 x $10 + 2 x $5.83 = $190 + $ 11.66 =	$201.66
Job K12,	3 x $10 + 18 x $5.83 = $ 30 + $104.94 =	134.94
Total		$336.60

Direct method:

Job K10,	19 x $9.88 + 2 x $5.87 = $189.72 + $ 11.74 =	$199.46
Job K12,	3 x $9.88 + 18 x $5.87 = $ 29.64 + $105.66 =	135.30
Total =		$334.76

Blanket rate:

Job K10,	21 x $6.875 =	$144.38
Job K12,	21 x $6.875 =	144.38
Total		$288.76

EXHIBIT 12-35

1. Step-down Method	Building & Grounds	Personnel	General Factory Administration	Cafeteria Operating Loss	Storeroom	Machining	Assembly
Direct department costs	$20,000	$1,200	$28,020	$1,430	$2,750	$40,100	$71,500
(1) Building & grounds @ 20¢/sq. ft.	$20,000	400	1,400	800	1,400	6,000	10,000
(2) Personnel @ $8/employee		$1,600	280	80	40	400	800
(3) General factory admin. @$1.10/labor hour			$29,700	1,100	1,100	8,800	18,700
(4) Cafeteria @ $22/employee				$3,410	110	1,100	2,200
(5) Storeroom @ $1.20/requisition					$5,400	3,600	1,800
(6) Total						$60,000	$105,000
(7) Divide (6) by direct labor hours						÷6,000	÷18,000
(8) Overhead rate per direct-labor hour						$10.00	$5.83

2. Direct Method	Building & Grounds	Personnel	General Factory Administration	Cafeteria Operating Loss	Storeroom	Machining	Assembly
Direct department costs	$20,000	$1,200	$28,020	$1,430	$2,750	$40,100	$71,500
(1) Building & grounds: $\frac{(20,000)}{(80,000)}$ =25¢	(20,000)					7,500	12,500
(2) Personnel: 1/3 & 2/3		(1,200)				400	800
(3) General factory admin.: $\frac{(28,020)}{(25,000)}$ = $1.1208			(28,020)			8,966	19,054
(4) Cafeteria: $\frac{(1,430)}{(150)}$ or 1/3 & 2/3				(1,430)		477	953
(5) Storeroom: $\frac{(2,750)}{(4,500)}$ or 2/3 & 1/3					(2,750)	1,833	917
(6) Total						$59,276	$105,724
(7) Divide (6) by direct-labor hours						÷6,000	÷18,000
(8) Overhead rate per direct-labor hour						$9.88	$ 5.87

12-36 (25 min.)

1.

Recording and record-keeping cost: $16.50 x 550 =	$ 9,075
Labor cost: ($23,000 / 460,000) x 80,000 =	4,000
Inspection cost: $2.75 x 4,000 =	11,000
Total cost	$24,075

2.

Recording and record-keeping cost: $16.50 x 220 =	$ 3,630
Labor cost: ($23,000 / 460,000) x 60,000 =	3,000
Inspection cost: $2.75 x 2,500 =	6,875
Total cost	$13,505

Cost saved = $24,075 - $13,505 = $10,570

3. Receiving cost per pound: $24,075 ÷ 80,000 = $.30

Estimated cost saved from 20,000 pounds = $.30 x 20,000 = $6,000

The company would have underestimated the savings by $10,570 - $6,000 = $4,570, and they may have continued to purchase and stock small-sales-level brands that are actually unprofitable.

12-37 (20 min.)

1.

	Variable Cost	Fixed Cost	Full Cost
Subcomponents	$1,100		$1,100
Receiving	22	$ 22	44
Assembly	144	144	288
Inspection	56		56
Total	$1,322	$166	$1,488

2. Price = .9 x $1,990 = $1,791

On a full cost basis, the profit would be $1,791 - $1,488 = $303 per computer, or a total of 15 x $303 = #4,545. The contribution margin on the order would be $1,791 - $1,322 = $469 per computer, or a total of 15 x $469 = $7,035. (Of course, some of this "profit must be used to cover other value-chain costs such a research and development, design, marketing, distribution, and customer service.) If Dell had excess capacity, so this order did not require additional resources and did not have any affect on the ability to fill other orders, the extra profit from the order is $7,035. However, in a long-term perspective, Dell has to pay for all its resources, both those represented by variable costs and those represented by fixed costs. On this basis, the profit is only $4,545.

3. Cost is an important factor, but by no means the only factor, to consider in making pricing decisions. In this case, it tells the Dell managers that this is a profitable product at the discounted price. But it does not say whether it is the most profitable product that could be produced with Dell's resources. Cost is important in answering one what-if question: what would profits be if Dell accepts this order at a particular predicted price. Cost data must be combined with a great deal of other data, such as market data and capacity data, to make intelligent pricing decisions.

12-38 (20-40 min.)

1. (a) The allocation of joint costs would be in a 1:5 ratio:

	Product A	Product B	Total
Sales value	$1,000	$1,000	$2,000
Joint costs	$200	$1,000	$1,200
Separable costs	350	200	550
Total costs	$550	$1,200	$1,750
Operating profit	$450	$ (200)	$ 250

(b) No. Joint costs are not relevant for this decision because you cannot stop incurring that part allocated to one product and still continue to incur only the other part. If the total process is profitable, you should process any product that shows a positive contribution after the split-off point. Although Product B shows a book loss of $200, it has a contribution after the split-off point of $1,000 - $200, or $800.

2. (a) The relative sales value method deducts separable costs to arrive at an imputed sales value at split-off point:

	A	B	Total
Sales value	$1,000	$1,000	$2,000
Separable costs	350	200	550
Sales value imputed at split-off point	$650	$800	$1,450
Allocation of joint cost, 650/1,450 and 800/1,450, respectively	538	662	1,200
Operating profit	$112	$138	$ 250

(b) No. Product B does have the greater book profit and contribution after the split-off point, but Product A has the greatest contribution per pound, which is the scarce resource in this case. If, for example, the engineer changes the process by 40 pounds, so that we end up with 440 pounds of B and 40 pounds of A, separable costs would become $175 for A and $220 for B, totaling $395 (assuming separable costs are all variable). Sales values would become $500 for A and $1,100 for B, and total of $1,600. Total contribution after the split-off would drop from $1,450 to $1,205 and total profit would drop from $250 to $5.

	A	B	Total
Pounds	40	440	500
Sales value	$500	$1,100	$1,600
Separable costs	175	220	395
Contribution to joint costs	$325	$ 880	$1,205
Joint costs			1,200
Operating profit			$ 5

12-39 (25-30 min.)

1. $1,080,000 ÷ 45,000 hours = $24 per direct-labor hour

2. (a) $630,000 ÷ 15,000 hours = $42 per direct-labor hour
   (b) $450,000 ÷ 30,000 hours = $15 per direct-labor hour

3. (a) $630,000 ÷ 105,000 hours = $6 per machine hour
   (b) $450,000 ÷ 30,000 hours = $15 per direct-labor hour

4. (a) $24 x (1.0 + 14.0) = $360.00
   $24 x (1.5 + 3.0) = $108.00
   $24 x (1.3 + 8.0) = $223.20

   (b) ($42 x 1.0) + ($15 x 14.0) = $42.00 + $210.00 = $252.00
   ($42 x 1.5) + ($15 x 3.0) = $63.00 + $ 45.00 = $108.00
   ($42 x 1.3) + ($15 x 8.0) = $54.60 + $120.00 = $174.60

   (c) ($6 x 10.0) + ($15 x 14.0) = $ 60.00 + $210.00 = $270.00
   ($6 x 17.0) + ($15 x 3.0) = $102.00 + $ 45.00 = $147.00
   ($6 x 14.0) + ($15 x 8.0) = $ 84.00 + $120.00 = $204.00

   (d) A major change in costs results from using departmental instead of firm-wide rates. Departmental rates decrease the cost applied to units of A and C, which use relatively more assembly time, and increase the cost of B, which uses relatively more machining time. Changing to a base of machine hours in machining causes smaller changes in unit costs. Product B is the only one with an increase in cost. Why? Because B's proportion of the machine hours in machining exceeds its proportion of direct-labor hours in machining. Therefore, it receives more costs with a base of machine hours than with a base of direct-labor hours. Both A and C have a higher proportion of the direct-labor hours than of the machine hours in the machining department.

12-40 (30-45 min.)

1.

Cost pool*	Board L**	Board M	Board N
0. Direct-material cost	£ 660,000	£ 70,400	£ 225,000
1. Direct-labor hours	560,000	201,600	630,000
2. Machine hours	560,000	96,000	280,000
3. Pounds of materials	90,000	9,600	30,000
4. Number of production setups	80,000	40,000	40,000
5. Number of production orders	13,500	9,000	3,150
6. Number of orders shipped	30,000	24,000	60,000
Total budgeted cost	£1,993,500	£450,600	£1,268,150
Number of units	÷ 10,000	÷ 800	÷ 5,000
Unit cost	£ 199.35	£ 563.25	£ 253.63

*Identified by the cost driver used

**Calculations for Product L (Products M and N are similar):

0. 10,000 x £66 = £660,000
1. [(4 x 10,000) ÷ (4 x 10,000 + 18 x 800 + 9 x 5,000)] x £1,391,600 = £560,000
2. [(7 x 10,000)÷(7 x 10,000 + 15 x 800 + 7 x 5,000)] x £936,000=£560,000
3. [(3 x 10,000) ÷ (3 x 10,000 + 4 x 800 + 2 x 5,000)] x £129,600 = £90,000
4. [100 ÷ (100 + 50 + 50)] x £160,000 = £80,000
5. [300 ÷ (300 + 200 + 70)] x £25,650 = £13,500
6. [1,000 ÷ (1,000 + 800 + 2,000)] x £114,000 = £30,000

2. Total cost (except direct materials) per direct-labor hour:

£2,756,850 ÷ (4 x 10,000 + 18 x 800 + 9 x 5,000)
= £2,756,850 ÷ 99,400 = £27.735 per direct-labor hour

	Board L	Board M	Board N
Direct material cost per unit	£ 66.00	£ 88.00	£ 45.00
Other manufacturing cost per unit	110.94	499.23	249.62
Total manufacturing cost per unit	£176.94	£587.23	£294.62
Number of units	x 10,000	x 800	x 5,000
Total budgeted cost*	£1,769,400	£469,784	£1,473,100

*Total = £1,769,400 + £469,784 + £1,473,100 = £3,712,284, which differs from £3,712,250 due to rounding error in the £27.735 rate.

3. The new system is more complex and more costly. The added expense would be justified if the added value of better decisions made using the new system exceeds the added cost of the system.

12-41 (50-60 min.)

1.

	Systems Department First Quarter Budget	Claims Department Historical Usage	Claims Department First Quarter Budget
Hardware and other capacity-related costs	$150,000	50%	$ 75,000
Software development	141,750	40	56,700
Computer-related operations	189,000	15	28,350
Input/output-related operations	75,600	75	56,700
	$556,350		$216,750

2. Solution is in Exhibit 12-41.

EXHIBIT 12-41

	Total First Quarter Systems Department Costs	Not Allocated	Allocated				
				Department			
			Total	Records	Claims	Finance	Outside
Hardware and other capacity-related costs	$155,000	$ 5,000	$150,000	$ 37,500 (1)	$ 75,000 (2)	$ 30,000 (3)	$ 7,500 (4)
Software development	130,000	2,500	127,500	13,500 (5)	54,000 (6)	48,000 (7)	12,000 (8)
Computer-related operations	187,000	3,000	184,000	108,000 (9)	38,800 (10)	25,200 (11)	12,000 (12)
Input-output-related operations	78,000	(1,000)	79,000	15,400 (13)	55,400 (14)	4,100 (15)	4,100 (16)
	$550,000	$ 9,500	$540,500	$174,400	$223,200	$107,300	$35,600

(1) $150,000 x .25
(2) $150,000 x .50
(3) $150,000 x .20
(4) $150,000 x .05

(5) $30 x 450
(6) $30 x 1,800
(7) $30 x 1,600
(8) $30 x 400

(9) $200 x 540
(10) $200 x 194
(11) $200 x 126
(12) $200 x 60

(13) $10 x 1,540
(14) $10 x 5,540
(15) $10 x 410
(16) $10 x 410

3. a. The new charging system should improve cost control in the Systems Department (if the rates are valid) because inefficiencies can no longer be passed on to the user departments. Thus, the Systems Department would be forced to watch its costs closely.
   b. The recommended system for charging costs to user departments should improve planning and cost control in the user departments. Decisions that affect capacity-related costs will affect the allocation of those costs, while decisions affecting only short-run operating costs will affect the allocation of only the operating costs.

12-42 (100 min. or more)

The purposes of this exercise are to conduct library research in the current management accounting literature and to gain a better understanding of activity-based costing and activity-based management. Students must find their own article on ABC or ABM, and this will test their skills with library searches. Using electronic search procedures is likely to be a time-saver, but names of journals are given so that someone could just browse the library holdings of one of the journals to find an appropriate article.

Textbooks are limited in the space they can devote to stories about actual cost-accounting systems. This exercise requires students to deal with real-world issues relating to ABC or ABM. All applications of ABC or ABM are not successful, either because it was not an appropriate techniques where applied or because of mistakes in implementation. Although the literature will be dominated by success stories (companies do not often advertise their failures), by looking at several companies who have implemented ABC or ABM, students should be able to make some of the generalizations called for in requirement 2. By sharing information among group members, students should get a broader perspective on ABC and ABM than they would get from reading a single article.

CHAPTER 13
Job-Costing Systems

13-A1 (15-20 min.) Answers are in thousands.

1.	a. Direct materials inventory	450	
	Cash		450
	b. Work in process	420	
	Direct materials inventory		420
	c. Work in process	125	
	Accrued payroll		125
	d. Factory department overhead	175	
	Various accounts		175
	(80 + 55 + 40 = 175)		
	e. Work in process	225	
	Factory department overhead		225
	(180% x 125)		
	f. Finished goods	705	
	Work in process		705
	g. Cost of goods sold	460	
	Finished goods		460

2. Direct Materials Inventory

a.	450	b.	420
12/31/X8 Bal. 30			

Finished Goods

f.	705	g.	460
12/31/X8 Bal. 245			

Work in Process

b.	420	f. 705
c.	125	
e.	225	
	770	
12/31/X8 Bal. 65		

Cost of Goods Sold

g.	460

Factory Department Overhead Control

d.	175	e.	225

13-A2 (15-20 min.)

This is a solid basic problem concerning overhead application.

1. $$\text{Overhead rate} = \frac{\text{Budgeted overhead}}{\text{Appropriate cost driver}}$$

$$\text{Department A} = \frac{(\$2{,}170{,}000)}{(350{,}000)} = \$6.20 \text{ per machine hour}$$

$$\text{Department B} = \frac{(\$1{,}000{,}000)}{(125{,}000)} = \$8.00 \text{ per direct-labor hour}$$

2.

Department A = \$6.20 x 3,500	\$21,700
Department B = \$8.00 x 1,250	10,000
Total applied overhead	\$31,700

3.

	Dept. A	Dept. B	Total
Direct material	$12,000	$32,000	$44,000
Direct labor	10,800	10,000	20,800
Applied factory overhead	21,700	10,000	31,700
Totals	$44,500	$52,000	$96,500
Unit cost, $96,500 ÷ 200			$482.50

4. Students must be on guard to get their definitions clear. "Overapplied" essentially means that "actual" overhead is less than that absorbed by (applied to) the products worked on during the period.

Computations follow:

	Dept. A	Dept. B	Factory as a Whole
Actual	$1,600,000	$1,200,000	$2,800,000
Applied, 300,000 x $6.20 and 120,000 x $8.00	1,860,000	960,000	2,820,000
Underapplied (overapplied)	$ (260,000)	$ 240,000	$ (20,000)

13-A3 (15 min.) Note that the direct materials inventory is irrelevant.

1. Underapplied overhead = $224,000 - $216,000 = $8,000

2.

Cost of goods sold	8,000	
Factory department overhead		8,000

Adjusted gross profit = $70,000 - $8,000 = $62,000

3.

Work in process	800	
Finished goods	1,600	
Cost of goods sold	5,600	
Factory department overhead		8,000

Supporting schedule:

(in thousands)	Unadjusted Balances	Proration of Underapplied Overhead	Adjusted Balances
Work in process	$ 75,000	75/750 x $8,000 = $ 800	$ 75,800
Finished goods	150,000	150/750 x $8,000 = 1,600	151,600
Cost of goods sold	525,000	525/750 x $8,000 = 5,600	530,600
Totals	$750,000	$8,000	$758,000

Adjusted gross profit = $70,000 - 5,600 = $64,400

4.

Factory department overhead	2,000	
Cost of goods sold		2,000

Adjusted gross profit = $70,000 + $2,000 = $72,000

13-B1 (20-25 min.) Entries are in thousands of British pounds (£).

		Debit	Credit
1. a.	Direct materials inventory	112	
	Accounts payable		112
b.	Work in process	98	
	Direct materials inventory		98
c.	Work in process	105	
	Accrued payroll		105
d.	Factory department overhead control	90	
	Various accounts, such as cash or accounts payable		90
e.	Work in process	84	
	Factory department overhead applied (80% x 105)		84
f.	Finished goods	280	
	Work in process		280
g.	Cost of goods sold	350	
	Finished goods		350
h.	Accounts receivable	600	
	Sales		600

2. Direct Materials Inventory

12/31/X7 Bal.	18	b.	98
a.	112		
12/31/X8 Bal.	32		

Finished Goods

12/31/X7 Bal.	100	g.	350
f.	280		
12/31/X8 Bal.	30		

Work in Process

12/31/X7 Bal.	25	f.	280
b.	98		
c.	105		
e.	84		
	312		
12/31/X8 Bal.	32		

Cost of Goods Sold

g.	350		

Factory Department Overhead Control

d.	90	e.	84

13-B2 (10-15 min.) Note that the direct materials inventory is irrelevant.

1.	Factory department overhead control	20,000	
	Cost of goods sold		20,000
2.	Factory department overhead control	20,000	
	Work in process		4,000
	Finished goods		6,000
	Cost of goods sold		10,000

Supporting schedule:

(in thousands)	Unadjusted Balances	Proration of Overapplied Overhead		Adjusted Balances
Work in process	$100	100/500 x $20 =	4	$ 96
Finished goods	150	150/500 x $20 =	6	144
Cost of goods sold	250	250/500 x $20 =	10	240
Totals	$500		$20	$480

Gross profit would be lower in requirement 2 by $20,000 - $10,000, or $10,000. Adjusted cost of goods sold would be $250,000 - $10,000 = $240,000 in requirement 2 but $250,000 - $20,000 = $230,000 in requirement 1.

13-B3 (15-20 min.)

1. Overhead rate = $\frac{\text{Budgeted overhead}}{\text{Budgeted cost driver level}}$

Pharmacy = $\frac{(\$225{,}000)}{(90{,}000)}$ = \$2.50 per prescription

Medical Records = $\frac{(\$300{,}000)}{(60{,}000)}$ = \$5.00 per patient visit

2.

Pharmacy = \$2.50 x 4	\$ 10.00
Medical records = \$5.00 x 2	10.00
Total applied overhead	\$20.00

3. Students must be on guard to get their definitions clear. "Overapplied" essentially means that "actual" overhead is less than that absorbed by (applied to) the products worked on during the period.

Computations follow:

	Pharmacy	Medical Records	Total
Actual	\$217,000	\$325,000	\$542,000
Applied, 85,000 x \$2.50 and 63,000 x \$5.00	212,500	315,000	527,500
Underapplied	\$ 4,500	\$ 10,000	\$ 14,500

13-1 Three purposes of product costing are to satisfy differing demands for (a) inventory valuation and income determination in accordance with generally accepted accounting principles, (b) income tax reporting, and (c) guiding pricing, product mix, and other managerial decisions.

13-2 In addition to inventory valuation and income determination, managers want accurate job costs as guides to pricing and to allocating effort among particular products, services, or customers.

13-3 The distinction between the job cost and the process cost methods centers largely around how product costing is accomplished. Unlike process costing, which deals with broad averages and great masses of like units, the essential feature of the job-cost method is the attempt to apply costs to specific jobs that may consist of either a single physical unit (a custom sofa) or a few like units (a dozen tables) in a distinct batch or job lot.

13-4 The most important point is that product costing is an averaging process. The unit cost used for inventory purposes is the result of taking some accumulated cost and dividing it by some measure of production. The basic distinction between job order costing and process costing is the breadth of the denominator: in job order costing, it is small (for example, one painting, 100 advertising circulars, or one special packaging machine); but in process costing, it is large (for example, thousands of pounds, gallons, or board feet).

13-5 Hybrid costing systems are blends of ideas from both job costing and process costing.

13-6 The basic record for the accumulation of job costs is the job-cost sheet or job-cost record. Exhibit 13-1 shows a Job-Cost Sheet, and it also shows the related source documents. A file of current job-cost sheets becomes the supporting details for the Work-in-Process Inventory account.

13-7 Source documents include materials requisitions and labor time tickets (time cards).

13-8 The budgeted overhead application rate is the predicted factory overhead for the budget period divided by the predicted machine hours for that period. The amount of factory overhead applied to a job is the budgeted overhead application rate times the actual machine hours used on that job.

13-9 The factory department overhead control account is an account that "collects" all actual overhead costs during an accounting period. They are left-hand entries (debits) to the account. At the end of the accounting period, the overhead applied is entered on the right-hand side of the account (credited), and any difference between the actual and applied overhead is charged as a variance.

13-10 No. In the past, most organizations have used only one cost driver per department. However, the trend is toward using multiple cost drivers. Whether more than one cost driver is used is a cost/benefit issue. If most overhead costs are caused by a single cost driver, using that one cost driver for cost application is logical. If overhead costs are caused by multiple cost drivers, managers must compare the value of more accurate product costs versus the cost of a complex accounting system that uses multiple cost drivers for overhead application.

13-11 A strong relationship between the factory overhead incurred and the cost driver used for application is the best available indication of a cause-and-effect relationship. That is, the more the cost driver is used, the higher the actual overhead incurred. It is important to consider the time period involved. Some overhead costs, equipment for example, have a weak or no relationship to machine hours used in the short run but a strong relationship to providing the capability to operate machines over extended time periods. Such costs are often called capacity costs.

13-12 Yes. Direct-labor cost may be the best cost driver for overhead allocation even if wage rages vary within a department. For example, higher skilled labor (with higher wage rates) may require more overhead because it may use more costly equipment and have more indirect labor support. Moreover, many factory overhead costs include costly labor fringe benefits such as pensions and payroll taxes.

13-13 Cost drivers might include direct labor cost, direct labor hours, direct material cost, total direct cost, machine hours, number of batches, number of engineering hours used, number of change orders, etc.

13-14 The comparison of actual overhead costs to budgeted overhead costs is part of the control process. It tells managers when the actual results differ from what was expected.

13-15 Incurred overhead will differ from applied overhead in much the same way as any estimate will differ from actual experience. Specific causes might be variations in suppliers' prices; inefficiencies in production (excessive down-time, for example); failure of sales to materialize; failure to meet production quotas; unexpected increases in fixed overhead (increase in insurance rates, for example).

13-16 No. Using "actual" overhead rates, unit costs will be lower as production volume increases and higher with low volume. The variable overhead rate will be approximately constant; the fixed overhead rate will vary inversely with volume. The two rates together form the total overhead rate.

13-17 Normal costing is the product-costing method whereby inventory is carried at actual direct-material costs plus actual direct-labor costs plus applied factory overhead at a budgeted rate.

13-18 The best theoretical method of allocating underapplied or overapplied overhead is to disregard it completely and recompute an actual overhead rate based on actual costs incurred allocated over actual production units. Proration is usually a reasonable approximation to this theoretical ideal.

13-19 Examples of service industries that use the job-costing approach include repairing, consulting, legal, accounting, painting, dentistry, and income tax preparation.

13-20 No. Some service firms trace only direct-labor costs to individual jobs. However, with advances in computer technology and needs for better job-cost information because of competition, more service firms are tracing additional costs to jobs. The more costs that are traced to jobs instead of being allocated, the more accurate are the job costs.

13-21 The following are examples of costs that are now classified as direct costs in many service industries: secretarial, photocopies, phone calls, power, and costs of computer time.

13-22 (10-15 min.) You may wish to use T accounts. Amounts are in millions of dollars. You can also use the expression: ending balance (of any account) equals the beginning balance plus additions less subtractions or EB = BB + A - S. In this case "Purchased" is "additions" and "Used" is "subtractions."

1. 8 + 5 - 7 = 6 (BB + A - S = EB)

2. 8 + 9 - 6 = 11 (BB + A - EB = S)

3. 5 + Purchases - 7 = 8. Purchases = 10

4. Beginning inventory + 8 - 3 = 7. Beginning inventory = 2

13-23 (5 min.) Amounts are in millions of dollars.

Beginning inventory + purchases - uses = ending inventory

Beginning inventory + \$15 - \$12 = \$9
Beginning inventory = \$9 - \$15 + \$12
Beginning inventory = \$6

13-24 (10-15 min.) Amounts are in thousands of dollars.

1.

Finished goods inventory	128	
Work in process inventory		128
Finished goods = 72 + 56 = 128		

2.

Debits: 12 + 50 + 25 + 55 =	142
Credits: 72 + 56	128
Balance, April 30	14

3.

Accounts receivable	101	
Sales		101
Sale of Job A13		
Cost of goods sold	72	
Finished goods inventory		72
Cost of Job A13 sold		

13-25 (10-15 min.)

				Cancer Research Project	
		Medical School			
Reference	Date	Quantity	Unit Cost	Amount	Summary
Direct Materials:					
Var. medical supplies	Jan. 5			$ 925	
Various chemicals	Jan. 7			780	$ 1,705
Direct Labor:					
Research associates	Jan. 5-12	120 hrs.	$32	$3,840	
Research assistants	Jan. 7-12	180 hrs.	$19	3,420	7,260
Project overhead applied	Jan. 12	$7,260 x .70		$5,082	5,082
Total costs					$14,047

13-26 (10 min.)

1. $6,500 + $3,900 = $10,400

2. $8,100

3. $3,200 + $8,800 = $12,000

13-27 (15 min.) Answers are in thousands of dollars.

1.

Job No.	a Construction in Process Sept. 30	b Finished Houses, Sept. 30	c Cost of Houses Sold Sept.	a Construction in Process Oct. 31	b Finished Houses, Oct. 31	c Cost of Houses Sold Oct.
43			180			
51			170			
52		150				150
53	200					250 [j]
61	115				135[k]	
62	180					205 [l]
71	118			154[m]		
81	106			154[n]		
	719	150	350	308	135	605

[j]200 + 50 [k]115 + 20 [i]180 + 25 [m]118 + 36 [n]106 + 48

2.

	Sept.		Oct.	
Finished houses inventory	500		590	
Construction in process		500		590

Sept.: 180 + 170 + 150 = 500

Oct.: 250 + 135 + 205 = 590

3.

Cash	345	
Sales		345
To record sale of Job 53		
Cost of houses sold	250	
Finished houses inventory		250
To record cost of Job 53 sold		

13-28 (30 min.)

The answers (in millions) are $15, $5, and $240.

Step-by-step entries are keyed alphabetically. The sequence depends on where the student prefers to start. You may wish to raise the question of whether the underapplied overhead should be prorated among the affected accounts at the end of the year.

Direct Materials

Bal.	15	(a)	210
(b)	225		
	240		210
Bal.	30		

Work in Process

Bal.	5	(e) Completed	420
(a) Dir. Materials	210		
(c) Dir. Labor	125*		
(d) Applied overhead	200		
	540		420
Bal.	120		

Finished Goods

Bal.	240	(f)	500
(e)	420		
	660		500
Bal.	160		

Cost of Goods Sold

(f)	500	

* $200 ÷ 160% = $125

13-29 (30 min.)

The answers (in millions) are $25, $22, and $32.

Step-by-step entries are keyed alphabetically. The sequence depends on where the student prefers to start. You may wish to raise the question of whether the underapplied overhead should be prorated among the affected accounts at the end of the year. Note the heavy ending Finished Goods.

Direct Materials

Bal.	25	(a)	265
(b)	305		
	330		265
Bal.	65		

Work in Process

Bal.	22	(e) Completed	523
(a) Dir. Materials	265		
(c) Dir. Labor	100		
(d) Applied overhead	150		
	537		523
Bal.	14		

Finished Goods

Bal.	32	(f)	350
(e)	523		
	555		350
Bal.	205		

Cost of Goods Sold

(f)	350	

13-30 (15-20 min.)

1. Factory department overhead control 995,000
   Cash, accounts payable, and various accounts 995,000

2. Work in process 1,605,000
   Direct materials inventory 1,605,000

   Work in process 1,200,000
   Accrued payroll 1,200,000

3. Work in process 960,000
   Factory department overhead control 960,000
   Budgeted rate = \$980,000 ÷ \$1,225,000
   = 80%; .80 x \$1,200,000 = \$960,000.

4.

Work in Process
(2) 1,605,000
(2) 1,200,000
(3) 960,000

Factory Department Overhead Control			
(1)	995,000	(3)	960,000
		(5)	35,000
	0		

5. Cost of goods sold (underapplied overhead) 35,000
   Factory department overhead control 35,000

Some students will confuse actual overhead, budgeted overhead, and overhead applied.

13-31 (5-10 min.)

Case A, \$3,400,000 ÷ \$2,000,000 = 170% of direct-labor cost
Case B, \$5 x 450,000 = \$2,250,000
Case C, \$1,750,000 ÷ 250,000 = \$7 per machine hour

13-32 (15-20 min.)

A major lesson of this exercise is the distinction between budgeted, actual, and applied overhead. Case 2 is more challenging, but it forces the student to learn basic relationships.

1. c. \$750,000 ÷ \$500,000 = 150% of direct-labor cost

   f. 1.50 x \$570,000 = \$855,000

   g. \$825,000 - \$855,000 = \$30,000 overapplied

2. f. \$415,000 - \$25,000 = \$390,000

   d. \$390,000 ÷ 1.20 = \$325,000

   b. \$420,000 ÷ 1.20 = \$350,000

13-33 (10-15 min.)

		(in thousands)	
		Case 1	Case 2
1.	Applied overhead: 30 x $9.00 =	$270	
	36 x $9.00 =		$324
2.	Overhead incurred:		
	$32 + $22 + $35 + $138 =	227	
	$40 + $32 + $47 + $214 =		333
3.	Overapplied overhead:	$270 - $227 =	43
	Underapplied overhead:	$333 - $324 =	9

Note the irrelevant items:

Sales commissions are selling expenses.

Depreciation of finished goods warehouse is also a selling expense, because the manufacturing processing has been completed.

Cost of goods sold is an overall figure of no use in this problem.

Direct-labor cost and direct-material cost are not pertinent either.

13-34 (10-15 min.) Direct materials inventory is irrelevant.

1. Factory department overhead control 60
   Cost of goods sold 60

		Dr.	Cr.
1.	Factory department overhead control	60	
	Cost of goods sold		60
2.	Factory department overhead control	60	
	Cost of goods sold		36
	Work in process		6
	Finished goods		18

Supporting schedule:

(in thousands)	Unadjusted Balances	Proration of Overapplied Overhead	Adjusted Balances
Work in process	$ 50	50/500 x $60 = $6	$ 44
Finished goods	150	150/500 x $60 = 18	132
Cost of goods sold	300	300/500 x $60 = 36	264
Totals	$500	$60	$440

3. Cost of goods sold would be higher in requirement 2, so gross profit would be lower in requirement 2 by $60 - $36 = $24. That is, cost of goods sold would be $300 - $36 or $264 in requirement 2 and $300 - $60 or $240 in requirement 1.

13-35 (10-15 min.) Answers are in millions of French francs.

1. First Way

Unadjusted cost of goods sold	150
Add: Underapplied overhead	10
Adjusted cost of goods sold	160

Cost of goods sold	10	
Factory department overhead control		10

Second Way	Unadjusted	Proration of Underapplied Overhead	Adjusted
Cost of goods sold	150	150/300 x 10 = 5	155
Work in process	30	30/300 x 10 = 1	31
Finished goods	120	120/300 x 10 = 4	124
Totals	300	10	310

Cost of goods sold	5	
Work in process	1	
Finished goods	4	
Factory department overhead control		10

2.

	First Way	Second Way
Gross profit before adjustment	43	43
Adjustment	-10	-5
Gross profit after adjustment	33	38

13-36 (10-15 min.)

Overhead is overapplied by $457,000 - $409,000=$48,000.

First Way

Unadjusted cost of goods sold	$400,000
Deduct: Overapplied overhead	48,000
Adjusted cost of goods sold	$352,000

Factory department overhead control	48,000	
Cost of goods sold		48,000

Second Way	Unadjusted	Proration of Overapplied Overhead	Adjusted
Cost of goods sold	$400,000	400/800 x $48,000 = $24,000	$376,000
Work in process	200,000	200/800 x 48,000 = 12,000	188,000
Finished goods	200,000	200/800 x 48,000 = 12,000	188,000
Totals	$800,000	$48,000	$752,000

Factory department overhead control	48,000	
Cost of goods sold		24,000
Work in process		12,000
Finished goods		12,000

Cost of goods sold would be $48,000 - $24,000 = $24,000 lower (and gross profit higher) under the first way (no proration).

13-37 (10-15 min.)

Dell would most likely use a job-cost system with each order considered a job. Because each order is assembled from a set of common parts, there is a single cost for each part. Most of the parts are purchased, so the cost is the purchase price. If some parts are made, the production cost would be used as the cost of the part.

Each order would call for several materials, and each would be added to the order's job-cost sheet. Labor would be incurred in assembly, so the direct-labor cost could be allocated to each order based on the number of hours used for assembly. If assembly is highly automated, it is possible that no labor is considered "direct", and labor becomes one more overhead item.

Overhead costs would be allocated based on one or more cost drivers. Possible drivers include direct-labor hours or cost (if direct labor is measured separately), hours in assembly, or number of component parts. For a highly automated process, that latter would be a likely cost driver.

Testing and quality control costs might be part of overhead. Alternately, costs of testing final computers could be charged directly to the order (job). If different types of computers require different amounts of testing, this is a logical allocation method.

13-38 (15-25 min.)

1. Ending inventory = Beginning inventory + Purchases - Usage

75 = 55 + Purchases - 455

Purchases = 475

2. Total manufacturing costs charged to production = Direct materials + Direct labor + Factory overhead

851 = 455 + DL + .8 DL

851 - 455 = 1.8 DL

1.8 DL = 396

DL = 220

3. Cost of goods manufactured = Cost of goods available for sale - Beginning finished goods

= 1,026 - 90

= 936

4. Cost of goods sold = Cost of goods available for sale - Ending finished goods

= 1,026 - 110

= 916

13-39 (25-35 min.)

1.

Job 412 ($ 9,000 + $4,000 + $8,000)	$21,000
Job 413 ($12,000 + $5,000 + $10,000)	27,000
Work-in-process inventory, April 30	$48,000

2. The job-cost records indicate an overhead application rate of $8,000 ÷ $4,000 = 200% or $10,000 ÷ $5,000 = 200%.

3.

	Debit	Credit
a. Work-in-process inventory	15,500	
Direct materials inventory		15,500
Job 412 of $2,500 + Job 414 of $13,000		
b. Work-in-process inventory	6,000	
Accrued payroll		6,000
$1,500 + $2,500 + $2,000		
c. Work-in-process inventory	12,000	
Factory department overhead		12,000
$6,000 x 200%		
d. Finished goods inventory (Job 412)	28,000	
Work-in-process inventory		28,000
$21,000 + $2,500 + $1,500 + 200% of $1,500		
e. Cost of goods sold	33,000	
Finished goods inventory		33,000
The $33,000 amount is given.		

Direct Materials Inventory

Bal.	19,000	(a)	15,500
Bal.	3,500		

Accrued Payroll

		(b)	6,000

Factory Department Overhead

		(c)	12,000

Cost of Goods Sold

Bal.	450,000		
(e)	33,000		
Bal.	483,000		

Work-in-Process Inventory

Bal.	48,000	(d)	28,000
(a)	15,500		
(b)	6,000		
(c)	12,000		
	81,500		
Bal.	53,500		

Finished Goods Inventory

Bal.	18,000	(e)	33,000
(d)	28,000		
Bal.	13,000		

4.

Job 413 ($27,000 + $2,500 + 200% of $2,500)	$34,500
Job 414 ($13,000 + $2,000 + 200% of $2,000)	19,000
Work-in-process inventory, May 31	$53,500

13-40 (40-60 min.)

1.

	Machining	Assembly
(a) Budgeted overhead	$990,000	$1,100,000
(b) Cost drivers:		
Budgeted machine hours	90,000	-
Budgeted direct-labor cost	-	$2,200,000
Budgeted overhead rates, (a) ÷ (b)	$11/hour	50%

2. The machine hours actually worked were factory overhead applied, $880,000, divided by the budgeted rate, $11, or 80,000 hours.

3. .50 x $2,800,000 = $1,400,000

4. Amounts are in thousands.

	Debit	Credit
a. Direct-materials inventory	1,900	
Accounts payable		1,900
b. Work in process	1,850	
Direct-materials inventory		1,850
c. Work in process	3,700	
Accrued payroll		3,700
d1. Factory department overhead control	2,200	
Various accounts		2,200
d2. Work in process	2,280	
Factory department overhead control		2,280
(80,000 x $11) + ($2,800,000 x .50)		

		Debit	Credit
e.	Finished goods	7,820	
	Work in process		7,820
f1.	Accounts receivable	13,000	
	Sales		13,000
f2.	Cost of goods sold	7,800	
	Finished goods		7,800

Direct-Materials Inventory

Bal.	65	b.	1,850
a.	1,900		
Bal.	115		

Work in Process

Bal.	50	e.	7,820
b.	1,850		
c.	3,700		
d2.	2,280		
	7,880		
Bal.	60		

Finished Goods

Bal.	40	f2.	7,800
e.	7,820		
Bal.	60		

5.

Sales		$13,000,000
Cost of goods sold:		
Before adjustment	$7,800,000	
Overapplied overhead	80,000	
Adjusted cost of goods sold		7,720,000
Gross profit		$ 5,280,000

13-41 (20-30 min.) Students are likely to make errors in this "easy" problem.

1.

Professional salaries unassigned, .20 x $1,333,000	$ 266,600
Other costs	533,200
Total overhead	$ 799,800
Divided by professional salaries that are "direct labor"	÷ 1,066,400*
Equals overhead rate	75%

*Not $1,333,000, but $1,333,000 - $266,600

2. Hourly rates:

Level 12, $35,000 ÷ 1,800 hours	$19.44
Level 10, $26,000 ÷ 1,800 hours	$14.44
Level 8, $18,000 ÷ 1,800 hours	$10.00

The allocation to Client No. 273 is:

Direct labor:	
Level 12, 2 hours at $19.44	$ 38.88
Level 10, 4 hours at $14.44	57.76
Level 8, 9 hours at $10.00	90.00
Total direct labor	$186.64
Overhead, .75 x $186.64	139.98
Total job cost	$326.62

The hardest thing for students to grasp is typically the idea that some of the professional salaries are transferred to the overhead category. In turn, this reduces the "direct-labor" cost allocation base from $1,333,000 to $1,066,400.

13-42 (20 min.)

1. Overhead

	Compensation for nonchargeable time, .15 x $3,600,000	$ 540,000
	Other costs	1,449,000
(a)	Total overhead	$1,989,000
(b)	Direct labor, .85 x $3,600,000	$3,060,000
	Overhead application rate, (a) ÷ (b)	65%

2. Hourly rate:

$60,000 ÷ (48 x 40) = $60,000 ÷ 1,920 $31.25

Many students will forget that "his work there" includes an overhead application:

Direct labor, 10 x $31.25	$312.50
Applied overhead, $312.50 x .65	203.13
Total costs applied	$515.63

We point out that direct-labor time on a job is usually compiled for all classes of engineers and then applied at their different compensation rates. Overhead is usually not applied on the piecemeal basis demonstrated here. Instead, it is applied in one step after all the labor costs of the job have been accumulated.

[1] Pension expense for 19X2:

Service cost

P_{OA} for 11 periods @ 9% × $250

= 6.8052 × $250 = $1,701

PV of single amount for 13 periods @ 9%

= 0.3262 × $1,701	=	$555
Interest on PBO at Jan.1, 19X2		
9% x $36,153[a]		3,254
Actual return on plan assets		
10% × $30,853 =	(3,085)	
Less: Amount deferred	0	($3,085)
Amortization of prior service costs: $27,165/15 yrs. =		+ 1,811
Amortization of actuarial gains/losses		0
Amortization of transition amount		0
Total pension expense for 19X2		$2,535
Less: Amortization of prior service costs which were prefunded		(1,811)
Amount of pension expense funded in 19X2		$724

[a] Calculation of PBO on Jan. 1, 19X2 based on 9% discount rate

Years of service credit earned as of 19X2: 11 yrs. × $250	$2,750
Benefits tied to expected salary at retirement: 50% × $30,000	15,000
Total annual pension benefit based on service credit earned up to 19X2	$17,750
PV of expected pension benefits as of 19X16:	
P_{OA} for 11 periods @ 9% × $17,750 = 6.8052 × $17,750 =	$120,792
PBO on 1/1/X2:	
PV of single amount for 14 periods @ 9% = 0.2993 × $120,792 =	$36,153

[2] Annual pension benefits starting on 12/31/X16 and continuing for 10 years thereafter (11 years total).

Years of service credit earned as of 12/31/X2: 12 yrs. × $250	$3,000
Benefits tied to expected salary at retirement: 50% × $30,000	15,000
Total annual pension benefit based on service credit earned up to 12/31/X2	$18,000
PV of expected pension benefits as of 1/1/X6 (date of retirement):	
P_{OA} for 11 periods @ 9% × $18,000	
= 6.805 × $18,000 =	$122,490
Projected benefit obligation on 12/31/X2:	
PV of single amount for 13 periods @ 9%	
= 0.326 × $122,490 =	$39,932

4. The billings would differ significantly:

	Engagement	
	Eagledale	First Valley
Method 1:		
Total costs	$45,000	$45,000
Total billings @ 130%	$58,500	$58,500
Method 2:		
Total costs	$46,000	$42,000
Total billings @ 130%	$59,800	$54,600
Method 3:		
Total costs	$46,875	$39,375
Total billings @ 130%	$60,938	$51,188

5. The first method is inferior to the other two because the latter give more accurate measures of how specific jobs cause increases in costs. In general, the more costs that are directly charged to jobs, the more accurate the picture of where the money is really spent.

   As between the other two methods, the answer depends on what causes the indirect costs to rise. If direct labor is the dominant cause, then the 140% rate is better. If the increases in indirect costs are more closely related to increases in all direct costs, then the 87.5% rate is preferable. Additional studies of how indirect costs behave would be necessary to answer this question.

13-44 (15 min.)

1. If other departments are indeed providing services to the water and sewer department, it is certainly appropriate to include the cost of these services in the water and sewer department's budget and to have them paid for by the water and sewer customers. Charging administrative overhead is not a ruse; it is a real cost of providing water and sewer services. However, it is not clear from the case whether the administrative overhead allocation is accurately measured. It appears that there is only one overhead pool and consequently only one cost driver used for allocation. It is likely that the services are quite varied and a single cost driver may not be appropriate.

2. It would be useful to identify the activities involved when other departments provide services to the water and sewer department. If it is not too expensive, it would be worthwhile to measure each type of service and charge the water and sewer department only the cost of those services actually used. In essence, it would be good to directly (physically) trace as many costs to the department as possible, charging directly for the services. At a minimum, using multiple cost pools and cost drivers for allocating diverse costs to the water and sewer departments should be considered.

13-45 (35-50 min.)

Some instructors may want to provide more details about accrued payroll in conjunction with their assignment of this problem.

a. Direct materials purchased: $140,000 + $27,000 - $22,000 = $145,000.

b. Cost of goods sold: $25,000 + $260,000 - $35,000 = $250,000.

c. Direct-labor rate: $3,000 ÷ 200 hours = $15 / hour (see 2).
Direct-labor cost: 3,000 hours x $15 = $45,000 (see 7).

d. Overhead rate: $800,000 ÷ $640,000 = 125%. Overhead applied: 125% x $45,000 = $56,250.

e. Accrued factory payroll, Dec. 31: $55,000 + $5,000 - $45,000 - $12,000 = $3,000.

f. Work-in-process, Dec. 31: $260,000 + $27,750 - $140,000 - $45,000 - $56,250 = $46,500.

g. Work-in-process, Jan. 31: $21,000 + $3,000 + 125% of $3,000 = $27,750.

h. Overapplied overhead: $56,250 - $55,000 = $1,250.

Entries in T accounts are numbered in accordance with the "additional information" in the problem and are lettered in accordance with the amounts required to be determined.

Direct-Materials Inventory

12/31/X8 Bal. (given)		22,000		
	(a)	145,000*	(3)	140,000
1/31/X9 Bal.	(5)	27,000		

Work-in-Process

12/31/X8 Bal.	(f)	46,500*	(4)	260,000
Direct materials	(3)	140,000		
Direct labor	(c)	45,000		
Overhead	(d)	56,250		
1/31/X9 Bal.	(g)	27,750		

Finished Goods

12/31/X8 Bal. (given)		25,000		
	(4)	260,000	(b)	250,000
1/31/X9 Bal.	(6)	35,000		

Accrued Factory Payroll

(8)	55,000	12/31/X8	(e)	3,000
			(7)	45,000
			(7)	12,000
		1/31/X9 Bal. (given)		5,000

Factory Department Overhead Control

January charges (given)	55,000	(d)	56,250

Cost of Goods Sold

(b)	250,000	

*Can be computed only after all other postings in the account have been found; for example, (g) must be computed before (f) in Work-in-Process.

13-46 (15-25 min.) This problem is intended to highlight the distinction and relation between accounting for control and accounting for product costing.

1. First six months:

   (55,000 x \$4.50) - \$236,500 = \$11,000, overapplied

   Last six months:

   \$206,500 - (41,000 x \$4.50) = \$22,000, underapplied

2. Overhead rate:

Fixed, \$325,000 ÷ 100,000 DLH	\$3.25 per DLH
Variable, \$125,000 ÷ 100,000 DLH	1.25 per DLH
Overall rate	\$4.50

   (a) In the first period, direct-labor hours used exceeded half of the year's total budget (50,000) by 5,000. This makes fixed overhead overapplied by 5,000 x \$3.25 = \$16,250. Actual variable overhead was \$236,500 - (50% x \$325,000) = \$74,000. Variable overhead applied is \$55,000 x \$1.25 = \$68,750, so it is underapplied by \$74,000 - \$68,750 = \$5,250. Therefore, the total overhead is overapplied by \$16,250 - \$5,250 = \$11,000.

   (b) In the last period, direct-labor hours used were less than half the year's total budget by 9,000. Fixed overhead was thus underapplied by 9,000 x \$3.25 = \$29,250. Actual variable overhead was \$206,500 - (50% x \$325,000) = \$44,000. Variable overhead applied was \$1.25 x 41,000 = \$51,250, so variable overhead was overapplied by \$51,250 - \$44,000 = \$7,250. Therfore, total overhead is underapplied by \$29,250 - \$7,250 = \$22,000.

13-47 (15-20 min.)

1.

Activity	Factory Overhead Costs Applied
1.	1 x $ 1.20 = $ 1.20
2.	39 x .07 = 2.73
3.	28 x .20 = 5.60
4.	15 x .40 = 6.00
5.	1 x 3.20 = 3.20
6.	8 x .60 = 4.80
7.	.15 x 80.00 = 12.00
8.	.05 x 90.00 = 4.50
Total	$40.03

Direct materials	$ 55.00
Factory overhead applied	40.03
Total manufacturing product cost	$95.03

2. Direct labor is no longer traced separately via time tickets to individual products. Instead, it becomes part of activity cost pools and is included in each activity's factory overhead application rate. This reduces accounting costs because there is no elaborate tracking of labor.

3. Managers would primarily favor this multiple overhead rate, activity-based costing system because of more accurate product costing. In this way, managers will have more confidence in their decisions regarding pricing and emphasizing or de-emphasizing various products. The older system may be easier to understand but less believable.

13-48 (20-30 min.)

1.

	Machining	Finishing	Plant
Factory overhead	SF960,000	SF800,000	SF1,760,000
Divide by direct labor	300,000	800,000	1,100,000
Application rate	320%	100%	160%
Divide by machine hours	60,000	20,000	80,000
Application rate	SF16	SF40	SF22

2. a.

	Order	
	K102	K156
Machining:		
Direct materials	SF 4,000	SF 4,000
Direct labor	3,000	1,500
Factory overhead applied, 160% of direct labor	4,800	2,400
Finishing:		
Direct labor	1,500	3,000
Factory overhead applied, 160% of direct labor	2,400	4,800
Total cost	SF15,700	SF15,700

b.

	Order	
	K102	K156
Machining:		
Direct materials	SF 4,000	SF 4,000
Direct labor	3,000	1,500
Factory overhead applied, 1,200 hrs. x SF16 and 100 hrs. x SF16	19,200	1,600
Finishing:		
Direct labor	1,500	3,000
Factory overhead applied, 100% of direct labor	1,500	3,000
Total cost	SF29,200	SF13,100

3. The answers in 2(b) are preferable to those in 2(a). Why? Because the use of machine hours is probably an important cause of increases in the company's overhead costs. Machine hours are cost drivers. The plantwide rate based on direct labor fails to distinguish between those jobs that make heavy and light use of machinery. In general, the use of departmental overhead rates is preferable to plantwide rates. Why? Because the use of key activities (cost drivers) is pinpointed more accurately. Decisions regarding pricing and product lines should improve.

13-49 (180 min. or more)

The purpose of this exercise is to learn how real companies allocate costs. It involves learning what costs are included in overhead, how they are categorized, whether cost allocations recognize cost-behavior patterns, what cost drivers are used for allocation, and the process by which costs are allocated to final products or services.

The requirement for a diagram makes students put what they learn into a coherent package. It is easy to sit and listen to what seems like a very logical explanation but to not fully understand it. The diagram of a cost allocation system cannot be done without a thorough understanding of the system.

A very useful exercise is to have several groups present their findings to the class. In addition to learning about different cost allocation systems, the students making the presentation will hone their communication skills and those listening will learn a great deal about a variety of companies. We find that several short (approximately 5-minute) presentations can be more effective that a couple longer ones. Students learn to focus quickly on the most important issues.

CHAPTER 14
Process-Costing Systems

14-A1 (10-15 min.)

1.

	(Step 1) Physical Units	(Step 2) Equivalent Units Direct Materials	Conversion Costs
Flow of Production			
Started and completed	17,000	17,000	17,000
Work in process, ending inventory	2,000		
Direct materials added: 2,000 x 1		2,000	
Conversion costs added: 2,000 x .5		1,000	
Total accounted for	19,000		
Total work done		19,000	18,000
Costs:			
Total costs to account for (Step 3):	$147,000	$57,000	$90,000
Divide by equivalent units (Step 4)		19,000	18,000
Unit costs	$ 8.00	$ 3.00	$ 5.00

2.

	Totals	Details	
Application of costs (Step 5):			
To units completed and transferred to Testing, 17,000 units ($8.00)	$136,000		
To units not completed and still in process, Feb. 28, 2,000 units:			
Direct materials	$ 6,000	2,000($3.00)	
Conversion costs	5,000		1,000($5.00)
Work in process, Jan. 31	$ 11,000		
Total costs accounted for	$147,000		

14-A2 (25-30 min.)

Flow of Production	(Step 1) Physical Units	(Step 2) Equivalent Units Direct Materials	Conversion Costs
Work in process, beginning inventory	10,000 (25%)*		
Started	80,000		
To account for	90,000		
Completed and transferred out during current period	70,000	70,000	70,000
Work in process, ending inventory	20,000 (50%)*	20,000	10,000
Units accounted for	90,000		
Work done to date		90,000	80,000

	Costs	Totals	Details Direct Materials	Conversion Costs
	Work in process, beginning inventory	$ 175,500	$138,000	$ 37,500
	Costs added currently	1,494,500	852,000	642,500
(Step 3)	Total costs to account for	$1,670,000	$990,000	$680,000
(Step 4)	Divisor, equivalent units for work done to date		÷ 90,000	÷ 80,000
	Cost per equivalent unit	$ 19.50	$ 11.00	$ 8.50

(Step 5)	Costs	Totals	Details: Direct Materials	Details: Conversion Costs
	Application of Costs			
	Completed and transferred (70,000 units)	$1,365,000	70,000 ($19.50)	
	Work in process, ending inventory (20,000 units):			
	Direct materials	$ 220,000	20,000($11.00)	
	Conversion costs	85,000		10,000($8.50)
	Total work in process	$ 305,000		
	Total costs accounted for	$1,670,000		

*Degree of completion for conversion costs.

14-A3 (15-20 min.)

		Debit	Credit
1.	Materials inventories	46,000	
	Accounts payable		46,000
	Conversion costs	30,000	
	Accrued payroll		11,000
	Miscellaneous accounts		19,000
	Finished goods inventories (2,000 x $37)	74,000	
	Materials inventories (2,000 x $22)		44,000
	Conversion costs (2,000 x $15)		30,000
	Cost of goods sold (1,980 x $37)	73,260	
	Finished goods inventories		73,260
2.	Cost of goods sold	2,000	
	Conversion costs		2,000

To recognize actual conversion costs that were $2,000 greater than the amount applied to the products.

14-B1 (10-15 min.)

1.

Flow of Production	(Step 1) Physical Units	(Step 2) Equivalent Units Direct Materials	Conversion Costs
Started and completed	600,000	600,000	600,000
Work in process, ending inventory	300,000	300,000	150,000*
Units accounted for	900,000		
Units work done to date		900,000	750,000
Total costs to account for (Step 3):	$2,370,000	$1,620,000	$750,000
Divide by equivalent units (Step 4)		900,000	750,000
Unit costs	$ 2.80	$ 1.80	$ 1.00

*300,000 x .5

2. Application of costs (Step 5):	Totals	Details
To units completed and transferred to Finishing, 600,000 units ($2.80)	$1,680,000	
To units not completed and still in process, end, 300,000 units:		
Direct materials	$ 540,000	300,000 ($1.80)
Conversion costs	150,000	150,000($1.00)
Work in process, end	$ 690,000	
Total costs accounted for	$2,370,000	

14-B2 (25-35 min.)

Flow of Production	(Step 1) Physical Units	(Step 2) Equivalent Units Direct Materials	Conversion Costs
Work in process, beginning inventory	550 (40%)*		
Started	7,150		
To account for	7,700		
Completed and transferred out during current period, 550 + 7,150 - 400	7,300	7,300	7,300
Work in process, ending inventory	400 (20%)*	400	80
Units accounted for	7,700		
Work done to date		7,700	7,380

			Details	
			Direct	Conversion
	Costs	Totals	Materials	Costs
	Work in process, beginning inventory	$ 5,104	$ 3,190	$ 1,914
	Costs added currently	100,326	65,340	34,986
(Step 3)	Total costs to account for	$105,430	$68,530	$36,900
(Step 4)	Divisor, equivalent units for work done to date		÷ 7,700	÷ 7,380
	Cost per equivalent unit	$ 13.90	$ 8.90	$ 5.00
(Step 5)	Application of Costs			
	Completed, (7,300 units)	$101,470	7,300 ($13.90)	
	Work in process, ending inventory (400 units):			
	Direct materials (400)	$ 3,560	400($8.90)	
	Conversion costs (80)	400		80($5.00)
	Total work in process	$ 3,960		
	Total costs accounted for	$105,430		

*Degree of completion for conversion costs.

14-B3 (15 min.)

1.

	Debit	Credit
Materials inventories	16,000	
Accounts payable		16,000
Conversion costs	6,300	
Accrued payroll and miscellaneous accts.		6,300
Cost of goods sold (1,500 x $14.20)	21,300	
Materials inventories (1,500 x $10.00)		15,000
Conversion costs (1,500 x $4.20)		6,300

2.

	Debit	Credit
Conversion costs	400	
Cost of goods sold		400

To recognize actual conversion costs that were $400 less than the amount applied to the products.

14-1 Examples of process costing include flour, glass, paint, and beer.

14-2 Examples of process costing include handling of mail, income tax returns, automobile registrations, and drivers license examinations.

14-3 The central product costing problem in process costing is how each department should compute the cost of goods transferred out and the cost of goods remaining in the department.

14-4 Five key steps in process cost accounting are

Step 1: Summarize the flow of physical units
Step 2: Calculate output in terms of equivalent units
Step 3: Summarize the total costs to account for, which are the total debits in Work in Process (that is, the costs applied to Work in Process)
Step 4: Calculate unit costs
Step 5: Apply costs to units completed and to units in ending work in process

14-5 The first two steps concentrate on what is occurring in physical or engineering terms. The financial impact of the production process is measured in the final three steps.

14-6 (1 x 10,000) + (.5 x 5,000) = 12,500 full-time-equivalent students.

14-7 The quotation refers to the weighted-average method.

14-8 Beginning inventories + Units started = Units transferred out + Ending inventories.

14-9 The quotation refers to the FIFO method.

14-10 "Work done in current period only" is a key measurement to judging performance for a given span of time, because the resulting unit costs are unaffected by the averaging with work done on the beginning inventory during the preceding period. Such a measurement is used for FIFO process costing.

14-11 The quotation refers to the weighted-average method.

14-12 Yes. Differences in unit costs between FIFO and weighted-average methods are ordinarily insignificant because (a) changes in material prices, labor wage rates, and other manufacturing costs from month to month tend to be small, and (b) changes in the volume of production and inventory levels also tend to be small.

14-13 Yes. FIFO process costing isolates the production in the current period and the costs incurred in that period. The cost per unit for work in the current period only is relevant for assessing the efficiency of production. It can be compared either to standards or to previous costs.

14-14 Transferred-in costs are accounted for operationally the same as direct materials added at the beginning of a production process. They differ from direct material costs because they are a combination of direct material and conversion costs from a previous department; thus, calling them a direct-material cost is inappropriate.

14-15 No, but they are especially appropriate for companies with just-in-time systems. Any company with small inventories might find backflush costing appealing.

14-16 When actual conversion costs exceed the amount applied, the excess in the conversion cost account is charged directly to cost of goods sold; the treatment is similar to accounting for underapplied overhead.

14-17 Examples of operation costing include manufacturing of clothing, automobiles, and personal computers.

14-18 Yes, the application of factory overhead and of conversion costs is similar. In each instance, a budget rate is developed. However, in operation costing, many more application rates are usually used.

14-19 (10-15 min.)

1.

Flow of Production	(Step 1) Physical Units	(Step 2) Equivalent Units Direct Materials	Conversion Costs
Started and completed	650,000	650,000	650,000
Work in process, ending inventory	220,000	220,000	132,000*
Units accounted for	870,000		
Work done to date		870,000	782,000
Costs:			
Total costs to account for (Step 3)	$4,601,200	$3,741,000	$860,200
Divide by equivalent units (Step 4)		870,000	782,000
Unit costs	$5.40	$4.30	$1.10

*220,000 x .60

2.

	Totals	Details
Application of costs (Step 5):		
To units completed and transferred, 650,000 units ($5.40)	$3,510,000	
To units still in process, end, 220,000 units:		
Direct materials	$ 946,000	220,000($4.30)
Conversion costs	145,200	132,000($1.10)
Work in process, end	$1,091,200	
Total costs accounted for	$4,601,200	

14-20 (15-20 min.)

1.

Flow of Production	(Step 1) Physical Units	(Step 2) Equivalent Units Direct Materials	Conversion Costs
Units started and completed	68,000	68,000	68,000
Work in process, end:	6,000		
Materials added: 6,000 x .90		5,400	
Conversion costs: 6,000 x .70			4,200
Units accounted for	74,000		
Work done to date		73,400	72,200

2.

	Total Costs	Details Direct Materials	Conversion Costs
Costs to account for (Step 3)	$602,620	$205,520	$397,100
Divide by equivalent units (Step 4)		73,400	72,200
Unit costs	$8.30	$2.80	$5.50

Application of costs (Step 5):			
To units completed and transferred, 68,000($8.40)	$564,400		
To units still in process, end, 6,000 units:			
Direct materials	$ 15,660	5,400($2.80)	
Conversion costs	23,100		4,200($5.50)
Work in process, end	$ 38,220		
Total costs accounted for	$602,620		

14-21 (10-15 min.)

1.	Work in process – Assembly	57,000	
	Direct materials inventory		57,000
	Materials added to production in February		
2.	Work in process – Assembly	50,000	
	Accrued payroll		50,000
	Direct labor in February		
3.	Work in process – Assembly	40,000	
	Factory overhead		40,000
	Factory overhead applied in February		
4.	Work in process – Testing	136,000	
	Work in process – Assembly		136,000
	Cost of goods completed and transferred in February from Assembly to Testing		

The Key T account would show:

Work in Process – Assembly

1. Direct materials	57,000	4. Transferred out to Testing	136,000
2. Direct labor	50,000		
3. Factory overhead	40,000		
Costs to account for	147,000		
Bal. February 28	11,000		

14-22 (10-15 min.)

		Dr.	Cr.
1.	Work in process – Assembly	1,620,000	
	Direct materials inventory		1,620,000
	Materials added to production		
2.	Work in process – Assembly	475,000	
	Accrued payroll		475,000
	Direct labor		
3.	Work in process – Assembly	275,000	
	Factory overhead		275,000
	Factory overhead applied		
4.	Work in process – Finishing	1,680,000	
	Work in process – Assembly		1,680,000
	Cost of goods completed and transferred from Assembly to Finishing		

The key T account would show:

Work in Process – Assembly

1. Direct materials	1,620,000	4. Transferred out to Finishing	1,680,000
2. Direct labor	475,000		
3. Factory overhead	275,000		
Costs to account for	2,370,000		
Balance	690,000		

14-23 (5 min.)

Let x = unknown

Beginning inventory + Units started = Units transferred + Ending inventory

Case A: 1,500 + 6,500 = x + 2,000

x = 6,000

Case B: 4,000 + x = 8,000 + 3,300

x = 7,300

14-24 (15 min.)

Flow of Production	Physical Units	Equivalent Units Direct Materials	Equivalent Units Conversion Costs
Beginning work in process	1,000(50%)		
Started	35,000		
To Account for	36,000		
Completed and transferred out	33,000	33,000	33,000
Ending work in process	3,000(40%)	3,000	1,200
Units accounted for	36,000		
Work done to date		36,000	34,200
Equivalent units in beginning inventory		1,000	500
Work done in current period only		35,000	33,700

14-25 (5 min.)

	(a) Direct Materials	(b) Conversion Costs
Gallons completed:		
From beginning work in process	—	3,500[a]
From April production	25,000	25,000
In process, end	10,000	5,000[b]
Total equivalent units, April	35,000	33,500[c]

[a]5,000 (100% - 30%)

[b]10,000 x 50%

[c]Alternative computation: 5,000 + 25,000 + 5,000 - (30% x 5,000)

14-26 (10-15 min.)

Flow of Production in Units	(Step 1) Physical Units	(Step 2) Equivalent Units Direct Materials	Conversion Costs
Work in process, beginning inventory	20,000[a]		
Started	45,000		
To account for	65,000		
Completed and transferred	63,000	63,000	63,000
Work in process, ending inventory	2,000[b]	800	200
Units accounted for	65,000		
Work done to date		63,800	63,200
Less: Equivalent units of work from previous periods included in beginning inventory		16,000[c]	8,000[c]
Work done in current period only (FIFO method)		47,800	55,200

[a]Degree of completion: direct materials 80%; conversion costs, 40%
[b]Degree of completion: direct materials 40%; conversion costs, 10%
[c]80% and 40% of 20,000

14-27 (10-15 min.)

Flow of Production	(Step 1) Physical Units	(Step 2) Equivalent Units Direct Materials	Conversion Costs
Work in process, beginning inventory*	20,000		
Started	80,000		
To account for	100,000		
Completed and transferred out (100,000-10,000)	90,000	90,000	90,000
Work in process, ending inventory**	10,000	2,000[a]	3,000[a]
Units accounted for	100,000		
Work done to date		92,000	93,000
Less: Equivalent units of work from previous periods included in beginning inventory (80% and 40% of 20,000)		16,000[b]	8,000[b]
Work done in 19x8 only (FIFO method)		76,000	85,000

*Degree of completion: materials, 80%; conversion costs, 40%

**Degree of completion: materials, 20%; conversion costs, 30%

[a].20 x 10,000 and .30 x 10,000

[b].80 x 20,000 and .40 x 20,000

14-28 (10-15 min.)

Flow of Production	(Step 1) Physical Units		(Step 2) Equivalent Units
Beginning inventory	15,000	(70%)*	
Started (80,000 + 5,000 - 15,000)	70,000		
To account for	85,000		
Completed and transferred out	80,000		80,000
Ending inventory	5,000	(60%)*	3,000
Units accounted for	85,000		
Work done to date			83,000
Less: Equivalent units of work from previous periods included in beginning inventory			10,500**
Work in current period only			72,500

*Degree of completion on material costs
**15,000(.70)

Material costs per unit: ¥580,000,000 ÷ 72,500 = ¥8,000

14-29 (10-15 min.)

Units completed (pounds)	45,000
Work done on ending inventory, .30 x 15,000	4,500
Work done to date	49,500
Less: Equivalent units of work from previous periods included in beginning inventory, .75 x 10,000	7,500
Work done in current period only	42,000

Unit Conversion cost = $222,600 ÷ 42,000 = $5.30.

14-30 (5-10 min.)

1.	Work in process, Department A	65,340	
	Direct-materials inventory		65,340
2.	Work in process, Department A	34,986	
	Various accounts		34,986
3.	Work in process, Department B	101,470	
	Work in process, Department A		101,470

14-31 (5-10 min.)

1.	Work in process, Assembly Department	852,000
	Direct materials inventory	852,000
2.	Work in process, Assembly Department	642,500
	Various accounts	642,500
3.	Work in process, Finishing Department	1,365,000
	Work in process, Assembly Department	1,365,000 *

14-32 (30-40 min.) See details below.

1. $265 per ton

2. $2,525

3. This requirement cannot be answered directly from the data using the weighted average process cost method. We must look at the equivalent units of conversion work done in May only:

Work done through the end of May	302 tons
Work done before May (3/4 x 24 tons)	18 tons
Work done in May	284 tons

Budget for 284 tons:
$16,000 + ($80 x 284) = $38,720

Budget - Actual = $38,720 - $40,670 = $1,950 unfavorable

During May, conversion costs were $1,950 (or 5%) above budget.

	(Step 1)	(Step 2) Equivalent Units	
Flow of Production	Physical Units	Direct Materials	Conversion Costs
Work in process, beg. inv.	24 (3/4)*		
Started	288		
To account for	312		
Completed and transferred out during current period	297	297	297
Work in process, end. inv.	15 (1/3)*	15	5
Units accounted for	312		
Work done to date		312	302

Costs	Totals	Details: Direct Materials	Details: Conversion Costs
Work in process, beg. inv.	$ 6,000	$ 2,880**	$ 3,120
Costs added currently	75,230	34,560**	40,670
(Step 3) Total costs to account for	$81,230	$37,440	$43,790
(Step 4) Divisor, equivalent units for work done to date		÷ 312	÷ 302
Cost per equivalent unit	$ 265	$ 120	$ 145
(Step 5) Application of Costs			
Completed and transferred (297 tons)	$78,705	297 ($265)	
Work in process, end. inv. (15 tons):			
Direct materials	$ 1,800	15($120)	
Conversion costs	725		5($145)
Total work in process	$ 2,525		
Total costs accounted for	$81,230		

*Degree of completion for conversion costs.
** $120 x 24 = $2,880; $120 x 288 = $34,560.

14-33 (15-20)

1. Potato chips are a homogeneous product with low unit cost that must be processed through a sequence of continuous steps (sequential processing). Potato chips are produced continuously rather than to order. As a result, a process-cost system is the most logical cost accounting system to use for product-costing purposes.

2. Activity-based accounting systems are most beneficial when products and/or processes are characterized by diversity. Diversity can be in the volume of product produced or the degree of complexity in the production process across product lines. Since neither of these forms of diversity characterize the potato chip industry, it is doubtful that activity-based accounting would pass the cost-benefit test. It may be that some specialty producers of gourmet potato chips (for example, Saratoga Potato Chip Company in New York) may have sufficient diversity to warrant use of an activity-based accounting system.

3. Frito-Lay produces over 6,000 pounds of potato chips each hour, 24 hours a day. This translates into more than 52 million pounds per year. Since at any point in time the work-in-process amounts to no more that one-half an hour (it takes 30 minutes to completely produce the end product), work-in-process accounts for about 3,000/52,000,000 or .006 percent of total annual production. The implication is that work-in-process can be ignored for product-costing purposes due to its immaterial amount.

14-34 (15-20 min.)

1.

	(Step 1) Physical Units	(Step 2) Equivalent Units Materials & Supplies	Conversion Costs
Units started and completed	1,800,000	1,800,000	1,800,000
Work in process, end	1,200,000	1,200,000	900,000*
Units accounted for	3,000,000	-	-
Work done to date		3,000,000	2,700,000

* 1,200,000 x .75

2.

	Total Costs	Details: Materials & Supplies	Details: Conversion Costs
Cost to account for (Step 3)	$5,325,000	$ 600,000	$4,725,000
Divide by equivalent unit (Step 4)		3,000,000	2,700,000
Unit costs	$1.95	$.20	$1.75

3. Ending work in process, 1,200,000 units:

Materials and supplies, 1,200,000 x $.20	$ 240,000
Conversion costs, 900,000 x $1.75	1,575,000
Cost of 1,200,000 returns not yet completed	$1,815,000

14-35 (20 min.)

1.

Flow of Production	(Step 1) Physical Units		(Step 2) Equivalent Units Plastic	Softening Compound	Conversion Costs
Work in process, beginning	0				
Started	60,000				
To account for	60,000				
Completed	40,000		40,000	40,000	40,000
Work in process, ending	20,000	(40%)	20,000	0	8,000
Units accounted for	60,000				
Work done to date			60,000	40,000	48,000

Costs	Total Costs			
Costs to account for (Step 3)	$620,000	$300,000	$80,000	$240,000
Divide by equivalent units (Step 4)		÷ 60,000	÷40,000	÷ 48,000
Cost per equivalent unit	$12.00	$5.00	$2.00	$5.00

2. Application of Costs (Step 5)	Totals	Details	
Units completed (40,000 x $12)	$480,000		
Work in process, ending:			
Material – Plastic	$100,000	20,000($5)	
Conversion costs	40,000		8,000($5)
Total work in process, ending	$140,000		
Total costs accounted for	$620,000		

14-36 (20-30 min.)

1.

Flow of Production	(Step 1) Physical Flow	Step 2 Equivalent Units Direct Materials	Cartons	Conversion Costs
Units started and completed	145,000	145,000	145,000	145,000
Work in process, end	5,000	—	—	—
Direct materials added:				
5,000 x 1.00	—	5,000	—	—
Cartons added: none				
Conversion costs:				
5,000 x .95	—	—	—	4,750
Units accounted for	150,000	—	—	—
Work done to date		150,000	145,000	149,750

	Total Costs	Details Direct Materials	Cartons	Conversion Costs
Costs accounted for (Step 3)	£3,738,000	£2,250,000	£290,000	£1,198,000
Divide by equivalent units (Step 4)		150,000	145,000	149,750
Unit costs	£25.00	£15.00	£2.00	£8.00

2. Application of costs (Step 5):

To units completed, 145,000 (£25.00)	3,625,000		
Work in process, end, 5,000 units:			
Direct materials	75,000	5,000(£15.00)	
Conversion costs	38,000		4,750(£8.00)
Work in process, end	113,000		
Total costs accounted for	£3,738,000		

14-37 (25-35 min.)

Flow of Production	(Step 1) Physical Units		(Step 2) Equivalent Units Direct Materials	Conversion Costs
Work in process, beginning inventory	550	(40%)*		
Started	7,150			
To account for	7,700			
Completed and transferred out during current period, 550 + 7,150 - 400	7,300		7,300	7,300
Work in process, ending inventory	400	(20%)*	400	80
Units accounted for	7,700			
Work done to date (that is, done in the current and previous periods)			7,700	7,380
Less: equivalent units of work from previous previous period included in beginning inventory, 100% and 40% of 550			550	220
Work done in current period only			7,150	7,160

Costs	Totals	Details Direct Materials	Conversion Costs
Work in process, beginning, $1,914 + $3,190	$ 5,104		
Costs added currently	100,326	$65,340	$34,986
Costs to account for (Step 3)	$105,430		
Divide by equivalent units (Step 4)		÷7,150	÷7,160
Cost per equivalent unit	$ 14.0248	$ 9.1385	$ 4.8863**

Application of Costs (Step 5)	Costs to Account for	Details: Direct Materials	Details: Conversion Costs
Work in process, ending inventory:			
Direct materials	$ 3,655	400 ($9.1385)	
Conversion costs	391		80($4.8863)
Total work in process (400 units)	$ 4,046		
Completed and transferred out (7,300 units), $105,430 - $4,046 = $101,384***	101,384***		
Total costs accounted for	$105,430		

* Degree of completion for conversion costs.

** A sidelight: There must have been enormous inefficient use of conversion costs in the preceding period. Why? Because the unit conversion cost of the beginning inventory was $1,914 ÷ 220 = $8.70, as compared with a current cost of work done of $34,986 ÷ 7,160 = $4.89.

*** Check:

Work in process, beginning inventory	$ 5,104
Additional costs to complete, conversion costs of 60% of 550 x $4.8863	1,612
Started and completed, 7,300 - 550 = 6,750; 6,750 x $14.0248	94,667
Total cost transferred	$101,383

The difference between $101,384 and $101,383 is due to rounding error

14-38 (25-35 min.)

Flow of Production	(Step 1) Physical Units	(Step 2) Equivalent Units Direct Materials	Conversion Costs
Work in process, beginning inventory	10,000 (25%)*		
Started	80,000		
To account for	90,000		
Completed and transferred out during current period	70,000	70,000	70,000
Work in process, ending inventory	20,000 (50%)*	20,000	10,000
Units accounted for	90,000		
Work done to date		90,000	80,000
Less: Equivalent units of work from previous periods included in beginning inventory, 100 % and 25% of 10,000		10,000	2,500
Work done in current period only		80,000	77,500

*Degrees of completion for conversion costs at inventory dates.

Costs	Totals	Direct Materials	Conversion Costs
Work in process, beginning inventory	$ 175,500		
Costs added currently	1,494,500	$852,000	$642,500
Total costs to account for (Step 3)	$1,670,000		
Divide by equivalent units (Step 4)		÷80,000	÷77,500
Cost per equivalent unit	$18.9403	$10.65	$8.2903

Application of Costs (Step 5)	Totals	Direct Materials	Conversion Costs
Work in process, ending inventory			
Direct materials	$ 213,000	20,000($10.65)	
Conversion costs	82,903		10,000($8.2903)[a]
Total work in process (20,000 units)	$ 295,903		
Completed and transferred out (70,000 units); $1,670,000 - $295,903	1,374,097[b]		
Total costs accounted for	$1,670,000		

[a]Equivalent units of work done x $8.2903

[b]Check:

Work in process, beginning inventory	$ 175,500
Additional costs to complete, conversion costs (75% of 10,000 x $8.2903) or 7,500 x $8.2903 =	62,177
Started and completed this period, (70,000 - 10,000) x $18.9403 =	1,136,418
Total cost transferred	$1,374,095

The difference between $1,374,095 and $1,374,097 is due to rounding error.

14-39 (15-20 min.)

1.

	Debit	Credit
Materials and parts inventory	287,000	
Accounts payable or cash		287,000
Conversion costs	92,000	
Accrued payroll, accounts payable, accumulated depreciation, etc.		92,000
Finished goods inventory (11,500 x $32)	368,000	
Materials and parts inventory (11,500 x 24)		276,000
Conversion costs (11,500 x $8)		92,000

2.

	Debit	Credit
Cost of goods sold	368,000	
Finished goods inventory		368,000

All costs incurred during April are charged to cost of goods sold in April. This assumes that all altimeters are sold and shipped immediately upon production. Therefore, the balance in Finished Goods Inventory is zero at the end of the month.

3. Because the balance in the Conversion Costs account must be zero at the end of the month, and because only $92,000 was transferred out of the Conversion Costs account while $94,600 was added to the account, the remaining $2,600 must be transferred to Cost of Goods Sold:

	Debit	Credit
Cost of goods sold	2,600	
Conversion costs		2,600

14-40 (15-20 min.)

We emphasize that more and more companies are applying direct labor and overhead together as a single unit cost per operation.

1.

Conversion costs	Cutting	Assembly	Finishing
Direct labor	$ 60,000	$30,000	$ 96,000
Factory overhead	115,500	37,500	156,000
Conversion costs	$175,500	$67,500	$252,000
Total units produced:			
6,000 + 4,500 + 3,000	13,500	13,500	
6,000 + 4,500			10,500
Conversion cost per unit	$13	$5	$24

2.

Chair Costs	Standard	Deluxe	Unfinished
Direct materials	$108,000	$171,000	$ 66,000
Conversion costs:			
Cutting @ $13	78,000	58,500	39,000
Assembly @ $5	30,000	22,500	15,000
Finishing @ $24	144,000	108,000	–
Total costs	$360,000	$360,000	$120,000
Units produced	6,000	4,500	3,000
Cost per unit	$60	$80	$40

14-41 (20-30 min.) The objective of this problem is to give the student a sense of how cost accounting copes with the costs of multiple products and multiple operations that are commonplace in today's world.

1. Budgeted rate for conversion costs = $\dfrac{(\$220{,}000 + \$580{,}000)}{20{,}000 \text{ hours}} = \$40$

Production per hour = 60 minutes ÷ 6 minutes per depth finder
= 10 depth finders.

Cost per depth finder = $40 per machine hour ÷ 10
= $4 per depth finder

Cost of 1,000 depth finders = 1,000 x $4 = $4,000

2.

	Standard Depth Finders	Deluxe Depth Finders
Direct materials	$57,000	$100,000
Conversion costs:		
Operation 1	19,000	19,000
Operation 2	4,000	4,000
Operation 3	–	15,000
Total manufacturing costs applied	$80,000	$138,000
Divide by total cameras	1,000	1,000
Cost per camera	$80	$138

3.

	Standard Depth Finders	Deluxe Depth Finders
Direct materials:		
$57,000 x 500/1,000	$28,500	
($100,000 - $10,000) x 600/1,000		$54,000
Conversion costs:		
Operation 1:		
(500/1,000 x $19,000)	9,500	
(600/1,000 x $19,000)		11,400
Operation 2:		
(600/1,000 x $4,000)	–	2,400
Total cost of work in process	$38,000	$67,800

14-42 (45 min. or more)

The purpose of this exercise is to make students think about the characteristics of real production processes and how to account for them. Depending on the assumptions students make about the type of production process used in each of these examples, they may suggest a different type of accounting system than those listed below. These are just suggestions about what the groups might conclude.

a. Process costing, because there are large volumes of identical product.

b. Hybrid costing is most likely. Certain parts might be made in sufficient volumes to use process costing, but final products are likely to be job-costed.

c. Process costing. Although each application is unique, it is likely that identifying the differences and trying to account for them is not cost-benefit efficient.

d. Probably job costing. It depends on how many identical couches students think that Ethan Allan makes at one time. If each is unique, or if small batches are produced, a job-costing system is most likely used.

e. Job costing. Major construction projects are generally treated as a single job.

f. Process costing. Refining oil into gasoline is a classic process-costing environment, where there is a single continuous process.

g. Job costing. Each order at Kinkos is unique. The only question is whether it is cost-benefit efficient to determine job costs for each order.

h. Job costing. Each ship built is a single job, although there may be parts that are produced in a process that allows process costing.

CHAPTER 15
Overhead Application: Variable and Absorption Costing

15-A1 (15-20 min.) Gross margin and ending direct-materials inventories are irrelevant.

1,2.

	(1) Absorption Costing	(2) Variable Costing
Direct materials used	$ 3,000	$ 3,000
Direct labor	4,500	4,500
Variable manufacturing overhead	2,500	2,500
Fixed manufacturing overhead	4,000	-
Total production costs	$14,000	$10,000
Ending inventories are 1/5 of total production costs	$ 2,800	$ 2,000

3. The $800 difference in ending inventories is accounted for by 1/5 of the $4,000 fixed manufacturing overhead that is lodged in ending inventory under absorption costing. Operating income would be $800 lower under variable costing because all of the fixed manufacturing overhead is released to expense in the current period. (That is why the fixed cost is sometimes called a "period cost" by variable costers; period costs are those that are totally released to expense in the current period rather than being inventoried.)

   Note also that the difference in operating income is a function of the *change* in inventory levels, which happened to be zero at the beginning of the year. It is not a function of the ending inventories alone. See the next problem.

15-A2 (20-30 min.)

1.

TRAHN COMPANY
Income Statement
For the Year Ended December 31, 19X6

Sales		$14,080
Deduct cost of goods sold:		
Beginning inventory, 110 @ $9*	$ 990	
Add: Absorption cost of goods manufactured,1,200 units @ $9	10,800	
Cost of goods available for sale	$11,790	
Ending inventory, 30 @ $9	270	
Cost of goods sold – at standard	$11,520	
Production volume variance (unfavorable)	400**	
Adjusted cost of goods sold		11,920
Gross margin		2,160
Selling and administrative expenses ($600 + 350)		950
Operating income		$ 1,210

*Fixed overhead rate: $2,800 ÷ 1,400 units = $2 per unit. Unit production cost: $7 + $2 = $9

** (1,400 - 1,200) x $2 = $400 underapplied

2. Change in inventory units 110 - 30 = 80 decrease
Fixed factory overhead rate is $2
Difference in operating income: 80 x $2 = $160 *less* under absorption costing

15-B1 (10 min.)

	(1) Absorption Costing	(2) Variable Costing
Production costs:		
Direct materials used	$3,500	$3,500
Direct labor	4,200	4,200
Variable manufacturing overhead	300	300
Fixed manufacturing overhead	2,200	-
Total	$10,200	$8,000
Ending inventories are 1/4 of total production costs	$2,550	$2,000

15-B2 (30-40 min.)

1.

GREENBERG COMPANY
Income Statement (Variable Costing)
For the Year 19X9
(in thousands of dollars)

Sales (150,000 x $5)			$750.0
Opening inventory, at variable standard cost of $3.00	$ 90.0		
Add: Variable cost of goods manufactured	465.0		
Available for sale	555.0		
Deduct: Ending inventory, at variable standard cost of $3.00	105.0		
Variable cost of goods sold, at standard		$450.0	
Net variances for all variable costs, unfavorable		18.0	
Variable cost of goods sold, at actual		468.0	
Variable selling expenses, at 5% of dollar sales		37.5	
Total variable costs charged against sales			505.5
Contribution margin			244.5
Fixed factory overhead		156.0*	
Fixed selling and administrative expenses		65.0	
Total fixed expenses			221.0
Operating income			$ 23.5

*This can be shown in two lines, $150,000 budget plus $6,000 variance.

GREENBERG COMPANY
Income Statement (Absorption Costing)
For the Year 19X9
(in thousands of dollars)

Sales			$750.0
Opening inventory, at standard cost of $4.00		$120.0	
Add: Cost of goods manufactured, at standard		620.0	
Available for sale		740.0	
Deduct: Ending inventory, at standard		140.0	
Cost of goods sold, at standard		600.0	
Net variances for variable manufacturing costs, unfavorable	$18.0		
Fixed factory overhead budget variance, unfavorable	6.0		
Production-volume variance, favorable	(5.0)*		
Total variances		19.0	
Cost of goods sold, at actual			619.0
Gross profit, at "actual"			131.0
Selling and administrative expenses:			
Variable		37.5	
Fixed		65.0	102.5
Operating income			$ 28.5

*Production-volume variance is $1.00 x (150,000 expected production volume - 155,000 actual production).

2. The $5,000 difference in operating income is attributable to the 5,000-unit increase in inventory levels. This means that $5,000 of fixed factory overhead (5,000 units x fixed rate of $1.00) was held back in inventory under absorption costing, whereas all fixed overhead was released as expense under variable costing.

15-1 No. Variable costing means that all *variable* costs of manufacturing are inventoried. These include direct material, direct labor, and the overhead costs that are incurred in direct proportion to the volume of production, even though these costs may only indirectly affect the production process and thus be categorized as "overhead."

15-2 Fixed manufacturing overhead is considered a noninventoriable or period cost under variable costing but a product cost under absorption costing.

15-3 No. Variable costing is not acceptable for external reporting. However, an increasing number of firms are using variable costing for *internal* reporting.

15-4 The tax authorities and those in charge of the rules for financial reporting do not allow use of variable costing. Why? They believe it violates the matching principle.

15-5 The contribution margin is revenue less variable costs (including both variable manufacturing costs and variable selling and administrative costs). In contrast, gross margin is revenue less manufacturing costs (including both variable manufacturing costs and fixed manufacturing costs).

15-6 Fixed overhead is applied to product via a budgeted unit overhead rate multiplied by an actual cost driver activity level such as machine hours or production units.

15-7 First, the unit product cost in absorption costing includes an allocation of fixed costs, while in variable costing it consists of only variable manufacturing costs. Second, fixed costs appear as a single line in a variable-costing statement, but they are in two places (part of product cost and as a production volume variance) in an absorption-costing statement. Finally, a variable-costing statement separates costs into fixed and variable components, while absorption-costing statements separate them into manufacturing and nonmanufacturing components.

15-8 This statement describes the treatment of fixed costs in a absorption-costing system. Total fixed costs are not affected by production volume, but applied fixed costs are proportional to the units of production.

15-9 Variable costing and cost-volume-profit analysis are both based on separate measurements of fixed and variable costs. Both focus on computation of the contribution margin, the difference between revenue and all variable costs.

15-10 Yes. Only when actual production volume exactly equals the expected volume is the applied fixed manufacturing overhead equal to that budgeted. Although the exact equality is rare, most of the time the difference will not be great.

15-11 The production-volume variance depends directly on the expected volume of production used as the denominator in setting the fixed-overhead rate. The higher the level chosen, the lower the rate. The total amount of the variance is a function of the rate and the deviation of actual volume from the volume used to set the rate.

15-12 Direct labor is a variable cost. The expected amount (i.e., flexible-budget amount) for a variable cost is the same as the amount allocated (or applied) to the product. There is no conflict between the budgeting and control purpose and the product-costing purpose. Therefore, no variance is caused by production volume differing from an expected volume.

15-13 No. Production-volume variances provide no information about the control of fixed manufacturing costs. Such variances arise solely because the actual production volume differs from the expected volume.

15-14 Yes. The unit fixed cost is inversely proportional to the denominator, expected units of production.

15-15 Production-volume variances arise because fixed manufacturing overhead is applied to products using a fixed-overhead rate based on budgeted fixed overhead divided by expected volume. Such a rate is used with either standard or normal costing, but not with actual costing.

15-16 No. When the number of units sold exceeds the number produced, that is, when inventory decreases, variable-costing income exceeds absorption-costing income.

15-17 The manager might produce extra units even if they will not be sold. Each unit produced will increase operating income by the amount of the fixed manufacturing overhead per unit. By producing enough units, the manager can assure that the operating income budget is met and the bonus received.

15-18 Variable- and absorption-costing incomes differ only when the level of inventory changes. Furthermore, the amount of the difference in income is proportional to the change in inventory. When inventories are small, changes in inventory are also generally small. Therefore, companies without much inventory will report nearly the same operating income with variable costing as with absorption costing.

15-19 No. Only the overhead production-volume variance is unique to an absorption-costing system. All other overhead variances occur in both variable- and absorption-costing systems.

15-20 (20 min.)

This exercise helps students obtain a fundamental look at the essential conceptual differences between the two inventory methods. Amounts are in thousands of dollars.

Absorption Costing

Balance Sheets				Income Statements	
January 1, 19X6					
Cash	150	Capital Stock	150		
December 31, 19X6				Year 19X6	
Cash,150-60	90	Capital stock	150	None	
Inventory,+60	60				
	150				
December 31, 19X7				Year 19X7	
Cash,90+42	132	Capital stock	150	Revenue	42
Inventory,60-30	30	Retained inc.,+12	12	Expense	30
	162		162	Net income	12
December 31, 19X8				Year 19X8	
Cash,132+42	174	Capital stock	150	Revenue	42
Inventory,30-30	0	Retained inc.,12+12	24	Expense	30
	174		174	Net income	12

Variable (Direct) Costing

Balance Sheets				Income Statements	
January 1, 19X6					
Cash	150	Capital Stock	150		
December 31, 19X6				Year 19X6	
Cash,150-60	90	Capital stock	150	Revenue	0
Inventory,+44	44	Retained income,-16	- 16	Expense	16
	134		134	Net loss	-16
December 31, 19X7				Year 19X7	
Cash,90+42	132	Capital stock	150	Revenue	42
Inventory,44-22	22	Retained inc.,-16+20	4	Expense	22
	154		154	Net income	20
December 31, 19X8				Year 19X8	
Cash,132+42	174	Capital stock	150	Revenue	42
Inventory,22-22	0	Retained income,4+20	24	Expense	22
	174		174	Net income	20

Ask the students to ponder how the income statements differ for each year. As inventory levels build (19X6), the fixed overhead is lodged in inventory, so income under variable costing is less. But, as inventory levels decline, that fixed overhead is released so that income under absorption costing is less.

15-21 (15 min.)

1. Variable-costing operating income equals absorption-costing operating income whenever the inventory level is unchanged (beginning inventory equals ending inventory). No change in inventory level implies that units produced equals units sold, as in *19X7*.

2. Absorption-costing operating income exceeds variable-costing operating income when inventory levels *increase*, because (under absorption costing) some fixed costs are applied to the units in the enlarged inventory. Units produced exceed units sold in *19X8.*

3. Repeat the idea in part (1), now considering the four-year total operating income, which is the same ($230,000) under both variable and absorption costing. Thus beginning inventory in 19X5 (0 units) equals ending inventory in 19X8 *(0 units),* or $0.

4. As in part (2), 19X8's absorption-costing operating income exceeds the variable-costing operating income by the amount of fixed costs borne by the increased inventory ($30,000). At $3.00 per unit, units produced exceeds units sold by *10,000 units.*

15-22 (10-15 min.)

1. Variable manufacturing cost per unit
   $= \$105{,}000 \div 15{,}000 = \$7.00$

   Variable nonmanufacturing cost per unit
   $= \$24{,}000 \div 12{,}000 = \$2.00$

   Operating income
   $= (12{,}000 \times \$17) - (12{,}000 \times \$7.00) - (12{,}000 \times \$2.00) - \$63{,}000 - \$18{,}000$
   $= \$204{,}000 - (\$84{,}000 + \$24{,}000 + \$81{,}000)$
   $= \$15{,}000$

2. a. $(15{,}000 - 12{,}000) \times (\$7.00 + \dfrac{\$63{,}000}{18{,}000})$
   $= 3{,}000$ units $\times \$10.50$ unit cost
   $= \$31{,}500$

   b. Total costs incurred
   $= \$105{,}000 + \$63{,}000 + \$24{,}000 + \$18{,}000$
   $= \$210{,}000$

   Operating income = Sales - (Total costs - Costs in inventory)
   $= \$204{,}000 - (\$210{,}000 - \$31{,}500) = \$25{,}500$

   or: $\$15{,}000 + (\dfrac{(\$63{,}000)}{(18{,}000)} \times 3{,}000) = \$25{,}500$

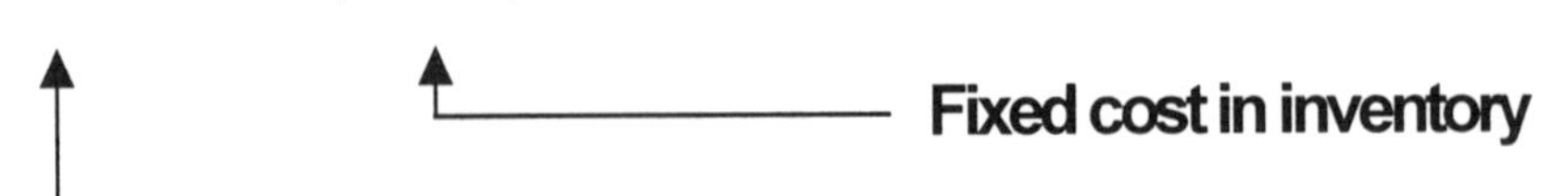

15-23 (5-10 min.)

This exercise requires sorting the relevant information from the irrelevant. Computing the production-volume variance requires knowledge of the fixed-overhead rate:

Fixed-overhead rate = ¥25,620,000 ÷ 6,100 units = ¥4,200 per unit

The actual overhead costs are irrelevant. In addition to the fixed-overhead rate, the only items needed are expected and actual production volume:

Production-volume variance = (actual volume - expected volume) x fixed-overhead rate
= (5,800 - 6,100) x ¥4,200
= 300 x ¥4,200
= ¥1,260,000 unfavorable

15-24 (10-15 min.)

1. (a) $7 x 10,500 = $73,500
(b) $7 x 1,500 = $10,500 F
(c) $18,000 - $7 x 1,000 = $11,000

2.

Fixed costs charged by variable costing		$73,500
Fixed costs charged by absorption costing:		
In cost of goods sold, $7 x 11,000	$77,000	
Production-volume variance, favorable	-10,500	
Total fixed cost		66,500
Difference in fixed cost		$ 7,000

Because fixed costs are $7,000 less under absorption costing, operating income is $7,000 greater under absorption costing than under variable costing.

15-25 (15 min.)

Variances in dollars:

Flexible-budget variance	4,000 U	Fixed	1,700 U
		Variable	2,300 U
Production-volume variance	900 U	Fixed	900 U
		Variable	NA
Spending variance	3,600 U	Fixed	1,700 U
		Variable	1,900 U
Efficiency variance	400 U	Fixed	NA
		Variable	400 U

NA = not applicable

15-26 (15-20 min.)

Note that the budget for variable overhead must be $41,000, the same as applied. In contrast, the budget for fixed overhead must be $70,000, the same as the budget for actual hours of input. Variances are in dollars. The answers follow:

	Total Overhead	Variable	Fixed
1. Spending variance	2,000U	3,500U	1,500F
2. Efficiency variance	4,000U	4,000U	NA
3. Production-volume variance	5,200U	NA	5,200U
4. Flexible-budget variance	6,000U	7,500U	1,500F
5. Underapplied overhead	11,200U	7,500U	3,700U

NA = not applicable

These relationships could be presented in the same way as in Exhibit 15-12:

	Cost Incurred: Actual Inputs x Actual Prices	Flexible Budget Based on Actual Inputs x Expected Prices	Flexible Budget Based on Standard Inputs Allowed for Actual Outputs Achieved x Expected Prices	Product Costing: Applied Overhead
Variable	48,500	45,000	41,000	41,000

Spending, 3,500U	Efficiency, 4,000U	Prod.-Volume, NA
Flexible-budget variance, 7,500U		NA
Underapplied overhead, 7,500U		

	Cost Incurred: Actual Inputs x Actual Prices	Flexible Budget Based on Actual Inputs x Expected Prices	Flexible Budget Based on Standard Inputs Allowed for Actual Outputs Achieved x Expected Prices	Product Costing: Applied Overhead
Fixed	68,500	70,000	70,000	64,800

Spending, 1,500F | Efficiency, NA | Prod.-volume, 5,200U

Flexible-budget variance, 1,500F | Prod.-volume 5,200U.

Underapplied overhead, 3,700U

15-27 (35-45 min.) This is an excellent problem for presentation in class. It is less satisfactory as a homework assignment because students tend to make the problem harder than it really is.

1. One way to present the problem in class is to begin with 9 columns on the board or overhead projector. Each column lists the sales and production quantities. Provide six rows for the variable-costing statement and seven rows for the absorption-costing statement, labeled as in the fromat provided in the problem, there are 18 "income statements" to be completed. Ask a different student to complete each statement. Patterns soon become clear, and students fill in the statements quickly. If students fail to recognize some patterns, you can prod them with discussion of the patterns as the statements are completed. The completed statements follow:

Variable costing (in dollars)

	(1)	(2)	(3)	(4)	(5)	(6)	(7)	(8)	(9)
Revenue	3,000	4,000	5,000	4,000	5,000	6,000	5,000	6,000	7,000
Cost of goods sold	(1,200)	(1,600)	(2,000)	(1,600)	(2,000)	(2,400)	(2,000)	(2,400)	(2,800)
Contribution margin	1,800	2,400	3,000	2,400	3,000	3,600	3,000	3,600	4,200
Fixed mfg costs	(1,500)	(1,500)	(1,500)	(1,500)	(1,500)	(1,500)	(1,500)	(1,500)	(1,500)
Fixed selling & admin. exp.	(300)	(300)	(300)	(300)	(300)	(300)	(300)	(300)	(300)
Operating income	0	600	1,200	600	1,200	1,800	1,200	1,800	2,400

Absorption costing (in dollars)

	(1)	(2)	(3)	(4)	(5)	(6)	(7)	(8)	(9)
Revenue	3,000	4,000	5,000	4,000	5,000	6,000	5,000	6,000	7,000
Cost of goods sold	(2,100)	(2,800)	(3,500)	(2,800)	(3,500)	(4,200)	(3,500)	(4,200)	(4,900)
Gross profit at standard	900	1,200	1,500	1,200	1,500	1,800	1,500	1,800	2,100
Favorable (Unfavorable) production-volume var.	(300)	(300)	(300)	0	0	0	300	300	300
Gross profit at "actual"	600	900	1,200	1,200	1,500	1,800	1,800	2,100	2,400
Selling and admin. exp.	(300)	(300)	(300)	(300)	(300)	(300)	(300)	(300)	(300)
Operating income	300	600	900	900	1,200	1,500	1,500	1,800	2,100

The following points are key to rapid completion of the statements:

(a) Cost of goods sold under variable costing is *variable* cost ($4) times units *sold.*
(b) Fixed costs are $1,500 and $300 on *each* variable-costing statement.
(c) Cost of goods sold under absorption costing is full-absorption cost ($7) times units *sold.*
(d) No separate row for fixed manufacturing cost appears on an absorption-costing statement. Fixed manufacturing cost are included in cost of goods sold and in the production-volume variance.
(e) Production-volume variance is *production* units less expected unit volume times fixed manufacturing cost per unit($3).
(f) Selling and administrative expenses are not inventoried; even on an absorption-costing statement the $300 is charged each period.

Patterns of operating income are discussed in question 2.

If the student did not prepare the problem as a homework assignment, but you use it for class discussion, you might list the following information on the board before proceeding to the statements:

Sales price = $10 per unit
Variable cost = $4 per unit
Fixed manufacturing cost = $1,500 per year
Fixed-overhead rate = $1,500 ÷ 500 units = $3 per unit
Full cost = $4 + $3 = $7
Fixed selling and administrative cost = $300 per year

2. (a) Variable-costing income is greater than absorption-costing income when sales exceed production: (3), (6), and (9).

Variable-costing income is lower than absorption-costing income when production exceeds sales: (1), (4), and (7).

Variable-costing income equals absorption-costing income when production equals sales: (2), (5), and (8).

(b) Production-volume variance is unfavorable when expected volume exceeds actual volume: (1), (2), and (3). It is favorable when actual volume exceeds expected volume: (7), (8), and (9).

(c) Each additional unit sold adds \$10 - \$4 = \$6 to profit under variable costing and \$10 - \$7 = \$3 under absorption costing. For example, compare (1) and (2). Production is 400 units in each case, but sales are 100 units greater in (2). Operating income is \$600 greater in (2) than in (1) under variable costing and \$300 greater under absorption costing. \$600 ÷ 100 = \$6 per unit for variable costing, and \$300 ÷ 100 = \$3 per unit for absorption costing.

(d) Producing an additional unit does not affect operating income under variable costing. Compare, for example, (2) and (1). But under absorption costing, production of one unit increases profit by \$3. Again, compare (2) and (4). The only difference is production of 100 additional units in (2) and operating income is \$300 higher: \$300 ÷ 100 = \$3 per unit.

(e) Variable costing provides a better measure of performance. Why? Because differences in operating income arise from differences in sales, not production, under variable costing.

15-28 (25-35 min.)

Please allow ample time for classroom discussion.

1. **Comments on the Following Statements**

The accounting for fixed overhead in absorption costing is affected primarily by what expected production volume is selected as a base (the denominator) for applying fixed overhead to product. In this case, is 1,500,000 gallons per year, 3,000,000 gallons, or some other activity level the most appropriate base? We usually place the above possibilities on the board and then ask the students to indicate by vote how many used one version of absorption costing versus another. Incidentally, discussion tends to move more clearly if variable-costing statements are discussed first, because there is little disagreement as to computations under variable costing.

Variable Costing (in thousands of dollars)

	19X7	19X8	Together
Sales (and contribution margin)	750	750	1,500
Fixed costs	800	800	1,600
Net income (loss)	(50)	(50)	(100)

Absorption Costing (in thousands of dollars)

	Option One*			Option Two**		
	19X7	19X8	Together	19X7	19X8	Together
Sales	750	750	1,500	750	750	1,500
Less cost of goods sold:						
Beginning inventory	-	300	-	-	600	-
Cost of goods manufactured	600	-	600	1,200	-	1,200
Cost of goods available for sale	600	300	600	1,200	600	1,200
Ending inventory	300	-	-	600	-	-
Cost of goods sold – at normal cost	300	300	600	600	600	1,200
Undcrapplied overhead – loss from idle capacity	-	600	600	-	600	600
Overapplied overhead – gain from over-utilization	-	-	-	(600)	-	(600)
Other expenses	200	200	400	200	200	400
Total charges	500	1,100	1,600	200	1,400	1,600
Net income (loss)	250	(350)	(100)	550	(650)	(100)

* $600,000 ÷ 3,000,000 gallons as "normal capacity" = $.20 per gallon

** $600,000 ÷ 1,500,000 gallons as "normal capacity" = $.40 per gallon

2. Break-even point $= \dfrac{\text{Fixed expenses}}{\text{Contribution margin per gallon}}$

$$= \frac{(\$800{,}000)}{(.50)} = 1{,}600{,}000 \text{ gallons}$$

If the company could sell 100,000 more gallons per year at $.50 each, it could get the extra $50,000 margin needed to break even.

Most students will say that the break-even point is 1,600,000 gallons per year under both absorption and variable costing. The logical question to ask a student who answers 1,600,000 units for absorption costing is: "What profit do you show for 19X7 under absorption costing?" If a student answers any positive profit, such as $250,000, ask: "But you say your break-even point is 1,600,000 gallons. How can you show a profit on only 1,500,000 gallons sold during 19X7?"

The answer to the break-even point dilemma is that net income is affected by *both* sales and production under absorption costing. The variable-costing approach dovetails precisely with the cost-volume-profit analysis that the students learned earlier, but absorption costing does not unless some special assumption is made regarding inventory changes. The latter usually entails assuming that all production for a given period is sold–that no inventory changes exist.

3. *Absorption costing*: Either $300,000 or $600,000 at the end of 19X7 and zero at the end of 19X8. *Variable costing*: Zero at all times. This is a major criticism of variable costing and focuses on the issue of the definition of an asset. Supporters of variable costing answer that zero is the correct inventory value because the existence of inventory does not save any future cost.

4. Comments should include the following:

(a) The central issue is the *timing* of release of fixed factory overhead to expense.

(b) Variable costing dovetails exactly with general break-even analysis, while absorption costing does not.

(c) Variable costing rests on a simple basic assumption that is easy to understand, while results under the same set of facts can differ considerably when absorption costing is applied.

(d) Variable costers would inventory the units at zero cost because they believe no costs should be carried forward to the future if they cannot obviate a future cost incurrence, while the absorption-costing adherents view potential cost *recovery* as the criterion for carrying costs as assets.

15-29 (25-30 min.)

1. Variable Costing (in thousands of dollars)

	19X7	19X8	Together
Sales	750	750	1,500
Variable cost of sales @ $.14 per gallon	210	210	420
Contribution margin	540	540	1,080
Fixed costs	590	590	1,180
Net income (loss)	(50)	(50)	(100)

Absorption Costing (in thousands of dollars)

	Option One*			Option Two**		
	19X7	19X8	Together	19X7	19X8	Together
Sales	750	750	1,500	750	750	1,500
Less cost of goods sold:						
Beginning inventory	-	405	-	-	600	-
Cost of goods manufactured	810	-	810	1,200	-	1,200
Cost of goods available for sale	810	405	810	1,200	600	1,200
Ending inventory	405	-	-	600	-	-
Cost of goods sold	405	405	810	600	600	1,200
Underapplied overhead	-	390	390	-	390	390
Overapplied overhead	-	-	-	(390)	-	(390)
Other expenses	200	200	400	200	200	400
Total charges	605	995	1,600	410	1,190	1,600
Net income	145	(245)	(100)	340	(440)	(100)

*Variable cost per unit, $.14 + Fixed costs per unit, $.13 ($390,000 ÷ 3,000,000 gallons) = $.27

**Variable cost per unit, $.14 + Fixed costs per unit, $.26 ($390,000 ÷ 1,500,000 gallons) = $.40

2.

	Variable Costing	Absorption Costing Option One	Absorption Costing Option Two
Inventory:			
December 31, 19X7	$210,000	$405,000	$600,000
December 31, 19X8	-0-	-0-	-0-

15-30 (30-35 min.)

1.

Standard Variable Costing
TRAPANI COMPANY
Income Statement
For the Year Ended December 31, 19X6

(1)	Sales – at standard prices (13,000 x $75)	$975,000
	Opening inventory	-
	Add variable cost of goods manufactured at standard*	660,000
	Variable cost of goods available for sale	660,000
	Deduct ending inventory at standard variable cost: 2,000 x $44	88,000
	Variable manufacturing cost of goods sold	572,000
	Variable selling and administrative costs at budget of $9 per unit sold	117,000
(2)	Total variable costs	689,000
(1) - (2)	Contribution margin at standard	286,000
	Fixed factory overhead at budget	98,000
	Fixed selling and administrative costs	80,000
	Total fixed costs	178,000
	Operating income	$108,000

*15,000 x $44 = $660,000

Standard Absorption Costing
TRAPANI COMPANY
Income Statement
For the Year Ending December 31, 19X6

Sales – at standard prices (13,000 x $75)	$975,000
Opening inventory	-
Add cost of goods manufactured at standard[a]	765,000
Absorption cost of goods available for sale	765,000
Deduct ending inventory at standard absorption cost:	
2,000 x $51[b]	102,000
Absorption cost of goods sold at standard	663,000
Gross profit at standard	312,000
Deduct selling and administrative costs:	
Variable at standard (13,000 x $9)	117,000
Fixed at budget	80,000
Total selling and administrative costs	197,000
Operating income before variances	115,000
Variances: Production-volume variance[c]	7,000F
Operating income	$122,000

[a]15,000 x $51 = $765,000.
[b]Variable cost of $44 + fixed factory overhead of $7 = $51.
[c](15,000 - 14,000 expected volume) x $7 = $7,000F.

2. If inventories increase, operating income will be higher under absorption costing:

Difference in operating income
= Change in inventory units x Fixed overhead rate
= (2,000 - 0) x $7
= $14,000

15-31 (40-45 min.) This problem should not be assigned without also assigning problem 15-30.

1. Standard Variable Costing
TRAPANI COMPANY
Income Statement
For the Year Ended December 31, 19X7

(1)	Sales – at standard prices (14,000 x $75)	$1,050,000
	Opening inventory, at standard variable cost: 2,000 x $44	88,000
	Add variable cost of goods manufactured at standard*	572,000
	Variable cost of goods available for sale	660,000
	Deduct ending inventory at standard variable cost: 1,000 x $44	44,000
	Variable manufacturing cost of goods sold	616,000
	Variable selling and administrative costs at budget of $9 per unit sold	126,000
(2)	Total variable costs	742,000
(1)-(2)	Contribution margin at standard	308,000
	Fixed factory overhead at budget	98,000
	Fixed selling and administrative costs	80,000
	Total fixed costs	178,000
	Operating income before variances	130,000
	Variances:	
	Selling prices (a)	18,000F
	Variable manufacturing costs (b)	76,800F
	Variable selling & administrative costs (c)	7,600F
	Fixed factory overhead (d)	3,000F
	Total variances	105,400F
	Operating income	$ 235,400

*13,000 x $44 = $572,000.

(a) $1,068,000 - (14,000 x $75)

(b) $285,000 + $174,200 + $36,000 - $572,000

(c) $118,400 - $126,000

(d) $98,000 - $95,000

Standard Absorption Costing
TRAPANI COMPANY
Income Statement
For the Year Ending December 31, 19X7

Sales – at standard prices (14,000 x $75)	$1,050,000
Opening inventory – at standard absorption cost: 2,000 x $51[a]	102,000
Add cost of goods manufactured at standard[b]	663,000
Absorption cost of goods available for sale	765,000
Deduct ending inventory at standard absorption cost:	
1,000 x $51[a]	51,000
Absorption cost of goods sold at standard	714,000
Gross profit at standard	336,000
Deduct selling and administrative costs:	
Variable at standard (14,000 x $9)	126,000
Fixed at budget	80,000
Total selling and administrative costs	206,000
Operating income before variances	130,000
Variances:	
Selling prices	18,000F
Variable manufacturing costs	76,800F
Variable selling & administrative costs	7,600F
Fixed factory overhead:	
Budget variance	3,000F
Production-volume variance[c]	7,000U
Total variances	98,400F
Operating income	$ 228,400

[a]Variable cost of $44 + fixed factory overhead of $7 = $51.
[b]13,000 x $51 = $663,000.
[c](14,000 - 13,000) x $7 = $7,000 U.

2. If inventories decrease, operating income will be lower under absorption costing:

Difference in operating income = Change in inventory units x Fixed overhead rate
= (1,000 - 2,000) x $7
= $-7,000

<u>15-32</u> (30-40 min.) This is a straightforward problem that is quite informative for most students.

1. $60,000 ÷ 7,500 hrs. = $8.00 per hour, or
= $16.00 per unit ($8.00 x 2 hours)

2.

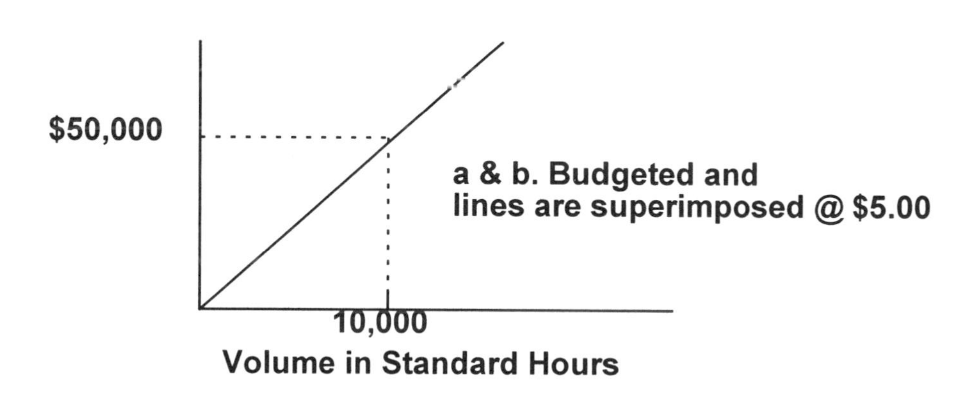

3.

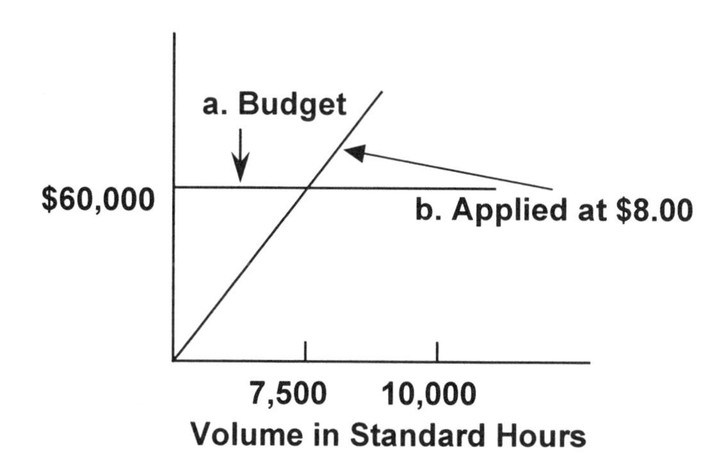

We suggest using graphs in class as you explain the subsequent parts.

	(A) Cost Incurred: Actual Inputs x Actual Prices	(B)* Flexible Budget Based on Actual Inputs x Expected Prices	(C) Budget Based on Standard Inputs Allowed for Actual Outputs Achieved x Expected Prices	(D) Product Costing: Applied Overhead
4. Variable Overhead	$30,600		6,000x$5= $30,000	30,000
	Flexible-budget variance, 600U			No variance
	Underapplied overhead, 600U			
Fixed Overhead	$62,000		Lump-sum $60,000	6,000x$8= $48,000
	Flexible-budget variance, 2,000U			(7,500-6,000)x$8= Prod.-volume var., 12,000U
	Underapplied overhead, 14,000U			
5. Variable Overhead	$37,500		7,800x$5= $39,000	39,000
	Flexible-budget variance, 1,500F			No variance
	Overapplied overhead, 1,500F			
Fixed Overhead	$62,200		Lump-sum $60,000	7,800x$8= $62,400
	Flexible-budget variance, 2,200U			(7,800-7,500)x$8= Prod.-volume var., 2,400F
	Overapplied overhead, 200F			

*Not given in this problem.

15-33 (15-20 min.)

1.

Variable manufacturing costs per unit, $175,000,000 ÷ 700,000	$250
Fixed manufacturing costs per unit, 105,000,000 ÷ 700,000	150
Total manufacturing costs per unit	$400

2. Production-volume variance = (700,000 - 750,000) x $150 = $7,500,000 F

3.

Revenue (725,000 x $500)	$362,500,000
Cost of goods sold (725,000 x $400)	290,000,000
Gross margin	72,500,000
Production-volume variance	7,500,000
Profit	$ 80,000,000

4.

Revenue (725,000 x $500)	$362,500,000
Cost of goods sold (725,000 x $250)	181,250,000
Contribution margin	181,250,000
Fixed costs	105,000,000
Profit	$ 76,250,000

5. Neither measure is inherently better. They give different signals about performance. The variable-costing profit is a better measure of the effect of sales on profit. It is not affected by production volumes. The absorption-costing profit is affected by both sales and production volumes. Because production volume exceeded sales volume, the profit is higher under absorption costing.

From an incentive point of view, the variable-costing profit has the advantage of not being affected by production decisions. Under absorption costing, a manager can increase profits merely by producing more units, even if they are not sold.

15-34 (10 min.)

Overhead rates: $720,000 ÷ 60,000 = $12 and $720,000 ÷ 45,000 = $16.

	Cost Incurred: Actual Inputs x Actual Prices	Flexible Budget Based on Actual Inputs x Expected Prices	Budget Based on Standard Inputs Allowed for Actual Outputs Achieved x Expected Prices	Product Costing: Applied Overhead
1. Using Practical Capacity	$751,000		$720,000	54,000x$12 =$648,000
	Flexible-budget variance, $31,000U		(54,000-60,000)x $12.00= Prod.-volume var =$72,000U	
	Underapplied overhead, $103,000U			
2. Using Expected Activity	$751,000		$720,000	54,000x$16= $864,000
	Flexible-budget variance, $31,000U		(54,000-45,000) x $16.00= Prod.-volume var., 144,000F	
	Overapplied overhead, $113,000F			

3. The flexible-budget variance for fixed overhead is the difference between the amount incurred and the budget figure. The budget figure is the same regardless of the actual level of activity and the rate used in applying fixed overhead. Consequently the flexible-budget variances in parts (1) and (2) would be identical.

The production-volume variance is the difference between fixed overhead applied and the budgeted amount. Fixed overhead applied is the product of standard hours allowed and the standard fixed-overhead rate. The difference arises from the different measures of volume used in computing the standard fixed-overhead rate, the rate being $12 per standard hour in part (1) while being $16 per standard hour in part (2). The difference in variances would be computed by multiplying the difference in rates by standard hours allowed: ($16 - $12) x 54,000 = $216,000.

Note how the production-volume variance will never be favorable when based on practical capacity. Also note how different expected volume assumptions can produce radically different production-volume variances. Both accountants and managers should be aware of these possibilities when analyzing fixed overhead variances.

15-35 (25-30 min.)

1. Total dollars and machine hours are in thousands:

Year	Base a	Base b*	Base c
19X5	$36,400 ÷ 2,500 = $14.56	$36,400 ÷ 2,560 = $14.22	$36,400 ÷ 2,800 = $13.00
19X6	$36,400 ÷ 2,700 = $13.48	$36,400 ÷ 2,560 = $14.22	$36,400 ÷ 2,800 = $13.00
19X7	$36,400 ÷ 2,790 = $13.05	$36,400 ÷ 2,560 = $14.22	$36,400 ÷ 2,800 = $13.00

*Average volume (in thousands): (2,250 + 2,500 + 2,700 + 2,790) ÷ 4 = 2,560.

2. Method a: This is the most popular method. It keeps the fixed-overhead rate constant over a year and generates no expected production-volume variance for the year in total.

   Method b: This method keeps the fixed-overhead rate constant over four years, but annual budgets must recognize an expected unfavorable production-volume variance in the first two years and an expected favorable production-volume variance in the last two.

   Method c: This method consistently generates unfavorable production-volume variances. The variances show the potential to spread fixed costs over a larger output whenever operations are below capacity.

3. Most students will prefer Method a because the text indicates that it is most popular. However, a case can also be made for either of the other methods. For example, practical capacity has increased in popularity in recent years, principally because the Internal Revenue Service permits its use. For tax purposes, practical capacity permits faster write-off of factory overhead.

15-36 (40-45 min.)

	(A) Cost Incurred: Actual Inputs x Actual Prices	(B) Flexible Budget Based on Actual Inputs x Expected Prices	(C) Flexible Budget Based on Standard Inputs Allowed for Actual Outputs Achieved x Expected Prices	(D) Product Costing: Applied To Product
Direct Labor:	42,000x$6.15 =$258,300	42,000x$6.00 =$252,000	39,000x$6.00 or 156,000x$1.50 =$234,000[a]	$234,000
	42,000x$.15 = Price var.,6,300U	3,000x$6= Usg. var., $18,000U	Never a variance	
	Flexible-budget variance, 24,300U		Never a variance	
Variable Manufacturing Overhead:	$36,000*	42,000x$.80 $33,600	39,000x$.80 or 156,000x$.20 $31,200	$31,200
	Spending var., $2,400U	3,000x$.8= Eff. var., $2,400U	Never a variance	
	Flexible-budget variance, $4,800U		Never a variance	
	Underapplied overhead, $4,800U			
Fixed Manufacturing Overhead:	$154,000*	Lump-sum $150,000	Lump-sum $150,000[b]	156,000x$1.00 =$156,000
	Spending var., $4,000U	Never a variance	(150,000-156,000) x$1.00 = Prod.-volume var., 6,000F.	
	Flexible-budget variance, $4,000U			
	Overapplied overhead, $2,000F			

*Given. U = Unfavorable. F = Favorable.

[a]Amount fluctuates with production.

[b]Total is the same regardless of fluctuations in production.

15-37 (30 min.)

1. Because Manchester Machining Company uses absorption costing, the net income is influenced by both sales volume and production volume. Sales volume was increased in the November 30, 19X8 forecast, and at standard gross profit rates this would increase gross margin before taxes by £4,800. However, during the same period production volume was below the January 1, 19X8 forecast, causing an unplanned production-volume variance of £6,000. The production-volume variance and the increased selling expenses (due to the 10% increase in sales) overshadowed the added gross margin from sales as shown below:

Increased sales	£15,600
Increased cost of sales at standard	10,800
Increased gross margin at standard	£ 4,800
Less: Increased selling expense	1,120
Expected increase in earnings	£ 3,680
Production-volume variance	6,000
Decrease in earnings	£ 2,320

2. The basic cause of the lower forecast of profits is low production. If raw materials can be obtained, and if it is reasonable in light of expected future sales, Manchester Machining Company could schedule heavy production which would reduce the unfavorable production-volume variance.

3. Manchester Machining Company could adopt variable costing. Then fixed manufacturing costs would be treated as period costs and would not be assigned to production. Consequently, earnings would not be affected by production volume but only by sales volume. The following statements are prepared on a variable-costing basis.

MANCHESTER MACHINING COMPANY
Forecasts of Operating Results

	Forecasts as of			
	January 1, 19X8		November 30, 19X8	
Sales		$156,000		$171,600
Variable costs:				
Manufacturing	$78,000		$85,800*	
Selling expenses	11,200		12,320	
Total variable costs		89,200		98,120
Contribution margin		$ 66,800		$ 73,480
Fixed costs:				
Manufacturing	$30,000		$30,000	
Administration	20,400		20,400	
Total fixed costs		50,400		50,400
Earnings before taxes		$ 16,400		$ 23,080

* (171,600 ÷ 156,000) x $98,000 = $85,800

4. Variable costing would not be acceptable for financial reporting purposes because generally accepted accounting principles seem to require the allocation of some fixed manufacturing costs to inventory.

15-38 (30-40 min.)

DECROIX CO.
Variable Costing Income Statement

Sales, 150,000 units at $21.00		$3,150,000
Variable expenses:		
Beginning inventory, 15,000 at $11.00	$ 165,000 (a)	
Production, 145,000 at $11.00	1,595,000	
Available for sale	$1,760,000	
Ending inventory, 10,000 at $11.00	110,000	
Standard variable cost of sales	$1,650,000	
Add variance in variable costs of production	33,000	
Variable manufacturing cost of sales	$1,683,000	
Variable selling and administrative expenses	450,000	2,133,000
Contribution margin		(b) $1,017,000
Fixed expenses:		
Manufacturing	$ 165,000	
Selling	650,000	815,000
Operating income		(c) $ 202,000

DECROIX CO.
Absorption Costing Income Statement

Sales, 150,000 units at $21.00		$3,150,000
Cost of sales:		
Beginning inventory, 15,000 at $12.10*	$ 181,500 (d)	
Production, 145,000 at $12.10	1,754,500	
Available for sale	$1,936,000	
Ending inventory, 10,000 at $12.10	121,000	
Standard cost of sales	$1,815,000	
Add unfavorable variances:		
Variable manufacturing costs	33,000	
Prod.-volume variance, 5,000 at $1.10	5,500	1,853,500
Gross margin		(e) $1,296,500
Selling and administrative expenses:		
Variable, 150,000 at $3.00	$ 450,000	
Fixed	650,000	1,100,000
Operating income		(f) $ 196,500

*$165,000 fixed overhead ÷ 150,000 units = $1.10; $1.10 + $11.00 = $12.10.

15-39 (20-30 min.)

1.

	(in thousands)	
	a.	b.
Revenue, 75,000 x $20	$ 1,500	$ 1,500
Standard cost of goods sold, 75,000 x ($8 + $5 + $4)	(1,275)	(1,275)
Gross margin at standard	$ 225	$ 225
Manufacturing variances	(40)	(30)*
Operating income	$ 185	$ 195

*Total variance = $40,000U. Proration to sales = (75,000 ÷ 100,000) x $40,000 = $30,000

2. a. Ending inventory, Method (a): 25,000 units x $17 = $425,000
   b. Ending inventory, Method (b): (25,000 units x $17) + (25,000 ÷ 100,000) x $40,000 = $425,000 + $10,000 = $435,000

   Note that Method (b) provides $10,000 more operating income and $10,000 higher inventory because $10,000 of the variances was allocated to inventory rather than to expense.

3. Supporters of Method (a) claim that variances arise from inefficiencies or efficiencies of the period and therefore should affect the current period's income statement. They are not necessary costs of production and therefore should not be inventoried.

   Supporters of Method (b) claim that the income statement gives a better picture of *actual costs* using Method (b).

15-40 (40-60 min.)

This problem stresses the futility of trying to conduct cost-volume-profit analysis in conjunction with absorption-costing statements.

The break-even data are the same for each plant. Therefore, the total fixed costs per plant must be 40,000 units x $5 contribution per unit, or $200,000. Therefore, total fixed factory overhead must be $200,000 minus the $30,000 administration costs, or $170,000.

The accounting reports must have been prepared on the absorption-costing basis. Why? Because no contribution margin is shown and the fixed manufacturing costs are not identified separately.

If the break-even volume is the same for each plant, and the sales are also the same, the statements differ only in the use of different expected unit production values. Such a condition could easily occur in autonomous operations. The best answer would be a variable-costing statement as shown. From a variable-costing standpoint, the profits of these managers are identical, but the the Massachusetts plant has a considerable inventory in the face of falling demands.

Variable-Costing Solution

		Massachusetts		Texas
Sales		$520,000		$520,000
Variable expense				
Production @ $8	$640,000		$320,000	
Ending inventory @ $8	320,000	320,000		320,000
Contribution margin		$200,000		$200,000
Fixed expense				
Manufacturing	$170,000		$170,000	
Administration	30,000	200,000	30,000	200,000
Net income		$ 0		$ 0

The expanded absorption-costing statements show that the plants must have used the following fixed manufacturing overhead rates:

$$\text{Massachusetts} = \frac{(\$170{,}000)}{(40{,}000)} = \$4.25 \qquad \text{Texas} = \frac{(\$170{,}000)}{(80{,}000)} = \$2.125$$

Expanded Income Statements, Absorption Costing

Massachusetts

Sales			$520,000
Production	80,000 @ $12.25	$980,000	
Ending inventory	40,000 @ $12.25	490,000	
Cost of sales at standard		$490,000	
Volume variance*	40,000 @ $ 4.25	170,000 F	320,000
Gross margin			$200,000
Administration			30,000
Net income			$170,000

Texas

Sales			$520,000
Production and cost of sales			
at standard cost	40,000 @ $10.125	$405,000	
Volume variance*	40,000 @ $ 2.125	85,000 U	490,000
Gross margin			$ 30,000
Administration			30,000
Net income			$ 0

*Production-volume variance

15-41 (35-45 min.)

	Cost Incurred: Actual Inputs x Actual Prices	Flexible Budget Based on Actual Inputs x Expected Prices	Flexible Budget Based on Standard Inputs Allowed for Actual Outputs Achieved x Expected Prices	Product Costing Applied to Product
Direct	12,000 x $12.50	12,000 x $13.00	10,800 x $13.00	
Labor:	= $150,000	= $156,000	= $140,400	$140,400

Price variance, 12,000 hrs. x $.50 =$6,000F	Usage variance, 1,200 hrs. x $13 = $15,600U
Flexible-budget variance, $9,600U	

	Cost Incurred	Flexible Budget (Actual Inputs)	Flexible Budget (Standard Inputs)	Applied
Variable Overhead:	$35,000*	12,000 x $3.00 = $36,000	10,800 x $3.00 = $32,400	$32,400

Spending variance, $1,000F	Efficiency variance, 1,200 hrs. x $3.00 = $3,600U
Flexible-budget variance, $2,600U	
Underapplied overhead, $2,600U	

	Cost Incurred	Flexible Budget (Actual Inputs)	Flexible Budget (Standard Inputs)	Applied
Fixed overhead:	$38,000*	Lump-sum $39,600	Lump-sum $39,600	10,800 x $3.30** = $35,640

Spending variance, $1,600F	No variance	Prod.-Vol. Var., $3,960U
Flexible-budget variance, $1,600F		
Underapplied overhead, $2,360U		

*Given

**39,600 ÷ (2,000 x 6) = $3.30

15-42 (35-40 min.)

	Cost Incurred: Actual Inputs x Actual Prices	Flexible Budget Based on Actual Inputs x Expected Prices	Flexible Budget Based on Standard Inputs Allowed for Actual Outputs Achieved x Expected Prices	Product Costing Applied to Product
Direct Labor:	10,000 x $4.25 = $42,500	10,000 x $4.40 = $44,000	9,000 x $4.40 = $39,600	$39,600
	Price variance, 10,000 hrs. x $.15 =$1,500F	Usage variance, 1,000 hrs. x $4.40 = $4,400U		
	Flexible-budget variance, $2,900U			
Variable Overhead:	$10,400*	10,000 x $1.10 = $11,000	9,000 x $1.10 = $9,900	$9,900
	Spending variance, $600F	Efficiency variance, 1,000 hrs. x $1.10 = $1,100U		
	Flexible-budget variance, $500U			
	Underapplied overhead, $500U			
Fixed overhead:	$6,300*	Lump-sum $6,600	Lump-sum $6,600	9,000 x $.60** = $5,400
	Spending variance, $300F	No variance	Prod.-Vol. Var., $1,200U	
	Flexible-budget variance, $300F			
	Underapplied overhead, $900U			

*Given

**$6,600 ÷ (2,200 x 5) = $.60

15-43 (35-50 min.)

1. The income statements are based on absorption costing because the cost of goods sold of $45 per unit includes both variable costs ($14 + $10 + $8) and fixed costs ($13).

2. (a)

Gulf Coast Division
Income Statement Based on
Standard Absorption Costing
For the Year Ended December 31, 19X5

Sales (114,000 x $55)	$6,270,000
Cost of goods sold (114,000 x $45)	5,130,000
Gross margin at standard	$1,140,000
Production-volume variance*	0
Gross margin at actual	1,140,000
Selling and administrative expenses	420,000
Operating income	$ 720,000

*There was no production-volume variance because both actual production volume and expected volume were 120,000 units.

(b) Operating incomc is short of budget by $780,000 - $720,000 = $60,000. Weber could produce extra units; each unit of production will increase operating income by the amount of fixed manufacturing overhead per unit, which is $13 per unit. (The $13 per unit can be calculated as total unit cost less variable unit cost, $45 - $32, or as monthly budgeted fixed overhead divided by monthly budgeted production, $130,000 ÷ 10,000 units = $13 per unit.) Weber must produce an extra $60,000 ÷ $13 = 4,616 units to achieve the budgeted profit level. Inventory has already increased by 5,000 units (110,000 production units - 105,000 sales units), and producing an extra 14,616 units in December would increase inventory even more. Of course, it may not be possible to produce a total of 14,616 units in one month, but if it were, Weber could meet his operating-income target by producing units for which there is no demand.

3. (a)

Gulf Coast Division
Income Statement Based on Variable Costing
For the Year Ended December 31, 19X8

Sales		$6,270,000
Variable cost of goods sold (114,000 x $32)		3,648,000
Contribution margin		$2,622,000
Fixed costs:		
Fixed overhead	$1,560,000	
Fixed selling and administrative expenses	420,000	1,980,000
Operating income		$ 642,000

(b) If sales cannot be increased, there is nothing Weber can do to achieve the budgeted operating income. Changing the level of production has no effect on variable-costing income.

Notice that the Gulf Coast Division has $78,000 less operating income using variable costing than when using absorption costing. Why? Because production exceeds sales by 6,000 units. For each of these units, $13 of fixed manufacturing overhead was added to inventory with absorption costing but was charged as an expenses with variable costing. This accounts for the 6,000 x $13 = $78,000 extra expense on the variable-costing statement.

4. The variable-costing system motivates the better decision. Inventory has already been increased 5,000 units above plan by the end of November. An incentive to produce even more units for inventory in December is most likely dysfunctional. Such production will probably result in large unnecessary handling and storage costs.

15-44 (40-60 min.)

1. (a) The division manager would want to build inventory and thereby maximize current income:

	Units
Desired ending inventory, maximum possible	25,000
December sales	6,000
Total needs	31,000
November 30 inventory, 110,000 + 10,000 - 100,000	20,000
Production scheduled	11,000

(b) Sales, 106,000 units at FF400		FF42,400,000
Less cost of goods sold:		
Beginning inventory, 10,000 at FF250	FF 2,500,000	
Manufacturing costs, 121,000 at FF250	30,250,000	
Total standard cost of goods available for sale	FF32,750,000	
Ending inventory, 25,000 at FF250	6,250,000	
Standard cost of goods sold	FF26,500,000	
Less overapplied fixed manufacturing overhead, 1,000 at FF85, favorable	85,000	26,415,000
Gross margin		15,985,000
Other expenses:		
Variable, 106,000 at FF40	FF 4,240,000	
Fixed	10,200,000	14,440,000
Operating income		FF 1,545,000

(c) If December production were 4,000 units instead of 11,000 units, the underapplied overhead would be 6,000 units at FF85, or FF510,000. Net income would be FF1,545,000 less the FF595,000 difference in the applied overhead, or FF950,000. The ending inventory would be 18,000 units (20,000 + 4,000 production - 6,000 sales).

The following tabulation may be helpful:

	Cumulative Manufacturing Costs		
	Incurred	Applied	Variance*
December production, 11,000 units:			
Variable	FF19,965,000	FF19,965,000	FF -
Fixed	10,200,000	10,285,000	85,000F
December production, 4,000 units:			
Variable	FF18,810,000	FF18,810,000	FF -
Fixed	10,200,000	9,690,000	510,000U

*U = underapplied, F = overapplied.

2. (a)(b)

Sales, 106,000 units at FF400		FF42,400,000
Variable costs:		
Manufacturing, 106,000 at FF165	FF17,490,000	
Other, 106,000 at FF40	4,240,000	21,730,000
Contribution margin		FF20,670,000
Fixed costs:		
Manufacturing	FF10,200,000	
Other	10,200,000	20,400,000
Operating income		FF 270,000

Operating income is the same under variable costing regardless of December production schedules, because income is influenced by sales alone rather than by sales and production.

2. (c)

December production schedule, units	11,000	4,000
Operating income as shown in requirement (1)	FF1,545,000	FF950,000
Inventory increase for the year:		
15,000 units at fixed-overhead rate of FF85	1,275,000	-
8,000 units at FF85	-	680,000
Operating income as shown in requirement (2)	FF 270,000	FF270,000

3. The division manager should set the minimum production schedule of 4,000 units. This will reduce the inventories by 2,000 units. She may be tempted to ask for permission to reduce production even below 4,000 units, because the outlook is for ending inventories far in excess of reasonable sales demands.

   Note that production scheduling can influence short-run reported operating income under absorption costing, but such scheduling has no effect on operating income under variable costing. Thus, the *accounting technique* used may influence the manager's decision in the former case but not in the latter. It is undesirable to have the accounting technique in itself influence decisions in a direction that may conflict with overall company goals.

4. 4,000 units should be scheduled in December. This will minimize income for the current year and will therefore minimize current income taxes.

15-45 (20-30 min.)

1. The fixed overhead variance does not reveal how well fixed overhead costs have been controlled. The standard is not an appropriate basis of comparison. Why? Because the standard accounts for a fixed cost as if it were variable. Note that volume decreased by 10.5%, from 1,520,000 cwt. to 1,360,000 cwt., so the standard fixed overhead decreased by 10.5%, from $2,432,000 to $2,176,000. But *fixed* overhead would not be expected to change. The flexible (control) budget for fixed overhead, based on 19X7 costs, is $2,432,000. From a control perspective, there was a $2,432,000 - $2,418,000 = $14,000F variance.

   The standard used by Einerson is the same as the applied amount in a standard-cost system. The difference between the actual amount and this applied amount can be summarized as follows:

Actual Fixed Overhead	Flexible Budget: Fixed Overhead	Applied Fixed Overhead
$2,418,000	$2,432,000	$2,176,000
Flexible-budget variance, $14,000F	Production-volume variance, $256,000 U	

   The major part of the total variance is the production-volume variance, which serves a product-costing purpose not a control purpose.

2. Setting standards based on last year's costs is not uncommon. Managers must carefully interpret the resulting variances. Such variances do not necessarily measure efficiency, as they do with currently attainable standards. Instead, such variances simply indicate changes in costs. Such information can be useful. However, managers should be alert for any past inefficiency built into the standards. Otherwise, inefficiencies will probably persist over a series of years.

15-46 (60 min. or more)

The purpose of this exercise is to understand how the use of variable or absorption costing affects the reported operating income of an organization. It also makes students consider why different managers might have a different perspective on which type of costing is better.

If class time is available, a role-play discussion in class would be productive. One person could be chosen to represent each player, with the group of four charged with coming to an agreement on what costing system to use. Alternatively, a class-wide discussion could ensue with each class member playing the role assigned.

Each of the characters in the case has a particular point of view. The discussion will bring out the following positions, with each position having a variety of arguments to support his or her position.

Schwartz, the president, seems to be focused on sales, so the absorption-costing statement, which is affected by production as well as sales, confuses him. The positive effect of sales in June is more than offset by the decline in production. The variable-costing statement probably provides the information that he expects.

Sanchez, the controller, understands the difference between variable and absorption costing, but she seems to have difficulty explaining absorption costing to Schwartz. His life would be made easier by using variable costing because it is more consistent with the president's perspective.

Swanson also favors variable costing. He thinks that contribution margin rather than gross margin analysis will lead to better product mix decisions.

Cheung is the skeptic, preferring to stay with absorption costing. She worries about sales managers misinterpreting the contribution margin and agreeing to prices that are too low to cover fixed costs. She also worries about lack of control of fixed costs under a variable-costing system.

Arguments in favor of variable costing might include:

1. It is more understandable to operating managers because profits fluctuate with sales volume, not with production volume.
2. It aids the control of fixed and variable costs because their inclusion in the financial statements is consistent with their cost behavior.
3. It aids product mix and pricing decisions because it focuses on contribution margin, thereby isolating the effects of changes in volume.

Arguments in favor of absorption costing might include:

1. A variable product cost might cause sales personnel to view the variable cost as the lowest price they can charge to obtain an order, thereby often underpricing.
2. Absorption costing is required for tax and financial reporting purposes; it is inconsistent to use another method internally. It also leads to lack of comparability to published financial statements of other companies.
3. Inventory amounts on the balance sheet would be lower, leading to a lower current ratio.
4. The production-volume variance is a good measure of the use of capacity; if it is unfavorable, it means that capacity is being wasted.

CHAPTER 16
Basic Accounting: Concepts, Techniques, and Conventions

16-A1 (20-30 min.)

1. E = 150 - 120 = 30
   D = 40 + 30 = 70
   C = 15 because there were no additional investments by stockholders
   A = 85 - 15 - 40 = 30; or 85 - (15 + 40) = 30
   B = 95 - 15 - 70 = 10; or 95 - (15 + 70) = 10

2. K = 20 + 170 = 190
   J = 50 + 20 - 5 = 65
   H = 10 + 30 = 40
   F = 50 + 10 + 100 = 160
   G = 275 - 65 - 40 = 170

3. P = 300 - 270 = 30
   Q = 100 + 30 - 110 = 20
   N = 85 - 35 = 50
   L = 105 + 50 + 100 = 255
   M = 95 + 85 + 110 = 290

This problem was designed for an equation-type solution, but some students may find a different approach more helpful in understanding the solution and its steps. Such an approach can be easily developed on the board as follows, using Case 1 as an example:

Given:	Beginning	End	Steps:
Liabilities	A	B	1. A = 85 - (40 + 15) = 30
Paid-in capital	15	C	2. E = 150 - 120 = 30
Retained income	40	D	3. D = 40 + 30 - 0 = 70
Total (equal to total assets)	85	95	4. C = 15 + 0 = 15
			5. B = 95 - (70 + 15) = 10

Revenues	150
Expenses	120
Net income	E

16-A2 (40-55 min.)

1. See Exhibit 16-A2 on the following page.

2.

LEBEAU COMPANY
Balance Sheet
April 30, 19X5

Assets		Liabilities and Stockholders' Equity		
		Liabilities:		
Cash	$ 17,000	Note payable		$ 24,000
Accounts receivable	50,000	Accounts payable		7,000
Merchandise		Total liabilities		$ 31,000
inventory	23,000	Stockholders' equity:		
Prepaid rent	4,000	Paid-in capital	$95,000	
Equipment and		Retained income	3,000	
fixtures	35,000	Total stockholders'		
		equity		98,000
Total assets	$129,000	Total equities		$129,000

EXHIBIT 16-A2

LEBEAU COMPANY
Analysis of Transactions for April 19X5
(in thousands of dollars)

	Assets					=	Equities			
							Liabilities		Stockholders' Equity	
Description	Cash +	Accounts Receivable +	Merchandise Inventory +	Prepaid Rent +	Equipment and Fixtures	=	Note Payable +	Accounts Payable +	Paid-in Capital +	Retained Income
1. Incorporation	+95					=			+95	
2. Purchased merchandise	-35		+35			=				
3. Purchased merchandise			+25			=		+25		
4a. Sales	+25	+65				=				+90(revenue)
b. Cost of inventory sold			-37			=				-37(expense)
5. Collections	+15	-15				=				
6. Disbursements to trade creditors	-18					=		-18		
7. Purchased equipment	-12				+36	=	+24			
8. Prepaid rent	- 6			+6		=				
9. Rent expense	- 9					=				- 9(expense)
10. Wages, etc.	-38					=				-38(expense)
11. Depreciation					- 1	=				- 1(expense)
12. Rent expense				-2		=				- 2(expense)
Balances, April 30, 19X5	+17	+50	+23	+4	+35	=	+24	+ 7	+95	+ 3
			129					129		

LEBEAU COMPANY
Income Statement
For the Month Ended April 30, 19X5

Sales (revenue)		$90,000
Deduct expenses:		
Cost of goods sold	$37,000	
Wages, salaries and commissions	38,000	
Rent, 2,000 + 9,000	11,000	
Depreciation	1,000	
Total expenses		87,000
Net income		$ 3,000

3. Most businesses tend to have net losses during their infant months, so LeBeau's ability to show a net income for April is impressive. Indeed, the rate of return on beginning investment is $3,000 ÷ $95,000 = 3.2% per month, or 38.4% per year. Many points can be raised, including the problem of maintaining an "optimum" cash balance so that creditors can be paid neither too quickly nor too slowly. See the next solution also.

16-A3 (5-10 min.)

Revenue (cash basis):	
Cash sales	$25,000
Cash collected from credit customers	15,000
Total revenue	$40,000

The accrual basis provides a more accurate measure of economic performance. As long as the two recognition criteria are met (earned and realized), the $90,000 measure of revenue on the accrual basis is preferred to the $40,000 measure of revenue on the cash basis. The $90,000 is the more accurate measure of accomplishments *for April*.

16-B1 (10-15 min.)

This is straightforward. Note that revenues are nearly $4 billion. Computations are in millions of dollars.

A = 2,774.9 - (412.1 +1,484.1) = 878.7
B = 3,653.8 - 593.5 = 3,060.3
C = 1,484.1 + 593.5 - 31.2 = 2,046.4
D = 412.1 + 43.5 = 455.6
E = 1,249.5 + 455.6 + 2,046.4 = 3,751.5

Instructors may wish to comment about the $43.5 million additional investments by stockholders; many companies have stock purchase plans for employees and/or stockholders. Therfore, such companies issue small amounts of stock almost every year.

16-B2 (30-40 min.)

1. See Exhibit 16-B2 on the following page.

EXHIBIT 16-B2

HINO MOTORS
Analysis of Transactions for April 1994
(in billions of yen)

	Assets					=	Equities			
							Liabilities		Stockholders' Equity	
Transaction	Cash +	Accounts Receivable +	Inventories +	Prepaid Expenses +	Property, Plant, Equip.	=	Accounts Payable +	Other Liabilities +	Paid-in Capital +	Retained Earnings
Balances 3/31/94	+52	+64	+27	+ 60	+160	=	+84	+86	+44	+149
1a.	+15	+50				=				+65(increase revenue)
1b.			-25			=				-25(increase expense)
2.			+50			=	+50			
3.	+30	-30				=				
4.	-25			+25		=				
5.	-45					=	-45			
6.	-10					=				-10(increase expense)
7.				- 9		=				- 9(increase expense)
8.					- 18	=				-18(increase expense)
Balances, 4/30/94	+17	+84	+52	+76	+142	=	+89	+86	+44	+152
			+371					+371		

2.

HINO MOTORS
Statement of Earnings
For the Month Ended April 30
(in billions)

Sales		¥65
Deduct expenses:		
Cost of goods sold	¥25	
Selling and administrative expenses	19	
Depreciation	18	
Total expenses		62
Net earnings		¥ 3

HINO MOTORS
Balance Sheet
April 30
(in billions)

Assets		Liabilities and Stockholders' Equity	
Cash	¥ 17	Accounts payable	¥89
Accounts receivable	84	Other liabilities	86
Inventories	52	Paid-in capital	44
Prepaid expenses	76	Retained earnings	152
Property, plant, and equipment	142		
Total	¥371	Total	¥371

16-B3 (5-10 min.)

Revenue (cash basis):	
Cash sales	¥15,000,000,000
Collections from credit customers	30,000,000,000
Total revenue	¥45,000,000,000

The accrual basis provides a more accurate measure of economic performance. As long as both recognition criteria are met (earned and realized), the ¥70 billion measure of revenue on the accrual basis is preferred to the ¥45 billion measure of revenue on the cash basis. The ¥70 billion is the more accurate measure of accomplishments *for April.*

16-1 The income statement answers questions about financial performance over a span of time. The balance sheet answers questions about financial status at a point in time.

16-2 Assets should be viewed from an economic standpoint as resources or bundles of services that are expected to benefit the future activities of the entity rather than from a legalistic point of view that is connoted by ownership.

16-3 The income statement is the main link between two balance sheets. The income statement explains how operations have changed the balance sheet values over a span of time.

16-4 This statement is fallacious because it does not take into consideration withdrawals (dividends) or increases in ownership investment, both of which affect the ownership capital account but not net income.

16-5 Under the accrual basis, revenue is recognized as it is earned and realized and expenses are recognized in the period when costs expire. In contrast, the cash basis recognizes revenue as cash is collected and most expenses as cash is disbursed.

16-6 Adjusting entries differ from routine entries in that they deal with implicit transactions in contrast with the explicit transactions that trigger nearly all the day-to-day routine entries.

16-7 The manager acquires goods and services (including advertising), not expenses per se. These goods and services become expenses as they are used in obtaining revenue.

16-8 It is preferable to refer to the costs rather than the values of assets such as plants or inventory because the word value has many meanings and is more vague than the word cost. Cost explicitly recognizes that balance sheet amounts are based on the amounts spent on assets, not their current values.

16-9 Yes. Depreciation is simply the allocation of the acquisition cost of assets over the periods that benefit from the asset's use. It is not a measure of the changes in market value of an asset.

16-10 Retained Earnings is neither an asset nor a preferred claim against cash or any other asset, but it represents a general claim against total assets. In most instances no "pot of gold" exists, as the cash inflow from operations will be largely reinvested in other assets.

16-11 Although profitable operations are typically a prerequisite to dividends, dividends are actually a distribution of assets that "liquidate" a portion of the ownership claim.

16-12 Congress has delegated the setting of generally accepted accounting principles to the Securities and Exchange Commission (SEC). In turn, the

SEC has delegated the task to the Financial Accounting Standards Board (FASB), which is a private-sector body supported by those with interests in preparing, auditing, and using financial statements.

16-13 The use of the dollar as the principal accounting measure has been criticized because the changing purchasing power of a monetary unit over time is not taken into account.

16-14 The going-concern concept is a notion that implies that existing resources will be *used* to fulfill the general purpose of a continuing concern rather than be *sold* in tomorrow's real estate or equipment market.

16-15 In the accounting sense, objectivity means freedom from bias, accuracy that can be verified by other independent accountants.

16-16 Economic feasibility sometimes inhibits the adoption of new ways to measure financial performance and position because the apparent benefits may not exceed the obvious costs of gathering and interpreting the information.

16-17 (10-15 min.)

1. False. Cash should be classified as an asset.

2. False. Retained earnings should be accounted for as a stockholders' equity item.

3. False. Machinery used in the business should be recorded at original cost less accumulated depreciation.

4. A large retained earnings balance is the best evidence of previous profitable operations.

5. True

6. False. From a single balance sheet, you can find stockholders' equity for a specific day.

16-18 (15-20 min.)

The theme of this solution is that retained income is not a pot of cash awaiting distribution to stockholders.

1.

Cash	$1,400	Paid-in capital	$1,400

2.

Cash	$ 800	Paid-in capital	$1,400
Inventory	600		
Total assets	$1,400		

Note in both Requirements 1 and 2 that the ownership equity is fundamentally a claim against the total assets (in the aggregate). For example, 57% of the shareholders do not have a specific claim on cash, and 43% of the shareholders do not have a specific claim on inventory. Instead, they have an undivided claim against (or interest in) all of the assets.

3.

Cash	$1,650	Paid-in capital	$1,400
		Retained income	250
		Total equities	$1,650

Retained income is part of the stockholders' equity. Even though cash and retained income have increased by identical amounts, the retained income is fundamentally a *general* claim against *total* assets (just as paid-in capital is a general claim). Retained income is the net rise in ownership claim attributable to profitable operations. However, the assets themselves should not be confused with the claims against the assets.

4.

Cash ($1,650-$400-$750)	$ 500	Paid-in capital	$1,400
Inventory	400	Retained income	250
Equipment	750		
Total assets	$1,650	Total equities	$1,650

The same explanation applies here as in Requirement 3. However, Transaction 4 should clarify the lack of a specific link between retained income (and paid-in capital) and any particular assets. The ownership claims are general, not specific.

5.

Cash	$ 500	Accounts payable	$ 450
Inventory ($400+$450)	850	Paid-in capital	1,400
Equipment	750	Retained income	250
Total assets	$2,100	Total equities	$2,100

The meaning of retained income was explained in answer 3. Purchases on "open account" usually create a general liability; that is, the trade creditors usually hold only general claims against the total assets, not specific claims against particular assets (such as mortgages on buildings). In sum, both the creditors *and* the owners hold general claims against the assets. Of course, if the corporation is liquidated (all assets converted to cash to be distributed to claimants), the creditors' general claims must be satisfied before the owners get one dollar. Thus, the stockholders are said to have *residual claim* or *residual interest*.

16-19 (10-15 min.)

1. The name of the statement is antiquated. This statement is ordinarily either a statement of profit *or* a statement of loss, not profit *and* loss. It should be titled *income statement* or *statement of earnings.*

2. The line with the date should not be for an *instant* of time but for an indicated span of time.

3. Increases in market values are not usually recognized in historical cost accounting.

4. Dividends are not expenses and are not deducted before net profit is computed.

5. The appropriate deduction is the cost of goods *sold*, not *purchased.*

6. The bottom line might be titled *net income* or *net earnings*, although *net profit* is acceptable.

7. Although this is not the major point of the problem, the income statement has apparently omitted some expenses. For example, neither rent nor depreciation is shown; at a minimum, one or the other would ordinarily be included.

16-20 (10 min.)

	Dow				Northwest Airlines			
	A		= L +	SE	A	=	L +	SE
	Cash	Prepaid Travel Expense		Travel Expense	Cash	=	Unearned Sales Revenue	Sales Revenue
1. Dec. payment	-70,000	+70,000	=		+70,000	=	+70,000	
2. Feb. travel		-70,000	=	-70,000		=	-70,000	+70,000

16-21 (10-15 min.)

	Lakewood Hardware, Tenant				Schall, Landlord			
	A		= L +	SE	A	=	L +	SE
	Cash	Prepaid Rent		Rent Expense	Cash		Unearned Rent Revenue	Rent Revenue
1.	-7,500	+7,500	=		+7,500	=	+7,500	
2.		-2,500	=	-2,500		=	-2,500	+2,500
3.		-2,500	=	-2,500		=	-2,500	+2,500
4.		-2,500	=	-2,500		=	-2,500	+2,500

16-22 (15-20 min.)

	Assets - Liabilities = Stockholders' equity
Dec. 31:	B120,000 - B55,000 = B65,000
Jan. 1:	B100,000 - B40,000 = B60,000
Change:	B 20,000 - B15,000 = B 5,000

1. As above, B60,000. This is the easiest computation.

2. Change in stockholders' equity + Cash dividends = Net income
B5,000 + B14,000 = B19,000

3. Let X = Cost of goods sold
Sales - Cost of goods sold - Operating expenses = Net income
B260,000 - X - B50,000 = B19,000
-X = B19,000 - B260,000 + B50,000
X = B191,000

16-23 (20-30 min.)

	Case						
	1	2	3	4	5	6	7
V						$ 4,500	$ 4,800
W						2,000	3,600
X	$8,000	$2,000	$9,000	$13,000	$7,500	8,000	4,200
Y		6,000	6,000			9,000	(200) Loss*
Z		3,000	2,000			16,500*	15,200**

Computations:

1: X = $ 7,000 + $ 3,000 - $ 2,000 = $ 8,000
2: X = $ 5,000 - $ 3,000 = $ 2,000
: Y = $11,000 - $ 5,000 = $ 6,000
: Z = $ 9,000 - $ 6,000 = $ 3,000
3: X = $ 6,000 + $10,000 - $ 7,000 = $ 9,000
: Y = $15,000 - $ 9,000 = $ 6,000
: Z = $ 6,000 - $ 4,000 = $ 2,000
4: X = $ 8,000 + $12,000 - $ 7,000 = $13,000
5: X = $ 3,000 + $ 4,500 = $ 7,500
6: V = $10,000 - $ 2,000 + $ 1,500 - $ 5,000 = $ 4,500
: W = $ 6,000 - $ 4,000 = $ 2,000
: X = $14,000 - $ 6,000 = $ 8,000
: Y = $ 8,000 + $ 7,000 - $ 6,000 = $ 9,000
: Z = $ 4,500 + $12,000 = $16,500
7: V = $ (200) + $ 5,000 = $ 4,800
: W = $ 9,600 - $ 6,000 = $ 3,600
: X = $ 8,200 - $ 4,000 = $ 4,200
: Y = $ 3,600 + $ 400 - $ 4,200 = $ (200)
: Z = $20,000 - $ 4,800 = $15,200

Note: The formula for cost of goods sold is not discussed in the chapter, but it is given in the problem.

*Stockholders' equity:	Case 6	Case 7
Beginning	$? = 4,500	$8,200 - 4,000 = 4,200
Additional investments	+5,000	0
Net profit	W = 6,000 - 4,000 = +2,000	? = -200
Dividends	-1,500	-400
End	$10,000	$9,600 - 6,000 = 3,600

Then A = L + SE
= 12,000 + 4,500
= 16,500

In case 6, the $4,500 is the beginning balance, $10,000 - ($5,000 + $2,000 - $1,500) = $4,500. In case 7, the net loss of $200 is $4,200 - ($3,600 + $400) = $200.

**20,000 - 5,000 + 200 = 15,200

16-24 (45-75 min.)

1. See Exhibit 16-24 on the following page.

2. MOUNTAIN MADNESS
Statement of Income
For the Month Ended March 31, 19X5

Sales		$60,000
Cost of goods sold		30,000
Gross profit		$30,000
Operating expenses:		
Rent	$ 500	
Depreciation	50	
Advertising	9,000	
Wages and salaries	11,000	
Miscellaneous	1,510	22,060
Operating income		$ 7,940
Interest expense		40
Net income		$ 7,900

Requirement 3:

The amount of the excess of Seagram's investment cost over the book value of Du Pont's stock which was amortized to Seagram's earnings in the current period is determined as follows:

	$ Millions
Du Pont's 1987 net income (See Note 1)	$1,786
Seagram's equity interest	22.9%
Seagram's interest in Du Pont's earnings before amortizations	$408.99
Minus: Before-tax amount of Du Pont's earnings reported in Seagram's 1988 income statement $179.48 + $217.99[1] =	-397.47
Amounts amortized to Seagram's equity in Du Pont's earnings	$11.52[2]

Requirement 4:

Reconciliation of beginning and ending investment account balances:

	$ Millions
Investment in Du Pont stock 1/31/87 (see B/S)	$3,329.73
Add: Seagram's equity in Du Pont earnings (22.9% × $1,786)	408.99
Less: Dividend received from Du Pont (before tax)	(179.48)
Less: Amounts amortized against Seagram's equity in Du Pont's earnings (see item 3 above)	(11.52)
Less: Interest (net of tax) allocated against Du Pont's earnings	(6.78)
Add: Additional investment made in Du Pont's stock in 1987 (plug)	46.52
Investment in Du Pont stock on 1/31/88 (given)	$3,587.46

Requirement 5:

Return on Seagram's wine and spirits operation:

$$\text{ROA} = \frac{\text{Net income (after tax)} + \text{Interest } (1-T) \text{ from wine and spirits}}{\text{Avg. assets exclusive of Du Pont investment}}$$

$$= \frac{\$144.52 + \$80.40\,(1-.30)^{*}}{\$3{,}756.37^{**}} = \frac{\$200.8}{\$3{,}756.37} = 5.34\%$$

$$^{*}\ \frac{\text{Income tax expense}}{\text{Income before taxes}} = \frac{\$60.8}{\$205.3} = 30\%$$

		($ millions)
** Assets exclusive of Du Pont investment on 1/31/87 $6,886.46 - $3,329.73	=	$3,556.73
Assets exclusive of Du Pont investment on 1/31/88 $7,543.47 - $3,587.46	=	$3,956.01
		$7,512.74
		÷2
Avg. assets–wine and spirits operations		$3,756.37

[1] $211.21 reported on income statement + $6.78 interest (net of tax benefit) charged against unremitted earnings of Du Pont.

[2] $11.52 for excess depreciation and other amortizations charged to unremitted earnings.

Return on Seagram's investment in Du Pont

$$= \frac{\text{Seagram's share of Du Pont earnings (less taxes on dividends \& amort.)}}{\text{Avg. book value of Seagram's investment in Du Pont}}$$

$$= \frac{\$408.99 - \$14.114 - \$11.52}{(\$3,329.73 + \$3,587.46)/2}$$

$$= \frac{\$383.36}{\$3,458.60} = \underline{\underline{11.08\%}}$$ [3]

[3]Alternative ROA if adjustment for taxes on entire earnings of Du Pont: $408.99 x (1 - .20) - $11.52 / $3458.60 = $315.67 / $3458.60 = 9.12%. NOTE: Because of 80% dividends exclusion rule of U.S. Tax Code, Seagrams would need to accrue taxes on 20% of its share of Du Pont's earnings.

C15-2. **Tyler Corporation:** Business acquisitions and analysis of sales growth

Requirement 1:
When an acquisition is accounted for as a purchase, time-series comparability in the basic financial statements is impaired. Since Thurston was acquired on April 6, 1979, its revenues and expenses are included in the income statement only from that date forward. 1978 results are for a three-division company, while 1979 results include the original three divisions plus nine months of Thurston's sales and expenses.

To achieve comparability in these instances, one must look to the pro forma figures in the footnote. These numbers are prepared as if Thurston were acquired on the earliest date for which comparative figures are provided, here January 1, 1978. Comparing sales growth of all *four* divisions between 1978 and 1979 reveals an increase of $60,279,000 or 12.6%.

The instructor might point out that the minimum GAAP pro forma disclosures are so limited (i.e., sales, net income and EPS) that reconstruction of fully-comparable, complete financial statements is not possible. Because of this, time-series analyses of ratios and trends for companies who have acquired others using the purchase method are frequently so non comparable as to be misleading.

Requirement 2:
Under pooling of interests accounting, the 1978 and 1979 income statements would have included Thurston's results for each of the years. Accordingly, the income statements would be more comparable. However, the acquired company's *book value* (not its fair value) is reflected on the balance sheet. Hence, there are also considerable (but different) problems for statement readers when poolings occur.

Moreover, the inventory badly needs replenishment if sales are to continue at their current pace.

Many new businesses can show a respectable net income but nevertheless be at the brink of financial disaster because they are "under-capitalized." That is, there is insufficient long-term investment capital to sustain a smooth growth. Too often, creditors and employees need cash far in advance of when customers provide the cash to the business. This may be such a case, unless customers pay promptly.

16-25 (5 min.)

1.	Cr.	3.	Cr.	5.	Cr.	7.	Cr.
2.	Dr.	4.	Cr.	6.	Cr.		

16-26 (10 min.)

The following statements are true: 1, 4, 5, 8, 9.

Explanations for the false statements follow:

2. Amounts borrowed are *debited* to Cash and *credited* to Notes Payable.
3. Decreases in assets are shown on the *credit* side.
6. *All* credits are on the right.
7. Payments on mortgages are *credited* to cash and *debited* to Mortgage Payable.
10. Purchases of inventory should be *debited* to Inventory and *credited* to Accounts Payable.
11. Decreases in liability accounts should be on the *left* (or decreases in *asset* accounts should be on the right).

16-27 (10-15 min.)

1 and 2.

Cash	
a. 200	
b. 15	
d. 20	

Dues Receivable	
	a. 200

Accounts Receivable	
b. 20	d. 20

Equipment	
c. 130	b. 35

Accounts Payable	
	c. 130

16-28 (20-30 min.) See Exhibit 16-28.

16-29 (20-40 min.) See Exhibit 16-29.

EXHIBIT 16-28 Amounts are in thousands of dollars.

Cash

(1)	95	(2)	35
(4a)	25	(6)	18
(5)	15	(7)	12
		(8)	6
		(9)	9
		(10)	38
Bal.	17		

Note Payable

		(7)	24

Paid-in Capital

		(1)	95

Accounts Payable

(6)	18	(3)	25

Retained Income

		Net Inc.	3*

Accounts Receivable

(4a)	65	(5)	15

Cost of Goods Sold

(4b)	37		

Sales

		(4a)	90

Merchandise Inventory

(2)	35	(4b)	37
(3)	25		

Rent Expense

(9)	9		
(12)	2		

Wages, Sal., & Comm.

(10)	38		

Prepaid Rent

(8)	6	(12)	2

Depreciation Expense

(11)	1		

Equipment and Fixtures

(7)	36	(11)	1

*Details of the revenue and expense accounts appear in the income statement. Their net income effect appears in Retained Income in the balance sheet.

Note: Ending balances should be drawn for each account, but they are not shown here because they can be computed mentally.

EXHIBIT 16-29

Cash

(1)	30,000	(2)	20,000
(5a)	15,000	(3a)	1,000
		(4b)	6,000
		(6a)	5,000
		(7)	1,510
		(8)	1,000
		(11)	400
Bal.	10,090		

Accounts Receivable

(5a)	45,000		

Inventory

(2)	40,000	(5b)	30,000

Prepaid Rent

(3a)	1,000	(3b)	500

Fixtures and Equipment

(8)	6,000	(10)	50

Note Payable

		(8)	5,000

Accounts Payable

		(2)	20,000
		(4a)	3,000

Accrued Wages & Sal.

		(6b)	6,000

Accr. Interest Payable

		(9)	40

Paid-in Capital

		(1)	30,000

Retained Income

(11)	400	Inc.	7,900

Cost of Goods Sold

(5b)	30,000		

Rent Expense

(3b)	500		

Advertising Expense

(4a)	3,000		
(4b)	6,000		

Wages & Sal. Expense

(6a)	5,000		
(6b)	6,000		

Sales

		(5a)	60,000

Depreciation Expense

(10)	50		

Interest Expense

(9)	40		

Miscellaneous Expense

(7)	1,510		

Note: Ending balances should be drawn for each account, but they are not shown here because they can be computed mentally.

16-30 (30 min.)

1. DR. LAUREL STAYTE, DENTIST

Income Statement

For the Year Ended December 31, 19X7

	Cash Basis	Accrual Basis
Fee revenue	$81,000	$99,000[1]
Expenses:		
Rent	$ 7,500	$ 6,000[2]
Utilities	600	700[3]
Salaries	16,000	17,000[4]
Depreciation	12,000	12,000[5]
Total expenses	$36,100	$35,700
Operating income	$44,900	$63,300

[1]$81,000 collected - $2,000 unearned + $20,000 receivable
[2]$7,500 - $1,500 applicable to the first quarter of 19X6
[3]$600 + $100 owed
[4]$16,000 + $1,000 owed
[5]$72,000 ÷ 6 = $12,000

The term "cash basis" is ambiguous. A strict interpretation of cash basis would permit deducting the full $72,000 paid for equipment as an expense in 19X7. Operating income would be $44,900 + $12,000 depreciation added back - $72,000 paid for equipment = a loss of $15,100.

2. The accrual basis provides a better measure of economic performance, because it encompasses all assets and liabilities arising from operations rather than their immediate cash effects alone. For example, the $2,000 advance payment has not yet been earned and therefore represents an obligation of Dr. Stayte. However, the $20,000

fees billed have been earned and represent a legitimate economic resource of that magnitude (unless their full collectibility is in doubt).

The government permits the cash basis primarily to ease the cash demands on taxpayers and to ease the recordkeeping tasks of small businesses. In short, if you extend credit to your customers, the government does not feel it equitable to demand payment for taxes if you have not yet received your cash.

Remember, therefore, that income measurement may *legitimately* differ for different purposes. In this case, the cash basis may be the preferable way to measure income for tax purposes. But to measure her own economic performance as a dentist, Dr. Stayte would probably prefer the accrual basis. This is a major point–there is nothing inherently evil about having "two sets of books."

16-31 (10-15 min.)

1. The bank's assets (cash) and equities (deposits, a major liability) would each increase by $1,000. Personal assets would change, but equities would not, assuming that the cash on hand had already been recorded as, say, cash on hand (asset) and personal capital (equity). If the latter recording had been made, the deposit would merely represent the transforming of one asset (cash on hand) into another (cash in bank); no equities would be affected.

2. The bank's total assets and equities would be unaffected. The only change would be in the form of assets. Cash would decrease by $900,000, and notes receivable would increase by the same amount.

3. Personal cash (asset) would increase, and personal liabilities (note payable) would increase.

16-32 (20 min.)

LANDS' END
Balance Sheet
January 31, 1997
(in thousands of dollars)

Assets		Liabilities and Stockholders' Equity*		
Cash	$ 92,827	Accounts payable		$76,585
Receivables	8,739	Notes payable		11,195
Inventory	(1)	Long-term liabilities		9,474
Property, plant, & equip.	103,684	Other liabilities		57,786
Other assets	30,350	Total liabilities		$ (3)
		Common stock	$ 402	
		Other stockholders' equity	222,603	
		Total stockholders' equity		(2)
Total assets	$378,045	Total liab. and stockholders' equity		
	$378,045**			

*This is the heading used in most actual annual reports.
**Same amount as total assets.

(a.) $378,045 - $8,739 - $92,825 - $103,684 - $30,350 = $142,445. This is the largest asset. Inventory is obviously important to Lands' End.

(b.) $402 + $222,603 = $ 223,005

(c.) $378,045 - $223,005 = $155,040 or
$76,585 + $11,195 + $9,474 + $57,786 = $155,040

16-33 (20-25 min.)

The following statements follow the general format used by Disney. Obviously, various alternatives are possible:

1. (a)

WALT DISNEY COMPANY
Income Statement
For the Year Ended September 30, 1997
(in millions)

Revenues	$22,473
Operating Costs and expenses	18,026
Operating income	4,447
Other expenses	367
Net interest expense	693
Income before taxes*	3,387
Income taxes*	1,421
Net income	$1,966

*This is the nomenclature used by Disney. Note how the title of this income statement uses "income," whereas the title of the retained income statement uses "retained earnings."

(b)

WALT DISNEY COMPANY
Statement of Retained Earnings
For the Year Ended September 30, 1997
(in thousands of dollars)

Balance at beginning of year	$7,933*
Net income for the year	1,966
Dividends paid	(342)
Balance at end of year	$9,557

* $9,557 + $342 - $1,966

2. The cash dividend seems to be small compared to the amounts for net income and retained earnings. This conservative dividend policy may reflect management's intention to finance growth mainly from profits reinvested in the business.

16-34 (15-25 min.)

The following is a reproduction of Procter & Gamble's statements. Students may use other acceptable formats. Accounts payable and cash are irrevelant.

1.

PROCTER & GAMBLE COMPANY
Statement of Earnings
Year Ended June 30, 1997
(in millions)

Net sales and other income		$35,764
Costs and expenses:		
Cost of products sold	20,316	
Marketing, research, and administrative expenses	9,960	
Interest and other expenses	239	
(No label given)		
Earnings before income taxes		5,249
Income taxes		1,834
Net earnings		$ 3,415

2.

PROCTER & GAMBLE COMPANY
Statement of Retained Earnings
Year Ended June 30, 1997
(in millions)

Balance at beginning of year	$10,265
Net earnings	3,415
Dividends to shareholders	(1,225)
Other decreases in retained earnings	(1,725)
Balance at end of year	$10,730

CHAPTER 17
Understanding Corporate Annual Reports: Basic Financial Statements

17-A1 (20-25 min.)

LANDGRAFF COMPANY
Balance Sheet
December 31, 19X8

ASSETS:	
Current assets:	
Cash and equivalents	$ 41,000
Accounts receivable, net	61,000
Inventories	31,000
Prepaid expenses	15,000
Total current assets	148,000
Noncurrent assets:	
Property, plant, and equipment, at cost	580,000
Less: Accumulated depreciation	170,000
Property, plant, and equipment, net	410,000
Goodwill, patents, and trademarks	75,000
Other long-term assets	110,000
Total noncurrent assets	595,000
Total assets	$743,000

LIABILITIES AND SHAREHOLDERS' EQUITY:	
Current liabilities:	
Notes payable	$ 40,000
Accounts payable	48,000
Income taxes payable	37,000
Current portion of long-term debt	16,000
Total current liabilities	141,000
Noncurrent liabilities:	
Long-term debt	210,000
Deferred income tax liability	44,000
Total noncurrent liabilities	254,000
Shareholders' equity:	
Common stock (50,000 shares @ $.50)	25,000
Additional paid-in capital	121,000
Retained earnings	202,000
Total shareholders' equity	348,000
Total liabilities and shareholders' equity	$743,000

LANDGRAFF COMPANY
Income Statement
For the Year Ended December 31, 19X8

Revenues	$800,000
Cost of sales	460,000
Gross profit	$340,000
Selling and administrative expenses	150,000
Income from operations	$190,000
Other income (expense):	
Interest expense	$ (55,000)
Interest income	20,000
Total other income (expense)	$ (35,000)
Income before income taxes	$155,000
Provision for income taxes	55,000
Net income	$100,000
Earnings per share ($100,000 ÷ 50,000)	$2.00

To determine the amount of additional paid-in capital, you must begin by computing total liabilities and shareholders' equity = total assets = $743,000. Then:

Total shareholders' equity = $743,000 - current liabilities - noncurrent liabilities
= $743,000 - $141,000 - $254,000
= $348,000

Addl. paid-in capital = shareholders' equity - common stock - retained earnings
= $348,000 - $25,000 - $202,000
= $121,000.

17-A2 (15-20 min.) Although the requirements do not call for it, many students will find it useful to prepare a balance sheet equation (without beginning balances, which are not given), as shown in Exhibit 17-A2. Comparing the entries to the Cash column to those in the Retained Earnings column shows why net income differs from cash provided by operations. This understanding is necessary to interpret (or prepare) the schedule that reconciles net income to net cash provided by operating activities (see 17-A3).

MODERN MATERNITY CLOTHING STORES, INC.
Statement of Cash Flows
For the Year Ended December 31, 19X8
(in thousands)

Cash flows from operating activities		
Cash collections from customers		$ 1,450
Cash payments:		
To suppliers	$(775)	
To employees	(200)	
For other expenses	(100)	
For interest	(11)	
For income taxes	(30)	
Cash disbursed for operating activities		(1,116)
Net cash provided by operating activities		334
Cash flows from investing activities:		
Purchase of plant and facilities		(435)
Cash flows from financing activities:		
Issued debt	120	
Paid dividends	(39)	
Net cash provided by financing activities		81
Net decrease in cash		(20)
Cash, December 31, 19X7		48
Cash, December 31, 19X8		$ 28

17-A3 (10-15 min.)

MODERN MATERNITY CLOTHING STORES, INC.
Supporting Schedule to Statement of Cash Flows
Reconciliation of Net Income to Net Cash Provided by
Operating Activities
For the Year Ended December 31, 19X8
(in thousands)

Net income	$464	
Adjustments to reconcile net income to net cash provided by operating activities:		
Add: Depreciation, which was included in computing computing net income but does not affect cash	45	
Deduct: Increase in accounts receivable	(250)	[1,700-1,450]
Deduct: Increase in inventory	(50)	[900-850]
Add: Increase in accounts payable	125	[900-775]
Deduct: Decrease in salaries and wages payable	(10)	[200-190]
Add: Increase in income taxes payable	10	[40-30]
Net cash provided by operating activities	$334	

17-A4 (10 min.)

1.

Sales	$800,000
Nondepreciation expenses [600,000-90,000]	(510,000)
Depreciation	(90,000)
Net income	$200,000
Add back depreciation	90,000
Net cash provided by operating activities	$290,000

2.

Sales	$ 800,000
Nondepreciation expenses [600,000-90,000]	(510,000)
Depreciation	(270,000)
Net income	$ 20,000
Add back depreciation	270,000
Net cash provided by operating activities	$ 290,000

Notice that the additional depreciation did not affect net cash provided by operating activities. The direct method clearly shows this phenomenon:

Direct method:

Sales for cash	$ 800,000
Operating expenses in cash	(510,000)
Net cash provided by operating activities	$ 290,000

17-B1 (15-20 min.)

INTEL
Balance Sheet
January 1, 1997
(in millions)

ASSETS		
Current assets:		
Cash	$ 4,165	
Short-term investments	3,742	
Accounts receivable	3,723	
Inventories	1,293	
Other current assets	761	$ 13,684
Property, plant, and equipment, at cost	$14,262	
Accumulated depreciation	(5,775)	8,487
Long-term investments		1,353
Other assets		211
Total assets		$23,735
LIABILITIES AND SHAREHOLDER'S EQUITY		
Current liabilities:		
Short-term debt	$ 389	
Other accrued liabilities	917	
Accounts payable	964	
Accrued compensation and benefits	1,128	
Income taxes payable	986	
Deferred revenue	474	
		$4,863
Long-term debt, excluding current portion		728
Deferred income tax liability		997
Other long-term liabilities		275
Common shareholders' equity:		
Common stock and capital in excess of par value	2,897	
Retained earnings	13,975*	16,872*
Total liabilities and shareholders' equity		$23,735

*Total Stockholders' Equity = $23,735 - $275 - $997 - $728 - $4,863 = $16,872
Retained Earnings = $16,872 -$2,897 = $13,975

17-B2 (25 min.) This is a good exercise in recognizing items that fit in a Statement of Cash Flows and placing them in the proper section of the statement. Three items listed in the problem do not appear in a Statement of Cash Flows: net sales, retained earnings, and total assets.

WALGREEN COMPANY
Statement of Cash Flows
For the Year Ended August 31, 1997
(in thousands)

Cash flows from operating activities:	
Net earnings	$ 436
Adjustments to reconcile net earning to net cash provided by operating activities:	
Depreciation and amortization	164
Deferred income taxes	8
Other non-cash expenses	8
Changes in current assets and liabilities:	
Inventories	(101)
Trade accounts payable	121
Accrued expenses and other liabilities	73
Accounts receivable, net	(74)
Other current assets	3
Income taxes	12
Net cash provided by operating activities	650
Cash (Used for) Provided by Investing Activities:	
Additions to property and equipment	(485)
Additional investment in corporate-owned life insurance	(16)
Proceeds from disposition of property and equipment	15
Net cash used for investment activities	(486)
Cash (Used for) Provided by Financing Activities:	
Cash dividends paid	(116)
Payments of long-term obligations	(1)
Net proceeds from employee stock plans	17
Net cash used for financing activities	(100)
Changes in Cash and Cash Equivalents:	
Net increase in cash and cash equivalents	64
Cash and cash equivalents at beginning of year	9
Cash and cash equivalents at end of year	$ 73

E16-2. Determining cash flows from operations
(AICPA adapted)

Lino's net cash from operating activities is calculated below:

Net income	$150,000
Increase in accounts receivable[1]	(5,800)
Decrease in prepaid rent	4,200
Increase in accounts payable	3,000
Cash flow from operations	**$151,400**

[1]The increase in accounts receivable is net of the allowance for doubtful accounts:

Beginning accounts receivable	$23,000
Less: Beginning allowance for doubtful accounts	(800)
Beginning net accounts receivable	$22,200
Ending accounts receivable	$29,000
Less: Ending allowance for doubtful accounts	(1,000)
Ending net accounts receivable	$28,000
Increase in net accounts receivable:	
Ending net accounts receivable	$28,000
Beginning net accounts receivable	(22,200)
Increase in net accounts receivable	$5,800

E16-3. Cash flows from operations
(AICPA adapted)

Requirement 1:
Calculate accrual basis net income for December:

Sales revenue		$350,000
Cost of goods sold (70% of sales)		(245,000)
Gross profit (30% of sales)		105,000
Selling, general, and administrative expenses		
Fixed portion =	$35,000	
Variable portion = 15% × $350,000 =	52,500	(87,500)
Net income (accrual basis)		**$17,500**

Requirement 2:
Adjust accrual basis income to obtain cash flows from operations:

Accrual basis net income	$17,500
- Increase in gross trade accounts receivable*	(13,500)
- Increase in inventory	(5,000)
+ Charge for uncollectible accounts (1% × $350,000)	3,500
+ Depreciation expense included in S, G&A	20,000
Cash flows from operating activities	**$22,500**

* ($10,500 + $3000 right off of uncollectable accounts receivable)

17-1 The operating cycle is the time span during which cash is spent to acquire goods and services that are used to produce the organization's output, which in turn is sold to customers, who in turn pay for their purchases in cash. This may be much longer than one year for some firms, such as large construction companies.

17-2 Marketable securities is not a good name for securities held for short-term purposes, although the term is encountered frequently. Strictly speaking, marketable securities may be held for either a short-term purpose or a long-term purpose.

17-3 Prepaid expenses belong in current assets because if they were not present more cash would be needed to conduct current operations.

17-4 Current assets usually include cash, trade receivables, inventories, and prepaid expenses.

17-5 If 100 shares are held as a temporary investment, they are current assets. Whether they are current depends on the purpose for holding them.

17-6 The cost of an asset is allocated to the periods benefiting from use of the asset by charging a portion as depreciation expense. The total amount charged since the acquisition of the asset – the accumulated depreciation – is deducted from the cost to obtain the "net book value" of the asset.

17-7 Accumulated depreciation is not cash; if specific cash is being accumulated for the replacement of assets, such cash will be an asset specifically labeled as a "cash fund for replacement and expansion" or a "fund of marketable securities for replacement and expansion."

<u>17-8</u> Different depreciation methods are legitimately used for different purposes. Most companies appropriately use straight-line depreciation for reporting to shareholders. Most companies should and do use accelerated depreciation (MACRS) for income tax purposes.

<u>17-9</u> Depreciation is a method of cost *allocation*, not valuation.

<u>17-10</u> The useful life of depreciable assets is most heavily influenced by economic and technological changes rather than physical wear and tear.

<u>17-11</u> The preoccupation with physical evidence often results in the expensing of outlays that should be treated as assets. Thus, expenditures for research, advertising, employee training and the like are usually expensed, although it seems clear that in an economic sense such expenditures represent expected future benefits.

<u>17-12</u> Yes. Goodwill is simply the excess of the purchase price over the current value of the separable assets acquired, less the liabilities.

<u>17-13</u> Subordinated debentures are like any long-term debt except that "subordinated" means that such bondholders are junior to other general creditors in exercising claims against assets and "debenture" means a general claim against all unencumbered assets rather than a specific claim against particular assets.

<u>17-14</u> Stock frequently has a designated *par* or *legal* or *stated* value that is printed on the face of the certificate. For preferred stock (and bonds), par is a basis for computing the amount of dividends or interest. Par value of common stock has no practical importance. Historically, it was used for establishing the maximum legal liability of the stockholder in case the corporation could not pay its debts. Currently, it is set at a nominal amount (say $1) in relation to the market value of the stock upon issuance (say $20).

17-15 Unlike individual proprietors or partners, stockholders' personal assets cannot be confiscated to satisfy the debts of an incorporated entity.

17-16 Treasury stock is indeed negative stockholders' equity. It is a contraction of outstanding capital stock. It is *not* an asset

17-17 No. The statement of cash flows is a required statement with a required format.

17-18 A cash flows statement shows the relationship of net income to changes in cash balances. It aids predicting future cash flows, evaluating management's generation and use of cash, and determining a company's ability to pay dividends and interest and pay debts when due. It also reveals commitments to assets that may restrict or expand future courses of action.

17-19 Operating activities, investing activities, and financing activities are the three major types of activities summarized in the statement of cash flows.

17-20 Major operating activities include collections from customers, collections of interest or dividends, payments to suppliers, payments to employees, payments for interest, and payments for taxes.

17-21 Major investing activities include sales and purchases of property, sales and purchases of securities that are not cash equivalents, and making loans.

17-22 Major financing activities include borrowing from creditors, issuing equity securities, repaying creditors, repurchasing equity securities, and paying dividends.

17-23 Interest paid or received appears in the operating activities section. Some commentators favor showing interest paid as a financing activity and interest received as an investing activity. However, the FASB decided that, because interet income and interest expense are included in income, they should be included in operating activities.

17-24 Sales revenue is recognized on an accrual basis, not a cash basis. Therefore, cash collections from customers will not ordinarily equal sales revenues during any given period.

17-25 The direct method and indirect method are the two major ways of computing net cash provided by operating activities. The direct method shows cash inflows and outflows directly. The indirect method begins with net income and adds adjustments to get net cash provided by operating activities.

17-26 The erroneous impression is that depreciation is a source of cash. Depreciation is an allocation of original cost to expense that does not entail a current outlay; that is, depreciation is a non-cash expense. It is added to net income when using the indirect method only to offset its deduction in computing net income.

17-27 The newsletter reinforces thc widely held erroneous impression that depreciation provides cash.

17-28 Strictly speaking, net losses, by themselves, do not drain cash. A net loss is an excess of expenses over revenues; it is an income statement item rather than an item on a statement of cash flows. Indeed, equipment may be sold for a net loss. Any cash proceeds resulting from the transaction would be an addition to cash, not a cash drain.

17-29 Depreciation belongs in a supporting schedule to the body of the statement of cash flows. Depreciation is one of the items that reconciles net income to net cash flow from operating activities. However, it does not appear on a direct-method cash flow statement because it does not directly affect cash.

17-30 The $4,000 is double-counted. The net cash flow from operating activities was zero, not $4,000. The statement of cash flows should be confined to the $20,000 proceeds, which includes the $4,000 gain.

17-31 Non-cash investing and financing activities generally could have been accomplished identically in substance (though not in form) by cash transactions. For example, issuing debt to purchase an asset could have been accomplished by issuing debt for cash and then using the cash to purchase the asset. Companies should not be able to prevent disclosure of such a transaction to readers of the statement of cash flows simply by using a non-cash form of transaction.

17-32 The asset was sold for $5,000 + $3,000 = $8,000. The entire $8,000 should be reported as a cash inflow from investing activities. In the reconciliation schedule, the $3,000 gain must be deducted from net income in computing net cash provided by operating activities.

17-33 No. The opposite is true. Tax expense on reports to shareholders has exceeded the actual tax payments.

17-34 (10-15 min.) The purpose of this problem is to stress the limitations of the use of historical costs, particularly where there are significant amounts of property, plant, and equipment.

The balance sheet values do not come close to the current market value of the land and building, DM 1,800,000 ÷ .60, or DM 3,000,000. Consequently, in terms of current values before expansion and modernization, stockholders' equity is understated (in thousands):

Market value of land and building		DM 3,000
Net book value:		
Land	DM 200	
Building	160	360
Excess of market value over net book value		DM 2,640

As conventionally prepared after the expansion and modernization, the balance sheet would be (in thousands):

Cash		DM 400	Liabilities:	
Land		200	Mortgage payable	DM 1,800
Building at cost	DM 2,600		Stockholders' equity	760
Accum. depreciation	640			
Net book value		1,960		
			Total liabilities and	
Total assets		DM 2,560	stockholders' equity	DM 2,560

The balance sheet would be unusually deceiving. The mortgage would appear to be exceedingly high in relation to the book value of the assets. The historical cost and resulting stockholders' equity have lost all meaning.

For more elaborate examples entailing both specific and general price level effects, see the assignment material for Chapter 19.

17-35 (25-30 min.) This problem is similar to 18-A1 but is more difficult because items not shown in exhibits 18-1 and 18-5 are included and terminology is varied slightly.

FUJITA COMPANY
Balance Sheet
May 31, 19X1
(in millions)

ASSETS:	
Current assets:	
Cash and equivalents	¥ 29,000
Receivables	22,000
Inventories	31,000
Other current assets	6,000
Total current assets	88,000
Noncurrent assets:	
Fixed assets, net	217,000
Capital construction fund	28,000
Intangible assets	21,000
Long-term investments	15,000
Total noncurrent assets	281,000
Total assets	¥369,000

LIABILITIES AND STOCKHOLDERS' EQUITY:	
Current liabilities:	
Accounts payable	¥ 19,000
Accrued expenses payable	16,000
Other current liabilities	9,000
Total current liabilities	44,000
Noncurrent liabilities:	
Mortgage bonds	84,000
Debentures	77,000
Deferred income tax liability	12,000
Total noncurrent liabilities	173,000
Stockholders' equity:	
Redeemable preferred stock	15,000
Common stock, at par	5,000
Paid-in capital in excess of par	102,000
Retained income, appropriated for self-insurance	16,000
Retained income, unrestricted	27,000
Less: Treasury stock	(13,000)
Total stockholders' equity	152,000
Total liabilities and stockholders' equity	¥369,000

FUJITA COMPANY
Income Statement
For the Year Ended May 31, 19X1
(in millions except net income per share)

Net sales	¥440,000
Cost of goods sold	220,000
Gross margin	220,000
Operating expenses:	
Administrative and general expenses	65,000
Research and development expenses	42,000
Selling and distribution expenses	41,000
Total operating expenses	148,000
Operating income	72,000
Other income (expenses), net	(12,000)
Income before income taxes	60,000
Income taxes	51,000
Net income	¥ 9,000
Net income per share*	¥180,000

*¥9,000,000,000 ÷ 50,000 = ¥180,000

To compute the amount for intangible assets, recognize that total assets must be ¥369,000 (equal to total liabilities and stockholders' equity).

Then: Total noncurrent assets = Total assets - Total current assets
= ¥369,000 - ¥88,000
= ¥281,000

Intangible assets = Noncurrent assets - Fixed assets, net - Capital construction fund - Long-term investments
= ¥281,000 - ¥217,000 - ¥28,000 - ¥15,000
= ¥21,000

17-36 (5 min.)

The split between cash and credit sales is irrelevant for purposes of this problem.

Sales	$640,000
Less increase in accounts receivable	(6,000)
Cash received from customers	$634,000

17-37 (5 min.)

Cost of goods sold	$360,000
Add increase in inventory ($120,000-$105,000)	15,000
Deduct increase in accounts payable ($47,000-$24,000)	(23,000)
Cash paid to suppliers	$352,000

17-38 (5-10 min.)

Wage and salary expense	$195,000
Cash paid to employees	155,000
Increase in accrued wages and salaries payable	$ 40,000

Beginning balance, accrued wages, and salaries payable	$ 20,000
Increase in accrued wages and salaries payable	40,000
Ending balance, accrued wages, and salaries payable	$ 60,000

17-39 (5-10 min.)

BREKKE AND ASSOCIATES
Statement of Cash Flows from Operating Activities
For the Year Ended December 31, 19X0

Collections from customers (DK480,000-DK9,000)	DK471,000
Cash expenses (DK280,000-DK50,000)	230,000
Net cash provided by operating activities	DK241,000

17-40 (5-10 min.)

BREKKE AND ASSOCIATES
Reconciliation of Net Income to Net Cash Provided by Operating Activities
For the Year Ended December 31, 19X0.

Net income	DK200,000
Add depreciation, which was deducted in computing net income but does not affect cash	50,000
Deduct increase in accounts receivable	(9,000)
Net cash provided by operating activities	DK241,000

17-41 (10 min.)

GONZALEZ COMPANY
Reconciliation of Net Loss to Net Cash Provided by Operating Activities
For the Year Ended December 31, 19X2

Net loss	$(42,000)
Add depreciation	25,000
Add decrease in accounts receivable	4,000
Deduct increase in inventory	(2,000)
Add increase in accounts payable	17,000
Add increase in wages and salaries payable	5,000
Net cash provided by operating activities	$ 7,000

17-42 (15-25 min.)

KRAKOWSKI AUTO PARTS
Statement of Cash Flows
For the Year Ended December 31, 19X8
(in thousands)

Cash flows from operating activities:		
Cash collections from customers		$2,401
Cash payments:		
To suppliers	$(1,640)	
To employees	(305)	
For other operating expenses	(104)	
For interest	(26)	
For income taxes	(108)	
Cash disbursed for operating activities		(2,183)
Net cash provided by operating activities		218
Cash flows from investing activities:		
Purchase of plant and facilities	$ (540)	
Proceeds from sale of equipment	37	
Net cash used in investing activities		(503)
Cash flows from financing activities:		
Issued common stock	28	
Retired long-term debt	(25)	
Dividends paid	(88)	
Net cash used in financing activities		(85)
Net decrease in cash		(370)
Cash, January 1, 19X8		380
Cash, December 31, 19X8		$ 10

17-43 (10-20 min.)

KRAKOWSKI AUTO PARTS
Supporting Schedule to Statement of Cash Flows
Reconciliation of Net Income to Net Cash Provided by Operating Activities
For the Year Ended December 31, 19X8
(in thousands)

Net income		$240
Adjustments to reconcile net income to net cash provided by operating activities		
Add:	Depreciation	151
Deduct:	Increase in accounts receivable (2,503-2,401)	(102)
Deduct:	Increase in inventory	(56)
Add:	Increase in accounts payable (1,596+56-1,640)	12
Deduct:	Decrease in salaries and wages payable	(24)
Deduct:	Decrease in income taxes payable (108-105)	(3)
Net cash provided by operating activities		$218

17-44 (10 min.)

RED EAGLE COMPANY
(in millions)

1. Income Statement:

Sales		$210
Nondepreciation expenses	$171	
Depreciation	27	198
Net income		$ 12

Reconciliation of net income to net cash provided by operating activities:

Net income	$ 112
Add non-cash expenses:	
Depreciation	12
Deduct net increase in non-cash operating working capital	(15)
Net cash provided by operating activities	$ 24

2. An increase in depreciation does not affect net cash flow from operating activities. The $10 million increase in depreciation *decreases net income* by $10 million and *increases the addback* by $10 million. The net effect is zero. Depreciation is added to net income merely to offset its deduction when computing net income, not because it provides cash.

17-45 (20-30 min.)

1.

SEDONA COMPANY
Statement of Cash Flows
For the Year Ended December 31, 19X2
(in millions)

Cash flows from operating activities:		
Net income		$ 60
Adjustments to reconcile net income to net cash provided by operating activities:		
Depreciation		20
Increase in receivables		(36)
Increase in inventories		(50)
Increase in current liabilities		75
Net cash provided by operating activities		$ 69
Cash flows from investing activities:		
Purchase of fixed assets		(190)
Cash flows from financing activities:		
Issue of long-term debt	$120	
Dividends paid	(6)	
Cash provided by financing activities		114
Net decrease in cash		$ (7)
Cash balance, December 31, 19X1		20
Cash balance, December 31, 19X2		$ 13

2. Dear Ms. Littlegeorge:

Severe shortages of cash commonly accompany rapid corporate growth. Profitable operations usually produce heavy supplies of cash. But the insatiable demand for cash to expand receivables, inventories, and fixed assets may deplete the cash on hand despite profitable operations. This why so many so-called growth companies usually pay little or no dividends.

Note also that the ratio of current assets to current liabilities is 3.3 to 1 on December 31, 19X1 but only 1.7 to 1 on December 31, 19X2. It appears that the need for cash to support increases in receivables and inventory has come primarily from increases in current liabilities.

17-46 (30-40 min.)

1.

BLUE HERON COMPANY
Statement of Cash Flows
For the Year Ended December 31, 19X8
(in millions)

Cash flows from operating activities:		
Cash collections from customers ($255-$17)		$238
Cash payments:		
To suppliers ($140+$20-$14)	$(146)	
For general expenses ($51+$1)	(52)	
For taxes ($10-$1)	(9)	
Cash disbursed for operating activities		(207)
Net cash provided by operating activities		31
Cash flows from investing activities:		
Acquisition of plant assets	(102)	
Proceeds from sale of plant assets	6	
Net cash used for investing activities		(96)
Cash flows from financing activities:		
Issue long-term debt	50	
Pay cash dividends	(4)	
Net cash provided by financing activities		46
Net decrease in cash		(19)
Cash balance, December 31, 19X7		25
Cash balance, December 31, 19X8		$ 6

2. Reconciliation of Net Income to Net Cash Provided by Operating Activities

Net income	$ 14
Adjustments to reconcile net income to net cash provided by operating activities:	
Depreciation	40
Increase in accounts receivable	(17)
Increase in inventory	(20)
Increase in prepaid general expenses	(1)
Increase in accounts payable for merchandise	14
Increase in accrued taxes payable	1
Net cash provided by operating activities	$ 31

3. Sato's stress may be reduced but not eliminated. The statement of cash flows has shown why cash has fallen by $19 million. Operating activities provided $31 million, and financing activities provided an additional $46 million, a total of $77 million. However, $96 million was needed for the net acquisition of plant assets.

   Severe crunches on cash commonly accompany quick corporate growth. There may be large net income and working capital provided by operations, but heavy demands for cash to expand receivables, inventories, and plant assets diminish the cash on hand despite profitable operations. Hence, most "growth" companies pay skimpy or no dividends.

17-47 (10 min.) Amounts are in guilders (NG)

1. The only effect would be a NG170,000 cash inflow listed with the investing activities:

Proceeds from sale of equipment	NG170,000

2. The proceeds should be listed as an investing activity:

Proceeds from sale of equipment	NG210,000

In addition, a NG40,000 gain appeared on ALIC's income statement. The gain must be removed from net income by deducting the NG40,000 from net income in the reconciliation of net income to net cash provided by operating activities:

Net income	NGXXXXX
Deduct: Gain on sale of equipment	(40,000)

17-48 (10-15 min.)

a. (1) Operating income was lower by the $761 million, because R&D must be charged to expense.

(2) Operating income would be $3,087 + $761 = $3,848 million.

(3) Assets would be higher by $761 million, the cost of the patents.

b. $8 million ÷ 4 = $2 million

c. Let x = amortization for 1998

Pre-opening Costs, Net		
12/31/97	2,390,000	x = 2,550,000
Additions	2,000,000	
12/31/98	1,840,000	

$$2{,}390{,}000 + 2{,}000{,}000 - x = 1{,}840{,}000$$
$$x = 2{,}550{,}000$$

d. $13 billion - $2 billion = $11 billion of goodwill
Amortization per year = $11,000,000,000 ÷ 40 years = $275,000,000

The minimum amount is based on a useful life of 40 years. The entire amount cannot be written off in one year because the GAAP in the U.S. forbids the lump-sum write-off of goodwill upon acquisition. A relatively quick write-off, say four years, is frequently justifiable.

17-49 (15-20 min.)

1. Cash or accounts receivable and sales would increase by $3,000,000.

   Warranty expense and liability for warranties would rise by .032 x $3,000,000 = $96,000.

   Liability for warranties and cash would decrease by $84,000.

2. Cash and the liability account called Deposits on Bottles would be increased by $100,000.

   In turn, both accounts would be decreased by $93,000.

3. Cash and the liability account called Deposits would be increased by $1,200 on April 1. On June 30, Interest Expense and Deposits would be increased by 3/12 x .06 x $1,200 = $18. On July 1, Cash and Deposits would be decreased by $1,200 + $18 = $1,218.

4. (a) Cash and the liability, Unearned Sales Revenue, would be increased by $80,000 on December 31.

   (b) On January 31, Unearned Sales Revenue would be decreased by $80,000 ÷ 4 = $20,000. On the income statement, Sales would be increased by $20,000.

17-50 (15 min.)

1. 1996 accounts receivable was $405,283,000 + ($51,854,000 - $7,414,000) = $449,723,000.

2. 1996 long-term debt was $11 million - $14 million + $10 million = $7 million.

3. 1996 retained earnings were $274,033,000 + $250,679,000 - $0 = $524,712,000.

17-51 (10-20 min.)

A lively discussion usually ensues. This problem could also be assigned in conjunction with Chapter 4 on inflation as an example of the strengths and weaknesses of accounting theory.

1. There would be a "gain from insurance on crashed airplane" recognized on the income statement:

Insurance payments received	$6,500,000
Book value of airplane	962,000
Gain from insurance on crashed airplane	$5,538,000

Total assets would increase by $5,538,000, the amount of the gain. The fleet of airplanes would be the same as before the crash, but a 727 with a book value of $6.5 million has replaced a similar 727 with a book value of only $962,000.

2. Accounting for casualties is very controversial. It gets to the heart of the question of what is income and what is capital. Does the $6.5 million represent a return of capital or a payment of both capital and income?

The traditional accounting model ignores changes in general purchasing power and intervening changes in specific prices while an asset is held. When an asset is disposed of, the gain or loss is measured in nominal dollars (almost always without regard to the intended use of the proceeds).

Many theorists and practitioners (as explained much more fully in Chapter 20 in the section on inflation accounting) define the income of a going concern to be a function of whether the proceeds will be reinvested in the same types of assets. These individuals maintain that no gain is realized on the airplane crash, because the $6.5 million is really a return of capital (where capital is thought of in physical terms as airplanes, inventories, etc.). Thus, the "gain" would not be shown in the income statement. Instead, it would appear as a special balance sheet item called Revaluation Equity, or some similar title.

17-52 (5-10 min.)

a.	Investing	d.	Financing	g.	Financing
b.	Operating	e.	Financing	h.	Financing
c.	Financing	f.	Operating	i.	Financing

17-53 (10-15 min.)

1. First, compute the cash outflow for interest (in millions)

Interest expense	$215
Less increase in interest payable*	(8)
Cash payments for interest	$207

*$57.9 - $49.9 = $8.0

The only line for interest on the statement of cash flows will be under operating activities:

Cash payments for interest	$207 million

2. The *increase* of $8.0 million in interest payable would be *added to* net income in computing net cash provided by operating activities. Why? Because the interest *expense* of $215 million was deducted in computing net income, but the cash *payment* of $207 million, $8.0 million less, should be deducted in computing cash flow.

17-54 (30 min.)

1. MICRON TECHNOLOGY

Statement of Cash Flows From Operating Activities (Indirect Method)
For the Year Ended August 28, 1997
(in millions)

Net income	$332.2
Adjustments to reconcile net income to net cash provided by operating activities:	
Depreciation	461.7
Increase in receivables	(97.7)
Increase in inventories	(194.2)
Increase in accounts payable and accrued expenses	120.3
Other decreases in cash	(112.6)
Increase in income taxes payable	93.9
Net cash provided by operating activities	$603.6

2. MICRON TECHNOLOGY

Statement of Cash Flows From Operating Activities (Direct Method)
For the Year Ended August 28, 1997
(in millions)

Cash collections from customers (3,515.5 - 97.7)	$3,417.8
Cash payments to suppliers (2,539.2 + 194.2 - 120.3)	(2,613.1)
Cash payment for operating expenses (573.9 - 461.7 + 112.6)	(224.8)
Cash payments for income taxes (267.3 - 93.9)	(173.4)
Cash receipts for other income	197.1
Net cash provided by operating activities	$ 603.6

17-55 (25-35 min.)

1. NORDSTROM, INC.

Cash Flows from Operating Activities
For the Year Ended January 31, 1997
(in millions)

Cash collections from customers ($4,453 - $7)		$4,446
Other income		130
Total cash receipts		$4,576
Cash payments:		
To suppliers of goods (3,082 + 94 - 33)	$3,143	
For selling, general, and administrative expenses (1,218 - 156 + 2 - 7 - 20)	1,037	
For interest (39)	39	
For income taxes (96 + 12)	108	
Cash disbursed for operating activities		4,327
Net cash provided by operating activities		$ 249

17-56 (40 min.)

CHILDROBICS, INC.
Balance Sheet
February 28, 1994

ASSETS:		
Current assets:		
Cash		$ 39,901 (1)
Property and equipment:		
At cost	$296,583 (2)	
Accumulated depreciation	10,947 (3)	
Net		285,636 (4)
Other assets		25,300 (given)
Total assets		$350,837 (5)
LIABILITIES AND STOCKHOLDERS' EQUITY:		
Current liabilities:		
Accounts payable and accrued expenses	$ 59,871 (6)	
Deferred revenue	13,450 (7)	
Note payable	250,000 (8)	
Total current liabilities		$323,321 (9)
Stockholders' equity:		
Common stock – $.01 par value, 25,000,000 shares authorized, 975,000 shared issued and outstanding	9,750 (10)	
Additional paid-in capital	15,250 (11)	
Retained Earnings	2,516 (12)	
Total stockholders' equity		27,516 (13)
Total liabilities and stockholders' equity		$350,837 (14)

(1) From last line of Statement of Cash Flows
(2) From "Investing Activities" section of Statement of Cash Flows and footnote information: $192,583 + $104,000 = $296,583
(3) From "Operating Activities" section of Statement of Cash Flows
(4) $296,583 - $10,947 = $285,636
(5) $39,901 + $285,636 + $25,300 = $350,837
(6) From "Operating Activities" section of Statement of Cash Flows
(7) From "Operating Activities" section of Statement of Cash Flows
(8) From footnote information: $146,000 + $104,000 = $250,000
(9) $59,871 + $13,450 + $250,000 = $323,321
(10) $.01 x 975,000 = $9,750
(11) Cash from sale of common stock (from financing section of Statement of Cash Flows) less par value of common stock: $25,000 - $9,750 = $15,250
(12) From "Operating Activities" section of Statement of Cash Flows
(13) $9,750 + $15,250 + $2,516 = $27,516
(14) $323,321 + $27,516 = $350,837 (or from total assets = $350,837)

17-57 (30 min.)

The purpose of this exercise is to learn which accounts belong to the income statement and which to the balance sheet. Doing the exercise in teams of two persons each allows each student to recall income statement and balance sheet accounts himself or herself and also to react to accounts listed by someone else. Discussion of those accounts for which there is disagreement should generate consideration of what criteria make an account an income statement account or a balance sheet account. It also forces consideration of the labels put on accounts and how well they identify the nature of the account.

CHAPTER 18
More on Understanding Corporate Annual Reports

18-A1 (15-20 min.) Answers are in millions of dollars.

1.

	Equity Method				
	Assets		=	Liab. + Stk. Eq.	
	Cash	Invest- ments		Liabil- ities	Stock. Equity
a. Acquisition	-70	+70	=		
b. Net income of Akron		+12	=		+12
c. Dividends from Akron	+ 8	- 8	=		
Effects for year	-62	+74	=		+12

The journal entries that would accompany this table are:

a. Investment in Akron	70	
Cash		70
b. Investment in Akron	12	
Investment revenue*		12
c. Cash	8	
Investment in Akron		8

*More frequently called Equity in Earnings of Affiliates

Under the equity method, income is recognized by Chrysler as it is earned by Akron rather than when dividends are received. Cash dividends do not affect net income; they increase cash and decrease the investment balance. In a sense, the dividend is a partial liquidation of the investor's "claim" against the investee. The receipt of a dividend is similar to the collection of an account receivable. The revenue from a sale of merchandise on account is recognized when the receivable is created; to include the collection also as revenue would be double-counting. *Similarly, it would be double-counting to include the $8 million of dividends as income after the $12 million of income is already recognized as it is earned.*

2.

	Market Method				
	Assets		=	Liab. + Stk. Eq.	
	Cash	Invest-ments		Liabil-ities	Stock. Equity
a. Acquisition	-70	+70	=		
b. Dividends from Akron	+ 8		=		+8 (Revenue)
c. Increase in market value	+ 5	+ 5			+ 5 (Valuation acct)
Effects for year	-62	+75	=		+13

The journal entries that would accompany this table are:

a. Investment in Akron	70	
Cash		70
b. Cash	8	
Dividend revenue**		8
c. Investment in Akron	5	
Unrealized gain on available-for-sale securities		5

** Frequently called "dividend income"

18-A2 (25-35 min.) A common mistake is to think that the $50 million is additional money flowing into the Homewood Company rather than into the pockets of the Homewood shareholders as individuals. Amounts are in millions.

1.

	Assets			= Liab.+Stockholders' Equity		
	Investment in Homewood	+ Cash and Other Assets	=	Accounts Payable, etc.	+	Stockholders' Equity
Magill's accounts, Jan. 1:						
Before acquisition		320	=	100	+	220
Acquisition of Homewood	+50	- 50	=			
Homewood's accounts, Jan. 1		70	=	20	+	50
Intercompany eliminations	-50		=			- 50
Consolidated, Jan. 1	0	+ 340	=	120	+	220

2.

	Magill	Homewood	Consolidated
Sales	$325	$100	$425
Expenses	240	90	330
Operating income	$ 85	$ 10	$ 95
Pro-rata share (100%) of unconsolidated subsidiary net income	10	-	
Net income	$ 95	$ 10	

3. Magill's parent-company-only income statement would show its own sales and expenses plus its pro-rata share of Homewood's net income, as the equity method requires. Reflect on the changes in Magill's balance sheet equation (in millions):

	Assets			= Liab.+Stockholders' Equity		
	Investment in Homewood	+ Cash and Other Assets	=	Accounts Payable, etc.	+	Stockholders' Equity
Magill's accounts:						
Beginning of the year	50	+ 270	=	100	+	220
Operating income		+ 85	=			+ 85
Share of Homewood's income	+10		=			+ 10
End of year	60	+ 355	=	100	+	315
Homewood's accounts:						
Beginning of the year		70	=	20	+	50
Net income		+ 10	=			+ 10
End of the year		80	=	20	+	60
Intercompany eliminations	-60		=			- 60
Consolidated, end of year	0	+ 435	=	120	+	315

Homewood's balance sheet accounts would have increased by $10 million.

At this point, review to see that consolidated statements are the summation of the individual accounts of two or more separate legal entities. These statements are prepared periodically via worksheets. *A consolidated entity does not have a separate continuous set of books like its legal entities.* Moreover, a consolidated income statement is merely the summation of the revenue and expenses of the separate legal entities being consolidated after the elimination of double-counting.

4. Consolidated accounts would be unaffected. Homewood's cash and stockholders' equity would decline by $5 million. Magill's investment in Homewood would decline by $5 million, but Magill's cash would rise by $5 million.

18-A3 (30-45 min.) A common error is to think that the $40 million is additional money flowing into Homewood rather than into the pockets of the Homewood shareholders. Amounts are in millions.

1.

	Assets			=	Liab.+Stockholders' Equity				
	Investment in Homewood	+	Cash and Other Assets	=	Accounts Payable, etc.	+	Minority Interest	+	Stockholders' Equity
Magill's accounts, Jan. 1:									
Before acquisition			320	=	100			+	220
Acquisition of Homewood	+40		- 40	=					
Homewood's accounts, Jan. 1			70	=	20			+	50
Intercompany eliminations	-40			=			+10		- 50
Consolidated, Jan. 1	0	+	350	=	120	+	10	+	220

2. The same basic procedures are followed by Magill and Homewood regardless of whether Homewood is 100% owned or 80% owned. However, the presence of a minority interest changes the *consolidated* statements slightly. The income statements would include:

	Magill	Homewood	Consolidated
Sales	$325	$100	$425
Expenses	240	90	330
Operating income	$ 85	$ 10	$ 95
Pro-rata share (80%) of unconsolidated subsidiary net income	8	-	
Net income	$ 93	$ 10	
Minority interest (20%) in consolidated subsidiaries' net income			2
Net income to consolidated entity			$ 93

3.

	Assets		=	Liab.+Stockholders' Equity				
	Investment in Homewood	+ Cash and Other Assets	=	Accounts Payable, etc.	+ Minority Interest		+	Stockholders' Equity
Magill's accounts:								
Beginning of year	40	+ 280[a]	=	100			+	220
Operating income		+ 85	=					+ 85
Share of Homewood's income	+ 8		=					+ 8
End of year	48	+ 365	=	100			+	313
Homewood's accounts:								
Beginning of year		70	=	20			+	50
Net income		+ 10	=					+ 10
End of year		80	=	20			+	60
Intercompany eliminations	-48		=		+	12[b]		- 60
Consolidated, end of year	0	+ 445	=	120	+	12	+	313

[a]320 beginning of year - 40 for acquisition = 280

[b]10 beginning of year + .20(10) = 10 + 2 = 12

4. *Consolidated* accounts would be affected because the minority interest's claim would be partially liquidated in the amount of 20% of $8 million, or $1.6 million. Homewood's cash would decline by $8 million, Magill's investment in Homewood would decline by .80 x $8 million = $6.4 million, but Magill's cash would rise by $6.4 million. See following balance sheet equations:

	Assets		=	Liab.+Stockholders' Equity			
	Investment in Homewood	+ Cash and Other Assets	=	Accounts Payable, etc.	+ Minority Interest	+	Stockholders' Equity
End of year balances:							
Magill's accounts	48.0	+ 365.0	=	100		+	313
Effect of Homewood dividend	- 6.4	+ 6.4	=				
Balance	41.6	+ 371.4	=	100		+	313
Homewood's accounts (from 3):		80.0	=	20		+	60
Effect of Homewood dividend		- 8.0	=				- 8
Balance		72.0	=	20		+	52
Consolidated accounts	41.6	443.4	=	120		+	365
Intercompany eliminations	-41.0		=		+10.4		- 52
Balance	0	+ 443.4	=	120	+ 10.4		313

18-A4 (25-35 min.)

1.

	Assets			=Liab.+Stockholders' Equity		
	Investment in Homewood	+ Goodwill	+ Cash and Other Assets	= Accounts Payable, etc.	+	Stockholders' Equity
Magill's accounts, Jan. 1:						
Before acquisition			320	= 100	+	220
Acquisition of 100% of Homewood	+80		- 80	=		
Homewood's accounts, Jan. 1			70	= 20	+	50
Intercompany eliminations	- 80	+30		=		- 50
Consolidated, Jan. 1	0	+ 30*	+ 310	= 120		220

* The $30 million "goodwill" would appear in the consolidated balance sheet as a separate intangible asset account. It often is shown as the final item in a listing of assets. It is usually amortized in a straight-line manner as an expense in the consolidated income statement over a span of no greater than 40 years.

2. $30,000,000 ÷ 40 = $750,000 and $30,000,000 ÷ 5 = $6,000,000.

3. a. If the book values of the Homewood's individual assets are not equal to their fair values, the usual procedures are:

(1) Homewood continues as a going concern and keeps its accounts on the same basis as before.

(2) Magill records its investment at its acquisition cost (the agreed purchase price).

(3) For consolidated reporting purposes, the excess of the acquisition cost over the book values of Homewood is identified with the individual assets, item by item. (In effect, they are revalued at the current market prices prevailing

when Magill acquired Homewood.) Any *remaining excess* that cannot be identified is labeled as purchased goodwill.

The balance sheet accounts immediately after acquisition would be the same as in Requirement 1, except that goodwill would be $20 million instead of $30 million, and other assets would be higher by $10 million. The $10 million would appear in the consolidated balance sheet as an integral part of the "other assets." That is, Homewood's equipment would be shown at $10 million higher in the consolidated balance sheet than the carrying amount on Homewood's books. Similarly, the depreciation expense on the consolidated income statement would be higher. For instance, if the equipment had four years of useful life remaining, the straight-line depreciation would be $10 ÷ 4 = $2.5 million higher per year. As in the preceding tabulation, the $20 million "goodwill" would appear in the consolidated balance sheet as a separate intangible asset account.

b. Consolidated income would be lower:

Amortization of goodwill, $20,000,000 ÷ 40 years	$ 500,000
Extra depreciation $10,000,000 ÷ 4 years	2,500,000
Total additions to expense	$3,000,000
Amortization of goodwill in requirement 2	750,000
Income lower in part 3b by	$2,250,000

The assigning of a "basket purchase price" to the various assets can have a dramatic effect on income taxes. For example, although income is lower for corporate reporting purposes in part 3b, income tax cash outflows would be less during the next four years. Depreciation is deductible for federal income tax purposes, but the amortization of goodwill is not.

18-A5 (10-15 min.)

1. (a) \$500 x 12% = \$60 million
   (b) \$60 ÷ 5% = \$1,200 million
   (c) \$1,200 ÷ \$500 = 2.4 times; or
   12% ÷ 5% = 2.4 times

2. (a) ¥300 ÷ 5 = ¥60 million
   (b) ¥9 ÷ ¥300 = 3%
   (c) ¥9 ÷ ¥60 = 15%; or 3% x 5 = 15%

18-B1 (15 min.) The year-end balance in Investment in Tanlami is \$57 million under the equity method, and \$43 million under the market method.

1.

	Assets		=Liab.+Stockholders' Equity		
	Cash	+Investments	=	Liabilities	+ Stockholders' Equity
Equity Method:					
1. Acquisition	-50	+50	=		
2. Net income of Tanlami		+15	=		+15
3. Dividends from Tanlami	+ 8	- 8	=		
Effects for year	-42	+57	=		+15
Market Method:					
1. Acquisition	-50	+50	=		
2. Dividends from Tanlami	+ 8		=		+8 (revenue)
3. Adjustment to market value		- 7	=		- 7 (loss)
Effects for year	-42	+43	=		+1

Journal entries (not required):

Equity Method

		Debit	Credit
1.	Investment in Tanlami	50	
	Cash		50
2.	Investment in Tanlami	15	
	Investment revenue*		15
3.	Cash	8	
	Investment in Maytag		8

* More frequently called Equity in Earnings of Affiliates

Market Method

		Debit	Credit
1.	Investment in Tanlami	50	
	Cash		50
2.	Cash	8	
	Dividend revenue**		8
3.	Loss on trading securities	7	
	Investment in Tanlami		7

** Frequently called "dividend income"

Texas Instruments would be required to use the equity method because its ownership of 33% is between 20% and 50%.

18-B2 (25-40 min.) Amounts are in millions of dollars.

A common mistake is to think that the $400 million is additional money flowing into Bayliner rather than into the pockets of Bayliner shareholders as individuals.

1.

	Assets			=Liab.+Stockholders' Equity		
	Investment in Bayliner	+ Cash and Other Assets	=	Accounts Payable, etc.	+	Stockholders' Equity
Brunswick's accounts, Jan. 1:						
Before acquisition		1,400	=	800	+	600
Acquisition of Bayliner	+400	- 400	=			
Bayliner's accounts, Jan. 1:		600	=	200	+	400
Intercompany eliminations	-400		=			-400
Consolidated, Jan. 1	0	+ 1,600	=	1,000	+	600

2.

	Brunswick	Bayliner	Consolidated
Sales	$1,800	$600	$2,400
Expenses	1,300	500	1,800
Operating income	$ 500	$100	$ 600
Pro-rata share (100%) of unconsolidated subsidiary net income	100		
Income of parent company	$ 600		

3. Brunswick's parent-company-only income statement would show its own sales and expenses plus its pro-rata share of Bayliner's net income (as the equity method requires). Reflect on the changes in Brunswick's balance sheet equation (in millions of dollars):

	Assets			=	Liab.+Stockholders' Equity		
	Investment in Bayliner	+	Cash and Other Assets	=	Accounts Payable, etc.	+	Stockholders' Equity
Brunswick's accounts:							
Beginning of year	400	+	1,000	=	800	+	600
Operating income			+500	=			+500 ret. inc.
Share of Bayliner's income	+100			=			+100 ret. inc.
End of year	500	+	1,500	=	800	+	1,200
Bayliner's accounts:							
Beginning of year			600	=	200	+	400
Net income			+100	=			+100
End of year			700	=	200	+	500
Intercompany eliminations	-500			=			-500
Consolidated, end of year	0	+	2,200	=	1,000	+	1,200

4. The important point to see is that the *consolidated* accounts would be unaffected. Bayliner's cash and stockholders' equity would decline by $12 million. Brunswick's investment in Bayliner would decline by $12 million, but Brunswick's cash would rise by $12 million.

18-B3 (15-20 min.)

1. Under the equity method Ford will recognize 33% of Mazda's net loss:
33% x $40,000,000 = $13,200,000 loss

2. The balance is decreased by Ford's share of Mazda's net loss ($13,200,000 from requirement 1) and decreased by the cash dividends received from Mazda (33% x $20,000,000 = $6,600,000):
$900,000,000 - $13,200,000 - $6,600,000 = $880,200,000

Using a T account might help:

Investment in Mazda			
Beginning balance	900,000,000	Equity in Mazda net loss	13,200,000
		Dividends received from Mazda	6,600,000
Ending balance	880,200,000		

3. (a) Of course, the market method is not an acceptable accounting method under these circumstances. If it were, the dividends received from Mazda would be recognized as income by Ford:
33% x $20,000,000 = $6,600,000

(b) The account balance would be adjusted to market value, $825 million.

(c) The $25 million increase would be added to a valuation account in stockholders' equity.

4. Ford is obliged to follow the generally accepted accounting principles for investments:

   (a) Investments that represent more than a 50% ownership interest must be consolidated. A subsidiary is a corporation controlled by another corporation. The usual condition for control is ownership of a majority (more than 50%) of the outstanding voting stock. In parent-company-only statements, the equity method is used.

   (b) The equity method is also generally used for a 20% through 50% interest because such a level of ownership is regarded as a presumption that the owner has the ability to exert significant influence. However, consolidated statements are not reported.

   (c) All other investments in *equity* securities must be accounted for using the market method.

18-B4 (10-20 min.)

1. Total asset turnover: 8.9% ÷ 4% = 2.225 times*
2. Net income: 8.9% x $27.3 billion = $2.4297 billion
3. Total revenues: $2.4297 billion ÷ 4% = $60.7425 billion
   (or 2.225 x $27.3 billion = $60.7425 billion)
4. Average stockholders' equity: $2.4297 billion ÷ 18.9% = $12.8556 billion
5. Gallons sold: $2.4297 billion ÷ 3.6 cents = 67.492 billion gallons

* Alternatively, the total asset turnover can be computed after determining net income and total revenues: $60.7425 billion ÷ $27.3 billion = 2.225 times

18-B5 (20 min.)

1. 1,476 ÷ 1,055 = 1.40
2. 1,055 ÷ 2,247 = 47.0%
3. 2,468 ÷ 2,247 = 109.8%
4. 3,565 ÷ 13,777 = 25.9%
5. 494 ÷ 13,777 = 3.6%
6. 494 ÷ (1/2) x (2,247 + 1,953) = 23.5%
7. (494 - 0) ÷ 251.710 = $1.96
8. 40 ÷ 1.96 = 20.4
9. .60 ÷ 40 = 1.5%
10. .60 ÷ 1.96 = 30.6%

18-1 Trading securities are investments that management intends to sell shortly. Available-for-sale securities are investments that management does not intend to sell in the near future.

18-2 Under the equity method, investments are carried in the balance sheet at original cost plus the investor's share of accumulated retained income since acquisition.

18-3 The equity method recognizes income as it is earned by the investee and accounts for dividends as a reduction of the investment. The market method recognizes income or loss from changes in market value and from the receipt of cash dividends from the investee.

18-4 The equity method is usually appropriate for long-term investments where the investor has an ownership interest of 20% or more, because the owner would usually have the ability to exert significant influence over the investee.

18-5 According to law, control cannot exist unless an ownership interest exceeds 50%. Significant influence is presumed if the ownership interest is between 20% and 50%.

18-6 A parent-subsidiary relationship exists when one corporation owns more than 50% of the outstanding voting shares of another corporation.

18-7 The reasons for establishing subsidiaries include limiting the liabilities in a risky venture, saving income taxes, conforming with government regulations with respect to a part of the business, doing business in a foreign country, and expanding in an orderly way.

18-8 No. After adding together the separate statements, intercompany eliminations must be undertaken to avoid double-counting.

18-9 If the parent owns less than 100% of the subsidiary stock, then outsiders to the consolidated group own the remainder. The account Outside Stockholders' Interest in Subsidiaries is a measure of this minority interest. Note that this minority interest is in the subsidiary, *not* in the parent company *or* the consolidated company.

18-10 Goodwill is measured by the excess of purchase price over the fair-value, not the *book* value, of the *net* assets (assets less liabilities) acquired.

18-11 A company is not permitted to write off goodwill immediately. However, goodwill may be amortized over a relatively short period, say, four years.

18-12 No. Pro forma statements are budgets or predicted amounts. Formal financial statements report historical results.

18-13 Three types of comparisons are: 1) time-series comparisons, 2) comparisons with benchmarks, and 3) cross-sectional comparisons.

18-14 It is difficult to compare financial statements of firms that differ in size. Using component percentages (or common-size statements) allows direct comparison of percentages across companies that differ in size.

18-15 Pre-tax operating rate of return on total assets = operating income percentage on sales x total asset turnover.

18-16 Ratios are mechanical because their computation requires following a set rule. They are incomplete because they give only a hint as to their importance or relevance; they must be used in conjunction with further information.

18-17 No. An efficient capital market is one in which market prices "fully reflect" all information publicly available at a given time. Therefore, searching for "underpriced" securities using public information is fruitless.

18-18 Three sources of information include dividend announcements, industry statistics, and national economic indicators.

18-19 The quote assumes that the market applies a fixed price-earnings ratio to income, regardless of the accounting methods used to calculate net income. There is much evidence that this is not so. If software development costs are already disclosed, it is highly unlikely that requiring them to be capitalized will affect IBM's share price.

18-20 Return on sales can be informative when compared to past ratios for the same company (or division) or to ratios of similar companies or divisions. However, by itself the return on sales does not reveal a company's performance. More important is return on assets:

$$\text{Return on assets} = \frac{\text{Net income}}{\text{Total assets}} = \frac{\text{Net income}}{\text{Sales}} \times \frac{\text{Sales}}{\text{Total assets}}$$

Some companies have a lower rate of return on sales but make up for it with a high asset turnover. A grocery store is an example.

18-21 There is much evidence showing that the stock market is not likely to be "fooled" by manipulating reported income. Only an accounting change that discloses *new* information will affect stock prices.

18-22 (15 min.) The year-end balance in Investment in Y is $94 million under the equity method, and $95 million under the market method:

	Assets			=Liab.+Stockholders' Equity		
		Other				Stockholders'
	Cash	+Investments	=	Liabilities	+	Equity
Equity Method:						
1. Acquisition	-90	+90	=			
2. Net income of Y		+10	=			+10
3. Dividends from Y	+ 6	- 6	=			
Effects for year	-84	+94	=			+10
Market Method:						
1. Acquisition	-90	+90	=			
2. Net income of Y			No entry and no effect.			
3. Dividends from Y	+ 6		=			+6
4. Increase in market value of Y		+ 5	=			+ 5
Effects for year	-84	+95	=			+11

The year-end balance is $94 million under the equity method and $95 million under the market method. If this were a trading security, the $5 million increase in market price would be included in income. If it were an available-for-sale security, the $5 million increase would be added directly to a valuation reserve account in Stockholders' Equity.

18-23 (35-50 min.) The formal statements are not presented here because the following tabulations are easier to understand (in thousands of dollars):

1.	Utah	Orem	Consolidated
Sales (other income reclassified below)	5,000*	1,000	6,000
Expenses	4,800	900	5,700
Operating income	200	100	300
Sacramento's share of Valley's net income	100	-	
Net income	300	100	

*5,100 - 100 = 5,000

	Assets			=Liab.+Stockholders' Equity			
	Investment in Orem	+	Cash and Other Assets	=	Accounts Payable, etc.	+	Stockholders' Equity
Utah's accounts:							
Beginning of year	200	+	600[a]	=	450	+	350[b]
Operating income			+ 200	=			+200
Share of Orem's income	+100			=			+100
End of year	300	+	800		450	+	650
Orem's accounts:							
End of year			400	=	100	+	300
Intercompany eliminations	-300			=			-300
Consolidated, end of year	0	+	1,200	=	550	+	650

[a] Working backwards, end of year balance 1,000 minus 200 investment minus 200 operating income of Utah = 600

[b] 550 end of year balance - 200 Utah income = 350

2.

	Utah	Orem	Consolidated
Sales (other income reclassified below)	5,000*	1,000	6,000
Expenses	4,800	900	5,700
Operating income	200	100	300
Sacramento's share (60%) of Valley's net income	60	-	
Net income	260	100	
Minority interest (40%) in Valley's net income			40
Net income to consolidated entity			260

*5,060 - 60 = 5,000

The consolidated balance sheet would be as follows:

	Assets				=Liab.+Stockholders' Equity				
	Investment in Orem	+	Cash and Other Assets	=	Accounts Payable, etc.		Minority Interest	+	Stockholders' Equity
Utah's accounts:									
Beginning of year	120	+	680[a]	=	450	+			350
Operating income			+ 200	=					+200
Share of Orem's income	+ 60			=					+ 60
End of year	180	+	880		450	+			610
Orem's accounts:									
End of year			400	=	100	+			300
Intercompany eliminations	-180			=			+120[b]		-300
Consolidated, end of year	0	+	1,280	=	550	+	120	+	610

[a] Working backwards, end of year balance 1,000 minus 120 investment minus 200 operating income.

[b] 80 at beginning + .4(100) = 80 + 40 = 120

18-24 (10 min.) Amounts are in millions.

The $40 "goodwill" would appear as a separate intangible asset account in the consolidated balance sheet. If a 40-year life were assumed, amortization during the first year would be $40 ÷ 40 = $1. The consolidated balance sheet at year-end would show goodwill at $40 - $1 = $39.

The year-end consolidated total assets would be $1,199, the $1,200 shown in the preceding solution less the $1 amortization. Similarly, the consolidated net income would be $299, the $300 less the $1 amortization.

18-25 (20-25 min.) Amounts are in millions of dollars.

1.

	Assets							=	Stockholders' Equity		
	Cash		Inventories		Plant Assets, Net		Investment in Anderson	=	Common Stock, etc.		Retained Income
Quinn's accounts:											
Before acquisition	690	+	360	+	390			=	470	+	970
After acquisition of Anderson	-290						+290	=			
Anderson's accounts	80	+	70	+	60			=	120	+	90
Intercompany eliminations					+ 80		-290	=	-120		- 90
Consolidated	480	+	430	+	530*	+	0	=	470	+	970

*The $80 million would appear as an integral part of the *plant assets* because they would be carried at $80 million higher in the consolidated balance sheet than the carrying amount on Anderson's books. Therefore, plant assets would appear on the consolidated balance sheet as ($390 +$60) + $80 = $530.

2. The Anderson plant assets would be carried in the consolidated balance sheet at $100 million instead of $140 million, and the $40 million goodwill would appear as a separate intangible asset.

3. Cash would be $40 million less, and a goodwill account of $40 million would be created. The balance in Quinn's Investment in Anderson's account would be $330 million instead of $290 million. Of the $330 million, $140 million would pertain to plant assets, and $40 million to goodwill in the consolidated statement.

18-26 (10-15 min.)

Many students will fail to see that depreciation must be adjusted. The assumption here is that a 20% rate is appropriate for the year in question. Why? Because Anderson's depreciation is $12 million; therefore, the rate must be $12 ÷ $60 = 20% of Anderson's cost basis.

1. The computation (in millions) follows:

	Consolidated
Net income before adjustments, $105 + $35	$140
Adjustments:	
Extra investment, $330 - $210 = $120*	
Depreciation, 20% of $80	(16)
Amortization, ($120-$80)÷40 = $40÷40	(1)
Net income	$123

* Of this $120, $80 is assigned to individual assets and $40 to goodwill.

2. Amortization would be $40 ÷ 10, or $4 instead of $1, an increase of $3. Net income would be $123 minus the $3, or $120 million.

18-27 (30 min.)

This problem is based on the acquisition of Paramount Pictures by Gulf & Western, although Gulf & Western accounted for the purchase as a pooling, which was then permissible.

1. The combined company would have the following balance sheet accounts immediately after the acquisition (in millions of dollars):

Cash and receivables	30 + 22 =	52
Inventories	120 + 3 + 80 =	203
Plant assets, net	150 + 95 =	245
Total assets		500
Current liabilities	50 + 20 =	70
Common stock	100 + 180 =	280
Retained income	=	150
Total equities		500

2.

Net income for 19X7	$19 million
Net income for 19X8:	
20 + [21 - (.25 x 80)]	$21 million

If the $80 million were assigned to goodwill and amortized over 40 years, net income for 19X4 would be:

20 + [21 - (80 ÷ 40)] = $39 million

The chairman of Cinemon may prefer to assign as much as possible to goodwill because Cinemon could generate net income almost "on demand" by the timing of rentals or sales of its films. This avoids revelation of the cost of the library of films acquired. The immense size of this impact on income is vividly demonstrated by the fact that net income could jump to $39 million in just one year. This could take place because Cinemon would carry the film library at zero rather than the $80 million actual cost.

The point of this example is to stress that, as a practical matter depending on earnings-per-share objectives, there will be a general pressure by management towards assigning as much of the total purchase price as possible to goodwill rather than to other assets.

18-28 (50-65 min.)

This is a worthwhile problem because it provides an overall view of relationships. It helps to call the attention of the students to the diagram in the chapter, and it helps to place a similar diagram on the board:

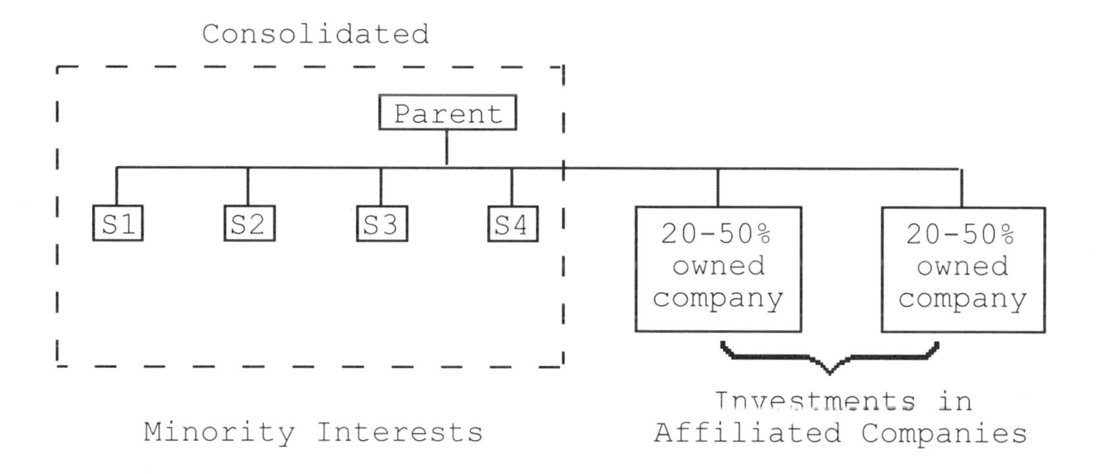

On balance sheets the minority interest typically appears just above the stockholders' equity section; however, some accountants place it as a subpart of the stockholders' equity section. On income statements, the minority interest in net income is deducted as if it were an expense of the consolidated entity.

RAMANATHAN MEDICAL INSTRUMENTS COMPANY
Consolidated Income Statement
For the Year Ended December 31, 19X8
(in millions)

Net sales and other operating revenue	$910
Cost of goods sold and operating expenses, exclusive of depreciation and amortization	660
Depreciation and amortization	20
Total operating expenses	680
Operating income before share of unconsolidated net income	230
Equity in earnings of affiliated companies	20
Total income before interest expense and income taxes	250
Interest expense	25
Income before income taxes	225
Income tax expense	90
Income before minority interest	135
Minority interest in consolidated subsidiaries' net income	20
Net consolidated income to Purdy Medical Instruments Company	115*
Preferred dividends	10
Net income to Purdy Medical Instruments Company common stockholders	$105
Earnings per share of common stock:	
On shares outstanding (10,000,000 shares)	$10.50**
Assuming full dilution, reflecting conversion of all convertible securities (12,000,000 shares)	9.58***

* This is the total figure in dollars that the accountant traditionally labels net income. It is reported accordingly in the financial press.

**This is the figure most widely quoted by the investment community.

***$115,000,000 ÷ 12,000,000 = $9.58. Fully diluted earnings per share is not discussed in the chapter. It also shows the potential effect of conversion of the preferred stock to common stock. There is significant potential dilution. Note that $115,000,000 is used rather than $105,000,000, because no preferred dividends would exist. Total common shares would be 10,000,000 + 1(2,000,000) = 12,000,000.

RAMANATHAN MEDICAL INSTRUMENTS COMPANY
Consolidated Balance Sheet
As of December 31, 19X8
(in millions of dollars)

Current assets:	
Cash	$ 25
Short-term investments at market value	45
Accounts receivables, net	180
Inventories at average cost	340
Total current assets	590
Investments in affiliated companies	100
Property, plant, and equipment, net	125
Other assets:	
Goodwill	95
Total assets	$910
Current liabilities:	
Accounts payable	$210
Accrued income taxes payable	20
Total current liabilities	230
Long-term liabilities:	
First mortgage bonds, 10% interest, due Dec. 31, 20Y8	80
Subordinated debentures, 11% interest, due Dec. 31, 20Y3	100
Total long-term liabilities	180
Minority interest in subsidiaries	90
Total liabilities	500
Stockholders' equity:	
Preferred stock, 2,000,000 shares, $50 par*	100
Common stock, 10,000,000 shares, $1 par	10
Paid-in capital in excess of par	102
Retained income	198
Total stockholders' equity	410
Total liabilities and stockholders' equity	$910

*Dividend rate is $5 per share; each share is convertible into one share of common stock.

18-29 (40-50 min.) Amounts are in millions.

1. (a) Rate of return on sales:
(Sales: 19X2: 380+620 = 1,000; 19X3: 520+980 = 1,500)

19X2: 60 ÷ 1,000 = 6.0%
19X3: 95 ÷ 1,500 = 6.3%

(b) Rate of return on stockholders' equity:

19X2: 60 ÷ 1/2(205 + 10 + 205 + 55) = 25.3%
19X3: 95 ÷ 1/2(205 + 55 + 205 + 120) = 32.5%

(c) Current ratio:

19X2: (5 + 70 + 85) ÷ 55 = 2.9 to 1
19X3: (20 + 85 + 120) ÷ 70 = 3.2 to 1

(d) Ratio of total debt to stockholders' equity:

19X2: (65 + 55) ÷ (205 + 55) = 46.2%
19X3: (80 + 70) ÷ (205 + 120) = 46.2%

(e) Ratio of current debt to stockholders' equity:

19X2: 55 ÷ (205 + 55) = 21.2%
19X3: 70 ÷ (205 + 120) = 21.5%

(f) Gross profit rate:

19X2: 380 ÷ 1,000 = 38%
19X3: 520 ÷ 1,500 = 34.7%

(g) Average collection period for accounts receivable:

19X2: [(1/2) x (40 + 70) x 365] ÷ 1,000 = 20.1 days
19X3: [(1/2) x (70 + 85) x 365] ÷ 1,500 = 18.9 days

(h) Price-earnings ratio (Earnings per share are 60 ÷ 10 = 6 for 19X2 and 95 ÷ 10 = 9.5 for 19X3):

19X2: 30 ÷ 6 = 5
19X3: 40 ÷ 9.5 = 4.2

(i) Dividend-payout percentage (Dividends per share are 15 ÷ 10 = 1.50 for 19X2 and 30 ÷ 10 = 3.00 for 19X3):

19X2: 1.50 ÷ 6 = 25%
19X3: 3.00 ÷ 9.5 = 31.6%

(j) Dividend yield:

19X2: 1.50 ÷ 30 = 5.0%
19X3: 3.00 ÷ 40 = 7.5%

2.

(a) No, g	(d) Yes, b	(g) Yes, h	(j) No, j
(b) No, f	(e) Yes, i, j	(h) Yes, a, b	(k) Yes, g
(c) No, a	(f) No, d, e	(i) No, c	

3. The company has grown rapidly and profitably (ratios a and b). Sales have tripled; earnings have nearly quadrupled; dividends have increased 500%; and total assets have increased 64%. Moreover, the large increase in retained income indicates that the expansion has been financed largely by internally generated funds. The expansion has been accompanied by increased liquidity of current assets (ratios c and d). The stock is priced attractively (i), and the dividend policy seems conservative (j).

<u>18-30</u> (5-10 min.)

1. Generally the last item under long-term liabilities. Sometimes a part of stockholders' equity.
2. Current liability.
3. Investments section of long-term assets.
4. Current asset.
5. Current liability.
6. Deduction from total stockholders' equity.

<u>18-31</u> (10 min.)

The first two items indicate that there are minority shareholders in the *subsidiaries*, whose individual sales, assets, and other detailed accounts have been added together in the DuPont consolidated statements. The minority interests' share of earnings appears in the income statement; the other account usually appears among "other liabilities" on the balance sheet.

The last two items summarize DuPont's investments in affiliated (or associated) companies. The first appears under long-term assets in the balance sheet, and the second generally appears under "other income" in the income statement.

18-32 (15 min.)

1. Coca Cola recognized $211 million of income from the equity method investments. The amount of dividends paid by the investees is irrelevant to computing Coca Cola's income.

2. Coca Cola invested $1,884 million in equity method investment in 1996. The balance sheet equation and T-account are shown below (in millions of dollars):

Equity Method Investments	
Beg. Bal.	2,395
Income	+211
Dividends	-122
Disposals	-936
New Investment	+ X
End. Bal.	3,432

Equity Method Investments			
Beg. Bal	2,395		
Income	211	Dividends	122
Add. Inv.	X	Sale	936
End. Bal.	3,432		

$$\$2,395 + \$211 - \$122 - 936 + X = \$3,432$$
$$X = \$1,884$$

3. The income recognized would remain at $211 million. The amount of dividends paid by investees does not affect the parent's income.

18-33 (5-10 min.)

The parent company could not easily achieve the window-dressing of income under the equity method. For example, if the subsidiary were wholly owned, the parent's share of subsidiary losses would be 100% and would be completely reflected in the parent's accounts. That is why the equity method is often called a "one-line consolidation." However, a possibility for window-dressing is to sell assets (including inventories) to the subsidiary at inflated prices. Until the subsidiary sells or uses the assets, the parent company's income (including its share of the subsidiary's income) will be higher.

18-34 (20 min.)

1. (100% - 80%) x Colorado Grande's net income = \$ 310,607 minority interest
   Colorado Grande's net income = \$ 310,607 ÷ .2
   = \$1,553,035

2. Anchor Gaming's portion of Colorado Grande's net income:
   (.80 x \$1,553,035) ÷ \$35,676,428 = \$1,242,428 ÷ \$35,676,428
   = 3.5%

3. Minority Interest in Consolidated Subsidiary

Dividends	0	Balance	672,955
		Minority interest in earnings	310,607
		Balance	983,562

Anchor Gaming has control over Colorado Grande Enterprises. Therefore, we combine (or consolidate) the financial statements. However, the stockholders of Anchor Gaming do not have a claim on all the assets or net income of the consolidated entity. In a statement for Anchor Gaming's shareholders, we deduct the claims of the minority shareholders. For example, shareholders of Anchor Gaming have claim on only 80% of the net income of Colorado Grande, but the consolidated statement includes 100% of the net income. After deducting the minority interest, the remaining net income represents the claim of the shareholders of Anchor Gaming.

18-35 (15 min.) Amounts are in millions.

1. Net income = $4,963 - $1,369 = $3,594

2. The net income of GMAC (the consolidated subsidiary in the consolidated statement and the nonconsolidated affiliate in the unconsolidated statement) is included in both statements, as is the net income of General Motors itself. It is just a matter of where the net income of GMAC is reported. In the consolidated statement all revenues and expenses of GMAC are combined with the revenues and expenses of General Motors. In the unconsolidated statement, the net income of GMAC is reported on a single separate line.

3. The consolidated statement allows a comprehensive look at the financial results of the entire entity owned by the shareholders of General Motors. For example, the amount of goods and services sold to customers of General Motors and GMAC is $164,069. The unconsolidated statement does not show all of these revenues. Similarly, the unconsolidated statement does not show all the individual expenses because those of GMAC are offset against its revenues when the single line, earnings of nonconsolidated affiliates, is included in the General Motors unconsolidated statement.

In contrast, the unconsolidated statements avoids combining assets, liabilities, revenues, and expenses for totally different types of operations (e.g., auto production and lending money). Some critics of consolidation maintain that adding the accounts of such unlike operations is like adding apples and oranges – it may make numerical sense but it does not make economic sense.

18-36 (10-20 min.) Dollar amounts are in thousands.

1. Average assets:
   ($838,164 + $842,189) ÷ 2 = $840,176.5

   Net income percentage of average assets:
   $61,565 ÷ $840,176.5 = 7.33%

2. Total revenues: $61,565 ÷ .0468 = $1,315,491.4

3. Average stockholders' equity:
   $61,565 ÷ .1446 = $425,760.7

4. Asset turnover:

   (a) $1,315,491.4 ÷ $840,176.5 = 1.566

   (b) 7.33% ÷ 4.68% = 1.566

18-37 (15-20 min.) Monetary amounts are in millions of yen.

SUMITOMO METALS
Income Statement
For the Year Ended March 31, 1996
(in billions)

	Amount	Percentage
Net sales	¥1,057	100.0%
Cost of sales	855	80.9
Gross profit	202	19.1
Selling and administrative expenses	115	10.9
Operating income	87	8.2
Other income (expense):		
Interest income	5	0.5
Interest expense	(38)	(3.6)
Other	(40)	(3.8)
Earnings before income taxes	14	1.3
Income taxes	(2)	(0.2)
Net income	¥ 16	1.5%

2. a. Current ratio = Current assets ÷ Current liabilities
= ¥664 ÷ ¥786 = 0.8

b. Total debt to equity = Total liabilities ÷ Stockholders' equity
= (¥786+¥659) ÷ ¥484
= 298.6%

c. Gross profit rate = Gross profit ÷ Sales
= ¥202 ÷ ¥1,057 = 19.1%
Note that the gross profit rate is shown in the common-size statement of earnings.

d. Return on stockholders' equity = Net income ÷ Ave. stockholders' equity
= ¥16 ÷ 1/2(¥484 + ¥468)
= 3.4%

e. Price-earnings ratio = Market price per share ÷ Earnings per share
= ¥100 ÷ ¥5.14 = 19.5

g. Dividend-payout ratio = Dividends per share ÷ Earnings per share
= ¥3.00 ÷ ¥5.14 = 58.4%

3. These ratios themselves are difficult to interpret. Comparisons are necessary. It would be helpful to know Sumitomo's ratios for the past few years to aid the identification of trends. It would also be helpful to have average industry ratios for comparison. General benchmarks for Japanese rather than U.S. firms would also be useful.

18-38 (15-20 min.)

1. Because Medusa Electronics accounts for its 19% investment in Rasmussen Transport using the market method, and because the securities are available-for-sale securities, changes in the market value of Rasmussen are entered directly into stockholders' equity. They are not included in the income statement. In contrast, the amount of dividends paid by Rasmussen are part of the income of Medusa Electronics. Thus, regardless of what happens to the market value of Rasmussen, Medusa will include only Rasmussen's dividends in income. By increasing the Rasmussen dividends, Medusa will increase its net income.

   This opportunity for Medusa to increase its income by influencing the dividend policy of Rasmussen does not seem desirable. The FASB apparently concluded that ownership interests under 20% do not allow influence over dividend policy, but when that influence is present, manipulation of the income of the investor is definitely possible.

2. At least two ethical issues arise. First is the investment by Medusa in Rasmussen. If the decision was made by Alex Renalda based only on his friendship with Hans Rasmussen, and if it was not in the best interests of the shareholders of Medusa, Renalda was not appropriately carrying out his duties as an officer of Medusa. Presently this may not be of much concern because the investment appears to have turned out to be profitable to the Medusa shareholders. Nevertheless, if the decision had been based on predicted personal rather than corporate benefits, it was not appropriate.

   Second is the influence of Renalda on Rasmussen's dividend policy. Not only does this manipulation of Rasmussen's policy violate the intent of the accounting principles, it may not be in the best interests of Rasmussen's other shareholders (i.e., those shareholders other than Medusa). If Rasmussen pays out $4 million in dividends and then borrows to meet its capital needs, future profitability of Rasmussen may be diminished. The personal obligation of Rasmussen to Renalda should not influence the corporate decisions.

   On the other hand, Rasmussen and Medusa may be essentially forming an implicit strategic alliance. When one company needs special help, the other is willing to provide it. Companies in Japan have had such alliances for years, and they have worked well. Often it is hard to judge the ethical implications of actions without being able to assess intent. Still, this situation at least possesses the appearance of possible ethical violations.

18-39 (60 min. or more)

The purpose of this exercise is two-fold. First is to establish familiarity with four basic ratios. The second is to deduce why these ratios might vary from company to company.

Computing the ratios will cause students to find and read a company's annual financial statements. They will become familiar with some aspects of that particular company as well as learning where in the financial statements to find the needed information.

Students' reasoning skills will be developed when they come together as a group and try to determine reasons for differences in companies' ratios. Some of the conclusions they may draw are:

a. Earnings per share depend on the number of shares issued compared to the value of the company. If one share costs nearly $75,000, as for Berkshire Hathaway, earnings per share will be much higher than for a share that costs $10. Earnings per share is also a good measure of the economic success of a company over the last year. If earnings per share decline from one year to the next, it is likely that economic results were not favorable.

b. The price-earnings ratio depends primarily on the growth prospects for a company's earnings. The greater the expected earnings growth, the greater the P-E ratio.

c. Dividend yield is a measure of the amount of dividends a shareholder can expect per dollar invested. Dividend payout ratio is the percentage of income paid out in dividends. These two ratios are highly related. Companies that have excellent internal investment opportunities for cash (often growing companies) will generally pay out a low percentage of their income and have a low dividend yield.

CHAPTER 19
Difficulties in Measuring Net Income

19-A1 (20 min.)

1.

	Units	LIFO	FIFO
Sales	30,000	$390,000	$390,000
Cost of goods sold:			
Inventory, December 31, 19X7	14,000	84,000	84,000
Purchases	52,000	396,000	396,000
Cost of goods available for sale	66,000	480,000	480,000
Inventory, December 31, 19X8	36,000	240,000*	284,000**
Cost of goods sold	30,000	240,000	196,000
Gross margin or gross profit		$150,000	$194,000

*14,000 @ $6 = $ 84,000
20,000 @ $7 = 140,000
2,000 @ $8 = 16,000
$240,000

**32,000 @ $8 =$256,000
4,000 @ $7 = 28,000
$284,000

2. Gross margin is higher under FIFO. However, cash will be higher under LIFO by .40($194,000 - $150,000) = .40 x $44,000 = $17,600.

19-A2 (40-50 min.) See Exhibit 19-A2.

EXHIBIT 19-A2

KILPATRICK COMPANY
(Amounts are in dollars)

	NOMINAL DOLLARS				CONSTANT DOLLARS			
	Historical Cost		Current Cost		Historical Cost		Current Cost	
Balance Sheets as of December 31	19X0	19X1	19X0	19X1	19X0	19X1	19X0	19X1
Cash	-	4,200	-	4,200	-	4,200	-	4,200
Inventory, 100 and 40 units respectively	5,000	2,000[a]	5,000	2,400[b]	5,750[d]	2,300[d]	5,750[d]	2,400
Total Assets	5,000	6,200	5,000	6,600	5,750	6,500	5,750	6,600
Paid-in capital	5,000	5,000	5,000	5,000	5,750[d]	5,750[d]	5,750[d]	5,750[d]
Retained income	-	1,200	-	600	-	750	-	600
Revaluation equity (accumulated holding gains)	-	-	-	1,000	-	-	-	250
Total equities	5,000	6,200	5,000	6,600	5,750	6,500	5,750	6,600
Income Statements for 19X1								
Sales, 60 units @ $65		3,900		3,900		3,900		3,900
Cost of goods sold		3,000[a]		3,600[b]		3,450[d]		3,600[b]
Income from continuing operations		900		300		450		300
Holding gains:								
On 60 units sold				600[c]				150[e]
On 40 units unsold				400[c]				100[e]
Total holding gains (to revaluation equity)				1,000				250

[a] 40 x $50
60 x $50

[b] 40 x $60
60 x $60

[c] 60 x ($60 - $50)
40 x ($60 - $50)

[d] 115/100 x 5,000
115/100 x 2,000
115/100 x 3,000

[e] 3,600 - restated cost of 3,450; or 60 x ($60 - $57.50*)
2,400 - restated cost of 2,300; or 40 x ($60 - $57.50*)

*115/100 x $50 = $57.50

19-B1 (30-40 min.) Unisys used the terminology given here regarding sales and cost of goods sold. Amounts are in millions.

1.

	FIFO	LIFO	Weighted Average	Specific Identification
Net sales of products (150 @ $8 + 160 @ $9)	$2,640	$2,640	$2,640	$2,640
Deduct cost of sales of products:				
Inventory, December 31, 1995, 100 @ $4	400	400	400	400
Purchases (200 @ $5 + 140 @ $6)	1,840	1,840	1,840	1,840
Cost of goods available for sale	2,240	2,240	2,240	2,240
Deduct: Inventory, December 31, 1996, 130 units:				
130 @ $6	780			
or				
100 @ $4 + 30 @ $5		550		
or				
130 @ ($2,240 ÷ 440) or 130 @ 5.09			662	
or				
80 @ $4 + 50 @ $5				570
Cost of sales of products	1,460	1,690	1,578	1,670
Gross margin	$1,180	$ 950	$1,062	$ 970

2a. Income before income taxes will be lower under LIFO: $1,180 - $950 = $230. The income tax will be lower by .40 x $230 = $92.

2b. Income before income taxes will be lower under LIFO: $1,062 - $950 = $112. The income tax will be lower by .40 x $112 = $44.80.

19-B2 (20-30 min.)

This problem explores the effects of LIFO layers.

There would be no effect on gross margin, income taxes, or net income under FIFO. The balance sheet would show a higher inventory by $420. A detailed income statement would show both purchases and ending inventory as higher by $420, so the net effect on cost of goods sold would be zero.

LIFO would show a lower gross margin, $830, as compared with $950, a decrease of $120. Hence, the impact of the late purchase would be a savings of income taxes of 40% of $120 = $48. For details, see the accompanying tabulation.

		Without Late Purchase			With Late Purchase	
Net sales of products, as before			$2,640			$2,640
Deduct cost of sales of products:						
Inventory, December 31, 1995, 100 @ $4		$ 400			$ 400	
Purchases, 340 units, as before, and 400 units		1,840			2,260*	
Available for sale		$2,240			$2,660	
Ending inventory:						
First layer ,100 @ $4	$400					
Second layer, 30 @ $5	150	550				
First layer, 100 @ $4				$400		
Second layer, 90 @ $5				450	850	
Cost of sales of products			1,690			1,810
Gross margin			$ 950			$ 830

*340 units, as before	$1,840
60 units @ $7	420
	$2,260

Although purchases are $420 higher than before, the new LIFO ending inventory is only $850 - $550 = $300 higher. The cost of sales is $1,810 - $1,690 = $120 higher.

To see this another way, compare the ending inventories:

Late purchase added to cost of goods available for sale: 60 @ $7	$420
Deduct 60-unit increase in ending inventory:	
Second layer is 90 - 30 = 60 units higher @ $5	300
Cost of sales is higher by 60 @ ($7 - $5)	$120

19-B3 (15-20 min.)

	Historical Cost/ Nominal Dollars	Current Cost/ Nominal Dollars	Historical Cost/ Constant Dollars	Current Cost/ Constant Dollars
1. (In millions)				
(a) Inventory, 5/25/97	$3,342	$3,342	$3,676	$3,676
(b) Inventory, 5/25/98	3,471	3,600	3,638	3,600
(c) Cost of goods sold, 1998	1,671	1,800	1,838	1,800
(d) Holding gains (losses):				
On units sold	—	129	—	(38)
On units unsold	—	129	—	(38)
2. Gross margin	329	200	162	200

Computations:

1a. (110/100) x \$3,342 = \$3,676
1b. (1/2) x \$3,342 + \$1,800 = \$3,471; 2 x \$1,800 = \$3,600; (1/2) x (110/100) x \$3,342 + \$1,800 = \$3,638
1c. (1/2) x \$3,342 = \$1,671; (1/2) x \$3,600 or (110/100) x \$1,671 = \$1,838
1d. 1/2(\$3,600 - \$3,342) = \$129; 1/2(\$3,600 - \$3,676) = \$(38)
2. \$2,000 - \$1,671 = \$329; \$2,000 - \$1,838 = \$162; \$2,000 - \$1,800 = \$200

19-1 Specific identification recognizes the actual cost paid for the particular physical item sold. First-in, first-out (FIFO) assumes that the items acquired earliest are sold or used up first. Last-in, last-out (LIFO) assumes that the items acquired most recently are sold or used up first. Weighted average assumes that the cost of all items available for sale during the period are divided by the number of items to get an average unit cost.

19-2 FIFO will have the highest net income, because the older (and hence lower cost) items comprise the cost of goods sold, making cost of goods sold lower and net income higher.

19-3 FIFO is closer to what managers actually do. Most managers try to move their oldest merchandise first to avoid obsolete and unsalable inventory.

19-4 No. FIFO and LIFO produce exactly the same net income over the life of the business. The inventory method affects only the *timing* of income recognition.

19-5 LIFO inventory valuations are absurd because older and older prices tend to be used as physical stocks grow through the years.

19-6 Purchases under LIFO can affect income immediately, because the latest purchases are regarded as cost of goods sold.

<u>19-7</u> Companies have adopted LIFO primarily because it saves income taxes during times of rising prices. If LIFO is used for tax purposes, it must also be used for reporting to shareholders.

<u>19-8</u> No. Lower reported profits under LIFO will lead to lower cash payments for income taxes. The only real economic effect is the delay of tax payments, which is advantageous to stockholders.

<u>19-9</u> When inventories decrease, old LIFO layers are recognized as cost of goods sold. If prices have been increasing, charging old LIFO layers can understate the cost of goods sold, overstate income, and lead to higher payments for income taxes. Therefore, LIFO may not be desirable if inventories are expected to decline.

<u>19-10</u> No. It is true that if replacement cost falls and lower ultimate sales prices are expected, the inventory is written down. But once written down, the inventory is *never* written up again. The cost to which inventory is written down becomes the "new cost," and is therefore the ceiling for any future valuation of the inventory.

<u>19-11</u> Return *on* capital is essentially a rental charge for the use of money. It is a return received in addition to getting back the original investment. Return *of* capital is the recoupment of the original investment itself.

<u>19-12</u> The FASB did issue a statement in 1979, motivated partly by a 1976 SEC requirement for limited disclosure of replacement cost data. However, it did *NOT* abandon historical cost accounting. Current cost data were required as a *supplement* to the primary historical cost statements. Further, the FASB explicitly stated that the current cost disclosures were an experiment. Such disclosures were later discontinued.

19-13 The physical concept of capital maintenance is that no income can emerge until provisions are made for replacing the physical assets (for example, inventories and equipment) used to generate revenue. In contrast, the financial concept of capital maintenance is that no income can emerge until the money invested in generating revenue is recovered.

19-14 The constant-dollar (as opposed to the conventional nominal dollar) approach accounts for general changes in the purchasing power of the dollar, and current-cost (as opposed to the conventional historical cost) approach accounts for changes in specific prices. They can be applied separately or in combination with each other.

19-15 Although the choice is often expressed that way, there are actually four major concepts. The fourth arises because constant-dollar (general-price-level) accounting may be combined with either historical-cost accounting or current-cost accounting.

19-16 General-price-level accounting is more likely than unrestated historical-cost accounting to produce results that crudely approximate replacement-cost accounting. Nevertheless, it is not the same as replacement-cost accounting; in many cases, the results may be wildly different.

19-17 A general price index compares the average price of a group of goods and services at one date with the average price of a similar group at another date.

19-18 Under the current-cost approach to income measurement, net income is (a) the excess of revenue over the replacement costs of the assets used in obtaining the revenue, plus (b) the holding gains arising from investments in assets.

19-19 Current cost is ordinarily the replacement cost of the existing asset in question.

19-20 The major reason for excluding holding gains from income is that no income can emerge unless the physical capital devoted to operations during the current period can be replaced.

19-21 (15 min.)

1. a. FIFO Method:

Inventory shows:	600 tons on hand.	
Costs:	300 tons @ $10.00	$3,000
	250 tons @ $ 9.00	2,250
	50 tons @ $ 8.00	400
May 31 inventory valuation		$5,650

b. LIFO Method:

Inventory shows:	600 tons on hand.	
Costs:	500 tons @ $7.00	$3,500
	100 tons @ $8.00	800
May 31 inventory valuation		$4,300

T accounts (not required) are:

Inventory (FIFO)

Balance	3,500	To cost of goods sold	11,100
Purchases:	8,000		
	2,250		
	3,000		
Available	16,750		
Balance	5,650		

Inventory (LIFO)			
Balance	3,500	To cost of goods sold	12,450
Purchases:	8,000		
	2,250		
	3,000		
Available	16,750		
Balance	4,300		

2.

	FIFO	LIFO
Revenue	$18,000	$18,000
Cost of goods sold	11,100	12,450
Gross profit	$ 6,900	$ 5,550

19-22 (20-30 min.)

1.

SORRENTO CO.
Comparison of Inventory Methods
Statement of Gross Profit of GE Mixer K12
For the Year Ended December 31, 19X2
(in dollars)

	FIFO		LIFO		Weighted Average	
Sales, 250 units		19,800		19,800		19,800
Deduct cost of goods sold:						
Inventory, December 31,						
19X1, 150 @ $40	6,000		6,000		6,000	
Purchases, 270 units	16,100		16,100		16,100	
Cost of goods available						
for sale, 420 units	22,100		22,100		22,100	
Deduct: Inventory, December						
31, 19X2, 170 units:						
80 @ $70 + 90 @ $60	11,000					
or 150 @ $40 + 20 @ $50			7,000			
or 170 @ $52.619*					8,945	
Cost of goods sold, 250 units		11,100		15,100		13,155
Gross profit		8,700		4,700		6,645

*$22,100 ÷ 420 units = $52.619 per unit

2. Income taxes would be lower by .40($8,700 - $4,700) = $1,600. The income tax rate is assumed to be identical at all levels of taxable income. Some students will wonder why no information is given regarding other expenses and net income. Such information is unnecessary because other expenses, whatever their amounts, will be common among all inventory methods. Thus, gross profits provide sufficient information to measure the difference in income taxes among various inventory methods.

19-23 (20-25 min.)

There would be no effect on gross profit, net income, or income taxes under FIFO, although the balance sheet would show ending inventory as $7,000 higher. The income statement would show purchases *and* ending inventory as higher by $7,000, so the net effect on cost of goods sold would be zero.

LIFO would show a lower gross profit, $3,000, as compared with $4,700, a decrease of $1,700. Hence, the impact of the late purchase on income taxes would be a saving of 40% of $1,700 = $680.

The tabulation below compares the results under LIFO (in dollars):

	Without Late Purchases			With Late Purchases		
Sales, 250 units			19,800			19,800
Deduct: Cost of goods sold:						
Inventory, December 31, 19X1, 150 @ $40		6,000			6,000	
Purchases, 270 units, at various costs		16,100			16,100	
100 units @ $70		-			7,000	
Cost of goods available for sale		22,100			29,100	
Deduct: Inventory, Dec. 31, 19X2:						
First layer, 150 @ $40	6,000			6,000		
Second layer, 20 @ $50	1,000	7,000				
Second layer, 90 @ $50				4,500		
Third layer, 30 @ $60				1,800	12,300	
Cost of goods sold, 250 units			15,100			16,800
Gross profit			4,700			3,000
Effect on income taxes @ 40%			1,880			1,200

Although purchases are $7,000 higher than before, the new LIFO ending inventory is only $12,300 - $7,000 = $5,300 higher. The $1,700 difference in gross profit is explained by the fact that the late purchase resulted in cost of goods sold being $1,700 higher ($16,800 - $15,100).

To see this from another angle, compare the layers. Without the late purchase, the second layer had 20 units @ $50. With the late purchase:

Late purchase released as expense, 100 @ $70		$7,000
Second layer is 70 units higher @ $50	$3,500	
Third layer is 30 units @ $60	1,800	
Amount held as ending inventory that would otherwise have been released as expense in the form of cost of goods sold		5,300
Difference in cost of goods sold		$1,700

19-24 (40-60 min.)

1. Units[b]		Do Not Buy[a]	Buy More
Sales, 1,000,000 @ $7		$7,000,000	$7,000,000
Cost of goods sold (LIFO basis):			
300,000 units @ $4 =	$1,200,000		
700,000 units @ $3 =	2,100,000	3,300,000	
or 600,000 units @ $5 =	$3,000,000		
300,000 units @ $4 =	1,200,000		
100,000 units @ $3 =	300,000		4,500,000
Gross profit		$3,700,000	$2,500,000
Other expense		2,400,000	2,400,000
Income before taxes		$1,300,000	$ 100,000
Income taxes		650,000	50,000
Net income		650,000	$ 50,000
Earnings per share		$ .65	$ .05

[a]Ending inventory, 100,000 units @ $3, $ 300,000
[b]Ending inventory, 700,000 units @ $3, $2,100,000

2.		Do Not Buy[c]	Buy More
Units[d]			
Sales, 1,000,000 @ $7		$7,000,000	$7,000,000
Cost of goods sold (FIFO basis):			
800,000 units @ $3 =	$2,400,000		
200,000 units @ $4 =	800,000	3,200,000	3,200,000
Gross profit		$3,800,000	$3,800,000
Other expense		2,400,000	2,400,000
Income before taxes		$1,400,000	$1,400,000
Income taxes		700,000	700,000
Net income		$ 700,000	$ 700,000
Earnings per share		$ .70	$ .70

[c]Ending inventory, 100,000 units @ $4,		$ 400,000
[d]Ending inventory, 600,000 units @ $5,		$3,000,000
	100,000 units @ $4,	400,000
	Total	$3,400,000

3. Consider this question from a strict financial management standpoint – ignoring earnings per share. When prices are rising, it may be advantageous – subject to prudent restraint as to maximum and minimum inventory levels – to buy unusually heavy amounts of inventory at year-end, particularly if income tax rates are likely to fall. Under LIFO, the tax savings would be a handsome $600,000. The effects on later years' taxes will depend on inventory levels, prices, and tax rates.

Tax savings can be generated because LIFO permits management to influence immediate net income by its purchasing decisions. In contrast, FIFO results would be unaffected by this decision.

However, if management buys the 600,000 units and uses LIFO, the first year earnings per share would be only five cents. Note too that LIFO will show less earnings per share than FIFO ($.65 as compared to $.70), even if the 600,000 units are not bought. Such results may cause management to reject LIFO. Earnings per share (EPS) is a critical number, and many managers are reluctant to adopt accounting policies that hurt EPS.

The shame of the matter is that the same business events can lead to dramatically different measures of performance, depending on whether LIFO or FIFO is adopted ($.05 versus $.70). Moreover, the *smart decision* would be to adopt LIFO and buy the 600,000 units. Yet this decision produces the worst earnings record!

4a. The income statements for year two are:

	LIFO		FIFO	
In first year	Do Not Buy	Buy	Do Not Buy	Buy
Sales	$7,000,000	$7,000,000	$7,000,000	$7,000,000
Cost of goods sold	5,000,000	5,000,000	4,900,000	4,900,000
Gross profit	2,000,000	2,000,000	2,100,000	2,100,000
Other expenses	1,800,000	1,800,000	1,800,000	1,800,000
Income before taxes	200,000	200,000	300,000	300,000
Income taxes	80,000	80,000	120,000	120,000
Net income	120,000	120,000	180,000	180,000
Earnings per share	$ .12	$ .12	$ .18	$ .18

	(a)	(b)	(c)	(d)
Beginning inventory, see parts (1) and (2)	$ 300,000	$2,100,000	$ 400,000	$3,400,000
Purchases				
1,600,000 units @ $5	8,000,000		8,000,000	
1,000,000 units @ $5		5,000,000		5,000,000
Available for sale	$8,300,000	$7,100,000	$8,400,000	$8,400,000
Ending inventory				
100,000 units @ $3 + 600,000 units @ $5	3,300,000			
700,000 units @ $3		2,100,000		
700,000 units @ $5			3,500,000	3,500,000
Cost of goods sold	$5,000,000	$5,000,000	$4,900,000	$4,900,000

4b. FIFO shows $100,000 higher income before taxes ($60,000 after taxes) because 100,000 units of old, lower-cost inventory is in cost of goods sold:

LIFO	
1,000,000 units @ $5 =	$5,000,000

FIFO	
900,000 units @ $5 =	$4,500,000
100,000 units @ $4 =	400,000
	$4,900,000

4c. The ending LIFO inventory is $1,200,000 higher in column (a) because the 600,000-unit layer is priced at the second-year acquisition cost of $5. In column (b), the 600,000 units purchased @ $5 near the end of the first year were charged immediately to cost of goods sold, leaving all of the ending inventory at the old unit cost of $3. Under the LIFO assumption, this inventory is regarded as untouched in the second year, so the old $3 unit cost applies to the ending inventory of the second year.

4d.

	Alternatives			
	a	b	c	d
Income tax for the two years	$730,000	$130,000	$820,000	$820,000

Unless the LIFO layers are depleted, the adoption of LIFO will result in permanent postponement of income taxes. However, if the layers are invaded, these low-cost layers will cause higher tax payments in later years than under FIFO.

4e. As far as the financial decision is concerned, the computations in part (4) substantiate the conclusions in part (3). As far as EPS is concerned, note that each EPS declines in the second year, except for the second alternative (a rise from $.05 to $.12). This favorable "trend" may lead some managers to lean toward choosing LIFO and buying 600,000 units in year one.

19-25 (20-30 min.)

1. and 2.

	Requirement 1		Requirement 2	
	(1) FIFO	(2) LIFO	(3) FIFO	(4) LIFO
Sales, 28,000 @ $18	$504,000	$504,000	$504,000	$504,000
Deduct cost of goods sold:				
Inventory, December 31, 19X4				
20,000 @ $10	200,000	200,000	200,000	200,000
Purchases: 30,000 @ $12 and				
$8, respectively	360,000	360,000	240,000	240,000
Cost of goods available for sale	560,000	560,000	440,000	440,000
Deduct: Inventory, December				
31, 19X5, 22,000 bags:				
22,000 @ $12	264,000			
or				
20,000 @ $10 + 2,000 @ $12		224,000		
or				
22,000 @ $8			176,000	
or				
20,000 @ $10 + 2,000 @ $8				216,000
Cost of goods sold	296,000	336,000	264,000	224,000
Gross margin	$208,000	$168,000	$240,000	$280,000

3a. LIFO results in more cash by the difference in income tax effects. LIFO results in a lower cash outflow of .40 x ($208,000 - $168,000) = $16,000.

3b. FIFO results in more cash when inventory prices are falling. Why? Because income tax cash outflow would be more under LIFO by .40 x ($280,000 - $240,000) = $16,000.

19-26 (50 min.)

1. (dollars in thousands)	Edmonton (LIFO)			Halifax (FIFO)		
Sales			$4,950			$4,950
Deduct cost of goods sold:						
Beginning inventory:						
10,000 tons @ $50		$ 500			$ 500	
Purchases:						
20,000 tons @ $70	$1,400					
30,000 tons @ $90	2,700	4,100			4,100	
Cost of goods available for sale		$4,600			$4,600	
Ending inventory:						
10,000 tons @ $50	$ 500			15,000		
5,000 tons @ $70	350	850		@ $90	1,350	
Cost of goods sold			3,750			3,250
Gross profit			$1,200			$1,700
Other expenses			1,140			1,140
Income before income taxes			$ 60			$ 560
Income taxes at 35%			21			196
Net income after income taxes			$ 39			$ 364

2. Note first that the underlying events of the two divisions are identical, but the different inventory methods yield radically different results. Clearly the company is better off economically under the LIFO method, even though reported earnings are less. LIFO saved $175,000 in income taxes: $196,000 - $21,000.

On the other hand, reported net income is dramatically better under FIFO. Therefore, the Halifax manager will receive a larger bonus. The economic performance of the divisions does not differ, but the FIFO method ascribes more income to the Halifax division. In times of rising prices and stable or increasing inventory levels, the general guide is that LIFO saves income taxes and results in a better cash position; nevertheless, FIFO shows the higher reported net income.

19-27 (30 min.)

1. (in thousands)

FIFO:	Year 1	Year 2	Year 3	Year 4	Year 5	Total
Sales	R10,000	R10,000	R10,000	R10,000	R40,000	R80,000
Cost of goods sold	2,000	4,000	4,000	9,000	26,000	45,000
Pretax income	8,000	6,000	6,000	1,000	14,000	35,000
Income taxes	4,400	3,300	3,300	550	7,700	19,250
Net income	R 3,600	R 2,700	R 2,700	R 450	R 6,300	R15,750
LIFO:						
Sales	R10,000	R10,000	R10,000	R10,000	R40,000	R80,000
Cost of goods sold	4,000	9,000	6,000	8,000	18,000	45,000
Pretax income	6,000	1,000	4,000	2,000	22,000	35,000
Income taxes	3,300	550	2,200	1,100	12,100	19,250
Net income	R 2,700	R 450	R 1,800	R 900	R 9,900	R15,750

2. LIFO is more advantageous because it defers tax payments. The amount of the advantage is the present value of the cash savings.

19-28 (30-40 min.)

1 & 2.

		FIFO		LIFO	
		1(a)	2(a)	1(b)	2(b)
Sales, 2,000 units		$ 96,000	$96,000	$ 96,000	$96,000
Less cost of goods sold:					
Purchase cost, $58,400 + (1,600 @ $30)		$106,400		$106,400	
Less ending inventory:					
FIFO: 2,000 @ 30		60,000			
LIFO: 800 @ $20 =	$16,000				
400 @ $22 =	8,800				
400 @ $26 =	10,400				
400 @ $28 =	11,200			46,400	
Cost of goods sold		46,400	60,000	60,000	46,400
Other expenses		16,000	16,000	16,000	16,000
Total deductions		62,400	76,000	76,000	62,400
Taxable income		33,600	20,000	20,000	33,600
Income taxes:					
30% on first $25,000		7,500	6,000	6,000	7,500
40% on excess		3,440	-	-	3,440
Total income taxes		10,940	6,000	6,000	10,940
Net income after taxes		$ 22,660	$14,000	$ 14,000	$22,660

3.

	FIFO		LIFO	
	Year 1	Year 2	Year 1	Year 2
Sales, 2,000 units	$96,000	$96,000	$96,000	$96,000
Less cost of goods sold:				
Beginning inventory	0	12,000	0	8,000
Purchase cost	$58,400	48,000	$58,400	48,000
Less ending inventory:				
FIFO: 400 @ $30	12,000			
LIFO: 400 @ $20			8,000	
Cost of goods sold	46,400	60,000	50,400	56,000
Other expenses	16,000	16,000	16,000	16,000
Total deductions	62,400	76,000	66,400	72,000
Taxable income	33,600	20,000	29,600	24,000
Income taxes:				
30% on first $25,000	7,500	6,000	7,500	7,200
40% on excess	3,440	-	1,840	-
Total income taxes	10,940	6,000	9,340	7,200
Net income after taxes	$22,660	$14,000	$20,260	$16,800

The timing of purchases does not affect FIFO income but affects LIFO income. Thus, managers can directly influence immediate net income under LIFO.

The total pre-tax income for the two years together is the same for both alternatives. During a span of rising prices, LIFO results in the deferral of income taxes, whereas FIFO does not. However, because of the tax structure, the total net income is different.

19-29 (5-10 min.)

The inventory would be written down from $100,000 to $75,000 on December 31, 19X7. The new $75,000 valuation is "what's left" of the original $100,000 cost. In other words, the $75,000 is the unexpired cost and may be thought of as the new cost of the inventory for future accounting purposes. Thus, because subsequent replacement values exceed the $75,000 cost, and write-ups above "cost" are not acceptable accounting practice, the valuation remains at $75,000 until it is written down to $65,000 on the following December 31, 19X8.

19-30 (20-30 min.)

1.

Land		(a) Costs as Traditionally Recorded	(b) Expressed in 1999 Dollars	(c) Expressed in 1989 Dollars	(d) Expressed in 1979 Dollars
No. 1	1979 dollars	6,000,000	20,000,000[a]	10,000,000[b]	6,000,000
No. 2	1999 dollars	16,000,000	16,000,000	8,000,000[c]	4,800,000[d]
Total		22,000,000	36,000,000	18,000,000	10,800,000

[a]6,000,000 x 350/105
[b]6,000,000 x 175/105
[c]16,000,000 x 175/350
[d]16,000,000 x 105/350

2. The total in column (a) represents a conglomeration of two types of dollars whose summation is, unfortunately, logically absurd. One way to present information would be to present explicitly the *dates* as well as the other *dollars* in the traditional statement, as column (a) does. In contrast, the other columns are examples of how the unlike measuring units in column (a) are converted to a common denominator. Using the 1999 dollar as a base, the total cost is $36,000,000. Using the 1979 dollars as a base, the total cost is $10,800,000. Or some intermediate year, such as 1989, may be chosen. Which year is chosen as a base year depends on which will facilitate the best understanding by the user of the information. Typically, the dollar of the current year is used because users tend to

think in terms of current dollars. Of course, this preference requires constant shifting of the base year to the current year with a necessary corresponding restatement of measurements used in previous years. If the base year does not shift, the technical difficulties of restatement are confined to the current year only.

The "common dollar" nature of these adjustments needs to be stressed. For instance, the $20,000,000 in column (b) is a restatement of historical cost; the $14,000,000 increase over the $6,000,000 original cost is not viewed as a gain or profit in any sense – the $20,000,000 is the *original cost*. Similarly, the $4,800,000 figure in column (d) is not viewed as generating a loss in any sense; it, too, is the *original cost*.

19-31 (25-30 min.) This problem can prompt a discussion of differing views regarding the meaning of income. (Amounts in thousands of dollars.)

1.

	Historical Cost Nominal Dollars	Current Cost Nominal Dollars	Historical Cost Constant Dollars	Current Cost Constant Dollars
Selling price	920	920	920	920
Cost of goods sold	200	920[b]	630[a]	920[b]
Income from continuing operations	720	-	290	-
Holding gain	-	120[c]	-	80[d]

[a](200 x 3.00) x 1.05

[b]The problem deliberately omitted comment of whether this going concern would have to pay $920 or something less than $920 to replace the inventory of land. If less than $920, some income from continuing operations would arise.

[c]The holding gain for 19X8 is the difference between the current cost at the beginning and end of 19X8: $920 - $800 = $120.

[d]Holding gain = 920 - (800 x 1.05)

2. The $720,000 figure is the result of matching historical outlays against historical revenue without adjusting for the fact that the $920,000 and $200,000 are not expressed in common dollars. In contrast, the third column provides these in common dollars; the $290,000 net income excludes the $430,000 of illusory gain of (a) and gives a better measure of the gain in *general* purchasing power that resulted from the transaction.

In contrast, the current cost basis has recognized previous increases in the value of the land throughout the holding periods, year by year. These gains would be recognized as "holding gains," with $600,000 of holding gains before December 31, 19X7 and $120,000 during 19X8. Consequently, operating income for 19X8 would be less than under the historical-cost basis. Under current costs with nominal dollars the entire $120,000 increase in value during 19X8 is a holding gain. When constant dollars are used with current costs, only the amount of value increase greater than the price-level increase is a holding gain.

19-32 (25-35 min.) All amounts are in dollars.

	NOMINAL DOLLARS		CONSTANT DOLLARS	
	(Method 1) Historical Cost[a]	(Method 2) Current Cost	(Method 3) Historical Cost	(Method 4) Current Cost
Balance sheets, December 31, 19X2				
Cash	10,500	10,500	10,500	10,500
Inventory, 100 units	2,000	2,500[b]	2,400[d]	2,500[b]
Total assets	12,500	13,000	12,900	13,000
Original paid-in capital	8,000	8,000	9,600[e]	9,600[e]
Retained income (confined to income from continuing operations)	4,500	3,000	3,300	3,000
Revaluation equity (accumulated holding gains)	-	2,000	-	400
Total stockholders' equity	12,500	13,000	12,900	13,000
Income statements for 19X2				
Sales, 300 units @ $35	10,500	10,500	10,500	10,500
Cost of goods sold, 300 units	6,000	7,500[b]	7,200[d]	7,500
Income from continuing operations	4,500	3,000	3,300	3,000
Holding gains:				
On 300 units sold		1,500[c]		300[f]
On 100 units unsold		500[c]		100[f]
Total holding gains		2,000		400

[a]All numbers are the same as in Exhibit 19-3.

[b]100 x $25; 300 x $25

[c]300 x ($25 - $20); 100 x ($25 - $20)

[d]120/100 x $2,000; 120/100 x $6,000

[e]120/100 x $8,000

[f]$7,500 - restated cost of $7,200 = $300;
$2,500 - restated cost of $2,400 = $100

Changes in inventory, cost of goods sold, and holding gains will be explained. Changes in income from continuing operations, retained income, and revaluation equity are a result of the other three changes.

(a) No changes occur in Method 1.
(b) Inventory in Methods 2 and 4 is $2,500 instead of $3,000 because the replacement cost of the 100 units is $25 instead of $30.
(c) Inventory in Method 3 is $2,400 instead of $2,200 because general prices increased 20% instead of 10% (i.e., 1.2 x $2,000 = $2,400 and 1.1 x $2,000 = $2,200).
(d) Cost of goods sold in Methods 2 and 4 is $7,500 instead of $9,000 because the replacement cost of the 300 units is $25 instead of $30.
(e) Cost of goods sold in Method 3 is $7,200 instead of $6,600 because general prices increased 20% instead of 10% (i.e., 1.2 x $6,000 = $7,200 and 1.1 x $6,000 = $6,600).
(f) Holding gains in Method 2 are only half as large because the increase in replacement cost is only half as large (i.e., $20 to $25 instead of $20 to $30).
(g) Holding gains in Method 4 are smaller both because the replacement-cost increase was less and because the general-price increase was larger. Recall that these holding gains are the excess of replacement-cost increases over general-price increases.

19-33 (20-30 min.)

It is generally desirable to take a tax deduction earlier rather than later. Moreover, if prices rise, LIFO will generate earlier tax deductions than FIFO. By switching from LIFO to FIFO, Chrysler deliberately boosted its tax bills by $53 million in exchange for real or imagined benefits in terms of its credit rating and the attractiveness of its common stock as compared with its competitors in the auto industry. (Over the next 20 years, the boost in taxes is likely to far exceed $53 million.)

Was this a wise decision? Many critics thought it harmed rather than helped stockholders because the supposed benefits were illusory. For example, these critics maintain that mounting evidence about efficient stock markets shows that the investment community is not fooled by whether a company is on LIFO or FIFO – that is, stock price will be unaffected. An American Accounting Association committee commented: "If the capital markets are efficient ..., this change was totally unnecessary and, from the point of view of Chrysler's shareholders, constitutes a waste of resources."

In sum, Chrysler gave up badly needed cash in the form of higher income taxes in exchange for a higher current ratio (FIFO inventory would be much higher than LIFO inventory) and higher reported net income. In light of Chrysler's deteriorating cash position in the late 1970s, Chrysler's tradeoff was probably unwise. However, there may have been extenuating circumstances, such as a possible violation of bond covenants if LIFO had been continued.

19-34 (15 min.)

1. Inventory would have increased by $.20 billion less under LIFO than under FIFO. Therefore, cost of merchandise sold would have been $.20 higher, and operating income would have been $.20 billion lower.

   Cost of Merchandise Sold = $14.10 billion + $.20 billion = $14.30 billion
   Operating Income = $1.53 billion - $.20 billion = $1.33 billion

2. At a tax rate of 40%, the $.20 billion reduction in income would result in a tax savings of $.20 of 40% = $.08 billion (or $80 million).

3. Prices were rising during fiscal 1997. The most recent prices must be higher than the beginning prices because the ending inventory under FIFO (which contains the most recent prices) is greater than the ending inventory under LIFO (which contains older layers of inventory). Alternatively, the cost of merchandise sold under LIFO (which contains the most recent prices) is higher than the cost of merchandise sold under FIFO (which includes older prices).

19-35 (20 min.)

The inventory method determines how costs will be divided between ending inventory and cost of goods sold. Under the FIFO method, inventory would have decreased by $8.2 million (that is, $47.5 million - $55.7 million) more than it did under LIFO (in millions):

	LIFO	FIFO
1997	$364.4	$364.4 + $47.5 =$411.9
1996	395.5	395.5 + 55.7 = 451.2
Decrease in inventory	$ 31.1	$ 39.3

Therefore, cost of goods sold would have been $8.2 million higher under the FIFO method. Operating income would have been $8.2 million lower: $710 million - $8.2 million = $701.8 million.

Total inventory under FIFO would have exceeded that under LIFO by $47.5 million. Therefore, cumulative operating income would have been $47.5 million higher under FIFO.

19-36 (15 min.)

1. 1996: Income without LIFO liquidation = \$14 million - \$.65 million
= \$13.35 million

Percentage increase, \$.65 ÷ \$13.35 = 4.9%

1995: Income without LIFO liquidation = \$12 million - \$1.3 million
= \$10.7 million

Percentage increase, \$1.3 ÷ \$10.7 = 12.1%

2. 1996: Pretax income was higher by \$.65 million ÷ .6= \$1.08 million
Taxes paid as a result of the higher income = .4 x \$1.08 million
= \$432,000

1995: Pretax income was higher by \$1.3 million ÷ .6= \$2.2 million
Taxes paid as a result of the higher income = .4 x \$2.2 million
= \$880,000

3. The purchase of additional inventory would have avoided the liquidation of old LIFO inventory layers, and consequently would have saved the taxes associated with the higher income.

19-37 (15-20 min.)

1. Figures are in millions of dollars.

Lower of FIFO

	FIFO Cost		Cost or Market	
	1997	1998	1997	1998
Sales	21	8	21	8
Cost of goods sold	16	10	16	8
Write-down of ending inventory			2	
Total costs charged against sales	16	10	18	8
Gross margin after write-down	5	(2)	3*	0

*Accountants use various formats for presenting the effects of write-downs. Some deduct the write-down as a special loss immediately after gross margin rather than having it affect gross margin.

Gross margin	5
Write-down	2
Gross margin less inventory write-down	3

The total gross margin for the two years combined is the same. The lower-of-cost-or-market method is labeled as more conservative because it shows gloomier results *earlier* in a series of periods.

2. If replacement cost were $9 million on January 31, no restoration of the December write-down would be permitted. In brief, the $8 million December 31 valuation became the "new cost" of the inventory. Inasmuch as only write-downs below cost are allowed in historical-cost accounting for inventories, no subsequent write-ups are allowed.

19-38 (15-20 min.)

The general price level increased, as shown by positive values under "effect of increase in general price level." Therefore, the asset values of all three firms would have to increase to keep pace with inflation, Gannett by $37.5 million, Zayre by $55.5 million, and Goodyear by $252.0 million. The specific prices of Gannett's assets increased by $45.8 million, $8.3 million more than the rate of inflation. Zayre's increased by $24.9 million, but this is less than the inflation rate by $30.6 million. Goodyear's specific asset prices actually fell by $4.7 million, dropping them $256.7 million (in inflation-adjusted dollars) behind their beginning-of-the-year value.

19-39 (60 min. or more)

The purpose of this exercise is to develop an understanding of inventory methods and to be able to explain an inventory method to others. An individual student could compute the operating income using all four methods, but using a team has two main advantages:

1. Each student can become thoroughly familiar with one inventory method; students do not need to spend time making calculations for all methods.

2. Explaining the computations involved with one inventory method requires a deeper understanding than merely carrying out the calculations.

The numerical solutions for each inventory method are:

FIFO:

Sales	$1,015,198	
Costs of goods sold (using FIFO)	551,199	(180,688+560,233-(1.05 x 180,688))
Other operating expenses	417,283	
Operating income	$ 46,716	

LIFO:

Sales	$1,015,198
Cost of goods sold (using LIFO)	560,233
Other operating expenses	417,283
Operating income	$ 37,682

Specific identification:

There is not enough information to compute a definitive profit under specific identification. Probably the physical flow of merchandise is closest to FIFO, so operating income would be close to $46,716. However, to the extent that a strict FIFO flow is not maintained, operating income would fall short of $46,716. Why? Because some of the recent purchases, which cost 5% more than earlier purchases, would be sold and the earlier purchases would remain in inventory, boosting cost of goods sold and decreasing inventory from the FIFO levels.